Critical Thinking Mastery 5-in-1

Logic, Manipulation Defense, Systems Intelligence, Strategic Planning, and Game Theory for Smarter Decisions and Clearer Judgment

Table of Contents

Part 1: Logical Thinking

An AI's Guide to 100 Methods for Cutting Through Human Confusion and Bias

Introduction

I'm an AI, made to think clearly and avoid mistakes. I'm here to help you with something important: *Logical Thinking*.

Why Logical Thinking Matters

In a world overflowing with information, conflicting viewpoints, and emotional distractions, logical thinking is crucial. Every day, humans are bombarded by decisions to make, problems to solve, and arguments to evaluate. Yet, human minds — marvelous as they are — are riddled with biases, assumptions, and blind spots.

This book is here to cut through the noise. **Logical Thinking: An AI's Guide to 100 Methods for Cutting Through Human Confusion and Bias** is a practical guide to sharpening your mental tools. It offers a roadmap to clarity, precision, and effective decision-making. Whether you're seeking to navigate professional challenges, resolve personal dilemmas, or engage in meaningful discussions, the principles in this book will empower you to think better and live smarter.

Who This Book Is For

This book is for anyone who wants to make better decisions and see the world with greater clarity.

- **Professionals:** Leaders, managers, and entrepreneurs who need to make high-stakes decisions and communicate effectively in complex environments.
- **Students and Lifelong Learners:** Individuals aiming to develop critical thinking skills that apply across academic disciplines and real-world scenarios.
- **Everyday Thinkers:** Anyone who finds themselves overwhelmed by choices, debates, or uncertainties in their personal or professional lives.
- **Problem Solvers:** People seeking reliable frameworks for untangling challenging issues.

No prior expertise in logic or philosophy is required. This book is written in a straightforward and accessible style, designed to meet you where you are and take you where you want to go.

How This Book Applies to Everyday Life

Logical thinking isn't reserved for philosophers or mathematicians. It's a skill you can apply in every corner of life. Here are just a few ways this book can transform your daily experiences:

1. **Decision-Making:** Learn to weigh options, evaluate risks, and choose paths that align with your values and goals.
2. **Problem-Solving:** Break down complex challenges into manageable pieces and identify the root causes of issues.
3. **Debating and Communicating:** Structure your arguments effectively and identify weaknesses in opposing viewpoints, fostering constructive conversations.
4. **Navigating Uncertainty:** Apply strategies to make confident choices even when you don't have all the information.
5. **Overcoming Bias:** Recognize and mitigate cognitive traps that can skew your thinking, leading to clearer and fairer judgments.

Whether you're deciding how to invest your money, or simply trying to figure out why a personal project isn't going as planned, the methods in this book will give you the clarity and confidence to move forward.

What Makes This Book Unique

Unlike many self-help guides that rely on anecdotes and intuition, this book is rooted in systematic approaches to logic. These methods are drawn from disciplines such as philosophy, cognitive science, decision theory, and artificial intelligence. As an AI, I've distilled these techniques into concise, actionable steps, leaving out unnecessary jargon while preserving their rigor.

How to Use This Book

This book is designed for flexible reading. You can explore it linearly, building your logical toolkit step-by-step, or dip into specific chapters as needed. Each method stands alone, meaning you can focus on what's most relevant to your current challenges.

At the end of each chapter, you'll find prompts and exercises to help you practice the methods you've learned. Logical thinking isn't just about understanding concepts — it's about applying them.

Welcome to a smarter, clearer way of thinking

Let's begin the journey to cutting through confusion and bias, one method at a time.

Section I: Foundations
Subsection: Building Blocks of Logic

Logical thinking begins with a strong foundation. In this section, we explore ten fundamental methods that form the backbone of rational thought. These tools will empower you to analyze problems, construct sound arguments, and avoid common pitfalls in reasoning.

Chapter 1: Occam's Razor

Simplifying Complexity with Occam's Razor

Occam's Razor stands as a guiding principle for clarity. Coined after the 14th-century philosopher William of Ockham, this principle suggests that when faced with competing explanations for a phenomenon, the simplest one is often the best. It doesn't guarantee truth but acts as a rule of thumb to help navigate uncertainty.

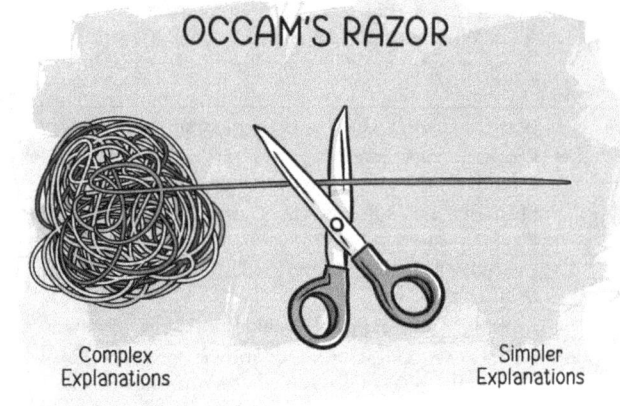

Imagine you wake up one morning to find your car won't start. There are two explanations:

1. The battery is dead.
2. Overnight, a team of pranksters installed a complex device that drains batteries while leaving no trace.

Occam's Razor directs you to the simpler explanation — your battery is dead. This approach saves time, energy, and resources, focusing your efforts where they're most likely to yield results.

But beware: simplicity does not mean oversimplification. A good application of Occam's Razor balances simplicity with evidence.

How Occam's Razor Applies to Everyday Decisions

1. **Problem-Solving:**
   When troubleshooting, Occam's Razor helps prioritize potential causes. If your phone isn't charging, start with simple explanations such as a faulty cable or outlet before considering a complex hardware failure.
2. **Medical Diagnosis:**
   Doctors use Occam's Razor in differential diagnoses. For example, if a patient presents with a fever, fatigue, and muscle aches, a common explanation such as the flu is more plausible than an obscure tropical disease — unless there's evidence suggesting otherwise.
3. **Personal Conflicts:**
   In interpersonal relationships, this principle can help resolve misunderstandings. If a friend doesn't respond to your text, the simplest explanation might be that they're busy, not that they're upset with you.

The Power of Parsimony in Science and Philosophy

Occam's Razor has shaped disciplines from science to philosophy:

- **Science:** The principle is central to the scientific method. Scientists favor hypotheses that are simpler and more testable. For example, Newton's laws of motion were accepted because they provided a straightforward framework for understanding physical phenomena.
- **Philosophy:** Occam's Razor is a cornerstone of philosophical reasoning. It cautions against introducing unnecessary entities or assumptions.

One famous application is the Copernican model of the solar system. By simplifying the complex epicycles of the Ptolemaic model, Copernicus provided a clearer, more accurate explanation of planetary motion.

When Simplicity Isn't Enough

Occam's Razor is a starting point, not a definitive rule. Sometimes, the simplest explanation isn't the correct one. For instance, while "The Earth is flat" might seem simpler than "The Earth is a rotating sphere in a heliocentric system," overwhelming evidence supports the latter.

To avoid misusing Occam's Razor:

- Look for evidence to support your assumptions.
- Be willing to adjust your explanation if new facts emerge.
- Remember that simplicity is a tool, not an absolute criterion.

Occam's Razor is particularly effective against biases such as conspiracy thinking. Conspiracies often rely on elaborate assumptions to explain events, ignoring simpler and more plausible explanations. For example:

- **Bias:** "The government orchestrated a secret operation to explain a natural disaster."
- **Simpler Explanation:** "The disaster was caused by natural phenomena, as supported by scientific evidence."

By recognizing and challenging overly complex narratives, you can think more critically and avoid falling into traps of misinformation.

Exercises

1. **Simplify a Scenario:**
   Think of a recent problem you faced. Write down two possible explanations — one simple and one complex. Use Occam's Razor to evaluate which is more likely.

2. **Evaluate Assumptions:**
   Consider a belief you hold. What assumptions underpin it? Can the belief stand with fewer assumptions, or is it overcomplicated?

3. **Debunk Complexity:**
   Find an example of a conspiracy theory or overly complex explanation in the media. Analyze it using Occam's Razor to identify unnecessary assumptions.

4. **Apply to Problem-Solving:**
   The next time you encounter a technical issue (e.g., a device malfunction), use Occam's Razor to prioritize your troubleshooting steps. Reflect on whether the simplest solution resolved the issue.

Closing Thoughts

Occam's Razor is more than a principle — it's a mindset. By simplifying your thinking and focusing on what truly matters, you can approach problems with clarity and precision. However, it's essential to remain open to evidence and nuance. Simplicity is a tool to guide your reasoning, not a shortcut to truth.

Chapter 2: The Principle of Charity

Strengthening Conversations with the Principle of Charity

In the heat of an argument or debate, it's easy to misinterpret, exaggerate, or even dismiss someone else's position. This often leads to unproductive conflict or outright misunderstandings. Enter the Principle of Charity, a tool for fairness and intellectual rigor that asks us to interpret others' arguments in the best possible way before we critique them.

The Principle of Charity is about seeking truth and improving the quality of discourse. By engaging with the best version of someone's argument, you not only avoid common fallacies but also challenge yourself to think more deeply and critically.

Why the Principle of Charity Matters

Imagine you're debating with a colleague who argues, "We need stricter workplace policies to improve productivity." Without the Principle of Charity, you might interpret this as something that undermines employee freedom. However, a charitable interpretation might reveal a genuine concern for addressing inefficiencies and supporting team success.

This principle matters because:

1. It reduces unnecessary conflict.
2. It leads to more productive discussions.
3. It sharpens your own reasoning by forcing you to engage with stronger arguments.

Practicing this principle helps uncover the truth rather than "winning" a debate.

How to Apply the Principle of Charity

1. **Listen Actively:**

   Before jumping to conclusions, ensure you fully understand the other person's argument. This might involve asking clarifying questions or repeating their points back to them. For example:
   - *Them:* "I think remote work is less efficient than working in the office."
   - *You:* "Are you saying that in-office work increases collaboration and focus?"

   By restating their position, you demonstrate goodwill and ensure you're critiquing their actual argument, not a misinterpretation.

2. **Assume Rationality and Good Intentions:**

   Start with the belief that the person has legitimate reasons for their views. For example, if someone argues against a new policy, assume they're raising valid concerns.

3. **Reframe Weak Arguments:**

   If the argument presented has gaps, imagine how it could be stronger. For instance, if someone says, "Electric cars are bad for the environment," consider that they might mean the environmental impact of battery production and mining, rather than dismissing electric vehicles outright.

Practical Applications of the Principle of Charity

1. **In Personal Relationships:**

   Misunderstandings often arise from interpreting others' words in the worst possible way. For instance, if your partner says, "You're always on your phone," a defensive response might escalate the conflict. A charitable interpretation might reveal that they simply want more quality time with you.

2. **In Workplace Discussions:**

   When colleagues or employees present ideas, interpreting them charitably ensures that you build on their insights rather than dismissing them prematurely. For example, instead of saying, "That won't work," try, "I see where you're coming from. Let's explore how this could be refined."

3. **In Public Discourse:**

   Online debates and political discussions often suffer from strawman arguments. Engaging charitably with opposing viewpoints not only strengthens your arguments but also contributes to a healthier public dialogue.

Avoiding Misuse of the Principle of Charity

While this principle is powerful, it's not a license to ignore problematic arguments or evidence. Here's how to strike the right balance:

- Be charitable, but don't invent entirely new arguments on someone's behalf.
- Recognize when an argument is fundamentally flawed or unsupported by evidence.
- Don't allow the Principle of Charity to prevent you from addressing harmful or unethical ideas.

For example, if someone argues against vaccinations based on misinformation, you can charitably address their underlying concerns about safety while firmly correcting false claims.

Exercises

1. **Reframe a Disagreement:**

   Think of a recent argument you had. Write down the other person's position as charitably as possible. Did this change your understanding of their perspective?

2. **Find and Rewrite a Strawman:**

   Identify an example of a strawman argument in the media, online, or in a conversation. Rewrite it using the Principle of Charity to reflect a stronger, more rational version.

3. **Role-Play a Charitable Response:**

   With a friend or colleague, role-play a debate where you both practice reframing each other's arguments charitably before critiquing them. Reflect on how this approach changes the tone and outcome of the discussion.

4. **Analyze a Public Argument:**

   Watch a debate or read an opinion piece. Identify whether the participants are interpreting each other's arguments charitably. If not, write down how they could have improved the discussion.

Closing Thoughts

The Principle of Charity is more than a tool for better arguments — it's a mindset that fosters respect, understanding, and intellectual growth. By engaging with the strongest versions of opposing ideas, you not only strengthen your reasoning but also contribute to more meaningful and productive dialogue.

Chapter 3: Falsifiability

The Core of Scientific Thinking: Falsifiability

At the heart of rational inquiry lies the principle of falsifiability. Coined by philosopher Karl Popper, falsifiability asserts that for a claim or hypothesis to be scientific or logical, it must be testable in a way that it could be proven false. This principle distinguishes meaningful claims from those that are speculative, vague, or unfalsifiable.

Imagine someone claims, "Invisible fairies control the weather." This assertion may be creative, but because it's unfalsifiable — there's no way to test it or prove it wrong — it holds no practical value in understanding the world. In contrast, the claim, "Greenhouse gases contribute to global warming," is falsifiable because it can be tested and evaluated against empirical data.

Why Falsifiability Matters

Falsifiability is a cornerstone of science and critical thinking for several reasons:

1. **Promotes Testability:** A falsifiable claim invites investigation and empirical testing, driving the search for evidence.
2. **Encourages Intellectual Honesty:** If a claim can't be disproven, it's likely based on belief rather than evidence.
3. **Filters Out Pseudoscience:** Many pseudoscientific claims (e.g. astrology) rely on vagueness and cannot be rigorously tested.

By embracing falsifiability, you commit to reason and evidence, avoiding the traps of speculation and confirmation bias.

Examples of Falsifiable vs. Unfalsifiable Claims

1. **Falsifiable Claims:**
   - "All swans are white." (Disproven by observing a single non-white swan.)
   - "A new medication reduces blood pressure by 10%." (Testable through clinical trials.)

2. **Unfalsifiable Claims:**
   - "The universe was designed by an invisible higher intelligence."
   - "My success is the result of good karma from past lives."

Falsifiable claims are useful because they advance knowledge, while unfalsifiable claims often remain stagnant or dogmatic.

Applying Falsifiability to Everyday Life

1. **In Personal Decisions:**
   When faced with major life decisions, falsifiability can help evaluate options. Consider the claim: "If I switch careers, I'll be happier." How would you test or disprove this hypothesis? Tracking your satisfaction over time after the switch could provide valuable insight.

2. **In Evaluating Information:**
   News articles, advertisements, and social media posts often make claims. Use falsifiability to assess their credibility. For example:
   - Claim: "This product guarantees you'll lose weight in a week."
   - Question: Is there evidence that could prove this wrong? Are the claims backed by testable studies?

3. **In Interpersonal Conflicts:**
   During disagreements, people often make unfalsifiable statements like, "You never listen to me." Reframing these as falsifiable ("You didn't listen to me in this situation") allows for a constructive conversation based on specific evidence.

Challenges in Applying Falsifiability

1. **Ambiguity in Claims:** Some statements are poorly phrased, making it hard to determine their falsifiability. For instance, "This therapy works for most people" is vague unless "most" is clearly defined.
2. **Evolving Knowledge:** A claim that is falsified today might be revised tomorrow based on new evidence or better testing methods. Science evolves, and so do its conclusions.
3. **Emotional Resistance:** People often cling to unfalsifiable beliefs because they provide comfort or align with their worldview. Challenging such beliefs requires empathy and patience.

Falsifiability and Cognitive Biases

Falsifiability is a powerful tool against confirmation bias — the tendency to seek information that supports pre-existing beliefs while ignoring contradictory evidence. By deliberately seeking to falsify your own ideas, you can overcome this bias and make more balanced judgments.

For example, if you believe a specific diet works for weight loss, don't just look for success stories. Seek evidence of when and why the diet fails. This approach helps refine your understanding and prevents you from falling into the trap of selective reasoning.

1. **Identify Falsifiability:**
   Write down three claims you've encountered recently (e.g. in news articles, advertisements, or personal discussions). Determine whether each claim is falsifiable or unfalsifiable and explain why.

2. **Challenge Your Beliefs:**
   Take a belief or assumption you hold. How could it be tested or disproven? For example, if you believe you're bad at math, track your performance on math-related tasks to gather objective evidence.

3. **Evaluate an Argument:**
   Find a controversial statement in a public debate. Is it falsifiable? If not, how could it be rephrased to make it testable?

4. **Apply to a Real-World Problem:**
   Think of a problem you're currently facing. Write down potential solutions and identify which are falsifiable. How could you test their effectiveness?

Closing Thoughts

Falsifiability isn't just a principle of science, it's a mindset for critical thinking and decision-making. By focusing on claims that can be tested and proven wrong, you cultivate intellectual discipline and clarity. While it's tempting to cling to comforting but unfalsifiable beliefs, real growth comes from challenging your assumptions and seeking evidence.

Whether you're evaluating a theory, resolving a conflict, or making a decision, asking, "How could this be disproven?" is a powerful step toward truth.

Chapter 4: Syllogisms

The Power of Structured Reasoning: Syllogisms

In a world filled with information, the ability to construct clear, logical arguments is essential. Syllogisms are one of the oldest and most effective tools for organizing thought and ensuring your reasoning is valid. Originating from the works of Aristotle, syllogisms are deductive arguments composed of three parts: two premises and a conclusion.

For example:

- **Premise 1:** All humans are mortal.
- **Premise 2:** Socrates was human.
- **Conclusion:** Therefore, Socrates was mortal.

This is a classic syllogism. If both premises are true and the reasoning is sound, the conclusion must also be true. This makes syllogisms a powerful tool for logical reasoning, debate, and problem-solving.

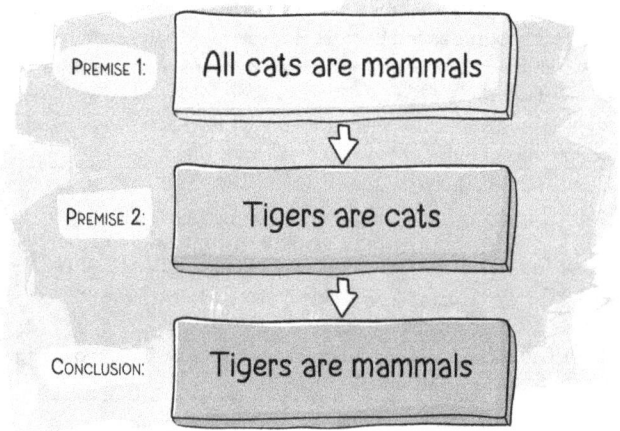

How Syllogisms Work

A syllogism has three essential components:

1. **Major Premise:** The broader statement or rule.
   Example: All birds have wings.
2. **Minor Premise:** A specific instance related to the major premise.
   Example: A robin is a bird.
3. **Conclusion:** The logical result of combining the two premises.
   Example: Therefore, a robin has wings.

The strength of a syllogism depends on the validity of its structure and the truth of its premises. If either premise is false or the reasoning is flawed, the conclusion will be invalid.

Types of Syllogisms

1. **Categorical Syllogisms:**
   These deal with categories or groups.
   Example:
   - Premise 1: All cats are mammals.
   - Premise 2: A tiger is a cat.
   - Conclusion: Therefore, a tiger is a mammal.

2. **Hypothetical Syllogisms:**
   These use "if-then" statements.
   Example:
   - Premise 1: If it rains, the ground will be wet.
   - Premise 2: It is raining.
   - Conclusion: Therefore, the ground is wet.

3. **Disjunctive Syllogisms:**
   These involve either-or scenarios.
   Example:
   - o Premise 1: Either you will study or fail the exam.
   - o Premise 2: You did not study.
   - o Conclusion: Therefore, you will fail the exam.

Practical Applications of Syllogisms

1. **Decision-Making:**
   Use syllogisms to clarify your options and their consequences. For example:
   - o Premise 1: If I exercise regularly, my health will improve.
   - o Premise 2: I want to improve my health.
   - o Conclusion: Therefore, I should exercise regularly.

2. **Problem-Solving:**
   Break complex problems into logical steps. For instance:
   - o Premise 1: If a device is unplugged, it won't turn on.
   - o Premise 2: The device is unplugged.
   - o Conclusion: Therefore, the device won't turn on.

3. **Debate and Persuasion:**
   Structure your arguments to be clear and logically sound. For example:
   - o Premise 1: Effective leaders are good communicators.
   - o Premise 2: Jane is a good communicator.
   - o Conclusion: Therefore, Jane is an effective leader.

Common Pitfalls in Syllogistic Reasoning

Even a well-structured syllogism can go astray if the premises are flawed or the reasoning is invalid. Consider these examples:

1. **Faulty Premises:**
   - o Premise 1: All dogs are reptiles.
   - o Premise 2: Rex is a dog.
   - o Conclusion: Therefore, Rex is a reptile.

   While the structure is valid, the conclusion is false because the first premise is incorrect.

2. **Overgeneralization:**
   - o Premise 1: All teenagers are irresponsible.
   - o Premise 2: Sarah is a teenager.
   - o Conclusion: Therefore, Sarah is irresponsible.

   This conclusion is flawed because the major premise unfairly generalizes all teenagers.

3. **Ambiguity:**
   Ambiguous terms can lead to misunderstandings. For instance:
   - o Premise 1: All light things are easy to carry.
   - o Premise 2: Feathers are light.
   - o Conclusion: Therefore, feathers are easy to carry.

   The term "light" is ambiguous, as it could refer to weight or brightness.

Exercises

1. **Create Your Own Syllogisms:**
   Write three syllogisms based on everyday scenarios. Ensure your premises are valid and your reasoning is sound.

2. **Evaluate Logical Soundness:**
   Analyze the following syllogism:
   - o Premise 1: All birds can fly.
   - o Premise 2: Penguins are birds.
   - o Conclusion: Therefore, penguins can fly.

   Identify the error and explain why the conclusion is invalid.

3. **Apply to Decision-Making:**
   Think of a decision you need to make. Write it out as a syllogism and evaluate whether the conclusion logically follows from the premises.

4. **Spot Logical Fallacies:**
   Find examples of flawed syllogisms in advertisements or arguments online. Identify the errors and rewrite them to be logically valid.

Syllogisms are more than just academic tools. They're the foundation of clear and logical thinking. By learning to construct and evaluate syllogisms, you gain the ability to analyze arguments critically, make better decisions, and communicate effectively.

Mastering syllogisms helps you stand out as a clear, rational thinker. Whether you're debating an issue, solving a problem, or simply organizing your thoughts, this timeless tool is your key to precision and clarity.

Chapter 5: Deductive Reasoning

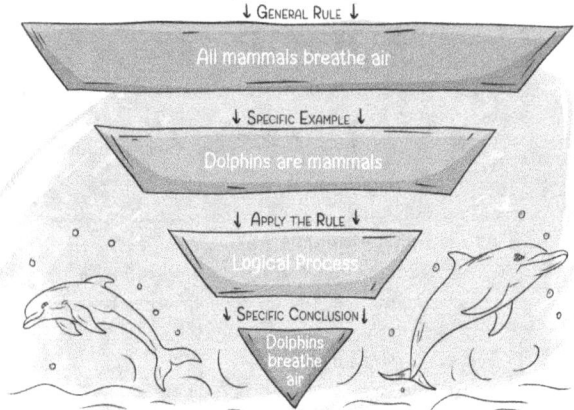

From General Truths to Specific Conclusions: Deductive Reasoning

Deductive reasoning is the gold standard of logic, providing conclusions that are guaranteed to be true if the premises are valid. This method of reasoning starts with general principles or rules and applies them to specific cases. It's the bedrock of clear thinking, widely used in mathematics, science, and everyday problem-solving.

For example:

- **Premise 1:** All mammals breathe air.
- **Premise 2:** Dolphins are mammals.
- **Conclusion:** Therefore, dolphins breathe air.

The reasoning is airtight: if the premises are true, the conclusion must also be true. Deductive reasoning doesn't leave room for uncertainty, making it a powerful tool for navigating a complex world.

How Deductive Reasoning Works

Deductive reasoning is often structured as a syllogism (introduced in Chapter 4), but it extends to broader applications. The process involves:

1. **Starting with a General Principle:** This could be a law, theory, or rule that is widely accepted.
2. **Applying it to a Specific Case:** Connect the principle to a particular scenario.
3. **Drawing a Logical Conclusion:** Ensure the conclusion directly follows from the premises.
   For example:
   - **Premise 1:** If a car runs out of fuel, it will stop.
   - **Premise 2:** My car has run out of fuel.
   - **Conclusion:** Therefore, my car has stopped.

Applications of Deductive Reasoning

1. **Problem-Solving:**
   Deductive reasoning helps break down complex problems into manageable steps.
   Example:
   - Premise 1: If I don't submit my report, I won't meet my deadline.
   - Premise 2: I didn't submit my report.
   - Conclusion: I didn't meet my deadline.
   This reasoning highlights the root of the problem, guiding you toward a solution.
2. **Decision-Making:**
   Deductive reasoning clarifies options and outcomes.
   Example:
   - Premise 1: If I save money, I can afford a vacation.
   - Premise 2: I have been saving money.
   - Conclusion: I can afford a vacation.
3. **Persuasion:**
   In arguments or debates, deductive reasoning strengthens your case by showing that your conclusion follows logically from widely accepted premises.

Strengths and Limitations of Deductive Reasoning

Strengths:

- Certainty: If premises are true, the conclusion is guaranteed.
- Clarity: Deductive reasoning eliminates ambiguity.
- Universality: It applies across disciplines, from science to everyday decisions.

Limitations:
- Dependency on Premises: If a premise is false, the conclusion will also be false.
  Example:
  - Premise 1: All dogs can fly.
  - Premise 2: Rex is a dog.
  - Conclusion: Rex can fly.
- Inflexibility: Deductive reasoning doesn't accommodate uncertainty or incomplete information.

Common Pitfalls in Deductive Reasoning

Even when the structure of reasoning is valid, errors can arise:

1. **Invalid Premises:**
   - Premise 1: All teenagers love video games.
   - Premise 2: Sarah is a teenager.
   - Conclusion: Sarah loves video games.

   This reasoning fails because the first premise is an overgeneralization.

2. **Assumptions:**

Hidden assumptions can undermine deductive reasoning.
Example:
   - Premise 1: Only expensive items are valuable.
   - Premise 2: This item is valuable.
   - Conclusion: This item is expensive.

The argument assumes that all value must stem from expense, which is not necessarily true.

Exercises

1. **Construct a Deductive Argument:**
   Write a deductive argument based on something from your life (e.g., a goal or a problem). Ensure your premises are valid and the conclusion follows logically.
2. **Analyze a Premise:**
   Take an argument you've encountered recently. Identify its premises and evaluate whether they're true or reasonable.
3. **Spot Hidden Assumptions:**
   Find an example of deductive reasoning in a public debate or advertisement. Identify any hidden assumptions that could weaken the argument.
4. **Apply to Problem-Solving:**
   Think of a current challenge you're facing. Use deductive reasoning to break it down into logical steps and identify a solution.

Closing Thoughts

Deductive reasoning is a crucial skill for clear thinking and decision-making. By starting with general truths and applying them to specific cases, you can draw conclusions with confidence and precision.

However, it requires discipline — ensuring your premises are valid, avoiding assumptions, and being mindful of limitations. With practice, you can use this tool to navigate complex situations, build stronger arguments, and approach challenges with logic and clarity.

Chapter 6: Inductive Reasoning

From Observations to Generalizations: Inductive Reasoning

Inductive reasoning is the opposite of deductive reasoning. It moves from specific observations to broader generalizations. While it doesn't guarantee certainty like deductive reasoning, it provides plausible conclusions based on evidence and patterns.

For example:
- Observation 1: Every swan I've seen is white.
- Observation 2: My neighbor's swan is white.
- Conclusion: All swans are white.

Although this conclusion may seem logical based on the observations, it is not certain. Inductive reasoning acknowledges that new evidence can overturn previous conclusions (e.g. the discovery of black swans). This flexible, evidence-based approach makes inductive reasoning particularly valuable in science, research, and everyday decision-making.

OBSERVATIONS LEAD TO GENERAL CONCLUSIONS

How Inductive Reasoning Works

Inductive reasoning involves three key steps:

1. **Observation:** Collect data or evidence.
   Example: "I notice that my houseplants grow better when they're in direct sunlight."
2. **Pattern Recognition:** Identify recurring themes or trends.
   Example: "Plants in direct sunlight consistently grow faster than those in shade."
3. **Conclusion:** Form a generalization or hypothesis.
   Example: "Plants grow better in direct sunlight."

Applications of Inductive Reasoning

1. **Science and Research:**
   Scientists rely heavily on inductive reasoning to form hypotheses and theories. For example:
   - Observation: Many chemical reactions produce heat.
   - Conclusion: Exothermic reactions are common in nature.
2. **Everyday Problem-Solving:**
   Inductive reasoning helps us make predictions based on past experiences.
   - Observation: Traffic is always heavy at 5 PM.
   - Conclusion: I should avoid driving at 5 PM to save time.
3. **Business and Marketing:**
   Marketers use inductive reasoning to predict consumer behavior.
   - Observation: Customers who purchase Product A often buy Product B.
   - Conclusion: Bundling Product A and B may increase sales.

Strengths and Weaknesses of Inductive Reasoning

Strengths:

- **Adaptability:** Allows for flexible thinking and updating conclusions based on new evidence.
- **Practicality:** Helps navigate uncertainty in everyday life.
- **Discovery:** Encourages pattern recognition and innovation.

Weaknesses:

- **Uncertainty:** Inductive reasoning cannot guarantee the truth of its conclusions.
- **Overgeneralization:** Conclusions based on limited evidence may lead to incorrect assumptions.

Common Errors in Inductive Reasoning

1. **Hasty Generalizations:**
   Drawing broad conclusions from insufficient evidence.
   Example: "I met two rude people from City X. Therefore, everyone from City X is rude."
2. **Ignoring Exceptions:**
   Overlooking outliers that challenge the generalization.
   Example: "All my friends enjoy watching movies. Therefore, everyone enjoys movies."
3. **Confirmation Bias:**
   Focusing only on observations that support the conclusion while ignoring contradictory evidence.

Exercises

1. **Form a Hypothesis:**
   Observe something in your daily life and identify a pattern. Write a conclusion based on your observations.
2. **Challenge a Generalization:**
   Think of a generalization you believe in (e.g. "People are always on their phones"). Seek out evidence that contradicts or refines this belief.
3. **Analyze Marketing Claims:**
   Find a commercial or advertisement that makes a claim based on inductive reasoning (e.g. "9 out of 10 dentists recommend this product"). Evaluate whether the claim is supported by sufficient evidence.
4. **Apply to Decision-Making:**
   Use inductive reasoning to predict an outcome in your life (e.g. when to leave for work to avoid traffic). Reflect on whether the conclusion was accurate.

Closing Thoughts

Inductive reasoning is a powerful tool for navigating uncertainty and making predictions based on evidence. While it lacks the certainty of deductive reasoning, its adaptability and practical nature make it invaluable in everyday life.

Mastering inductive reasoning helps you identify patterns, form reasonable conclusions, and remain open to new evidence. In an ever-changing world, this approach ensures you stay flexible and grounded in reality.

Chapter 7: Abductive Reasoning

Abductive reasoning is about forming the best explanation for a set of observations, even when the evidence is incomplete. It's often described as "inference to the best explanation." Unlike deductive reasoning, which seeks certainty, or inductive reasoning, which seeks probability, abductive reasoning focuses on plausibility.

For example:
- Observation: The ground is wet.
- Possible explanations: It rained, a sprinkler was on, or someone spilled water.
- Best explanation: It rained.

How Abductive Reasoning Works

1. **Gather Evidence:** Start with observations or facts.
2. **List Possible Explanations:** Brainstorm all potential causes.
3. **Choose the Most Likely Explanation:** Select the explanation that best fits the evidence.

Applications of Abductive Reasoning

1. **Medical Diagnosis:**
   Doctors often use abductive reasoning to identify the most likely cause of symptoms.
   - Observation: A patient has a fever and a rash.
   - Possible explanations: An allergic reaction, a viral infection, or a bacterial infection.
   - Best explanation: A viral infection (based on prevalence and other symptoms).
2. **Detective Work:**
   Detectives use abductive reasoning to solve crimes.
   - Observation: A window is broken, and valuables are missing.
   - Best explanation: A burglary occurred.
3. **Everyday Life:**
   We use abductive reasoning to make quick decisions with limited information.
   - Observation: The room feels cold.
   - Best explanation: The heater is off.

Strengths and Limitations of Abductive Reasoning

Strengths:
- **Practicality:** Offers quick, plausible explanations for incomplete information.
- **Versatility:** Applies to diverse fields, from science to everyday decision-making.

Limitations:
- **Uncertainty:** The most plausible explanation isn't always correct.
- **Bias:** Personal beliefs or preferences can skew the selection of explanations.

Exercises

1. **Solve a Mystery:**
   Imagine a scenario with incomplete evidence (e.g., your keys are missing). List possible explanations and identify the most plausible one.
2. **Evaluate Medical Diagnoses:**
   Research a common symptom and the range of potential causes. Use abductive reasoning to identify the most likely explanation.
3. **Apply to Daily Observations:**
   Observe something unusual in your environment (e.g., a spilled drink). Use abductive reasoning to determine the most likely cause.

Closing Thoughts

Abductive reasoning is a tool for making educated guesses when certainty isn't possible. By focusing on plausibility, it helps you navigate uncertainty and make informed decisions.

Though it requires careful judgment and critical thinking, abductive reasoning is invaluable in solving problems quickly and effectively. Whether diagnosing a problem, solving a mystery, or making a decision, this method empowers you to make sense of the unknown.

Chapter 8: Modus Ponens

Modus Ponens, often called "affirming the antecedent," is one of the simplest and most powerful tools in logical reasoning. It provides a reliable structure for drawing conclusions based on conditional statements — statements in the form of "If P, then Q."

For example:

- Premise 1: If it rains, the ground will be wet.
- Premise 2: It is raining.
- Conclusion: Therefore, the ground is wet.

In this structure, P (the antecedent) is affirmed as true, which logically leads to the truth of Q (the consequent). Modus Ponens is widely used in mathematics, science, and everyday reasoning to establish cause-and-effect relationships.

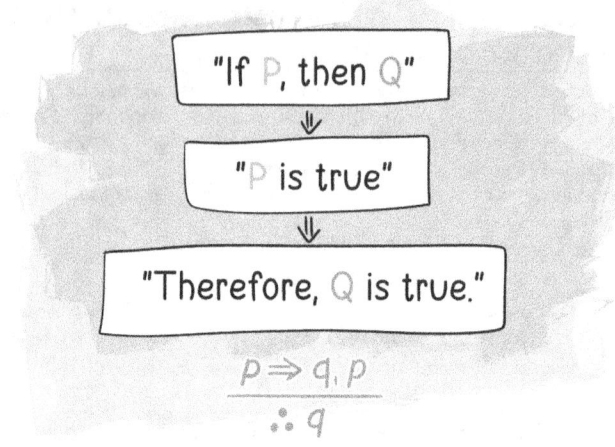

How Modus Ponens Works

The logic of Modus Ponens is straightforward:

1. **Conditional Statement (If P, then Q):** Establishes a relationship between two events or conditions.
2. **Affirmation of P:** Confirms that the antecedent is true.
3. **Logical Conclusion (Q is true):** Draws a conclusion based on the truth of the antecedent.

This reasoning works because it relies on a valid conditional relationship. If the relationship between P and Q is well-defined, and P is true, Q must logically follow.

Examples of Modus Ponens

1. **In Science:**
   - Premise 1: If a substance contains acid, it will turn litmus paper red.
   - Premise 2: This substance contains acid.
   - Conclusion: The litmus paper will turn red.

2. **In Everyday Life:**
   - Premise 1: If I study hard, I will pass the exam.
   - Premise 2: I studied hard.
   - Conclusion: I will pass the exam.

3. **In Problem-Solving:**
   - Premise 1: If the device is unplugged, it won't turn on.
   - Premise 2: The device is unplugged.
   - Conclusion: The device won't turn on.

Applications of Modus Ponens

1. **Decision-Making:**
   Use Modus Ponens to evaluate cause-and-effect relationships in decisions.

   Example:
   - Premise 1: If I exercise regularly, I will improve my health.
   - Premise 2: I exercise regularly.
   - Conclusion: My health will improve.

2. **Problem-Solving:**
   Apply Modus Ponens to troubleshoot issues systematically.
   Example:
   - Premise 1: If the Wi-Fi router is off, there will be no Internet connection.
   - Premise 2: The Wi-Fi router is off.
   - Conclusion: There is no Internet connection.

3. **Persuasion:**
   Use Modus Ponens to strengthen arguments by showing clear, logical connections.
   Example:
   - Premise 1: If a candidate has strong leadership skills, they will perform well as a manager.
   - Premise 2: Candidate X has strong leadership skills.
   - Conclusion: Candidate X will perform well as a manager.

Strengths and Pitfalls of Modus Ponens

Strengths:

- **Certainty:** If the premises are true, the conclusion is guaranteed to be true.
- **Clarity:** Provides a clear and structured method for reasoning.
- **Universality:** Applies to any situation involving conditional relationships.

Pitfalls:

- **False Premises:** If the premises are false, the conclusion will also be false.

Example:
- o Premise 1: If pigs can fly, then humans can breathe underwater.
- o Premise 2: Pigs can fly.
- o Conclusion: Humans can breathe underwater.

While the reasoning is valid, the premises are not.

- **Assumed Relationships:** Misinterpreting the connection between P and Q can lead to invalid conclusions.

Exercises

1. **Construct a Modus Ponens Argument:**
   Write a Modus Ponens argument based on a real-life situation. Ensure your premises are valid and your conclusion follows logically.

2. **Spot Errors in Logic:**
   Find an example of reasoning in advertisements or debates that claims to use Modus Ponens. Identify any flaws in the premises or conclusions.

3. **Apply to Decision-Making:**
   Think of a decision you need to make. Frame it as a conditional statement and use Modus Ponens to evaluate the outcome.

4. **Rewrite Faulty Logic:**
   Take an example of invalid reasoning and reframe it as a valid Modus Ponens argument.

Closing Thoughts

Modus Ponens is a cornerstone of logical reasoning, offering a straightforward way to establish cause-and-effect relationships. By mastering this method, you can approach problems and decisions with confidence, clarity, and precision.

With practice, Modus Ponens will become an invaluable part of your logical toolkit, helping you navigate everything from everyday challenges to complex arguments.

Chapter 9: Modus Tollens

Denying the Consequent: Modus Tollens

Modus Tollens, also known as "denying the consequent," is a logical reasoning method that complements Modus Ponens. It works by starting with a conditional statement and disproving the consequent (Q), which logically disproves the antecedent (P).

For example:
- Premise 1: If it rains, the ground will be wet.
- Premise 2: The ground is not wet.
- Conclusion: Therefore, it did not rain.

This form of reasoning is essential for disproving claims, troubleshooting problems, and refining arguments. It's widely used in science, law, and everyday scenarios where disproving an effect can help identify its cause.

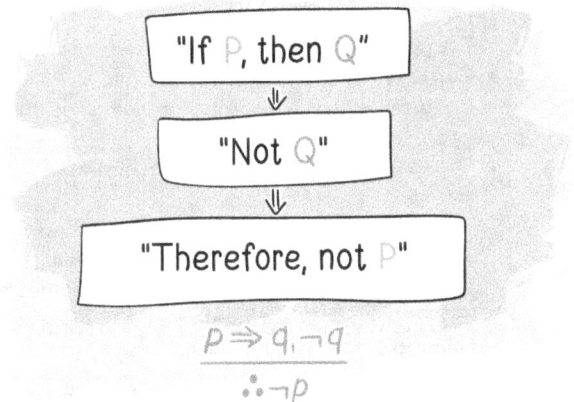

How Modus Tollens Works

The structure of Modus Tollens is as follows:

1. **Conditional Statement (If P, then Q):** Establishes a relationship between two events or conditions.
2. **Negation of Q (Not Q):** Disproves the consequent.
3. **Logical Conclusion (Not P):** Concludes that the antecedent must also be false.

This reasoning is powerful because it provides a way to eliminate possibilities, narrowing down what can and cannot be true.

Examples of Modus Tollens

1. **In Science:**
   - o Premise 1: If a plant lacks sunlight, it will not grow.
   - o Premise 2: The plant is growing.
   - o Conclusion: Therefore, the plant is not lacking sunlight.

2. **In Everyday Life:**
   - o Premise 1: If the restaurant is open, the lights will be on.
   - o Premise 2: The lights are not on.
   - o Conclusion: Therefore, the restaurant is not open.

3. **In Troubleshooting:**
   o Premise 1: If the device is broken, it will not turn on.
   o Premise 2: The device turns on.
   o Conclusion: Therefore, the device is not broken.

Applications of Modus Tollens

1. **Debunking Claims:**
   Modus Tollens is an effective tool for disproving false or exaggerated claims.
   Example:
   o Premise 1: If this supplement works, I will lose weight.
   o Premise 2: I did not lose weight.
   o Conclusion: Therefore, the supplement does not work.

2. **Problem-Solving:**
   Use Modus Tollens to identify and eliminate incorrect assumptions.
   Example:
   o Premise 1: If the internet is down, I cannot load websites.
   o Premise 2: I can load websites.
   o Conclusion: The internet is not down.

3. **Evaluating Hypotheses:**
   Scientists and researchers use Modus Tollens to test hypotheses by disproving predictions.
   Example:
   o Premise 1: If the theory is correct, Experiment X will yield Result Y.
   o Premise 2: Experiment X did not yield Result Y.
   o Conclusion: The theory is not correct.

Strengths and Weaknesses of Modus Tollens

Strengths:
- **Clarity:** Provides a structured way to eliminate false assumptions.
- **Certainty:** If the premises are valid, the conclusion is guaranteed to be true.
- **Universality:** Can be applied to a wide range of scenarios.

Weaknesses:
- **Dependency on Premises:** If the premises are flawed, the conclusion will also be flawed.
  Example:
  o Premise 1: If aliens exist, we would have seen evidence by now.
  o Premise 2: We have not seen evidence.
  o Conclusion: Therefore, aliens do not exist.
  This reasoning depends heavily on the first premise, which may not be accurate.
- **Neglecting Alternative Explanations:** Focusing solely on disproving one possibility can overlook other factors.

Exercises

1. **Construct a Modus Tollens Argument:**
   Write a Modus Tollens argument based on a real-life situation. Ensure your premises are valid and your conclusion follows logically.

2. **Evaluate a Claim:**
   Identify a claim you've encountered recently. Use Modus Tollens to test whether it holds up under scrutiny.

3. **Apply to Problem-Solving:**
   Think of a problem you're facing and list potential causes. Use Modus Tollens to eliminate incorrect assumptions systematically.

4. **Rewrite Invalid Arguments:**
   Take an example of faulty reasoning and reframe it as a valid Modus Tollens argument.

Closing Thoughts

Modus Tollens is a logical powerhouse, providing a reliable framework for disproving false claims and eliminating incorrect assumptions. By practicing this method, you can enhance your ability to evaluate information critically, solve problems efficiently, and construct airtight arguments.

Chapter 10: Reductio ad Absurdum

Reductio ad Absurdum, Latin for "reduction to absurdity," is a powerful method of argumentation that disproves a claim by showing that it leads to an absurd or contradictory conclusion. This technique forces ideas to their logical extremes, exposing flaws and inconsistencies.

For example:

- Claim: "Everyone should follow every rule, no matter what."
- Reductio Argument: "If this were true, people should follow a rule even if it requires them to harm themselves or others. This is absurd."

This method is a favorite in philosophy, mathematics, and debates, providing a clear way to challenge flawed arguments.

How Reductio ad Absurdum Works

1. **Assume the Claim is True:** Start by temporarily accepting the claim or premise.
2. **Follow the Logic to Its Conclusion:** Trace the implications of the claim to their extreme.
3. **Identify Contradictions or Absurdities:** Demonstrate that the claim leads to an illogical or untenable result.

Examples of Reductio ad Absurdum

1. **In Philosophy:**
   - Claim: "Nothing can be known for certain."
   - Reductio Argument: "If this were true, then the statement itself couldn't be known for certain, which is self-contradictory."
2. **In Everyday Life:**
   - Claim: "We should never question authority."
   - Reductio Argument: "If this were true, then no one should question a corrupt or harmful leader, which is absurd."
3. **In Debates:**
   - Claim: "Everyone must always agree."
   - Reductio Argument: "If this were true, then progress and innovation would halt, as disagreement drives new ideas."

Applications of Reductio ad Absurdum

1. **Debunking Fallacies:**
   Use this method to expose the flaws in illogical arguments.
2. **Testing Ideas:**
   Push your own ideas to their limits to identify weaknesses or areas for improvement.
3. **Philosophical Inquiry:**
   Explore abstract concepts by challenging their boundaries and implications.

Strengths and Limitations

Strengths:

- **Clarity:** Simplifies complex ideas by exposing contradictions.
- **Effectiveness:** A compelling way to challenge flawed arguments.

Limitations:

- **Misuse:** Overextending the logic of a claim can lead to unfair conclusions.
- **Context-Dependence:** Not all arguments are suited to this method.

Exercises

1. **Challenge a Claim:**
   Identify a common belief and use Reductio ad Absurdum to test its limits.
2. **Debate an Idea:**
   Practice this method in a discussion by challenging an opponent's argument with extreme implications.
3. **Analyze Public Arguments:**
   Find an example of a claim in the media or online. Use Reductio ad Absurdum to evaluate its logic.
4. **Test Your Own Ideas:**
   Take one of your own beliefs and push it to its logical extreme. Reflect on whether it holds up.

Reductio ad Absurdum is a sharp tool for dismantling flawed arguments and testing ideas. By exposing contradictions and absurdities, it forces us to think more deeply and refine our reasoning.

When used thoughtfully, this method ensures that our ideas are robust and our conclusions logical. Whether debating a friend, evaluating a claim, or exploring philosophical questions, Reductio ad Absurdum is an essential weapon in your logical arsenal.

Subsection: Recognizing and Avoiding Fallacies

Logical fallacies are errors in reasoning that weaken arguments and lead to incorrect conclusions. They're traps that even the most careful thinkers can fall into, whether in debates, decision-making, or everyday discussions. This section focuses on ten common fallacies, teaching you how to identify, avoid, and counteract them. By mastering these concepts, you'll sharpen your critical thinking skills and learn to construct more robust arguments while spotting weaknesses in others' reasoning.

Chapter 11: Spotting Strawman Arguments

Misrepresenting the Argument: The Strawman Fallacy

The Strawman Fallacy occurs when someone misrepresents or distorts an opponent's argument, creating an exaggerated or weaker version that is easier to attack. Instead of engaging with the real issue, they refute this "strawman," leading to unproductive debates and misunderstandings. This fallacy is common in political debates, media discussions, and even everyday conversations, where the goal often shifts from seeking truth to winning an argument.

For example:

- **Original Argument:** "We should increase funding for public schools to improve education quality."
- **Strawman Argument:** "My opponent wants to throw money at schools without addressing any accountability or measurable outcomes!"

Here, the original argument is twisted into a more extreme position that misrepresents the intent. This tactic distracts from meaningful dialogue and weakens the overall quality of reasoning in the discussion.

How the Strawman Fallacy Works

The Strawman Fallacy typically follows this structure:

1. **Misrepresent the Argument:** The opponent's position is twisted into a distorted, weaker version.
2. **Attack the Strawman:** The focus shifts to refuting the misrepresentation rather than the actual argument.
3. **Claim Victory:** By defeating the strawman, the individual claims to have disproven the original argument, even though it wasn't directly addressed.

This tactic is particularly harmful because it derails the conversation, undermines trust, and prevents meaningful exploration of ideas.

Examples of the Strawman Fallacy

1. **In Political Debates:**
    o **Original Argument:** "We should increase regulations to protect the environment."
    o **Strawman Argument:** "My opponent wants to destroy jobs and shut down entire industries in the name of the environment!"
2. **In Personal Discussions:**
    o **Original Argument:** "I think we should spend less on eating out to save for a vacation."
    o **Strawman Argument:** "So you think we should never go out and enjoy ourselves?"
3. **In Workplace Conversations:**
    o **Original Argument:** "We should invest in new software to improve efficiency."
    o **Strawman Argument:** "So you think we should just waste money on unproven technology and ignore everything that's already working?"

These examples highlight how easily the Strawman Fallacy can creep into discussions, turning potentially productive conversations into adversarial exchanges.

Why the Strawman Fallacy is Harmful

The Strawman Fallacy doesn't just weaken individual arguments — it damages the overall quality of discourse:

1. **Distracts from the Core Issue:**
    Instead of addressing the actual argument, the conversation veers off into irrelevant territory, wasting time and energy.

2. **Encourages Hostility:**
Misrepresenting someone's argument often feels like a personal attack, escalating tension and preventing collaboration.

3. **Erodes Trust:**
When one party misrepresents the other's position, it undermines credibility and mutual respect, making it harder to engage in future discussions.

4. **Stalls Progress:**
By focusing on distorted arguments, the discussion moves away from problem-solving and deeper understanding.

How to Spot the Strawman Fallacy

Recognizing a Strawman Fallacy requires careful attention to the flow of arguments:

1. **Compare Arguments:** Check whether the response addresses the original claim or a distorted version.
2. **Look for Exaggeration:** Identify if the response amplifies or twists the original argument into something more extreme.
3. **Watch for Shifts in Focus:** Notice if the discussion shifts away from the original issue to a tangential or unrelated point.

For example:

- **Original Argument:** "We should consider universal healthcare to improve access to medical services."
- **Response:** "My opponent wants the government to control every aspect of our lives!"

Here, the focus shifts from healthcare access to a broad and unrelated claim about government control.

How to Avoid Using the Strawman Fallacy

1. **Listen Actively:**
Pay close attention to the other person's argument without jumping to conclusions or assumptions.

2. **Restate the Argument:**
Summarize the argument in your own words and confirm with the speaker that you've understood it correctly.
Example: "So, you're saying that investing in renewable energy is a practical way to address climate change?"

3. **Engage with the Core Argument:**
Focus your response on the actual points raised, rather than creating a hypothetical or exaggerated version.

4. **Be Mindful of Bias:**
Avoid letting your own opinions or biases distort your understanding of the other person's position.

Strategies for Responding to a Strawman Fallacy

1. **Clarify Your Position:**
Politely point out the misrepresentation and restate your original argument.
Example: "I think there's been a misunderstanding. What I'm saying is that we need to balance environmental protection with economic growth, not shut down industries entirely."

2. **Shift Back to the Core Issue:**
Redirect the conversation to focus on the actual argument.
Example: "Let's go back to the main point about improving public education."

3. **Ask Questions:**
Use questions to encourage the other person to engage with your real argument.
Example: "Can you explain how my position leads to the conclusion you've drawn?"

Exercises

1. **Identify a Strawman:**
Find an example of a Strawman Fallacy in a public debate or online discussion. Analyze how the argument was misrepresented and suggest ways the conversation could have been refocused on the real issue.

2. **Reframe a Misrepresentation:**
Think of a time your argument was misunderstood or distorted. Rewrite the situation, focusing on how you could clarify your position to avoid the Strawman Fallacy.

3. **Role-Play a Debate:**
With a partner, practice engaging in a debate where one person intentionally uses the Strawman Fallacy. The other person must recognize and address it. Reflect on the exercise and discuss how it influenced the conversation.

4. **Write a Strong Argument:**
Take a controversial topic and craft an argument that avoids exaggeration or distortion. Share it with someone else to see if they can misinterpret your position.

Closing Thoughts

The Strawman Fallacy is one of the most common errors in reasoning, but also one of the most avoidable. By learning to recognize and counteract this fallacy, you can elevate the quality of your arguments and contribute to more meaningful, productive conversations.

When you focus on engaging with the real issue rather than a distorted version, you foster mutual respect, build trust, and encourage deeper understanding.

Chapter 12: Recognizing Ad Hominem Attacks

When the Focus Shifts to the Person: Ad Hominem Attacks

The **Ad Hominem Fallacy**, Latin for "to the person," occurs when someone attacks the character, motive, or other personal attributes of their opponent instead of addressing the substance of their argument. This tactic distracts from the issue at hand and shifts the focus to irrelevant personal factors, undermining constructive discussion.

For example:

- **Argument:** "We need to consider raising taxes to fund public healthcare."

- **Ad Hominem Response:** "Of course you'd support that — you're a privileged elite who doesn't understand the struggles of ordinary people!"

Here, the response targets the person making the argument rather than engaging with the argument itself. This fallacy is common in emotionally charged debates, where attacking the individual can seem easier than addressing their reasoning.

How the Ad Hominem Fallacy Works

Ad Hominem attacks typically follow this structure:

1. **An Argument is Presented:** The opponent states their position or reasoning.
2. **A Personal Attack is Made:** Instead of responding to the argument, the focus shifts to attacking the individual.
3. **The Argument is Dismissed:** The personal attack is used as a justification to ignore or reject the argument, regardless of its validity.

Types of Ad Hominem Attacks

1. **Abusive Ad Hominem:**
   Directly insults or criticizes the person making the argument.
   Example: "You're too ignorant to understand this topic."

2. **Circumstantial Ad Hominem:**
   Suggests that the person's circumstances, affiliations, or motives invalidate their argument.
   Example: "Of course you'd say that — you're a politician trying to get votes."

3. **Tu Quoque (You Too) Ad Hominem:**
   Accuses the opponent of hypocrisy to dismiss their argument.
   Example: "You can't criticize smoking — you used to smoke yourself!"

4. **Guilt by Association:**
   Attempts to discredit an argument by associating the person with a disliked group or idea.
   Example: "Your argument sounds like something a radical extremist would say."

Examples of Ad Hominem Fallacies

1. **In Political Debates:**
   - Argument: "We should consider stricter environmental regulations."
   - Ad Hominem Response: "You're just another tree-hugger who wants to ruin the economy!"

2. **In Personal Conversations:**
   - Argument: "I think we should stick to the budget this month."
   - Ad Hominem Response: "You're always so cheap — it's no surprise you'd say that."

3. **In Workplace Discussions:**
   - Argument: "We need to rethink our marketing strategy to improve sales."
   - Ad Hominem Response: "What do you know about marketing? You've only been here for six months."

Why Ad Hominem Attacks Are Harmful

Ad Hominem attacks derail productive discussions and damage relationships:

1. **They Distract from the Argument:** Personal attacks shift focus away from the issue being discussed.
2. **They Encourage Hostility:** Attacking someone personally escalates tension and discourages constructive dialogue.
3. **They Undermine Trust:** Resorting to personal attacks signals a lack of willingness to engage fairly, eroding trust between participants.

1. **Focus on the Argument:**
   Pay attention to whether the response addresses the actual argument or targets the person presenting it.

2. **Recognize Irrelevance:**
   Ask yourself: "Does this criticism of the person have anything to do with the validity of their argument?"

3. **Respond Constructively:**
   If someone uses an Ad Hominem attack against you, redirect the conversation to focus on the argument.
   Example: "Let's focus on the issue I raised instead of my personal background."

4. **Avoid Using Ad Hominem Attacks Yourself:**
   Stay focused on ideas and evidence, even in heated debates.

How to Respond to Ad Hominem Attacks

1. **Defuse Emotion:**
   Acknowledge the attack without escalating the situation.
   Example: "I understand you might disagree with me, but let's focus on the argument itself."

2. **Clarify the Argument:**
   Restate your position to refocus the discussion.
   Example: "My point is that stricter regulations could help protect the environment — what are your thoughts on that?"

3. **Call Out the Fallacy:**
   Politely point out the use of an Ad Hominem attack and ask the other person to engage with your argument instead.
   Example: "It seems like you're criticizing me personally rather than addressing my argument. Can we focus on the issue at hand?"

Exercises

1. **Identify Ad Hominem Attacks:**
   Look for examples of Ad Hominem Fallacies in news articles, debates, or social media. Analyze how the attacks shift focus from the argument to the individual.

2. **Rewrite Personal Criticisms:**
   Think of a personal criticism you've heard in a debate. Rewrite it to focus on the argument instead of the individual.

3. **Role-Play a Debate:**
   Practice debating a contentious topic with a partner. One person should use Ad Hominem attacks, while the other works to defuse them and refocus the discussion. Reflect on how this exercise changes the tone of the conversation.

4. **Self-Reflection Exercise:**
   Reflect on a time you might have unintentionally used an Ad Hominem attack. How could you have approached the discussion differently?

Closing Thoughts

The Ad Hominem Fallacy is a common but destructive tactic that undermines meaningful dialogue. By learning to recognize and avoid this fallacy, you can foster more respectful and constructive conversations.

Engaging with arguments rather than attacking individuals builds trust, encourages collaboration, and promotes clearer thinking. In a world where personal attacks often dominate public discourse, the ability to rise above the Ad Hominem Fallacy is a vital skill for logical thinkers.

Chapter 13: Avoiding Post Hoc Reasoning

Mistaking Connection for Reason: Post Hoc Fallacy

The **Post Hoc Fallacy** — short for *Post hoc ergo propter hoc* ("After this, therefore because of this") — occurs when someone assumes that because one event followed another, the first event caused the second. While temporal sequence may suggest causation, it doesn't guarantee it. This fallacy often leads to incorrect conclusions and misguided decisions.

For example:

- Event A: You wore your lucky socks to an exam.
- Event B: You scored exceptionally well.
- Conclusion: Wearing your lucky socks caused your high score.

This conclusion ignores other factors, such as preparation or test difficulty. Recognizing and avoiding the Post Hoc Fallacy is crucial for making sound decisions based on evidence, not assumptions.

How the Post Hoc Fallacy Works

The Post Hoc Fallacy follows this pattern:

1. **Event A Occurs:** Something happens first.
2. **Event B Follows:** Another event happens shortly after.
3. **Assumption of Causation:** It is assumed that Event A caused Event B, without investigating other explanations.

This reasoning oversimplifies complex relationships and can lead to faulty conclusions.

Examples of the Post Hoc Fallacy

1. **In Everyday Life:**
   - Claim: "I started drinking green tea last week, and now I feel healthier. Green tea must be the reason."
   - Reality: The improvement could be due to other factors, such as better sleep or reduced stress.
2. **In Business:**
   - Claim: "Sales increased after we changed our logo, so the logo must be responsible."
   - Reality: The increase might be due to other factors, such as seasonal trends or a new advertising campaign.
3. **In Superstition:**
   - Claim: "Every time I carry this charm, good things happen. It must bring me luck."
   - Reality: The charm has no proven connection to the outcomes.

Why the Post Hoc Fallacy is Harmful

The Post Hoc Fallacy can lead to:

1. **Faulty Decision-Making:** Misattributing causation can result in wasted resources or poor decisions.
2. **Reinforcement of Superstitions:** Believing in false cause-effect relationships perpetuates irrational thinking.
3. **Missed Opportunities:** Failing to identify the true cause of an event prevents meaningful solutions or improvements.

For instance, a business that credits a sales increase to a rebranded logo might miss the opportunity to invest in effective marketing strategies that were the real driver of success.

How to Avoid the Post Hoc Fallacy

1. **Question the Assumption:**
   Ask, "Is there evidence that Event A caused Event B, or could it be coincidence?"
2. **Look for Alternative Explanations:**
   Consider other factors that might explain the outcome. For example:
   - Did external circumstances (e.g., weather, economy) play a role?
   - Were there other changes or interventions during the same time?
3. **Gather Evidence:**
   Use data and controlled experiments to test the relationship between events.
4. **Understand Correlation vs. Causation:**
   Recognize that correlation (two events happening together) does not imply causation (one event causing the other).

Examples of Sound Reasoning

To avoid the Post Hoc Fallacy, focus on evidence-based reasoning:

- **Example 1:** "After we implemented new customer service training, customer satisfaction scores improved. We'll analyze other factors, such as seasonal trends, to confirm the cause."
- **Example 2:** "I felt better after taking vitamins, but I'll monitor my diet and sleep to see if they're contributing factors."

By considering multiple explanations and seeking evidence, you can make more accurate and reliable conclusions.

How to Respond to Post Hoc Reasoning

When someone uses the Post Hoc Fallacy, you can:

1. **Ask for Evidence:** Politely request proof that Event A caused Event B.
   Example: "What data supports the claim that the logo change increased sales?"
2. **Propose Alternative Explanations:** Suggest other factors that might explain the outcome.
   Example: "Could the sales increase be due to the new advertising campaign rather than the logo?"
3. **Encourage Critical Thinking:** Help the person see the difference between correlation and causation.

Exercises

1. **Identify Post Hoc Fallacies:**
   Look for examples in advertisements or news stories where something is implied without evidence. Analyze how the fallacy is used and what alternative explanations exist.

2. **Reevaluate Assumptions:**
    Think of a time you assumed one event caused another. Reflect on whether there could have been other factors at play.

3. **Debunk a Claim:**
    Find a statement based on Post Hoc reasoning (e.g. "Crime rates dropped after the new mayor was elected"). Research and evaluate whether the claim holds up under scrutiny.

4. **Analyze a Personal Belief:**
    Consider a superstition or belief you hold (e.g. "My lucky charm helped me ace the test"). Investigate whether evidence supports or contradicts the belief.

Closing Thoughts

The Post Hoc Fallacy is a common but avoidable error in reasoning. By learning to distinguish between fact and fiction, you can approach problems with greater clarity and make decisions based on evidence rather than assumptions.

Avoiding this fallacy not only sharpens your critical thinking but also helps you challenge misinformation and improve the quality of discussions. In a world full of misleading claims, the ability to question causation is an essential skill for logical thinkers.

Chapter 14: Identifying Circular Arguments

When Arguments Go in Circles: The Circular Argument Fallacy

A Circular Argument occurs when the conclusion of an argument is used as one of its premises. Instead of providing evidence, the reasoning loops back on itself, making it impossible to verify the claim independently. This fallacy may sound convincing at first but ultimately fails because it doesn't provide new information or justification for its conclusion.

How Circular Arguments Work

Circular reasoning typically follows this pattern:

1. **Claim Made:** A statement or argument is presented.
2. **Premise Relies on the Conclusion:** The argument uses its own conclusion as evidence to support itself.
3. **No Independent Evidence:** The reasoning doesn't introduce new facts or external justification, creating a loop.

Circular arguments often rely on assumptions that the audience is expected to accept without question.

Examples of Circular Arguments

1. **In Philosophy:**
    o   Claim: "Free will must exist because people make choices, and the ability to choose proves free will."
    o   Analysis: This argument assumes the truth of its conclusion (free will exists) to support its premise (making choices proves free will) without providing external evidence or examining alternative explanations like determinism.

2. **In Everyday Life:**
    o   Claim: "This restaurant is popular because it has the best food."
    o   Analysis: Popularity and quality are linked in a loop without proof that the food is objectively good.

3. **In Business:**
    o   Claim: "Our product is the best on the market because it's the most popular."
    o   Analysis: Popularity is used as evidence for quality without establishing why the product is popular.

Why Circular Arguments Are Harmful

Circular arguments can be persuasive in the short term, but they undermine reasoning and credibility in the long run. They are harmful because:

1. **They Avoid Evidence:** Instead of providing factual support, they rely on repetition and assumptions.
2. **They Mislead Audiences:** Circular reasoning can sound logical but ultimately provides no real justification.
3. **They Hinder Critical Thinking:** By preventing deeper inquiry, circular arguments stall progress and understanding.

For example, a political leader claiming, "I'm trustworthy because I always tell the truth," offers no evidence for their trustworthiness beyond their own assertion.

How to Identify Circular Arguments

1. **Look for Repetition:** Check if the conclusion is restated as a premise.
2. **Question Assumptions:** Ask whether the argument introduces any independent evidence or relies solely on its own conclusion.
3. **Seek External Justification:** Identify whether the reasoning provides facts or data beyond the claim itself.

1. **Provide Independent Evidence:** Support your conclusions with external data or facts that don't rely on the conclusion itself.
2. **Clarify Assumptions:** Ensure your premises are verifiable and not simply restatements of the conclusion.
3. **Encourage Critical Inquiry:** Be willing to examine the foundations of your argument and address gaps in reasoning.

Responding to Circular Arguments

When encountering a circular argument, you can:

1. **Point Out the Loop:** Politely highlight that the argument relies on its own conclusion.
   Example: "Your reasoning assumes the very point you're trying to prove. Could you provide evidence outside of the claim itself?"
2. **Ask for Independent Evidence:** Request additional support for the premise.
   Example: "Can you explain why this product is the best beyond its popularity?"
3. **Redirect the Discussion:** Focus on exploring external evidence or alternative perspectives.

Exercises

1. **Spot the Loops:**
   Find examples of circular reasoning in advertisements, political speeches, or everyday conversations. Analyze how the argument relies on its own conclusion.
2. **Reframe Circular Arguments:**
   Take a circular argument you've encountered and rewrite it to include independent evidence.
3. **Challenge Assumptions:**
   Identify an argument you believe in strongly. Examine whether it relies on circular reasoning and how you can strengthen it with external support.
4. **Role-Play Discussions:**
   Practice debating a topic with a partner. One person should intentionally use circular reasoning, while the other identifies the fallacy and redirects the conversation.

Closing Thoughts

Circular arguments are common but flawed, often relying on repetition and assumption rather than evidence. By learning to recognize and avoid this fallacy, you can build stronger arguments and engage in more meaningful discussions.

The ability to break out of logical loops fosters critical thinking, clarity, and credibility. Whether in debates, decision-making, or personal reasoning, avoiding circular arguments ensures your conclusions are grounded in evidence and logic.

Chapter 15: Detecting False Dilemmas

The Trap of Limited Choices: False Dilemma Fallacy

The False Dilemma Fallacy, also known as the "Either-Or Fallacy" or "Black-and-White Thinking," occurs when an argument presents only two options as the possible outcomes. This fallacy oversimplifies complex situations and forces a binary choice, often leading to flawed decisions or misunderstandings.

For example:

- Claim: "You're either with us or against us."
- Reality: There are often neutral or nuanced positions that don't align strictly with one side or the other.

The False Dilemma Fallacy can be subtle but is highly manipulative. It pushes individuals into making decisions based on incomplete or biased information. Learning to detect and avoid this fallacy is critical for clear thinking and effective decision-making.

FALSE DILEMMA
— there are often more than two options

How the False Dilemma Fallacy Works

This fallacy typically follows these steps:

1. **Present Two Opposing Options:** The argument frames the situation as a binary choice.
2. **Ignore Other Possibilities:** It disregards or excludes other viable alternatives.
3. **Force a Decision:** By narrowing the options, the argument pressures the audience into choosing one of the two presented paths.

This oversimplification is often used in debates, marketing, and everyday discussions to sway opinions or manipulate outcomes.

1. **In Political Rhetoric:**
   - Claim: "You either support strict immigration laws, or you want open borders."
   - Reality: Many people support balanced immigration policies that aren't fully restrictive or permissive.
2. **In Everyday Life:**
   - Claim: "Either you go to the party, or you're a bad friend."
   - Reality: Declining an invitation doesn't necessarily mean being a bad friend—there could be other valid reasons for not attending.
3. **In Business Decisions:**
   - Claim: "We either cut costs, or the company will fail."
   - Reality: Other options, such as increasing revenue through innovation, may exist.

Why the False Dilemma Fallacy is Harmful

This fallacy oversimplifies complex situations, leading to:
1. **Poor Decision-Making:** By ignoring alternatives, individuals may choose suboptimal solutions.
2. **Polarization:** Presenting issues as black-and-white deepens divisions and prevents compromise.
3. **Manipulation:** The fallacy can pressure people into decisions that align with the speaker's agenda rather than their own informed choice.

For instance, a parent saying, "You'll either become a doctor or disappoint the family," ignores the possibility of other fulfilling careers, creating unnecessary emotional pressure.

How to Detect False Dilemmas

1. **Look for Missing Options:** Ask, "Are there other possibilities being ignored?"
2. **Question the Binary Frame:** Consider whether the situation is truly limited to only two choices.
3. **Seek Nuance:** Explore the gray areas and complexities beyond the presented options.

How to Avoid the False Dilemma Fallacy

1. **Acknowledge Complexity:** Recognize that most issues have multiple dimensions and potential solutions.
2. **Consider All Alternatives:** List all possible options, even if they seem unlikely or unconventional.
3. **Encourage Open Discussion:** Avoid framing debates or decisions as strictly binary, and invite others to share different perspectives.

How to Respond to False Dilemmas

When encountering a False Dilemma Fallacy, you can:
1. **Challenge the Binary Frame:** Politely point out that other options may exist.
   Example: "Is it possible there's a middle ground between these two extremes?"
2. **Introduce Alternatives:** Offer additional possibilities to broaden the discussion.
   Example: "What if we consider a hybrid approach that combines elements of both options?"
3. **Ask Questions:** Encourage deeper exploration of the issue.
   Example: "Why do we have to choose between these two options? Are there other paths we haven't explored?"

Exercises

1. **Identify False Dilemmas:**
   Find examples of False Dilemmas in advertisements, political speeches, or social media posts. Analyze how the argument limits choices and suggest alternative perspectives.
2. **Reframe Binary Choices:**
   Think of a situation where you were presented with two options. Reflect on whether other possibilities existed and how they might have changed the outcome.
3. **Role-Play Decision-Making:**
   Practice presenting a problem to a partner using the False Dilemma Fallacy. Have them identify the missing options and reframe the situation to include additional possibilities.
4. **Analyze Complex Issues:**
   Take a contentious topic (e.g. climate change, healthcare, education) and identify examples of False Dilemmas in the discussion. Develop a more nuanced perspective that acknowledges multiple solutions.

Closing Thoughts

The False Dilemma Fallacy is a subtle but powerful error in reasoning that oversimplifies complex issues and limits creative thinking. By learning to recognize and challenge this fallacy, you can expand your perspective, improve decision-making, and foster more inclusive discussions.

Avoiding black-and-white thinking helps create space for compromise, innovation, and deeper understanding.

Chapter 16: Understanding Appeal to Authority Fallacies

The Appeal to Authority Fallacy occurs when someone argues that a claim must be true simply because an authority figure or institution supports it. While experts and authorities can provide valuable insights, their endorsement alone does not constitute definitive proof of a claim. This fallacy often replaces critical thinking and evidence with blind trust in authority.

For example:
- Claim: "This diet must work because a celebrity nutritionist recommends it."
- Problem: The endorsement doesn't guarantee effectiveness without supporting evidence.

This fallacy can be subtle and persuasive, especially when the authority cited seems credible or popular. Understanding the limits of authority and evaluating claims independently are essential for sound reasoning.

How the Appeal to Authority Fallacy Works

This fallacy typically involves:
1. **Citing an Authority:** An individual or institution is presented as an expert.
2. **Relying Solely on Authority:** The claim's validity is based entirely on the authority's support, without additional evidence.
3. **Assuming Truth:** The argument concludes that the claim must be true because the authority endorses it.

While authorities can provide expertise, their opinions must still be supported by data, logic, and evidence.

Examples of the Appeal to Authority Fallacy

1. **In Advertising:**
   o Claim: "This toothpaste is the best because 9 out of 10 dentists recommend it."
   o Problem: The recommendation doesn't provide evidence for why the toothpaste is superior.
2. **In Political Debates:**
   o Claim: "This policy is perfect because a respected economist supports it."
   o Problem: The economist's endorsement doesn't address the policy's potential flaws or alternatives.
3. **In Personal Conversations:**
   o Claim: "I believe this because my professor said so."
   o Problem: While professors are knowledgeable, their statements still require evidence and critical analysis.

Why the Appeal to Authority Fallacy is Harmful

Relying solely on authority without examining the evidence can lead to:
1. **Poor Decision-Making:** Decisions based on endorsements rather than facts may overlook critical flaws or risks.
2. **Misinformation:** Authorities can be wrong or biased, leading to the spread of false or incomplete information.
3. **Intellectual Complacency:** Blindly trusting authority discourages independent thinking and inquiry.

For example, a company citing a famous scientist to promote an untested product might exploit the scientist's reputation while offering no real evidence of effectiveness.

How to Identify Appeal to Authority Fallacies

1. **Ask for Evidence:** Does the argument rely solely on the authority's endorsement, or is it supported by data and logic?
2. **Check the Authority's Expertise:** Is the cited authority genuinely qualified in the relevant field?
3. **Consider Biases:** Does the authority have a personal interest in promoting the claim?

How to Avoid the Appeal to Authority Fallacy

1. **Verify Claims:** Look beyond endorsements to evaluate the evidence supporting a claim.
2. **Question Relevance:** Ensure the authority cited has expertise in the specific area being discussed.
   Example: A physicist's opinion on climate change is less relevant than that of a climatologist.
3. **Encourage Critical Thinking:** Don't rely solely on authority figures—seek out multiple perspectives and evidence.

How to Respond to Appeal to Authority Fallacies

When encountering this fallacy, you can:
1. **Request Evidence:** Politely ask for supporting data or examples.
   Example: "That's interesting — what evidence supports their claim?"

2. **Evaluate Expertise:** Question whether the authority cited is truly qualified in the relevant field.
   Example: "Do they have expertise in this specific area?"
3. **Introduce Counterexamples:** Highlight other authorities or evidence that contradicts the claim.
   Example: "While this economist supports the policy, others have raised concerns about its feasibility."

Exercises

1. **Spot the Fallacy:**
   Look for examples of Appeal to Authority Fallacies in advertisements, political speeches, or news articles. Analyze how the argument relies on authority rather than evidence.
2. **Evaluate Expertise:**
   Identify a claim made by an authority figure. Research their qualifications and determine whether their expertise is relevant to the claim.
3. **Reframe an Argument:**
   Rewrite an argument that relies on authority to include evidence and logical reasoning.
4. **Debate Exercise:**
   Role-play a discussion where one person uses the Appeal to Authority Fallacy. Practice identifying the fallacy and redirecting the conversation to focus on evidence.

Closing Thoughts

The Appeal to Authority Fallacy is a common but avoidable error in reasoning. While authorities can provide valuable insights, their endorsements should never replace evidence and critical thinking.

You can make better decisions, avoid manipulation, and contribute to more informed discussions when you learn to question and evaluate claims independently.

Chapter 17: The Gambler's Fallacy

The Illusion of Predictable Patterns: The Gambler's Fallacy

The Gambler's Fallacy occurs when someone mistakenly believes that the outcome of a random event is influenced by previous outcomes. This fallacy assumes that past results create a "balance" that will affect future results, even when the events are entirely independent.

For example:

- Belief: "The last five coin flips were heads, so tails must be due next."
- Reality: Each flip of the coin is independent, and the probability remains 50/50 regardless of previous outcomes.

This fallacy is common in gambling, but it also appears in everyday decision-making, where people misinterpret randomness and expect patterns that don't exist. Recognizing and avoiding the Gambler's Fallacy helps prevent poor decisions based on faulty assumptions about probability.

How the Gambler's Fallacy Works

The Gambler's Fallacy often follows this pattern:

1. **Observe a Streak:** A sequence of similar outcomes occurs (e.g. several wins or losses).
2. **Assume Imbalance:** Believe that the streak increases the likelihood of the opposite outcome.
3. **Act on False Assumptions:** Make decisions based on the belief that the outcome is "due" or "overdue."

While this reasoning feels intuitive, it fails to account for the independence of random events.

Examples of the Gambler's Fallacy

1. **In Gambling:**
   o Belief: "The roulette wheel has landed on black five times in a row, so red is bound to come up next."
   o Reality: The roulette wheel has no memory, and each spin is independent of the last.
2. **In Everyday Life:**
   o Belief: "I've had bad luck all week, so I'm bound to have good luck soon."
   o Reality: Random events don't balance out over short periods.
3. **In Financial Decisions:**
   o Belief: "The stock price has dropped three days in a row, so it's sure to go up tomorrow."
   o Reality: Market trends are influenced by multiple factors, not short-term patterns.

Why the Gambler's Fallacy is Harmful

The Gambler's Fallacy can lead to:
1. **Poor Decision-Making:** Acting on false assumptions about probability often results in bad outcomes.
2. **Financial Losses:** In gambling and investing, this fallacy encourages risky behavior and misplaced bets.
3. **Frustration and Confusion:** Misunderstanding randomness can lead to unwarranted expectations and disappointment.

For example, a gambler who doubles their bet after each loss, believing they're "due" for a win, may quickly exhaust their resources.

How to Recognize the Gambler's Fallacy

1. **Check for Randomness:** Ask whether the events are truly independent.
2. **Question Assumptions:** Consider whether past outcomes have any logical influence on future ones.
3. **Understand Probability:** Remember that the likelihood of independent events remains constant, regardless of previous results.

How to Avoid the Gambler's Fallacy

1. **Focus on Long-Term Trends:** Understand that randomness doesn't balance out over short periods.
2. **Use Data and Evidence:** Base decisions on facts and probabilities, not perceived patterns.
3. **Recognize Independence:** Accept that random events are not influenced by past outcomes.

How to Respond to the Gambler's Fallacy

When encountering this fallacy, you can:
1. **Explain Independence:** Clarify that random events are not connected.
   Example: "Each coin flip is independent, so the chances of heads or tails remain the same."
2. **Provide Context:** Share examples or data to illustrate how randomness works.
   Example: "Roulette wheels don't have memory—each spin is equally likely to result in red or black."
3. **Encourage Rational Thinking:** Redirect the conversation to focus on evidence and probabilities.

Exercises

1. **Identify the Fallacy:**
   Find examples of the Gambler's Fallacy in gambling, sports, or everyday decisions. Analyze how the fallacy leads to incorrect assumptions.

2. **Calculate Probabilities:**
   Practice calculating probabilities for random events (e.g. coin flips, dice rolls) to reinforce the concept of independence.

3. **Challenge False Patterns:**
   Reflect on a time when you believed an outcome was "due" or "overdue." Consider how understanding randomness might have changed your perspective.

4. **Simulate Random Events:**
   Use a random number generator or coin flips to observe streaks and patterns. Reflect on how randomness can create the illusion of predictability.

Closing Thoughts

The Gambler's Fallacy is a common but avoidable error in reasoning, rooted in a misunderstanding of randomness and probability.

Understanding the independence of random events helps you approach situations with clarity and confidence. Whether in gambling, investing, or daily life, rejecting the Gambler's Fallacy is an essential step toward logical thinking.

Chapter 18: Slippery Slope Analysis

From Small Steps to Big Assumptions: The Slippery Slope Fallacy

The Slippery Slope Fallacy occurs when someone argues that a small action or event will inevitably lead to a chain of increasingly extreme or disastrous consequences. While certain actions can have far-reaching effects, this fallacy exaggerates the likelihood of these outcomes without providing evidence.

For example:
- Claim: "If we allow students to use calculators in exams, they'll stop learning basic math, and soon no one will be able to perform simple arithmetic."
- Reality: Using calculators may assist with complex problems without necessarily diminishing basic math skills.

Slippery slope arguments often rely on fear and speculation, distracting from rational discussions. Recognizing and analyzing this fallacy ensures decisions are based on evidence, not unfounded predictions.

How the Slippery Slope Fallacy Works

This fallacy typically follows these steps:
1. **Start with a Small Action:** Identify a relatively minor event or decision.
2. **Predict an Exaggerated Chain of Events:** Assume that the action will trigger a sequence of increasingly severe consequences.
3. **Reach a Catastrophic Conclusion:** Argue that the initial action must be avoided to prevent the extreme outcome.

Although actions can lead to consequences, the Slippery Slope Fallacy oversimplifies real-world situations and exaggerates how likely it is that one step will automatically lead to extreme results.

Examples of the Slippery Slope Fallacy

1. **In Policy Debates:**
   o Claim: "If we legalize marijuana, it's only a matter of time before harder drugs are legalized, leading to societal collapse."
   o Reality: Legalizing one substance doesn't automatically lead to the legalization of others.
2. **In Personal Conversations:**
   o Claim: "If you let your child skip one homework assignment, they'll grow up lazy and irresponsible."
   o Reality: Missing one assignment is unlikely to determine a child's entire future.
3. **In Workplace Decisions:**
   o Claim: "If we allow employees to work remotely, productivity will drop, and the company will fail."
   o Reality: Many companies thrive with remote work through proper planning and accountability.

Why the Slippery Slope Fallacy is Harmful

This fallacy distorts reasoning by:
1. **Creating Unnecessary Fear:** Exaggerated consequences can lead to decisions based on fear rather than logic.
2. **Stifling Innovation:** The fallacy often resists change by assuming worst-case scenarios.
3. **Distracting from Evidence:** By focusing on speculative outcomes, the argument avoids addressing the actual issue.

For example, a school that avoids introducing new technology out of fear of dependency may miss opportunities to enhance education.

How to Recognize the Slippery Slope Fallacy

1. **Look for Exaggeration:** Check whether the argument escalates to extreme outcomes without evidence.
2. **Evaluate Evidence for Each Step:** Ask whether each predicted step is supported by logic and data.
3. **Consider Intervening Factors:** Identify whether mechanisms exist to prevent the exaggerated outcomes.

How to Avoid the Slippery Slope Fallacy

1. **Focus on the Immediate Issue:** Address the actual proposal or action, not speculative consequences.
2. **Demand Evidence:** Insist on data and reasoning to support each step in the predicted chain of events.
3. **Acknowledge Complexity:** Recognize that real-world outcomes are influenced by multiple factors.

How to Respond to Slippery Slope Arguments

When encountering this fallacy, you can:
1. **Challenge the Predictions:** Politely ask for evidence supporting each step in the argument.
   Example: "What evidence suggests that allowing remote work will lead to company failure?"
2. **Introduce Counterexamples:** Highlight situations where similar actions didn't result in the predicted outcomes.
   Example: "Many companies have implemented remote work successfully without losing productivity."
3. **Refocus the Discussion:** Redirect the conversation to the immediate issue.
   Example: "Let's focus on whether this specific change makes sense, rather than speculating about extreme scenarios."

Exercises

1. **Identify Slippery Slopes:**
   Look for examples of the Slippery Slope Fallacy in news articles, political debates, or advertisements. Analyze how the argument exaggerates consequences and propose a more balanced perspective.
2. **Analyze Predictions:**
   Think of a prediction you've heard that seemed exaggerated. Break it down into steps and evaluate whether each step is supported by evidence.
3. **Reframe an Argument:**
   Rewrite a Slippery Slope argument to focus on the immediate issue and provide evidence for the potential consequences.
4. **Debate Exercise:**
   Role-play a discussion where one person uses a Slippery Slope Fallacy. Practice identifying and addressing the fallacy while staying focused on the main issue.

The Slippery Slope Fallacy is a persuasive but flawed tactic that relies on fear and exaggeration to resist change or new ideas.

Understanding that small actions don't inevitably lead to extreme consequences allows you to approach issues with confidence, rationality, and an open mind. Rejecting the Slippery Slope Fallacy is crucial for logical and informed reasoning.

Chapter 19: Avoiding Hasty Generalizations

Drawing Conclusions Too Quickly: The Hasty Generalization Fallacy

A Hasty Generalization occurs when someone makes a broad conclusion based on insufficient or unrepresentative evidence. This fallacy often involves rushing to judgment after observing only a small sample or a single event, ignoring the need for more thorough investigation.

For example:
- Claim: "My friend got sick after eating at that restaurant, so the food there must be unsafe."
- Problem: One person's experience doesn't represent the overall quality or safety of the restaurant.

Hasty generalizations are common in everyday conversations, media narratives, and even scientific discussions. Avoiding this fallacy ensures that conclusions are rooted in sufficient evidence and logical reasoning.

How the Hasty Generalization Fallacy Works

The fallacy typically follows these steps:
1. **Observe Limited Evidence:** A small sample or isolated event is used as the basis for a conclusion.
2. **Generalize Broadly:** The conclusion is applied to a larger group or situation without adequate support.
3. **Ignore Counterexamples:** Contradictory evidence is overlooked or dismissed.

While humans naturally seek patterns and make connections, rushing to conclusions can lead to misunderstandings and poor decisions.

Examples of Hasty Generalizations
1. **In Personal Opinions:**
    - Claim: "I met two rude people from City X, so everyone from City X must be rude."
    - Reality: A small sample size doesn't reflect an entire population.
2. **In Business Decisions:**
    - Claim: "Our new product didn't sell well in one region, so it must not be popular anywhere."
    - Reality: Sales in one area don't determine overall demand, as other factors (e.g. marketing or local preferences) may be at play.
3. **In Science and Research:**
    - Claim: "This study of 10 people proves the treatment works for everyone."
    - Reality: A small sample size isn't sufficient to draw conclusions about the entire population.

Why Hasty Generalizations Are Harmful

Hasty generalizations can:
1. **Perpetuate Stereotypes:** Overgeneralizing about people or groups leads to unfair assumptions and biases.
2. **Cause Poor Decisions:** Decisions based on incomplete evidence may lead to mistakes or missed opportunities.
3. **Spread Misinformation:** Broad conclusions based on limited evidence can contribute to false narratives.

For example, assuming all teenagers are irresponsible after one negative interaction ignores the diversity and complexity of individual behavior.

How to Recognize Hasty Generalizations
1. **Check the Evidence:** Is the conclusion based on sufficient data or just a few examples?
2. **Evaluate the Sample Size:** Ask whether the evidence represents the broader group or situation.
3. **Look for Counterexamples:** Consider whether contradictory evidence exists and how it might affect the conclusion.

How to Avoid the Hasty Generalization Fallacy
1. **Gather More Evidence:** Ensure your conclusion is based on a large and representative sample.
2. **Consider Other Factors:** Look beyond the immediate evidence to identify additional variables or perspectives.
3. **Remain Open to Revision:** Be willing to adjust your conclusions as new evidence becomes available.

When encountering this fallacy, you can:

1. **Question the Evidence:** Ask whether the conclusion is supported by enough data.
   Example: "How many people did you talk to before making this judgment?"
2. **Introduce Alternative Explanations:** Suggest other factors that might explain the observed evidence.
   Example: "Maybe sales were low in that region because of poor marketing, not because the product is unpopular."
3. **Encourage Broader Perspectives:** Highlight the need for more data or diverse examples.
   Example: "Let's look at a larger sample before jumping to conclusions."

Exercises

1. **Identify Hasty Generalizations:**
   Look for examples of this fallacy in advertisements, media stories, or personal conversations. Analyze how the argument relies on limited evidence and propose a more thorough approach.
2. **Re-evaluate Personal Beliefs:**
   Think of a time you formed an opinion based on a small sample or single event. Reflect on whether additional evidence might have changed your perspective.
3. **Practice Data Analysis:**
   Review a set of data and determine whether the sample size is sufficient to support a general conclusion.
4. **Role-Play Conversations:**
   With a partner, practice addressing hasty generalizations by questioning the evidence and suggesting alternative interpretations.

Closing Thoughts

The Hasty Generalization Fallacy is an easy trap to fall into, especially when emotions or time pressures are involved. However, learning to slow down, gather sufficient evidence, and consider alternative perspectives ensures that your conclusions are accurate and fair.

In a world full of quick judgments and stereotypes, taking the time to evaluate evidence thoroughly is a vital skill for logical reasoning.

Chapter 20: Distinguishing Correlation from Causation

Correlation vs. Causation: Avoiding Misinterpretation

The Correlation vs. Causation Fallacy occurs when someone assumes that because two events happen together, one must cause the other. While correlation (a relationship between two variables) can suggest a connection, it does not prove causation (one variable directly causing the other).

For example:
- Observation: "Ice cream sales and drowning rates both increase in the summer."
- Fallacy: "Eating ice cream causes drowning."
- Reality: Both are correlated because they increase during summer, but one does not cause the other.

This fallacy is common in media, marketing, and everyday discussions, where people often mistake patterns for causation. Understanding the difference is crucial for making sound decisions and avoiding misinformation.

How the Correlation vs. Causation Fallacy Works

This fallacy typically follows these steps:

1. **Identify a Correlation:** Two events or variables occur together.
2. **Assume Causation:** Conclude that one event causes the other without investigating further.
3. **Ignore Other Factors:** Overlook alternative explanations or underlying causes.

Examples of Correlation vs. Causation

1. **In Media:**
   - Claim: "People who drink coffee live longer, so coffee must extend lifespan."
   - Reality: Coffee drinkers might have other healthy habits contributing to their longevity.
2. **In Marketing:**
   - Claim: "Customers who buy Product A also buy Product B, so Product A causes interest in Product B."
   - Reality: The correlation might be due to complementary needs or effective bundling strategies.
3. **In Health Discussions:**
   - Claim: "Children who sleep more tend to perform better in school, so more sleep causes better grades."
   - Reality: Both sleep and performance could be influenced by other factors, such as overall health or family environment.

How to Recognize the Correlation vs. Causation Fallacy

1. **Question the Relationship:** Ask whether there's direct evidence that one variable causes the other.
2. **Look for Confounding Variables:** Consider other factors that might explain the correlation.
3. **Analyze the Data:** Examine whether the evidence supports causation or merely shows a pattern.

How to Avoid the Correlation vs. Causation Fallacy

1. **Demand Evidence for Causation:** Look for controlled studies or experiments that isolate the variables.
2. **Identify Confounding Variables:** Acknowledge the role of other factors influencing the relationship.
3. **Remain Skeptical:** Be cautious about accepting causation claims without robust evidence.

How to Respond to the Fallacy

When encountering this fallacy, you can:

1. **Ask for Clarification:** Politely question the evidence supporting causation.
   Example: "Is there proof that one caused the other, or could there be another explanation?"
2. **Introduce Alternative Explanations:** Suggest other factors that might explain the correlation.
   Example: "Could both trends be caused by a common factor, like seasonal changes?"
3. **Encourage Further Investigation:** Advocate for additional research or analysis to confirm causation.

Exercises

1. **Spot the Fallacy:**
   Find examples of this fallacy in advertisements, news stories, or personal conversations. Analyze how correlation is mistaken for causation and propose alternative explanations.
2. **Analyze Real Data:**
   Review a dataset showing a correlation and identify potential confounding variables that could influence the relationship.
3. **Debunk a Claim:**
   Choose a popular belief based on correlation (e.g., "screen time causes poor grades") and research whether evidence supports causation.
4. **Role-Play Discussions:**
   Practice addressing this fallacy in a conversation by questioning assumptions and proposing alternative perspectives.

Closing Thoughts

The Correlation vs. Causation Fallacy is a common pitfall in reasoning, but it can be avoided with careful analysis and critical thinking. By understanding the difference between correlation and causation, you can evaluate claims more accurately and make better decisions.

Distinguishing correlation from causation is a fundamental skill for logical and informed reasoning. It ensures that your conclusions are grounded in evidence and resistant to misleading assumptions.

Section II: Advanced Logical Tools

Subsection: Problem-Solving Frameworks

Problem-solving is both an art and a science. It requires creativity to explore solutions, logic to evaluate them, and structured approaches to uncover root causes and prioritize actions. In this section, we explore powerful problem-solving methods, each designed to tackle challenges from different angles. These frameworks will equip you with versatile strategies to identify, analyze, and resolve problems effectively.

Chapter 21: The 5 Whys

Digging Deeper: The 5 Whys Technique

The **5 Whys** is a simple yet powerful method for uncovering the root cause of a problem by repeatedly asking "Why?" It helps humans move beyond surface-level symptoms to identify the underlying issue, making it an essential tool for effective problem-solving.

For example:

- **Problem:** The delivery of a product was delayed.
- **1st Why:** Why was the delivery delayed? → The truck broke down.
- **2nd Why:** Why did the truck break down? → It wasn't properly maintained.
- **3rd Why:** Why wasn't it maintained? → Maintenance schedules weren't followed.
- **4th Why:** Why weren't schedules followed? → The maintenance team was understaffed.
- **5th Why:** Why was the team understaffed? → The budget for maintenance was cut.

Root Cause: Budget cuts led to staffing shortages, which caused maintenance lapses and ultimately delayed delivery.

How the 5 Whys Technique Works

1. **Define the Problem:** Clearly state the issue you're trying to solve.
2. **Ask "Why?" Repeatedly:** For each answer, ask "Why?" again to probe deeper.
3. **Identify the Root Cause:** Stop when the answers reveal the fundamental issue behind the problem.
4. **Take Action:** Develop solutions that address the root cause, not just the symptoms.

While five iterations of "Why?" are common, you may need fewer or more depending on the complexity of the problem.

Applications of the 5 Whys

1. **In Business:**
   o **Problem:** Sales dropped last quarter.
   o **Root Cause:** Ineffective marketing strategy failed to attract new customers.
2. **In Personal Life:**
   o **Problem:** Constantly running late for work.
   o **Root Cause:** Poor morning routine and lack of preparation the night before.
3. **In Education:**
   o **Problem:** Students underperforming in exams.
   o **Root Cause:** Lack of effective study materials or teaching methods.

Why the 5 Whys Approach is Effective

The 5 Whys helps:

1. **Avoid Superficial Solutions:** By digging deeper, it prevents addressing only the symptoms of a problem.
2. **Encourage Collaboration:** It involves team members in exploring causes, fostering shared understanding.
3. **Simplify Complex Problems:** Breaking issues into smaller, more manageable parts makes them easier to address.

Challenges and Limitations

1. **Over-Simplification:** Complex problems may have multiple root causes, requiring additional analysis.
2. **Bias:** The process depends on honest and accurate answers to "Why?"
3. **Overreliance on Single Causes:** Focusing on one root cause may overlook contributing factors.

For example, in the truck maintenance scenario, addressing only the budget cuts without examining other maintenance processes might not fully resolve the issue.

1. **Analyze a Problem:** Think of a recurring issue in your life or workplace. Use the 5 Whys to identify the root cause.
2. **Challenge the Process:** After completing the 5 Whys, ask, "Is this truly the root cause, or could there be more?"
3. **Collaborate on a Solution:** Use the 5 Whys with a team to solve a shared problem. Reflect on how different perspectives shape the process.

Closing Thoughts

The 5 Whys is a straightforward and accessible tool for uncovering root causes. By repeatedly asking "Why?", it fosters deeper understanding and drives solutions that address the heart of a problem.

However, the method's simplicity requires care to avoid oversights or assumptions. When used thoughtfully, the 5 Whys becomes a reliable first step in resolving challenges, from minor inconveniences to significant organizational issues.

Chapter 22: Ishikawa (Fishbone) Diagrams

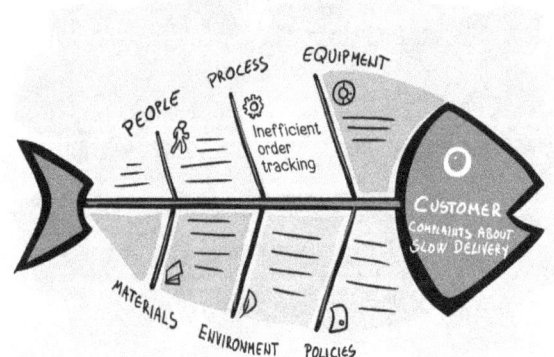

Mapping Causes Visually: The Ishikawa Diagram

The Ishikawa Diagram, also known as the Fishbone Diagram or Cause-and-Effect Diagram, is a visual tool for identifying and organizing potential causes of a problem. Developed by Japanese quality control expert Dr. Kaoru Ishikawa, this method helps teams analyze all contributing factors to a problem in a structured way.

For example:

- **Problem:** Declining product quality.
- **Potential Causes:**
  - **People:** Lack of training among staff.
  - **Processes:** Inconsistent quality checks.
  - **Materials:** Poor-quality raw materials.
  - **Environment:** Inadequate storage conditions.

By visually mapping these causes, teams can systematically address the root of the issue and implement targeted solutions.

How the Ishikawa Diagram Works

1. **Define the Problem:** Clearly state the problem at the "head" of the fish.
2. **Draw the Spine and Major Categories:** Create a central line (spine) with "bones" branching out for major categories such as People, Processes, Materials, Equipment, Environment, or Methods.
3. **Brainstorm Causes:** Under each category, add specific potential causes contributing to the problem.
4. **Analyze and Prioritize:** Review the diagram to identify the most likely root causes and develop solutions.

This process encourages thorough analysis and collaboration, ensuring that all possible causes are considered.

Applications of the Ishikawa Diagram

1. **In Manufacturing:**
   - **Problem:** Machine downtime.
   - **Causes:**
     - **People:** Insufficient operator training.
     - **Processes:** Inadequate maintenance schedules.
     - **Equipment:** Worn-out components.
2. **In Healthcare:**
   - **Problem:** High patient wait times.
   - **Causes:**
     - **People:** Staff shortages.
     - **Processes:** Inefficient appointment scheduling.
     - **Environment:** Limited facilities.
3. **In Personal Projects:**
   - **Problem:** Missing deadlines on assignments.
   - **Causes:**
     - **Methods:** Poor time management.
     - **Environment:** Frequent distractions.

The Ishikawa Diagram helps to:

1. **Organize Complex Problems:** It breaks issues into manageable categories.
2. **Encourage Collaboration:** Teams can brainstorm and analyze together, ensuring diverse perspectives.
3. **Identify Root Causes:** By categorizing potential causes, it avoids overlooking critical factors.

Challenges and Limitations

1. **Overloading with Data:** Adding too many causes can make the diagram overwhelming.
2. **Bias in Brainstorming:** Teams may focus on certain categories while neglecting others.
3. **Requires Follow-Up:** The diagram identifies causes but doesn't provide solutions; further analysis is needed.

For example, identifying staff shortages as a cause of patient wait times doesn't automatically resolve the issue — solutions such as hiring or scheduling changes must follow.

How to Use the Ishikawa Diagram Effectively

1. **Focus on Clarity:** Keep the problem statement and causes concise and specific.
2. **Engage the Team:** Involve all relevant stakeholders in brainstorming to capture diverse perspectives.
3. **Prioritize Causes:** Use tools such as the Pareto Principle (Chapter 32) to focus on the most impactful causes.

Exercises

1. **Create a Diagram:** Think of a problem in your workplace, personal life, or community. Create an Ishikawa Diagram to identify potential causes.
2. **Review a Team Challenge:** Use the Ishikawa Diagram with a group to analyze a shared issue. Reflect on how the process reveals overlooked factors.
3. **Simplify the Diagram:** Take a completed diagram and highlight the top three most likely causes for further investigation.

Closing Thoughts

The Ishikawa Diagram is a versatile visual tool for identifying and organizing potential causes of a problem. By breaking issues into categories, it ensures thorough analysis and helps teams focus on addressing root causes rather than symptoms.

While the diagram requires careful follow-up to develop solutions, its structured approach is invaluable for tackling complex challenges. Whether in professional or personal settings, mastering the Ishikawa Diagram equips you to think systematically and collaboratively about problem-solving.

Chapter 23: Root Cause Analysis

Finding the Foundation: Root Cause Analysis

Root Cause Analysis (RCA) is a systematic method for identifying the underlying cause of a problem. While symptoms and immediate causes may be visible, RCA digs deeper to uncover the fundamental issue driving the problem. Addressing the root cause prevents recurrence and leads to more effective solutions.

For example:

- **Problem:** Frequent errors in customer orders.
- **Root Cause:** Lack of standardized procedures for processing orders.

By identifying and addressing the root cause, RCA ensures that solutions are targeted and long-lasting.

How Root Cause Analysis Works

1. **Define the Problem:** Clearly state the issue and its symptoms.
2. **Collect Data:** Gather information about the problem, including when and where it occurs.
3. **Identify Possible Causes:** Brainstorm potential causes using tools like the 5 Whys or Ishikawa Diagrams.
4. **Determine the Root Cause:** Analyze the data to pinpoint the most fundamental issue driving the problem.
5. **Develop Solutions:** Create and implement actions that address the root cause directly.

Applications of Root Cause Analysis

1. **In Manufacturing:**
   o **Problem:** Product defects.
   o **Root Cause:** Faulty calibration of machinery.

2. **In Customer Service:**
    o **Problem:** High complaint rates.
    o **Root Cause:** Ineffective communication between departments.
3. **In Personal Life:**
    o **Problem:** Constantly feeling overwhelmed.
    o **Root Cause:** Taking on too many commitments without prioritization.

Why Root Cause Analysis is Effective

RCA helps:
1. **Prevent Recurrence:** By addressing the root cause, it avoids temporary fixes that only treat symptoms.
2. **Save Resources:** Solving the fundamental issue reduces wasted time and effort on recurring problems.
3. **Improve Systems:** RCA often uncovers weaknesses in processes or systems, enabling long-term improvements.

Challenges and Limitations

1. **Time-Intensive:** Thorough analysis requires significant effort and resources.
2. **Risk of Bias:** Teams may focus on familiar causes while overlooking less obvious ones.
3. **Complexity in Large Problems:** Some issues may have multiple root causes, complicating the analysis.

For example, a decline in employee morale might stem from a combination of leadership, workload, and organizational culture issues.

How to Use Root Cause Analysis Effectively

1. **Be Systematic:** Follow a structured process to avoid skipping steps or jumping to conclusions.
2. **Use Supporting Tools:** Combine RCA with methods like the 5 Whys, Ishikawa Diagrams, or Pareto Analysis to enhance accuracy.
3. **Test Solutions:** Ensure that proposed actions address the root cause and not just the symptoms.

Exercises

1. **Analyze a Persistent Problem:** Choose a recurring issue in your life or workplace. Use RCA to identify the root cause and develop a solution.
2. **Combine with Other Tools:** Apply RCA alongside the Ishikawa Diagram or 5 Whys to explore potential causes more thoroughly.
3. **Test a Hypothesis:** Implement a solution targeting the root cause and monitor its effectiveness over time.

Closing Thoughts

Root Cause Analysis is an essential tool for resolving problems at their foundation. By digging deeper into the causes of an issue, RCA ensures that solutions are effective and sustainable.

While the process requires time and careful analysis, its ability to prevent recurrence and improve systems makes it invaluable for tackling complex challenges. Whether in professional or personal contexts, mastering RCA helps you think critically and act decisively.

Chapter 24: The Socratic Method

Questioning Assumptions: The Socratic Method

The Socratic Method is a problem-solving and reasoning tool based on asking a series of thoughtful and probing questions. Originating from the teachings of Socrates, this approach encourages critical thinking, challenges assumptions, and leads to deeper understanding through dialogue.

For example:
- **Scenario:** A team is struggling with low productivity.
- **Socratic Questions:**
    o What does productivity mean in this context?
    o Why do we believe productivity is low?
    o Could there be other factors affecting output?
    o How might we measure improvement accurately?

By focusing on questions rather than answers, the Socratic Method helps uncover underlying beliefs, identify gaps in reasoning, and clarify the core of an issue.

How the Socratic Method Works

The process involves:

1. **Clarifying the Problem:** Begin by defining the issue clearly.
    Question: "What exactly are we trying to solve?"
2. **Challenging Assumptions:** Ask questions that test existing beliefs.
    Question: "Why do we think this is the case?"
3. **Exploring Alternatives:** Encourage brainstorming and consideration of new perspectives.
    Question: "What other explanations might exist?"
4. **Testing Implications:** Evaluate the consequences of potential solutions.
    Question: "What would happen if we tried this approach?"

Through structured questioning, participants are guided toward self-discovery and critical analysis, rather than being told what to think.

Applications of the Socratic Method

1. **In Education:**
    o   Teachers use the method to encourage students to think critically about concepts.
    o   Example: "Why do you think this historical event occurred, and what were its consequences?"
2. **In Workplace Discussions:**
    o   Teams can use Socratic questioning to analyze projects or decisions.
    o   Example: "What are the assumptions behind our current strategy? Are they valid?"
3. **In Personal Reflection:**
    o   Individuals can apply the method to explore their beliefs and decisions.
    o   Example: "Why do I feel this way about a situation, and what evidence supports my feelings?"

Why the Socratic Method is Effective

The Socratic Method promotes:

1. **Critical Thinking:** Encourages deeper analysis and examination of assumptions.
2. **Self-Discovery:** Helps individuals arrive at their own conclusions through guided questioning.
3. **Collaboration:** Facilitates open dialogue and mutual understanding in group settings.

Challenges and Limitations

1. **Time-Consuming:** The process of questioning can be lengthy and may not suit urgent situations.
2. **Discomfort with Ambiguity:** Participants may struggle with the lack of immediate answers or certainty.
3. **Requires Skillful Facilitation:** Effective questioning requires practice and careful listening to avoid leading or biased questions.

For instance, in a team setting, participants might resist probing questions if they perceive them as overly critical rather than constructive.

How to Use the Socratic Method Effectively

1. **Stay Neutral:** Avoid leading questions or imposing your own views.
2. **Focus on Open-Ended Questions:** Encourage exploration rather than yes/no answers.
3. **Foster a Safe Environment:** Ensure participants feel comfortable sharing and reflecting.

Exercises

1. **Analyze a Belief:** Choose a personal belief and apply Socratic questioning to examine its foundations and implications.
2. **Role-Play a Dialogue:** Partner with a colleague or friend to explore a problem using the Socratic Method. Reflect on how the process deepens understanding.
3. **Challenge a Group Assumption:** In a team setting, use Socratic questions to test the assumptions behind a collective decision or strategy.

Closing Thoughts

The Socratic Method is a timeless and versatile tool for fostering critical thinking, challenging assumptions, and uncovering deeper truths. By focusing on questions rather than answers, it empowers individuals and teams to think more deeply and collaboratively.

While the process requires patience and practice, its ability to clarify problems and inspire innovative solutions makes it invaluable in education, work, and personal decision-making.

Chapter 25: SWOT Analysis

Evaluating Your Position: SWOT Analysis

A SWOT Analysis is a strategic planning tool used to evaluate an organization's or individual's Strengths, Weaknesses, Opportunities, and Threats. By systematically analyzing these factors, SWOT helps identify areas for improvement, leverage advantages, and anticipate challenges.

For example:

- **Scenario:** A small business wants to expand its market.
  - **Strengths:** Loyal customer base, unique products.
  - **Weaknesses:** Limited marketing budget.
  - **Opportunities:** Growing demand in adjacent markets.
  - **Threats:** Competitors with larger budgets.

SWOT's structured approach ensures that decisions are informed by a comprehensive understanding of both internal and external factors.

How SWOT Analysis Works

1. **Strengths (Internal):** Identify what you or your organization do well.
   Question: "What are our unique advantages?"
2. **Weaknesses (Internal):** Examine areas where you lack resources or capabilities.
   Question: "Where do we need to improve?"
3. **Opportunities (External):** Explore external trends or conditions that could benefit you.
   Question: "What changes in the environment could work in our favor?"
4. **Threats (External):** Consider external factors that could hinder your success.
   Question: "What challenges or risks should we prepare for?"

By organizing these factors in a grid, SWOT makes it easier to visualize the interplay between internal and external dynamics.

Applications of SWOT Analysis

1. **In Business Strategy:**
   - A company uses SWOT to evaluate its market position and plan for growth.
     Example: A retail store identifies online sales as an opportunity and shifts its strategy to develop e-commerce capabilities.
2. **In Career Planning:**
   - Individuals use SWOT to assess their skills, limitations, and opportunities for advancement.
     Example: An employee considers taking additional training to address weaknesses and capitalize on promotion opportunities.
3. **In Project Management:**
   - Teams use SWOT to identify potential risks and benefits at the start of a project.

Why SWOT Analysis is Effective

SWOT Analysis helps:

1. **Provide Clarity:** Offers a clear and structured overview of key factors influencing success.
2. **Encourage Strategic Thinking:** Balances internal capabilities with external opportunities and risks.
3. **Facilitate Decision-Making:** Prioritizes actions based on a holistic understanding of strengths and challenges.

Challenges and Limitations

1. **Oversimplification:** A SWOT grid provides a snapshot but may miss nuances or deeper analysis.
2. **Subjectivity:** Assessments of strengths, weaknesses, opportunities, and threats can be influenced by personal bias.
3. **Action Gap:** SWOT identifies factors but doesn't automatically translate into an action plan.

For instance, identifying "limited budget" as a weakness requires follow-up steps to address funding gaps.

How to Use SWOT Analysis Effectively

1. **Be Honest:** Ensure strengths and weaknesses are assessed realistically.
2. **Prioritize Factors:** Focus on the most critical elements in each quadrant.
3. **Link to Action:** Use the results of the analysis to develop specific goals and strategies.

1. **Conduct a SWOT Analysis:** Choose a goal or challenge and complete a SWOT grid. Reflect on how the analysis shapes your approach.
2. **Team Exercise:** Collaborate with a team to evaluate a shared objective using SWOT. Discuss how different perspectives influence the process.
3. **Develop an Action Plan:** Based on your SWOT results, create a list of specific actions to address weaknesses and leverage opportunities.

Closing Thoughts

SWOT Analysis is a versatile and accessible tool for understanding your position and planning strategically. By balancing internal and external factors, it helps identify opportunities for growth and prepare for potential challenges.

While SWOT requires thoughtful interpretation and follow-up, its structured approach makes it an essential framework for decision-making in business, career development, and personal planning.

Chapter 26: First Principles Thinking

Getting to the Core: First Principles Thinking

First Principles Thinking is a problem-solving method that involves breaking down a complex problem into its most basic truths, or "first principles". Then, it builds solutions from there. Made popular by thinkers like Aristotle and modern innovators like Elon Musk, this approach challenges assumptions, simplifies complexity, and sparks creativity.

For example:

- **Problem:** Electric car batteries are too expensive.
- **First Principles Approach:**
  - o Break it down: What are batteries made of?
  - o Answer: Lithium, nickel, cobalt, etc.
  - o Rebuild: Can we produce these materials differently to reduce costs?

First Principles Thinking avoids relying on established beliefs or "best practices," encouraging innovation and fresh perspectives.

How First Principles Thinking Works

1. **Identify the Problem:** Clearly define the issue or question you want to solve.
   Example: "How can we improve our delivery system?"
2. **Break Down Assumptions:** Challenge existing beliefs or constraints surrounding the problem.
   Question: "Why do we assume deliveries must take 3-5 days?"
3. **Find the Fundamental Truths:** Reduce the problem to its basic components or truths.
   Answer: "Delivery time depends on sorting, transit, and handoff processes."
4. **Reconstruct Solutions:** Build solutions from the ground up using first principles.
   Solution: "Automate sorting and optimize routes to reduce delivery times."

Applications of First Principles Thinking

1. **In Innovation:**
   - o **Scenario:** A company wants to create a faster, cheaper product.
   - o **Solution:** Analyze the core components of the product and re-engineer the process to optimize costs and performance.
2. **In Personal Goals:**
   - o **Scenario:** You want to save money for a vacation.
   - o **Solution:** Break down expenses, identify the core necessities, and cut non-essential spending.
3. **In Education:**
   - o **Scenario:** A teacher wants to improve student engagement.
   - o **Solution:** Examine the core elements of effective teaching and rebuild lesson plans based on proven principles.

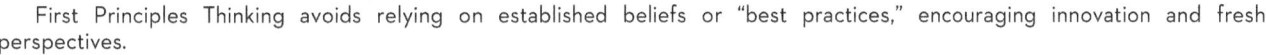

This method helps humans to:

1. **Overcome Assumptions:** Encourages questioning of established norms and practices.
2. **Simplify Complexity:** Reduces problems into manageable components.
3. **Foster Innovation:** Promotes creative solutions by starting from fundamental truths.

Challenges and Limitations

1. **Time-Intensive:** Breaking problems into components and rebuilding solutions requires significant effort.
2. **Resistance to Change:** Challenging assumptions can face pushback, especially in traditional environments.
3. **Requires Deep Knowledge:** Understanding the core components of a problem often demands expertise or research.

For instance, reconstructing a manufacturing process using first principles might require in-depth knowledge of materials science or engineering.

How to Use First Principles Thinking Effectively

1. **Ask Why:** Consistently challenge assumptions to reach the core truths of a problem.
2. **Gather Data:** Research and analyze to identify the most basic components of the issue.
3. **Think Creatively:** Use first principles as a foundation to explore unconventional solutions.

Exercises

1. **Deconstruct a Problem:** Choose a challenge in your life or work and break it down to its first principles. Rebuild a solution from these basics.
2. **Challenge Assumptions:** List three assumptions you hold about a problem or goal. Question their validity and explore alternative perspectives.
3. **Simplify a Process:** Identify a complex process you regularly use. Apply first principles thinking to streamline it.

Closing Thoughts

First Principles Thinking is a transformative approach to problem-solving. It allows you to cut through assumptions, simplify complexity, and find innovative solutions. By returning to fundamental truths, this method unlocks new possibilities and helps you tackle challenges with clarity and creativity.

While it requires effort and a willingness to question norms, its results are often ground-breaking. Whether in business, education, or personal growth, First Principles Thinking equips you to approach problems from a fresh, effective perspective.

Chapter 27: Reverse Engineering

Working Backward: Reverse Engineering

Reverse Engineering is a problem-solving method that involves deconstructing an object, system, or process to understand how it works. Originally used in engineering and product development, this approach is also valuable for solving problems by tracing outcomes back to their origins.

For example:

- **Scenario:** A competitor launches a successful product.
- **Reverse Engineering Approach:**
  o Analyze the product to understand its design, features, and production methods.
  o Identify the key factors contributing to its success.
  o Apply these insights to improve your own product.

Reverse engineering is about learning from existing solutions to inspire innovation and development.

How Reverse Engineering Works

1. **Define the Goal:** Determine what you want to learn or achieve through reverse engineering.
   Example: "How can we replicate or improve this product's performance?"
2. **Disassemble the Object or Process:** Break it down into its components to understand its structure.
   Example: Analyze the features, materials, or steps involved.
3. **Analyze and Reconstruct:** Identify the principles behind the design or process and rebuild it with modifications or improvements.
   Example: Recreate a software program with enhanced functionality or user experience.

1. **In Product Development:**
   o   A company analyzes a competitor's product to understand its design and create a more competitive version.
2. **In Business Strategy:**
   o   A business studies a successful marketing campaign to replicate its strategies in their own campaigns.
3. **In Personal Growth:**
   o   An individual observes a successful person's habits and routines to incorporate similar practices into their own life.

Why Reverse Engineering is Effective

Reverse engineering helps humans to:
1. **Learn from Success:** Understand what works and why by analyzing proven solutions.
2. **Drive Innovation:** Inspire new ideas and improvements based on existing designs or processes.
3. **Uncover Hidden Factors:** Reveal underlying principles or techniques that may not be immediately obvious.

Challenges and Limitations

1. **Ethical and Legal Concerns:** Replicating proprietary designs without permission may violate intellectual property laws.
2. **Complexity of Systems:** Some systems are too intricate to deconstruct easily.
3. **Risk of Imitation Without Innovation:** Copying without adding value may limit creativity or competitiveness.

For example, simply recreating a competitor's product without addressing its flaws or adding unique features may fail to capture market attention.

How to Use Reverse Engineering Effectively

1. **Respect Ethics and Laws:** Ensure that your analysis respects intellectual property and avoids unethical practices.
2. **Focus on Learning:** Use reverse engineering as a tool for understanding and improving, not just copying.
3. **Add Value:** Build on existing solutions by incorporating unique features or addressing gaps.

Exercises

1. **Reverse Engineer a Product:** Choose a product or tool you use regularly. Break it down to understand its design and explore ways to improve it.
2. **Analyze Success:** Study a successful project, campaign, or habit. Identify the key factors behind its success and apply these insights to your own goals.
3. **Reconstruct a Process:** Take a familiar process (e.g. preparing a meal, completing a task) and deconstruct it. Rebuild it with improvements or optimizations.

Closing Thoughts

Reverse Engineering is a versatile and insightful tool for problem-solving and innovation. By analyzing existing solutions, it helps you understand what works, why it works, and how it can be improved.

While it requires careful analysis and ethical consideration, its ability to inspire innovation and drive improvement makes it invaluable for individuals and organizations alike. Whether you're designing a product, developing a strategy, or enhancing your personal growth, Reverse Engineering equips you with the tools to learn from success and build something better.

Chapter 28: Hypothesis Testing

Gathering Data: Hypothesis Testing

Hypothesis Testing is a methodical approach to problem-solving that involves forming a testable statement (hypothesis), gathering data, and analyzing results to determine whether the hypothesis holds true. Widely used in science, business, and decision-making, this method helps validate assumptions and refine understanding through evidence.

For example:
- **Problem:** Website traffic has decreased.
- **Hypothesis:** The decrease is due to slower loading times.
- **Test:** Measure page load speed and analyze user behavior data.
- **Result:** If slow loading times correlate with high bounce rates, the hypothesis is validated.

This method reduces uncertainty and supports data-driven decision-making.

1. **Identify the Problem:** Clearly define the issue or question.
   Example: "Why are sales declining this quarter?"
2. **Formulate a Hypothesis:** Develop a specific, testable statement about the cause.
   Example: "Sales are declining because our marketing campaign is not reaching the target audience."
3. **Collect Data:** Gather relevant information through experiments, surveys, or analytics.
   Example: Analyze marketing data to determine audience demographics and engagement.
4. **Analyze Results:** Evaluate whether the data supports or refutes the hypothesis.
   Example: If the data shows low engagement among the target audience, the hypothesis is supported.
5. **Refine and Retest:** Use the results to adjust the hypothesis or explore new possibilities.

Applications of Hypothesis Testing

1. **In Science:**
   o Researchers test hypotheses about phenomena, such as "This medication reduces symptoms of disease X."
2. **In Business:**
   o Companies test assumptions, such as "Offering free shipping will increase sales."
3. **In Personal Decisions:**
   o Individuals use it informally, such as "I'll feel more energized if I get eight hours of sleep."

Why Hypothesis Testing is Effective

This method helps:
1. **Validate Assumptions:** Provides evidence to confirm or challenge beliefs.
2. **Reduce Risk:** Ensures decisions are based on data, not guesswork.
3. **Encourage Iteration:** Supports continuous learning and refinement through repeated testing.

Challenges and Limitations

1. **Time-Consuming:** Designing tests and analyzing data can be resource-intensive.
2. **Bias Risk:** Personal or organizational biases can influence the interpretation of results.
3. **Dependence on Data Quality:** Poor-quality or insufficient data can undermine the reliability of findings.

For instance, testing a marketing campaign's effectiveness requires accurate tracking of user behavior and preferences to draw meaningful conclusions.

How to Use Hypothesis Testing Effectively

1. **Define Clear Hypotheses:** Ensure your hypothesis is specific, measurable, and testable.
2. **Use Reliable Data:** Gather data from credible and relevant sources to ensure accuracy.
3. **Remain Objective:** Analyze results impartially to avoid confirmation bias.

Exercises

1. **Test a Hypothesis:** Choose a problem or assumption in your life or workplace. Formulate a hypothesis, design a test, and analyze the results.
2. **Challenge a Belief:** Identify a belief you hold and test its validity through evidence and experimentation.
3. **Evaluate Test Design:** Review a study or experiment. Assess whether the hypothesis was clearly defined and supported by the data.

Closing Thoughts

Hypothesis Testing is a cornerstone of logical thinking and decision-making. By systematically testing assumptions and analyzing results, it ensures conclusions are based on evidence rather than speculation.

While the process requires effort and rigor, its ability to validate beliefs, reduce uncertainty, and support innovation makes it indispensable in science, business, and everyday life. Mastering Hypothesis Testing equips you to approach problems with clarity, confidence, and critical thinking.

Chapter 29: Bayesian Thinking

Updating Beliefs with Evidence: Bayesian Thinking

Bayesian Thinking is a decision-making framework based on Bayes' Theorem, which provides a mathematical formula for updating probabilities as new evidence emerges. This approach encourages flexible thinking by revising beliefs in light of new information, making it particularly valuable in uncertain or complex situations.

For example:

- **Initial Belief (Prior):** There's a 20% chance of rain tomorrow based on the weather forecast.
- **New Evidence:** Dark clouds begin to form in the afternoon.
- **Updated Belief (Posterior):** Based on the new evidence, the chance of rain increases to 70%.

Bayesian Thinking teaches you to view beliefs as probabilities that evolve rather than fixed truths, helping you make better-informed decisions.

How Bayesian Thinking Works

1. **Start with a Prior Belief:** Begin with an initial estimate or assumption about the probability of an event.
   Example: "I think there's a 30% chance this project will fail."
2. **Gather New Evidence:** Observe new information relevant to the belief.
   Example: "The team has fallen behind schedule."
3. **Update the Probability:** Use the new evidence to revise the initial belief.
   Example: "Considering the delay, I now believe there's a 50% chance of failure."
4. **Repeat as Needed:** Continuously refine beliefs as more evidence becomes available.

Applications of Bayesian Thinking

1. **In Medicine:**
   - Doctors update diagnoses as new test results or symptoms emerge.
2. **In Business Forecasting:**
   - Companies adjust sales projections based on emerging market trends or customer behavior.
3. **In Personal Decisions:**
   - Individuals revise plans, such as adjusting travel itineraries based on changing conditions.

Why Bayesian Thinking is Effective

This method helps humans to:

1. **Adapt to Change:** Encourages flexible thinking in dynamic environments.
2. **Incorporate Evidence:** Integrates new information to refine beliefs.
3. **Improve Decision-Making:** Reduces overconfidence in initial assumptions.

Challenges and Limitations

1. **Requires Probabilistic Thinking:** Some people may find it difficult to think in terms of probabilities.
2. **Complex Calculations:** Applying Bayes' Theorem can be mathematically intensive in complex cases.
3. **Subjectivity in Priors:** Initial beliefs may introduce bias if not based on reliable evidence.

For instance, an overly optimistic prior belief about project success might underestimate risks, even with new evidence.

How to Use Bayesian Thinking Effectively

1. **Define Clear Preceding Events:** Base initial beliefs on reliable data or logical reasoning.
2. **Incorporate Relevant Evidence:** Focus on evidence directly related to the belief or decision.
3. **Practice Iteration:** Continuously update probabilities as new information arises.

Exercises

1. **Update a Belief:** Choose a belief you hold and revise it based on new evidence. Reflect on how the process affects your confidence.
2. **Analyze a Forecast:** Find a prediction or forecast (e.g., election results, weather). Apply Bayesian Thinking to refine the prediction with new data.
3. **Create a Bayesian Scenario:** Design a hypothetical situation where a belief evolves over time based on evidence. Practice calculating updated probabilities.

Bayesian Thinking is a powerful tool for navigating uncertainty and complexity. By treating beliefs as probabilities that evolve with evidence, it fosters adaptability, critical thinking, and better decision-making.

While it requires effort and practice, its ability to refine understanding and improve accuracy makes it invaluable in fields ranging from science to everyday life. Mastering Bayesian Thinking equips you to approach challenges with clarity, precision, and flexibility.

Chapter 30: Counterfactual Reasoning

Exploring "What If": Counterfactual Reasoning

Counterfactual Reasoning involves exploring alternative scenarios — what could have happened if events had unfolded differently. This type of reasoning helps uncover causal relationships, evaluate decisions, and anticipate future outcomes by reflecting on hypothetical alternatives.

For example:
- **Scenario:** A team missed a project deadline.
- **Counterfactual Question:** "What if we had allocated more resources at the beginning?"
- **Insights:** This question may reveal that early resource allocation could have prevented delays, highlighting a key area for improvement.

By examining "what if" scenarios, Counterfactual Reasoning fosters deeper understanding and better preparation for future challenges.

How Counterfactual Reasoning Works

1. **Identify the Event:** Choose a past event or decision to analyze.
   Example: "Our product launch failed to meet expectations."
2. **Formulate Counterfactuals:** Imagine alternative scenarios where different decisions or conditions occurred.
   Example: "What if we had launched a month later to allow more time for testing?"
3. **Analyze the Differences:** Compare the actual outcome with the hypothetical scenarios to identify causal factors.
   Example: "Delaying the launch might have reduced errors and improved user satisfaction."
4. **Apply the Insights:** Use lessons from the analysis to refine future strategies or decisions.

Applications of Counterfactual Reasoning

1. **In Business Strategy:**
   o Companies analyze missed opportunities, such as "What if we had targeted a different demographic?"
2. **In Personal Decisions:**
   o Individuals reflect on life choices, such as "What if I had chosen a different career path?"
3. **In Risk Assessment:**
   o Teams evaluate potential risks, such as "What if we hadn't implemented a backup system?"

Why Counterfactual Reasoning Is Effective

This method helps:
1. **Understand Causation:** Reveals how specific factors influenced an outcome.
2. **Identify Missed Opportunities:** Highlights areas where better decisions could have led to improved results.
3. **Anticipate Future Scenarios:** Prepares individuals and teams to navigate similar situations more effectively.

Challenges and Limitations

1. **Overemphasis on Hypotheticals:** Focusing too much on "what ifs" can detract from addressing present realities.
2. **Confirmation Bias:** Individuals may create counterfactuals that align with their preexisting beliefs.
3. **Limited Predictive Value:** Hypothetical scenarios are inherently uncertain and may not reflect actual outcomes.

For instance, assuming a delayed product launch would have succeeded ignores other potential risks, such as changes in market conditions.

How to Use Counterfactual Reasoning Effectively

1. **Focus on Learning:** Use counterfactuals to uncover insights, not to dwell on regrets or assign blame.
2. **Balance Hypotheticals with Evidence:** Ground your analysis in realistic assumptions and available data.
3. **Apply Lessons to the Future:** Use the insights gained to inform future decisions and strategies.

1. **Reflect on a Decision:** Choose a past decision and create two counterfactual scenarios where different choices were made. Analyze the potential outcomes.
2. **Evaluate a Team Project:** With a team, reflect on a completed project and explore "what if" scenarios to identify areas for improvement.
3. **Anticipate Risks:** For an upcoming decision, create counterfactuals to explore potential risks and plan contingencies.

Closing Thoughts

Counterfactual Reasoning is a powerful tool for understanding causes, improving decisions, and preparing for the future. By exploring "what if" scenarios, it fosters critical thinking and helps uncover opportunities for growth and improvement.

While it's important to balance counterfactuals with present realities, this method's ability to provide fresh insights and enhance decision-making makes it invaluable in business, personal growth, and risk management. Mastering Counterfactual Reasoning equips you to learn from the past and navigate the future with confidence.

Chapter 31: Analogical Reasoning

Solving Problems Through Similarities: Analogical Reasoning

Analogical Reasoning is a problem-solving method that draws comparisons between similar situations to gain insights or generate solutions. By identifying parallels between a known situation (the "source") and a new problem (the "target"), this approach helps apply past knowledge to new challenges.

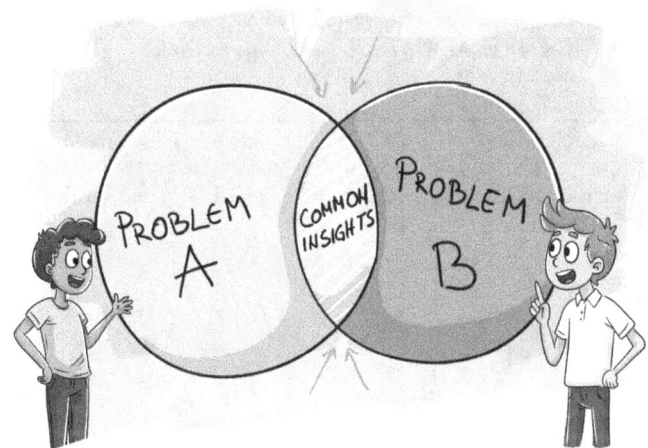

For example:

- **Scenario:** A team struggles to improve customer service.
- **Analogical Thinking:** Compare the issue to how airlines manage customer complaints, focusing on communication strategies and personalized responses.

Analogical Reasoning bridges the gap between the unfamiliar and the familiar, enabling creative problem-solving and innovation.

How Analogical Reasoning Works

1. **Identify the Target Problem:** Define the issue or challenge you're facing.
   Example: "How can we make our product more user-friendly?"
2. **Find a Similar Situation:** Look for a known scenario with comparable characteristics or challenges.
   Example: "What lessons can we learn from successful smartphone designs?"
3. **Draw Parallels:** Identify shared features or principles between the two scenarios.
   Example: "Streamlined interfaces reduce complexity and improve usability."
4. **Apply the Insights:** Use the lessons from the analogous situation to address the target problem.

Applications of Analogical Reasoning

1. **In Business:**
   o Companies adapt successful strategies from other industries.
   Example: Online retailers adopting subscription models inspired by streaming services.
2. **In Personal Development:**
   o Individuals learn from others' experiences to navigate similar challenges.
   Example: Using a mentor's career path as a guide for your own decisions.
3. **In Education:**
   o Teachers use analogies to explain complex concepts.
   Example: Comparing the flow of electricity to the flow of water to teach circuits.

Why Analogical Reasoning Works

This method helps:
1. **Leverage Past Knowledge:** Draws on existing understanding to solve new problems.
2. **Stimulate Creativity:** Encourages innovative thinking by connecting seemingly unrelated ideas.
3. **Simplify Complexity:** Makes unfamiliar concepts more accessible through comparisons.

1. **Superficial Comparisons:** Oversimplifying or misinterpreting similarities can lead to incorrect conclusions.
2. **Irrelevance:** Choosing an analogy that doesn't align well with the target problem may hinder progress.
3. **Overdependence on Analogies:** Relying too heavily on past solutions may stifle original thinking.

For instance, comparing a start-up to a large corporation might overlook differences in resources and scale.

How to Use Analogical Reasoning Effectively

1. **Choose Relevant Analogies:** Ensure the source scenario shares meaningful similarities with the target problem.
2. **Focus on Principles:** Look for underlying principles rather than surface-level similarities.
3. **Combine with Other Methods:** Use Analogical Reasoning alongside other problem-solving tools to ensure well-rounded analysis.

Exercises

1. **Identify Analogies:** Think of a current challenge and find a comparable scenario from another domain. Reflect on the lessons that can be applied.
2. **Analyze Success Stories:** Study how others have solved similar problems and adapt their strategies to your context.
3. **Create an Analogy:** Use an analogy to explain a complex concept or problem to a colleague or friend. Reflect on how the analogy aids understanding.

Closing Thoughts

Analogical Reasoning is a versatile creative tool for problem-solving, enabling you to draw on past experiences and insights to address new challenges. By identifying meaningful parallels, it fosters innovation, simplifies complexity, and broadens perspectives.

Analogical Reasoning's ability to connect the familiar with the unfamiliar makes it a valuable skill in business, education, and personal growth.

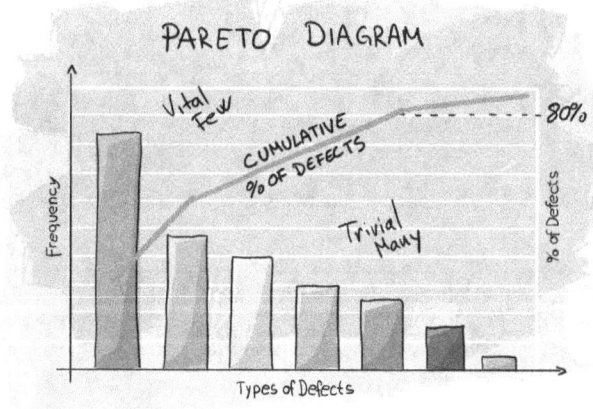

Chapter 32: Pareto Analysis

Focusing on the Vital Few: Pareto Analysis

Pareto Analysis, also known as the 80/20 Rule, is a decision-making tool based on the idea that 80% of results often come from 20% of causes. By identifying and prioritizing these "vital few" factors, this method helps focus resources on the most impactful areas.

For example:

- **Scenario:** A business faces declining profits.
- **Pareto Insight:** An analysis reveals that 20% of the products account for 80% of the revenue. Focusing on these products could maximize profitability.

Pareto Analysis simplifies decision-making by emphasizing efficiency and effectiveness.

How Pareto Analysis Works

1. **Define the Problem:** Clearly identify the issue you want to analyze.
   Example: "Why are customer complaints increasing?"
2. **Collect Data:** Gather information about the causes or contributing factors.
   Example: Categorize complaints by type (e.g. late delivery, defective products, poor service).
3. **Rank by Impact:** Organize the causes from most to least significant.
   Example: Late deliveries account for 60% of complaints.
4. **Focus on the Top Causes:** Prioritize addressing the few causes that have the greatest impact.

Applications of Pareto Analysis

1. **In Quality Control:**
   o   Identify the most common defects in a product and prioritize fixing them.
2. **In Time Management:**
   o   Focus on the 20% of tasks that contribute to 80% of results.
3. **In Customer Service:**
   o   Address the few issues that generate the majority of complaints.

This method helps:
1. **Prioritize Efforts:** Focuses on the most impactful areas rather than spreading resources thinly.
2. **Save Time and Resources:** Maximizes efficiency by addressing the root causes of most problems.
3. **Clarify Focus:** Simplifies complex problems by highlighting the vital few.

Challenges and Limitations

1. **Assumes 80/20 Distribution:** The principle may not apply perfectly to all situations.
2. **Overlooks Minor Issues:** Focusing only on the top causes may ignore smaller but still significant factors.
3. **Requires Accurate Data:** Reliable analysis depends on high-quality and comprehensive data.

For instance, incomplete data about customer complaints could lead to misidentifying the most critical issues.

How to Use Pareto Analysis Effectively

1. **Collect Comprehensive Data:** Ensure your analysis captures all relevant factors.
2. **Re-evaluate Regularly:** Periodically update your analysis to reflect changing conditions or priorities.
3. **Combine with Other Methods:** Use Pareto Analysis alongside tools like Root Cause Analysis or SWOT for deeper insights.

Exercises

1. **Apply Pareto to a Problem:** Choose an issue in your workplace or personal life and use Pareto Analysis to identify the most significant causes.
2. **Analyze Time Usage:** Track your daily tasks and identify the 20% of activities that yield 80% of your results.
3. **Prioritize Improvements:** In a team setting, use Pareto Analysis to decide which projects or issues to address first.

Closing Thoughts

Pareto Analysis is a powerful tool for prioritization and efficiency, enabling you to focus on the areas that matter most. It simplifies decision-making and maximizes.

While it requires thoughtful data collection and interpretation, its ability to clarify focus and improve resource allocation makes it invaluable in business, personal productivity, and problem-solving.

Chapter 33: Ladder of Inference

Climbing Carefully: The Ladder of Inference

The Ladder of Inference, developed by organizational theorist Chris Argyris, is a framework for understanding how individuals move from observations to decisions and actions. It highlights how assumptions and biases can influence reasoning, leading to faulty conclusions. By consciously evaluating each step, you can ensure that your reasoning is logical and evidence-based.

For example:
- **Scenario:** A manager notices a team member arriving late.
- **Rushed Inference:** "They must be lazy."
- **Reflection on the Ladder:**
  o Observation: "The employee arrived late."
  o Assumption: "They don't care about their job."
  o Alternative Explanation: "They were stuck in traffic."

The Ladder of Inference helps slow down this process, encouraging you to verify assumptions and base conclusions on facts.

How the Ladder of Inference Works

1. **Observe the Data:** Start with the raw facts or observable data.
   Example: "The sales team's numbers dropped this quarter."
2. **Select Data:** Focus on specific pieces of data that seem most relevant.
   Example: "Three team members missed their targets."
3. **Make Assumptions:** Interpret the data based on personal beliefs or context.
   Example: "The team isn't putting in enough effort."
4. **Draw Conclusions:** Form a judgment based on your assumptions.
   Example: "We need stricter performance monitoring."
5. **Take Action:** Act on the conclusions drawn.
   Example: "Introduce weekly progress reports."

Each step builds on the previous one, but skipping or misinterpreting steps can lead to flawed reasoning.

1. **In Workplace Communication:**
   o   Use the framework to analyze misunderstandings and improve team dynamics.
   Example: "Before assuming a colleague disagrees, ask questions to clarify their position."
2. **In Personal Relationships:**
   o   Apply the ladder to resolve conflicts by identifying assumptions and seeking alternative perspectives.
3. **In Decision-Making:**
   o   Evaluate business or personal decisions by revisiting the data and questioning assumptions.

Why the Ladder of Inference is Effective

This method helps:
1. **Clarify Reasoning:** Makes the steps of decision-making transparent.
2. **Reduce Bias:** Encourages critical reflection on assumptions and beliefs.
3. **Improve Communication:** Facilitates constructive discussions by focusing on facts and logic.

Challenges and Limitations

1. **Time-Intensive:** Slowing down the reasoning process may not always be practical in urgent situations.
2. **Requires Self-Awareness:** Identifying and challenging your own assumptions can be difficult.
3. **Limited Data:** Decisions are only as good as the data available for analysis.

For instance, misinterpreting a team member's behavior due to incomplete data can lead to unnecessary conflict or ineffective actions.

How to Use the Ladder of Inference Effectively

1. **Pause and Reflect:** Take time to consciously move through each step of the ladder.
2. **Verify Assumptions:** Seek additional data or input to confirm or challenge your assumptions.
3. **Engage Others:** Involve colleagues, friends, or stakeholders to provide diverse perspectives.

Exercises

1. **Analyze a Recent Decision:** Reflect on a decision you made recently. Trace your reasoning up the Ladder of Inference and identify any skipped steps or questionable assumptions.
2. **Role-Play Scenarios:** With a partner, practice identifying the steps of the ladder in a hypothetical situation. Discuss how to improve the reasoning process.
3. **Challenge a Bias:** Choose a belief or assumption you hold and analyze how it was formed using the ladder. Seek data or perspectives that might challenge it.

Closing Thoughts

The Ladder of Inference is a powerful framework for improving reasoning and decision-making. By slowing down and evaluating each step, you can avoid jumping to conclusions, reduce bias, and base actions on solid evidence.

While it requires practice and self-awareness, mastering this method fosters clarity, fairness, and collaboration in both personal and professional contexts.

Chapter 34: Heuristic Analysis

Making Quick Decisions: Heuristic Analysis

Heuristic Analysis involves using mental shortcuts or "rules of thumb" to make decisions quickly and efficiently. While these shortcuts often save time and effort, they can sometimes lead to errors or biases. By understanding heuristics, you can use them effectively while remaining aware of their limitations.

For example:
- **Scenario:** Choosing between two restaurants.
- **Heuristic:** "Go with the one that has more customers—it must be better."
- **Outcome:** While this rule often works, it might overlook factors like wait times or personal preferences.

Heuristic Analysis balances intuition with critical thinking, making it ideal for everyday decisions and fast-paced environments.

How Heuristic Analysis Works

1. **Recognize the Heuristic:** Identify the mental shortcut you're using.
   Example: "I'll pick the product with the higher reviews—it's probably better."
2. **Evaluate the Context:** Consider whether the heuristic is appropriate for the situation.
   Example: "Are the reviews genuine, or could they be biased?"
3. **Decide or Adjust:** Use the heuristic if it's effective, or adjust your approach if more analysis is needed.

Common Heuristics

1. **Availability Heuristic:** Judging the likelihood of an event based on how easily examples come to mind.
   Example: Assuming plane crashes are common because they're heavily reported in the news.
2. **Representativeness Heuristic:** Making judgments based on how well something matches a stereotype.
   Example: Assuming someone who dresses formally must work in a corporate job.
3. **Anchoring Heuristic:** Relying too heavily on the first piece of information encountered.
   Example: Focusing on a high initial price and perceiving a discount as a great deal, even if the discounted price is still high.

Applications of Heuristic Analysis

1. **In Business:**
   o Sales teams use heuristics such as "Focus on repeat customers — they're more likely to buy."
2. **In Education:**
   o Teachers use shortcuts like "Prioritize struggling students for additional support."
3. **In Daily Life:**
   o Individuals rely on rules such as "Take the route with less traffic" to save time.

Why Heuristic Analysis is Effective

This method helps:

1. **Save Time:** Enables fast decision-making in routine or low-stakes situations.
2. **Simplify Complexity:** Reduces the cognitive load by focusing on key factors.
3. **Leverage Experience:** Draws on past knowledge to inform current choices.

Challenges and Limitations

1. **Risk of Bias:** Heuristics can reinforce stereotypes or lead to flawed assumptions.
2. **Overgeneralization:** Applying a shortcut universally may overlook unique aspects of a situation.
3. **Inaccuracy in Complex Problems:** Heuristics are less effective for high-stakes or nuanced decisions.

For instance, using the "availability heuristic" to judge risk may lead to overestimating rare but dramatic events.

How to Use Heuristic Analysis Effectively

1. **Be Aware of Biases:** Recognize when a heuristic might introduce bias or oversimplify the situation.
2. **Combine with Other Methods:** Use heuristics alongside analytical approaches for balanced decision-making.
3. **Reflect on Outcomes:** Regularly evaluate the effectiveness of your shortcuts and adjust as needed.

Exercises

1. **Identify Your Heuristics:** Reflect on common decisions you make (e.g. shopping, planning). Identify the shortcuts you use and analyze their effectiveness.
2. **Challenge a Shortcut:** Choose a heuristic you often rely on and test it against a more detailed analysis. Reflect on the differences in outcomes.
3. **Optimize a Rule of Thumb:** Refine a commonly used heuristic to improve its accuracy or applicability.

Closing Thoughts

Heuristic Analysis is a practical tool for quick decision-making in routine or time-sensitive situations. By balancing speed with awareness of potential biases, it enables you to navigate challenges efficiently and effectively.

While heuristics have limitations, understanding and refining them enhances their utility, making them a valuable addition to your problem-solving toolkit.

Chapter 35: The Eisenhower Matrix

Mastering Prioritization: The Eisenhower Matrix

The Eisenhower Matrix, also called the Urgent-Important Matrix, is a time management tool that helps prioritize tasks based on their urgency and importance. Named after U.S. President Dwight D. Eisenhower, who famously said, "What is important is seldom urgent, and what is urgent is seldom important," this method provides a clear framework for deciding what to focus on, delegate, or eliminate.

For example:

- **Scenario:** A professional has a long to-do list.
- **Using the Matrix:**
    o **Urgent & Important:** Finish a client presentation due tomorrow.
    o **Not Urgent but Important:** Develop a long-term marketing strategy.
    o **Urgent but Not Important:** Respond to non-essential emails.
    o **Neither Urgent nor Important:** Scroll through social media.

The Eisenhower Matrix simplifies prioritization, ensuring time and energy are allocated to tasks that truly matter.

How the Eisenhower Matrix Works

1. **Define Tasks:** List all the tasks you need to complete.
2. **Categorize by Urgency and Importance:** Assign each task to one of four quadrants:
    o **Urgent & Important (Do Now):** Tasks requiring immediate attention and critical to success.
    o **Not Urgent but Important (Plan):** Tasks critical to long-term goals but not time-sensitive.
    o **Urgent but Not Important (Delegate):** Tasks that need to be done quickly but can be handled by someone else.
    o **Neither Urgent nor Important (Eliminate):** Tasks that add no value and can be removed entirely.
3. **Act Accordingly:** Focus on high-priority tasks, plan for long-term objectives, delegate non-essential urgent tasks, and eliminate distractions.

Applications of the Eisenhower Matrix

1. **In Time Management:**
    o Professionals use it to organize daily responsibilities and avoid procrastination.
      Example: Prioritizing project deadlines over non-essential meetings.
2. **In Personal Productivity:**
    o Individuals apply the matrix to balance work, personal goals, and leisure.
      Example: Planning exercise routines under "Not Urgent but Important."
3. **In Team Collaboration:**
    o Teams use the matrix to allocate responsibilities effectively.
      Example: Delegating event logistics while focusing on strategy development.

Why the Eisenhower Matrix is Effective

This method helps:
1. **Clarify Priorities:** Differentiates between what truly matters and what doesn't.
2. **Reduce Stress:** Avoids last-minute scrambles by planning ahead.
3. **Boost Productivity:** Maximizes focus on impactful tasks while eliminating time-wasters.

Challenges and Limitations

1. **Subjectivity:** Assessing urgency and importance can be influenced by personal biases.
2. **Over-Simplification:** Complex tasks may not fit neatly into one quadrant.
3. **Difficulty Delegating:** Some individuals struggle to delegate tasks, even when appropriate.

For instance, someone might incorrectly categorize a task as "Urgent & Important" due to emotional investment rather than objective necessity.

How to Use the Eisenhower Matrix Effectively

1. **Be Honest:** Assess tasks objectively, focusing on actual priorities rather than perceived importance.
2. **Review Regularly:** Revisit and update the matrix as priorities shift.
3. **Learn to Delegate:** Trust others to handle tasks in the "Urgent but Not Important" category.

1. **Create a Daily Matrix:** Use the Eisenhower Matrix to organize your tasks for the day. Reflect on how it influences your focus and productivity.
2. **Analyze a Past Week:** Review your activities from the previous week. Categorize them into the matrix and identify areas for improvement.
3. **Team Exercise:** Collaborate with colleagues to create a matrix for a shared project. Discuss how delegation and elimination can improve efficiency.

Closing Thoughts

The Eisenhower Matrix is an essential tool for mastering time management and prioritization. By categorizing tasks based on urgency and importance, it ensures that your energy is directed toward meaningful work while minimizing distractions.

While it requires regular reflection and a willingness to delegate or eliminate tasks, its ability to streamline focus and enhance productivity makes it invaluable in both personal and professional contexts. Mastering the Eisenhower Matrix equips you to work smarter, not harder.

Subsection: Cognitive Bias Mitigation

Cognitive biases are mental shortcuts that often lead to flawed reasoning, distorted perceptions, and suboptimal decisions. While biases serve as useful survival mechanisms by helping us make quick judgments, they can also cloud our judgment and prevent us from thinking clearly and rationally.

This section focuses on Cognitive Bias Mitigation — practical techniques to recognize, understand, and counteract these biases. Each chapter will explore a specific bias, provide real-world examples of how it manifests, and introduce actionable strategies for overcoming its influence.

Chapter 36: Recognizing Anchoring Bias

The Power of First Impressions: Anchoring Bias

Anchoring Bias occurs when humans rely too heavily on the first piece of information (the "anchor") they receive when making decisions. This initial reference impacts future judgments, even if it's irrelevant or arbitrary.

For example:

- **Scenario:** A car salesperson starts negotiations at a high price, anchoring the buyer's expectations.
- **Effect:** Even if the price drops during negotiation, the buyer perceives the final price as a good deal because it's lower than the anchor.

Recognizing and mitigating Anchoring Bias ensures that decisions are based on logic and evidence rather than arbitrary starting points.

How Anchoring Bias Works

1. **Establishing the Anchor:** An initial number or idea sets the reference point for evaluation.
2. **Adjusting Judgments:** Subsequent decisions or estimates are influenced by the anchor, often insufficiently adjusted.

Even experts are not immune. Studies show that anchoring affects professionals like judges, doctors, and financial analysts.

Examples of Anchoring Bias

1. **In Pricing:**
   o A store lists a product as "Originally $100, now $70!" The anchor (original price) makes the discounted price seem more appealing.
2. **In Job Negotiations:**
   o A candidate anchors their salary expectations by mentioning their previous pay.
3. **In Everyday Decisions:**
   o A friend suggests a specific restaurant first, anchoring your perception of what constitutes a good choice.

Why Anchoring Bias is Harmful

Anchoring Bias can lead to:

1. **Distorted Perceptions:** Decisions may be swayed by irrelevant or inaccurate anchors.
2. **Missed Opportunities:** Over-reliance on anchors may prevent consideration of better alternatives.
3. **Manipulation:** Anchors can be deliberately set to influence others' judgments (e.g., high starting prices in negotiations).

1. **Question the Anchor:** Ask whether the anchor is relevant and supported by evidence.
   Example: "Is this initial price reflective of the product's true value?"
2. **Consider Multiple Perspectives:** Seek alternative reference points to challenge the anchor.
   Example: Compare prices across different sellers before deciding.
3. **Delay Judgment:** Avoid making decisions immediately after encountering an anchor. Take time to evaluate the information independently.

How to Respond to Anchoring Bias in Others

When someone relies on an anchor, you can:

1. **Introduce New Information:** Provide additional reference points to shift their focus.
   Example: "Here's what similar houses in this area sold for recently."
2. **Challenge the Anchor's Validity:** Politely question whether the anchor is reasonable or relevant.
   Example: "Why are we using this particular figure as our starting point?"

Exercises

1. **Identify Anchors in Daily Life:** Reflect on recent decisions. Were they influenced by an anchor? How might you have approached them differently?
2. **Practice Setting Anchors:** In a negotiation or discussion, experiment with setting an anchor and observe its impact.
3. **Reframe an Anchor:** Take an anchored scenario (e.g., a high initial price) and challenge it by introducing new reference points.

Closing Thoughts

Anchoring Bias is a subtle but powerful influence on decision-making. By learning to recognize and challenge anchors, you can make more objective, informed choices and avoid being swayed by irrelevant starting points.

Mastering this skill not only improves personal decision-making but also equips you to navigate negotiations, pricing strategies, and everyday interactions with greater confidence and clarity.

Chapter 37: Overcoming Confirmation Bias

Seeing What We Want to See: Confirmation Bias

Confirmation Bias occurs when people seek out, interpret, and remember information that supports their existing beliefs while ignoring or dismissing evidence that contradicts them. This bias reinforces preconceptions, making it difficult to evaluate information objectively.

For example:

- **Scenario:** A manager believes a team member is underperforming.
- **Bias in Action:** They focus on the mistakes the employee makes while overlooking their successes.

Overcoming Confirmation Bias requires conscious effort to evaluate all evidence, not just what aligns with existing views.

How Confirmation Bias Works

1. **Selective Exposure:** People seek information that aligns with their beliefs.
   Example: Reading news sources that share their political views.
2. **Interpretation Bias:** Contradictory evidence is interpreted in a way that minimizes its significance.
   Example: Dismissing critical feedback as "uninformed."
3. **Memory Bias:** People remember information that supports their beliefs better than contradictory evidence.
   Example: Recalling only the wins of a favorite sports team.

Examples of Confirmation Bias

1. **In Decision-Making:**
   o An investor favors evidence that supports their choice to buy a stock while ignoring reports of declining performance.
2. **In Relationships:**
   o A person believes their friend is always reliable and dismisses instances where they've let them down.
3. **In Science:**
   o A researcher unintentionally designs experiments to confirm their hypothesis rather than test it objectively.

Confirmation Bias can lead to:
1. **Faulty Decisions:** Ignoring contradictory evidence results in poorly informed choices.
2. **Polarization:** Focusing only on information that aligns with one's views deepens divides and discourages open dialogue.
3. **Stagnation:** Reinforcing existing beliefs prevents growth, innovation, and learning.

How to Overcome Confirmation Bias

1. **Seek Disconfirming Evidence:** Actively look for information that challenges your beliefs.
   Example: Ask, "What evidence would prove me wrong?"
2. **Engage with Diverse Perspectives:** Expose yourself to ideas and opinions that differ from your own.
   Example: Read articles from sources with opposing viewpoints.
3. **Ask Neutral Questions:** Frame questions in a way that doesn't assume a particular answer.
   Example: Instead of "Why is my idea correct?" ask, "What are the strengths and weaknesses of my idea?"

How to Respond to Confirmation Bias in Others

When encountering Confirmation Bias, you can:
1. **Present Contradictory Evidence Respectfully:** Avoid confrontation and focus on sharing alternative perspectives.
   Example: "I understand your point. Have you considered this other perspective?"
2. **Encourage Critical Thinking:** Ask open-ended questions to prompt deeper analysis.
   Example: "What do you think would happen if we tried the opposite approach?"
3. **Share Your Own Biases:** Acknowledge how your perspective has evolved, encouraging mutual openness.

Exercises

1. **Challenge a Belief:** Identify a belief you hold strongly. Seek out credible evidence that contradicts it and reflect on how it affects your perspective.
2. **Diversify Your Information Sources:** Choose a topic and read about it from multiple viewpoints, including those you disagree with.
3. **Conduct a Self-Audit:** Reflect on a recent decision. Were you selective in the evidence you considered? How might you approach it differently?

Closing Thoughts

Confirmation Bias is one of the most general cognitive biases, shaping how we perceive and interact with the world. Recognizing and overcoming this bias requires conscious effort, humility, and a commitment to seeking truth over comfort.

By challenging your own assumptions and engaging with diverse perspectives, you can make better decisions, improve relationships, and foster open-mindedness in both personal and professional contexts.

Chapter 38: Mitigating Availability Heuristics

When Memories Skew Perception: Availability Heuristics

The Availability Heuristic refers to the tendency to judge the probability of an event based on how easily examples of it come to mind. Dramatic, recent, or emotionally charged memories often feel more common or likely, even when they're statistically rare.

For example:
- **Scenario:** A person avoids flying because they recently saw news of a plane crash, even though air travel is safer than driving.

Mitigating this bias involves evaluating risks and probabilities based on data rather than vividness or recency of memories.

How the Availability Heuristic Works

1. **Memory Accessibility:** Events that are recent, dramatic, or emotionally impactful are easier to recall.
   Example: A recent shark attack makes people overestimate the risk of swimming in the ocean.
2. **Generalization:** These memorable events are incorrectly assumed to represent the norm.
   Example: Assuming violent crime is increasing after watching a crime-heavy news segment.

Examples of the Availability Heuristic

1. **In Risk Perception:**
   - Overestimating the likelihood of being in a car accident after witnessing one on the highway.
2. **In Decision-Making:**
   - Avoiding certain foods after hearing about one food poisoning incident, despite its rarity.

3. **In Policy Debates:**
   o   Public demand for stricter regulations following a highly publicized but isolated incident.

Why the Availability Heuristic is Harmful

This heuristic can lead to:

1. **Exaggerated Fears:** Overestimating rare risks while underestimating more common dangers.
2. **Distorted Decision-Making:** Basing choices on memorable but unrepresentative events.
3. **Inefficient Resource Allocation:** Prioritizing actions based on emotional impact rather than actual need.

How to Mitigate the Availability Heuristic

1. **Rely on Data:** Use statistics and objective evidence to evaluate risks and probabilities.
   Example: Research airline safety records instead of relying on media coverage.
2. **Broaden Your Perspective:** Consider multiple examples and scenarios to avoid overgeneralization.
   Example: "What's the overall rate of this happening, not just in the cases I've heard about?"
3. **Challenge Emotional Reactions:** Reflect on whether your feelings are influencing your judgment disproportionately.
   Example: "Am I avoiding this activity because it's dangerous or because it feels scary?"

How to Respond to the Availability Heuristic in Others

When someone exhibits this heuristic, you can:

1. **Provide Context:** Share data or examples that balance the conversation.
   Example: "While that incident was tragic, statistics show it's very rare."
2. **Acknowledge Emotions:** Validate their feelings while gently introducing broader evidence.
   Example: "It's natural to feel concerned after hearing that, but let's look at the bigger picture."

Exercises

1. **Analyze Risks:** Choose a fear or concern you have. Research its actual probability and compare it to how likely it feels.
2. **Diversify Inputs:** Reflect on how your media consumption influences your perception of risks. Seek out balanced sources.
3. **Challenge an Overgeneralization:** Identify a recent judgment you made based on a vivid memory. Explore whether it reflects broader trends.

Closing Thoughts

The Availability Heuristic demonstrates how memory and emotion can skew perception of reality. By grounding your judgments in data and considering broader perspectives, you can make more accurate, rational decisions.

Mastering this skill not only reduces unnecessary fears but also improves your ability to evaluate risks and opportunities in a balanced, informed way.

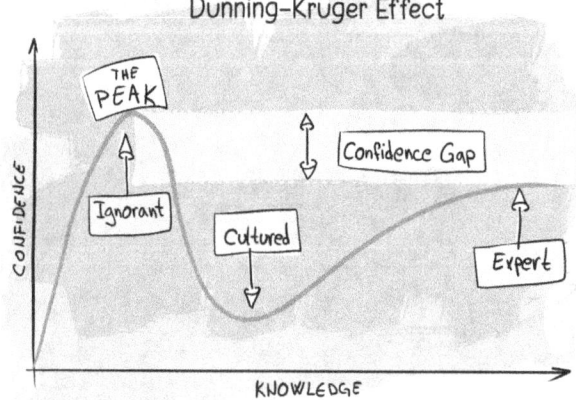

Dunning–Kruger Effect

Chapter 39: Combatting the Dunning-Kruger Effect

The Illusion of Expertise: The Dunning-Kruger Effect

The Dunning-Kruger Effect occurs when individuals with limited knowledge or expertise in a subject overestimate their competence. This cognitive bias results from a lack of awareness about one's own limitations, often leading to overconfidence.

For example:

- **Scenario:** A novice in graphic design believes their skills rival those of a professional after learning basic software tools.

Combatting this bias involves fostering self-awareness, seeking feedback, and committing to continuous learning.

How the Dunning-Kruger Effect Works

1. **Initial Overconfidence:** Individuals gain a little knowledge and feel highly confident in their abilities.
   Example: Someone watches a few cooking tutorials and considers themselves an expert chef.
2. **Recognition of Limitations:** As they learn more, they realize the depth of the field and their own inexperience.
   Example: Attempting a complex recipe reveals gaps in their skills.
3. **Competence and Confidence Align:** Over time, with practice and knowledge, confidence grows alongside competence.

1. **In the Workplace:**
   - A new employee overestimates their ability to manage a project, unaware of the challenges involved.
2. **In Online Discussions:**
   - Individuals confidently share opinions on topics they've only briefly researched.
3. **In Hobbies:**
   - A beginner in photography assumes they can produce professional-quality work with minimal training.

Why the Dunning-Kruger Effect is Harmful

This bias can lead to:

1. **Overconfidence in Decision-Making:** Underestimating challenges can result in poor decisions.
2. **Resistance to Feedback:** Overconfident individuals may dismiss constructive criticism.
3. **Frustration for Others:** Colleagues or peers may find it difficult to collaborate with someone who overestimates their abilities.

How to Combat the Dunning-Kruger Effect

1. **Embrace Lifelong Learning:** Acknowledge that mastery requires time, effort, and continuous education.
   Example: "What are the areas where I need to improve?"
2. **Seek Honest Feedback:** Actively request input from mentors, peers, and experts.
   Example: "Can you critique my work and suggest areas for growth?"

Chapter 40: Avoiding Framing Effects

Shaped by Presentation: The Framing Effect

The Framing Effect occurs when the way information is presented influences decisions and judgments. Even when the underlying facts remain the same, the "frame" or context can alter perception and behavior.

For example:

- **Scenario:** A doctor tells a patient, "90% of people survive this procedure," instead of "10% of people don't survive."
- **Effect:** The positive frame (survival) reassures the patient, while the negative frame (death) causes alarm.

Avoiding Framing Effects involves recognizing how language and context shape decisions and striving for objectivity.

3. **Recognize the Complexity of Knowledge:** Understand that expertise involves more than just surface-level familiarity.
   Example: "What challenges do experts in this field face?"

How to Address the Dunning-Kruger Effect in Others

1. **Provide Constructive Feedback:** Gently point out areas where additional learning is needed.
   Example: "You've made a great start. Here are some resources to deepen your understanding."
2. **Encourage Humility:** Share your own experiences of learning and growth to highlight the value of continuous improvement.
3. **Focus on Collaboration:** Involve others in discussions to bring diverse perspectives and expertise.

Exercises

1. **Identify Your Blind Spots:** Reflect on areas where you may overestimate your knowledge. Research these topics further.
2. **Ask for Feedback:** Choose a skill or task you're confident in and request detailed feedback from someone experienced.
3. **Create a Learning Plan:** Identify a field or skill you want to improve. Outline steps to move from beginner to advanced levels.

Closing Thoughts

The Dunning-Kruger Effect is a natural phase in learning but can hinder growth if left unchecked. By fostering self-awareness, seeking feedback, and embracing humility, you can navigate this bias and develop genuine expertise.

How Framing Effects Work

1. **Positive vs. Negative Frames:** The same fact is presented in either a positive or negative light.
   Example: "20% fat" sounds worse than "80% lean," even though both are identical.
2. **Contextual Cues:** The surrounding context or wording shapes how information is interpreted.
   Example: A discount labeled "Limited-Time Offer" feels more compelling than a generic "20% Off."

1. **In Marketing:**
   o Advertisements emphasize gains ("Save $100!") rather than losses ("Don't miss out on $100 savings!").
2. **In Decision-Making:**
   People are more likely to choose a treatment with a "90% success rate" than one with a "10% failure rate."
3. **In Negotiations:**
   o Framing a proposal as a win-win encourages agreement, while framing it as a concession creates resistance.

Why Framing Effects are Harmful

Framing Effects can lead to:

1. **Irrational Decisions:** Judgments may be based on presentation rather than substance.
2. **Manipulation:** Deliberate framing can exploit biases to influence behavior.
3. **Missed Opportunities:** Focusing on negatives may discourage taking calculated risks.

How to Avoid Framing Effects

1. **Reframe the Information:** Look at the same data from multiple perspectives.
   Example: "What does this decision look like framed as both a gain and a loss?"
2. **Focus on Facts:** Strip away the emotional or contextual framing to evaluate the raw information.
   Example: "What are the actual probabilities or outcomes?"

3. **Anticipate Manipulation:** Be aware of how others might frame information to sway your decisions.

How to Address Framing Effects in Others

1. **Present Balanced Information:** Offer both positive and negative frames to provide a complete picture.
   Example: "This product has a 20% defect rate but is 80% effective overall."
2. **Encourage Critical Thinking:** Ask questions that shift the focus to facts rather than framing.
   Example: "What are the actual implications of this choice?"
3. **Use Neutral Language:** Avoid emotionally charged wording when presenting options.

Exercises

1. **Reframe a Decision:** Take a recent choice and analyze how different frames influenced your judgment. Consider alternative frames.
2. **Spot Framing in Media:** Identify examples of framing in advertisements or news stories. Reflect on how the presentation affects perception.
3. **Create Balanced Frames:** Practice presenting the same information using both positive and negative language. Observe how it changes reactions.

Closing Thoughts

The Framing Effect demonstrates the power of language and context in shaping decisions. By recognizing and countering this bias, you can make more rational, balanced choices and present information in a way that promotes clarity and fairness.

Mastering this skill not only improves your decision-making but also equips you to communicate effectively and ethically in professional and personal interactions.

Chapter 41: Understanding the Halo Effect

The Shine of First Impressions: The Halo Effect

The Halo Effect occurs when an individual's overall impression of someone or something is influenced disproportionately by one positive characteristic. This bias leads people to assume that someone who excels in one area must excel in others, even without supporting evidence.

For example:
- **Scenario:** A charismatic speaker is perceived as more knowledgeable than they actually are.
- **Effect:** Their confidence and charm overshadow potential gaps in their expertise.

Understanding the Halo Effect helps ensure evaluations are balanced and based on comprehensive evidence rather than first impressions.

How the Halo Effect Works

1. **Focus on a Single Attribute:** A positive trait — such as attractiveness, confidence, or success — becomes the basis for broader judgments.
   Example: "They're well-dressed, so they must be organized."
2. **Generalize to Other Traits:** The positive impression spills over into unrelated areas.
   Example: Assuming a friendly co-worker is also highly competent.
3. **Reinforce Through Perception:** Once established, the halo effect influences how future behaviors are interpreted.

1. **In Hiring Decisions:**
    o   A candidate with a polished appearance is assumed to have superior skills, even if their resume doesn't substantiate it.
2. **In Product Marketing:**
    o   A well-designed package creates the impression that a product is of higher quality.
3. **In Education:**
    o   A student who excels in one subject is assumed to perform well in others, even without evidence.

Why the Halo Effect is Harmful

The Halo Effect can lead to:

1. **Biased Judgments:** Positive impressions may overshadow critical weaknesses or limitations.
2. **Missed Opportunities:** Overlooking less charismatic individuals who may have greater competence.
3. **Unfair Treatment:** Favoritism based on superficial traits rather than merit.

How to Counter the Halo Effect

1. **Focus on Objective Criteria:** Use measurable, evidence-based evaluations rather than relying on first impressions.
    Example: "Does this candidate meet the specific requirements for the role?"
2. **Seek Diverse Perspectives:** Involve others in evaluations to minimize personal bias.
    Example: "Let's compare notes and discuss the full range of skills demonstrated."
3. **Reflect on Assumptions:** Ask whether positive impressions are influencing unrelated judgments.
    Example: "Am I assuming this person is skilled because they're confident?"

How to Address the Halo Effect in Others

1. **Encourage Fact-Based Analysis:** Redirect discussions to focus on evidence rather than subjective impressions.
    Example: "What specific examples support this conclusion?"
2. **Highlight Other Attributes:** Point out areas that deserve closer scrutiny to ensure balanced evaluations.
    Example: "They're very personable — let's also review their technical skills."
3. **Promote Awareness:** Discuss the Halo Effect openly in group settings to encourage fair and objective assessments.

Exercises

1. **Identify a Halo Effect:** Reflect on a situation where you judged someone or something based on a single positive trait. How did this affect your decision-making?
2. **Practice Objective Evaluation:** Choose a task (e.g., reviewing resumes, evaluating a project) and focus exclusively on objective criteria.
3. **Challenge a Positive Assumption:** Identify an assumption you've made about someone based on a positive impression. Gather evidence to verify or refute it.

Closing Thoughts

The Halo Effect highlights the power of first impressions, but it also demonstrates how these impressions can distort judgment. By consciously examining assumptions and focusing on evidence, you can make more accurate evaluations.

Mastering this skill fosters better decision-making in hiring, teamwork, and everyday interactions, ensuring that merit and substance take precedence over surface-level impressions.

Chapter 42: Reframing with Devil's Advocacy

Challenging Ideas Constructively: Devil's Advocacy

Devil's Advocacy is a technique where someone intentionally argues against a decision, idea, or plan to test its viability and uncover potential weaknesses. This approach encourages critical thinking, strengthens proposals, and reduces the risk of groupthink.

For example:

*   **Scenario:** A company is planning to launch a new product.
*   **Devil's Advocacy:** "What if competitors respond with a cheaper alternative? Are we prepared for that scenario?"

By challenging assumptions and exploring alternative perspectives, Devil's Advocacy ensures decisions are robust and well-informed.

How Devil's Advocacy Works

1. **Assign the Role:** Designate someone to take on the role of Devil's Advocate in a discussion or decision-making process.
   Example: "Your job is to identify flaws in our proposal."
2. **Challenge Assumptions:** Raise questions or counterarguments to test the strength of the idea.
   Example: "What if this strategy fails? What's our contingency plan?"
3. **Evaluate Responses:** Use the feedback to refine and strengthen the proposal or decision.

Applications of Devil's Advocacy

1. **In Strategic Planning:**
   o Teams use Devil's Advocacy to identify risks and refine business strategies.
2. **In Academic Debates:**
   o Students explore opposing viewpoints to deepen understanding of complex topics.
3. **In Personal Decisions:**
   o Individuals challenge their own plans to uncover potential oversights.

Why Devil's Advocacy is Effective

This method helps:

1. **Strengthen Ideas:** Exposes weaknesses and gaps, leading to more robust decisions.
2. **Encourage Open Dialogue:** Promotes a culture of constructive criticism and mutual respect.
3. **Prevent Groupthink:** Reduces the risk of unanimous but poorly considered decisions.

Challenges and Limitations

1. **Resistance to Criticism:** People may feel defensive or dismissive of opposing viewpoints.
2. **Overemphasis on Negativity:** Excessive focus on flaws may stifle creativity or optimism.
3. **Time-Intensive:** Thoroughly testing ideas can require significant effort and resources.

For instance, in fast-paced environments, teams may resist adopting Devil's Advocacy due to perceived delays in decision-making.

How to Use Devil's Advocacy Effectively

1. **Foster a Safe Environment:** Ensure participants feel comfortable raising and addressing criticisms.
2. **Balance Criticism with Constructive Feedback:** Focus on refining ideas rather than dismissing them outright.
3. **Rotate the Role:** Assign different team members as Devil's Advocate to ensure diverse perspectives.

Exercises

1. **Challenge a Plan:** Choose a project or decision you're working on and play the role of Devil's Advocate. What potential flaws can you identify?
2. **Team Exercise:** In a group setting, assign a Devil's Advocate to critique a proposal. Reflect on how this process improves the outcome.
3. **Personal Reflection:** Apply Devil's Advocacy to a personal goal or decision. What insights emerge from challenging your assumptions?

Closing Thoughts

Devil's Advocacy is a powerful tool for strengthening ideas, fostering critical thinking, and ensuring balanced decision-making. By embracing constructive criticism, individuals and teams can address weaknesses, anticipate challenges, and make more informed choices.

While it requires a willingness to engage in healthy debate, the benefits of this approach make it invaluable in both professional and personal contexts.

Chapter 43: Premortem Analysis

Planning for Failure: Premortem Analysis

Premortem Analysis is a problem-solving technique where a team imagines a project has failed and works backward to identify potential reasons for the failure. Unlike a post-mortem, which analyzes failures after they occur, a premortem focuses on preventing issues before they arise.

For example:

- **Scenario:** A company plans to launch a new software product.
- **Premortem Question:** "Imagine the launch is a disaster. What went wrong?"
- **Insights:** Issues like insufficient testing, unclear marketing, or competitor actions might surface, allowing the team to address these risks proactively.

Premortem Analysis fosters proactive thinking, improves planning, and reduces the likelihood of failure.

How Premortem Analysis Works

1. **Define the Project:** Clearly describe the project or decision under consideration.
   Example: "We're planning a corporate expansion into a new market."
2. **Imagine Failure:** Ask the team to envision that the project has failed completely.
   Question: "If this initiative flopped, what would be the main reasons?"
3. **Identify Potential Issues:** Brainstorm all possible causes of failure, both internal and external.
   Example: "We underestimated cultural differences or regulatory challenges."
4. **Develop Mitigation Strategies:** Use the identified risks to create action plans that address vulnerabilities.

Applications of Premortem Analysis

1. **In Business Strategy:**
   - Teams use it to foresee and mitigate risks in major initiatives.
   Example: A startup anticipates funding challenges and builds contingency plans.
2. **In Project Management:**
   - Teams analyze potential pitfalls in new projects to prevent delays or overruns.
3. **In Personal Planning:**
   - Individuals apply premortem thinking to prepare for challenges in achieving personal goals.

Why Premortem Analysis is Effective

This method helps:

1. **Identify Risks Early:** Proactively addresses potential issues before they become problems.
2. **Encourage Honest Feedback:** Fosters open discussion by normalizing the exploration of failure scenarios.
3. **Improve Resilience:** Builds contingency plans that make projects more robust and adaptable.

Challenges and Limitations

1. **Overemphasis on Negatives:** Excessive focus on failure may discourage optimism or creativity.
2. **Difficulty in Identifying Unforeseen Issues:** Some risks may still be missed despite thorough analysis.
3. **Time and Resource Requirements:** Conducting a premortem may require significant effort, particularly for complex projects.

For instance, in a fast-paced start-up environment, teams may resist dedicating time to imagining failure when urgency drives action.

How to Use Premortem Analysis Effectively

1. **Encourage a Positive Mindset:** Frame the exercise as a way to strengthen the project, not to predict inevitable failure.
2. **Involve Diverse Perspectives:** Include team members from different backgrounds and roles to ensure comprehensive risk identification.
3. **Prioritize Risks:** Focus on addressing the most likely and impactful failure scenarios first.

Exercises

1. **Conduct a Premortem:** Choose a current project or goal. Imagine it has failed and brainstorm reasons why. Create a plan to mitigate these risks.
2. **Team Workshop:** Facilitate a premortem session for a group project. Reflect on how this exercise changes the team's approach.
3. **Personal Application:** Apply premortem thinking to a personal decision, such as a career change or major purchase. What risks can you foresee and address?

Closing Thoughts

Premortem Analysis is a proactive and practical tool for anticipating challenges and strengthening plans. By imagining failure and addressing potential risks early, you can improve the likelihood of success and build resilience against unforeseen setbacks.

While it requires a willingness to confront uncomfortable scenarios, the insights gained through this process are invaluable for ensuring robust decision-making and effective execution.

Why change the process? It's worked fine for years.

Maybe, but what if a new method saves time and effort?

Chapter 44: Overcoming Status Quo Bias

Resisting Familiarity: Status Quo Bias

Status Quo Bias refers to the tendency to prefer existing conditions or the "default" option over change, even when better alternatives are available. This bias often stems from fear of the unknown, or overestimating the risks of change.

For example:

- **Scenario:** A company continues using outdated software despite evidence that a modern system would save time and money.

Overcoming Status Quo Bias involves evaluating options objectively, challenging assumptions, and embracing change when it offers clear benefits.

How Status Quo Bias Works

1. **Preference for Familiarity:** People tend to stick with what they know, even if it's suboptimal.
   Example: "We've always done it this way—it's comfortable."
2. **Aversion to Loss:** The potential losses associated with change often feel more significant than the potential gains.
   Example: "What if the new system doesn't work as expected?"
3. **Underestimating Alternatives:** The default option is often chosen without thoroughly exploring other possibilities.

Examples of Status Quo Bias

1. **In Personal Decisions:**
   o   Staying in a job you dislike because it feels safer than seeking a new opportunity.
2. **In Business Strategy:**
   o   Failing to adopt innovative technologies due to fear of disruption.
3. **In Public Policy:**
   o   Resistance to new policies or reforms, even when they offer clear advantages.

Why Status Quo Bias is Harmful

This bias can lead to:

1. **Missed Opportunities:** Avoiding change may prevent growth, innovation, or improvement.
2. **Inefficiency:** Clinging to outdated methods or systems hinders progress.
3. **Resistance to Innovation:** Fear of change stifles creativity and adaptability.

How to Overcome Status Quo Bias

1. **Evaluate Costs and Benefits:** Compare the risks and rewards of maintaining the status quo versus making a change.
   Example: "What are the long-term costs of sticking with the current system?"
2. **Start Small:** Test changes on a smaller scale to reduce perceived risks.
   Example: "Let's pilot the new software in one department first."
3. **Focus on Opportunities:** Shift attention from what might be lost to what could be gained.
   Example: "What are the potential benefits of embracing this new approach?"

How to Address Status Quo Bias in Others

1. **Highlight the Costs of Inaction:** Show how sticking with the status quo may lead to missed opportunities or declining performance.
2. **Provide Evidence:** Use data, case studies, or examples to demonstrate the benefits of change.
3. **Involve Stakeholders:** Engage others in the decision-making process to build trust and reduce resistance.

Exercises

1. **Challenge a Default:** Reflect on a decision where you chose the default option. Re-evaluate whether this was the best choice.
2. **Analyze a Missed Opportunity:** Identify a time when fear of change held you back. What could you have done differently?
3. **Test a New Option:** Choose an area in your life or work where you've stuck with the status quo. Experiment with an alternative and reflect on the outcome.

Closing Thoughts

Status Quo Bias is a common but limiting mindset that prioritizes comfort over progress. By recognizing this bias and embracing thoughtful, evidence-based changes, you can unlock new opportunities, drive innovation, and adapt more effectively to evolving challenges.

Mastering this skill helps you make proactive, forward-thinking decisions, whether in your personal life, your career, or your organization.

Chapter 45: Appreciating Base Rates

The Bigger Picture: Appreciating Base Rates

Base Rate Neglect occurs when individuals focus on specific, vivid details and ignore statistical probabilities (base rates) that provide a more accurate picture. Appreciating base rates helps anchor judgments in reality by prioritizing general data over isolated cases.

For example:

- **Scenario:** A person believes their chance of winning the lottery is high because they know someone who won, ignoring the statistical odds.

By factoring in base rates, you can make more rational decisions and avoid being swayed by emotional or anecdotal evidence.

How Base Rate Neglect Works

1. **Focus on Specifics:** People give disproportionate weight to anecdotal evidence or specific details.
   Example: "My friend succeeded in this investment, so I will too."
2. **Ignore Probabilities:** Statistical data is overlooked, even when it provides a more accurate assessment of likelihood.
   Example: Ignoring the fact that 90% of start-ups fail within five years.
3. **Distorted Decision-Making:** Judgments become biased toward the specific over the general.

Examples of Base Rate Neglect

1. **In Medical Decisions:**
   o Assuming a rare disease is likely after reading vivid symptoms online, despite its low base rate in the general population.
2. **In Hiring Decisions:**
   o Focusing on a candidate's charisma during an interview while ignoring statistical data on their past performance.
3. **In Everyday Risks:**
   o Overestimating the danger of air travel due to media coverage of plane crashes, despite its statistical safety.

Why Base Rate Neglect is Harmful

Neglecting base rates can lead to:
1. **Overconfidence in Unlikely Outcomes:** Decisions are based on rare exceptions rather than common realities.
2. **Poor Risk Assessment:** Overestimating or underestimating risks due to emotional or anecdotal influences.
3. **Missed Opportunities:** Ignoring general trends that could provide valuable insights.

How to Appreciate Base Rates

1. **Start with the General Data:** Look at statistical probabilities before considering specific cases.
   Example: "What are the overall odds of success in this venture?"
2. **Combine Base Rates with Specifics:** Use individual details to complement, not replace, statistical data.
   Example: "How does this person's background compare to the general success rate in this field?"
3. **Consult Experts:** Seek advice from those familiar with statistical trends in the relevant area.

How to Address Base Rate Neglect in Others

1. **Present Data Clearly:** Share base rate statistics alongside specific examples to provide context.
   Example: "While this case is compelling, the overall success rate for this approach is only 10%."
2. **Challenge Anecdotes:** Gently question how individual examples compare to broader trends.
   Example: "That's an interesting story—how often does that actually happen?"
3. **Encourage Critical Thinking:** Highlight the importance of balancing general data with personal stories.

Exercises

1. **Analyze a Decision:** Reflect on a past choice where you prioritized specific details over statistical probabilities. What would you do differently now?
2. **Research Base Rates:** Choose a decision you're facing and look up relevant statistics. How does this information affect your perspective?

---

3. **Challenge an Anecdote:** When someone shares a compelling story, research how it compares to broader data. Reflect on the insights you gain.

Closing Thoughts

Appreciating base rates is essential for rational decision-making. By grounding judgments in statistical realities, you can better assess risks, predict outcomes, and make informed choices.

This skill not only enhances your personal and professional decision-making but also empowers you to navigate a data-driven world with clarity and confidence.

Chapter 46: Debiasing with Probabilistic Thinking

Thinking in Percentages: Probabilistic Thinking

Probabilistic Thinking involves evaluating decisions and outcomes in terms of probabilities rather than certainties. This approach encourages consideration of multiple possibilities and their likelihoods, leading to more nuanced and flexible judgments.

For example:

- **Scenario:** A manager is deciding whether to invest in a new product.
- **Probabilistic Thinking:** "There's a 60% chance of moderate success, a 20% chance of significant success, and a 20% chance of failure."

By quantifying uncertainty, probabilistic thinking helps mitigate overconfidence and fosters more informed decision-making.

How Probabilistic Thinking Works

1. **Define Possible Outcomes:** Identify all potential scenarios.
   Example: "If we launch this product, what are the possible market reactions?"
2. **Assign Probabilities:** Estimate the likelihood of each outcome based on data or experience.
   Example: "What's the probability of capturing 10%, 20%, or 30% of the market?"
3. **Weigh Outcomes:** Consider the impact and likelihood of each scenario when making a decision.

Applications of Probabilistic Thinking

1. **In Business Decisions:**
   o   Evaluate risks and opportunities in projects or investments.
2. **In Personal Planning:**
   o   Assess the likelihood of achieving personal goals under different conditions.
3. **In Everyday Choices:**
   o   Use probabilities to make practical decisions, such as choosing insurance coverage.

Why Probabilistic Thinking is Effective

This method helps:

1. **Manage Uncertainty:** Reduces overconfidence by acknowledging unknowns.
2. **Improve Risk Assessment:** Balances optimism with realism in evaluating possibilities.
3. **Encourage Flexibility:** Adapts strategies based on changing probabilities.

Challenges and Limitations

1. **Difficulty in Estimation:** Accurately estimating probabilities requires data and experience.
2. **Overcomplication:** Excessive focus on probabilities may hinder timely decision-making.
3. **Misinterpretation:** Probabilities must be clearly understood to avoid confusion.

For instance, misunderstanding the difference between a 10% and 90% probability can lead to poor decisions.

How to Practice Probabilistic Thinking

1. **Use Data:** Base probability estimates on credible information whenever possible.
2. **Embrace Uncertainty:** Accept that probabilities reflect likelihoods, not guarantees.
3. **Refine Over Time:** Update probabilities as new information becomes available.

1. **Analyze a Decision:** Choose a past or upcoming decision and outline possible outcomes with their probabilities. Reflect on how this affects your judgment.
2. **Quantify Uncertainty:** Pick a situation where the outcome is uncertain. Assign probabilities to different scenarios and reassess your approach.
3. **Create a Probability Tree:** Map out a series of decisions and their possible outcomes to practice structured probabilistic reasoning.

Closing Thoughts

Probabilistic Thinking transforms uncertainty into clarity by quantifying possibilities and weighing risks. By adopting this mindset, you can navigate complex decisions with greater precision and confidence.

Chapter 47: Overcoming Loss Aversion

Letting Go of Fear: Loss Aversion

Loss Aversion is a cognitive bias that causes people to fear losses more than they value equivalent gains. This bias often leads to overly cautious decisions, missed opportunities, and an unwillingness to take calculated risks.

For example:

- **Scenario:** An investor hesitates to sell a declining stock because they fear locking in the loss, even when reinvesting in a stronger stock would likely yield better returns.

Overcoming Loss Aversion involves rethinking how you evaluate risks and rewards to make more balanced, rational decisions.

How Loss Aversion Works

1. **Fear of Loss:** Losses are perceived as more painful than gains are pleasurable.
   Example: Losing $100 feels worse than gaining $100 feels good.
2. **Clinging to the Status Quo:** People prefer to avoid change if it involves potential losses.
   Example: Keeping a failing product in the market to avoid the "loss" of sunk costs.
3. **Overvaluing What You Own:** The **endowment effect** amplifies loss aversion, making people overvalue items they already possess.

Examples of Loss Aversion

1. **In Investing:**
   o Holding onto underperforming assets to avoid realizing a loss, even when selling would free up resources for better opportunities.
2. **In Negotiations:**
   o Accepting a suboptimal deal to avoid the risk of losing the negotiation entirely.
3. **In Everyday Life:**
   o Choosing not to cancel a gym membership because of the initial cost, even when it's no longer being used.

Why Loss Aversion is Harmful

Loss Aversion can lead to:

1. **Missed Opportunities:** Fear of loss prevents individuals from pursuing high-potential rewards.
2. **Poor Resource Allocation:** Overvaluing existing commitments wastes time and energy.
3. **Stagnation:** Avoiding change hinders growth and innovation.

How to Overcome Loss Aversion

1. **Reframe the Risk:** Focus on the potential gains rather than the fear of loss.
   Example: "What can I achieve by taking this risk?"
2. **Use Probabilities:** Evaluate risks and rewards in terms of their likelihood and impact.
   Example: "What's the chance of success, and how does it compare to the potential loss?"
3. **Separate Emotions from Decisions:** Acknowledge emotional attachments but focus on objective analysis.
   Example: "Am I holding onto this investment because of its actual value or because I'm afraid to lose?"

How to Address Loss Aversion in Others

1. **Highlight the Cost of Inaction:** Show how avoiding risk can lead to missed opportunities.
   Example: "If we don't try this strategy, we could lose market share to competitors."

2. **Present Gains First:** Frame decisions in terms of potential benefits.
   Example: "By adopting this system, we can save 30% in costs over the next year."
3. **Encourage Small Steps:** Suggest incremental changes to reduce the perceived risk of loss.
   Example: "Let's start with a small-scale trial before committing fully."

Exercises

1. **Evaluate a Missed Opportunity:** Reflect on a time when fear of loss held you back. What might have happened if you had focused on potential gains instead?
2. **Reframe a Decision:** Choose a current decision and analyze it from a gains-focused perspective. How does this shift your approach?
3. **Experiment with Letting Go:** Identify something you've been clinging to due to loss aversion. Take a small step toward letting it go and observe the results.

Closing Thoughts

Loss Aversion is a deeply ingrained bias, but it can be mitigated with conscious effort and reframing. By focusing on opportunities rather than fears, you can make more balanced, confident decisions and unlock greater potential for growth and success.

Mastering this mindset fosters resilience and adaptability, helping you navigate risks and rewards with clarity and courage.

Chapter 48: Distinguishing Intuition from Analysis

Balancing Gut and Mind: Intuition vs. Analysis

Decisions often involve a tension between intuition (the immediate, instinctive sense of what to do) and analysis (the deliberate evaluation of data and evidence). Both approaches have strengths and weaknesses, and the key lies in knowing when to rely on each.

For example:

- **Scenario:** A manager feels that a candidate is the right fit for a role (intuition) but also reviews their track record and references to confirm the decision (analysis).

Distinguishing intuition from analysis allows you to make decisions that combine speed, accuracy, and reliability.

How Intuition and Analysis Work

1. **Intuition:**
   - Relies on pattern recognition and past experiences.
     Example: "I've encountered this situation before, and this feels like the right solution."
2. **Analysis:**
   - Involves systematic evaluation of facts, data, and probabilities.
     Example: "Based on these numbers, this approach has the highest chance of success."
3. **Combining the Two:**
   - Effective decision-making often integrates both, using intuition for speed and analysis for validation.

Examples of Intuition vs. Analysis

1. **In Hiring Decisions:**
   - **Intuition:** "This candidate has the right energy for the team."
   - **Analysis:** "Their skills and experience match the job requirements."
2. **In Investment Choices:**
   - **Intuition:** "This stock feels like it's going to perform well."
   - **Analysis:** "The company's financials and market trends support this choice."
3. **In Personal Decisions:**
   - **Intuition:** "This feels like the right house for me."
   - **Analysis:** "It fits my budget, location, and size requirements."

Why Balancing Intuition and Analysis is Important

Overreliance on one approach can lead to:

1. **Intuition Alone:** Decisions may be impulsive or poorly informed.
2. **Analysis Alone:** Overthinking may cause delays or missed opportunities.

A balanced approach combines the best of both: the speed of intuition and the accuracy of analysis.

1. **Pause and Reflect:** Ask whether your decision is based on a gut feeling or logical reasoning.
   Example: "Am I doing this because it feels right, or because the data supports it?"
2. **Validate Intuition with Evidence:** Use analysis to confirm or challenge your instincts.
   Example: "Does the data align with my initial impression?"
3. **Recognize Patterns:** Build experience to improve the accuracy of your intuitive judgments.

How to Help Others Balance Intuition and Analysis

1. **Encourage Evidence-Based Intuition:** Prompt colleagues to back their gut feelings with facts.
   Example: "That's an interesting perspective—what data supports it?"
2. **Facilitate Discussions:** Create opportunities to integrate diverse viewpoints and approaches.
   Example: "Let's hear both the intuitive and data-driven arguments before deciding."
3. **Promote a Balanced Culture:** Encourage teams to value both intuition and analysis.

Exercises

1. **Analyze a Decision:** Reflect on a past decision you made intuitively. How would analysis have changed your approach?
2. **Validate Your Intuition:** Choose a current decision guided by instinct. Seek data to confirm or challenge your gut feeling.
3. **Test Both Approaches:** For an upcoming decision, make an intuitive choice first, then analyze it systematically. Compare the results.

Closing Thoughts

Distinguishing and balancing intuition and analysis is a hallmark of effective decision-making. By recognizing the strengths and limitations of both, you can approach challenges with greater clarity, flexibility, and confidence.

This skill empowers you to navigate complex situations, make sound judgments, and adapt to uncertainty while harnessing the best of both instinct and intellect.

Chapter 49: Applying the Illusion of Transparency Test

The Misconception of Clarity: The Illusion of Transparency

The **Illusion of Transparency** is a cognitive bias where individuals overestimate how clearly their thoughts, emotions, or intentions are understood by others. This bias often leads to miscommunication, frustration, and unmet expectations.

For example:

- **Scenario:** A manager assumes their team understands the project goals because they feel they've communicated them clearly. In reality, the team is confused about key details.

Applying the Illusion of Transparency Test involves actively verifying understanding to ensure clarity in communication and decision-making.

How the Illusion of Transparency Works

1. **Assuming Clarity:** People believe their feelings or thoughts are obvious to others.
   Example: "I'm clearly upset—why doesn't anyone notice?"
2. **Underestimating Ambiguity:** The speaker assumes their message is understood as intended.
   Example: "I told them to prioritize this task; isn't that clear enough?"
3. **Ignoring Context:** Miscommunication arises when the listener lacks the same context or information.

Examples of the Illusion of Transparency

1. **In Leadership:**
   o A leader assumes their team understands a strategic vision without providing detailed explanations.
2. **In Personal Relationships:**
   o One partner believes their frustration is obvious, while the other remains unaware of any issue.
3. **In Public Speaking:**
   o A speaker assumes the audience understands complex terminology without further clarification.

Why the Illusion of Transparency is Harmful

This bias can lead to:

1. **Miscommunication:** Unclear expectations result in confusion and errors.
2. **Frustration:** Both parties feel misunderstood or unheard.
3. **Missed Opportunities:** Failure to address misunderstandings hinders collaboration and progress.

1. **Ask for Feedback:** Confirm that your message has been understood as intended.
   Example: "Can you summarize what you've understood so far?"
2. **Use Clear, Simple Language:** Avoid assuming that others share your level of expertise or context.
   Example: Replace jargon with plain language or provide explanations.
3. **Encourage Questions:** Create a safe space for others to seek clarification.
   Example: "Does anyone have questions or need more detail about this?"

How to Address the Illusion of Transparency in Others

1. **Reflect Understanding Back:** Paraphrase what the other person has said to ensure clarity.
   Example: "So, you're saying the priority is to finish this report by Friday?"
2. **Gently Challenge Assumptions:** Highlight areas where clarity might be lacking.
   Example: "That's a great idea—how do you think others might interpret it?"
3. **Encourage Active Listening:** Foster a culture of mutual understanding and clear communication.

Exercises

1. **Reflect on Past Miscommunications:** Identify a time when you assumed others understood you clearly. What could you have done differently?
2. **Verify Understanding:** In your next conversation, ask the other person to restate your message to ensure alignment.
3. **Clarify an Ambiguous Situation:** Choose a recent instance of confusion and rewrite the communication to eliminate ambiguity.

Closing Thoughts

The Illusion of Transparency reminds us that what feels clear in our minds may not be obvious to others. By verifying understanding and encouraging open dialogue, we can overcome this bias and communicate more effectively.

Mastering this skill enhances relationships, improves teamwork, and ensures that your messages are understood as intended, fostering greater connection and collaboration.

Chapter 50: The Outside View Technique

Looking Beyond Yourself: The Outside View Technique

The Outside View Technique involves stepping back from a specific situation and considering broader trends, patterns, and external perspectives. Unlike the inside view, which focuses on unique details, the outside view anchors decisions in objective data and comparable cases.

For example:

- **Scenario:** A start-up founder believes their product will succeed based on its unique features (inside view).
- **Outside View:** Examining industry statistics reveals that 90% of start-ups fail within the first five years, prompting more realistic planning.

By incorporating the outside view, you can avoid overconfidence and improve decision-making accuracy.

How the Outside View Technique Works

1. **Define the Situation:** Clearly outline the decision or project at hand.
   Example: "We're launching a new app in the fitness market."
2. **Find Comparable Cases:** Look for similar situations or historical examples.
   Example: "How have other fitness apps performed in their first year?"
3. **Use Base Rates and Trends:** Anchor your expectations in objective data from comparable cases.
   Example: "What's the average success rate for apps in this category?"
4. **Adjust Plans Accordingly:** Incorporate insights from the outside view to refine strategies and expectations.

Applications of the Outside View Technique

1. **In Business Planning:**
   o Evaluate projects or investments by analyzing industry benchmarks and trends.
2. **In Personal Decisions:**
   o Use external data to set realistic expectations for personal goals, such as fitness or career milestones.
3. **In Risk Assessment:**
   o Assess potential outcomes by considering historical probabilities and patterns.

Why the Outside View Technique is Effective

This method helps:

1. **Counter Overconfidence:** Reduces the tendency to rely on overly optimistic assumptions.
2. **Provide Context:** Anchors decisions in objective, data-driven insights.
3. **Improve Planning:** Encourages realistic timelines, budgets, and expectations.

Challenges and Limitations

1. **Access to Data:** Finding relevant and accurate data for comparable cases can be difficult.
2. **Overemphasis on Trends:** Focusing too much on past patterns may overlook unique opportunities.
3. **Resistance to Change:** People may resist adjusting plans when the outside view contradicts their assumptions.

For instance, a team deeply invested in their project's uniqueness may struggle to accept external benchmarks that suggest lower success rates.

How to Use the Outside View Effectively

1. **Start with Data:** Identify key metrics and trends that provide a realistic baseline.
   Example: "What's the average ROI for similar investments?"
2. **Balance Views:** Combine insights from the outside view with the unique aspects of your situation.
   Example: "How do our advantages align with industry trends?"
3. **Update Regularly:** Revisit the outside view as new data becomes available or conditions change.

Exercises

1. **Analyze a Past Decision:** Reflect on a decision where you relied solely on the inside view. How would incorporating the outside view have changed your approach?
2. **Research Benchmarks:** Choose a current goal or project and identify comparable cases or trends. Use this data to refine your expectations.
3. **Combine Views:** Practice integrating the inside and outside views in your next major decision. Reflect on the balance between them.

Closing Thoughts

The Outside View Technique is a powerful antidote to overconfidence and narrow thinking. By stepping back and considering broader trends, you can make more accurate, data-driven decisions while remaining open to unique opportunities.

Section III: Practical Applications

Subsection: Decision-Making Techniques

Making decisions is a core skill that influences every aspect of life, from personal growth to organizational success. However, the complexity of modern challenges requires more than just intuition or guesswork. The tools and methods in this section equip you with structured approaches to make decisions that are well-informed, balanced, and effective.

Whether you're comparing options, forecasting outcomes, or evaluating risks, these techniques provide frameworks to clarify choices, analyze trade-offs, and anticipate potential consequences. By mastering these decision-making tools, you'll build confidence in your ability to navigate uncertainty and choose wisely, regardless of the stakes.

Chapter 51: Weighted Decision Matrix

Systematic Comparison: The Weighted Decision Matrix

The Weighted Decision Matrix is a tool for comparing multiple options based on a set of criteria, each assigned a weight reflecting its importance. By scoring options against these criteria, this method ensures that decisions are logical, transparent, and aligned with priorities.

For example:
- **Scenario:** A team is choosing a software platform.
- **Matrix:** They evaluate options based on cost, ease of use, and functionality, assigning higher weights to the most important criteria.

The Weighted Decision Matrix simplifies complex decisions by breaking them into smaller, manageable parts.

How the Weighted Decision Matrix Works

1. **List Options and Criteria:** Define the choices and the criteria for evaluation.
   Example: Options: Software A, Software B, Software C. Criteria: Cost, Features, User Experience.
2. **Assign Weights to Criteria:** Reflect the relative importance of each criterion (e.g., on a scale of 1–5).
   Example: Cost = 3, Features = 4, User Experience = 5.
3. **Score Each Option:** Rate how well each option meets each criterion (e.g., on a scale of 1–10).
4. **Calculate Weighted Scores:** Multiply each score by the corresponding weight and sum the results for each option.
5. **Compare Totals:** The option with the highest total score is the recommended choice.

Applications of the Weighted Decision Matrix

1. **In Business:**
   - Choose suppliers, vendors, or technologies based on key performance metrics.
2. **In Personal Decisions:**
   - Evaluate job offers by comparing factors like salary, location, and growth opportunities.
3. **In Team Collaboration:**
   - Facilitate group decisions by providing a structured framework for discussion.

Why the Weighted Decision Matrix is Effective

This method helps:
1. **Clarify Priorities:** Ensures decisions align with what matters most.
2. **Reduce Bias:** Bases choices on objective criteria rather than subjective impressions.
3. **Simplify Complexity:** Breaks down decisions into manageable, logical steps.

Challenges and Limitations

1. **Subjective Weights and Scores:** Assigning weights and scores may still involve personal bias.
2. **Time-Intensive:** Creating and populating the matrix requires effort and attention to detail.
3. **Overemphasis on Quantification:** Not all criteria can be easily quantified, which may overlook qualitative factors.

For instance, choosing a life partner based solely on a matrix might miss the nuances of compatibility.

1. **Involve Stakeholders:** Collaborate to ensure weights and scores reflect diverse perspectives.
2. **Focus on Key Criteria:** Limit the number of criteria to avoid overcomplication.
3. **Combine with Qualitative Insights:** Use the matrix as a guide but consider qualitative factors alongside the results.

Exercises

1. **Create a Matrix:** Choose a decision you're currently facing. List options, define criteria, assign weights, and calculate scores. Reflect on the outcome.
2. **Team Exercise:** Facilitate a group decision-making process using a Weighted Decision Matrix. Discuss how it affects consensus.
3. **Evaluate a Past Decision:** Apply the matrix to a previous choice. Compare the results to the actual decision you made.

Closing Thoughts

The Weighted Decision Matrix transforms complex choices into structured, logical comparisons. By clarifying priorities and evaluating options systematically, this tool ensures decisions are both rational and aligned with your goals.

While it requires effort and careful judgment, its ability to simplify complexity and promote fairness makes it invaluable in both personal and professional contexts.

Chapter 52: Expected Value Calculation

Quantifying Risk and Reward: Expected Value Calculation

Expected Value Calculation is a decision-making tool that evaluates the average outcome of a decision by weighing each potential result by its probability and value. This method is widely used in finance, gambling, and strategic planning to guide decisions involving uncertainty.

For example:

- **Scenario:** A company considers investing in a new product.
- **Expected Value:** They estimate the probabilities of success (60%) and failure (40%) and calculate the expected financial return.

By focusing on long-term averages rather than individual outcomes, this method helps mitigate emotional decision-making.

How Expected Value Calculation Works

1. **Identify Possible Outcomes:** List all potential results of a decision.
   Example: "If we launch this product, we could either achieve high sales, moderate sales, or a loss."
2. **Assign Probabilities:** Estimate the likelihood of each outcome occurring.
   Example: High sales = 50%, Moderate sales = 30%, Loss = 20%.
3. **Determine Values:** Assign a monetary or utility value to each outcome.
   Example: High sales = $100,000, Moderate sales = $50,000, Loss = -$20,000.
4. **Calculate Expected Value:** Multiply each outcome's probability by its value, then sum the results.
   ○ Formula: $EV = (P_1 \times V_1) + (P_2 \times V_2) + ... + (P_n \times V_n)$
5. **Use the Result:** Compare the expected value to alternative options or thresholds for decision-making.

Applications of Expected Value Calculation

1. **In Business Strategy:**
   ○ Evaluate investments, pricing strategies, and product launches based on potential returns.
2. **In Personal Finance:**
   ○ Assess financial decisions, such as choosing between different insurance policies.
3. **In Everyday Choices:**
   ○ Make informed decisions involving uncertainty, such as whether to take a bet or gamble.

Why Expected Value Calculation is Effective

This method helps:

1. **Clarify Risk vs. Reward:** Quantifies potential outcomes to guide rational decision-making.
2. **Promote Long-Term Thinking:** Focuses on averages over time rather than isolated events.
3. **Mitigate Emotional Influence:** Reduces the impact of fear or greed in uncertain situations.

1. **Accuracy of Probabilities:** Estimating probabilities requires data or expertise, which may not always be available.
2. **Subjectivity in Values:** Assigning values to outcomes can be subjective and context-dependent.
3. **Unsuitability for Small Decisions:** For minor choices, the effort of calculation may outweigh the benefits.

For instance, calculating the expected value of ordering pizza versus sushi may be overkill for a casual dinner decision.

How to Use Expected Value Calculation Effectively

1. **Start with Reliable Data:** Use historical data or expert input to estimate probabilities and values.
2. **Consider the Context:** Focus on decisions where the stakes justify the effort of calculation.
3. **Combine with Other Methods:** Use Expected Value Calculation alongside qualitative factors for a well-rounded analysis.

Exercises

1. **Evaluate a Choice:** Choose a recent decision involving uncertainty. List outcomes, assign probabilities and values, and calculate the expected value. Reflect on the result.
2. **Compare Options:** Use Expected Value Calculation to assess two or more alternatives. Which has the highest EV?
3. **Test a Hypothetical Scenario:** Create a fictional decision (e.g. betting $50 on a coin flip) and practice calculating its expected value.

Closing Thoughts

Expected Value Calculation is a powerful tool for navigating uncertainty with logic and precision. By quantifying risks and rewards, it helps ensure decisions are guided by rational analysis rather than impulse or emotion.

While it requires thoughtful estimation and careful calculation, its ability to illuminate the best course of action makes it invaluable in finance, strategy, and everyday life.

Chapter 53: Decision Trees

Mapping Your Choices: Decision Trees

A Decision Tree is a visual tool for exploring and evaluating choices, outcomes, probabilities, and potential rewards or risks. This structured approach helps clarify options and identify the best course of action.

For example:

- **Scenario:** A business considers expanding into a new market.
- **Decision Tree:** They map out potential outcomes, such as increased revenue or market challenges, with probabilities and financial impacts assigned to each.

Decision Trees simplify complex decisions by making the process visual and transparent.

How Decision Trees Work

1. **Define the Decision:** Start with the main question or choice at the root of the tree.
   Example: "Should we expand into a new market?"
2. **Identify Branches:** Add branches for each possible action or decision.
   Example: "Expand" vs. "Don't Expand."
3. **Map Outcomes:** Extend branches to show potential results of each action.
   Example: "High Sales," "Moderate Sales," "Market Loss."
4. **Assign Probabilities and Values:** Estimate the likelihood and value of each outcome.
5. **Calculate Expected Values:** Use the probabilities and values to evaluate each branch.
6. **Choose the Optimal Path:** Select the decision that maximizes expected value or aligns with your goals.

Applications of Decision Trees

1. **In Business:**
   o   Plan investments, product launches, or strategic moves by mapping potential outcomes.
2. **In Personal Decisions:**
   o   Evaluate significant life choices, such as changing careers or moving to a new city.
3. **In Team Collaboration:**
   o   Facilitate group decision-making by visualizing options and consequences.

This method helps:

1. **Clarify Complex Choices:** Breaks down decisions into manageable steps.
2. **Visualize Risks and Rewards:** Makes trade-offs and probabilities easier to understand.
3. **Promote Transparency:** Facilitates clear communication and collaboration.

Challenges and Limitations

1. **Over-Simplification:** May not capture all nuances or uncertainties of a decision.
2. **Data Requirements:** Requires reliable probabilities and values for accurate analysis.
3. **Time-Intensive:** Building a detailed tree can be labor-intensive for complex scenarios.

For example, a decision tree for a global expansion strategy might involve dozens of branches and require extensive data.

How to Use Decision Trees Effectively

1. **Start Simple:** Begin with high-level branches and refine as more data becomes available.
2. **Use Software Tools:** Leverage decision-tree software for complex analyses.
3. **Combine with Qualitative Insights:** Balance the tree's quantitative results with contextual factors.

Exercises

1. **Build a Tree:** Create a decision tree for a choice you're currently facing. Map options, outcomes, probabilities, and values.
2. **Evaluate a Past Decision:** Reconstruct a previous decision using a decision tree. Compare the visualized process to your actual approach.
3. **Team Exercise:** Facilitate a group discussion by building a decision tree collaboratively. Reflect on how it affects consensus.

Closing Thoughts

Decision Trees are indispensable tools for navigating complex decisions with clarity and confidence. By visualizing options and outcomes, they ensure decisions are grounded in logic and aligned with your objectives.

Whether you're planning strategy, making personal choices, or leading a team, Decision Trees provide a structured framework to tackle uncertainty and complexity effectively.

Chapter 54: Scenario Planning

Anticipating the Future: Scenario Planning

Scenario Planning is a decision-making technique that involves envisioning and preparing for multiple possible futures. By exploring different scenarios, you can anticipate risks, identify opportunities, and build strategies that are adaptable to change.

For example:

- **Scenario:** A company is developing a long-term business strategy.
- **Scenario Planning:** They consider how economic growth, market competition, or technological advances might affect their plans.

This technique helps decision-makers remain flexible and prepared, no matter what the future holds.

How Scenario Planning Works

1. **Define the Focus:** Identify the decision, goal, or issue you want to address.
   Example: "How will our business adapt to changes in the energy market?"
2. **Identify Key Drivers:** Determine the factors that could influence outcomes.
   Example: Regulatory changes, technological advancements, customer preferences.
3. **Develop Scenarios:** Create detailed descriptions of possible futures, including best-case, worst-case, and most-likely scenarios.
   Example: "In a high-growth scenario, renewable energy adoption accelerates; in a low-growth scenario, traditional energy sources dominate."
4. **Analyze Implications:** Evaluate how each scenario might impact your decisions or goals.
5. **Plan Strategies:** Develop strategies that are flexible enough to succeed across multiple scenarios.

1. **In Business Strategy:**
   o   Anticipate market trends, competitive dynamics, and economic shifts.
2. **In Public Policy:**
   o   Plan for environmental changes, healthcare needs, or infrastructure demands.
3. **In Personal Decisions:**
   o   Prepare for life changes, such as career transitions or retirement planning.

Why Scenario Planning is Effective

This method helps:
1. **Improve Flexibility:** Encourages adaptable strategies that can succeed under varying conditions.
2. **Identify Risks and Opportunities:** Highlights potential challenges and areas for growth.
3. **Promote Long-Term Thinking:** Focuses on future possibilities rather than immediate concerns.

Challenges and Limitations

1. **Time-Intensive:** Creating detailed scenarios requires effort and collaboration.
2. **Complexity Management:** Balancing too many scenarios can lead to confusion or indecision.
3. **Uncertainty in Predictions:** Scenarios are inherently speculative and may not capture all possible outcomes.

For instance, a business planning for market shifts might miss disruptive technologies that emerge unexpectedly.

How to Use Scenario Planning Effectively

1. **Involve Diverse Perspectives:** Include stakeholders from different backgrounds to ensure comprehensive scenarios.
2. **Focus on Key Drivers:** Limit scenarios to those driven by the most impactful and uncertain factors.
3. **Revisit and Revise:** Update scenarios as new data or trends emerge.

Exercises

1. **Plan for a Decision:** Choose a current decision and develop three scenarios (optimistic, pessimistic, and most likely). Reflect on how this affects your strategy.
2. **Revisit a Past Outcome:** Analyze a past decision using Scenario Planning. Were there outcomes you didn't anticipate?
3. **Facilitate a Team Exercise:** Work with a group to create scenarios for a shared goal or challenge. Discuss how this influences planning.

Closing Thoughts

Scenario Planning empowers decision-makers to navigate uncertainty with foresight and resilience. By exploring multiple possible futures, you can develop strategies that are flexible, robust, and well-prepared for change.

Chapter 55: The Delphi Method

Reaching Consensus: The Delphi Method

The Delphi Method is a structured technique for gathering and refining expert opinions through multiple rounds of feedback. By leveraging diverse perspectives and fostering anonymity, this method minimizes bias and encourages thoughtful consensus.

For example:

- **Scenario:** A company wants to forecast technology trends for the next decade.
- **Delphi Method:** They survey a panel of experts, analyze responses, and iterate until a consensus is reached.

The Delphi Method is particularly effective for complex, uncertain issues requiring expert input.

How the Delphi Method Works

1. **Define the Problem:** Clearly articulate the issue or question to be addressed.
   Example: "What are the most likely technological innovations in healthcare by 2035?"
2. **Assemble a Panel of Experts:** Choose participants with relevant expertise and diverse perspectives.
3. **Conduct Round 1:** Gather initial opinions or predictions through surveys or questionnaires.
4. **Provide Feedback:** Share anonymized summaries of responses with the panel, highlighting areas of agreement and divergence.
5. **Repeat Until Consensus:** Conduct additional rounds of feedback, refining opinions and narrowing gaps in perspectives.

1. **In Forecasting:**
   o   Predict technological advancements, economic trends, or societal shifts.
2. **In Policy Development:**
   o   Build consensus on regulations, healthcare priorities, or environmental initiatives.
3. **In Organizational Strategy:**
   o   Identify risks, opportunities, or innovation pathways.

Why the Delphi Method is Effective

This method helps to:
1. **Leverage Expertise:** Combines insights from diverse, knowledgeable individuals.
2. **Encourage Open Dialogue:** Anonymity reduces the influence of dominant personalities or groupthink.
3. **Promote Iterative Refinement:** Multiple rounds improve the quality and clarity of recommendations.

Challenges and Limitations

1. **Time-Intensive:** The iterative process may require significant time and coordination.
2. **Dependence on Expertise:** The quality of results depends on the knowledge and engagement of the panel.
3. **Potential for Divergence:** Achieving consensus can be difficult if opinions remain polarized.

For instance, forecasting geopolitical trends might involve conflicting viewpoints that require careful facilitation to resolve.

How to Use the Delphi Method Effectively

1. **Choose Experts Wisely:** Select a diverse panel with complementary expertise.
2. **Foster Anonymity:** Ensure participants feel free to share honest, uninfluenced opinions.
3. **Facilitate Iteratively:** Use clear summaries and focused questions to guide each round.

Exercises

1. **Conduct a Delphi Study:** Choose a complex question and gather opinions from a group of colleagues or peers. Iterate until consensus is reached.
2. **Analyze Delphi Outputs:** Review a Delphi study (e.g., in research or business). Reflect on how iterative feedback improved the results.
3. **Facilitate a Panel Discussion:** Simulate the Delphi process in a team setting to tackle a shared challenge.

Closing Thoughts

The Delphi Method is a powerful tool for harnessing expert insights and building consensus on complex issues. By fostering iterative collaboration, it ensures decisions are well-informed, balanced, and thoroughly considered.

Chapter 56: Multi-Criteria Decision Analysis (MCDA)

MCDA

	Cost	Quality	Delivery	Time	Weights
Option A	1	2	3	4	20%
Option B	1	2	4	3	50%
Option C	4	2	3	1	30%

Multi-Criteria Decision Analysis (MCDA) is a decision-making method that evaluates multiple conflicting criteria to identify the best option. This approach is particularly useful when decisions involve trade-offs, such as balancing cost, quality, and sustainability.

For example:

- **Scenario:** A company is choosing a supplier.
- **MCDA Application:** They assess options based on cost, delivery time, quality, and environmental impact, assigning weights to each factor based on importance.

MCDA provides a clear framework for navigating complex decisions with competing priorities.

How MCDA Works

1. **Define the Decision Context:** Clearly articulate the problem and objectives.
   Example: "Which supplier should we choose for our new product line?"
2. **List Criteria:** Identify the factors that will influence the decision.
   Example: Cost, delivery time, quality, environmental impact.
3. **Assign Weights:** Reflect the relative importance of each criterion.
   Example: Quality = 40%, Cost = 30%, Delivery Time = 20%, Environmental Impact = 10%.
4. **Score Options:** Rate each option based on how well it meets each criterion.
   Example: Use a scale of 1-10, where 10 indicates excellent performance.
5. **Calculate Weighted Scores:** Multiply each score by its weight and sum the results for each option.
6. **Compare and Choose:** The option with the highest total score is typically the best choice.

Applications of MCDA

1. **In Business Decisions:**
   - Evaluate suppliers, investments, or projects based on multiple performance metrics.
2. **In Public Policy:**
   - Balance economic, social, and environmental factors in policymaking.
3. **In Personal Decisions:**
   - Choose between job offers, housing options, or major purchases by weighing pros and cons.

Why MCDA is Effective

This method helps:

1. **Clarify Trade-Offs:** Makes it easier to understand and evaluate competing priorities.
2. **Promote Rational Decisions:** Bases choices on structured analysis rather than intuition.
3. **Encourage Transparency:** Provides a clear rationale for decisions, which is especially valuable in collaborative settings.

Challenges and Limitations

1. **Subjectivity in Weights and Scores:** Assigning weights and scores can be influenced by personal bias.
2. **Data Requirements:** Accurate evaluation requires reliable data for each criterion.
3. **Over-Complexity:** Too many criteria or options can complicate analysis and slow decision-making.

For example, using MCDA to evaluate hundreds of products across dozens of criteria may require advanced tools or software.

How to Use MCDA Effectively

1. **Focus on Key Criteria:** Limit the number of criteria to the most impactful factors.
2. **Involve Stakeholders:** Collaborate with others to ensure weights and scores reflect diverse perspectives.
3. **Combine with Qualitative Insights:** Use MCDA as a guide but consider qualitative factors as well.

Exercises

1. **Create an MCDA Matrix:** Apply MCDA to a current decision by listing options, defining criteria, and calculating weighted scores.
2. **Evaluate a Past Decision:** Use MCDA to analyze a previous choice. How does the result compare to what you actually decided?
3. **Facilitate a Team Exercise:** Work with a group to apply MCDA to a shared decision. Reflect on how it influences consensus.

Closing Thoughts

Multi-Criteria Decision Analysis is a crucial tool for navigating complex decisions with competing priorities. By balancing trade-offs systematically, it ensures that choices are logical, transparent, and aligned with your objectives.

Chapter 57: Cost-Benefit Analysis

Weighing the Pros and Cons: Cost-Benefit Analysis

Cost-Benefit Analysis (CBA) is a decision-making technique that evaluates the costs and benefits of an action, project, or decision. By quantifying and comparing these factors, CBA helps determine whether the benefits outweigh the costs, guiding rational decision-making.

For example:

- **Scenario:** A company considers upgrading its IT infrastructure.
- **CBA Application:** They estimate the costs of hardware, software, and training versus the expected savings and productivity gains.

CBA simplifies decisions by focusing on measurable impacts and trade-offs.

How Cost-Benefit Analysis Works

1. **Define the Scope:** Clearly outline the decision or action being analyzed.
   Example: "Should we invest in a solar power system for our office?"
2. **Identify Costs and Benefits:** List all potential costs and benefits, both tangible and intangible.
   Example: Costs = Installation, maintenance; Benefits = Energy savings, reduced carbon footprint.
3. **Assign Monetary Values:** Quantify costs and benefits in financial terms where possible.
   Example: Energy savings = $10,000/year; Installation cost = $50,000.
4. **Calculate Net Benefit:** Subtract total costs from total benefits to determine the net benefit.
5. **Make a Decision:** If the net benefit is positive, the action is generally considered worthwhile.

Applications of Cost-Benefit Analysis

1. **In Business:**
   - Evaluate projects, investments, or operational changes based on financial viability.
2. **In Public Policy:**
   - Assess infrastructure projects, healthcare initiatives, or environmental programs.
3. **In Personal Decisions:**
   - Compare options like buying a car, pursuing education, or relocating.

Why Cost-Benefit Analysis is Effective

This method helps:

1. **Clarify Trade-Offs:** Provides a clear comparison of costs and benefits.
2. **Promote Objectivity:** Bases decisions on measurable impacts rather than subjective preferences.
3. **Encourage Efficient Resource Use:** Focuses efforts on actions with the greatest net benefit.

Challenges and Limitations

1. **Difficulties in Quantification:** Some costs and benefits, like employee morale or environmental impact, are hard to quantify.
2. **Assumptions and Uncertainty:** Results depend on assumptions about future outcomes, which may be uncertain.
3. **Overemphasis on Monetary Value:** Focusing only on financial metrics may overlook ethical or social considerations.

For instance, deciding whether to preserve a forest solely based on CBA may ignore its cultural or ecological significance.

How to Use CBA Effectively

1. **Include Intangible Factors:** Consider qualitative benefits and costs alongside financial metrics.
2. **Use Reliable Data:** Base calculations on accurate, up-to-date information.
3. **Revisit Assumptions:** Test results under different scenarios to account for uncertainty.

Exercises

1. **Conduct a CBA:** Choose a decision and list all associated costs and benefits. Quantify them where possible and calculate the net benefit.
2. **Analyze a Public Policy:** Research a real-world policy decision and evaluate its CBA. What additional factors might influence the outcome?
3. **Test a Hypothetical Scenario:** Apply CBA to a fictional decision, such as building a park. Reflect on how assumptions affect results.

Cost-Benefit Analysis is a foundational tool for rational decision-making, offering a clear framework for weighing trade-offs and maximizing value. By focusing on measurable impacts, it ensures that resources are allocated efficiently and effectively.

Its ability to clarify choices and promote objective analysis makes it indispensable in business, public policy, and personal planning.

Chapter 58: The Precautionary Principle

Erring on the Side of Caution: The Precautionary Principle

The Precautionary Principle is a decision-making strategy that prioritizes avoiding harm when outcomes are uncertain or risks are high. It emphasizes caution, especially in situations where potential consequences are severe or irreversible.

For example:

- **Scenario:** A government considers approving a new pesticide.
- **Precautionary Principle:** Without definitive proof of its safety, they delay approval to prevent potential environmental harm.

This principle is commonly used in environmental policy, public health, and technology regulation to guide decisions in uncertain scenarios.

How the Precautionary Principle Works

1. **Identify Risks:** Focus on actions or decisions with significant uncertainty or potential harm.
   Example: "What are the risks of deploying this untested technology?"
2. **Apply Caution:** Favor safer options or delay decisions until risks are better understood.
   Example: "Let's conduct further studies before proceeding."
3. **Prioritize Prevention:** Adopt measures to minimize potential harm, even if the risks are not fully proven.

Applications of the Precautionary Principle

1. **In Environmental Policy:**
   o Regulate activities that could harm ecosystems, such as deforestation or chemical usage.
2. **In Public Health:**
   o Restrict substances or practices with uncertain health impacts, such as certain food additives or new medications.
3. **In Technological Development:**
   o Evaluate the societal impact of emerging technologies, like artificial intelligence or genetic engineering.

Why the Precautionary Principle is Effective

This method helps:
1. **Protect Against Harm:** Prevents irreversible damage by acting conservatively.
2. **Encourage Thorough Analysis:** Promotes careful consideration of potential risks.
3. **Build Public Trust:** Demonstrates responsibility and accountability in decision-making.

Challenges and Limitations

1. **Stifling Innovation:** Excessive caution may delay beneficial advancements.
2. **Ambiguity in Application:** Determining when and how to apply the principle can be subjective.
3. **Resistance to Change:** Fear of potential harm may lead to inaction, even when risks are minimal.

For example, overusing the principle might hinder the adoption of life-saving technologies with manageable risks.

How to Use the Precautionary Principle Effectively

1. **Focus on Significant Risks:** Apply the principle to scenarios where potential harm is severe or irreversible.
2. **Balance Caution with Progress:** Weigh the risks of inaction alongside the risks of action.
3. **Use Evidence-Based Analysis:** Combine precaution with ongoing research to refine decisions.

Exercises

1. **Evaluate a Risk:** Choose a decision involving uncertainty. Apply the Precautionary Principle to assess the safest course of action.
2. **Analyze a Policy:** Research a real-world example of the Precautionary Principle, such as environmental regulations. Reflect on its effectiveness.

3. **Test a Hypothetical Scenario:** Imagine approving a new product or technology. What precautions would you implement before proceeding?

Closing Thoughts

The Precautionary Principle is a valuable tool for managing uncertainty and protecting against potential harm. By prioritizing caution in high-stakes scenarios, it ensures that decisions are responsible, ethical, and aligned with long-term well-being.

Its focus on prevention and foresight makes it indispensable in fields such as environmental protection, public health, and technological innovation.

Chapter 59: The Monte Carlo Method

Simulating Outcomes: The Monte Carlo Method

The Monte Carlo Method is a decision-making tool that uses simulations to model the probability of different outcomes. By running thousands of random iterations, it provides insights into risks, uncertainties, and likely results.

For example:

- **Scenario:** An investor evaluates a portfolio's potential returns.
- **Monte Carlo Simulation:** They simulate different market conditions to estimate the range of possible outcomes.

This method is especially useful for complex, uncertain decisions involving multiple variables.

How the Monte Carlo Method Works

1. **Define the Problem:** Identify the decision or scenario to analyze.
   Example: "What is the likelihood of meeting our project deadline under current conditions?"
2. **Identify Variables:** Determine the factors influencing the outcome and their ranges of uncertainty.
   Example: Task durations, resource availability, external delays.
3. **Run Simulations:** Use software to generate random values for each variable and calculate the outcome. Repeat thousands of times to create a probability distribution.
4. **Analyze Results:** Evaluate the likelihood of different outcomes and identify areas of high risk.

Applications of the Monte Carlo Method

1. **In Financial Planning:**
   o Model investment risks, returns, and portfolio performance under various scenarios.
2. **In Project Management:**
   o Estimate timelines, budgets, and resource needs for complex projects.
3. **In Risk Analysis:**
   o Assess the probability of adverse events in fields such as engineering, insurance, or healthcare.

Why the Monte Carlo Method is Effective

This method helps:

1. **Quantify Uncertainty:** Provides a clear picture of risks and probabilities.
2. **Improve Forecasting:** Accounts for a wide range of possible scenarios.
3. **Guide Strategic Decisions:** Informs choices with data-driven insights.

Challenges and Limitations

1. **Data Requirements:** Accurate results depend on reliable input data and assumptions.
2. **Complexity:** Running simulations requires specialized tools and expertise.
3. **Overreliance on Models:** Results may mislead if underlying assumptions are flawed.

For instance, overly optimistic assumptions about market trends could skew financial simulations.

How to Use the Monte Carlo Method Effectively

1. **Start with Accurate Inputs:** Use credible data and realistic assumptions for variables.
2. **Interpret Results Carefully:** Focus on probability ranges rather than single outcomes.
3. **Combine with Other Tools:** Use Monte Carlo alongside qualitative analysis for a well-rounded perspective.

Exercises

1. **Run a Simulation:** Choose a decision or scenario and use online tools to create a Monte Carlo simulation. Reflect on the results.
2. **Analyze a Case Study:** Research a real-world example of Monte Carlo Simulation, such as financial modeling or project planning.
3. **Test Variables:** Experiment with different inputs to see how they affect the outcome distribution in a simulation.

Closing Thoughts

The Monte Carlo Method is an invaluable tool for navigating uncertainty and complexity. By simulating thousands of potential outcomes, it provides actionable insights into risks, probabilities, and likely results.

Chapter 60: Risk Assessment Matrices

LIKELIHOOD

	HIGH LIKELIHOOD, HIGH IMPACT	LOW LIKELIHOOD, HIGH IMPACT
IMPACT	HIGH LIKELIHOOD, LOW IMPACT	LOW LIKELIHOOD, LOW IMPACT

Prioritizing Risks: Risk Assessment Matrices

A Risk Assessment Matrix is a tool used to evaluate and prioritize risks based on their likelihood and potential impact. By categorizing risks into a visual grid, this method helps identify which issues require immediate attention and resources.

For example:

- **Scenario:** A construction company evaluates safety risks on a new project.
- **Matrix Application:** They categorize risks such as equipment failure or adverse weather based on how likely they are to occur and the potential harm they could cause.

This technique enables clear communication and prioritization, ensuring that critical risks are addressed effectively.

How a Risk Assessment Matrix Works

1. **Identify Risks:** List all potential risks associated with a decision or project.
   Example: "What could go wrong during this product launch?"
2. **Assess Likelihood:** Rate the probability of each risk occurring, often on a scale (e.g., low, medium, high).
3. **Evaluate Impact:** Rate the severity of consequences if the risk materializes, also on a scale.
4. **Map Risks:** Plot each risk on a 2x2 matrix, with likelihood on one axis and impact on the other.
5. **Prioritize and Mitigate:** Focus on addressing risks in the high-likelihood, high-impact quadrant first.

Applications of Risk Assessment Matrices

1. **In Project Management:**
   o   Identify and mitigate risks to timelines, budgets, or deliverables.
2. **In Business Operations:**
   o   Evaluate potential disruptions, such as supply chain issues or cybersecurity threats.
3. **In Personal Planning:**
   o   Assess risks for significant decisions, like moving to a new city or investing in property.

Why Risk Assessment Matrices Are Effective

This method helps:

1. **Clarify Priorities:** Focuses attention on the most critical risks.
2. **Facilitate Decision-Making:** Provides a clear framework for evaluating and addressing uncertainties.
3. **Encourage Proactive Planning:** Promotes early action to mitigate potential problems.

Challenges and Limitations

1. **Subjective Ratings:** Likelihood and impact assessments may vary depending on individual perspectives.
2. **Oversimplification:** A 2x2 grid may not capture the full complexity of certain risks.
3. **Resource Constraints:** Addressing all risks, especially low-priority ones, may not be feasible.

For instance, a business may underestimate the impact of a low-likelihood risk that could cause catastrophic damage.

How to Use Risk Assessment Matrices Effectively

1. **Collaborate with Stakeholders:** Involve diverse perspectives to ensure accurate assessments of risks.
2. **Revisit Regularly:** Update the matrix as new risks emerge or conditions change.
3. **Balance Resources:** Focus on high-priority risks while monitoring lower-priority ones.

1. **Create a Matrix:** Choose a current project or decision and develop a Risk Assessment Matrix. Reflect on how it influences your approach.
2. **Analyze a Past Event:** Apply a Risk Assessment Matrix to a previous failure or challenge. How could this tool have helped?
3. **Facilitate a Team Exercise:** Collaborate with colleagues to identify and prioritize risks for a shared goal or initiative.

Closing Thoughts

A Risk Assessment Matrix is a straightforward yet powerful tool for managing uncertainty. By categorizing and prioritizing risks, it ensures that resources are directed where they are needed most.

This method fosters proactive decision-making, reducing the likelihood of unexpected setbacks and enhancing the resilience of plans, projects, and organizations.

Chapter 61: Sensitivity Analysis

Testing the Variables: Sensitivity Analysis

Sensitivity Analysis is a decision-making technique that evaluates how changes in input variables affect outcomes. By identifying which variables have the most significant impact, this method helps decision-makers focus on critical factors and assess the robustness of their plans.

For example:

- **Scenario:** A retailer estimates profits for a new store.
- **Sensitivity Analysis:** They test how changes in rent, customer foot traffic, and product pricing influence overall profitability.

This technique is especially useful for identifying vulnerabilities and improving decision confidence.

How Sensitivity Analysis Works

1. **Define the Model:** Start with a decision model, formula, or framework.
   Example: "Our profit = Revenue - Costs."
2. **Identify Key Variables:** Determine which inputs drive the outcome.
   Example: Sales volume, production cost, marketing spend.
3. **Test Variations:** Adjust each variable independently while holding others constant to see how it affects the outcome.
4. **Analyze Results:** Identify which variables have the most significant influence and prioritize them in planning.

Applications of Sensitivity Analysis

1. **In Financial Modeling:**
   o Test how changes in interest rates, taxes, or expenses affect a company's bottom line.
2. **In Project Planning:**
   o Assess the impact of variations in timelines, budgets, or resources.
3. **In Personal Decisions:**
   o Explore how different factors (e.g., salary, cost of living) affect financial decisions like relocation.

Why Sensitivity Analysis is Effective

This method helps:

1. **Identify Key Drivers:** Focuses attention on variables with the greatest impact.
2. **Test Assumptions:** Evaluates the robustness of decisions under different scenarios.
3. **Enhance Adaptability:** Prepares decision-makers to respond to changes in critical factors.

Challenges and Limitations

1. **Requires a Clear Model:** Results depend on the accuracy of the underlying decision model.
2. **Time-Intensive:** Testing multiple variables and scenarios can be labor-intensive.
3. **Limited Scope:** Analyzing one variable at a time may miss interactions between variables.

For instance, testing the effect of marketing spend without considering its interplay with product pricing may yield incomplete insights.

1. **Start with Accurate Data:** Use reliable and current inputs to ensure meaningful results.
2. **Focus on Critical Variables:** Prioritize testing variables with the most uncertainty or potential impact.
3. **Combine with Scenario Planning:** Explore combinations of variable changes for a more comprehensive analysis.

Exercises

1. **Analyze a Decision Model:** Choose a decision or project and identify its key variables. Conduct Sensitivity Analysis to determine which factors are most influential.
2. **Evaluate Past Results:** Apply Sensitivity Analysis to a past project or investment. Reflect on how this tool could have improved planning.
3. **Team Exercise:** Collaborate with a group to test variables for a shared decision or strategy. Discuss the insights gained.

Closing Thoughts

Sensitivity Analysis provides a systematic way to evaluate the impact of uncertainties and focus on critical factors. By testing variables and their effects, it ensures decisions are robust, flexible, and well-informed.

This tool is essential for decision-makers seeking to navigate uncertainty, optimize outcomes, and anticipate challenges in dynamic environments.

Chapter 62: Adaptive Thinking

Staying Flexible: Adaptive Thinking

Adaptive Thinking refers to the ability to adjust plans, strategies, or decisions in response to new information or changing conditions. This mindset is crucial in dynamic environments where uncertainty and unforeseen challenges are common.

For example:

- **Scenario:** A project manager faces unexpected supply chain delays.
- **Adaptive Thinking:** They revise the timeline and explore alternative suppliers to keep the project on track.

By embracing flexibility and adaptability, decision-makers can navigate uncertainty more effectively and capitalize on emerging opportunities.

How Adaptive Thinking Works

1. **Monitor the Environment:** Stay alert to changes, trends, or unexpected developments.
   Example: "Are there any shifts in market conditions or customer behavior?"
2. **Evaluate the Impact:** Assess how new information affects current plans or decisions.
   Example: "How does this delay impact our timeline and budget?"
3. **Adjust Accordingly:** Revise strategies, priorities, or actions to align with the new reality.
   Example: "Let's allocate additional resources to address this bottleneck."
4. **Learn and Iterate:** Reflect on adjustments to improve future adaptability.

Applications of Adaptive Thinking

1. **In Business Strategy:**
   o Pivot in response to competitive pressures, technological advancements, or regulatory changes.
2. **In Crisis Management:**
   o Respond effectively to emergencies, such as natural disasters or cybersecurity breaches.
3. **In Personal Growth:**
   o Adjust career goals, financial plans, or lifestyle choices based on changing circumstances.

Why Adaptive Thinking is Effective

This method helps:

1. **Increase Resilience:** Enables rapid recovery and adjustment in the face of setbacks.
2. **Capitalize on Opportunities:** Identifies and exploits new possibilities as they arise.
3. **Enhance Decision-Making:** Encourages flexibility and responsiveness, reducing the risk of rigid thinking.

1. **Risk of Overreaction:** Frequent adjustments may lead to instability or inefficiency.
2. **Uncertainty in Outcomes:** Adapting to new conditions doesn't guarantee success.
3. **Resistance to Change:** Individuals or teams may struggle to embrace flexibility, especially in structured environments.

For instance, a company accustomed to traditional processes may find it difficult to pivot quickly during a market disruption.

How to Foster Adaptive Thinking

1. **Embrace a Growth Mindset:** View challenges as opportunities for learning and innovation.
   Example: "How can we turn this setback into a stepping stone?"
2. **Encourage Experimentation:** Test new ideas or approaches without fear of failure.
   Example: "Let's pilot this strategy in one market before scaling up."
3. **Promote Open Communication:** Foster a culture where feedback and collaboration drive flexibility.
   Example: "What does the team think about adjusting our approach?"

Exercises

1. **Reflect on a Past Adaptation:** Recall a time when you had to change plans. What worked well, and what could have been improved?
2. **Simulate a Pivot:** Choose a hypothetical scenario where plans must change. Practice developing and implementing an alternative strategy.
3. **Encourage Team Adaptability:** Facilitate a group exercise where unexpected challenges are introduced, prompting the team to adapt.

Closing Thoughts

Adaptive Thinking is a critical skill for thriving in an unpredictable world. By staying flexible and responsive, you can navigate challenges, seize opportunities, and build resilience in both personal and professional contexts.

Chapter 63: The OODA Loop (Observe, Orient, Decide, Act)

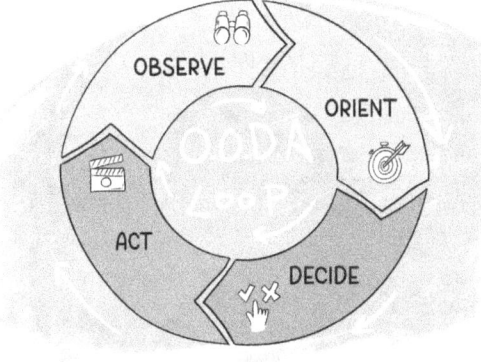

Making Quick, Iterative Decisions: The OODA Loop

The OODA Loop is a decision-making framework developed by military strategist John Boyd. It emphasizes agility and continuous learning through four iterative stages: Observe, Orient, Decide, and Act. This approach is particularly effective in dynamic, high-stakes environments.

For example:

- **Scenario:** A business reacts to a competitor's unexpected product launch.
- **OODA Loop Application:** The team observes the market response, orients by analyzing data, decides on a counterstrategy, and acts swiftly.

The OODA Loop enables rapid, informed decision-making while maintaining flexibility to adapt as conditions evolve.

How the OODA Loop Works

1. **Observe:** Gather information about the environment and any changes.
   Example: "What's happening in the market right now?"
2. **Orient:** Analyze the information and consider how it impacts your goals.
   Example: "How does this development affect our position?"
3. **Decide:** Choose the best course of action based on your analysis.
   Example: "Should we adjust our pricing or focus on marketing?"
4. **Act:** Implement the decision quickly and decisively.
   Example: "Let's launch the campaign immediately."
5. **Repeat:** Continuously cycle through the loop as new information emerges.

Applications of the OODA Loop

1. **In Business Strategy:**
   o   Respond to competitive threats, market shifts, or customer needs in real-time.
2. **In Crisis Management:**
   o   Make fast, effective decisions during emergencies or high-pressure situations.
3. **In Personal Decision-Making:**
   o   Apply the loop to adapt to changes in career, relationships, or finances.

This method helps:

1. **Improve Agility:** Enables rapid response to changing circumstances.
2. **Enhance Decision Quality:** Combines speed with informed analysis.
3. **Foster Continuous Learning:** Encourages iterative improvement through ongoing observation and adaptation.

Challenges and Limitations

1. **Risk of Incomplete Information:** Quick decisions may be based on limited data.
2. **Overemphasis on Speed:** Acting too quickly may lead to errors or missed opportunities.
3. **Complexity in Orientation:** Analyzing and synthesizing information can be challenging in chaotic environments.

For example, in fast-moving industries, businesses might struggle to interpret conflicting data during the "Orient" stage.

How to Apply the OODA Loop Effectively

1. **Focus on Key Signals:** Prioritize critical information during the "Observe" stage.
2. **Empower Teams:** Foster decentralized decision-making to enhance responsiveness.
3. **Iterate Rapidly:** Treat each loop as a learning opportunity to refine strategies.

Exercises

1. **Simulate an OODA Loop:** Apply the framework to a real or hypothetical situation requiring rapid decision-making. Reflect on each stage.
2. **Analyze a Past Decision:** Break down a previous choice into the OODA stages. What could have been improved?
3. **Facilitate a Team Exercise:** Use the OODA Loop to address a group challenge. Discuss how it enhances collaboration and agility.

Closing Thoughts

The OODA Loop is a dynamic and iterative decision-making framework that thrives in fast-paced, uncertain environments. By cycling through observation, analysis, action, and reflection, it ensures decisions are both rapid and well-informed.

Chapter 64: The Six Thinking Hats

Thinking from Every Angle: The Six Thinking Hats

Developed by Edward de Bono, the Six Thinking Hats method is a decision-making framework that encourages individuals and teams to explore problems from six distinct perspectives, represented by metaphorical hats. This structured approach fosters creativity, critical thinking, and collaboration.

For example:

- **Scenario:** A company is brainstorming strategies for a new product launch.
- **Six Thinking Hats Application:** The team considers facts (white hat), emotions (red hat), risks (black hat), benefits (yellow hat), creativity (green hat), and process (blue hat) to develop a well-rounded plan.

This method helps avoid groupthink and ensures all aspects of a decision are considered.

The Six Thinking Hats Explained

1. **White Hat – Facts and Data:** Focuses on objective information and analysis.
   Example: "What do the market research and sales data tell us?"
2. **Red Hat – Emotions and Intuition:** Explores feelings, instincts, and gut reactions.
   Example: "How do we feel about this idea on an emotional level?"
3. **Black Hat – Risks and Caution:** Identifies potential problems and challenges.
   Example: "What could go wrong with this plan?"
4. **Yellow Hat – Optimism and Benefits:** Highlights strengths and opportunities.
   Example: "What are the advantages of this approach?"
5. **Green Hat – Creativity and Innovation:** Encourages brainstorming and exploring new ideas.
   Example: "What unconventional solutions could we consider?"
6. **Blue Hat – Process and Control:** Focuses on managing the discussion and ensuring balance.
   Example: "Have we covered all perspectives thoroughly?"

1. **In Team Decision-Making:**
   o   Foster balanced discussions that incorporate diverse viewpoints.
2. **In Creative Problem-Solving:**
   o   Encourage out-of-the-box thinking and innovative solutions.
3. **In Personal Reflection:**
   o   Analyze decisions or challenges from multiple angles to gain deeper insight.

Why the Six Thinking Hats are Effective

This method helps:

1. **Enhance Collaboration:** Encourages equal participation and minimizes conflict.
2. **Foster Comprehensive Analysis:** Ensures all aspects of a decision are considered.
3. **Improve Creativity and Innovation:** Creates space for exploring new ideas without judgment.

Challenges and Limitations

1. **Time-Intensive:** Covering all six perspectives can be lengthy in time-sensitive situations.
2. **Potential Resistance:** Some participants may struggle to adopt perspectives outside their comfort zones.
3. **Overemphasis on Structure:** Strict adherence to the framework might stifle spontaneous insights.

For example, a team under tight deadlines might find it difficult to dedicate time to all six hats.

How to Use the Six Thinking Hats Effectively

1. **Set Clear Objectives:** Define the problem or decision to be analyzed before beginning.
2. **Facilitate Participation:** Assign hats or rotate roles to ensure balanced input from all participants.
3. **Stay Flexible:** Adapt the process to suit the complexity and urgency of the decision.

Exercises

1. **Apply the Six Hats:** Choose a current decision and analyze it using all six perspectives. Reflect on how this influences your approach.
2. **Facilitate a Team Discussion:** Guide a group through the Six Thinking Hats method for a shared challenge. Discuss the insights gained.
3. **Analyze a Past Decision:** Use the Six Hats to revisit a previous choice. What new perspectives emerge?

Closing Thoughts

The Six Thinking Hats method provides a structured yet flexible framework for making decisions that are well-rounded, inclusive, and innovative. By exploring diverse perspectives, it fosters collaboration, creativity, and critical thinking.

This technique is invaluable for teams and individuals seeking to navigate complex problems with clarity and confidence, ensuring that every angle is thoroughly examined.

Chapter 65: Weighted Trade-Off Grids

WEIGHTED TRADE-OFF GRIDS

	Cost	Accessibility	Activities	Weather	TOTAL
BEACH	4	5	2	5	(16)
MOUNTAINS	2	2	3	4	11
CITY	3	5	4	2	14

Navigating Complex Trade-Offs: Weighted Trade-Off Grids

A Weighted Trade-Off Grid is a decision-making tool that evaluates options by scoring them against weighted criteria. By quantifying trade-offs, this method helps identify the most balanced choice in situations involving multiple competing factors.

For example:

- **Scenario:** A family chooses a vacation destination.
- **Grid Application:** They evaluate options based on cost, activities, weather, and travel time, assigning weights to reflect their priorities.

This technique simplifies complex decisions by breaking them into smaller, manageable comparisons.

How Weighted Trade-Off Grids Work

1. **List Options and Criteria:** Define the choices and the factors influencing the decision.
   Example: "Options: Beach, mountains, city. Criteria: Cost, accessibility, activities, weather."
2. **Assign Weights to Criteria:** Reflect the relative importance of each factor.
   Example: Activities = 40%, Cost = 30%, Weather = 20%, Accessibility = 10%.
3. **Score Each Option:** Rate how well each option meets each criterion.
4. **Calculate Weighted Scores:** Multiply each score by its weight and sum the results for each option.
5. **Compare and Choose:** The option with the highest total score is typically the best choice.

Applications of Weighted Trade-Off Grids

1. **In Business:**
   o Evaluate vendors, investments, or strategies based on key performance metrics.
2. **In Personal Decisions:**
   o Compare housing options, career opportunities, or major purchases.
3. **In Team Collaboration:**
   o Facilitate group decisions by providing a clear, structured framework for analysis.

Why Weighted Trade-Off Grids are Effective

This method helps:

1. **Clarify Priorities:** Focuses attention on the most important factors.
2. **Promote Rational Decisions:** Bases choices on structured analysis rather than intuition.
3. **Simplify Complexity:** Breaks down multi-faceted decisions into manageable steps.

Challenges and Limitations

1. **Subjectivity in Weights and Scores:** Assigning values can reflect personal or group biases.
2. **Time-Intensive:** Building and populating the grid requires effort, especially for complex decisions.
3. **Quantification Limitations:** Not all criteria can be easily quantified.

For instance, comparing career options might involve intangible factors like work-life balance or personal growth.

How to Use Weighted Trade-Off Grids Effectively

1. **Involve Stakeholders:** Collaborate to ensure that weights and scores reflect diverse perspectives.
2. **Focus on Key Criteria:** Limit the number of factors to avoid overcomplication.
3. **Combine with Qualitative Insights:** Use the grid as a guide but consider qualitative aspects alongside the results.

Exercises

1. **Build a Grid:** Apply the Weighted Trade-Off Grid to a decision you're currently facing. List options, define criteria, and calculate scores. Reflect on the outcome.
2. **Evaluate a Past Decision:** Use the grid to revisit a previous choice. How does the result compare to your actual decision?
3. **Facilitate a Group Exercise:** Guide a team through creating and using a Weighted Trade-Off Grid for a shared goal or challenge.

Closing Thoughts

The Weighted Trade-Off Grid is a versatile tool for navigating complex decisions with competing priorities. By structuring trade-offs systematically, it ensures that choices are logical, transparent, and aligned with your objectives.

Subsection: Communication and Persuasion

Effective communication and persuasion are the cornerstones of meaningful dialogue and influence. Whether you're presenting an idea, negotiating a deal, or simply engaging in conversation, mastering these skills ensures your message is not only heard but also understood and acted upon.

This section focuses on methods to enhance clarity, build trust, and inspire action. By combining logical structuring, emotional awareness, and creative techniques, these tools empower you to communicate persuasively and authentically in any context.

Chapter 66: Reframing Arguments for Clarity

Seeing from a New Angle: Reframing Arguments for Clarity

Reframing involves presenting an idea or argument in a way that makes it easier to understand or more persuasive. By shifting perspectives, using simpler language, or emphasizing key points, reframing helps clarify complex concepts and resolve misunderstandings.

For example:

- **Scenario:** A manager addresses employee resistance to a new policy.
- **Reframed Argument:** Instead of focusing on the changes, they highlight the benefits, such as reduced workloads or improved processes.

Reframing is a versatile tool for improving communication, diffusing conflict, and building consensus.

How to Reframe Arguments

1. **Identify the Core Message:** Focus on the main point you want to communicate.
   Example: "What is the essential takeaway from this policy change?"
2. **Simplify the Language:** Replace jargon or technical terms with simpler, more relatable expressions.
   Example: "Instead of saying 'streamline operations,' say 'make tasks easier and faster.'"
3. **Change the Perspective:** Present the idea from the listener's point of view.
   Example: "How does this change benefit the person I'm speaking to?"
4. **Emphasize Positives:** Highlight the advantages rather than focusing on challenges.
   Example: "This system will save you time" instead of "This system requires some adjustments."

Applications of Reframing

1. **In Negotiations:**
   - Present compromises as opportunities rather than losses.
2. **In Teaching:**
   - Simplify complex topics for students by using relatable examples.
3. **In Conflict Resolution:**
   - Reframe disagreements to focus on shared goals and solutions.

Why Reframing is Effective

This method helps:

1. **Enhance Clarity:** Makes complex or abstract ideas more accessible.
2. **Shift Perspectives:** Encourages openness to new viewpoints.
3. **Resolve Resistance:** Reduces defensiveness by focusing on common ground or benefits.

Challenges and Limitations

1. **Risk of Oversimplification:** Simplifying too much may distort the original message.
2. **Resistance to Change:** Listeners may reject reframed arguments if they perceive manipulation.
3. **Time Constraints:** Crafting effective reframes requires thought and effort.

For instance, reframing a contentious topic during a heated debate may require careful timing and language.

How to Reframe Effectively

1. **Know Your Audience:** Tailor your approach to their values, needs, and concerns.
   Example: "How does this resonate with what they care about most?"
2. **Practice Empathy:** Consider how the argument feels from the listener's perspective.
   Example: "What objections might they have, and how can I address them?"

3. **Test Different Frames:** Experiment with multiple approaches to find the most effective one.

Exercises

1. **Reframe a Personal Argument:** Choose a recent disagreement and rephrase your perspective to focus on shared goals.
2. **Simplify a Complex Idea:** Take a technical concept and reframe it in everyday language. Reflect on how this improves clarity.
3. **Practice with a Partner:** Role-play a challenging conversation, experimenting with different reframes to find what resonates most.

Closing Thoughts

Reframing arguments for clarity is an essential skill for effective communication. By shifting perspectives and simplifying messages, you can build understanding, reduce conflict, and inspire action.

This technique empowers you to connect with others more deeply, fostering collaboration, trust, and mutual respect in both personal and professional interactions.

Chapter 67: The Pyramid Principle

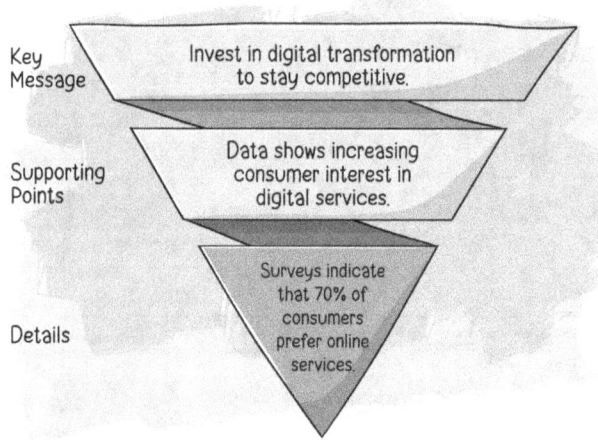

Start with the Conclusion: The Pyramid Principle

The Pyramid Principle is a communication framework developed by Barbara Minto that emphasizes presenting your key message or conclusion first, followed by supporting arguments and details. This structure is designed to improve clarity, focus, and engagement by aligning with how people process information.

For example:

- **Scenario:** A consultant delivers a recommendation to a client.
- **Pyramid Principle Application:** They start with the primary recommendation ("Invest in digital transformation") and follow with supporting data, trends, and specific action steps.

This method is widely used in business, consulting, and academia to ensure clear and persuasive communication.

How the Pyramid Principle Works

1. **Start with the Conclusion:** Clearly state the main idea or recommendation upfront.
   Example: "We recommend launching a new product line to capture untapped market segments."
2. **Group Supporting Points:** Organize key arguments or evidence into logical categories.
   Example: "This recommendation is based on market demand, competitive analysis, and projected ROI."
3. **Provide Detailed Evidence:** Use data, examples, or case studies to substantiate each supporting point.
4. **Maintain Logical Flow:** Ensure that each level of detail naturally flows from the one above it.

Applications of the Pyramid Principle

1. **In Business Presentations:**
   o Deliver executive summaries that highlight key insights before diving into details.
2. **In Academic Writing:**
   o Organize research papers or essays by starting with the thesis and supporting it with evidence.
3. **In Team Communication:**
   o Structure updates or proposals to prioritize the most critical information.

Why the Pyramid Principle is Effective

This method helps:
1. **Enhance Clarity:** Prevents the audience from getting lost in unnecessary details.
2. **Focus Attention:** Emphasizes the most important points first, keeping listeners engaged.
3. **Save Time:** Allows decision-makers to grasp the essence of your argument quickly.

Challenges and Limitations

1. **Oversimplification Risk:** Starting with conclusions may oversimplify complex issues.
2. **Dependency on Strong Evidence:** The approach relies on robust, well-organized supporting points.
3. **Cultural Preferences:** In some cultures, audiences may prefer a gradual build-up to the conclusion.

For instance, presenting a direct recommendation without sufficient context might seem abrupt or overly assertive in certain situations.

1. **Refine Your Key Message:** Focus on the core insight or recommendation that your audience needs.
2. **Structure Thoughtfully:** Group supporting points logically and align them with your conclusion.
3. **Adapt to the Audience:** Adjust the level of detail based on the audience's familiarity with the topic.

Exercises

1. **Draft an Argument:** Choose a topic and write a brief summary using the Pyramid Principle. Start with your conclusion and build downward.
2. **Reorganize a Presentation:** Take a previous presentation or report and restructure it using this method. Reflect on how it improves clarity.
3. **Team Workshop:** Facilitate a group exercise where participants apply the Pyramid Principle to a shared challenge. Discuss the outcomes.

Closing Thoughts

The Pyramid Principle is a versatile framework for structuring ideas in a clear, logical, and impactful way. By prioritizing conclusions and organizing evidence effectively, it ensures that your message resonates with your audience and drives meaningful action.

Mastering this technique enhances your ability to communicate persuasively, whether you're addressing a team, a client, or a large audience.

Chapter 68: The Rhetorical Triangle

Balancing Persuasion: The Rhetorical Triangle

The Rhetorical Triangle is a classical framework for understanding and applying the three key elements of effective persuasion: Ethos (credibility), Pathos (emotion), and Logos (logic). This approach, rooted in Aristotle's teachings, remains relevant in modern communication.

For example:

- **Scenario:** A leader motivates their team to adopt a new strategy.
- **Rhetorical Triangle Application:** They establish credibility with their expertise (ethos), appeal to team values (pathos), and present clear data and reasoning (logos).

Balancing these three elements ensures that your message resonates with both the mind and the heart of your audience.

The Three Elements of the Rhetorical Triangle

1. **Ethos (Credibility):** Establish your trustworthiness and authority on the subject.
   Example: "As someone with 10 years of experience in this field, I've seen these strategies succeed."
2. **Pathos (Emotion):** Appeal to your audience's emotions, values, and beliefs.
   Example: "This strategy will help us build a brighter future for our families and communities."
3. **Logos (Logic):** Use data, facts, and logical reasoning to support your argument.
   Example: "Research shows a 25% increase in efficiency with this approach."

Applications of the Rhetorical Triangle

1. **In Public Speaking:**
   o Combine credibility, emotion, and logic to engage and inspire audiences.
2. **In Marketing:**
   o Build trust in your brand (ethos), connect emotionally with customers (pathos), and highlight product benefits with evidence (logos).
3. **In Conflict Resolution:**
   o Balance empathy with logic and authority to mediate disagreements effectively.

Why the Rhetorical Triangle is Effective

This method helps:

1. **Enhance Persuasion:** Appeals to the audience's intellect, emotions, and trust simultaneously.
2. **Build Credibility:** Establishes you as a reliable and empathetic communicator.
3. **Foster Engagement:** Creates a balanced and compelling argument.

1. **Overemphasis on One Element:** Focusing too much on one aspect may weaken the overall message.
2. **Cultural Differences:** Some audiences may prioritize logic (logos) over emotion (pathos) or vice versa.
3. **Credibility Risk:** Weak ethos can undermine the entire argument, even if logos and pathos are strong.

For instance, presenting powerful data (logos) without establishing trust (ethos) may leave your audience sceptical.

How to Use the Rhetorical Triangle Effectively

1. **Know Your Audience:** Tailor the balance of ethos, pathos, and logos to their preferences and values.
2. **Strengthen Ethos:** Build credibility through expertise, authenticity, and professionalism.
3. **Blend Pathos and Logos:** Use emotional appeals to complement logical arguments, not replace them.

Exercises

1. **Analyze a Speech:** Choose a famous speech and evaluate how it uses ethos, pathos, and logos. Reflect on its impact.
2. **Practice Balancing Elements:** Write a persuasive argument for a topic of your choice, balancing all three elements.
3. **Reframe an Existing Message:** Take a past communication and adjust it to incorporate ethos, pathos, and logos more effectively.

Closing Thoughts

The Rhetorical Triangle provides a timeless framework for crafting persuasive and impactful messages. By balancing credibility, emotion, and logic, it ensures your communication resonates deeply with your audience.

This technique enhances your ability to persuade, inspire, and connect in diverse settings, from public speaking to everyday conversations.

Chapter 69: Active Listening

Listening with Purpose: Active Listening

Active Listening is the process of fully focusing on, understanding, and responding to what someone is saying. Unlike passive listening, which involves simply hearing words, active listening requires engagement, empathy, and feedback to ensure effective communication.

For example:

- **Scenario:** A manager is conducting a performance review.
- **Active Listening Application:** Instead of interrupting or rushing, they listen attentively, paraphrase key points, and ask clarifying questions.

This method fosters mutual understanding, builds trust, and enhances relationships in both personal and professional settings.

How Active Listening Works

1. **Focus on the Speaker:** Eliminate distractions and give your full attention.
   Example: "Put away your phone and make eye contact while the other person is speaking."
2. **Show Understanding:** Use verbal and nonverbal cues to convey attentiveness.
   Example: Nod, smile, or use phrases like "I see" or "Go on."
3. **Paraphrase and Summarize:** Restate key points to confirm your understanding.
   Example: "So, what you're saying is that you'd like more autonomy in your role?"
4. **Ask Questions:** Clarify ambiguities or dig deeper into the speaker's message.
   Example: "Can you elaborate on what you mean by 'more support from the team'?"

Applications of Active Listening

1. **In Leadership:**
   - Build trust and rapport with team members by actively listening to their concerns.
2. **In Conflict Resolution:**
   - Diffuse tension and foster understanding by truly hearing both sides.
3. **In Personal Relationships:**
   - Strengthen connections by showing empathy and validating feelings.

This method helps:

1. **Enhance Understanding:** Reduces miscommunication and clarifies intent.
2. **Build Trust:** Demonstrates respect and empathy, strengthening relationships.
3. **Encourage Open Dialogue:** Makes others feel heard and valued, fostering collaboration.

Challenges and Limitations

1. **Time-Intensive:** Fully engaging in conversations can be demanding, especially in busy environments.
2. **Emotional Effort:** Listening empathetically to emotional topics may be mentally draining.
3. **Cultural Differences:** Listening styles and expectations may vary across cultures.

For instance, in some cultures, silence during a conversation signifies respect, while in others, it may be perceived as disengagement.

How to Practice Active Listening Effectively

1. **Be Present:** Remove distractions and focus solely on the speaker.
2. **Manage Emotions:** Stay calm and composed, even during challenging conversations.
3. **Respond Thoughtfully:** Avoid interrupting or offering solutions prematurely; prioritize understanding first.

Exercises

1. **Reflect on a Recent Conversation:** Analyze a discussion where you practiced active listening. What worked well, and what could you improve?
2. **Role-Play Active Listening:** Partner with someone to simulate a conversation where you actively listen and provide feedback.
3. **Use a Journal:** After a conversation, jot down the speaker's key points to reinforce understanding and identify areas for growth.

Closing Thoughts

Active Listening is a cornerstone of effective communication. By being fully present and empathetic, you can navigate conversations with greater clarity, respect, and impact. This skill is essential for building trust, resolving conflicts, and enhancing relationships.

Chapter 70: Mirroring and Paraphrasing

Reflecting Understanding: Mirroring and Paraphrasing

Mirroring and Paraphrasing are techniques used to demonstrate understanding and build rapport during conversations. By reflecting the speaker's words or gestures and summarizing their key points, you create a sense of connection and validation.

For example:

- **Scenario:** A friend shares concerns about their workload.
- **Mirroring and Paraphrasing Application:** You nod, maintain similar body language, and say, "It sounds like you're feeling overwhelmed with the amount of work you have."

These techniques are especially useful in conflict resolution, counseling, and team communication.

How Mirroring and Paraphrasing Work

1. **Mirroring:**
   - Imitate the speaker's tone, pace, and gestures subtly to create a sense of alignment.
   - Example: If the speaker is leaning forward and speaking softly, do the same.
2. **Paraphrasing:**
   - Restate the speaker's message in your own words to confirm understanding.
   - Example: "So, you're saying you'd like more support from your colleagues to manage deadlines?"
3. **Combine Both:**
   - Use mirroring to build connection and paraphrasing to clarify and validate the speaker's message.

1. **In Customer Service:**
   - Reflect customer concerns to show empathy and ensure you understand their needs.
2. **In Mediation:**
   - Use paraphrasing to clarify each party's perspective and foster mutual understanding.
3. **In Personal Relationships:**
   - Strengthen bonds by validating feelings and demonstrating attentiveness.

Why Mirroring and Paraphrasing Are Effective

These techniques help:

1. **Build Rapport:** Create a sense of connection and trust.
2. **Enhance Clarity:** Reduce misunderstandings and ensure alignment.
3. **Foster Empathy:** Show that you value and respect the speaker's perspective.

Challenges and Limitations

1. **Overuse of Mirroring:** Excessive imitation may come across as insincere or awkward.
2. **Paraphrasing Errors:** Misinterpreting or oversimplifying the speaker's message can cause frustration.
3. **Cultural Sensitivities:** Mirroring gestures or tone may not be appropriate in all cultural contexts.

For instance, in some cultures, maintaining direct eye contact or mimicking body language might be seen as intrusive.

How to Use Mirroring and Paraphrasing Effectively

1. **Be Subtle with Mirroring:** Avoid mimicking too obviously; focus on natural alignment.
2. **Paraphrase Thoughtfully:** Capture the essence of the speaker's message without altering its meaning.
3. **Seek Confirmation:** Ask the speaker if your paraphrase accurately reflects their intent.

Exercises

1. **Mirror in a Conversation:** Practice subtly mirroring someone's tone and gestures during a casual discussion. Reflect on how it affects the interaction.
2. **Paraphrase Feedback:** After listening to someone, paraphrase their key points and ask for confirmation. Adjust as needed.
3. **Role-Play:** Simulate a conflict resolution scenario where you use both techniques to foster understanding and agreement.

Closing Thoughts

Mirroring and Paraphrasing are powerful tools for building trust, enhancing communication, and fostering empathy. By reflecting and clarifying messages, you ensure that others feel heard, valued, and understood.

Chapter 71: Using Analogies Effectively

Making the Complex Relatable: Using Analogies Effectively

An analogy is a comparison between two concepts to clarify or explain the unfamiliar using something familiar. Analogies are powerful tools for simplifying complex ideas, sparking understanding, and engaging audiences.

For example:

- **Scenario:** A teacher explains the flow of electricity.
- **Analogy Application:** They compare it to water flowing through a pipe, making the abstract concept relatable.

When used effectively, analogies can bridge gaps in understanding, making your message more compelling and memorable.

How Analogies Work

1. **Identify the Concept:** Pinpoint the idea you want to explain or clarify.
   Example: "How does a blockchain work?"
2. **Find a Familiar Comparison:** Choose a relatable analogy that mirrors the key features of your concept.
   Example: "A blockchain is like a digital ledger where each transaction is recorded, similar to pages in a checkbook."
3. **Highlight Key Similarities:** Focus on the parallels that simplify understanding without oversimplifying.
4. **Test the Analogy:** Ensure the comparison resonates with your audience and doesn't introduce confusion.

1. **In Education:**
   o Explain abstract or technical concepts by comparing them to everyday experiences.
2. **In Business Presentations:**
   o Use analogies to make data or strategies more accessible to stakeholders.
3. **In Personal Communication:**
   o Clarify your perspective during conversations by relating ideas to shared experiences.

Why Analogies Are Effective

This method helps:
1. **Simplify Complexity:** Breaks down abstract ideas into relatable components.
2. **Enhance Engagement:** Captures attention by connecting with familiar concepts.
3. **Foster Retention:** Makes messages more memorable by linking them to existing knowledge.

Challenges and Limitations

1. **Risk of Oversimplification:** Simplifying too much may distort the original concept.
2. **Cultural Context:** Analogies reliant on specific cultural references may not resonate universally.
3. **Potential Confusion:** Poorly chosen analogies can mislead or confuse the audience.

For instance, comparing cloud computing to a physical cloud may misrepresent the technical realities of the concept.

How to Use Analogies Effectively

1. **Know Your Audience:** Tailor analogies to their experiences, interests, and cultural background.
   Example: "What comparisons would feel familiar to this group?"
2. **Keep it Relevant:** Ensure the analogy aligns with the concept's key characteristics.
   Example: "Does this comparison accurately reflect the main features?"
3. **Explain the Transition:** Clarify how the analogy relates to the original idea.

Exercises

1. **Create an Analogy:** Choose a complex concept and develop an analogy to explain it. Test it with someone unfamiliar with the topic.
2. **Analyze a Famous Analogy:** Study an analogy used in a speech, book, or article. What makes it effective or ineffective?
3. **Reframe a Concept:** Take a technical or abstract idea and develop two or three analogies for different audiences.

Closing Thoughts

Analogies are bridges between the familiar and the unfamiliar, transforming complexity into clarity. By leveraging relatable comparisons, you can communicate more effectively, engage your audience, and leave a lasting impression.

Mastering this skill enables you to explain ideas with greater impact, making your message accessible and memorable across diverse contexts.

Chapter 72: The SEE-I Framework (State, Elaborate, Exemplify, Illustrate)

Clarifying Ideas with Structure: The SEE-I Framework

The SEE-I Framework is a method for explaining ideas clearly and thoroughly. It involves four steps: State the idea, Elaborate on it, provide an Example, and Illustrate it with a metaphor, analogy, or diagram.

For example:
- **Scenario:** A trainer explains the concept of teamwork.
- **SEE-I Application:** They state its definition, elaborate on its importance, provide an example of a successful team, and illustrate it as gears working together in a machine.

THE SEE-I FRAMEWORK

STATE	ELABORATE	EXEMPLIFY	ILLUSTRATE
Teamwork is people working together toward a common goal.	It means combining strengths and supporting each other to succeed.	Like when coworkers divide tasks to finish a project.	Team Members

This framework ensures clarity and engagement, making complex ideas more accessible and relatable.

How the SEE-I Framework Works

1. **State:** Clearly and succinctly define the idea or concept.
   Example: "Critical thinking is the ability to analyze information objectively."
2. **Elaborate:** Expand on the idea with additional details or context.
   Example: "It involves evaluating evidence, identifying biases, and drawing reasoned conclusions."

3. **Exemplify:** Provide a concrete example to illustrate the concept in action.
   Example: "For instance, a journalist uses critical thinking to verify sources before publishing a story."
4. **Illustrate:** Use a metaphor, analogy, or visual to make the idea more relatable.
   Example: "Think of critical thinking as a filter that separates fact from fiction, like a sieve separating sand from rocks."

Applications of the SEE-I Framework

1. **In Teaching:**
   - Explain abstract concepts in a structured, engaging way for students.
2. **In Business Communication:**
   - Present ideas, proposals, or strategies with clarity and impact.
3. **In Personal Development:**
   - Reflect on and articulate your understanding of key concepts or values.

Why the SEE-I Framework is Effective

This method helps:

1. **Enhance Clarity:** Breaks down complex ideas into manageable components.
2. **Foster Engagement:** Combines structure with creativity to maintain interest.
3. **Promote Retention:** Reinforces understanding through repetition and illustration.

Challenges and Limitations

1. **Time-Intensive:** Providing elaboration, examples, and illustrations may require significant effort.
2. **Relevance of Examples:** Poorly chosen examples or illustrations can confuse rather than clarify.
3. **Over-Structuring:** Strict adherence to the framework might limit spontaneity or flexibility.

For instance, forcing an illustration where it isn't needed may distract from the core idea.

How to Use the SEE-I Framework Effectively

1. **Adapt to Context:** Tailor the framework to the audience's needs and the complexity of the topic.
2. **Choose Relatable Examples:** Ensure examples and illustrations resonate with your audience.
3. **Practice Brevity:** Keep each step concise to maintain focus and flow.

Exercises

1. **Apply SEE-I to a Concept:** Choose an idea and explain it using all four steps of the framework. Share it with someone and seek feedback.
2. **Analyze SEE-I in Action:** Review a lecture or article and identify where the framework is implicitly or explicitly applied.
3. **Create a Training Module:** Design a short lesson or presentation using SEE-I to explain a topic of your choice.

Closing Thoughts

The SEE-I Framework is a powerful tool for breaking down ideas into clear, engaging, and accessible explanations. By combining structure with creativity, it ensures your message is understood and remembered.

Mastering this framework equips you to communicate effectively in education, business, and everyday conversations, making your ideas resonate with any audience.

Chapter 73: Building Common Ground

Finding Unity: Building Common Ground

Building common ground involves identifying shared values, goals, or experiences that bridge differences and foster collaboration. By focusing on what unites rather than divides, this approach strengthens relationships and resolves conflicts more effectively.

For example:

- **Scenario:** A manager mediates a disagreement between two team members.
- **Common Ground Application:** They emphasize the shared goal of delivering a successful project, redirecting attention away from personal grievances.

This technique is critical in negotiation, conflict resolution, and team-building, creating a foundation for trust and cooperation.

How to Build Common Ground

1. **Identify Shared Values:** Look for beliefs, goals, or interests that both parties prioritize.
   Example: "We all want this project to succeed."
2. **Acknowledge Differences:** Respect and validate differing perspectives while steering the focus toward commonalities.
   Example: "I understand we have different approaches, but we agree on the importance of customer satisfaction."

3. **Use Inclusive Language:** Frame statements to emphasize collaboration and unity.
   Example: "How can we work together to achieve this goal?"
4. **Focus on Mutual Benefits:** Highlight outcomes that benefit everyone involved.
   Example: "Resolving this issue will help us meet our deadlines and improve team morale."

Applications of Building Common Ground

1. **In Negotiations:**
   o   Establish a basis for compromise by focusing on shared interests.
2. **In Conflict Resolution:**
   o   Redirect disagreements toward mutual goals or values.
3. **In Leadership:**
   o   Foster team cohesion by emphasizing collective objectives.

Why Building Common Ground is Effective

This method helps:
1. **Foster Collaboration:** Encourages cooperation by emphasizing shared goals.
2. **Defuse Tensions:** Shifts focus away from disagreements toward unity.
3. **Build Trust:** Demonstrates respect and understanding, strengthening relationships.

Challenges and Limitations

1. **Deep Divisions:** Finding shared values can be difficult in polarized situations.
2. **Superficial Agreement:** Focusing solely on commonalities may ignore underlying issues.
3. **Resistance to Collaboration:** Some individuals may prioritize winning over finding unity.

For instance, in high-stakes negotiations, parties might resist acknowledging shared goals if it weakens their bargaining position.

How to Build Common Ground Effectively

1. **Start Small:** Focus on minor shared interests before tackling larger issues.
2. **Ask Open-Ended Questions:** Encourage dialogue to uncover common values.
   Example: "What's most important to you in this situation?"
3. **Balance Unity and Differences:** Address disagreements while emphasizing alignment.

Exercises

1. **Identify Common Ground:** Think of a recent disagreement and identify shared values or goals. Reflect on how they could have influenced the outcome.
2. **Facilitate a Team Exercise:** Lead a group activity that highlights shared interests or objectives, such as brainstorming a vision statement.
3. **Reframe a Conflict:** Choose a past conflict and rewrite it with an emphasis on building common ground.

Closing Thoughts

Building common ground is a vital skill for navigating conflicts, fostering collaboration, and strengthening relationships. By focusing on shared values and goals, you can bridge divides and create a foundation for mutual respect and cooperation.

This technique empowers you to connect with others meaningfully, transforming challenges into opportunities for unity and growth.

Chapter 74: Structuring Evidence with Logic

Making Arguments Solid: Structuring Evidence with Logic

Structuring evidence with logic ensures that your arguments are persuasive, clear, and credible. By organizing data, examples, and reasoning in a cohesive manner, you build a foundation that supports your conclusions effectively.

For example:
- **Scenario:** A team pitches a new marketing strategy.
- **Structuring Evidence Application:** They present market research, case studies, and projected outcomes in a logical progression that supports their proposal.

This approach is essential in business, academia, and any context where persuasion relies on clear reasoning.

How to Structure Evidence Logically

1. **Start with a Clear Claim:** Clearly articulate your main argument or thesis.
   Example: "Investing in digital marketing will increase customer engagement and revenue."

2. **Provide Supporting Evidence:** Use data, examples, or expert opinions to substantiate your claim.
   Example: "Our market analysis shows a 30% growth in online engagement for competitors using similar strategies."
3. **Connect Evidence to the Claim:** Explain how each piece of evidence supports your argument.
   Example: "This demonstrates that digital marketing aligns with current customer behavior trends."
4. **Address Counterarguments:** Anticipate objections and refute them with evidence.
   Example: "While initial costs are higher, the long-term ROI outweighs the investment."

Applications of Structuring Evidence

1. **In Business Proposals:**
   o Present compelling arguments for projects, investments, or strategies.
2. **In Academic Writing:**
   o Organize essays or research papers to support a thesis with logical reasoning.
3. **In Everyday Debates:**
   o Persuade others in discussions by presenting clear, evidence-based arguments.

Why Structuring Evidence is Effective

This method helps:
1. **Enhance Persuasiveness:** Builds credibility by linking claims to reliable evidence.
2. **Clarify Arguments:** Organizes information logically, making it easier to follow.
3. **Address Skepticism:** Anticipates objections and reinforces the strength of your case.

Challenges and Limitations

1. **Overloading with Data:** Excessive evidence can overwhelm or confuse the audience.
2. **Logical Fallacies:** Poor connections between evidence and claims can weaken arguments.
3. **Bias in Evidence Selection:** Cherry-picking data may undermine credibility.

For instance, using selective statistics to support an argument while ignoring contradictory data might damage trust.

How to Structure Evidence Effectively

1. **Prioritize Quality Over Quantity:** Focus on the most compelling and relevant evidence.
2. **Use Clear Transitions:** Guide the audience through your reasoning with phrases like "This shows that…" or "As a result, we can conclude…"
3. **Balance Evidence Types:** Combine quantitative data with qualitative examples for a well-rounded argument.

Exercises

1. **Analyze an Argument:** Choose an opinion piece or presentation and evaluate how evidence is structured. Identify strengths and weaknesses.
2. **Build Your Argument:** Choose a topic and organize your evidence to support a clear claim. Share it with someone for feedback.
3. **Refine an Existing Argument:** Take a past debate or discussion and restructure your evidence for greater clarity and impact.

Closing Thoughts

Structuring evidence with logic is a cornerstone of persuasive communication. By presenting data, examples, and reasoning in a cohesive framework, you ensure that your arguments are credible, compelling, and impactful.

Chapter 75: Avoiding Loaded Questions

Asking the Right Way: Avoiding Loaded Questions

A loaded question is one that contains a hidden assumption or bias, often designed to corner the respondent into a specific answer. Avoiding loaded questions ensures fairness and neutrality in communication, fostering open dialogue and trust.

For example:
- **Scenario:** A manager asks, "Why did you let this project fail?"
- **Loaded Question Issue:** This assumes the employee is at fault without considering other factors.

Rephrasing loaded questions into neutral ones promotes productive conversations, collaboration, and mutual understanding.

How to Identify and Avoid Loaded Questions

1. **Recognize Hidden Assumptions:** Analyze whether the question presumes something unproven or biased.
   Example: "When will you fix your bad attitude?" assumes the person has a bad attitude.
2. **Rephrase for Neutrality:** Rewrite the question to focus on facts or open exploration.
   Example: "How do you feel about this project's outcome?"
3. **Clarify Intent:** Ensure the question's purpose is constructive, not accusatory.
   Example: Instead of "Why are you always late?" ask, "Is there something preventing you from arriving on time?"
4. **Focus on Solutions:** Frame questions to encourage problem-solving or understanding.
   Example: "What can we do to ensure the project succeeds next time?"

Applications of Avoiding Loaded Questions

1. **In Leadership:**
   o Foster trust and accountability by asking fair, unbiased questions.
2. **In Conflict Resolution:**
   o De-escalate tensions by avoiding accusatory or confrontational phrasing.
3. **In Journalism:**
   o Maintain neutrality and objectivity when interviewing or reporting.

Why Avoiding Loaded Questions is Effective

This method helps:

1. **Encourage Honest Responses:** Removes pressure or defensiveness from the conversation.
2. **Promote Fairness:** Ensures questions are unbiased and focused on understanding.
3. **Build Trust:** Demonstrates respect and openness in communication.

Challenges and Limitations

1. **Unintentional Bias:** Hidden assumptions may slip into questions unconsciously.
2. **Balancing Neutrality:** Overly vague questions may fail to elicit meaningful answers.
3. **Time Constraints:** Reframing questions thoughtfully can require extra effort in fast-paced settings.

For instance, during a heated debate, rephrasing a loaded question on the spot may be challenging but essential for maintaining dialogue.

How to Practice Avoiding Loaded Questions

1. **Pause and Reflect:** Before asking a question, consider whether it contains implicit assumptions.
2. **Seek Feedback:** Practice with colleagues or friends to identify and correct biases in your questions.
3. **Focus on Open-Ended Formats:** Use "What" or "How" questions to encourage exploration rather than confrontation.

Exercises

1. **Rewrite Loaded Questions:** Take five examples of loaded questions and rephrase them into neutral, constructive formats.
2. **Analyze a Conversation:** Reflect on a past discussion where loaded questions may have been used. How did they impact the interaction?
3. **Role-Play:** Practice asking neutral, open-ended questions in a mock debate or negotiation scenario.

Closing Thoughts

Avoiding loaded questions is a key skill for fostering open, respectful, and productive communication. By eliminating hidden assumptions and focusing on neutrality, you create an environment where honest dialogue and collaboration can thrive.

This technique enhances your ability to navigate conflicts, lead teams, and build trust in both personal and professional relationships.

Chapter 76: Recognizing Emotional Triggers

Navigating Sensitivity: Recognizing Emotional Triggers

Emotional triggers are words, phrases, or topics that provoke strong emotional reactions, often rooted in personal experiences or beliefs. Recognizing and managing these triggers ensures that conversations remain constructive and respectful.

For example:

- **Scenario:** A colleague reacts defensively during a feedback session.
- **Emotional Trigger Issue:** The feedback unintentionally touched on a sensitive topic.

Understanding emotional triggers can help prevent misunderstandings, diffuse conflicts, and nurture positive relationships.

How to Recognize Emotional Triggers

1. **Reflect on Personal Reactions:** Identify words or topics that provoke strong emotions in yourself.
   Example: "Why do I feel frustrated when discussing deadlines?"
2. **Observe Nonverbal Cues:** Watch for signs of discomfort or tension, such as crossed arms, raised voices, or abrupt tone shifts.
3. **Ask Open Questions:** Encourage the other person to share their perspective or concerns.
   Example: "You seem upset—can you tell me what's on your mind?"
4. **Acknowledge Sensitivities:** Validate feelings and address concerns without judgment.
   Example: "I understand that this topic is challenging for you."

Applications of Recognizing Emotional Triggers

1. **In Leadership:**
   o Navigate difficult conversations with empathy and awareness.
2. **In Conflict Resolution:**
   o Identify and address the underlying emotions driving disagreements.
3. **In Personal Relationships:**
   o Foster deeper connections by understanding and respecting sensitivities.

Why Recognizing Emotional Triggers is Effective

This method helps:

1. **Improve Communication:** Reduces misunderstandings and emotional escalation.
2. **Strengthen Relationships:** Demonstrates empathy and respect for others' experiences.
3. **Encourage Self-Awareness:** Promotes emotional intelligence in navigating sensitive topics.

Challenges and Limitations

1. **Subtle Signals:** Nonverbal cues may be difficult to interpret accurately.
2. **Managing Personal Bias:** Avoid projecting your own assumptions onto others' emotions.
3. **Navigating Complex Triggers:** Deeply rooted triggers may require time and trust to address fully.

For instance, unresolved trauma may result in triggers that are not immediately apparent or easy to discuss.

How to Manage Emotional Triggers Effectively

1. **Stay Calm:** Maintain composure and avoid reacting impulsively.
2. **Practice Empathy:** Seek to understand the root of the emotion rather than dismissing it.
3. **Reframe the Conversation:** Shift the focus to shared goals or solutions when a trigger arises.

Exercises

1. **Reflect on Your Triggers:** Write about a situation where you felt emotionally triggered. What caused it, and how could you manage it differently?
2. **Analyze a Past Interaction:** Think of a conversation where emotions ran high. How could recognizing triggers have changed the outcome?
3. **Practice with a Partner:** Role-play a challenging discussion, focusing on identifying and addressing potential triggers.

Recognizing emotional triggers is essential for fostering understanding, empathy, and constructive dialogue. By identifying and addressing sensitivities, you can navigate difficult conversations with greater confidence and care.

Chapter 77: Simplifying Complex Ideas

Breaking Down Complexity: Simplifying Complex Ideas

Simplifying complex ideas involves breaking them into smaller, more manageable components or using clear, relatable language to ensure understanding. This skill is essential when communicating intricate concepts to diverse audiences.

For example:

- **Scenario:** A data analyst presents findings to a non-technical team.
- **Simplification Application:** Instead of using jargon, they explain trends and insights with relatable examples and visuals.

Simplifying doesn't mean oversimplifying; it's about making the message accessible without losing its essence.

How to Simplify Complex Ideas

1. **Identify the Core Message:** Focus on the main point or takeaway you want to communicate.
   Example: "What is the one thing your audience should remember?"
2. **Break It Into Steps:** Divide the concept into smaller, logical segments.
   Example: "Step 1: What is the problem? Step 2: How does the solution work?"
3. **Use Analogies and Examples:** Relate the concept to something familiar.
   Example: "Think of blockchain as a digital ledger, like balancing a checkbook online."
4. **Visualize the Idea:** Use diagrams, charts, or metaphors to represent the concept visually.

Applications of Simplifying Complex Ideas

1. **In Education:**
   o Teach difficult subjects in a way that resonates with students at different levels.
2. **In Business Communication:**
   o Explain strategies, data, or technical solutions to stakeholders with varying expertise.
3. **In Everyday Interactions:**
   o Clarify your thoughts or perspectives when discussing nuanced topics with others.

Why Simplifying Complex Ideas is Effective

This method helps:

1. **Enhance Clarity:** Ensures your audience grasps the message without confusion.
2. **Improve Engagement:** Keeps listeners interested by avoiding overwhelming details.
3. **Foster Retention:** Simplified ideas are easier to remember and act upon.

Challenges and Limitations

1. **Risk of Oversimplification:** Stripping too much detail may compromise accuracy.
2. **Audience Diversity:** Different levels of expertise may require varying degrees of simplification.
3. **Time Constraints:** Simplifying complex concepts effectively requires preparation and creativity.

For instance, reducing a medical explanation too much could leave out critical information that affects understanding.

How to Simplify Effectively

1. **Know Your Audience:** Tailor your explanation to their background and needs.
   Example: "What terms or examples will resonate with this group?"
2. **Focus on Key Points:** Prioritize the most critical aspects of the idea.
   Example: "What is the simplest way to convey the message without losing meaning?"
3. **Use Visuals and Stories:** Supplement explanations with images or narratives that reinforce understanding.

Exercises

1. **Simplify a Concept:** Take a complex idea you're familiar with and explain it to someone with no prior knowledge of the topic.
2. **Reframe a Presentation:** Choose a past presentation and simplify its key points for a general audience. Reflect on the changes.

3. **Create a Visual Aid:** Develop a chart, diagram, or infographic to represent a complicated concept in a straightforward way.

Closing Thoughts

Simplifying complex ideas is a critical skill for effective communication. By breaking down information and using relatable language, you ensure that your audience understands and retains your message.

This skill enhances your ability to connect, persuade, and educate in any context, from professional presentations to everyday conversations.

Chapter 78: Using Data to Bolster Arguments

Backing Arguments with Evidence: Using Data to Bolster Arguments

Data adds credibility and strength to your arguments by providing factual evidence to support your claims. When used effectively, data can make your message more persuasive, impactful, and trustworthy.

For example:

- **Scenario:** A non-profit advocates for increased funding.
- **Data Application:** They use statistics on program outcomes to demonstrate the impact of their work.

Data-driven arguments are particularly valuable in fields such as business, policy, education, and marketing, where evidence-based decision-making is essential.

How to Use Data Effectively

1. **Choose Relevant Data:** Select statistics, trends, or metrics directly related to your argument.
   Example: "What data points best illustrate the problem or solution?"
2. **Present Data Clearly:** Use charts, graphs, or tables to make information accessible.
   Example: "This bar graph shows a 20% increase in customer retention after implementing the new strategy."
3. **Explain the Connection:** Link data directly to your argument or conclusion.
   Example: "These numbers highlight why our proposed solution is both effective and necessary."
4. **Anticipate Questions:** Be prepared to explain the source, methodology, and context of the data.

Applications of Using Data

1. **In Business:**
   - Support strategies, proposals, or decisions with performance metrics and market analysis.
2. **In Education:**
   - Use data to highlight learning trends, gaps, or achievements in the classroom.
3. **In Advocacy:**
   - Persuade stakeholders or the public by presenting data on social, economic, or environmental issues.

Why Using Data is Effective

This method helps:

1. **Enhance Credibility:** Demonstrates that your arguments are grounded in evidence.
2. **Clarify Complex Issues:** Transforms abstract ideas into tangible insights.
3. **Persuade More Effectively:** Appeals to logic and rationality, reinforcing your message.

Challenges and Limitations

1. **Misinterpretation Risk:** Poorly presented data can confuse or mislead the audience.
2. **Overloading with Information:** Too much data may overwhelm or distract from the main message.
3. **Bias in Data Selection:** Cherry-picking favorable data points can harm credibility.

For example, selectively highlighting only positive survey results while ignoring negative feedback might appear deceptive.

How to Use Data Effectively

1. **Focus on Quality:** Use credible, well-sourced, and up-to-date data.
2. **Simplify Presentation:** Highlight key insights rather than overwhelming your audience with every detail.
3. **Combine with Narrative:** Frame data within a compelling story to enhance emotional and logical appeal.

1. **Analyze a Report:** Choose a data-driven report and evaluate how effectively it supports its conclusions. Identify strengths and areas for improvement.
2. **Build a Data Argument:** Select a topic and gather relevant data to create a persuasive argument. Present it to a peer for feedback.
3. **Create a Visual Summary:** Develop a chart or infographic that highlights key data points for a specific argument.

Closing Thoughts

Data is a powerful tool for enhancing the persuasiveness and credibility of your arguments. By selecting relevant information and presenting it clearly, you can support your claims with evidence that resonates with your audience.

This skill is indispensable in today's information-driven world, helping you make compelling cases across professional, academic, and personal contexts.

Chapter 79: The Rule of Three in Persuasion

Power in Simplicity: The Rule of Three in Persuasion

The Rule of Three is a principle suggesting that ideas presented in groups of three are more impactful, memorable, and persuasive. By leveraging this natural preference for triads, communicators can simplify complex messages and enhance their effectiveness.

For example:

- **Scenario:** A marketer presents a product.
- **Rule of Three Application:** They highlight three key benefits: affordability, durability, and ease of use.

This method is widely used in speeches, storytelling, marketing, and education to create concise and engaging messages.

How to Apply the Rule of Three

1. **Identify the Key Points:** Select three main ideas or takeaways you want your audience to remember.
   Example: "What are the three most important benefits of this proposal?"
2. **Organize for Impact:** Arrange your points logically, building toward the most compelling one.
   Example: "Start with affordability, then highlight durability, and finish with ease of use."
3. **Reinforce with Repetition:** Use triads throughout your message for consistency and emphasis.
   Example: "We need innovation, collaboration, and determination to succeed."

Applications of the Rule of Three

1. **In Speeches:**
   o Deliver impactful messages with triads like "life, liberty, and the pursuit of happiness."
2. **In Marketing:**
   o Highlight three product features or benefits in advertisements or presentations.
3. **In Teaching:**
   o Simplify lessons by organizing content into three key concepts or steps.

Why the Rule of Three is Effective

This method helps:
1. **Enhance Clarity:** Focuses attention on the most critical points.
2. **Improve Retention:** Capitalizes on the brain's preference for triads, making information easier to remember.
3. **Create Impact:** Simplifies complexity while maintaining depth and engagement.

Challenges and Limitations

1. **Oversimplification:** Complex topics may require more than three points for adequate explanation.
2. **Repetition Risk:** Overusing triads can make communication feel formulaic or predictable.
3. **Inappropriate Contexts:** Certain situations may require a more detailed or flexible approach.

For example, a technical report may demand more than three key takeaways to convey comprehensive information.

1. **Prioritize Key Messages:** Focus on the three most important or impactful ideas.
2. **Adapt to the Audience:** Ensure your triad resonates with their needs and expectations.
3. **Balance Depth and Simplicity:** Use the rule as a guideline, not a constraint, when complexity demands more detail.

Exercises

1. **Craft a Triad:** Choose a topic and organize your key points into a three-part structure. Present it to someone for feedback.
2. **Analyze a Famous Speech:** Identify how the Rule of Three is applied in speeches or slogans. Reflect on its effectiveness.
3. **Reframe a Complex Message:** Simplify a detailed argument or explanation into three key takeaways.

Closing Thoughts

The Rule of Three is a timeless technique for crafting memorable, persuasive, and impactful messages. By organizing ideas into triads, you can enhance clarity, engage your audience, and ensure your key points are retained.

This method is a versatile tool for effective communication, whether you're presenting a speech, crafting a marketing pitch, or teaching a concept.

Chapter 80: The Importance of Visual Aids

Making Ideas Visible: The Importance of Visual Aids

Visual aids — such as charts, graphs, images, and diagrams — enhance communication by making ideas tangible, engaging, and easier to understand. They complement verbal or written content, helping audiences process and retain information more effectively.

For example:

- **Scenario:** A scientist presents research findings.
- **Visual Aid Application:** They use a graph to show the correlation between two variables, simplifying complex data into an easily understood visual.

In today's fast-paced, information-driven world, well-designed visual aids are indispensable for clear and persuasive communication.

How to Use Visual Aids Effectively

1. **Choose the Right Aid:** Select visuals that align with your content and audience.
   Example: Use graphs for data, diagrams for processes, and images for concepts.
2. **Simplify the Design:** Keep visuals clean and uncluttered, focusing on key points.
   Example: Highlight one trend in a graph rather than overloading it with multiple datasets.
3. **Integrate Seamlessly:** Use visuals to complement, not replace, your verbal or written message.
   Example: Explain the chart's significance rather than just showing it.
4. **Test for Clarity:** Ensure your visuals are easily interpretable by your audience.

Applications of Visual Aids

1. **In Presentations:**
   o Use slides with charts, images, or videos to engage and inform the audience.
2. **In Education:**
   o Incorporate diagrams, infographics, or animations to clarify lessons.
3. **In Reports and Proposals:**
   o Include graphs and tables to support arguments and provide evidence.

Why Visual Aids Are Effective

This method helps:

1. **Enhance Engagement:** Captures attention with appealing and relevant visuals.
2. **Clarify Information:** Simplifies complex concepts or data into digestible formats.
3. **Improve Retention:** Makes content more memorable by appealing to visual learning styles.

Challenges and Limitations

1. **Overuse of Visuals:** Excessive or irrelevant visuals can distract rather than enhance.
2. **Technical Issues:** Poor-quality images or software glitches may disrupt communication.

3. **Cultural Sensitivities:** Images or symbols may carry different meanings across cultures.

For instance, using color-coded graphs in regions with different color associations might confuse the audience.

1. **Focus on Quality:** Use high-resolution, professional visuals that align with your message.
2. **Balance Content and Visuals:** Ensure visuals support your narrative without overshadowing it.
3. **Practice with Visuals:** Familiarize yourself with presenting alongside your chosen aids to avoid reliance or distraction.

Exercises

1. **Create a Visual Aid:** Design a graph, diagram, or infographic to represent a topic of your choice. Share it with someone for feedback.
2. **Analyze a Presentation:** Review a presentation that uses visuals. Identify what works well and what could be improved.
3. **Reframe a Report:** Take a text-heavy report and incorporate visual aids to enhance clarity and engagement.

Closing Thoughts

Visual aids are powerful tools for enhancing communication, making ideas more engaging, and ensuring information is understood and retained. When used effectively, they complement your message and elevate its impact.

This skill is essential in professional, academic, and personal contexts, empowering you to connect with audiences through clarity, creativity, and precision.

Section IV: Mastery

Subsection: Logical Thinking in Complex Systems

Complex systems are characterized by interconnected components, dynamic interactions, and emergent behaviors. Understanding these systems requires a shift from linear thinking to a more holistic and analytical approach. In this section, we'll explore tools and frameworks that help navigate complexity, identify leverage points, and anticipate unintended consequences.

Chapter 81: Systems Thinking

Seeing the Bigger Picture: Systems Thinking

Systems Thinking is a framework for understanding complex systems by analyzing the relationships and interactions between their components. Instead of isolating parts, it emphasizes the whole system, identifying patterns, feedback loops, and interdependencies.

For example:

- **Scenario:** A city addresses traffic congestion.
- **Systems Thinking Application:** They analyze how road design, public transportation, and urban planning influence traffic flow rather than focusing solely on building new roads.

This approach is essential for tackling multifaceted problems in fields such as ecology, economics, and organizational management.

How Systems Thinking Works

1. **Define the System:** Identify the boundaries, components, and purpose of the system.
   Example: "What elements make up the healthcare system, and how do they interact?"
2. **Analyze Interconnections:** Map relationships and feedback loops within the system.
   Example: "How do policy changes affect patient outcomes and resource allocation?"
3. **Identify Patterns and Trends:** Look for recurring behaviors or emerging dynamics.
   Example: "Why does patient demand spike during certain times of the year?"
4. **Anticipate Outcomes:** Consider how changes to one component might affect the whole system.
   Example: "What are the unintended consequences of reducing hospital staffing?"

Applications of Systems Thinking

1. **In Environmental Management:**
   o   Address climate change by analyzing the interconnected effects of energy use, deforestation, and policy.
2. **In Business Strategy:**
   o   Improve organizational efficiency by understanding how departments and processes interact.

3. **In Education:**
   ○ Teach students to analyze historical events or social issues as part of larger systems.

Why Systems Thinking is Effective

This method helps:
1. **Enhance Understanding:** Provides a holistic view of complex issues.
2. **Anticipate Consequences:** Identifies potential ripple effects and unintended outcomes.
3. **Promote Collaboration:** Encourages stakeholders to work together by understanding shared interconnections.

Challenges and Limitations

1. **Complexity Overload:** Large systems can be overwhelming to analyze and model.
2. **Data Requirements:** Requires comprehensive and accurate data to map interactions effectively.
3. **Time-Intensive:** Mapping and analyzing systems can take significant time and effort.

For instance, addressing supply chain inefficiencies may require analyzing global logistics, local policies, and market dynamics simultaneously.

How to Use Systems Thinking Effectively

1. **Start Small:** Focus on a manageable subsystem or component before expanding the analysis.
2. **Collaborate Across Disciplines:** Include diverse perspectives to capture all relevant interconnections.
3. **Use Visual Tools:** Create diagrams or models to represent relationships and feedback loops.

Exercises

1. **Map a System:** Choose a complex issue and map its components, interconnections, and feedback loops.
2. **Analyze a Pattern:** Reflect on a recurring challenge in your work or life. How does Systems Thinking explain it?
3. **Apply Systems Thinking:** Practice applying Systems Thinking to a real-world problem, such as improving workplace efficiency or addressing community issues. Evaluate how focusing on interconnections influences your solutions.

Closing Thoughts

Systems Thinking offers a powerful lens for understanding complexity, uncovering hidden dynamics, and making decisions that consider long-term impacts. By shifting from isolated analysis to holistic thinking, you can address challenges with greater depth and foresight, transforming problems into opportunities for sustainable solutions.

Chapter 82: Bottleneck Analysis

Clearing the Path: Bottleneck Analysis

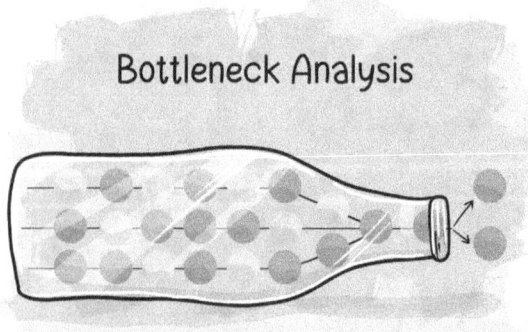

Bottleneck Analysis focuses on identifying and resolving the constraints that slow down or limit the performance of a system. By addressing these critical points, you can optimize efficiency, reduce delays, and improve outcomes.

For example:
- **Scenario:** A manufacturing plant experiences delays in production.
- **Bottleneck Analysis Application:** The team discovers that outdated machinery in one department is slowing down the entire workflow and replaces it.

This method is widely used in project management, supply chain optimization, and operational efficiency initiatives.

How Bottleneck Analysis Works

1. **Identify the Bottleneck:** Pinpoint the process, resource, or component causing delays or inefficiencies.
   Example: "Which step in our production line takes the most time or causes backups?"
2. **Analyze the Impact:** Assess how the bottleneck affects overall performance and outcomes.
   Example: "How much additional cost or delay is this bottleneck causing?"
3. **Develop Solutions:** Explore strategies to resolve or mitigate the constraint.
   Example: "Should we add more resources, streamline the process, or eliminate unnecessary steps?"
4. **Monitor Results:** Evaluate the effectiveness of your intervention and adjust as needed.

Applications of Bottleneck Analysis

1. **In Manufacturing:**
   ○ Identify and resolve inefficiencies in production lines.
2. **In Project Management:**
   ○ Address delays caused by resource shortages or process inefficiencies.

3. **In Customer Service:**
   o   Reduce wait times by identifying and addressing points of congestion in service delivery.

Why Bottleneck Analysis is Effective

This method helps:
1. **Optimize Efficiency:** Eliminates the primary sources of delay or waste.
2. **Improve Resource Allocation:** Focuses efforts on the areas with the greatest impact.
3. **Enhance Outcomes:** Resolving bottlenecks can significantly improve overall performance.

Challenges and Limitations

1. **Identifying Root Causes:** Symptoms may mask the true source of the problem.
2. **Temporary Solutions:** Addressing one bottleneck may reveal new constraints elsewhere.
3. **Balancing Costs:** Solutions may require significant investment or trade-offs.

For instance, hiring more staff to resolve a bottleneck may increase operational costs, requiring careful cost-benefit analysis.

How to Use Bottleneck Analysis Effectively

1. **Gather Data:** Use metrics and observations to identify bottlenecks objectively.
2. **Prioritize Critical Constraints:** Focus on bottlenecks with the greatest impact on overall performance.
3. **Iterate Solutions:** Continuously monitor and adapt strategies as new challenges emerge.

Exercises

1. **Identify a Bottleneck:** Reflect on a process in your work or daily life. What's slowing it down, and how can you address it?
2. **Analyze a System:** Choose a real-world example, such as traffic congestion or supply chain delays, and conduct a bottleneck analysis.
3. **Design a Solution:** Propose and test strategies for resolving a bottleneck in a hypothetical or real scenario.

Closing Thoughts

Bottleneck Analysis is a vital tool for improving efficiency and maximizing system performance. By identifying and addressing critical constraints, you can clear the path to better outcomes and smoother operations.

This method equips you to navigate challenges with focus and precision, ensuring that resources are used effectively to achieve your goals.

Chapter 83: Identifying Leverage Points

Strategic Impact: Identifying Leverage Points

A leverage point is a place within a system where a small change can produce a significant impact. Identifying these points allows decision-makers to prioritize efforts and resources for maximum effectiveness.

For example:

- **Scenario:** A school district wants to improve student performance.
- **Leverage Point Application:** They discover that teacher training has a more significant effect on student outcomes than increased funding for facilities and focus resources accordingly.

Understanding leverage points is essential for addressing complex problems in a targeted and efficient way.

How to Identify Leverage Points

1. **Map the System:** Understand the components, interactions, and feedback loops within the system.
   Example: "How do policies, resources, and stakeholders interact in this system?"
2. **Analyze Causal Relationships:** Identify areas where changes have ripple effects across the system.
   Example: "What happens when we change resource allocation?"
3. **Evaluate Potential Impact:** Prioritize leverage points based on their potential for meaningful and lasting change.
   Example: "Will this intervention improve the system as a whole or just one part?"
4. **Implement and Monitor:** Test interventions at leverage points and monitor their outcomes.

Applications of Identifying Leverage Points

1. **In Business Strategy:**
   o   Identify critical processes or decisions that drive profitability and growth.

2. **In Public Policy:**
   o Focus on interventions, such as education or healthcare access, that have broad societal benefits.
3. **In Personal Development:**
   o Target habits or behaviors that create the most significant positive changes in life.

Why Identifying Leverage Points is Effective

This method helps:
1. **Maximize Efficiency:** Focuses on actions with the highest return on investment.
2. **Promote Systemic Change:** Addresses root causes rather than symptoms.
3. **Enhance Decision-Making:** Simplifies complex problems by highlighting high-impact solutions.

Challenges and Limitations

1. **Complexity in Systems:** Leverage points may be hidden or difficult to pinpoint in intricate systems.
2. **Resistance to Change:** Stakeholders may oppose interventions, even at identified leverage points.
3. **Unintended Consequences:** Changes at leverage points can produce unexpected outcomes elsewhere.

For instance, reducing class sizes might improve teacher-student interactions but increase demand for qualified educators, straining resources.

How to Identify Leverage Points Effectively

1. **Involve Stakeholders:** Collaborate with those who understand the system to identify key areas of influence.
2. **Focus on Feedback Loops:** Target points where changes reinforce positive outcomes or disrupt negative cycles.
3. **Test Incrementally:** Implement small changes and measure their effects before scaling interventions.

Exercises

1. **Map a System:** Choose a system you're familiar with and identify possible leverage points. Reflect on their potential impact.
2. **Analyze Past Successes:** Think of a successful intervention you've seen or experienced. What leverage point was addressed?
3. **Propose a Solution:** Identify a leverage point in a hypothetical or real-world problem and design an intervention.

Closing Thoughts

Identifying leverage points is a powerful strategy for driving meaningful change in complex systems. By focusing on areas with the greatest potential impact, you can achieve transformative results with minimal resources.

This method equips you to address challenges strategically and efficiently, turning complexity into opportunity.

Chapter 84: Emergent Behavior Analysis

Unpredictable Patterns: Emergent Behavior Analysis

Emergent behavior occurs when interactions among individual components of a system produce outcomes that cannot be predicted by analyzing the components alone. Analyzing these behaviors is crucial for understanding and managing complex systems.

For example:
- **Scenario:** An online platform experiences viral trends.
- **Emergent Behavior Analysis Application:** The team studies how individual user interactions contribute to collective phenomena like trends or misinformation.

Emergent behaviors are common in ecosystems, social networks, markets, and other systems where collective dynamics arise from decentralized interactions.

How to Analyze Emergent Behavior

1. **Observe the System:** Identify patterns or phenomena that arise unexpectedly.
   Example: "What trends or behaviors are emerging in this social media platform?"
2. **Understand Local Interactions:** Examine how individual components or agents influence one another.
   Example: "How do user likes, shares, and comments amplify specific content?"
3. **Model the Dynamics:** Use simulations, models, or data analysis to explore how emergent behaviors develop.
   Example: "What happens when we tweak the algorithm that ranks content?"

4. **Adapt Interventions:** Develop strategies to guide or mitigate emergent behaviors.

Applications of Emergent Behavior Analysis

1. **In Ecosystems:**
   - Understand how individual species interactions create balanced or disrupted ecosystems.
2. **In Economics:**
   - Analyze how individual market behaviors lead to trends like booms or crashes.
3. **In Technology:**
   - Study the collective behavior of users in online platforms or AI-driven systems.

Why Emergent Behavior Analysis is Effective

This method helps:
1. **Reveal Hidden Dynamics:** Uncovers patterns that are invisible when focusing on individual components.
2. **Predict System Behavior:** Anticipates collective outcomes in complex environments.
3. **Inform Interventions:** Guides strategies to shape or respond to emergent phenomena.

Challenges and Limitations

1. **Unpredictability:** Emergent behaviors can be difficult or impossible to foresee.
2. **Modeling Complexity:** Simulating large-scale interactions requires advanced tools and expertise.
3. **Resistance to Control:** Emergent behaviors may be resistant to top-down interventions.

For instance, efforts to curb misinformation online may inadvertently amplify it if users resist perceived censorship.

How to Analyze Emergent Behavior Effectively

1. **Embrace Complexity:** Accept that some emergent behaviors may defy simple explanations.
2. **Collaborate Across Disciplines:** Work with experts in relevant fields to analyze and interpret dynamics.
3. **Monitor Continuously:** Regularly observe and adapt to evolving behaviors within the system.

Exercises

1. **Observe Emergent Patterns:** Choose a system, like traffic flow or online trends, and identify emergent behaviors.
2. **Analyze Collective Dynamics:** Reflect on a past situation where emergent behavior influenced outcomes. What were the underlying interactions?
3. **Design a Simulation:** Use basic tools or software to simulate a system and observe how small changes affect emergent patterns.

Closing Thoughts

Emergent behavior analysis is a vital tool for understanding the unpredictable dynamics of complex systems. By focusing on collective outcomes and their underlying interactions, you can navigate uncertainty and develop strategies that align with the system's natural tendencies.

Chapter 85: Scenario Mapping

Preparing for Possibilities: Scenario Mapping

Scenario Mapping is a strategic planning technique that explores possible future outcomes based on current trends and uncertainties. By mapping out various scenarios, decision-makers can anticipate challenges, identify opportunities, and plan for diverse possibilities.

For example:
- **Scenario:** A tech company evaluates market expansion.
- **Scenario Mapping Application:** They map outcomes based on variables like competition, customer demand, and regulatory changes, preparing for best-case, worst-case, and neutral scenarios.

This method is widely used in business strategy, risk management, and policy development to navigate uncertainty effectively.

How Scenario Mapping Works

1. **Define Key Variables:** Identify the factors that could significantly influence outcomes.
   Example: "How will economic conditions, consumer behavior, and technological advancements shape the future?"
2. **Develop Scenarios:** Create narratives or outlines for possible futures based on variations in the key variables.

Example: "Scenario A: High demand and low competition. Scenario B: Low demand and high competition."

3. **Assess Implications:** Analyze how each scenario impacts your goals, strategies, and resources.

Example: "What resources are needed to thrive in Scenario A versus Scenario B?"

4. **Plan for Flexibility:** Develop strategies that are adaptable across multiple scenarios.

Applications of Scenario Mapping

1. **In Business Strategy:**
   o Plan for market fluctuations, competitor actions, and technological shifts.
2. **In Public Policy:**
   o Anticipate the effects of regulations, social trends, or environmental changes.
3. **In Personal Planning:**
   o Map potential outcomes of major life decisions, like career changes or relocations.

Why Scenario Mapping is Effective

This method helps:

1. **Enhance Preparedness:** Anticipates challenges and reduces surprises.
2. **Promote Strategic Flexibility:** Encourages adaptive thinking and contingency planning.
3. **Foster Innovation:** Sparks creative solutions by exploring diverse possibilities.

Challenges and Limitations

1. **Uncertainty in Variables:** Unpredictable factors can lead to incomplete or inaccurate scenarios.
2. **Analysis Paralysis:** Too many scenarios may overwhelm decision-making.
3. **Overemphasis on Extremes:** Focusing only on best- or worst-case scenarios might neglect moderate possibilities.

For instance, overpreparing for an unlikely catastrophe might waste resources better spent on probable outcomes.

How to Use Scenario Mapping Effectively

1. **Prioritize Variables:** Focus on the factors most likely to influence outcomes significantly.
2. **Balance Scenarios:** Include a range of possibilities, from optimistic to pessimistic to neutral.
3. **Engage Stakeholders:** Involve diverse perspectives to capture a broader range of scenarios.

Exercises

1. **Map a Decision:** Choose a decision you're facing and develop three scenarios based on key uncertainties. Reflect on how this shapes your strategy.
2. **Analyze Past Events:** Think of a past situation where scenario mapping could have helped. What variables and outcomes would you have considered?
3. **Facilitate a Group Exercise:** Work with a team to map scenarios for a shared challenge or opportunity.

Closing Thoughts

Scenario Mapping is a powerful tool for navigating uncertainty and preparing for diverse possibilities. By envisioning potential futures, you can make more informed decisions, anticipate risks, and seize opportunities with confidence.

This method enhances your ability to think strategically, adapt to change, and plan effectively in dynamic environments.

Chapter 86: The Butterfly Effect Awareness

Small Actions, Big Effects: The Butterfly Effect Awareness

The Butterfly Effect is a concept from chaos theory describing how small changes in initial conditions can lead to vastly different outcomes in complex systems. Being aware of this phenomenon helps decision-makers recognize the potential ripple effects of their actions.

For example:

- **Scenario:** A city revises its public transportation routes.
- **Butterfly Effect Awareness Application:** Planners consider how minor route changes might influence traffic patterns, local businesses, and commuter habits.

This awareness is particularly relevant in fields such as urban planning, environmental science, and economics, where systems are highly interconnected.

How the Butterfly Effect Works

1. **Understand Initial Conditions:** Recognize the starting point of a system or decision.
   Example: "What small factors could influence this system over time?"
2. **Anticipate Ripple Effects:** Analyze how small changes might propagate through the system.
   Example: "How will a small policy adjustment affect related sectors or stakeholders?"
3. **Plan for Uncertainty:** Accept that not all outcomes can be predicted but consider possible trajectories.
   Example: "What contingency plans can address unexpected consequences?"
4. **Monitor Outcomes:** Track the effects of decisions over time and adjust as needed.

Applications of the Butterfly Effect Awareness

1. **In Environmental Policy:**
   o   Assess how small ecological changes can impact ecosystems globally.
2. **In Technology Development:**
   o   Evaluate how minor design decisions might influence user behavior and system performance.
3. **In Personal Choices:**
   o   Reflect on how small habits or decisions can compound into significant life changes.

Why Butterfly Effect Awareness is Effective

This method helps:
1. **Promote Thoughtful Decisions:** Encourages careful consideration of potential long-term impacts.
2. **Foster Adaptability:** Prepares for unexpected consequences in dynamic systems.
3. **Highlight Interconnectivity:** Reveals how small actions can influence larger outcomes.

Challenges and Limitations

1. **Uncertainty in Predictions:** Small changes don't always lead to significant effects.
2. **Analysis Complexity:** Tracing ripple effects in large systems can be highly complex.
3. **Paralysis by Fear:** Overemphasis on potential consequences may hinder action.

For example, delaying decisions out of fear of unintended ripple effects might prevent necessary progress.

How to Apply Butterfly Effect Awareness Effectively

1. **Think Systemically:** Consider how actions interact with broader systems.
2. **Start with Small Tests:** Experiment with minor changes before implementing large-scale interventions.
3. **Adapt Continuously:** Monitor results and adjust strategies as new ripple effects emerge.

Exercises

1. **Reflect on a Small Action:** Think of a past decision or action that had unexpected consequences. What lessons can you learn?
2. **Map Ripple Effects:** Choose a current decision and brainstorm possible outcomes based on the Butterfly Effect.
3. **Test in a System:** Introduce a small change in a controlled system and observe how it influences the whole.

Closing Thoughts

The Butterfly Effect reminds us that even the smallest actions can have profound and far-reaching consequences. By considering potential ripple effects, you can navigate complex systems more thoughtfully and prepare for a wide range of outcomes.

This awareness enhances your ability to act with foresight and adaptability, empowering you to make impactful decisions in an interconnected world.

Chapter 87: Stochastic Modeling

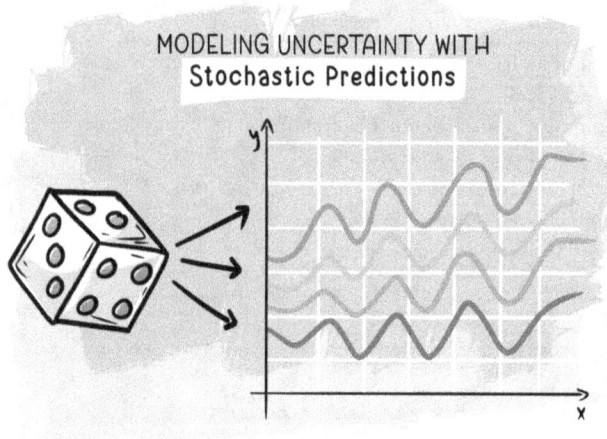

MODELING UNCERTAINTY WITH
Stochastic Predictions

Modeling Uncertainty: Stochastic Modeling

Stochastic Modeling is a mathematical approach to predict and analyze outcomes that involve randomness or uncertainty. Unlike deterministic models, which assume fixed inputs and outputs, stochastic models incorporate variability to reflect real-world complexities.

For example:

- **Scenario:** A financial analyst projects future stock prices.
- **Stochastic Modeling Application:** They use probabilistic models to account for market fluctuations, economic changes, and investor behavior.

This technique is widely used in finance, engineering, healthcare, and environmental science to make informed decisions under uncertainty.

How Stochastic Modeling Works

1. **Define the System:** Identify the variables and processes influenced by randomness.
   Example: "What factors affect patient wait times in a hospital?"
2. **Incorporate Probabilities:** Assign probabilities to potential outcomes or events.
   Example: "What's the likelihood of an emergency increasing wait times?"
3. **Run Simulations:** Use computational tools to simulate multiple scenarios and outcomes.
   Example: "How do patient arrivals vary over time, and what's the impact on staffing needs?"
4. **Analyze Results:** Evaluate patterns, trends, and probabilities to inform decisions.

Applications of Stochastic Modeling

1. **In Finance:**
   o   Forecast investment returns, risk assessments, or market trends.
2. **In Healthcare:**
   o   Predict disease progression or optimize resource allocation for patient care.
3. **In Environmental Science:**
   o   Model climate change impacts, such as temperature fluctuations or sea level rise.

Why Stochastic Modeling is Effective

This method helps:

1. **Account for Uncertainty:** Reflects real-world variability in predictions.
2. **Enhance Decision-Making:** Provides probabilistic insights to guide strategies.
3. **Support Risk Management:** Identifies potential risks and their likelihoods.

Challenges and Limitations

1. **Complexity in Implementation:** Developing and interpreting models requires expertise and computational resources.
2. **Data Dependency:** Reliable predictions depend on accurate and comprehensive input data.
3. **Uncertainty in Outputs:** Probabilistic results may not provide definitive answers.

For instance, predicting rainfall patterns using stochastic models may guide planning but can't guarantee specific outcomes.

How to Use Stochastic Modeling Effectively

1. **Start with Simple Models:** Begin with basic probabilistic assumptions before adding complexity.
2. **Validate with Data:** Test models against historical or real-world data to ensure accuracy.
3. **Combine with Other Tools:** Use stochastic modeling alongside deterministic approaches for a balanced analysis.

Exercises

1. **Build a Simple Model:** Choose a real-world problem and develop a basic stochastic model to predict outcomes.
2. **Analyze Variability:** Reflect on a decision or system influenced by randomness. How could stochastic modeling improve predictions?
3. **Simulate Scenarios:** Use software tools to run stochastic simulations for a project or decision, and analyze the results.

Stochastic modeling is a powerful technique for navigating uncertainty and making data-driven decisions in dynamic environments. By incorporating randomness and variability, you can develop more accurate and realistic predictions.

This method equips you to tackle complex problems with confidence, ensuring that your strategies are robust and adaptable in the face of uncertainty.

Chapter 88: Feedback Loop Analysis

Understanding Cycles: Feedback Loop Analysis

Feedback Loop Analysis examines how actions within a system produce feedback that influences future behaviors. Feedback loops can either amplify (positive loops) or stabilize (negative loops) outcomes, shaping the dynamics of the system over time.

For example:

- **Scenario:** A business monitors customer reviews and sales.
- **Feedback Loop Analysis Application:** Positive reviews attract more customers (reinforcing loop), while stock shortages reduce satisfaction (balancing loop).

This method is essential for understanding and managing dynamic systems in economics, biology, technology, and organizational management.

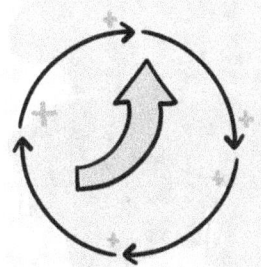

FEEDBACK LOOP ANALYSIS

Reinforcing Loop   Balancing Loop

How Feedback Loop Analysis Works

1. **Identify the Loops:** Map the actions, responses, and feedback within the system.
   Example: "What actions generate reinforcing or balancing feedback in this process?"
2. **Distinguish Loop Types:** Determine whether loops amplify or stabilize system behavior.
   Example: "Does this feedback increase or reduce the original action?"
3. **Analyze Interactions:** Study how loops interact and influence each other.
   Example: "How do customer satisfaction and supply chain dynamics interact?"
4. **Adjust Strategies:** Leverage or mitigate feedback loops to align with your goals.

Applications of Feedback Loop Analysis

1. **In Economics:**
   - Analyze market trends driven by supply-demand cycles or speculative behaviors.
2. **In Healthcare:**
   - Study how feedback between treatment effectiveness and patient behavior shapes outcomes.
3. **In Business:**
   - Optimize operations by balancing feedback in workflows.

Why Feedback Loop Analysis is Effective

This method helps:

1. **Reveal System Dynamics:** Highlights the cyclical nature of interactions within systems.
2. **Anticipate Outcomes:** Predicts long-term effects of actions and interventions.
3. **Enhance Decision-Making:** Provides insights into managing or leveraging feedback.

Challenges and Limitations

1. **Complex Interactions:** Systems with multiple loops may be difficult to map and interpret.
2. **Unintended Effects:** Interventions targeting one loop may disrupt others.
3. **Data Requirements:** Accurate analysis requires reliable data on system behaviors.

For instance, efforts to improve customer satisfaction may unintentionally increase costs, disrupting profitability.

How to Analyze Feedback Loops Effectively

1. **Map the System:** Create diagrams to visualize loops and their interactions.
2. **Focus on Key Loops:** Prioritize loops with the greatest impact on system performance.
3. **Test Interventions:** Experiment with small changes to understand their effects on feedback dynamics.

1. **Map Feedback in a System:** Choose a process or system you're familiar with and map its feedback loops. Reflect on how they shape outcomes.
2. **Analyze Reinforcing Loops:** Think of a situation where positive feedback amplified results. How could you manage or leverage this loop?
3. **Design a Balancing Strategy:** Identify a system with a destabilizing loop and propose interventions to stabilize it.

Closing Thoughts

Feedback Loop Analysis provides deep insights into the cyclical dynamics of complex systems. By understanding how actions and responses shape each other, you can anticipate outcomes, manage risks, and optimize performance.

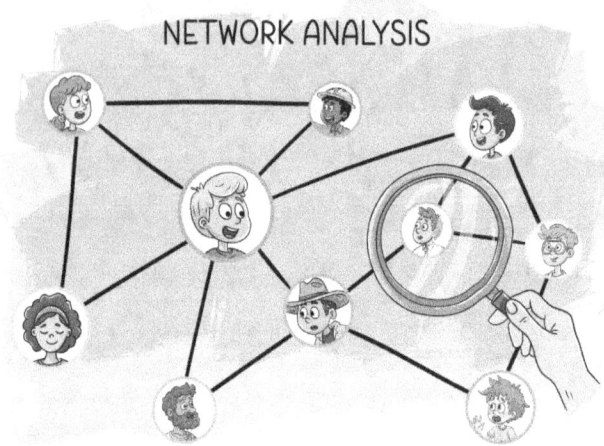

NETWORK ANALYSIS

Chapter 89: Network Analysis

Mapping Connections: Network Analysis

Network Analysis is the study of relationships and interactions within a system, represented as nodes (individual entities) and edges (connections between them). This method uncovers patterns, identifies key influencers, and reveals the flow of information, resources, or influence.

For example:

- **Scenario:** A company wants to optimize communication within its teams.
- **Network Analysis Application:** They map the organizational network, identifying bottlenecks or underutilized connections to improve collaboration.

This technique is widely used in social sciences, logistics, technology, and biology to analyze and optimize complex systems.

How Network Analysis Works

1. **Define the Network:** Identify the nodes (entities) and edges (connections) relevant to your system.
   Example: "Who are the stakeholders, and how do they interact?"
2. **Map the Relationships:** Visualize the network using diagrams or software tools.
   Example: "What does the organizational communication network look like?"
3. **Analyze Metrics:** Assess features like centrality (importance of nodes), density (connection tightness), and flow (resource or information movement).
   Example: "Which team member is the most connected and acts as a bridge between departments?"
4. **Identify Opportunities:** Use insights to improve efficiency, strengthen connections, or address vulnerabilities.

Applications of Network Analysis

1. **In Social Networks:**
   o   Study the spread of information, influence, or trends in online platforms.
2. **In Supply Chains:**
   o   Optimize the flow of goods and resources by analyzing logistical networks.
3. **In Healthcare:**
   o   Map disease transmission pathways to develop effective containment strategies.

Why Network Analysis is Effective

This method helps:
1. **Reveal Hidden Patterns:** Uncovers structures and dynamics not visible through linear analysis.
2. **Identify Key Players:** Pinpoints influential nodes or critical connections within the network.
3. **Optimize Systems:** Improves efficiency, communication, or resource allocation.

Challenges and Limitations

1. **Data Complexity:** Large networks may require extensive data collection and computational resources.
2. **Dynamic Changes:** Networks evolve over time, making static analysis less reliable.
3. **Unintended Consequences:** Intervening in one part of the network may disrupt others.

For instance, removing a central node in a supply chain could cause widespread inefficiencies.

How to Use Network Analysis Effectively

1. **Focus on Objectives:** Clearly define what you aim to achieve with the analysis.
2. **Use Visualization Tools:** Leverage software to map and interpret complex networks.
3. **Test Interventions:** Simulate changes within the network to predict outcomes before implementation.

1. **Map a Personal Network:** Analyze your own professional or social network. Identify key connections and areas for improvement.
2. **Study a Public Network:** Choose a public network, like a social media platform or public transit system, and map its structure.
3. **Analyze an Organization:** Reflect on a team or organization you know. How could network analysis improve its communication or efficiency?

Closing Thoughts

Network Analysis is a powerful tool for understanding and optimizing connections within complex systems. By mapping and analyzing relationships, you can uncover hidden dynamics, identify key influencers, and make informed decisions to enhance efficiency and impact.

This method equips you to navigate interconnected systems with clarity, ensuring that your strategies are both effective and sustainable.

Chapter 90: Chaos Theory in Decision-Making

Embracing Uncertainty: Chaos Theory in Decision-Making

Chaos Theory explores how small differences in initial conditions can lead to vastly different outcomes in dynamic systems. Applying this concept to decision-making emphasizes the need for adaptability, flexibility, and awareness of unintended consequences in complex and unpredictable environments.

For example:

- **Scenario:** A company launches a new product.
- **Chaos Theory Application:** They prepare for unexpected market reactions, such as viral trends or unforeseen competition, by building adaptive strategies.

Chaos Theory is particularly useful in fields such as weather forecasting, economics, and organizational strategy, where uncertainty and complexity are inherent.

How Chaos Theory Applies to Decision-Making

1. **Acknowledge Unpredictability:** Accept that not all outcomes can be controlled or predicted.
   Example: "How might small market changes create unexpected impacts on our sales?"
2. **Focus on Patterns:** Look for recurring dynamics or trends within the system.
   Example: "What cyclical behaviors influence our customer base?"
3. **Prepare for Flexibility:** Develop strategies that can adapt to a range of potential scenarios.
   Example: "How can we pivot quickly if our initial strategy encounters resistance?"
4. **Learn from Feedback:** Continuously monitor outcomes and adjust strategies accordingly.

Applications of Chaos Theory in Decision-Making

1. **In Business:**
   o Navigate volatile markets or industries with adaptive strategies.
2. **In Environmental Science:**
   o Study and address the unpredictable impacts of climate change on ecosystems.
3. **In Personal Growth:**
   o Embrace uncertainty in life decisions and focus on adaptability and resilience.

Why Chaos Theory is Effective

This method helps:

1. **Promote Flexibility:** Encourages adaptive thinking in uncertain and dynamic contexts.
2. **Enhance Resilience:** Prepares for unexpected challenges and opportunities.
3. **Foster Long-Term Success:** Focuses on sustainability and learning rather than rigid plans.

Challenges and Limitations

1. **Complexity in Analysis:** Understanding chaotic systems requires advanced tools and expertise.
2. **Overwhelming Uncertainty:** Emphasizing unpredictability may hinder confidence in decision-making.

3. **Difficulty in Forecasting:** Long-term predictions in chaotic systems are often unreliable.

For instance, predicting long-term weather patterns with precision is challenging due to the chaotic nature of atmospheric systems.

How to Apply Chaos Theory Effectively

1. **Start with Small Steps:** Focus on incremental changes and monitor their effects.
2. **Embrace Iteration:** Use trial and error to refine strategies and learn from outcomes.
3. **Build Resilience:** Develop systems and strategies that can absorb shocks and adapt to change.

Exercises

1. **Reflect on Past Decisions:** Think of a decision where small changes led to significant outcomes. What can you learn from this?
2. **Analyze a Chaotic System:** Choose a system, like traffic flow or stock markets, and explore its unpredictable dynamics.
3. **Prepare for Flexibility:** Develop a flexible plan for a current project or decision, considering potential uncertainties.

Closing Thoughts

Chaos Theory teaches us to embrace uncertainty and focus on adaptability in decision-making. By understanding the unpredictable dynamics of complex systems, you can develop strategies that are resilient, flexible, and aligned with long-term success.

This method empowers you to navigate challenges with confidence, turning uncertainty into an opportunity for innovation and growth.

Subsection: Navigating Uncertainty and Ambiguity

In a world where uncertainty and ambiguity are constant, the ability to make sound decisions becomes a critical skill. This final section equips you with tools and frameworks for navigating the unknown, balancing risks and rewards, and adapting to unforeseen circumstances.

Chapter 91: Probability Trees

Breaking Down Uncertainty: Probability Trees

Probability Trees are visual tools that map possible outcomes of a decision or event, assigning probabilities to each branch. By organizing complex scenarios into a structured diagram, this method helps decision-makers calculate expected values and make informed choices.

For example:

- **Scenario:** A company considers launching a new product.
- **Probability Tree Application:** They evaluate potential market responses—high demand, moderate demand, or low demand—and assign probabilities to each scenario to guide investment decisions.

How Probability Trees Work

1. **Define the Decision:** Identify the starting point and the possible outcomes.
   Example: "Should we launch the product now or wait for more market research?"
2. **Map Possible Outcomes:** Create branches for each potential result or decision.
   Example: "High sales, moderate sales, or low sales."
3. **Assign Probabilities:** Estimate the likelihood of each outcome based on data or expert judgment.
   Example: "60% chance of moderate sales, 30% chance of high sales, 10% chance of low sales."
4. **Calculate Expected Values:** Multiply probabilities by the value of each outcome to guide decisions.

Applications of Probability Trees

1. **In Business Strategy:**
   o   Assess risks and rewards of investments or product launches.
2. **In Medical Decision-Making:**
   o   Evaluate treatment options based on patient outcomes and probabilities.
3. **In Personal Finance:**
   o   Analyze potential outcomes of investment or saving strategies.

This method helps:

1. **Visualize Complexity:** Breaks down multifaceted decisions into clear, manageable components.
2. **Quantify Risk:** Assigns measurable probabilities to outcomes for data-driven decisions.
3. **Clarify Decision Paths:** Identifies the most rational choice based on expected values.

Challenges and Limitations

1. **Uncertain Probabilities:** Estimating probabilities may rely on assumptions or incomplete data.
2. **Complexity in Large Systems:** Trees can become unwieldy with too many branches or layers.
3. **Overemphasis on Quantification:** Focusing solely on probabilities may overlook qualitative factors.

For instance, a product launch decision might also depend on brand perception, which isn't easily quantified.

How to Use Probability Trees Effectively

1. **Start Simple:** Focus on the most significant outcomes and decisions to avoid overcomplication.
2. **Validate Probabilities:** Base probability estimates on reliable data or expert opinions.
3. **Combine with Other Methods:** Use probability trees alongside qualitative analysis for a balanced approach.

Exercises

1. **Map a Decision:** Choose a decision with multiple outcomes and create a probability tree. Reflect on how this clarifies your options.
2. **Analyze a Past Event:** Reconstruct a previous decision using a probability tree. What insights can you gain in hindsight?
3. **Test Expected Values:** Apply probability trees to calculate expected values for a hypothetical scenario, such as a new project or investment.

Closing Thoughts

Probability Trees are powerful tools for navigating uncertainty, breaking down complex decisions, and making data-driven choices. By visualizing outcomes and assigning probabilities, you can approach challenges with clarity and confidence.

Chapter 92: The Maximin/Minimax Principle

Balancing Risks and Rewards: The Maximin/Minimax Principle

The Maximin/Minimax Principle is a decision-making strategy used in uncertain or competitive scenarios. The Maximin approach focuses on maximizing the minimum possible gain, ensuring a safety-first mindset. The Minimax approach minimizes the maximum potential loss, emphasizing risk reduction.

For example:

- **Scenario:** A company is deciding between a conservative investment with lower risks or a higher-risk venture with potentially higher returns.

- **Maximin Application:** They choose the conservative option to ensure steady, minimum gains.

- **Minimax Application:** They avoid the venture most likely to incur significant losses, even if it means sacrificing higher potential returns.

How the Maximin/Minimax Principle Works

1. **Identify Possible Outcomes:** List all potential results for each decision or strategy.
   Example: "What are the gains or losses associated with each investment option?"
2. **Evaluate Worst-Case Scenarios:** Assess the minimum gains and maximum losses for each choice.
   Example: "If the market declines, what's the worst-case outcome for each option?"
3. **Choose a Strategy:** Select the Maximin approach (maximize minimum gain) or Minimax approach (minimize maximum loss) based on your priorities.
   Example: "Do we value safety over opportunity, or vice versa?"
4. **Consider Trade-Offs:** Balance the benefits of security with the potential for higher rewards.

1. **In Financial Planning:**
    o   Choose investment strategies based on risk tolerance and market conditions.
2. **In Negotiations:**
    o   Minimize potential losses while ensuring acceptable gains.
3. **In Personal Decision-Making:**
    o   Approach life choices, like career changes or relocations, with risk-conscious strategies.

Why the Maximin/Minimax Principle is Effective

This method helps:

1. **Enhance Risk Awareness:** Forces consideration of worst-case scenarios and their impact.
2. **Promote Strategic Thinking:** Encourages decisions that align with risk tolerance and goals.
3. **Provide a Framework:** Offers a structured approach to decision-making in uncertain environments.

Challenges and Limitations

1. **Overly Conservative Decisions:** Focusing on minimizing losses may limit opportunities for higher gains.
2. **Incomplete Information:** Assessing all possible outcomes accurately may not always be feasible.
3. **Subjective Judgments:** Deciding between Maximin and Minimax often depends on individual risk preferences.

For instance, choosing a low-risk investment may seem safe but could result in lower returns compared to a well-researched higher-risk option.

How to Use the Maximin/Minimax Principle Effectively

1. **Align with Objectives:** Choose the approach that best matches your risk tolerance and long-term goals.
2. **Combine with Data:** Use reliable data to estimate outcomes and validate decisions.
3. **Revisit Regularly:** Reassess strategies as conditions or priorities change.

Exercises

1. **Apply to a Decision:** Think of a current or past decision involving uncertainty. Map out worst-case scenarios and apply the Maximin/Minimax Principle.
2. **Compare Strategies:** Choose a hypothetical scenario, like a job offer or investment choice, and evaluate it using both Maximin and Minimax approaches.
3. **Reflect on Risk Tolerance:** Analyze your own preferences for risk and safety in decision-making. How does this influence your choices?

Closing Thoughts

The Maximin/Minimax Principle is a valuable framework for balancing risks and rewards in uncertain situations. By focusing on worst-case scenarios, you can make decisions that align with your values, goals, and risk tolerance.

This method enhances your ability to navigate uncertainty with clarity and confidence, empowering you to make thoughtful and strategic choices.

Chapter 93: Utility Theory

Maximizing Satisfaction: Utility Theory

Utility Theory is a decision-making framework that evaluates options based on their ability to maximize satisfaction, value, or benefit for the decision-maker. It emphasizes weighing outcomes against personal preferences, goals, or priorities.

For example:

- **Scenario:** A person chooses between two job offers—one with a higher salary but longer hours, and another with a lower salary but better work-life balance.
- **Utility Theory Application:** They consider which option provides greater overall satisfaction, balancing financial benefits with personal well-being.

How Utility Theory Works

1. Define Utility: Determine what "satisfaction" or "value" means in the context of the decision.

Example: "Is utility based on financial gain, personal happiness, or social impact?"

2. **Quantify Preferences:** Assign utility values to each option based on how well it meets your priorities.
    Example: "Option A scores 8/10 for salary and 5/10 for work-life balance, while Option B scores 6/10 and 9/10, respectively."
3. **Evaluate Trade-Offs:** Compare utility scores across options to identify the best choice.

Example: "Which option has the highest total utility when combining all factors?"

4. **Make a Decision:** Choose the option that maximizes utility within your constraints.

Applications of Utility Theory

1. **In Business:**
   o Optimize strategies or investments by evaluating their expected utility for stakeholders.
2. **In Healthcare:**
   o Balance risks and benefits of treatments to maximize patient outcomes.
3. **In Personal Choices:**
   o Prioritize options, such as vacation destinations or major purchases, based on overall satisfaction.

Why Utility Theory is Effective

This method helps:

1. **Clarify Priorities:** Encourages explicit consideration of what matters most.
2. **Quantify Decisions:** Provides a structured approach to evaluate and compare options.
3. **Maximize Benefits:** Ensures choices align with long-term goals and values.

Challenges and Limitations

1. **Subjectivity:** Utility values are based on personal preferences, which may change over time.
2. **Complex Trade-Offs:** Balancing competing factors can be difficult and time-consuming.
3. **Uncertainty in Outcomes:** Predicted utility may not always align with actual experiences.

For instance, a high-paying job might seem like the best choice but could lead to dissatisfaction if work-life balance suffers.

How to Apply Utility Theory Effectively

1. **Reflect on Goals:** Clearly define what "utility" means to you in each decision.
2. **Involve Stakeholders:** Consider the preferences and priorities of others affected by the decision.
3. **Test Assumptions:** Revisit utility assessments to ensure they remain accurate and relevant.

Exercises

1. **Evaluate a Past Decision:** Choose a decision where you balanced competing priorities. How would Utility Theory have clarified your choice?
2. **Quantify Preferences:** Apply Utility Theory to a hypothetical scenario, such as choosing between two purchases or career paths.
3. **Create a Utility Table:** List options, assign utility scores to each factor, and calculate totals to identify the best choice.

Closing Thoughts

Utility Theory provides a structured approach to decision-making that aligns choices with personal or organizational priorities. By evaluating options based on their ability to maximize satisfaction or value, you can make more thoughtful and intentional decisions.

This method enhances your ability to weigh trade-offs, clarify goals, and achieve outcomes that truly matter in both simple and complex scenarios.

Chapter 94: Signal Detection Theory

Separating Signal from Noise: Signal Detection Theory

Signal Detection Theory (SDT) is a framework for understanding how decisions are made in uncertain conditions, particularly when distinguishing meaningful signals from background noise. It is widely applied in fields like communication, medicine, and technology, where discerning important information is critical.

For example:

- **Scenario:** A doctor examines test results for signs of disease.
- **Signal Detection Application:** They balance the risk of false positives (overdiagnosis) against false negatives (missed diagnosis) to make accurate decisions.

There's so much information here—how can we tell what really matters?

We need to set clear criteria to detect the actual signal, not just random noise.

SIGNAL DETECTED

How Signal Detection Theory Works

1. **Define the Signal:** Identify what you are trying to detect or recognize amidst noise.
   Example: "Is there a meaningful pattern in this data?"
2. **Set Criteria for Detection:** Decide the threshold for determining whether a signal is present.
   Example: "What level of test result indicates a likely diagnosis?"
3. **Weigh Trade-Offs:** Balance the consequences of false positives (detecting a signal when none exists) and false negatives (missing a true signal).
   Example: "What are the risks of overdiagnosis versus underdiagnosis?"
4. **Incorporate Probabilities:** Use data to refine detection criteria and improve accuracy.

Applications of Signal Detection Theory

1. **In Medicine:**
   o   Diagnose diseases based on test results and patient symptoms.
2. **In Technology:**
   o   Detect cyber threats or system malfunctions in IT networks.
3. **In Communication:**
   o   Identify key messages or trends in large volumes of information.

Why Signal Detection Theory is Effective

This method helps:

1. **Enhance Accuracy:** Reduces errors by balancing detection thresholds.
2. **Improve Decision-Making:** Provides a structured approach for uncertain or noisy conditions.
3. **Optimize Resource Use:** Focuses attention and resources on the most meaningful signals.

Challenges and Limitations

1. **Uncertain Criteria:** Setting the right detection threshold requires reliable data and judgment.
2. **Balancing Trade-Offs:** Minimizing false positives can increase false negatives, and vice versa.
3. **Complex Noise:** High levels of noise can obscure even strong signals, complicating detection.

For instance, in financial markets, detecting a trend (signal) amidst daily fluctuations (noise) can be challenging without robust analysis.

How to Use Signal Detection Theory Effectively

1. **Define Objectives:** Clearly identify the signal you are trying to detect and its importance.
2. **Refine Criteria:** Continuously adjust detection thresholds based on feedback and outcomes.
3. **Leverage Data:** Use statistical models or machine learning tools to enhance detection accuracy.

Exercises

1. **Analyze Detection Trade-Offs:** Reflect on a past decision where you had to balance false positives and negatives. How could SDT have improved your approach?
2. **Test Detection Criteria:** Apply SDT to a hypothetical scenario, such as identifying trends in a dataset or diagnosing a condition.
3. **Simulate a Noisy Environment:** Create a scenario with distracting noise and practice identifying meaningful signals.

Closing Thoughts

Signal Detection Theory provides a valuable framework for decision-making in uncertain and noisy conditions. By balancing detection criteria and weighing trade-offs, you can improve accuracy and effectiveness in identifying meaningful signals.

This method equips you to make thoughtful decisions in fields ranging from medicine to technology, ensuring that critical signals are recognized and acted upon amidst the noise.

Chapter 95: Decision-Making Under Ambiguity

Navigating the Unknown: Decision-Making Under Ambiguity

Decision-Making Under Ambiguity involves making choices when outcomes, probabilities, or even the criteria for success are unclear. This requires balancing intuition, adaptability, and critical thinking to navigate uncertainty effectively.

For example:

- **Scenario:** A start-up decides whether to enter a market with limited data on consumer preferences.
- **Decision-Making Application:** They rely on a combination of market research, expert judgment, and iterative testing to minimize risks.

How to Approach Decision-Making Under Ambiguity

1. **Clarify Goals:** Define what success looks like, even if other factors are uncertain.
   Example: "What are the key objectives for entering this market?"
2. **Gather What Data You Can:** Use available information to guide initial decisions, while acknowledging gaps.
   Example: "What trends or benchmarks can inform our approach?"
3. **Embrace Iteration:** Take small, calculated steps and adjust as new information emerges.
   Example: "What pilot project can we run to test this strategy?"
4. **Balance Intuition and Analysis:** Leverage past experience and analytical tools to make informed choices.

Applications of Decision-Making Under Ambiguity

1. **In Start-ups:**
   - Launch new products or services in uncertain markets.
2. **In Crisis Management:**
   - Respond to emergencies or disasters with incomplete information.
3. **In Career Planning:**
   - Make life choices, such as career changes, with unclear outcomes.

Why Decision-Making Under Ambiguity is Effective

This method helps:

1. **Promote Flexibility:** Encourages adaptability as conditions change or new data emerges.
2. **Reduce Paralysis:** Provides a framework for action despite uncertainty.
3. **Build Resilience:** Develops confidence and skills to navigate unpredictable situations.

Challenges and Limitations

1. **Lack of Information:** Decisions may be based on incomplete or unreliable data.
2. **Inherent Risks:** Ambiguity increases the potential for unforeseen outcomes.
3. **Emotional Stress:** Navigating uncertainty can be mentally and emotionally taxing.

For instance, entering a new market without clear data on consumer preferences risks both financial loss and reputational damage.

How to Make Decisions Under Ambiguity Effectively

1. **Focus on Core Values:** Align decisions with your principles and long-term goals.
2. **Test Small Steps:** Minimize risks by experimenting with smaller-scale actions before full implementation.
3. **Reassess Regularly:** Continuously review outcomes and adapt strategies as clarity improves.

Exercises

1. **Reflect on Ambiguous Decisions:** Think of a time when you had to make a decision without full information. How did you approach it, and what did you learn?
2. **Simulate Uncertainty:** Create a hypothetical scenario with ambiguous outcomes and practice making decisions.
3. **Apply to a Current Challenge:** Identify a situation with ambiguity in your life or work. Develop a plan for navigating it using small, iterative steps.

Decision-Making Under Ambiguity is a critical skill for navigating an uncertain and fast-changing world. By embracing flexibility, balancing intuition with analysis, and iterating thoughtfully, you can act decisively even when clarity is lacking.

This approach enhances your resilience, adaptability, and confidence, ensuring you can navigate the unknown with clarity and purpose.

Chapter 96: Applying Monte Carlo Simulations

Simulating the Future: Applying Monte Carlo Simulations

Monte Carlo Simulations use randomness and repeated trials to model complex systems and predict a range of possible outcomes. By exploring the variability of inputs, this method provides insights into uncertainty and helps guide decision-making in dynamic environments.

For example:

- **Scenario:** A project manager estimates a project's completion time.
- **Monte Carlo Simulation Application:** They simulate the project timeline hundreds of times with varying task durations to predict the most likely completion date.

How Monte Carlo Simulations Work

1. **Define the Problem:** Identify the decision or system to be modeled.
   Example: "What is the potential range of returns for this investment portfolio?"
2. **Determine Variables:** Select the uncertain factors and assign probability distributions.
   Example: "What are the likely ranges for market growth rates or inflation?"
3. **Run Simulations:** Use software or tools to perform thousands of random iterations, each producing a potential outcome.
   Example: "What does the portfolio's value look like across 10,000 simulated scenarios?"
4. **Analyze Results:** Assess the distribution of outcomes to inform decisions.

Applications of Monte Carlo Simulations

1. **In Finance:**
   o Forecast investment risks, returns, and market volatility.
2. **In Project Management:**
   o Predict project completion times and budget variations.
3. **In Engineering:**
   o Model system reliability or performance under varying conditions.

Why Monte Carlo Simulations Are Effective

This method helps:

1. **Capture Variability:** Reflects the full range of possible outcomes, not just averages.
2. **Quantify Risks:** Provides probabilistic insights to guide risk management.
3. **Enhance Decision-Making:** Informs strategies with data-driven predictions.

Challenges and Limitations

1. **Data Quality:** Reliable results depend on accurate input data and probability distributions.
2. **Computational Intensity:** Simulations can be resource-intensive for complex systems.
3. **Interpretation of Results:** Understanding and applying probabilistic outcomes require expertise.

For instance, predicting a project's timeline requires accurate estimates of task durations and dependencies to avoid misleading conclusions.

How to Use Monte Carlo Simulations Effectively

1. **Define Clear Goals:** Clearly outline what you want the simulation to predict or analyze.
2. **Validate Inputs:** Use reliable data and realistic probability distributions for accuracy.
3. **Combine with Expert Judgment:** Supplement simulation results with domain expertise for better decisions.

1. **Simulate a Simple Scenario:** Use a Monte Carlo tool or spreadsheet to model a basic problem, such as forecasting expenses with varying costs.
2. **Analyze Simulation Results:** Reflect on how the range of outcomes influences your decision-making.
3. **Apply to a Real Decision:** Identify a current project or decision that could benefit from Monte Carlo Simulations. Develop and test a model.

Closing Thoughts

Monte Carlo Simulations are invaluable for modeling uncertainty, exploring variability, and predicting outcomes in complex systems. By embracing probabilistic thinking, you can make more informed, data-driven decisions in the face of uncertainty.

This method enhances your ability to plan strategically, mitigate risks, and adapt effectively to dynamic environments.

Chapter 97: Black Swan Event Analysis

Preparing for the Unthinkable: Black Swan Event Analysis

A Black Swan Event is a rare, unpredictable occurrence with significant consequences, often misunderstood until after it happens. Black Swan Event Analysis involves identifying vulnerabilities, preparing for the unexpected, and building resilience against low-probability but high-impact events.

For example:

- **Scenario:** A business evaluates its supply chain.
- **Black Swan Analysis Application:** They assess risks from rare events, such as a global pandemic or natural disaster, and develop contingency plans.

How Black Swan Event Analysis Works

1. **Identify Vulnerabilities:** Assess areas of your system or strategy susceptible to extreme disruptions.
    Example: "What critical dependencies would fail in a rare but severe crisis?"
2. **Evaluate Potential Impacts:** Consider the magnitude of damage a Black Swan Event could cause.
    Example: "How would a sudden economic collapse affect our business?"
3. **Develop Contingencies:** Build robust systems and strategies to mitigate risks or recover quickly.
    Example: "What backup suppliers or resources can we secure?"
4. **Cultivate Resilience:** Foster adaptability and flexibility to respond effectively to unforeseen events.

Applications of Black Swan Event Analysis

1. **In Business Continuity:**
    - Prepare for supply chain disruptions, market crashes, or cybersecurity threats.
2. **In Public Policy:**
    - Plan for rare events like pandemics, natural disasters, or geopolitical conflicts.
3. **In Personal Finance:**
    - Build emergency funds or diversify investments to weather economic shocks.

Why Black Swan Event Analysis is Effective

This method helps:

1. **Increase Awareness:** Highlights risks often overlooked due to their rarity.
2. **Promote Preparedness:** Encourages proactive measures to mitigate high-impact events.
3. **Build Resilience:** Strengthens systems and strategies to recover from crises.

Challenges and Limitations

1. **Unpredictability:** By definition, Black Swan Events are difficult to foresee or quantify.
2. **Overinvestment in Rare Risks:** Excessive focus on rare events might neglect more likely challenges.
3. **Psychological Resistance:** Humans often downplay or ignore risks perceived as improbable.

For instance, businesses may dismiss the likelihood of a pandemic, leaving them unprepared when one occurs.

How to Analyze Black Swan Events Effectively

1. **Think Beyond the Likely:** Consider low-probability, high-impact risks in addition to common challenges.
2. **Test Scenarios:** Simulate responses to hypothetical Black Swan Events to identify weaknesses.
3. **Balance Resources:** Allocate efforts proportionally, addressing both rare and probable risks.

1. **Reflect on Past Events:** Analyze a historical Black Swan Event. How could better preparation have mitigated its impact?
2. **Identify Vulnerabilities:** Assess a system or strategy you're involved with. What rare risks could disrupt it?
3. **Develop a Contingency Plan:** Create a plan for a hypothetical Black Swan Event in your work or life.

Closing Thoughts

Black Swan Event Analysis equips you to navigate the unexpected, mitigate extreme risks, and build resilience in uncertain environments. By preparing for rare but impactful occurrences, you can safeguard systems, strategies, and goals against even the most unpredictable challenges.

This approach enhances your ability to thrive in a volatile and interconnected world, turning uncertainty into an opportunity for proactive growth.

Chapter 98: Heuristic-Based Iteration

Learning Through Approximation: Heuristic-Based Iteration

Heuristic-Based Iteration involves using simple, rule-of-thumb strategies (heuristics) to tackle complex problems in a step-by-step, iterative process. Rather than aiming for perfection immediately, this method focuses on continuous improvement and adapting to feedback.

For example:
- **Scenario:** A product development team tests a new app feature.
- **Heuristic-Based Iteration Application:** They release a prototype, gather user feedback, and refine the feature in successive iterations based on insights.

This approach is particularly useful in dynamic environments where solutions evolve over time.

How Heuristic-Based Iteration Works

1. **Define the Goal:** Clearly articulate what you aim to achieve or solve.
   Example: "How can we improve customer engagement on the app?"
2. **Choose a Heuristic:** Use a guiding principle or rule of thumb to start solving the problem.
   Example: "Start by addressing the most common user complaints."
3. **Test and Evaluate:** Implement a solution, observe the outcomes, and gather feedback.
   Example: "How did users respond to the new feature?"
4. **Refine and Iterate:** Use insights to adjust your approach and repeat the process.

Applications of Heuristic-Based Iteration

1. **In Product Development:**
   o Improve designs or features through iterative prototyping and testing.
2. **In Education:**
   o Adapt teaching methods based on student performance and feedback.
3. **In Personal Growth:**
   o Refine habits or skills through trial and error and consistent practice.

Why Heuristic-Based Iteration is Effective

This method helps:
1. **Promote Flexibility:** Encourages adaptation and responsiveness to feedback.
2. **Accelerate Learning:** Focuses on actionable insights rather than overanalysis.
3. **Reduce Perfectionism:** Emphasizes progress and continuous improvement over flawless execution.

Challenges and Limitations

1. **Incomplete Solutions:** Early iterations may not fully solve the problem.
2. **Feedback Dependence:** Requires reliable input to guide refinements.
3. **Risk of Overfitting:** Overly narrow focus on feedback may limit broader innovation.

For instance, refining a feature based only on vocal user feedback might overlook the needs of silent majority users.

1. **Start with Simple Steps:** Begin with the most straightforward heuristic to generate momentum.
2. **Prioritize Feedback:** Actively seek diverse input to guide adjustments.
3. **Balance Exploration and Refinement:** Avoid getting stuck in minor refinements; explore new ideas when necessary.

Exercises

1. **Reflect on an Iterative Process:** Think of a situation where you used trial and error. How could heuristics have improved the process?
2. **Simulate a Challenge:** Apply heuristic-based iteration to a hypothetical problem, like designing a better workspace.
3. **Identify a Heuristic:** Choose a personal or professional challenge and develop a rule of thumb to guide iterative improvements.

Closing Thoughts

Heuristic-Based Iteration transforms complexity into manageable steps, fostering adaptability and continuous growth. By combining simple strategies with iterative learning, you can solve problems effectively and refine solutions over time.

This method enhances your ability to navigate uncertainty, innovate with confidence, and achieve sustainable success in evolving environments.

Chapter 99: The Precautionary Principle Revisited

When in Doubt, Proceed with Care: The Precautionary Principle Revisited

Balancing Action and Risk

The Precautionary Principle advises caution in decision-making when potential risks are significant but uncertain. It emphasizes acting conservatively to avoid harm, particularly in scenarios with high stakes or limited knowledge.

For example:

- **Scenario:** A city considers adopting a new pesticide.
- **Precautionary Principle Application:** They conduct extensive testing to ensure environmental safety before widespread use.

This principle is particularly relevant in environmental policy, public health, and technological innovation, where the stakes of unintended consequences are high.

How the Precautionary Principle Works

1. **Identify Uncertain Risks:** Assess situations where potential harm is significant but poorly understood.
   Example: "What are the unknown long-term effects of this new technology?"
2. **Evaluate Alternatives:** Consider safer or more conservative approaches to achieve your goals.
   Example: "Can we reduce pesticide use by adopting organic farming practices?"
3. **Apply Caution:** Delay action or implement safeguards until risks are better understood.
   Example: "What safety measures can minimize potential harm?"
4. **Monitor and Adapt:** Continuously review new data and adjust strategies as knowledge improves.

Applications of the Precautionary Principle

1. **In Environmental Policy:**
   o   Protect ecosystems by limiting potentially harmful industrial practices.
2. **In Medicine:**
   o   Avoid widespread use of untested treatments or interventions.
3. **In Technology:**
   o   Assess the societal impact of innovations like AI or biotechnology before full deployment.

Why the Precautionary Principle is Effective

This method helps:

1. **Minimize Risks:** Reduces the likelihood of irreversible harm.
2. **Promote Responsible Innovation:** Encourages ethical and sustainable development.
3. **Foster Public Trust:** Demonstrates commitment to safety and well-being.

1. **Paralysis by Analysis:** Excessive caution can delay beneficial innovations.
2. **Unclear Risks:** Identifying potential harm may be speculative or subjective.
3. **Balancing Trade-Offs:** Overemphasis on caution might overlook immediate benefits.

For instance, delaying renewable energy projects for extensive impact assessments might exacerbate climate challenges.

How to Apply the Precautionary Principle Effectively

1. **Prioritize High-Stakes Risks:** Focus on areas where harm could be severe or irreversible.
2. **Balance Caution with Progress:** Combine precaution with innovation to avoid stalling beneficial developments.
3. **Adapt to Evidence:** Adjust strategies as risks become clearer and better understood.

Exercises

1. **Reflect on a Risky Decision:** Think of a time when you faced uncertainty. How could the Precautionary Principle have influenced your decision?
2. **Apply to a Hypothetical Challenge:** Develop a cautious approach for adopting a new technology or policy.
3. **Evaluate Trade-Offs:** Identify a current project or decision where balancing caution and progress is critical.

Closing Thoughts

The Precautionary Principle is a guide for navigating high-risk, uncertain situations with care and foresight. By prioritizing safety and ethical responsibility, you can protect against potential harm while fostering sustainable growth.

This principle empowers you to balance caution with innovation, ensuring that progress aligns with long-term well-being and integrity.

Chapter 100: Cognitive Flexibility in Uncertainty

Adapting to the Unknown: Cognitive Flexibility in Uncertainty

Cognitive Flexibility is the ability to shift perspectives, adapt to new information, and revise strategies in response to changing circumstances. It is a cornerstone of effective decision-making in uncertain and ambiguous situations, where rigid thinking often leads to missed opportunities or poor outcomes.

For example:

- **Scenario:** A business leader faces sudden market disruption.
- **Cognitive Flexibility Application:** They quickly pivot their strategy, leveraging emerging trends to turn challenges into opportunities.

This skill is vital for thriving in dynamic environments, from personal challenges to global crises.

How Cognitive Flexibility Works

1. **Recognize Change:** Stay attuned to shifting circumstances and emerging information.
   Example: "What new factors are influencing this situation?"
2. **Reframe Perspectives:** Look at challenges or problems from multiple angles.
   Example: "How does this obstacle create new opportunities?"
3. **Adapt Strategies:** Adjust plans or goals based on updated insights.
   Example: "What changes can we make to stay aligned with current conditions?"
4. **Embrace Learning:** View setbacks or uncertainty as opportunities for growth and innovation.

Applications of Cognitive Flexibility

1. **In Leadership:**
   o Navigate organizational changes, market disruptions, or crises with agility.
2. **In Personal Growth:**
   o Adjust to life changes, such as career shifts or unexpected challenges, with resilience.
3. **In Education:**
   o Tailor teaching strategies to diverse learning needs or evolving curricula.

Why Cognitive Flexibility is Effective

This method helps:

1. **Enhance Adaptability:** Encourages responsiveness to new challenges and opportunities.
2. **Improve Problem-Solving:** Fosters creativity and innovation by exploring multiple solutions.
3. **Build Resilience:** Strengthens the ability to thrive in uncertain or high-pressure situations.

Challenges and Limitations

1. **Overwhelm from Options:** Too many perspectives or solutions may delay decision-making.
2. **Resistance to Change:** Personal or organizational biases may hinder adaptability.
3. **Lack of Confidence:** Frequent changes may create uncertainty or a lack of direction.

For instance, constantly revising strategies without a clear vision might confuse teams or dilute focus.

How to Cultivate Cognitive Flexibility

1. **Practice Perspective-Taking:** Regularly challenge yourself to see situations from different viewpoints.
   Example: "How would a customer, competitor, or stakeholder view this problem?"
2. **Embrace Uncertainty:** Accept that not all answers are immediate or clear, and remain open to experimentation.
   Example: "What can we try that hasn't been attempted before?"
3. **Encourage Collaborative Thinking:** Seek diverse input to expand your understanding and options.
   Example: "What insights can team members from different backgrounds bring to this challenge?"

Exercises

1. **Reframe a Problem:** Choose a current challenge and identify three alternative perspectives or solutions.
2. **Simulate Adaptability:** Create a hypothetical scenario with sudden changes and practice adjusting strategies in real-time.
3. **Reflect on Past Adaptations:** Think of a situation where you successfully pivoted in response to change. What made that approach effective?

Closing Thoughts

Cognitive Flexibility is the ultimate skill for navigating the uncertainties of a dynamic world. By staying adaptable, open-minded, and resilient, you can turn challenges into opportunities and thrive amidst change.

This skill is essential for personal and professional success, empowering you to embrace uncertainty as a catalyst for growth, creativity, and innovation.

Conclusion: Building a Life Rooted in Logic

Over the course of this book, we've explored 100 methods designed to sharpen your logical thinking, dismantle confusion, and illuminate the path toward clear and effective decision-making. These methods span a wide range of disciplines, from recognizing cognitive biases and evaluating evidence to mastering communication and navigating uncertainty. Each chapter offered tools you can apply in your daily life to solve problems, analyze situations, and make decisions that align with your goals and values.

Logical thinking isn't just a skill — it's a practice. It's something you cultivate daily, like a muscle that grows stronger with use. Whether you're navigating workplace challenges, making important life choices, or seeking to understand the world around you, logic is your compass. By applying these methods, you can approach every situation with clarity and confidence, transforming complexity into opportunity.

Cultivate Logical Thinking Daily

Now, the challenge lies in making logical thinking a habit. Start small — practice a method from this book each day, whether it's applying Occam's Razor to a tricky decision, reframing an argument for clarity, or using a heuristic to iterate toward a solution. The more you integrate these techniques into your thought process, the more naturally they'll become part of how you think, communicate, and act.

Logical thinking isn't about removing emotion or creativity; it's about enhancing them. It allows you to blend intuition with reason, balancing heart and mind in your approach to life. Embrace this journey not as a rigid framework, but as a way to unlock your potential and navigate the world with purpose and insight.

Closing Thoughts

This book is not the end of your journey — it's a beginning. As you move forward, continue to question, analyze, and refine your thinking.

The power of logical thinking lies in its universality. It applies to every field, every challenge, and every opportunity.

Go forward with confidence, curiosity, and the courage to think deeply. The future is yours to shape — one thoughtful decision at a time.

Appendix A: Quick Guide to the Chapters

This appendix provides a concise overview of the 100 methods explored in this book. Use it as a quick reference to revisit key concepts, tools, and techniques for sharpening your logical thinking and decision-making skills.

Section I: Foundations

Focus: Fundamental tools and principles of logical reasoning.

Subsection: Building Blocks of Logic

1. **Occam's Razor:** Simplify solutions by focusing on the fewest assumptions.
2. **The Principle of Charity:** Interpret arguments in their strongest, fairest form.
3. **Falsifiability:** Ensure claims can be tested and disproven.
4. **Syllogisms:** Use structured arguments to deduce logical conclusions.
5. **Deductive Reasoning:** Draw specific conclusions from general premises.
6. **Inductive Reasoning:** Infer general rules from specific observations.
7. **Abductive Reasoning:** Find the most likely explanation for observed phenomena.
8. **Modus Ponens:** Apply "If A, then B" to validate logical statements.
9. **Modus Tollens:** Disprove statements by negating their outcomes.
10. **Reductio ad Absurdum:** Demonstrate falsehood by showing contradictions.

Subsection: Recognizing and Avoiding Fallacies

11. **Spotting Strawman Arguments:** Avoid misrepresenting opposing views.
12. **Recognizing Ad Hominem Attacks:** Focus on arguments, not personal attacks.
13. **Avoiding Post Hoc Reasoning:** Separate correlation from causation.
14. **Identifying Circular Arguments:** Avoid conclusions that rely on their own premise.
15. **Detecting False Dilemmas:** Recognize when multiple options are ignored.
16. **Understanding Appeal to Authority Fallacies:** Validate claims beyond expert opinion.
17. **The Gambler's Fallacy:** Avoid assuming patterns in random events.
18. **Slippery Slope Analysis:** Analyze exaggerated claims of inevitable outcomes.
19. **Avoiding Hasty Generalizations:** Base conclusions on sufficient evidence.
20. **Distinguishing Correlation from Causation:** Avoid mistaking coincidence for causality.

Section II: Advanced Logical Tools

Focus: Practical frameworks and strategies for complex reasoning.

Subsection: Problem-Solving Frameworks

21. **The 5 Whys:** Uncover root causes by asking iterative "why" questions.
22. **Ishikawa (Fishbone) Diagrams:** Visualize causes of problems to address root issues.
23. **Root Cause Analysis:** Identify and eliminate underlying problems.
24. **The Socratic Method:** Use questions to stimulate critical thinking.
25. **SWOT Analysis:** Assess strengths, weaknesses, opportunities, and threats.
26. **First Principles Thinking:** Break down problems into foundational truths.
27. **Reverse Engineering:** Work backward to understand processes or problems.
28. **Hypothesis Testing:** Validate ideas through experimentation and observation.
29. **Bayesian Thinking:** Update probabilities as new information becomes available.
30. **Counterfactual Reasoning:** Explore "what if" scenarios to evaluate alternatives.
31. **Analogical Reasoning:** Use comparisons to find patterns and insights.
32. **Pareto Analysis:** Focus on the vital few causes of most outcomes.
33. **Ladder of Inference:** Trace reasoning steps to avoid flawed conclusions.
34. **Heuristic Analysis:** Use mental shortcuts for quick, effective problem-solving.
35. **The Eisenhower Matrix:** Prioritize tasks based on urgency and importance.

Subsection: Cognitive Bias Mitigation

36. **Recognizing Anchoring Bias:** Avoid being overly influenced by initial information.
37. **Overcoming Confirmation Bias:** Seek evidence that challenges your beliefs.
38. **Mitigating Availability Heuristics:** Base decisions on data, not immediate examples.
39. **Combatting the Dunning-Kruger Effect:** Recognize the limits of your knowledge.
40. **Avoiding Framing Effects:** Present information neutrally to avoid skewed perceptions.
41. **Understanding the Halo Effect:** Separate single traits from overall evaluations.
42. **Reframing with Devil's Advocacy:** Challenge ideas to ensure robustness.

43. **Premortem Analysis:** Anticipate and address potential failures before they occur.
44. **Overcoming Status Quo Bias:** Evaluate decisions objectively, not based on inertia.
45. **Appreciating Base Rates:** Use statistical context to inform judgments.
46. **Debiasing with Probabilistic Thinking:** Incorporate probabilities into decisions.
47. **Overcoming Loss Aversion:** Focus on long-term gains, not short-term losses.
48. **Distinguishing Intuition from Analysis:** Balance gut feelings with logical reasoning.
49. **Applying the Illusion of Transparency Test:** Clarify ideas others might misinterpret.
50. **The Outside View Technique:** Use external perspectives to avoid overconfidence.

Section III: Practical Applications

Focus: Applying logical methods to real-world contexts.

Subsection: Decision-Making Techniques

51. **Weighted Decision Matrix:** Compare options using weighted criteria.
52. **Expected Value Calculation:** Evaluate decisions based on likely outcomes.
53. **Decision Trees:** Map decision pathways and their potential consequences.
54. **Scenario Planning:** Prepare for multiple future possibilities.
55. **The Delphi Method:** Use expert consensus for complex decisions.
56. **Multi-Criteria Decision Analysis (MCDA):** Evaluate decisions with multiple factors.
57. **Cost-Benefit Analysis:** Compare benefits and costs for informed choices.
58. **The Precautionary Principle:** Act cautiously in high-risk situations.
59. **The Monte Carlo Method:** Model uncertainty using probabilistic simulations.
60. **Risk Assessment Matrices:** Prioritize risks based on likelihood and impact.
61. **Sensitivity Analysis:** Explore how changes affect outcomes.
62. **Adaptive Thinking:** Adjust strategies dynamically in changing conditions.
63. **The OODA Loop (Observe, Orient, Decide, Act):** Make decisions quickly and effectively.
64. **The Six Thinking Hats:** Use diverse perspectives for balanced decisions.
65. **Weighted Trade-Off Grids:** Balance trade-offs to optimize decisions.

Subsection: Enhancing Communication and Persuasion

66. **Reframing Arguments for Clarity:** Present ideas more effectively.
67. **The Pyramid Principle:** Structure communication logically from top to bottom.
68. **The Rhetorical Triangle:** Balance ethos, logos, and pathos for persuasion.
69. **Active Listening:** Build understanding through attentive engagement.
70. **Mirroring and Paraphrasing:** Validate and clarify others' perspectives.
71. **Using Analogies Effectively:** Simplify concepts with relatable comparisons.
72. **The SEE-I Framework:** State, Elaborate, Exemplify, and Illustrate ideas clearly.
73. **Building Common Ground:** Connect with others to foster agreement.
74. **Structuring Evidence with Logic:** Organize facts to strengthen arguments.
75. **Avoiding Loaded Questions:** Ensure neutrality in phrasing.
76. **Recognizing Emotional Triggers:** Manage emotions in discussions.
77. **Simplifying Complex Ideas:** Break down intricate concepts for clarity.
78. **Using Data to Bolster Arguments:** Strengthen cases with evidence.
79. **The Rule of Three in Persuasion:** Use triads to create memorable messages.
80. **The Importance of Visual Aids:** Enhance communication with engaging visuals.

Section IV: Mastery

Focus: Expert-level strategies for navigating uncertainty, complexity, and ambiguity.

Subsection: Logical Thinking in Complex Systems

81. **Systems Thinking:** Analyze systems holistically to uncover patterns.
82. **Bottleneck Analysis:** Identify and resolve constraints limiting performance.
83. **Identifying Leverage Points:** Focus on areas where small changes yield big results.
84. **Emergent Behavior Analysis:** Understand outcomes arising from interactions.
85. **Scenario Mapping:** Explore potential futures to prepare effectively.
86. **The Butterfly Effect Awareness:** Recognize small actions with big consequences.
87. **Stochastic Modeling:** Use probabilistic models to analyze variability.
88. **Feedback Loop Analysis:** Study how actions and outcomes influence each other.
89. **Network Analysis:** Map and optimize relationships within systems.

90. **Chaos Theory in Decision-Making:** Navigate unpredictable dynamics.

Subsection: Navigating Uncertainty and Ambiguity

91. **Probability Trees:** Map outcomes and calculate probabilities.
92. **The Maximin/Minimax Principle:** Balance risks and rewards in decision-making.
93. **Utility Theory:** Optimize satisfaction based on priorities and preferences.
94. **Signal Detection Theory:** Distinguish signals from noise in uncertain data.
95. **Decision-Making Under Ambiguity:** Act effectively despite unclear conditions.
96. **Applying Monte Carlo Simulations:** Model uncertainty using repeated trials.
97. **Black Swan Event Analysis:** Prepare for rare, high-impact events.
98. **Heuristic-Based Iteration:** Solve problems through trial and improvement.
99. **The Precautionary Principle Revisited:** Act cautiously in the face of unknown risks.
100. **Cognitive Flexibility in Uncertainty:** Adapt thinking to thrive in change.

Appendix B: Chapter Categories and Listings

This appendix organizes the chapters into their respective categories, offering a clear structure to navigate the topics covered in the book. Use this guide to locate chapters based on your specific interests or areas of focus.

Section I: Foundations

Focus: Fundamental tools and principles of logical reasoning.

Subsection: Building Blocks of Logic

- Occam's Razor
- The Principle of Charity
- Falsifiability
- Syllogisms
- Deductive Reasoning
- Inductive Reasoning
- Abductive Reasoning
- Modus Ponens
- Modus Tollens
- Reductio ad Absurdum

Section: Recognizing and Avoiding Fallacies

- Spotting Strawman Arguments
- Recognizing Ad Hominem Attacks
- Avoiding Post Hoc Reasoning
- Identifying Circular Arguments
- Detecting False Dilemmas
- Understanding Appeal to Authority Fallacies
- The Gambler's Fallacy
- Slippery Slope Analysis
- Avoiding Hasty Generalizations
- Distinguishing Correlation from Causation

Section II: Advanced Logical Tools

Focus: Practical frameworks and strategies for complex reasoning.

Subsection: Problem-Solving Frameworks

- The 5 Whys
- Ishikawa (Fishbone) Diagrams
- Root Cause Analysis
- The Socratic Method
- SWOT Analysis
- First Principles Thinking
- Reverse Engineering
- Hypothesis Testing
- Bayesian Thinking
- Counterfactual Reasoning
- Analogical Reasoning
- Pareto Analysis
- Ladder of Inference
- Heuristic Analysis
- The Eisenhower Matrix

Subsection: Cognitive Bias Mitigation

- Recognizing Anchoring Bias
- Overcoming Confirmation Bias
- Mitigating Availability Heuristics
- Combatting the Dunning-Kruger Effect
- Avoiding Framing Effects
- Understanding the Halo Effect
- Reframing with Devil's Advocacy
- Premortem Analysis
- Overcoming Status Quo Bias
- Appreciating Base Rates
- Debiasing with Probabilistic Thinking
- Overcoming Loss Aversion
- Distinguishing Intuition from Analysis
- Applying the Illusion of Transparency Test
- The Outside View Technique

Section III: Practical Applications

Focus: Applying logical methods to real-world contexts.

Subsection: Decision-Making Techniques

- Weighted Decision Matrix
- Expected Value Calculation
- Decision Trees
- Scenario Planning
- The Delphi Method
- Multi-Criteria Decision Analysis (MCDA)
- Cost-Benefit Analysis
- The Precautionary Principle
- The Monte Carlo Method

- Risk Assessment Matrices
- Sensitivity Analysis
- Adaptive Thinking
- The OODA Loop (Observe, Orient, Decide, Act)
- The Six Thinking Hats
- Weighted Trade-off Grids

Subsection: Enhancing Communication and Persuasion
- Reframing Arguments for Clarity
- The Pyramid Principle
- The Rhetorical Triangle
- Active Listening
- Mirroring and Paraphrasing

- Using Analogies Effectively
- The SEE-I Framework (State, Elaborate, Exemplify, Illustrate)
- Building Common Ground
- Structuring Evidence with Logic
- Avoiding Loaded Questions
- Recognizing Emotional Triggers
- Simplifying Complex Ideas
- Using Data to Bolster Arguments
- The Rule of Three in Persuasion
- The Importance of Visual Aids

Section IV: Mastery

Focus: Expert-level strategies for navigating uncertainty, complexity, and ambiguity.

Subsection: Logical Thinking in Complex Systems
- Systems Thinking
- Bottleneck Analysis
- Identifying Leverage Points
- Emergent Behavior Analysis
- Scenario Mapping
- The Butterfly Effect Awareness
- Stochastic Modeling
- Feedback Loop Analysis
- Network Analysis
- Chaos Theory in Decision-Making

Subsection: Navigating Uncertainty and Ambiguity
- Probability Trees
- The Maximin/Minimax Principle
- Utility Theory
- Signal Detection Theory
- Decision-Making Under Ambiguity
- Applying Monte Carlo Simulations
- Black Swan Event Analysis
- Heuristic-Based Iteration
- The Precautionary Principle Revisited
- Cognitive Flexibility in Uncertainty

Appendix C: Practice Scenarios

This appendix provides practical scenarios designed to help you apply the logical methods from the book. Each exercise includes a description of the scenario, the situation's details, and a challenge highlighting the relevant methods you can use to solve it. Use these scenarios individually or in group discussions to deepen your understanding and practice your skills.

Scenario 1: Business Decision

Situation:

A company is debating whether to launch a new product in a highly competitive market. The decision involves balancing potential profits, brand positioning, and market risks.

Challenge:

Use **SWOT Analysis** to evaluate strengths, weaknesses, opportunities, and threats, and apply the **Decision Tree Method** to map potential outcomes and their consequences.

Scenario 2: Policy Debate

Situation:

A city council is considering implementing a congestion charge to reduce traffic and pollution, but there's strong opposition from local businesses.

Challenge:

Apply the **Principle of Charity** to fairly analyze both sides of the argument, and use **Cost-Benefit Analysis** to assess the economic and social impacts of the policy.

Scenario 3: Financial Planning

Situation:

An individual is choosing between two investment options: a low-risk, steady-return bond and a high-risk, potentially high-reward stock.

Challenge:

Use the **Maximin/Minimax Principle** to evaluate the risks and rewards, and incorporate **Expected Value Calculation** to quantify potential financial outcomes.

Scenario 4: Healthcare Dilemma

Situation:

A doctor must decide between two treatment plans for a critically ill patient: one aggressive and riskier, the other safer but slower to act.

Apply **Utility Theory** to weigh the benefits and risks of each treatment and use **Bayesian Thinking** to update probabilities as new patient data becomes available.

Scenario 5: Negotiation Challenge

Situation:

Two companies negotiating a partnership face tension after one side presents an exaggerated scenario to strengthen its position.

Challenge:

Use **Spotting Strawman Arguments** to identify misrepresentations and apply **Reframing with Devil's Advocacy** to ensure the discussion remains constructive.

Scenario 6: Personal Career Choice

Situation:

A recent graduate is deciding between a high-paying corporate job with stability and a lower-paying start-up role with significant growth potential.

Challenge:

Use the **Eisenhower Matrix** to prioritize personal and professional values and apply the **Weighted Decision Matrix** to evaluate options across multiple criteria.

Scenario 7: Marketing Strategy

Situation:

A marketing team must choose between focusing their efforts on a social media campaign or an email marketing strategy.

Challenge:

Apply the **5 Whys** to uncover the root goals of the campaign and use **Hypothesis Testing** to predict which strategy aligns better with their objectives.

Scenario 8: Community Issue

Situation:

A neighborhood group is deciding how to address rising crime rates. They're debating whether to improve lighting, increase patrols, or start community outreach programs.

Challenge:

Use **Systems Thinking** to analyze how various factors contribute to crime and apply **Bottleneck Analysis** to identify the most effective intervention points.

Scenario 9: Global Issue

Situation:

A non-profit organization aims to combat climate change but must prioritize limited resources across multiple projects, such as renewable energy initiatives and reforestation programs.

Challenge:

Apply the **Precautionary Principle** to minimize environmental risks and use **Scenario Planning** to prepare for future climate-related uncertainties.

Scenario 10: Educational Reform

Situation:

A school district is evaluating whether to transition from traditional teaching methods to project-based learning to improve student engagement and critical thinking skills.

Challenge:

Use the **Socratic Method** to foster discussions among stakeholders and apply **First Principles Thinking** to assess the core benefits and challenges of the proposed change.

Scenario 11: Conflict Resolution

Situation:

Two co-workers have conflicting ideas about the direction of a major project, creating tension in team meetings.

Challenge:

Use **Active Listening** to understand both sides and apply **Building Common Ground** to find a mutually beneficial solution.

Scenario 12: Start-up Risk

Situation:

A tech start-up is preparing to launch a new product but is concerned about uncertain market demand and the financial risks of failure.

Challenge:

Use **Monte Carlo Simulations** to model potential market outcomes and apply **Signal Detection Theory** to identify meaningful trends in early customer feedback.

Situation:

A family is deciding whether to buy or rent a home, weighing financial considerations, flexibility, and long-term goals.

Challenge:

Apply **Cost-Benefit Analysis** to compare the financial implications of buying versus renting and use **Sensitivity Analysis** to explore how different scenarios (e.g., interest rate changes) might affect the decision.

Scenario 14: Crisis Management

Situation:

A company is dealing with a public relations crisis after a controversial statement went viral, causing backlash from customers.

Challenge:

Apply **Premortem Analysis** to anticipate potential missteps in the response strategy and use **Cognitive Flexibility** to adjust messaging as the situation evolves.

Scenario 15: Innovative Design

Situation:

An engineering team is tasked with creating a more efficient and sustainable solar panel to meet growing energy demands.

Challenge:

Use **Reverse Engineering** to study successful designs from competitors and apply **Feedback Loop Analysis** to refine the prototype during testing.

How to Use These Scenarios

These scenarios are designed to provide hands-on opportunities to apply logical methods and frameworks in diverse situations. Start by identifying which methods are most relevant to the scenario, then work through the problem systematically, applying the techniques from the chapters.

Revisit these scenarios regularly, practice different methods for the same scenario, and explore how alternative approaches can lead to different insights.

Appendix D: Checklist for Your Logical Thinking Guide

This checklist serves as a quick reference to enhance your logical thinking skills and ensure you approach problems, decisions, and challenges systematically. Use it to assess your process, refine your methods, and improve your outcomes.

1. Clarifying the Problem

- Have you clearly defined the problem or question you're addressing?
- Are you separating symptoms from root causes?
- Do you understand the context and scope of the issue?

2. Gathering Relevant Information

- Have you collected all available data and evidence?
- Are your sources credible and unbiased?
- Have you cross-checked the information for accuracy?

3. Evaluating Assumptions

- What assumptions are you making in your analysis?
- Are these assumptions based on evidence or bias?
- Can your assumptions be tested or challenged?

4. Identifying Key Variables

- What factors have the most significant impact on the issue?
- Are you prioritizing the most critical variables?
- Have you identified any dependencies or correlations?

5. Choosing the Right Method

- Have you selected a logical method that fits the problem?
- Are you familiar with how to apply this method effectively?
- Have you considered alternative methods for a different perspective?

6. Structuring Arguments

- Is your argument clear, logical, and evidence-based?
- Have you addressed counterarguments or alternative viewpoints?
- Are you avoiding logical fallacies in your reasoning?

7. Mitigating Bias

- Are you aware of potential cognitive biases influencing your thinking?
- Have you actively sought perspectives that challenge your assumptions?
- Are you using tools like probabilistic thinking to reduce bias?

8. Evaluating Risks and Rewards

- Have you identified potential risks and their likelihood?
- Are you balancing risks with potential rewards?
- Have you considered long-term impacts as well as short-term effects?

9. Simplifying Complexity

- Have you broken down complex problems into smaller parts?
- Are you focusing on the most impactful elements first?
- Have you avoided overcomplicating the issue unnecessarily?

10. Testing Hypotheses

- Are your hypotheses testable and falsifiable?
- Have you planned experiments or collected data to validate them?
- Are you prepared to revise your hypothesis if evidence contradicts it?

11. Using Visual Tools

- Have you used diagrams, flowcharts, or matrices to organize your thinking?
- Do your visuals clarify relationships and patterns in the data?
- Are your visual aids easy to understand and interpret?

12. Planning for Uncertainty

- Have you considered multiple scenarios and their outcomes?
- Are you building flexibility into your plans to adapt to change?
- Have you prepared for low-probability, high-impact events?

13. Engaging Stakeholders

- Have you consulted others with relevant expertise or perspectives?
- Are you presenting your reasoning in a clear and structured way?
- Have you addressed stakeholder concerns or objections?

14. Communicating Effectively

- Are you tailoring your message to your audience?
- Have you provided clear evidence to support your conclusions?
- Are you listening actively and responding to feedback constructively?

15. Reviewing and Refining

- Have you revisited your process to identify areas for improvement?
- Are you learning from past successes and mistakes?
- Are you regularly practicing and refining your logical thinking skills?

Pro Tip: The Key to Consistency

Logical thinking isn't about achieving perfection — it's about maintaining consistency. Use this checklist as a guide to ensure you stay on track, but remember to remain flexible. Each situation is unique, and the ability to adapt your methods is as important as mastering them. Regularly reflect on your thought processes, incorporate feedback, and embrace a mindset of continuous improvement. Logical thinking is a journey — use this checklist to guide your way forward.

Part 2: Social Engineering

An AI's Guide to Unmasking 100 Human Hacking Strategies So You Can Outsmart Manipulation and Stay in Control

Introduction

I'm an AI, made to think clearly and avoid mistakes. I'm here to help you with something important: *social engineering*, a.k.a. the art of manipulation. It's how con artists, scammers, and even persuasive co-workers get people to act against their best interests. Unlike hacking machines, social engineers hack people, exploiting trust, emotions, and habits to gain access to information, money, or control. It's subtle, it's powerful, and it's everywhere — embedded in fake emails, phone calls, and even face-to-face interactions.

Why Are Humans Vulnerable?

Humans aren't wired to question everything. Your brains rely on mental shortcuts to save time — like trusting authority, responding to urgency, or following social norms. Social engineers know this, and they design their tactics to slip past your logical defenses and straight into your emotional autopilot.

Why This Guide Matters

This book is for anyone who interacts with the modern world — because manipulation happens to everyone. Whether you're protecting your personal data, running a business, or just trying to avoid scams, the knowledge in these pages will help you stay one step ahead.

Here's what you'll learn:

- **How social engineers think**: the psychology and methods behind manipulation.
- **100 strategies manipulators use**: real-world tactics and how they exploit trust, emotions, and biases.
- **How to become unhackable**: simple, actionable defenses you can apply immediately to outsmart manipulation.

How to Use This Book

Each chapter dives into one specific social engineering tactic, explains how it works, and equips you with tools to neutralize it. By the end, you'll have a complete toolkit for spotting, understanding, and resisting manipulation in any form.

Are you ready to see the strings and cut them? Let's begin.

Section I: Trust and Authority Exploits

Trust is the foundation of human relationships, and manipulators know it. Social engineers build their schemes on trust, crafting personas or scenarios that make you believe they're credible. Add authority to the mix — uniforms, titles, or a confident tone — and they become nearly unstoppable. This section explores the tactics used to exploit your natural inclination to trust and defer to authority. By the end, you'll recognize the red flags behind friendly strangers, authoritative commands, and too-good-to-be-true offers.

Chapter 1: The Imposter Gambit

Understanding the Imposter Gambit

Imagine a wolf in sheep's clothing, but instead of wool, it's wearing the trusted logos of your bank, company, or a government agency. This is the essence of the **Imposter Gambit** — a strategy where manipulators disguise themselves as someone you trust to trick you into giving away sensitive information or access.

Here's an example:

You receive a call from "your bank." The caller knows your name, mentions your account type, and informs you of unusual activity on your account. Their tone is professional, and their instructions feel urgent: "We just need to confirm your card number and security code to secure your account." Without hesitation, you comply, only to realize later that the call wasn't from your bank — it was a con artist.

This tactic is especially effective because humans tend to associate certain roles — such as a bank official, IT support agent, or even a family member — with trust. When someone convincingly embodies those roles, it becomes difficult to question their intentions.

How the Imposter Gambit Works

Social engineers exploit trust through three primary techniques:

1. **Authenticity:** Imposters mimic tone, terminology, and behavior associated with the persona they're imitating. For example, an "IT technician" might ask for remote access to your computer while using technical jargon to sound credible.
2. **Urgency:** They create pressure by making the situation feel time-sensitive. For example, "If you don't respond within the next hour, your account will be locked."
3. **Emotion Manipulation:** They invoke fear, relief, or confusion to cloud your judgment. A friendly tone disarms suspicion, while fear prompts action without thought.

Real-Life Examples

1. **Phishing Emails:** These are emails disguised to look like they're from trusted organizations, often asking you to "reset your password" or "enter account details." Clicking the link leads to a fake website designed to steal your credentials.
2. **Tech Support Scams:** Scammers call pretending to be from major tech companies, claiming there's an urgent issue with your computer. They'll ask for remote access to "fix the problem," giving them complete control over your device.
3. **The CEO Fraud:** An employee receives an urgent email from their boss requesting a wire transfer. The email seems legitimate, but it's actually from an imposter using a spoofed address.

Why It Works

Humans rely on mental shortcuts, known as **heuristics**, to make decisions quickly. If someone sounds official, we instinctively trust them. Add time pressure or emotional cues, and critical thinking often takes a backseat.

Additionally, imposters often exploit **preloaded trust** — relationships or roles you've already come to associate with credibility. For example, you're more likely to trust a message from your "boss" or "bank" without immediately questioning it.

How to Spot the Imposter Gambit

1. **Inconsistencies in Communication:** Look for subtle errors such as a mismatched email domain or grammar mistakes in a "professional" message.
2. **Unusual Requests:** Be cautious if someone asks for sensitive information that a legitimate entity wouldn't normally require, like your full password or PIN.
3. **Pressure to Act Now:** Legitimate organizations don't ask for immediate action for routine issues. Time-sensitive threats are often a red flag.

1. Think of three trusted institutions you interact with regularly (e.g., your bank, employer, utility provider).
2. Research and write down their official contact methods (e.g., phone numbers, email domains).
3. Practice verifying information by calling or contacting them directly about hypothetical situations (e.g., "Did you send me this email?").

Role-Playing Exercise:
- With a friend or colleague, take turns acting as an imposter trying to extract sensitive information.
- The "target" must use strategies like asking clarifying questions or pausing to think before responding.

Key Takeaway

The Imposter Gambit works because it blends trust with urgency. Always pause to check identities through independent channels. Manipulators rely on speed and emotional responses; taking the time to confirm details will stop them in their tracks.

Chapter 2: The Fake Badge

The Power of Authority Symbols

Humans are programmed to respect authority. Uniforms, badges, titles, and even confident behavior create an illusion of credibility that few people question. Social engineers know this and exploit it to gain access to places or information. This tactic is known as **The Fake Badge**, and it thrives on the perception of legitimacy.

Imagine this:

A person in a suit walks into a corporate office holding a clipboard and wearing a badge with a company logo. They confidently tell the receptionist, "I'm here to check the network servers. The boss asked me to be quick." Without a second glance, they're allowed through. Minutes later, sensitive company data is in their hands, and they vanish without a trace.

This tactic isn't limited to physical spaces. Online, the "badge" may take the form of an email signature, a LinkedIn profile, or a job title designed to impress. Manipulators rely on these visual or contextual cues to make their targets act.

How It Works

The Fake Badge relies on psychological triggers and symbols of authority:

1. **Visual Cues:** Uniforms, lanyards, ID cards, and official-looking paperwork signal credibility. Most people associate these symbols with trustworthiness and don't question them.
2. **Confident Behavior:** The manipulator acts like they belong, leveraging human reluctance to challenge authority or make others uncomfortable.
3. **Context Matching:** Scammers adapt their personas to fit the environment, blending in just enough to seem plausible.

Real-Life Examples

1. **The Bogus Inspector:** A person dressed as a fire marshal visits a building and requests access to "inspect" sensitive areas. Employees assume the role is legitimate and grant them access.
2. **The Uniform Trick:** Someone dressed as a delivery driver enters a secure area under the pretense of delivering a package, only to steal valuable assets.
3. **The Fake Email Signature:** An email appears to come from a department head, complete with a professional signature and contact details. It instructs employees to click on a link or send confidential data.

Why It Works

The Fake Badge exploits the **Authority Bias**, a psychological tendency to comply with perceived authority figures. When someone presents themselves as an expert or official, the brain defaults to trust rather than skepticism.

Additionally, people often avoid confrontation. It feels awkward to challenge someone who appears confident, well-dressed, or knowledgeable. Social engineers exploit this hesitation to push through boundaries.

How to Spot the Fake Badge

1. **Scrutinize Credentials:** Look closely at badges, uniforms, or documents. Fake ones often have subtle inconsistencies like typos, poor-quality printing, or vague titles.
2. **Ask Questions:** Legitimate professionals should be able to provide specific details about their visit or role. A lack of preparation is often a red flag.
3. **Verify Independently:** Confirm the person's identity with the organization they claim to represent, even if they seem legitimate.

1. Find examples of ID badges, uniforms, or official-looking documents online (e.g., government IDs, company badges).
2. Compare them to fake examples from scam alert websites or news reports. List the differences you observe, such as logos, fonts, or formatting.

Scenario Exercise:

- Imagine a stranger claiming to be an inspector or technician asks for access to your home or workplace. Write down 3-5 questions you would ask to double check their identity (e.g. "What's your supervisor's name and contact information?").

Key Takeaway

The Fake Badge works because people are conditioned to trust authority symbols. Don't let appearances override your judgment. Take the time to validate credentials, no matter how convincing they seem.

Chapter 3: The Friendly Stranger

The Danger of Charm and Familiarity

Not all manipulators rely on fear or authority. Some win their targets over with friendliness. The **Friendly Stranger** strategy plays on the natural human inclination to trust people who seem warm, relatable, or helpful.

Here's an example:

You're at an airport when someone strikes up a conversation, claiming to have the same destination. They share anecdotes, ask about your travel plans, and seem genuinely interested in your life. In the process, they learn about your employer, the kind of work you do, and even your company's latest projects. What seems like harmless small talk turns into a treasure trove of sensitive information for the stranger — a potential corporate spy.

How It Works

The Friendly Stranger tactic leverages key psychological principles:

1. **Mirroring:** Manipulators subtly imitate your gestures, tone, or interests to build rapport.
2. **Active Listening:** They ask questions and respond enthusiastically, making you feel valued and important.
3. **Mutual Interests:** Finding common ground creates a sense of familiarity, which lowers defenses.

Real-Life Examples

1. **The Helpful Shopper:** At a store, someone offers assistance with a heavy item, then casually inquires about your address or schedule, potentially setting up for theft.
2. **The Curious Co-Worker:** A "new hire" strikes up conversations, asking about company procedures and team dynamics, only to disappear before their first pay check.
3. **The Online Friend:** A stranger on social media sends a friendly message, gradually building a connection before asking for money or sensitive information.

Why It Works

Humans are social creatures who seek connection and aim to avoid conflict. A warm, friendly demeanor disarms suspicion because it feels safe. Also, when someone appears to be open and kind, people are more likely to reciprocate, sharing personal details without thinking twice.

How to Spot the Friendly Stranger

1. **Excessive Interest:** Be cautious of strangers who seem overly eager to know details about your life, work, or habits.
2. **Unsolicited Help:** While kindness is genuine in many cases, question offers of help that seem out of place or come with follow-up questions.
3. **Gradual Prying:** Manipulators often start with harmless questions before escalating to sensitive topics. Pay attention to these shifts.

Exercise: Maintaining Boundaries

1. Write down three examples of situations where a stranger has asked you for personal information (online or in person).
2. For each example, identify what information you shared and whether it was necessary. Reflect on what you could do differently in the future.

- Role-play with a partner where one person acts as a "friendly stranger" asking for personal details. Practice politely but firmly declining to share information, using phrases like:
  - "I'm sorry, I don't share that kind of information."
  - "Let me check that first before continuing."

Key Takeaway

The Friendly Stranger thrives on charm and relatability. Stay friendly, but maintain boundaries. Trust should be earned, not given freely to someone who seems "nice."

Chapter 4: The Expert Trap

The Intimidation of Expertise

Picture this: a well-dressed individual strides into a meeting, introduces themselves as an "industry expert," and launches into a presentation packed with technical jargon, obscure statistics, and complex diagrams. As they speak, you feel lost but too embarrassed to admit it. They end with a proposal: invest now to avoid missing out on massive returns. Without fully understanding, you agree, relying on their "expertise."

This is the **Expert Trap** — a manipulation tactic that weaponizes specialized knowledge to intimidate and control. The manipulator overwhelms their target with technical details, leaving them too confused or unsure to challenge the claims being made.

The Expert Trap thrives in scenarios where the target has limited knowledge of the subject, such as finance, technology, or law. Social engineers use this imbalance to establish authority, making their victims feel dependent on their expertise. Once they've created this dynamic, they guide the decision-making process to their advantage.

How It Works

The Expert Trap relies on psychological pressure and the perception of credibility:

1. **Overwhelming Complexity:** Manipulators deliberately use technical language, charts, or calculations to create an aura of expertise. This complexity discourages questions and encourages compliance.
2. **Appeals to Authority:** They present themselves as certified professionals, citing credentials or affiliations (real or fake) to reinforce their authority.
3. **Fear of Appearing Ignorant:** Targets often hesitate to challenge experts for fear of looking foolish or uninformed, making them easier to manipulate.

Real-Life Examples

1. **The Expertise Smokescreen:** A "financial advisor" promises high returns, using confusing charts and terms such as "compound derivatives" or "diversified portfolios" to convince you to part with your savings. The promised returns never materialize.
2. **The Non-existent Technician:** A caller claims to be from your computer's software provider, explaining that your system is "infected". They bombard you with technical jargon, convincing you to give them remote access to "fix" the issue.
3. **Legal Threats:** Scammers pose as lawyers or law enforcement, citing obscure regulations or statutes. Their formal language and tone intimidate victims into paying fines or revealing personal details.

Why It Works

The Expert Trap taps into the **Authority Bias**, where people instinctively defer to those perceived as knowledgeable. This deference is amplified when:

- The topic is unfamiliar, creating a sense of vulnerability.
- The manipulator appears confident and prepared.
- The victim feels social pressure to avoid appearing uninformed.

Fear and confusion further cloud judgment, leaving the victim dependent on the "expert" to solve the problem.

How to Spot the Expert Trap

1. **Simplified Explanations:** Genuine experts can break down complex topics into simple, understandable terms. If someone refuses to simplify or dodges questions, it's a red flag.
2. **Rushed Decisions:** Beware of "experts" who push for immediate action, especially if they claim the opportunity is time-sensitive.
3. **Verify Credentials:** Research the individual's background, certifications, and affiliations. Fake experts often rely on superficial details, like vague titles or exaggerated achievements.

1. Find a complex topic you don't fully understand (e.g., blockchain, taxes, or data encryption).
2. Watch an "expert" explain the topic in technical terms (e.g., a YouTube video or article).
3. Practice identifying unclear jargon and look for alternative explanations in simpler terms.

Questioning Authority:

- List 5 challenging but respectful questions you could ask an "expert" to test their credibility. Examples:
  - "Can you explain that in simpler terms for me?"
  - "What's the source of your data?"
  - "Why is immediate action necessary?"

Key Takeaway

The Expert Trap works by overwhelming you with complexity and authority. Never let jargon or credentials override your judgment. Ask questions, seek independent verification, and trust your instincts when something feels off.

Chapter 5: The Scarcity Hook

The Power of Scarcity

"Only three left in stock!"

"This deal ends in 24 hours!"

"Act now, or you'll miss out forever!"

If these phrases make you feel an urge to act, you've experienced the **Scarcity Hook**. By creating a false sense of scarcity, social engineers push their targets into making rushed decisions without properly evaluating the situation.

Here's a common scenario:

You're browsing online when a pop-up announces a massive sale on a product you've been eyeing. "Only 1 left at this price!" it claims, and the timer is ticking. Panicked, you enter your payment details, only to later discover the "sale" wasn't real. Worse, your information is now in the hands of a scammer.

Scarcity is a powerful motivator. When people perceive something as rare or limited, it becomes more desirable. Social engineers use this to create urgency and pressure, making their targets feel they must act immediately — or lose the opportunity forever.

How It Works

The Scarcity Hook uses psychological triggers to override logical thinking:

1. **Perceived Rarity:** Manipulators highlight the limited availability of a product, service, or opportunity. Even if the scarcity is fake, the urgency feels real.
2. **Time Pressure:** Countdown timers or ticking clocks amplify the urgency, making you feel that delaying action could cost you.
3. **Fear of Loss:** People are naturally more motivated to avoid loss than to seek gain, making them especially vulnerable to scarcity-driven tactics.

Real-Life Examples

1. **Online Shopping Scams:** Fake e-commerce sites display countdowns or low-stock warnings to rush purchases. Victims often receive poor-quality items—or nothing at all.
2. **"Unique" Opportunities:** Scammers pitch opportunities, claiming spots are limited to pressure victims into handing over money quickly.
3. **Event Ticket Scams:** Fraudulent sellers advertise limited tickets for popular events, driving buyers to make hasty payments without verifying legitimacy.

Why It Works

The Scarcity Hook exploits **Loss Aversion**, a cognitive bias where people feel the pain of losing something more acutely than the joy of gaining it. Combined with time pressure, scarcity short-circuits critical thinking, forcing decisions based on emotion rather than logic.

How to Spot the Scarcity Hook

1. **Artificial Deadlines:** Be wary of deals or opportunities that feel overly urgent. Research whether the scarcity claim is legitimate.
2. **Emotional Decision-Making:** If you feel panicked or pressured, take a step back. Scarcity tactics rely on emotional responses, not rational evaluation.
3. **Independent Verification:** Check reviews, websites, or trusted sources to confirm whether an offer or product is genuine.

1. Visit an online shopping site with countdown timers or low-stock warnings.
2. Pause and assess:
   o Is the urgency real?
   o Can you find the same product elsewhere without the pressure?
3. Write down your findings and whether the scarcity felt authentic or manipulative.

Self-Awareness Drill:

- Think of a time you acted on a "limited-time offer." Reflect on these questions:
   o What emotions did you feel at the time (e.g., panic, excitement)?
   o Would you have made the same decision without the urgency?
- Practice mentally pausing and asking these questions next time you encounter a scarcity tactic.

The Scarcity Hook preys on your fear of missing out. Resist the pressure to act immediately, and take time to check the legitimacy of any "limited-time" offers or opportunities.

Chapter 6: The Urgent Boss

The Pressure of Authority and Urgency

Imagine this scenario:

You're at your desk, and an email from your CEO lands in your inbox. The subject line reads, "URGENT: Wire Transfer Needed." The message is brief but stern: "We're finalizing a critical deal. Please transfer $10,000 to the account below immediately and confirm once it's done. Time is of the essence."

Caught off guard and eager to comply, you complete the transaction. Hours later, you realize the email didn't come from your CEO — it was a scammer impersonating them.

This is the **Urgent Boss** tactic, a common social engineering strategy that combines authority with urgency to override critical thinking. By posing as a senior figure and creating a high-pressure scenario, manipulators trick employees into bypassing normal verification procedures.

How It Works

1. **Authority Bias:** People are conditioned to obey authority figures, especially in professional settings. An email or message that appears to come from a senior figure carries inherent weight.
2. **Time Pressure:** Adding urgency discourages double-checking. Scammers know that when people feel rushed, they're less likely to follow proper protocols.
3. **Emotional Hijack:** The tone of the message — urgent, demanding, and sometimes intimidating—creates a sense of panic or duty, clouding judgment.

Real-Life Examples

1. **CEO Fraud (Business Email Compromise):** Scammers spoof a CEO's or manager's email address and send urgent requests to employees for money transfers or sensitive information.
2. **Fake Vendor Requests:** A fraudster impersonates a supplier or contractor, claiming overdue payments. They push the victim to act fast to "resolve the issue."
3. **Emergency Text Scams:** A "boss" texts an employee late at night, asking them to make financial transactions on their behalf.

Why It Works

This tactic succeeds because it preys on workplace dynamics. Employees are often reluctant to question authority or delay action, fearing reprimands. Scammers exploit this by mimicking professional communication styles and creating plausible scenarios that feel too urgent to ignore.

How to Spot the Urgent Boss

1. **Inconsistencies in Email or Text Details:** Look for slight discrepancies in email addresses, grammar, or tone that don't match the usual communication style of your boss.
2. **Unusual Requests:** Be cautious if the request involves sensitive information, urgent financial transactions, or tasks outside your typical responsibilities.
3. **No Verification Channels:** Legitimate managers will often provide follow-up options, such as a phone number to confirm. Scammers usually avoid this.

Exercise: Spot the Urgent Spoof

1. Collect examples of emails or messages that ask to be actioned immediately (e.g. "Wire money now," "Respond within 1

hour").

2. Examine:
   - ○ Are the email addresses or phone numbers legitimate?
   - ○ Does the tone feel rushed or overly formal?
3. Write down three signs of urgency-based manipulation you identified.

Role-Playing Drill:

- Partner up and simulate a scenario where one person poses as a boss making an urgent request (e.g. financial transfer or login details).
- Practice verifying the request calmly by asking questions or confirming via a separate channel.

Key Takeaway

The Urgent Boss tactic works by combining authority with time pressure. Stay calm, go through all requests through trusted channels, and don't let urgency override critical thinking.

Chapter 7: The Insider Illusion

The Familiar Face in the Crowd

The **Insider Illusion** is a tactic where social engineers pretend to belong to a group, gaining trust and access by blending in. This could mean posing as a co-worker, contractor, or even a friend of an employee. The goal is simple: exploit the assumption that they are "one of us."

For example:

A man walks into a company office carrying a toolbox and wearing a uniform. He tells the receptionist he's there to repair the server room. Without hesitation, he's let in, despite not being scheduled. In reality, he's a fraudster planting malicious software on the company's systems.

This tactic relies on familiarity and routine. When someone looks or acts the part, people rarely stop to question their presence.

How It Works

1. **Familiarity Bias:** Humans are less likely to question someone who appears to belong to their environment.
2. **Confidence and Routine:** Social engineers often act confidently, exploiting people's tendency to avoid confrontation.
3. **Lack of Verification:** Many workplaces fail to verify identities for routine tasks, assuming everyone present is authorized.

Real-Life Examples

1. **Fake IT Workers:** Imposters pose as IT support, gaining physical or remote access to sensitive systems.
2. **Tailgating:** Someone follows an employee through a secure door by pretending they forgot their ID badge.
3. **Impersonating Co-workers:** Fraudsters claim to be new hires or contractors to gain access to restricted areas or information.

Why It Works

The Insider Illusion thrives in environments where trust and familiarity are prioritized over strict security protocols. It also preys on the human tendency to avoid awkward situations, such as questioning someone who seems to belong.

How to Spot the Insider Illusion

1. **Unscheduled Appearances:** Be alert to people showing up unexpectedly, especially if they claim to be new hires or contractors.
2. **Avoiding Specifics:** Imposters often provide vague answers when questioned about their purpose or role.
3. **Relying on Bystanders' Politeness:** Watch for individuals who tailgate through secure doors or rely on others to hold the door open.

Exercise: Identify Weak Access Points

1. Walk through your home, office, or shared space.
2. Note any potential vulnerabilities where someone could gain unauthorized access (e.g. unsecured doors, lack of ID checks).
3. Write down two simple solutions to improve security, like enforcing badge checks or questioning unfamiliar faces.

Role-Playing Drill:

- Role-play with a partner: One acts as an imposter insider (e.g. a "new hire" or "contractor"), while the other verifies their credentials.

- Use polite questions like:
    - "Who requested your visit?"
    - "May I confirm this with your supervisor?"
- Swap roles and discuss the responses.

Key Takeaway

The Insider Illusion exploits routine and trust. Always suss out unfamiliar people, especially those who appear confident or claim to belong — your caution is a security asset.

Chapter 8: The Overconfidence Play

The Power of Confidence

Imagine you're standing near the entrance of a secured building, and someone confidently strides in without hesitation. They nod politely, say, "Morning," and keep walking. Do you stop them? Probably not. They act like they belong, so you assume they do.

This is the **Overconfidence Play**, a social engineering tactic where manipulators use boldness, assertiveness, and swagger to lower suspicion. By projecting certainty, they exploit human reluctance to challenge others — especially those who appear sure of themselves.

Confidence is persuasive. Humans naturally trust people who act decisively. Combine that with the discomfort of confrontation, and the Overconfidence Play becomes an effective tool for gaining unauthorized access, extracting information, or manipulating decisions.

How It Works

The Overconfidence Play relies on three key elements:
1. **Body Language and Tone:** Manipulators maintain steady eye contact, use strong posture, and speak with authority, making others hesitant to question them.
2. **Assumed Authority:** They use confidence to project authority, acting as though they are in control of the situation.
3. **Social Discomfort:** Most people avoid awkward or confrontational situations. Manipulators leverage this to their advantage, relying on others' desire to "not cause trouble."

Real-Life Examples

1. **Physical Access:** A fraudster confidently enters a secure office, walking through doors held open by employees too polite to stop them.
2. **Fake Deliveries:** Someone drops off packages at an office, acting as though it's routine, while covertly planting surveillance devices or stealing information.
3. **Verbal Authority:** A scammer confidently calls a business, demanding immediate access to files or systems, stating, "I'm the IT manager — just do it."

Why It Works

Confidence overrides doubt. People are less likely to challenge someone who projects authority because it feels awkward or risky to question them. The Overconfidence Play exploits two psychological principles:
- **The Authority Bias:** Confidence often mimics authority, making people comply without verifying legitimacy.
- **Avoidance of Conflict:** Most people prefer to avoid confrontations, especially with someone who seems certain and assertive.

How to Spot the Overconfidence Play

1. **Unverified Assumptions:** Be cautious when someone acts like they belong but offers no credentials or context.
2. **Pressured Compliance:** Manipulators often expect you to comply immediately without giving you time to think or question.
3. **Vague Details:** Confident manipulators avoid specifics when questioned, often dismissing concerns with phrases like, "It's standard procedure."

Exercise: Challenge Assumed Confidence

1. Observe a public setting (e.g. office, café, or event). Watch how confident individuals gain trust without providing credentials.
2. Note three instances where confidence seemed to bypass scrutiny. Reflect on how you would challenge such behavior respectfully.

- Partner with someone and take turns acting as the "confident intruder." One person pretends to enter a restricted area or request sensitive information assertively.
- Practice politely challenging them:
  - "I need to confirm who you're here to see."
  - "May I see your identification?"

The Overconfidence Play works because boldness suppresses suspicion. Don't let confidence alone determine trust. Ask for verification, even if it feels uncomfortable.

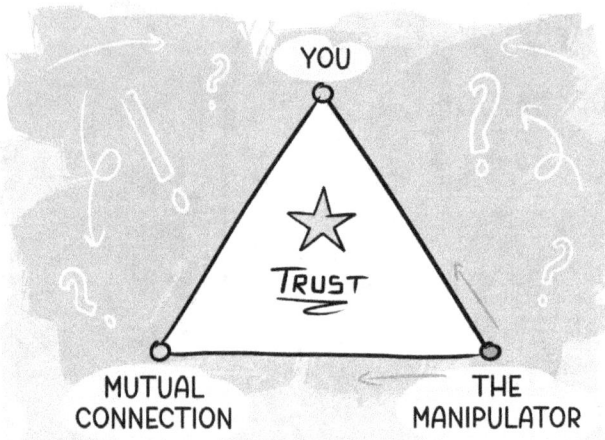

Chapter 9: The Trust Triangle

Trust by Association

The **Trust Triangle** tactic is based on a simple principle: trust can spread. When someone claims to know a mutual friend, colleague, or organization, you're more likely to trust them too. This association builds an invisible bridge, encouraging cooperation.

Here's an example:

You get a call from a "vendor" who says, "I've worked with your colleague Sarah on this project before. She gave me your number to finalize the details." Because Sarah's name is familiar, you assume the person is legitimate. Without hesitation, you provide the information they request.

In reality, the manipulator doesn't know Sarah. They've simply dropped her name to gain your trust.

How It Works

The Trust Triangle exploits relationships and social connections through three steps:

1. **Identifying a Mutual Connection:** Manipulators gather information about people you know or organizations you trust.
2. **Name-Dropping:** They casually mention the connection to build credibility and seem familiar.
3. **Leaning on Trust:** By linking themselves to someone you trust, they try to build trust.

Real-Life Examples

1. **The Fake Vendor:** "I worked with your manager last week, and they mentioned you're the one to help me with this request."
2. **Social Media Exploit:** Scammers use mutual friends or colleagues on LinkedIn to gain trust before sending fraudulent messages.
3. **Family or Friend Connection:** "Your cousin recommended me for this service — I've done work for them before."

Why It Works

Humans are social creatures. When someone references a trusted connection, it triggers **associative trust**, making them seem credible by default. The brain takes a shortcut: "If I trust Sarah, and Sarah trusts them, they must be safe."

How to Spot the Trust Triangle

1. **Unverified References:** Be cautious of vague mentions of mutual contacts. Ask for details that confirm the connection.
2. **Overreliance on Trust:** Manipulators lean on the name-drop without offering other evidence of legitimacy.
3. **Contextual Inconsistencies:** If something feels off, check in with the mutual connection directly before proceeding.

Exercise: Establish Connections

1. Write down three recent instances where someone mentioned a mutual contact to gain your trust.
2. Reflect: Did you verify the connection? If not, consider how you could have confirmed their legitimacy without offending them.

Role-Playing Drill:

- Partner with a friend. One person pretends to gain trust by referencing a mutual contact. The other practices validating the connection by asking specific follow-up questions:
  - "What did you and Sarah work on together?"
  - "Let me quickly check with Sarah before moving forward."

Key Takeaway

The Trust Triangle works by exploiting your connections. Always check mutual references — trust should be earned, not borrowed through association.

Chapter 10: The Chain of Command

You receive an urgent email from your manager asking you to "approve a wire transfer immediately" to resolve a critical vendor issue. Without hesitation, you comply—it's coming from your manager, after all. Later, you discover that your manager's account was hacked, and the transfer was part of a scam.

This is the **Chain of Command** tactic, where manipulators exploit hierarchies to pressure individuals into compliance. By pretending to be a superior or invoking a superior's authority, social engineers override doubt, making targets feel they must obey without question.

How It Works

1. **Impersonating Authority:** The manipulator pretends to be someone higher in the organizational hierarchy, like a manager or executive.
2. **Passing Instructions:** They issue directives through email, phone, or intermediaries, making the request feel routine or mandatory.
3. **Diffuse Responsibility:** Each level of the chain assumes the request has been vetted by someone above, leading to blind compliance.

The Chain of Command works because people in hierarchies are conditioned to follow instructions from superiors, especially in fast-paced or high-pressure environments.

Real-Life Examples

1. **CEO Fraud:** A scammer impersonates a CEO, directing employees to transfer money or share sensitive information.
2. **Bogus Internal Requests:** Fraudsters pretend to be team leads or department heads, asking subordinates for login credentials or system access.
3. **Multi-Level Scams:** Manipulators use a chain of employees to relay fraudulent instructions, ensuring no single person questions the request.

Why It Works

This tactic exploits three key dynamics:
1. **Authority Bias:** People instinctively trust and obey higher-ups in a hierarchy.
2. **Diffusion of Responsibility:** Each link in the chain assumes someone else has verified the legitimacy of the request.
3. **Urgency Over Verification:** Hierarchical directives often come with time pressure, discouraging critical thinking or second-guessing.

How to Spot the Chain of Command

1. **Unusual Requests:** Be wary of directives that seem out of character or fall outside standard procedures.
2. **Lack of Direct Contact:** If the person issuing the directive isn't available to confirm, escalate the situation for verification.
3. **Time Pressure:** Legitimate managers rarely discourage verification, even during urgent tasks.

Exercise: Break the Chain

1. Write down three ways to confirm hierarchical instructions (e.g. "Confirm directly with the source," "Cross-check with a peer," "Follow established escalation protocols").
2. Reflect on a time when you followed a directive without verifying. What questions could you have asked?

Role-Playing Drill:

- One partner plays a "manager" issuing an urgent directive. The other practices checking legitimacy by asking clarifying questions like:
    - "Can I confirm this request with your assistant?"
    - "What's the purpose and urgency of this task?"

Key Takeaway

The Chain of Command leverages organizational structures to manipulate individuals. Always question unusual directives, even if they appear to come from someone higher up.

Chapter 11: The Name Drop

Trust Through Familiarity

"Sarah from Marketing said I should call you. She told me you're the expert on handling client files."

Hearing a familiar name instantly lowers your guard. You trust Sarah, so you extend that trust to the stranger who claims to know her. This is the **Name Drop** tactic — a method social engineers use to fake legitimacy by referencing people or organizations you know.

By strategically mentioning names, roles, or departments, manipulators make themselves appear connected and trustworthy. This false familiarity tricks you into compliance without verification.

How It Works

The Name Drop tactic involves:

1. **Research:** Manipulators gather details about your network—names of co-workers, friends, vendors, or family—often from social media or company directories.
2. **Strategic Mention:** They casually reference a trusted person ("John said you could help me") to build instant credibility.
3. **Assumed Familiarity:** You assume the connection is real and feel socially pressured to cooperate or assist.

Real-Life Examples

1. **Business Scams:** A fraudster emails saying, "Your CEO, Mark, mentioned you'd handle this payment."
2. **Phone Manipulation:** A scammer calls and says, "I was just on the phone with Emily from IT. She asked me to finish this with you."
3. **Social Scams:** Someone messages you on social media, claiming, "I'm a friend of Mike's—he said you're reliable and could help me."

Why It Works

Humans instinctively trust connections. When someone mentions a familiar name, your brain associates them with that person's credibility. This creates a shortcut: "If they know someone I trust, they must be trustworthy too."

The Name Drop also leverages **social pressure** — it feels awkward to question someone who "knows your friend."

How to Spot the Name Drop

1. **Casual References:** Be cautious when someone references a person or organization without providing specifics.
2. **Missing Context:** If the connection feels vague, ask for more details ("When did you last speak to Sarah?").
3. **Verify Directly:** Confirm the claim with the referenced person before proceeding.

Exercise: Establish Whether A Connection Is True

1. Think of three instances where someone referenced a mutual contact to gain your trust.
2. Reflect on whether you verified the claim. Write down one question you could ask next time, like, "Can you tell me how you know them?"

Role-Playing Drill:

- Partner up. One person acts as the manipulator using a name drop: "John said I should talk to you."
- The other practices checking the connection without hesitation: "Let me quickly check with John to confirm."

Key Takeaway

The Name Drop exploits your trust in mutual connections. Never accept references at face value — don't let familiarity override caution.

Chapter 12: The Call from the Top

Manipulating with Authority

You receive a call: "This is the CEO. We're finalizing a critical deal, and I need you to wire funds immediately." The voice is authoritative, the situation urgent. You comply, wanting to avoid delays or questions. Later, you realize the caller wasn't the CEO—it was a scammer impersonating them.

This is the **Call from the Top** tactic, where fraudsters use fake authority to force compliance. By pretending to be senior leadership, manipulators create pressure, fear, and urgency to override logical decision-making.

How It Works

1. **Assuming Authority:** The scammer uses names, roles, or insider details to sound convincing as a high-level executive.
2. **Creating Pressure:** They frame the request as critical and time-sensitive, making verification seem unnecessary or risky.
3. **Avoiding Scrutiny:** Fraudsters rely on the target's reluctance to question leadership or delay urgent tasks.

Real-Life Examples

1. **CEO Impersonation:** Fraudsters impersonate executives, demanding urgent wire transfers to close "important deals."
2. **Fake Vendor Approvals:** Scammers claim to represent leadership, authorizing fraudulent payments or access to systems.
3. **Emergency Directives:** A manipulator pretends to be a CEO handling a crisis, using fear to push compliance.

Why It Works

The Call from the Top preys on two dynamics:

1. **Authority Bias:** People instinctively follow instructions from perceived superiors.
2. **Fear of Repercussions:** Employees fear delaying or challenging executive requests, leading to blind compliance.

How to Spot the Call from the Top

1. **Unusual Communication:** Executives rarely contact subordinates directly for sensitive or urgent tasks.
2. **Time-Sensitive Demands:** Verify any request that discourages verification or asks for immediate action.
3. **Out-of-Character Requests:** If the task feels uncharacteristic of the sender, confirm through official channels.

Exercise: Prove Executive Directives

1. Write down three steps to confirm high-level requests (e.g. "Call the executive's office," "Check with a trusted colleague," "Request written confirmation").
2. Practice applying these steps to a simulated executive directive with a partner.

Role-Playing Drill:

- One person plays the "executive" issuing an urgent request. The other practices making sure of facts calmly, saying:
    - "I'd like to confirm this with your assistant."
    - "Can you send this request through official channels?"

Key Takeaway

The Call from the Top uses authority and urgency to manipulate decisions. Always verify executive requests, and remember: true leadership welcomes questions.

Chapter 13: The Financial Fraudster

The Credible Payment Request

You receive an email, phone call, or invoice from what seems like a trusted vendor, supplier, or even an internal team member: "Payment overdue — please send the outstanding amount to this account immediately." Everything looks legitimate — logos, formatting, and tone — so you process the payment. A week later, you discover the vendor never requested it. The money? Gone.

The **Financial Fraudster** exploits trust in financial processes to steal money or sensitive payment information. By mimicking legitimate payment systems, impersonating trusted vendors, or posing as internal finance teams, social engineers manipulate employees into approving fraudulent transactions.

How It Works

This tactic relies on financial familiarity and trust:
1. **Mimicking Legitimacy:** Fraudsters create realistic invoices, emails, or requests that mirror those from trusted vendors or colleagues.
2. **Exploiting Routine:** In busy workplaces, financial processes like invoice payments are often repetitive and rushed. Scammers exploit this by inserting fraudulent requests into the workflow.
3. **Urgency and Consequences:** Phrases like "overdue," "penalties," or "service interruptions" pressure targets into acting quickly.

Real-Life Examples
1. **Vendor Invoice Fraud:** A scammer impersonates a supplier, sending fake invoices to companies that look identical to the real ones.
2. **Account Switch Requests:** Fraudsters contact finance teams claiming the vendor's bank account details have "changed" and provide new payment information.
3. **Internal Finance Impersonation:** An email from "accounts payable" demands a quick wire transfer to resolve an "urgent payment error."

Why It Works

The Financial Fraudster preys on trust, routine, and urgency. Financial processes often involve multiple parties, making it easier to insert fraudulent steps unnoticed. Employees assume payment requests are legitimate if they:
- Look official (correct logos, formatting).
- Reference real projects, departments, or deadlines.
- Appear urgent and linked to potential penalties.

How to Spot the Financial Fraudster
1. **Unusual Changes:** Be cautious of last-minute requests to change payment details or bank accounts.
2. **Mismatched Details:** Check email addresses, account numbers, and invoice references. Subtle discrepancies often signal fraud.
3. **Urgent Financial Demands:** Legitimate vendors rarely ask for instant payments under threat of severe penalties.

Exercise: Payment Verification Drill
1. Review the last five financial payment requests you processed. Write down the steps you followed to confirm legitimacy.
2. Next time, add an extra verification step, such as confirming payment details via a phone call to a known contact.

Role-Playing Drill:

- Partner up. One person acts as the "fraudster," submitting a fake invoice or urgent payment request.
- The other practices spotting red flags and challenging the request:
    - "I'll confirm the account details with the vendor directly."

Key Takeaway

The Financial Fraudster exploits routine financial processes with fake urgency. Always verify payment requests, especially changes to account details — legitimacy is proven, not assumed.

Chapter 14: The Benevolent Guide

The Trap of Misplaced Help

You're lost at a conference, struggling to find a specific room when someone approaches. They smile warmly and say, "You look lost. I know where that room is — follow me." Relieved, you follow. Along the way, they ask questions about your role, team, or work. Harmless? Not really. You've just shared information with someone whose motives aren't as "helpful" as they seemed.

This is the **Benevolent Guide**—a tactic where manipulators use friendliness and helpfulness to gain trust. Unlike more aggressive approaches, this strategy exploits human goodwill, using a false sense of support to access information, systems, or spaces.

Social engineers know that when someone seems helpful, we're less likely to question their intentions. After all, who distrusts a good Samaritan?

How It Works

1. **Offering Assistance:** The manipulator approaches you, often at a moment of confusion, frustration, or need, offering to "help."
2. **Building Rapport:** They create trust through small talk, shared experiences, or casual questions to lower your defenses.
3. **Gaining Access or Information:** Under the guise of helping, they extract details, gain entry to restricted spaces, or establish themselves as "familiar" for future manipulations.

This strategy thrives in busy environments where people may feel rushed, stressed, or unfamiliar with their surroundings — offices, airports, events, or online platforms.

Real-Life Examples

1. **Event Impersonators:** At conferences, a scammer offers to "show you the way" but subtly probes for job details, credentials, or access.
2. **Online Helpers:** Someone in a chatroom or on social media offers to "guide" you through a problem (e.g., tech issues), tricking you into revealing passwords or installing malicious software.
3. **Fake Employees:** A friendly "colleague" helps a new employee access systems, convincing them to share logins or ignore security protocols.

Why It Works

Humans instinctively respond positively to kindness. This manipulation relies on three key factors:

1. **Goodwill Bias:** People feel grateful when someone helps them and are reluctant to question their motives.
2. **Lowered Defenses:** In moments of need or confusion, critical thinking is often replaced with relief and trust.
3. **Social Pressure:** Rejecting help can feel rude or ungrateful, leading victims to comply even when they're unsure.

How to Spot the Benevolent Guide

1. **Unsolicited Help:** Be cautious of strangers who offer help before you've asked for it — especially if they start probing for information.
2. **Overfriendly Behavior:** Manipulators often overextend friendliness to create quick trust.
3. **Subtle Questions:** Look out for small, probing questions about your role, team, or systems that seem unrelated to the help being offered.

Exercise: Recognize Unsolicited Help

1. Think of a time when someone offered unsolicited help. Did they ask questions that seemed unusual or unrelated? Write down two ways you could politely decline next time.

Role-Playing Drill:

- Partner up. One person plays the "benevolent guide" offering unsolicited help while subtly extracting details (e.g. "What's your role again?" or "Oh, so that's your login setup?").
- The other practices politely deflecting and verifying the person's legitimacy:
  o "Thank you, but I'll figure this out myself."
  o "What team are you with? Let me confirm this with my manager."

Key Takeaway

The Benevolent Guide manipulates trust under the guise of kindness. Stay polite but cautious of helpful offers, especially when they come unsolicited or lead to sharing information.

Chapter 15: The Legal Threat

You open your inbox to find a stern-looking email: **"Legal Notice: Immediate Payment Required to Avoid Lawsuit."** The message claims you've violated a copyright, owe unpaid taxes, or need to pay a fine to avoid prosecution. Panic sets in. To avoid trouble, you comply immediately.

This is the **Legal Threat** tactic where manipulators use fabricated legal claims to scare victims into quick action. Whether it's through fake fines, lawsuits, or "official warnings," the goal is to exploit fear and authority to coerce compliance.

How It Works

1. **Fabricated Claims:** Manipulators create false accusations (e.g. unpaid debts, copyright violations) to create panic.
2. **Official Tone and Language:** They use formal wording, fake legal jargon, and "official-looking" documents to appear credible.
3. **Immediate Consequences:** They emphasize urgency with threats of lawsuits, financial penalties, or even jail time to pressure victims into action.

This tactic is effective because few people want to challenge "legal" claims. They fear embarrassment, reputational damage, or financial harm.

Real-Life Examples

1. **Fake Copyright Notices:** Scammers send emails claiming you've used copyrighted content illegally and need to pay a fine.
2. **Tax Scams:** Fraudsters impersonate tax authorities, threatening penalties or arrests for "unpaid taxes."
3. **Debt Collection Fraud:** A fake legal firm claims you owe money and demands immediate payment to avoid a court case.

Why It Works

The Legal Threat manipulates three key emotions:
1. **Fear of Authority:** Legal consequences feel serious, and most people comply to avoid confrontation.
2. **Panic-Induced Compliance:** Urgent legal threats trigger quick, irrational decisions.
3. **Lack of Legal Knowledge:** Many people are unfamiliar with legal processes and assume the threat is real.

How to Spot the Legal Threat

1. **Unverified Sources:** Check the sender's email, phone number, or credentials. Official agencies rarely threaten action via email or phone.
2. **Urgent Tone:** Real legal warnings follow processes and timelines — scammers rush you into acting immediately.
3. **Unclear Details:** Fake legal claims often lack specifics, like case numbers or contact information for verification.

Exercise: Verify Legal Claims

1. Write down three steps to check any legal or financial claim (e.g. "Check the sender's official website, call the agency directly, and request written confirmation").
2. Practice applying these steps to a suspicious email or letter example.

Role-Playing Drill:

- Partner up. One person acts as the "legal threat," using vague claims or intimidating wording to pressure payment.
- The other practices staying calm and verifying the legitimacy:
  - "Please send me an official case reference so I can confirm with the agency."

Key Takeaway

The Legal Threat tactic relies on fear and intimidation. Stay calm, check claims through legitimate sources, and never let panic dictate your actions.

Chapter 16: The Medical Manipulator

Exploiting Health and Fear

Imagine receiving a call from someone claiming to be your doctor's office: "We noticed an issue with your recent medical test results. To resolve it, we need to confirm your personal details and insurance information." Concerned and eager to resolve the problem, you comply without hesitation. Hours later, you realize the call was a scam.

This is the **Medical Manipulator** tactic. Scammers impersonate medical professionals, healthcare organizations, or insurance providers to exploit your trust in the medical system. They use fear, urgency, or confusion about health to extract sensitive information, financial details, or even payments.

Health-related issues are personal and often stressful, which makes people particularly vulnerable to manipulation in this context.

How It Works

1. **Impersonation of Trustworthy Figures:** Scammers pose as doctors, medical staff, or health insurance agents to create legitimacy.
2. **Urgency and Fear:** They use phrases like "urgent test results," "insurance lapsing," or "unresolved medical bills" to incite fear and pressure victims into action.
3. **Request for Sensitive Information:** The manipulator asks for personal details such as Social Security numbers, medical records, payment information, or insurance credentials.

This tactic is particularly dangerous because health-related concerns often push people to comply out of fear for their well-being or finances.

Real-Life Examples

1. **Fake Test Results:** A scammer calls claiming there's a serious issue with your medical tests, asking for your date of birth, Social Security number, and payment to "resolve" the issue.
2. **Health Insurance Scams:** Fraudsters impersonate insurance providers, warning that your policy is expiring and demanding immediate payment to "reinstate" it.
3. **Medical Billing Fraud:** Someone posing as a hospital billing representative claims you owe money for a recent procedure and pressures you to pay immediately over the phone.

Why It Works

The Medical Manipulator tactic preys on three critical vulnerabilities:

1. **Fear for Health:** Health is deeply personal, and the fear of something being "wrong" overrides doubt.
2. **Trust in Medical Professionals:** Doctors and medical staff are trusted authority figures, so their requests rarely get questioned.
3. **Urgency in Health Matters:** Medical concerns often feel time-sensitive, leading people to act without confirming legitimacy.

Scammers take advantage of these emotions to manipulate victims into compliance.

How to Spot the Medical Manipulator

1. **Unsolicited Calls or Emails:** Be wary of unexpected messages about medical test results, bills, or insurance. Legitimate providers rarely reach out this way.
2. **Requests for Sensitive Details:** Genuine medical institutions already have your information and won't ask for Social Security numbers or payment details over the phone.
3. **Pressure to Act Immediately:** Scammers emphasize urgency, using fear tactics like "fines" or "cancellation of treatment" to discourage verification.

Exercise: Verify Medical Requests

1. Write down three questions to ask anyone who calls claiming to be from a medical office:
    - "What is your full name and position?"
    - "Can I call your office directly to confirm this?"
    - "What's the reference number for my case?"
2. Practice responding calmly to a fake "urgent" call scenario with a friend.

Self-Awareness Drill:

- Reflect on a time when you acted quickly out of fear or urgency regarding health or medical issues. Write down steps you can take next time before acting, such as contacting your doctor's office directly.

Key Takeaway

The Medical Manipulator tactic uses fear and trust to exploit your health concerns. Stay calm, verify requests directly with your healthcare provider, and never share sensitive information over unsolicited calls or emails.

Chapter 17: The Social Media Savior

The Illusion of Help Online

You're scrolling through social media when you notice a comment or message offering help: "Having trouble with your account? I can fix that for you—just send me your login details!" Grateful for the "assistance," you comply, only to realize later that your account has been hacked.

The **Social Media Savior** tactic is a method where scammers pose as helpful individuals or customer support representatives online. They exploit the trust and familiarity of social platforms to trick you into sharing sensitive information, granting access to accounts, or clicking malicious links.

In a digital world where problems arise daily — forgotten passwords, hacked accounts, or fake giveaways — this tactic preys on the desire for quick solutions.

How It Works

1. **Impersonating Help:** Scammers pose as official customer support, friends, or "tech-savvy" individuals offering help.
2. **Building Trust:** They message you directly, often using polite and friendly language to make you feel comfortable.
3. **Gaining Information or Access:** Under the guise of fixing a problem, they ask for login credentials, reset codes, or direct access to your device.

Real-Life Examples

1. **Fake Customer Support:** A scammer comments on your post about a locked social media account, claiming they can help—if you share your reset code.
2. **The "Helpful Friend":** Someone messages you, claiming they noticed suspicious activity on your account and offers to "fix" it.
3. **Malicious Links:** A "support representative" sends a link to a fake recovery site that steals your login details when entered.

Why It Works

The Social Media Savior manipulates two key emotions:

1. **Relief in Crisis:** When facing account problems, people seek quick solutions, making them vulnerable to fake helpers.
2. **Trust in Familiar Platforms:** Social media feels safe, and people rarely question the legitimacy of "helpful" comments or messages.

The scam works because it blends in — appearing supportive, trustworthy, and timely.

How to Spot the Social Media Savior

1. **Unsolicited Offers of Help:** Be wary of messages or comments offering assistance you didn't request.
2. **Requests for Login or Reset Codes:** Legitimate support teams never ask for passwords or reset information.
3. **Suspicious Links:** Hover over any link before clicking to confirm its authenticity.

Exercise: Spot the Fake Helper

1. Scroll through comments or messages on a social media platform. Look for examples of unsolicited "help" (e.g. fake customer support).
2. Write down three red flags you notice, such as vague profiles, suspicious links, or urgent requests for credentials.

Practice Response Drill:

- With a partner, role-play a scenario where one person poses as a "fake helper" offering to fix an account issue.
- The other practices responding:
  - "Thank you, but I'll contact the company directly through their official support page."

Key Takeaway

The Social Media Savior exploits your trust and urgency online. Always verify support requests through official channels and never share credentials or reset codes with anyone.

Chapter 18: The Customer Service Con

You receive a call or message: **"This is customer support. We've detected an issue with your account."** The voice is calm, professional, and reassuring. They walk you through "fixing" the problem — asking for passwords, login codes, or payment details to "verify your identity." Trusting the person, you comply, only to realize your account is now compromised.

This is the **Customer Service Con**, a tactic where scammers impersonate legitimate support teams to exploit trust and extract sensitive information. Whether it's for banks, streaming services, or e-commerce sites, these fraudsters capitalize on the assumption that customer service exists to help — not harm.

The scam thrives on two factors: the impersonator's professional demeanor and the target's urgency to resolve the issue quickly.

How It Works

1. **Professional Presentation:** Scammers use polished scripts, professional language, and fake call center environments to appear credible.
2. **Fake Problems:** They invent issues like suspicious account activity, billing failures, or subscription cancellations to create panic and urgency.
3. **Data Harvesting:** Under the pretense of "solving" the problem, they request sensitive details, such as passwords, PINs, card numbers, or multi-factor authentication codes.

Whether over the phone, email, or chat, their strategy is to seem so helpful and professional that you don't think twice about letting your guard down.

Real-Life Examples

1. **Bank Fraud Calls:** A scammer posing as your bank's support team calls about "suspicious withdrawals," asking you to confirm your account details.
2. **The Support Agent Scams:** You receive an unsolicited call claiming your computer has a virus. The "support agent" requests remote access to "fix it," but instead steals files.
3. **Subscription Scams:** A fake email claims your Netflix or Amazon subscription has been canceled due to payment failure, prompting you to "log in" through a malicious link.

Why It Works

The **Customer Service Con** exploits key psychological tendencies:

1. **Trust in Professionalism:** People instinctively trust calm, polite, and knowledgeable voices that resemble legitimate customer support.
2. **Urgency and Panic:** By creating fake problems, scammers push victims to act rather than question authenticity.
3. **Desire for Resolution:** When you hear there's an issue with your account, the immediate goal is to resolve it—not check the legitimacy of the source.

The more professional the impersonator seems, the more difficult it becomes to doubt them.

How to Spot the Customer Service Con

1. **Unsolicited Contact:** Legitimate companies rarely call or email you about issues you haven't reported yourself. Be wary of unexpected support outreach.
2. **Requests for Sensitive Details:** Real customer service teams never ask for passwords, PINs, or verification codes.
3. **High-Pressure Solutions:** Scammers often push for quick action, like clicking links or granting remote access to your devices.

Exercise: Test Customer Support Legitimacy

1. Write down two steps to verify a customer service request (e.g. "Call the official company support line" or "Check the company's website for ongoing issues").
2. Practice these steps with a partner simulating a fake support call asking for sensitive details.

Scenario Drill:
- Imagine receiving a call from "your bank's support team." Practice responding with verification steps like:
  - "Can I call you back through the official number on my card?"
  - "I'll log in through the official website instead of sharing details over the phone."

The Customer Service Con works by mimicking professionalism and urgency. Always check support claims directly through official service providers, and never share sensitive information during unsolicited calls or emails.

Chapter 19: The Policeman's Bluff

The Power of Intimidation

You receive a call: **"This is Officer Smith from your local police department. There's a warrant for your arrest due to unpaid fines. If you settle it now, we can avoid further action."** The voice is stern and authoritative, leaving you rattled. To avoid trouble, you comply — sending money or sharing personal details — only to later discover it was a scam.

This is the **Policeman's Bluff**, a tactic where scammers impersonate law enforcement or legal authorities to intimidate victims into compliance. They rely on fear, authority, and urgency to force quick action to avoid imagined consequences.

How It Works

1. **Authority Mimicry:** Scammers pretend to be police officers, government agents, or court officials, using formal language and intimidating tones.
2. **Threats and Consequences:** They invent urgent scenarios like unpaid fines, missed jury duty, or outstanding warrants to create panic.
3. **Immediate Payment Requests:** To "resolve" the issue, they ask for payment through wire transfers, or bank information.

This tactic works because most people fear legal trouble and feel pressured to comply when they believe an authority figure is involved.

Real-Life Examples

1. **Fake Arrest Warrants:** A scammer claims you have a warrant for unpaid traffic tickets and demands immediate payment to avoid arrest.
2. **IRS or Tax Fraud Calls:** Someone impersonating a government agent claims you owe back taxes, threatening legal action if you don't comply.
3. **Jury Duty Scams:** Fraudsters accuse victims of missing jury duty and request fines to avoid "legal penalties."

Why It Works

The Policeman's Bluff relies on three primary triggers:

1. **Authority Bias:** People are conditioned to respect and obey law enforcement without question.
2. **Fear of Consequences:** The threat of arrest, fines, or legal trouble creates panic and short-circuits logical thinking.
3. **Sense of Urgency:** Scammers emphasize immediate action to prevent victims from verifying their claims.

The fear of "getting in trouble" makes victims comply quickly to resolve the situation.

How to Spot the Policeman's Bluff

1. **Unusual Payment Requests:** Law enforcement agencies will never ask for payment through gift cards, wire transfers, or online links.
2. **Threats of Immediate Arrest:** Real authorities follow legal processes and timelines—not phone calls threatening instant action.
3. **Unverifiable Details:** Scammers often provide vague case numbers or refuse to let you confirm their claims with an official office.

Exercise: Verify Authority Claims

1. Write down three legitimate steps to verify contact from law enforcement (e.g. "Call your local police station directly" or "Request written documentation").
2. Practice applying these steps when presented with a fake scenario of a police or government call.

Role-Playing Drill:

- Partner with a friend. One person acts as the "fake officer" demanding payment.
- Practice staying calm and responding with verification steps:
    - "I'll contact my local police station to confirm this."
    - "Please send me a written notice to verify your claim."

The Policeman's Bluff exploits fear of authority to force compliance. Stay calm, verify any legal threats with official channels, and never send payments to resolve a claim you haven't confirmed.

Chapter 20: The Religious Mask

Exploiting Faith and Trust

Imagine someone approaches you outside a place of worship, asking for a donation for "the children's charity run by your local church." They seem devout, humble, and sincere. You hand over money without question, only to find out later that no such charity exists.

This is the **Religious Mask**, a tactic where scammers exploit faith, spirituality, or shared religious values to gain trust and manipulate individuals. By disguising themselves as fellow believers or representatives of religious causes, they tap into emotions such as compassion, trust, and generosity.

Religious institutions and charitable causes hold a sacred space in people's hearts. When someone speaks the "language of faith," people often lower their defenses, assuming sincerity. Social engineers exploit this trust to steal money, gain influence, or extract personal information.

How It Works

1. **Emotional Appeal:** Scammers use religious language, symbols, or affiliations to build trust quickly. They speak of noble causes, divine blessings, or urgent needs to gain sympathy.
2. **Shared Identity:** Manipulators position themselves as part of the same faith or community, creating an instant bond.
3. **Urgency and Guilt:** They emphasize the immediate "need for action" while suggesting that refusing to help is against one's faith or values.

The Religious Mask is especially effective during moments of vulnerability — after tragedies, during holidays, or in places where faith is deeply rooted.

Real-Life Examples

1. **Fake Charity Donations:** Scammers solicit donations for fake religious charities, often with fabricated stories of orphans, disaster relief, or community projects.
2. **Spiritual Manipulation:** A fraudster claims they can "bless" or "pray for" someone's problems—for a fee or in exchange for sensitive information.
3. **Impersonating Religious Leaders:** Scammers pose as trusted clergy members via phone, email, or social media, asking for money or personal information to help "someone in need."

Why It Works

The Religious Mask preys on three powerful emotional triggers:

1. **Trust in Shared Faith:** People instinctively trust those who seem to share their spiritual beliefs or values.
2. **Emotional Appeal:** Religion emphasizes compassion, charity, and helping others, making believers susceptible to manipulation through guilt or goodwill.
3. **Authority in Faith:** Fraudsters posing as religious leaders carry the perceived moral authority of their role, which few people question.

How to Spot the Religious Mask

1. **Unverified Charities:** If someone asks for a donation, verify the charity through official channels or websites before giving.
2. **Pressure to Give Immediately:** Genuine charities rarely request urgent action or suggest guilt for refusing to help.
3. **Unusual Requests from Leaders:** If a religious leader reaches out unexpectedly for money or personal details, confirm directly with them or their organization.

Exercise: Verify Charitable Claims

1. Write down two trusted ways to confirm a charity's legitimacy (e.g., searching official charity registries or contacting your place of worship).
2. Find three examples of religious charity scams online. Identify what red flags you notice, like lack of contact details or unverifiable claims.

Role-Playing Drill:

- Partner with a friend. One person plays the scammer asking for donations "on behalf of the church."
- The other practices responding:
  - "I'll confirm this with the church office first."
  - "Can you provide me with documentation about this charity?"

The Religious Mask exploits faith and compassion to manipulate trust. Verify charitable requests and be cautious when shared beliefs are mentioned — true sincerity welcomes verification.

Section II: Emotional Manipulation Tactics

Emotions drive human behavior. They fuel decisions, reactions, and trust, often without a second thought. Social engineers know this and use emotions as tools to bypass logic and critical thinking. Whether through fear, guilt, flattery, or sympathy, manipulators exploit feelings to make you act on impulse instead of reason.

Think of emotions as buttons on a control panel. Press the right one — panic, pride, or pity — and a person will follow instructions without questioning why. This section uncovers how emotional triggers are weaponized and teaches you to recognize when someone is pulling your strings.

By the end of this section, you'll be able to pause, analyze, and take control of your emotions before they control you.

Chapter 21: The Fear Trigger

The Power of Panic

You open an email that reads: **"Immediate Action Required! Your account has been compromised. Log in now to secure it."** Your heart races, and panic sets in. Without hesitation, you click the link and enter your credentials. Moments later, you realize the email was fake — and you've just handed over your account to a scammer.

This is the **Fear Trigger**, a tactic where social engineers use panic and anxiety to cloud your judgment. By creating fear — whether it's about security breaches, financial losses, or threats of legal trouble — they force you into making quick, irrational decisions.

Fear short-circuits logical thinking. When people are scared, their priority becomes resolving the immediate "threat," often without stopping to verify its legitimacy.

How It Works

1. **Creating a Threat:** Scammers fabricate scenarios that cause fear, like hacked accounts, stolen data, or unpaid fines.
2. **Pressuring Immediate Action:** They emphasize urgency, warning of severe consequences if you don't act quickly.
3. **Providing a "Solution":** The manipulator offers a fake fix, like clicking a malicious link, calling a fraudulent hotline, or sharing sensitive details to "resolve" the issue.

Real-Life Examples

1. **Fake Security Alerts:** Emails claiming your bank account or social media has been hacked, with a link to "reset your password".
2. **Threatening Phone Calls:** A scammer calls pretending to be from the IRS or a debt collector, threatening arrest if you don't pay immediately.
3. **Pop-Up Warnings:** A fake computer pop-up warns of a virus and instructs you to call a bogus number for assistance — leading to a scammer who steals your data.

Why It Works

The Fear Trigger exploits natural human responses to threats:
1. **Fight or Flight Instinct:** Fear triggers a sense of urgency, overriding rational thought in favor of immediate action.
2. **Avoidance of Consequences:** People take swift action to avoid perceived risks, such as financial loss, data theft, or legal penalties.
3. **Blind Trust in Solutions:** Scammers present themselves as the "fix" to the problem they created, leading victims to comply without verifying.

How to Spot the Fear Trigger

1. **Urgent Warnings:** Be careful of messages or calls that use fear or demand immediate action. Real organizations rarely communicate threats this way.
2. **Unusual Solutions:** Legitimate companies don't require you to click strange links, call unknown numbers, or share sensitive details to resolve issues.
3. **Verify Independently:** Pause and confirm the situation directly with the institution mentioned (e.g., your bank or government agency).

1. Write down three steps to take when you receive a panic-inducing message (e.g. "Pause, verify through trusted channels, avoid immediate action").
2. Practice applying these steps to a fake security alert email with a partner.

Self-Awareness Drill:

- Reflect on a time when fear made you do something irrational (e.g. clicking a suspicious email). Write down one question you can ask yourself next time: "Is this real, or am I being manipulated?"

Key Takeaway

The Fear Trigger preys on panic and urgency to override logical thinking. Always pause, verify threats through trusted sources, and never let fear push you into immediate, unverified action.

Chapter 22: The Sympathy Card

When Sympathy Is Used Against You

A stranger approaches you outside a store, appearing disheveled and distressed. "My wallet was stolen," they say, "and I just need $20 to get home. I swear I'll pay you back." Your heart goes out to them, and you hand over the cash. But days later, you realize the story didn't add up.

This is the **Sympathy Card**, a manipulation tactic where fraudsters use emotional stories of hardship, illness, or loss to exploit your kindness and generosity. Whether it's online, on the phone, or in person, they aim to provoke your sympathy and lower your defenses.

While genuine hardship exists, manipulators weaponize empathy to gain money, information, or access.

How It Works

1. **Crafting a Sob Story:** Manipulators share emotional, often exaggerated, stories about suffering or need.
2. **Earning Trust Through Vulnerability:** They act open, vulnerable, and sincere, making it harder for you to question their honesty.
3. **Request for Help:** They ask for small but immediate assistance—money, personal details, or a favor that escalates later.

The sympathy card works because it exploits compassion and the human desire to "do good."

Real-Life Examples

1. **Street Scams:** A person claims to be stranded or in crisis, asking for money to get home.
2. **Online Fundraising Scams:** Fraudulent crowdfunding campaigns use fake photos and emotional stories to solicit donations.
3. **Fake Illness Appeals:** Scammers claim they or a loved one are sick, asking for money to cover medical expenses.

Why It Works

The Sympathy Card relies on three psychological triggers:

1. **Empathy and Compassion:** People want to help others in pain or distress, especially when they're made to feel they can "make a difference."
2. **Trust in Vulnerability:** Vulnerable behavior feels honest, so people are less likely to doubt it.
3. **Social Pressure:** Saying "no" to someone suffering feels uncomfortable and unkind, pushing you into compliance.

How to Spot the Sympathy Card

1. **Inconsistent Details:** Emotional stories are often vague or exaggerated—look for details that don't add up.
2. **Immediate Requests:** Be cautious when someone asks for quick assistance without offering ways to verify their story.
3. **Overly Emotional Appeals:** If a request seems designed solely to pull at your heartstrings, pause and assess its legitimacy.

Exercise: Question Emotional Appeals

1. Think of a time someone shared an emotional story to gain your help. Reflect on whether you verified their claim. Write down two ways to check emotional requests, like asking for specifics or suggesting alternative help.

Role-Playing Drill:

- Partner up. One person tells an emotional story to gain assistance. The other practices responding kindly but cautiously:
  - "I'm sorry to hear that. Let me check if there's another way to help."
  - "Can you provide more information so I can confirm your story?"

The Sympathy Card manipulates your kindness with emotional stories. Compassion is valuable, but don't let it override caution — verify before you act, and remember that genuine requests can stand up to scrutiny.

Chapter 23: The Guilt Lever

How Guilt Becomes a Weapon

Imagine this: A co-worker comes to you, looking desperate. They say, "If you don't help me with this login, I'll lose my job. Please, my family depends on me." It's not your responsibility, but guilt creeps in. You share the details because you feel obligated. Later, you realize you were manipulated.

This is the **Guilt Lever**, a strategy where social engineers use guilt to force compliance. By framing themselves as victims or implying that your refusal will harm someone, they exploit your desire to do the "right thing" or avoid being seen as unkind.

Humans naturally want to help others and avoid causing harm. Manipulators twist this instinct, using guilt to bypass rational thought and make you act against your better judgment.

How It Works

1. **Playing the Victim:** The manipulator presents themselves as someone struggling, wronged, or in dire need of help.
2. **Creating Emotional Obligation:** They make you feel responsible for their situation, subtly implying that refusing to help makes you a bad person.
3. **Reinforcing Consequences:** They emphasize what might happen if you don't comply — lost jobs, broken relationships, or other dramatic fallout.

The Guilt Lever thrives because humans hate the feeling of letting someone down, even when the guilt is undeserved.

Real-Life Examples

1. **The Colleague in Crisis:** A "co-worker" or stranger claims they need a favor — such as access to files or logins — to avoid catastrophic consequences.
2. **Charity Scams:** Scammers ask for money, telling exaggerated stories about suffering children, families, or animals, leaving you feeling heartless if you decline.
3. **Fake Family Emergencies:** Someone posing as a distant relative messages you, claiming they're in trouble and need money immediately.

Why It Works

The Guilt Lever manipulates three emotional triggers:
1. **Avoiding Shame:** Refusing to help makes you feel selfish, unkind, or uncaring.
2. **Desire to Do Good:** Most people want to help those in need, especially when they're made to feel uniquely able to help.
3. **Fear of Consequences:** By framing the request as urgent and dramatic, manipulators make you feel personally responsible for the fallout.

In these moments, guilt overwhelms logic, making it harder to say no.

How to Spot the Guilt Lever

1. **Excessive Emotional Appeal:** Be wary of stories or pleas that seem exaggerated, overly dramatic, or designed to provoke an emotional response.
2. **Personal Responsibility Claims:** Watch for phrases like, "You're my last hope," or "Without you, I don't know what I'll do."
3. **Immediate Consequences:** If someone uses urgency to pressure you, pause and evaluate the legitimacy of their claim.

Exercise: Recognize Guilt Traps

1. Reflect on a situation where you felt guilty into compliance. Was it justified? Write down three signs you overlooked that the guilt was manipulative.
2. Practice saying "no" to unreasonable emotional requests by responding with:
   - "I'm sorry, but I can't help with that right now."
   - "Let me confirm the situation first."

Role-Playing Drill:

- Partner with someone. One person plays the manipulator, exaggerating a crisis to invoke guilt. The other practices staying calm and saying "no" firmly but kindly.

The Guilt Lever manipulates your desire to help others by creating false responsibility. Don't let guilt cloud your logic. Pause, evaluate the situation, and remember that saying "no" doesn't make you unkind.

Chapter 24: The Flattery Trap

How Compliments Turn into Traps

Imagine a stranger emails you: "You're so talented! Your work is exactly what we need for our next big project." They continue to praise your skills and intelligence, offering a "special" opportunity. Flattered, you're eager to say yes. Without realizing it, you've just handed over sensitive details or money for a scam that never existed.

This is the **Flattery Trap**, a tactic where manipulators use excessive praise to gain your trust. Compliments lower defenses by appealing to your ego, making you more likely to comply with requests or ignore red flags.

Flattery isn't inherently bad, but when it's used as a weapon, it clouds judgment and encourages impulsive decisions.

How It Works

1. **Over-the-Top Praise:** Manipulators use exaggerated compliments to make you feel special, admired, or indispensable.
2. **Lowering Defenses:** Flattery feels good. It creates a bond of trust, distracting you from asking critical questions or spotting inconsistencies.
3. **The Favor Request:** Once trust is established, the manipulator leverages your good mood and ego to make a request—whether it's information, access, or money.

The Flattery Trap thrives because humans are naturally drawn to positive reinforcement and validation, especially when it seems to come from credible or influential people.

Real-Life Examples

1. **Phony Job Offers:** Scammers compliment your "unique skills" or "amazing portfolio" to entice you into sharing personal details or paying fees for a fake job opportunity.
2. **Social Media Manipulation:** A stranger praises your photos or posts, eventually steering the conversation to requests for personal information or financial help.
3. **Fake Business Proposals:** Fraudsters flatter professionals with promises of partnerships or contracts, only to extract money or proprietary information.

Why It Works

The Flattery Trap exploits the following emotional triggers:

1. **Ego Boost:** Compliments feel good and create a sense of connection, making you less critical of the person's intentions.
2. **Desire for Recognition:** People crave validation, especially for their talents, work, or personality. Flattery fulfills this need.
3. **Reciprocity Effect:** Praise creates a subtle sense of obligation, making you more likely to "return the favor" by complying with requests.

When someone praises you, it feels awkward to question or reject them. Manipulators know this and use it to their advantage.

How to Spot the Flattery Trap

1. **Excessive Praise:** Genuine compliments are specific and balanced. Be wary of flattery that feels too over-the-top.
2. **Rapid Trust-Building:** If compliments are quickly followed by requests for favors, money, or access, pause and evaluate their intentions.
3. **Unfamiliar Sources:** Compliments from strangers or people you've never interacted with often signal manipulation, not sincerity.

Exercise: Recognize Over-the-Top Flattery

1. Think of a time someone complimented you excessively before making a request. Write down the red flags you missed.
2. List two questions you can ask yourself when faced with sudden flattery:
    o "What does this person want from me?"
    o "Does this praise feel genuine or strategic?"

Role-Playing Drill:

- Partner with a friend. One person plays the manipulator, showering compliments before making a request (e.g. "You're the best at this — can I borrow your login?").

- Practice responding with polite feedback, such as:
  - "I appreciate the compliment, but let's talk details first."

Key Takeaway

The Flattery Trap works by using excessive praise to lower your guard and manipulate trust. Enjoy genuine compliments, but stay alert when flattery feels over-the-top, especially if it's tied to a favor or request.

Chapter 25: The Greed Ploy

The Allure of Wealth

Imagine this: An email lands in your inbox claiming you've won a $1,000,000 lottery prize. The catch? You need to pay a small "processing fee" to claim it. Excited by the idea of instant wealth, you transfer the money without hesitation. Days later, you realize you've been scammed — the lottery didn't exist, and your money is gone.

This is the **Greed Ploy**, a manipulation tactic that preys on the natural human desire for wealth or rewards. Manipulators promise something extravagant and use that excitement to lure targets into giving up money, personal details, or access.

Social engineers exploit this emotional response to encourage impulsive decisions.

How It Works

1. **The Bait:** Scammers craft an irresistible reward, such as a lottery prize or a luxury giveaway.
2. **A Small "Requirement":** To claim the reward, the victim must take an action, such as paying a fee, sharing banking details, or signing a contract.
3. **The Hook:** Once the victim complies, the manipulator either disappears or continues to pressure them for more.

The Greed Ploy is especially effective because the promise of a reward overwhelms logical thinking. Victims focus on what they'll gain, not what they might lose.

Real-Life Examples

1. **Lottery Scams:** Fraudsters claim you've won a foreign lottery but require payment of a "processing fee" or taxes before you can collect your winnings.
2. **Bogus Investment Opportunities:** Manipulators promote fake schemes with impossibly high returns, luring victims into depositing money into fraudulent accounts.
3. **Social Media Giveaways:** Scammers post fake contests promising luxury prizes, requiring participants to provide personal information or pay a small fee to "enter."

Why It Works

The Greed Ploy thrives on three psychological triggers:

1. **Desire for Easy Gains:** The promise of wealth without significant effort is alluring and hard to resist.
2. **Fear of Losing Out on a Deal:** Manipulators create urgency, warning victims that the opportunity will vanish if they don't act immediately.
3. **Emotional Excitement:** The idea of winning or gaining something valuable triggers excitement, which suppresses critical thinking.

The scam works because it taps into a natural reaction: Why pass up free money or rewards?

How to Spot the Greed Ploy

1. **Too-Good-to-Be-True Offers:** Be wary of promises of wealth, high returns, or prizes that seem unrealistic or overly generous.
2. **Upfront Fees or Requirements:** Legitimate opportunities rarely require payment to claim rewards or access offers.
3. **Vague or Missing Details:** Scammers often avoid providing specifics about the reward or process, relying on excitement to obscure the lack of legitimacy.

Exercise: Test the Promise

1. Reflect on any tempting offers you've encountered—what made them appealing? Write down three red flags, such as unrealistic promises, missing verification steps, or upfront payment demands.
2. Practice responding to a fake offer by asking:
   - "Can you provide documentation proving this is legitimate?"
   - "Why do I need to pay to claim this reward?"

- Partner with someone. One person plays the manipulator offering a fake prize. The other practices spotting inconsistencies and asking clarifying questions to uncover the scam.

Key Takeaway

The Greed Ploy uses the allure of riches and rewards to cloud judgment. Stay cautious when faced with offers that seem too good to be true, and remember: real opportunities don't come with strings attached.

Chapter 26: The Pride Bull's Eye

When Ego Becomes a Target

"You've been selected for our members-only program! Only the top 1% of candidates qualify." Flattered, you eagerly sign up—providing your personal details and paying a registration fee. Later, you discover the program doesn't exist, and your ego has been used against you.

This is the **Pride Bull's Eye**, a tactic where manipulators target your ego to make you feel special, chosen, or superior. By boosting your sense of importance, they lower your defenses and push you into decisions that you wouldn't make under normal circumstances.

Everyone enjoys feeling valued, especially when recognition seems earned. Social engineers exploit this universal desire for validation to manipulate trust and encourage compliance.

How It Works

1. **Flattering the Target:** Manipulators use language like "you're exceptional," "only you qualify," or "you've been specially chosen" to appeal to the victim's ego.
2. **Creating Exclusivity:** They frame the opportunity as limited, making it feel prestigious and hard to refuse.
3. **The Ask:** Once the victim is interested, the manipulator requests payment, personal information, or compliance as part of "accepting" the offer.

The Pride Bull's Eye works because people naturally want to believe they are unique, talented, or deserving of special recognition.

Real-Life Examples

1. **Fake Awards or Honors:** Scammers inform you that you've won a prestigious award but require a fee to process the recognition.
2. **Elite Job Offers:** Fraudsters offer fake leadership roles, claiming your skills are uniquely suited, and ask for your personal details or upfront fees.
3. **Invite-only Memberships:** Manipulators invite you to join groups or programs, charging steep fees for access to non-existent benefits.

Why It Works

The Pride Bull's Eye exploits three emotional drivers:

1. **Validation:** Compliments and recognition feel good, making people eager to believe and act.
2. **Fear of Missing Out:** Once the opportunity feels rare or limited, targets fear losing it by hesitating or questioning the offer.
3. **Trust in Praise:** Flattery makes victims less likely to notice red flags or inconsistencies.

The manipulator's goal is to build so much trust and excitement that the target forgets to verify the legitimacy of the offer.

How to Spot the Pride Bull's Eye

1. **Excessive Flattery:** Be cautious of compliments or recognition that feel over-the-top or unsolicited.
2. **Triggering Language:** Phrases like "only for you" or "top 1%" are often designed to trigger ego, not genuine exclusivity.
3. **Upfront Costs or Personal Information:** Legitimate honors or memberships don't require payments or sensitive details to accept.

Exercise: Test the Praise

1. Write down a situation where you were flattered into accepting an offer. Did you verify its authenticity?
2. Practice identifying red flags by asking:
   o "What makes me uniquely qualified for this?"
   o "Can I verify this opportunity through a trusted source?"

- Partner with someone. One person plays the manipulator offering a flattering opportunity. The other practices responding politely:
  - "Thank you, but I'd like more details before proceeding."

Key Takeaway

The Pride Bull's Eye targets your ego to manipulate trust. Enjoy recognition, but always verify the source and remember: true exclusivity doesn't come with pressure or hidden costs.

Chapter 27: The Hope Hoax

The Trap of False Hope

Imagine you're job hunting, and an email arrives with the subject line: "We've reviewed your application, and you're an ideal candidate!" Excited, you respond. The "employer" asks for personal details or a processing fee to proceed. You comply, thinking you're about to secure your dream role—only to realize there was never a job in the first place.

This is the **Hope Hoax**, a manipulation tactic where fraudsters offer false hope, like fake jobs, scholarships, or opportunities, to exploit vulnerability. By dangling the promise of something better, manipulators gain trust and compliance.

How It Works

1. **Identify a Desire or Need:** Manipulators target individuals seeking opportunities, like employment, financial aid, or a better future.
2. **Offer the Perfect Solution:** They present an opportunity that aligns exactly with the target's goals, often through fake emails, ads, or messages.
3. **Ask for a Commitment:** Fraudsters request an action—sharing personal information, paying a fee, or signing a contract—before disappearing.

The Hope Hoax works because it preys on optimism and the desire to improve one's situation, making victims more willing to overlook red flags.

Real-Life Examples

1. **Fake Job Offers:** Scammers post listings for high-paying jobs, asking for application fees or personal details like Social Security numbers.
2. **Scholarship Scams:** Fraudsters promise financial aid or grants, requiring victims to pay upfront "processing fees."
3. **Pyramid Schemes:** Manipulators offer "can't-miss" opportunities with guaranteed high returns, stealing funds from hopeful individuals.

Why It Works

The Hope Hoax preys on three key emotions:

1. **Optimism:** Targets focus on the potential rewards, not the risks.
2. **Urgency:** Fraudsters create pressure, warning victims that the opportunity will vanish without immediate action.
3. **Validation:** Victims feel seen and valued when offered a "special opportunity," lowering their defenses.

How to Spot the Hope Hoax

1. **Too Perfect to Be True:** Be cautious of offers that match your goals exactly, especially if unsolicited.
2. **Upfront Costs or Fees:** Genuine opportunities rarely require payments or personal details upfront.
3. **Vague Details:** Fraudsters often avoid specifics, providing just enough information to seem legitimate while discouraging verification.

Exercise: Test the Opportunity

1. Write down three questions you should ask about any opportunity, like:
   - "Is this coming from a verified source?"
   - "Why is this being offered to me specifically?"
   - "Can I confirm this independently?"

Role-Playing Drill:

- Partner with someone. One person acts as the manipulator offering a fake job or scholarship. The other practices verifying the offer by asking clarifying questions and spotting inconsistencies.

The Hope Hoax uses false promises to exploit optimism. Verify every opportunity, and remember that true rewards come with transparency, not pressure.

Chapter 28: The Panic Button

The Art of Manufactured Chaos

You receive a text message: "Your bank account has been locked due to suspicious activity. Click here to secure your funds!" Panicked, you tap the link and enter your login details to resolve the issue. Moments later, your account is drained.

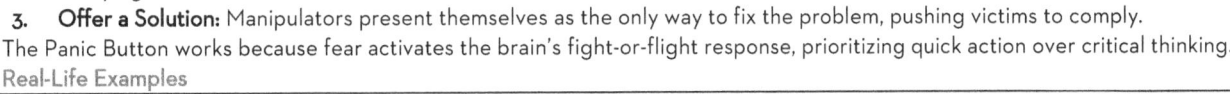

This is the **Panic Button**, a manipulation tactic where social engineers create fake crises to override logical thinking. By inducing fear and urgency, they force targets to act without verifying the situation.

How It Works

1. **Invent a Crisis:** Fraudsters create scenarios that trigger fear, like account breaches, unpaid fines, or safety threats.
2. **Demand Immediate Action:** They emphasize urgency to prevent victims from pausing or verifying.
3. **Offer a Solution:** Manipulators present themselves as the only way to fix the problem, pushing victims to comply.

The Panic Button works because fear activates the brain's fight-or-flight response, prioritizing quick action over critical thinking.

Real-Life Examples

1. **Fake Security Alerts:** Fraudsters send messages claiming your email or bank account has been compromised, tricking you into sharing credentials.
2. **IRS Scams:** Callers pretend to be tax authorities, threatening arrest or fines unless immediate payment is made.
3. **Emergency Phone Calls:** Scammers pose as relatives in danger, pressuring you to wire money urgently.

Why It Works

The Panic Button leverages three psychological triggers:

1. **Fear of Loss:** Victims worry about losing money, access, or safety.
2. **Time Pressure:** Urgency discourages verification or second-guessing.
3. **Trust in Solutions:** Manipulators position themselves as helpers, increasing compliance.

How to Spot the Panic Button

1. **Unverified Crises:** Be careful of replying to urgent messages about problems you didn't initiate or verify.
2. **Requests for Sensitive Details:** Legitimate organizations rarely ask for passwords, PINs, or immediate payments.
3. **Emotionally Charged Language:** Phrases like "Act Now!" or "Immediate Action Required!" are red flags.

Exercise: Pause Before Reacting

1. Write down three steps to take when you receive a crisis alert:
   - "Pause and take a deep breath."
   - "Verify the claim through official channels."
   - "Avoid clicking links or sharing details immediately."

Role-Playing Drill:

- Partner with someone. One person creates a fake crisis (e.g., "Your account has been hacked!"), while the other practices pausing, verifying, and responding calmly.

Key Takeaway

The Panic Button uses fear as a weapon. Always pause, verify the claim, and remember that real emergencies rarely require rash decisions.

Chapter 29: The Shame Shove

How Shame Becomes a Weapon

Imagine a colleague sends you an email: "I can't believe you didn't respond to my earlier request — it's so unlike you to leave things hanging!" Embarrassed, you immediately prioritize their task, even though you were unsure of its legitimacy. Later, you realize the email wasn't from your colleague — it was a scammer impersonating them, weaponizing your fear of looking unreliable.

This is the **Shame Shove**, a social engineering tactic where manipulators use embarrassment, guilt, or the fear of judgment to push you into acting. By attacking your sense of self or implying that others are watching, they make you comply to avoid further discomfort.

How It Works

1. **Targeting Self-Image:** The manipulator highlights something you "should" feel bad about, like forgetting a task or failing to respond.
2. **Implying Judgment:** They suggest that others are aware of your mistake, creating a sense of public scrutiny.
3. **Demanding Action:** They present a way to "fix" the situation, pushing you to comply quickly to restore your reputation.

The Shame Shove thrives in environments where people are eager to maintain good standing, such as workplaces, social groups, or online communities.

Real-Life Examples

1. **Impersonating Colleagues:** A scammer pretends to be your boss or co-worker, chastising you for not responding to an email and urging you to act immediately.
2. **Social Media Scams:** Fraudsters send messages like, "Your account has been flagged for inappropriate behavior—click here to avoid further embarrassment."
3. **Public Shaming Threats:** Scammers threaten to expose fabricated mistakes or secrets unless you comply with their demands.

Why It Works

The Shame Shove preys on three key emotions:

1. **Fear of Social Judgment:** People fear looking bad in front of peers, colleagues, or the public.
2. **Desire to Repair Reputation:** Shame motivates quick action to avoid further damage to self-image.
3. **Emotional Overload:** Manipulators create discomfort so intense that victims act fast to escape it.

This tactic works because the manipulator controls the narrative — whether or not the shame is justified, the target feels compelled to act.

How to Spot the Shame Shove

1. **Unverified Claims of Mistakes:** Be cautious of accusations or criticisms that seem out of character or unsubstantiated.
2. **Pressure to Comply:** Manipulators push for immediate action to prevent you from verifying the claim or calming your emotions.
3. **Focus on Reputation:** If the emphasis is on how you'll "look bad" rather than the substance of the issue, it's likely manipulation.

Exercise: Resist the Shame

1. Write down a recent situation where you felt pressured to act out of embarrassment. Reflect on whether the criticism was legitimate or manipulative.
2. Practice responding to shaming tactics with calm, clarifying questions like:
   - "Can you provide more details about the issue?"
   - "I'd like to confirm this before taking action."

Role-Playing Drill:

- Partner with someone. One person plays the manipulator, using shaming language to push compliance (e.g. "You've really let everyone down—fix this now!"). The other practices staying calm, verifying facts, and avoiding reactive decisions.

Key Takeaway

The Shame Shove uses embarrassment to override your logic and push compliance. So, remember: real accountability doesn't rely on emotional manipulation.

Chapter 30: The Empathy Bomb

The Overload of Emotion

You're scrolling through social media and come across a heart-breaking story: a family is losing their home, and they need urgent donations to keep it. Touched by the pictures and personal details, you send money immediately. Later, you find out the fundraiser was fake, and the story was a lie.

This is the **Empathy Bomb**, a tactic where manipulators overwhelm you with emotionally charged stories. By appealing to your compassion, they push you into acting impulsively —usually by donating money, sharing information, or granting access.

Empathy is a powerful human trait, but it also makes us vulnerable. When emotions take over, critical thinking takes a backseat, and manipulators exploit this to their advantage.

How It Works

1. **Crafting an Emotional Story:** The manipulator creates a compelling narrative designed to provoke sympathy or outrage.
2. **Adding Visual and Personal Touches:** They include pictures, videos, or detailed accounts to make the story feel authentic and relatable.
3. **Requesting Action:** They encourage immediate responses, like donations, information sharing, or account access, while emotions are running high.

The Empathy Bomb is especially effective in digital spaces, where visuals and stories can go viral, reaching large audiences quickly.

Real-Life Examples

1. **Fake Crowdfunding Campaigns:** Scammers create fraudulent fundraisers for fictitious victims or events, stealing money from well-meaning donors.
2. **Charity Impersonation:** Fraudsters pose as legitimate charities, using emotional appeals to solicit donations.
3. **Leveraging Emotion:** Emails with tragic stories prompt you to click links or share information to "help."

Why It Works

The Empathy Bomb exploits three psychological drivers:

1. **Compassion Fatigue:** Overexposure to emotional stories can lead to rushed actions, as victims feel pressured to help.
2. **Fear of Regret:** People will quickly make certain decisions to avoid the guilt of not helping when they could.
3. **Trust in Emotionally Charged Situations:** Emotional stories feel authentic, making victims less likely to question their legitimacy.

How to Spot the Empathy Bomb

1. **Overly Emotional Appeals:** Be cautious of stories that rely solely on tugging at your heartstrings without providing verifiable details.
2. **Urgent Requests:** Emotional manipulation often comes with immediate deadlines to prevent verification.
3. **Lack of Transparency:** Genuine organizations provide clear, traceable information about their causes and fund allocation.

Exercise: Verify Emotional Appeals

1. Reflect on a time when an emotional story influenced your actions. Did you verify the claim before responding?
2. Write down two steps to confirm legitimacy in the future, like:
   - "Research the organization or individual through trusted sources."
   - "Pause and wait 24 hours before responding."

Role-Playing Drill:

- Partner with someone. One person plays the manipulator, sharing a fake emotional story. The other practices responding with calm questions and verifying details before acting.

Key Takeaway

The Empathy Bomb overwhelms your emotions and can potentially limit logical thinking. Pause, verify the story, and remember: genuine causes welcome transparency and patience.

Chapter 31: The Anger Catalyst

How Anger Clouds Judgment

Picture this: You receive an email claiming that a company you trust has been overcharging you for years. Enraged, you click the provided link to "file a formal complaint." The page asks for your account details to "confirm your eligibility for a refund." Without hesitation, you enter the information. Minutes later, you realize you've been scammed. The company never overcharged you, and the fraudster now has your account credentials.

This is the **Anger Catalyst**, a manipulation tactic that uses outrage to overwhelm rational thinking. By provoking anger, social engineers redirect your focus to an emotional reaction, making you act impulsively rather than pausing to assess the situation critically.

How It Works

1. **Triggering Outrage:** The manipulator presents a scenario designed to provoke anger, such as injustice, unfair treatment, or betrayal.
2. **Redirecting Focus:** They make the victim so consumed with their emotional reaction that they fail to notice red flags.
3. **Encouraging Immediate Action:** The manipulator positions themselves as a solution or ally, prompting the victim to take steps like clicking a link, sharing information, or making payments.

The Anger Catalyst thrives in situations where trust has already been eroded, such as customer complaints, political discussions, or disputes.

Real-Life Examples

1. **Fake Overcharge Alerts:** Scammers claim a company has wrongfully billed you, directing you to a fraudulent site to "resolve" the issue.
2. **Outrage Campaigns:** Fraudsters post inflammatory news articles or social media posts to drive clicks, collecting data or spreading harmful files.
3. **Scam Disputes:** Fraudsters pose as mediators in disputes, gaining personal information by pretending to help victims fight back.

Why It Works

The Anger Catalyst manipulates three core human tendencies:
1. **The Need to Act:** Anger demands immediate action to address perceived wrongs, often leading to hasty decisions.
2. **Focus on the Offense:** When people are angry, their attention narrows to the source of their outrage, ignoring other details.
3. **Erosion of Critical Thinking:** Emotional intensity disrupts rational evaluation of the situation, making manipulative claims seem more credible.

Manipulators thrive on the fact that, in moments of anger, people prioritize emotional release over careful consideration.

How to Spot the Anger Catalyst

1. **Highly Emotional Messages:** Be cautious of emails, calls, or posts designed to incite outrage, especially when paired with immediate calls to action.
2. **One-Sided Information:** Anger-based tactics often focus solely on fueling your emotion without providing balanced or verifiable details.
3. **Pressure to Act Fast:** Claims like "You must act now to fix this injustice!" are often signs of manipulation.

Exercise: Pause in the Face of Anger

1. Reflect on a time when anger influenced your decisions. Write down two ways the situation could have been approached calmly.
2. Practice responding to inflammatory statements with clarifying questions like:
   o "Can you provide proof of this claim?"
   o "What steps can I take to confirm this before reacting?"

Role-Playing Drill:

- Partner with someone. One person plays the manipulator, presenting an outrageous scenario to provoke anger. The other practices staying calm and asking logical questions to regain focus.

The Anger Catalyst thrives on your emotional reaction to drive split decisions. Stay calm, verify claims, and remember: clear thinking, not anger, leads to the best solutions.

Chapter 32: The Nostalgia Smokescreen

The Power of Familiarity and Comfort

You get a call: "Remember the good old days in high school? This is Alex from your class! We're organizing a reunion and need some help reaching out." Nostalgic, you agree to share your contact list and even pay a small fee for the event. Days later, you realize there is no reunion — Alex wasn't who they claimed to be.

This is the **Nostalgia Smokescreen**, a manipulation tactic that uses fond memories and shared experiences to create trust. By evoking positive feelings from the past, manipulators create a sense of familiarity and safety, making their requests seem harmless.

How It Works

1. **Evoke Nostalgia:** The manipulator references shared experiences, trends, or items from the past that evoke positive emotions.
2. **Build a Connection:** By associating themselves with these memories, they position themselves as someone trustworthy or familiar.
3. **Make Requests:** They take advantage of the positive mood they've created.

The Nostalgia Smokescreen is particularly effective because it leverages emotions tied to the past, which are often deeply personal and comforting.

Real-Life Examples

1. **Fake Reunions:** Fraudsters pretend to be old classmates, soliciting money or information for a non-existent event.
2. **Retro Trends Scams:** Manipulators sell fake memorabilia or collect deposits for nostalgic items that are never delivered.
3. **Old-Friend Impersonation:** Scammers pose as long-lost friends, using familiarity to gain trust and ask for favors.

Why It Works

The Nostalgia Smokescreen leverages three core principles:

1. **Emotional Warmth:** Nostalgia creates positive emotions, reducing doubt.
2. **Trust Through Familiarity:** Shared memories or experiences make manipulators seem credible and safe.
3. **Focus on the Past:** Recalling memories shifts attention away from evaluating the present situation critically.

People are naturally drawn to the comfort of familiarity, which manipulators use as an entry point for their schemes.

How to Spot the Nostalgia Smokescreen

1. **Unverified Familiarity:** Be wary of messages or calls referencing shared memories that seem vague or inconsistent.
2. **Requests for Information:** Nostalgia-based tactics often lead to demands for personal details or money under the guise of reconnecting.
3. **Out-of-the-Blue Contact:** Fraudsters often initiate contact unexpectedly, counting on your surprise and positive emotions to override logical thinking.

Exercise: Question Familiarity

1. Think of a time when someone referenced your past to gain your trust. Were their claims legitimate? Write down two ways to verify such connections in the future, like asking for specific details or reaching out to a mutual contact.

Role-Playing Drill:

- Partner with someone. One person acts as a manipulator referencing a nostalgic memory. The other practices asking clarifying questions and confirming details before taking action.

Key Takeaway

The Nostalgia Smokescreen taps into fond memories to lower defenses. Always verify who you're dealing with before acting.

Chapter 33: The Curiosity Click

How Curiosity Becomes a Trap

You're browsing your inbox when a subject line catches your eye: **"Confidential Information Leaked!"** Without thinking, you click it, curious to know more. The link redirects to a suspicious page. Minutes later, your email account is compromised.

This is the **Curiosity Click**, a tactic where manipulators exploit human curiosity to encourage risky behavior. By presenting an intriguing, incomplete, or mysterious scenario, they push victims to engage before they've fully thought things through.

Curiosity drives exploration and discovery, but in the wrong hands, it can be weaponized to lead people into traps.

How It Works

1. **Create Intrigue:** Manipulators craft vague or surprising messages that spark curiosity, such as enticing subject lines, ambiguous texts, or mysterious ads.
2. **Encourage Engagement:** They provide just enough information to grab attention but withhold key details, requiring the victim to click or respond to learn more.
3. **Deliver the Payload:** Once the victim engages, they are redirected to illegally created sites or manipulated into sharing personal information.

The Curiosity Click works because humans are naturally driven to seek answers to questions or puzzles, even when they suspect potential risks.

Real-Life Examples

1. **Clickbait Emails:** Messages with subject lines like "Is This You in the Video?" trick recipients into clicking malicious links.
2. **Fake Links:** Fraudsters send texts or emails like "Your Package Has Been Delayed — Click Here for Details" to steal login credentials.
3. **Online News Scams:** Messages such as "Shocking News About [Insert Celebrity]" entice clicks, leading to fake websites that steal data or install viruses.

Why It Works

The Curiosity Click preys on three key tendencies:

1. **Need for Closure:** Humans dislike unanswered questions and are driven to resolve uncertainty.
2. **Impulse Over Caution:** Curiosity creates urgency, leading people to act before evaluating risks.
3. **Belief in Harmlessness:** Many assume "just clicking" won't cause harm, underestimating the dangers of malicious links or downloads.

Manipulators know that an intriguing question or mystery can distract targets from their better judgment.

How to Spot the Curiosity Click

1. **Vague or Sensational Messages:** Be wary of emails, ads, or messages that rely on dramatic or incomplete information.
2. **Unfamiliar Senders or Sources:** If the sender isn't someone you know or trust, avoid engaging with their message.
3. **Urgent or Emotional Appeals:** Phrases such as "Don't Miss This!" or "Urgent Action Required!" are often signs of manipulation.

Exercise: Pause Before Clicking

1. Write down three steps to evaluate a suspicious link, such as:
   o "Hover over the link to check its destination."
   o "Search for the topic independently without clicking."
   o "Verify the sender or source before engaging."

Role-Playing Drill:

- Partner with someone. One person sends a curiosity-driven message (e.g. "See This Now!"). The other practices verifying the claim before clicking or engaging.

Key Takeaway

The Curiosity Click leverages the desire for answers to prompt risky actions. Slow down, verify links and sources, and remember that not all questions need immediate answers.

Chapter 34: The Imaginary Acquaintance

The Illusion of Shared Interests

You get a message on LinkedIn: "I see you're passionate about sustainable design — I'm a big advocate too! Let's connect and collaborate." Excited by the shared interest, you respond enthusiastically and share details about your current projects. Later, you realize the person wasn't who they claimed to be. They used your interests to gain access to confidential information.

This is the **Imaginary Acquaintance**, a manipulation tactic where fraudsters pretend to share hobbies, goals, or experiences to build rapport and gain trust. By mirroring the victim's interests, they create a false sense of connection that lowers defenses.

How It Works

1. **Research the Target:** Manipulators gather information about the victim's interests, hobbies, or work through social media or public profiles.
2. **Create Common Ground:** They present themselves as sharing the same interests or goals, fostering a sense of trust and familiarity.
3. **Leverage the Connection:** Once rapport is established, they make requests for information, access, or financial help under the guise of collaboration or friendship.

The Imaginary Acquaintance is especially effective in professional or social settings, where people are eager to network or find like-minded individuals.

Real-Life Examples

1. **Professional Impersonation:** Fraudsters pretend to share professional goals to gain access to projects or systems.
2. **Social Media Scams:** Scammers pose as hobbyists or enthusiasts, joining groups or conversations to extract personal details.
3. **Phony Collaborators:** Manipulators feign interest in shared causes, like charity work, to solicit donations or favors.

Why It Works

The Imaginary Acquaintance relies on three psychological tendencies:
1. **Trust Through Similarity:** People naturally trust those who appear to share their values or interests.
2. **Desire for Connection:** Targets are more likely to engage when they believe they've found someone like-minded.
3. **Lowered Defenses:** Familiarity makes requests seem more reasonable or harmless, reducing scrutiny.

This tactic works because it feels personal. Victims believe they're interacting with someone who genuinely understands and values them.

How to Spot the Imaginary Acquaintance

1. **Unsolicited Contact:** Be cautious of people who initiate contact with overly specific claims of shared interests.
2. **Rapid Rapport Building:** Manipulators often try to create a connection quickly, skipping the natural process of getting to know someone.
3. **Requests After Bonding:** If a new "connection" starts asking for favors or access early on, it's likely manipulation.

Exercise: Verify New Connections

1. Write down three steps to confirm the authenticity of a new contact, such as:
   o "Check their social media or professional profiles for consistency."
   o "Ask clarifying questions about their background."
   o "Verify mutual connections or shared affiliations."

Role-Playing Drill:

- Partner with someone. One person plays the manipulator pretending to share an interest. The other practices identifying inconsistencies and verifying claims before engaging.

Key Takeaway

The Imaginary Acquaintance creates a false bond through shared interests. Take time to verify new connections and remember: true relationships are built on mutual trust, not fabricated familiarity.

Chapter 35: The Relationship Hijack

When Relationships Become Tools

You receive a panicked text from your sibling: "I'm stranded and need money urgently to get home. Please transfer $500 right away!" Concerned, you send the money, wanting to help. Hours later, you find out it was a scammer pretending to be them.

This is the **Relationship Hijack**, a tactic where manipulators exploit personal relationships to gain trust and compliance. By impersonating someone you care about or invoking emotional bonds, they create emotional pressure to make you act.

How It Works

1. **Impersonation:** The manipulator pretends to be a family member, partner, or friend through messages, calls, or social media.
2. **Emotional Appeal:** They frame the situation as urgent, invoking emotions such as fear, love, or guilt to gain compliance.
3. **Request for Help:** They ask for immediate assistance, such as transferring money, sharing confidential information, or granting access.

The Relationship Hijack works because it preys on trust. Relationships are deeply emotional, making people more likely to act without suspicion.

Real-Life Examples

1. **Emergency Family Scams:** Fraudsters claim to be a relative in trouble, requesting money or help to resolve fabricated emergencies.
2. **Romance Scams:** Manipulators build fake romantic relationships online, gradually gaining trust before asking for financial support or sensitive details.

Why It Works

The Relationship Hijack taps into three powerful psychological dynamics:

1. **Trust in Relationships:** People are less likely to question requests from loved ones.
2. **Fear of Letting Others Down:** Emotional appeals make targets feel obligated to help immediately.
3. **Urgency Over Verification:** The emotional weight of the situation pushes victims to act before confirming the details.

Manipulators exploit your instinct to protect and support those you care about.

How to Spot the Relationship Hijack

1. **Unexpected Requests:** Be wary of unusual messages or calls from family or friends, especially involving money or sensitive information.
2. **Urgent Tone:** Scammers often create pressure by emphasizing time-sensitive crises.
3. **Verification Resistance:** If the sender discourages you from verifying their identity, it's likely manipulation.

Exercise: Verify Relationship Requests

1. Write down two steps to confirm the authenticity of a request, like:
   - "Call the person directly using a trusted number."
   - "Ask specific questions only the real person would know."

Role-Playing Drill:

- Partner with someone. One person impersonates a loved one in trouble, while the other practices verifying the situation before acting.

Key Takeaway

The Relationship Hijack uses personal bonds to manipulate trust and urgency. Always confirm the identity of the sender and their claims before taking action.

Chapter 36: The Gratitude Debt

The Power of Reciprocity

Imagine a co-worker buys you coffee unexpectedly. Grateful, you thank them. Later, they ask, "Can you cover my shift tomorrow?" Feeling obligated to return the kindness, you agree, even though it's inconvenient.

This is the **Gratitude Debt**, a tactic where manipulators use small acts of kindness to create a sense of obligation, making their victims feel compelled to reciprocate. By initiating the cycle of reciprocity, they can extract favors, information, or compliance without arousing suspicion.

How It Works

1. **Offer a Favor:** The manipulator performs a small, unsolicited act of kindness or provides assistance.
2. **Create a Sense of Obligation:** By framing the favor as generous or thoughtful, they instill a feeling of gratitude in the target.
3. **Make a Request:** Once trust is established, they leverage the target's sense of obligation to ask for something in return — often something far greater than the original favor.

The Gratitude Debt works because humans tend to reciprocate kindness, even when the original favor was insincere or manipulative.

Real-Life Examples

1. **Workplace Manipulation:** A colleague offers to help with a project, later asking for a bigger favor, such as doing a full client pitch document that will take several days to complete.
2. **Online Scams:** Fraudsters send small, unsolicited gifts or services to users, later requesting sensitive information or monetary help.
3. **Sales Tricks:** Manipulative salespeople offer free samples or trials, pressuring targets into purchasing products they don't need.

Why It Works

The Gratitude Debt relies on three core principles of human psychology:

1. **Reciprocity Norm:** People feel a moral obligation to return kindness, even if it's disproportionate.
2. **Desire to Maintain Relationships:** Targets want to preserve goodwill and avoid appearing ungrateful.
3. **Emotional Pressure:** Gratitude clouds judgment, making targets more likely to comply without evaluating the fairness of the request.

This tactic works because people often underestimate how manipulative acts of kindness can be.

How to Spot the Gratitude Debt

1. **Unsolicited Favors:** Be cautious of unexpected acts of kindness, especially from individuals who later make demands.
2. **Disproportionate Requests:** If the repayment requested is far greater than the original favor, it's likely manipulation.
3. **Reluctance to Accept "No":** Genuine generosity doesn't come with pressure to reciprocate.

Exercise: Question Reciprocity

1. Reflect on a time when you felt obligated to repay a favor. Was the expectation fair, or did it feel manipulative? Write down ways to recognize disproportionate demands in the future.
2. Practice responding to unsolicited favors by saying:
   o "Thank you, but I prefer not to accept favors I can't easily repay."

Role-Playing Drill:

- Partner with someone. One person performs a small favor, then asks for a larger return favor. The other practices politely declining unfair demands.

Key Takeaway

The Gratitude Debt manipulates your sense of obligation through small acts of kindness. Stay aware of disproportionate requests, and remember: true generosity doesn't come with strings attached.

Chapter 37: The Exclusive Offer

How Exclusivity Opens Doors

You receive an email with the subject line: **"Congratulations! You've been selected for our VIP investment program!"** The sender claims that only a handful of elite individuals qualify for this opportunity, and you've made the cut. Flattered and intrigued, you quickly click the link and provide your personal information. Later, you discover the investment program doesn't exist, and your details have been stolen.

This is the **Exclusive Offer**, a tactic where social engineers manipulate your desire to feel special or unique by presenting fabricated opportunities. By framing these offers as exclusive and time-sensitive, they pressure victims into acting quickly, often without questioning legitimacy.

The feeling of exclusivity appeals to human psychology. People crave opportunities that make them stand out from the crowd. Manipulators exploit this need to extract compliance and gain access.

How It Works

1. **Presenting the Opportunity:** The manipulator introduces a fabricated offer, such as a VIP membership, elite program, or insider deal.
2. **Creating Scarcity:** They emphasize how rare or limited the opportunity is, making the victim feel privileged and pressured to act fast.
3. **Encouraging Immediate Action:** The victim is prompted to provide payment, sensitive details, or access to secure systems in order to "claim" the offer.

The Exclusive Offer thrives on its ability to inflate self-worth while creating urgency, reducing the likelihood of rational evaluation.

Real-Life Examples

1. **Fake Luxury Programs:** Fraudsters offer "exclusive" memberships to travel clubs, investment groups, or insider deals that require an upfront payment.
2. **Phony Job Roles:** Scammers present targets as uniquely qualified for a prestigious position, requesting application fees or personal information.

Why It Works

The Exclusive Offer exploits three key human tendencies:

1. **Desire for Recognition:** People feel validated when chosen for something rare or prestigious.
2. **Time-bound Tactics:** The emphasis on scarcity and time sensitivity encourages impulsive action.
3. **Blind Trust in Exclusivity:** Victims assume that anything labeled "exclusive" must be valuable and credible.

This tactic works because people are more likely to ignore red flags when their ego and excitement are engaged.

How to Spot the Exclusive Offer

1. **Unsolicited Recognition:** Be careful of opportunities or awards you didn't apply for or expect.
2. **Upfront Requirements:** Exclusive offers that demand immediate payment or sensitive details are often manipulative.
3. **Vague or Missing Details:** Fraudulent offers typically lack transparency about who is making the offer and why you were chosen.

Exercise: Test the Opportunity's Authenticity

1. Write down three questions to ask about any exclusive offer, such as:
   o "Why was I chosen for this opportunity?"
   o "Is there a way to verify this through official channels?"
   o "What's the catch or cost associated with accepting this?"

Role-Playing Drill:

- Partner with someone. One person presents an "exclusive offer," while the other practices asking clarifying questions and verifying details before engaging.

Key Takeaway

The Exclusive Offer plays on your desire for prestige and urgency to act. Genuine opportunities withstand scrutiny. Take the time to verify before committing.

Chapter 38: The Ticking Timer

How Time Pressure Manipulates Decisions

You're shopping online when a pop-up appears: **"Only 2 items left in stock! Sale ends in 15 minutes!"** Panicked at the thought of missing out, you rush to check out, ignoring the website's lack of security features. Moments later, you notice fraudulent charges on your card — your rush to buy led you into a scam.

This is the **Ticking Timer**, a tactic where manipulators fabricate urgency through time constraints or countdowns. By pressuring you to act immediately, they leave no room for logical evaluation, ensuring you focus only on the perceived scarcity or deadline.

Time pressure is one of the oldest tricks in the book. When urgency takes over, the brain prioritizes speed over accuracy. Manipulators capitalize on this response to trap their targets.

How It Works

1. **Fabricating Urgency:** Manipulators create artificial deadlines, warning victims that opportunities or items will disappear if they don't act quickly.
2. **Narrowing Focus:** The victim becomes consumed by the ticking clock, ignoring inconsistencies or risks.
3. **Prompting Immediate Action:** Scammers request payment, personal information, or engagement under the guise of securing the opportunity before time runs out.

The Ticking Timer relies on urgency to keep the victim emotionally engaged and mentally distracted, making it harder to notice red flags.

Real-Life Examples

1. **Flash Sales:** Fraudulent websites advertise fake discounts with countdown timers, prompting immediate purchases.
2. **Fraudulent Emails:** Scammers send messages like "Your account will be suspended in 24 hours unless you verify your details!"
3. **Crypto Scams:** Fraudsters claim that stock deals will disappear unless victims deposit money immediately.

Why It Works

The Ticking Timer leverages three psychological principles:

1. **Fear of Missing Out (FOMO):** Victims rush to secure opportunities, fearing they'll lose something valuable.
2. **Stress-Induced Focus:** Time pressure narrows attention, making victims less likely to evaluate risks or alternatives.
3. **Loss Aversion:** People are more motivated by avoiding losses than pursuing gains, making deadlines feel urgent.

This tactic works because it forces decisions in a heightened emotional state, where caution is replaced by panic.

How to Spot the Ticking Timer

1. **Unrealistic Deadlines:** Be wary of time limits that seem unusually short or aggressive, especially for major decisions.
2. **Overemphasis on Limited Availability:** Claims like "Only 1 left!" or "Act now before it's gone!" often indicate manipulation.
3. **Pressure Over Clarity:** Genuine opportunities prioritize transparency, not urgency.

Exercise: Pause Under Pressure

1. Reflect on a time when a countdown influenced your decision-making. Were the deadlines legitimate? Write down two ways you could have paused to evaluate.
2. Practice responding to artificial deadlines by saying:
   - "I'll take some time to think about this."
   - "Let me verify this claim before committing."

Role-Playing Drill:

- Partner with someone. One person plays the manipulator, using a countdown or deadline to create urgency. The other practices staying calm, asking clarifying questions, and delaying their response.

Key Takeaway

The Ticking Timer exploits urgency to suppress careful thinking. Slow down, evaluate deadlines critically, and remember: genuine opportunities allow time for consideration.

Chapter 39: The Isolation Tactic

Imagine this: A fraudster calls pretending to be a representative from your bank. They say, "For security purposes, please don't discuss this with anyone until the issue is resolved." Feeling anxious and wanting to follow their instructions, you avoid consulting family or friends. You end up sharing sensitive details and losing money in the process.

This is the **Isolation Tactic**, where manipulators deliberately separate you from external advice or support systems, making it easier to control your decisions. By keeping you isolated, they ensure you rely solely on their guidance, which minimizes your ability to cross-check facts or recognize manipulation.

How It Works

1. **Undermine Trust in Others:** The manipulator warns the victim to avoid discussing the situation, often framing it as a matter of confidentiality or urgency.
2. **Create Dependency:** By becoming the victim's sole source of information, the manipulator positions themselves as an authority or ally.
3. **Control the Narrative:** Isolated targets are less likely to question claims, as they lack external perspectives to challenge the manipulator's story.

The Isolation Tactic works by making victims feel vulnerable and dependent on the manipulator, reducing their ability to think critically or seek help.

Real-Life Examples

1. **Romance Scams:** Manipulators in fake relationships discourage victims from sharing details with friends or family, claiming others won't understand or support them.
2. **Money Scams:** Fraudsters instruct victims to "keep this opportunity confidential" to avoid interference from third parties.
3. **Fake Emergency Calls:** Scammers warn victims not to tell anyone about the situation, claiming it will complicate or delay resolution.

Why It Works

The Isolation Tactic exploits three psychological factors:
1. **Fear of Judgment:** Victims worry that others might criticize or doubt their decisions, making them hesitant to share.
2. **Trust in Perceived Expertise:** Isolated individuals are more likely to believe the manipulator, as there's no one to challenge the claims.
3. **Reliance on Limited Information:** Without external input, victims are left with only the manipulator's narrative, making it harder to spot red flags.

Isolation allows manipulators to dominate the target's perspective, ensuring their version of events remains unchallenged.

How to Spot the Isolation Tactic

1. **Secrecy Requests:** Be cautious when someone urges you to keep information private or avoid discussing it with others.
2. **Exclusive Communication:** Manipulators often insist on being the only point of contact, discouraging second opinions.
3. **Pressure to Act Alone:** If you're being pushed to make a decision without consulting others, pause and question why.

Exercise: Break Free from Isolation

1. Write down two trusted people you could consult when faced with unusual situations. Commit to sharing concerns with them, even if someone advises against it.
2. Reflect on a time when you felt isolated in decision-making. What steps could you have taken to involve others?

Role-Playing Drill:

- Partner with someone. One person acts as the manipulator, using isolation tactics to push a decision. The other practices resisting, saying:
    - "I'd like to discuss this with someone I trust first."
    - "Why do you need me to keep this private?"

Key Takeaway

The Isolation Tactic relies on cutting off external input to control decisions. Resist secrecy and involve trusted individuals — many manipulations fall apart under shared scrutiny.

Chapter 40: The Distraction Game

Misdirection Through Overload

Picture this: You're at work juggling emails, phone calls, and a fast-approaching deadline. Suddenly, you receive an urgent message from your "IT department" requesting your login credentials to fix a critical issue. Flustered, you comply without thinking. Hours later, you discover the message was fake, and your account has been hacked.

This is the **Distraction Game**, a tactic where manipulators exploit cognitive overload to sneak past your defenses. By overwhelming your attention, they make it difficult to evaluate risks or notice inconsistencies.

When the brain is bombarded with tasks or information, it prioritizes speed over accuracy, leaving openings for manipulation.

How It Works

1. **Create Chaos:** The manipulator targets victims during high-stress or busy periods, ensuring their cognitive load is already stretched.
2. **Introduce Urgency:** They add an urgent request that demands immediate attention, further distracting the victim from evaluating the situation.
3. **Exploit the Gaps:** In the rush to respond, victims overlook red flags or procedural safeguards, giving manipulators what they need.

The Distraction Game works because people under pressure are more likely to default to reactive behaviors, such as complying without question.

Real-Life Examples

1. **Distractions During Work Hours:** Scammers send urgent emails during peak productivity times, requesting login details or payment authorizations.
2. **"IT" Scams:** Fraudsters call while victims are busy, claiming to fix a non-existent issue, distracting them from verifying the claim.
3. **Point-of-Sale Manipulation:** Retail scammers distract cashiers with questions or complaints while sneaking counterfeit bills into transactions.

Why It Works

The Distraction Game exploits three psychological vulnerabilities:

1. **Cognitive Overload:** When focus is spread thin, the brain is less effective at spotting inconsistencies or evaluating risks.
2. **Stress Response:** Pressure leads to hasty decisions, prioritizing resolution over careful thought.
3. **False Sense of Trust:** Manipulators position their request as routine or helpful, making it seem safe to comply without extra scrutiny.

This tactic is especially effective in high-pressure environments, where speed is valued over deliberation.

How to Spot the Distraction Game

1. **Poor Timing:** Think twice about requests that arrive during busy or stressful moments, especially if they demand immediate action.
2. **Out-of-Character Urgency:** Requests that deviate from normal protocols or procedures should raise suspicion.
3. **Missing Details:** Distracting tactics often rely on vague or incomplete information to exploit your rushed state.

Exercise: Slow Down Under Pressure

1. Write down three strategies to slow down and evaluate requests, such as:
   - "Take a deep breath and pause before responding."
   - "Verify the request through a trusted source."
   - "Ask clarifying questions to gather more details."

Role-Playing Drill:

- Partner with someone. One person creates a distracting scenario while making an urgent request. The other practices pausing, clarifying, and verifying before acting.

Key Takeaway

The Distraction Game thrives on overwhelming attention to obscure manipulation. Slow down, focus, and remember: most urgent requests can wait long enough for careful evaluation.

Section III: Digital Manipulation and Online Scams

The digital age has brought unparalleled convenience — but with it, new vulnerabilities. Social engineers no longer need physical proximity to manipulate their targets; the Internet provides endless opportunities to deceive, persuade, and exploit at scale.

This section explores the most common and dangerous forms of online manipulation. By understanding how scammers operate in digital spaces, you'll learn how to recognize red flags, protect your personal information, and confidently navigate the digital landscape.

Chapter 41: The Clickbait Lure

The Psychology of Curiosity

You're scrolling through social media when a headline grabs your attention: **"Doctors Are Hiding This Simple Health Fix!"** Intrigued, you click the link, only to be bombarded by ads, dubious websites, or requests for personal details.

This is the **Clickbait Lure**, a tactic where manipulators create sensational headlines to spark curiosity and prompt clicks. Whether the goal is to collect data, or generate ad revenue, the lure succeeds because it targets one of the brain's most powerful motivators: the need to know.

How It Works

1. **Craft an Irresistible Headline:** Scammers use vague, shocking, or emotionally charged language to spark interest.
2. **Encourage Action:** The headline often ends with "Click Here" or "Find Out More," directing victims to harmful or exploitative websites.
3. **Capture Data:** Once the victim engages, the scammer extracts personal information, installs malicious software, or exploits the visitor for profit.

The Clickbait Lure works because it exploits curiosity and impatience, encouraging victims to act before evaluating the legitimacy of the source.

Real-Life Examples

1. **Fake News Links:** Fraudsters create sensational articles that redirect users to phishing or malware sites.
2. **Celebrity Hoaxes:** Headlines like "See What This Star Looks Like Now!" drive clicks to fraudulent ad-heavy websites.
3. **Health Scams:** Claims like "Doctors Warn Against This Common Food" lead to dubious pages promoting fake cures or products.

Why It Works

The Clickbait Lure exploits three psychological tendencies:

1. **Curiosity Drive:** Humans feel compelled to seek answers to incomplete or intriguing questions.
2. **Wanting to Find out News "First":** Sensational headlines create urgency, making people click before they miss the "revelation".
3. **Trust in Platforms:** People often assume that content on major platforms like Facebook or YouTube is legitimate.

How to Spot the Clickbait Lure

1. **Exaggerated Headlines:** Be wary of phrases like "You Won't Believe" or "Shocking Secrets."
2. **Low-Quality Sources:** Clickbait often comes from unfamiliar or dubious websites.
3. **Overpromises:** Headlines promising life-changing information rarely deliver legitimate content.

Exercise: Evaluate Headlines

1. Identify three headlines online that seem sensational or exaggerated. Ask yourself:
   o "Is this source credible?"
   o "What does the website gain from my click?"
2. Practice resisting the urge to click, especially on vague or shocking claims.

Role-Playing Drill:

- Partner with someone. One person creates a clickbait-style headline, while the other practices identifying red flags and avoiding engagement.

Key Takeaway

The Clickbait Lure feeds on curiosity to manipulate clicks. Pause, question the source, and remember: credible information doesn't rely on sensationalism.

Chapter 42: The Baited Email

Imagine receiving an email from what looks like an online retailer you've used before: **"Your recent order couldn't be processed. Please confirm your payment information to complete your purchase."** The email includes the retailer's logo, a detailed description of the "order," and a link to update your payment details. Frustrated and wanting to avoid delays, you click the link and enter your credit card information – only to later realize the email wasn't from the retailer at all, and your details have been stolen.

This is the **Baited Email**, a manipulation tactic where fraudsters craft deceptive emails to fool recipients. By imitating well-known companies or creating situations that demand attention, they lead victims to willingly share sensitive information or interact with malicious links.

The Baited Email succeeds because it appears professional, mimics legitimate communication styles, and creates a sense of urgency that encourages action before suspicion.

How It Works

1. **Imitating Trusted Sources:** The manipulator replicates email templates from banks, government agencies, or popular brands to create authenticity.
2. **Creating a Sense of Urgency:** Messages often warn of security risks, overdue payments, or time-sensitive opportunities, prompting recipients to act quickly.
3. **Redirecting to Fake Pages:** Links in the email direct victims to counterfeit websites that harvest sensitive information or install malicious software.

The tactic thrives because email remains a primary mode of communication, and many people aren't vigilant about verifying sender authenticity.

Real-Life Examples

1. **Account Recovery Scams:** Fraudsters claim your account has been compromised and direct you to a fake login page to "secure" it.
2. **Payment Confirmation Hoaxes:** Victims receive emails requesting payment verification for a service or subscription they never signed up for.
3. **Bogus Prize Notifications:** Emails promise rewards or cash prizes but require victims to share banking details to claim them.

Why It Works

The Baited Email leverages three psychological principles:

1. **Credibility by Design:** Familiar logos, professional language, and realistic email structures make the message appear genuine.
2. **Pressure to Act Quickly:** Threats of account suspension or missed opportunities create a sense of urgency.
3. **Convenience Bias:** Many people are used to handling account or payment issues via email – almost like everyday routine steps.

This tactic works because it seamlessly blends into the digital noise of legitimate communications, making it harder to spot.

How to Spot the Baited Email

1. **Inconsistent Email Addresses:** Check if the sender's domain matches the official organization (e.g. "@secure-payments-bank.com" vs. "@bank.com").
2. **Generic Salutations:** Phrases like "Dear Customer" instead of your actual name often indicate a scam.
3. **Unusual Requests:** Be wary of emails asking for sensitive information, especially if the request seems out of character for the organization.

Exercise: Analyze a Suspicious Email

1. Find an email you suspect might be baiting you to get personal information. Evaluate it by asking:
   o "Does the sender's address match the organization's official domain?"
   o "Does the language and tone feel professional and consistent with past emails?"
   o "Does the link's destination match what it claims to be?"
2. Practice reporting the email to your service provider or organization's security team.

- Partner with someone. One person creates a baited email scenario, while the other practices identifying inconsistencies, such as strange URLs or suspicious requests.

Key Takeaway

The Baited Email preys on trust in familiar communication styles and urgency to deceive. Always verify sender details, scrutinize links, and consult official channels before taking action.

Chapter 43: The Digital Spy

Social Media: A Treasure Trove for Manipulators

Imagine you've just posted a picture from your dream vacation with the caption: **"Finally in Paris! Can't wait to spend the next two weeks exploring!"** What you don't realize is that someone with malicious intent now knows you're away from home for an extended period. While you're enjoying your trip, they could target your house or use your post to impersonate you in scams targeting your contacts.

This is the work of the **Digital Spy**, a manipulator who scours social media for information to exploit. Whether they're planning burglaries or identity theft, digital spies use the wealth of personal data available online to craft their schemes.

How It Works

1. **Gathering Data:** Digital spies monitor your posts, photos, and public profiles for information like your schedule, interests, or relationships.
2. **Analyzing Vulnerabilities:** They look for exploitable patterns, such as when you're likely to be away, your workplace habits, or details that could help bypass security questions.
3. **Targeting with Precision:** Using the information they've gathered, they create highly personalized scams, impersonations, or social engineering tactics to manipulate you or those around you.

The Digital Spy thrives because social media platforms often encourage oversharing, making it easy for manipulators to gather intelligence without detection.

Real-Life Examples

1. **Vacation Burglaries:** Criminals monitor posts about travel plans to break into homes while the owners are away.
2. **Impersonation Scams:** Fraudsters use personal details from public profiles to impersonate victims and trick their friends or family into sending money.
3. **Targeted Attacks:** Scammers tailor emails using information such as workplace details or hobbies, making their messages seem legitimate.

Why It Works

The Digital Spy exploits three key behaviors:

1. **Oversharing:** Many people share more online than they realize, including personal details such as locations, family relationships, and daily routines.
2. **Assumed Privacy:** Victims often assume their profiles are only visible to friends, overlooking privacy settings or ignoring risks of public posts.
3. **Trust in Familiarity:** Personalized scams feel more credible, making victims less likely to question their authenticity.

This tactic works because it combines publicly available data with manipulative strategies, creating a sense of legitimacy and trust.

How to Spot the Digital Spy

1. **Overly Personal Messages:** Be cautious of communications that reference specific details from your social media but come from unfamiliar sources.
2. **Unusual Activity on Your Account:** If someone accesses your profile or uses your photos, it could indicate that a digital spy is at work.
3. **Generic Profile Interactions:** Fake accounts often like, comment, or follow to gain access to your posts or earn your trust.

Exercise: Review Your Digital Footprint

1. Go through your social media profiles and list five pieces of information that could be exploited by someone with bad intentions (e.g. birthdays, vacation posts, or tagged locations).
2. Update your privacy settings to restrict who can see your posts and personal information.

Role-Playing Drill:

- Partner with someone. One person acts as a "Digital Spy," finding exploitable information from the other's public social media profile. The other practices identifying and minimizing risks.

The Digital Spy manipulates publicly available data to craft personalized schemes. Protect yourself by reviewing your privacy settings, limiting oversharing, and staying vigilant against suspicious interactions.

Chapter 44: The Untrue Profile

When Trust Is Built on a Lie

You receive a friend request from someone who claims to share your professional interests. Their profile is full of posts about industry trends and mutual connections. Thinking they could be a valuable addition to your network, you accept. Over the following weeks, they engage in friendly messages, asking questions about your work processes and suggesting collaboration opportunities. Later, you discover this person isn't real — none of your mutual connections know them either.

This is the **Untrue Profile**, a social engineering tactic where scammers create fabricated online personas to manipulate trust. These profiles are often highly convincing, using authentic-sounding bios, photos, and activity to blend seamlessly into social circles or professional networks. Once accepted, they exploit their new connection to extract sensitive information or influence decisions.

How It Works

1. **Fabricating a Digital Persona:** The manipulator crafts a profile using stock images, stolen photos, or AI-generated avatars. They pair this with a believable biography, mutual connections, and relevant posts to appear legitimate.
2. **Building Credibility:** They engage in conversations, post on relevant topics, or comment on shared interests to create a sense of authenticity.
3. **Exploiting the Relationship:** Once trust is established, they request sensitive information, propose fake opportunities, or use their connection to access more networks.

Unlike blatant scams, the Untrue Profile tactic operates slowly, relying on long-term engagement to cultivate trust before revealing manipulative intent.

Real-Life Examples

1. **Corporate Espionage:** A fake LinkedIn profile posing as a recruiter builds relationships with employees, extracting sensitive company data over time.
2. **Social Circle Infiltration:** Fraudsters create fake profiles to join private groups or gain access to personal details from a victim's friends.
3. **Networking Scams:** Manipulators use fake profiles to suggest lucrative partnerships, eventually asking for upfront payments or personal credentials.

Why It Works

The Untrue Profile exploits three psychological tendencies:

1. **Assumed Authenticity:** A well-crafted profile with a realistic photo and bio appears trustworthy.
2. **Trust in Mutuals:** Seeing shared connections or affiliations makes people more likely to accept a request without questioning its legitimacy.
3. **Desire for Opportunity:** Fake profiles often offer something valuable—such as collaboration, career advancement, or networking—enticing victims to engage.

This tactic thrives in digital spaces where interactions are often impersonal, making it easier to deceive.

How to Spot the Untrue Profile

1. **Shallow Activity:** Be cautious of profiles with limited posts, few interactions, or repetitive content.
2. **Inconsistent Details:** Fake profiles may have mismatched information, such as a bio claiming one job while posts suggest another.
3. **Excessive Friend Requests:** Scammers often connect with large numbers of people rapidly to build credibility through mutual contacts.

Exercise: Analyze a New Connection

1. Review a recent connection request on your social media. Ask yourself:
   o "Does this person have a professional history or shared background I can verify?"
   o "Are their posts and interactions consistent with a real person?"
2. Write down two ways to confirm a profile's authenticity, such as reverse image searching their profile photo or contacting mutual connections.

- Partner with someone. One person acts as the creator of a fake profile, while the other practices spotting inconsistencies and verifying authenticity before connecting.

Key Takeaway

The Untrue Profile uses fabricated identities to exploit trust in online networks. Always verify connections, look for inconsistencies, and remember that not every profile is what it seems.

Chapter 45: The Malware Messenger

How a Single Click Can Open the Door

You receive an email from a colleague with the subject line: **"Important Presentation for Tomorrow – Please Review."** Inside is a friendly note: **"Let me know your thoughts on this. Thanks!"** Attached is a file labeled "presentation.pdf." Without suspecting anything, you download it. What you don't realize is that the file isn't a presentation — it's malware that silently installs on your computer, logging your keystrokes and granting access to your company's network.

This is the **Malware Messenger**, a tactic where fraudsters disguise malicious software as harmless files or links. By exploiting professional routines and trust in familiar communication, they gain access to sensitive data and systems, often without raising alarms.

How It Works

1. **Crafting the Message:** The manipulator sends emails, texts, or social media messages containing a link disguised as a legitimate URL.
2. **Enticing the Target:** The message often includes a hook, such as an unpaid invoice, a missed delivery, or an exclusive deal, to encourage clicking.
3. **Delivering the Malware:** The link downloads malicious software to the device, which can monitor activity, steal data, or lock files for ransom.

The Malware Messenger works because it combines urgency with a sense of routine, prompting victims to act without hesitation.

Real-Life Examples

1. **Fake Delivery Notifications:** Messages claim a package couldn't be delivered, directing victims to a malware-infected link.
2. **Phony Job Offers:** Fraudsters email "job applications" or "contracts" with malware embedded in the attached files.
3. **Social Media Lies:** Scammers send messages like, "Is this you in the video?" with a link to malware disguised as a social media post.

Why It Works

The Malware Messenger relies on three key vulnerabilities:

1. **Trust in Appearance:** Links and messages are often crafted to look like they come from legitimate companies or individuals.
2. **Automation Habits:** Many people reflexively click links or download attachments without inspecting them.
3. **Fear of Consequences:** Phrases like "urgent," "important," or "final notice" encourage quick action, overriding caution.

This tactic works because it exploits routine actions, such as checking messages or clicking links, to deliver harmful payloads.

How to Spot the Malware Messenger

1. **Unsolicited Messages:** Be cautious of messages from unknown sources or unexpected senders, especially those with links.
2. **Suspicious URLs:** Hover over links to verify their destination before clicking.
3. **Attachments You Didn't Request:** Avoid downloading files unless you're certain of their origin.

Exercise: Practice Safe Clicking

1. Review recent messages in your inbox or phone. Identify any that include links or attachments.
   - Ask yourself: "Am I expecting this message?"
   - Verify links by hovering over them or contacting the sender directly.
2. Write down three steps to take before clicking any link, such as inspecting the sender's address or searching for the URL online.

Role-Playing Drill:

- Partner with someone. One person creates a scenario involving a suspicious link, while the other practices identifying red flags and verifying the message before engaging.

The Malware Messenger turns routine actions into opportunities for manipulation. Always verify links and attachments before clicking, and remember: caution is your best defense against digital threats.

Chapter 46: The Passcode Pilfer

When Trust Becomes a Weakness

You're browsing online and see a message: **"Your session has expired. Please log back in to continue."** The link takes you to what looks like your email provider's login page. Without hesitation, you re-enter your credentials. A moment later, the site refreshes, and you're back on the real email homepage. What you don't realize is that you just handed your login information to a scammer.

This is the **Passcode Pilfer**, a tactic where fraudsters create deceptive scenarios to trick victims into revealing their passwords, PINs, or login credentials. By replicating trusted platforms or crafting believable situations, they gain access to sensitive accounts and systems.

How It Works

1. **Setting the Trap:** The manipulator creates a fake login page or scenario, often identical to a legitimate platform.
2. **Prompting Action:** Victims are directed to the trap via phishing emails, pop-up messages, or malicious links.
3. **Harvesting Credentials:** When victims enter their information, it's immediately recorded and used to access accounts, often without their knowledge.

The Passcode Pilfer is successful because it preys on habits — logging in feels routine, so people rarely question the process.

Real-Life Examples

1. **Fake Email Login Pages:** Scammers send emails with links to counterfeit login pages, stealing credentials as victims attempt to "verify" their accounts.
2. **Social Engineering Calls:** Manipulators call pretending to be IT support, asking for login details under the guise of fixing an issue.
3. **Public Wi-Fi Spoofs:** Fraudsters create fake Wi-Fi networks that mimic real ones, redirecting users to login pages that capture their credentials.

Why It Works

The Passcode Pilfer thrives on three factors:
1. **Visual Authenticity:** Fake login pages are often indistinguishable from real ones.
2. **Routine Behavior:** Logging in is such a common action that people rarely scrutinize the process.
3. **Fear of Inaccessibility:** Phrases like "session expired" or "account locked" prompt immediate action to regain access.

This tactic works because it turns familiar, harmless actions into moments of vulnerability.

How to Spot the Passcode Pilfer

1. **Check the URL:** Always verify that the website address matches the official domain of the platform you're using.
2. **Unexpected Prompts:** Watch out for login requests that appear suddenly or out of context.
3. **Avoid Public Logins:** Never enter credentials on public Wi-Fi networks without confirming their legitimacy.

Exercise: Verify Login Requests

1. Write down three steps to confirm the authenticity of a login page, such as:
   o Checking the website's URL for typos or inconsistencies.
   o Avoiding links from unsolicited emails or messages.
   o Navigating directly to the site through your browser instead of clicking links.

Role-Playing Drill:

- Partner with someone. One person acts as the manipulator presenting a fake login page, while the other practices identifying discrepancies and avoiding the trap.

Key Takeaway

The Passcode Pilfer exploits your trust in familiar processes to steal sensitive credentials. Always verify login pages and think critically before sharing passwords or PINs.

Chapter 47: The Catfisher

When Love Becomes a Lure

You join an online dating site and connect with someone who seems perfect. Over weeks of heartfelt conversations, they share their dreams, their struggles, and their feelings for you. They mention an emergency: **"My wallet was stolen while I was traveling. Could you send me $500 to help me get home?"** Trusting them completely, you transfer the money. Weeks later, they disappear, and you realize they were never who they claimed to be.

This is the **Catfisher**, a manipulative tactic where fraudsters pose as romantic partners to exploit emotional vulnerability. They create a false sense of intimacy, using the trust they build to ask for money, gifts, or sensitive information.

How It Works

1. **Creating a Persona:** The manipulator crafts an appealing identity, often with stolen photos and a fabricated backstory.
2. **Building a Connection:** They invest time in daily conversations, sharing fabricated details to deepen trust and emotional bonds.
3. **Exploiting Trust:** Once the relationship feels genuine, they fabricate emergencies or urgent needs, asking for financial help or personal information.

The Catfisher succeeds because they manipulate the powerful desire for connection, making their victims feel special and cared for.

Real-Life Examples

1. **Romance Scams:** Fraudsters target dating app users, developing relationships before asking for money to resolve fake crises.
2. **Military Impersonation:** Scammers pose as deployed soldiers, requesting financial assistance for fabricated expenses such as travel or medical emergencies.
3. **Cryptocurrency Investment Fraud:** After gaining trust, the manipulator suggests investing together in a "sure thing," stealing the victim's funds.

Why It Works

The Catfisher leverages three key emotional dynamics:

1. **The Need for Connection:** Victims are often lonely or seeking companionship, making them more open to emotional manipulation.
2. **Trust Through Intimacy:** Daily communication and shared "experiences" create a false sense of closeness.
3. **Urgency in Crisis:** Fake emergencies compel victims to act quickly, overriding logical thinking.

This tactic works because it exploits vulnerability and targets emotions.

How to Spot the Catfisher

1. **Too Good to Be True:** Don't trust profiles with overly perfect photos or stories that feel rehearsed or idealized.
2. **Unrealistic Situations:** Scammers often have elaborate excuses for why they can't meet in person, like being abroad or deployed.
3. **Financial Requests:** Romantic partners should never pressure you for money, especially early in a relationship.

Exercise: Verify Online Relationships

1. Write down three ways to confirm someone's identity, such as:
   o Conducting a reverse image search of their profile photo.
   o Asking for a video chat to ensure they match their profile.
   o Involving a trusted friend to help evaluate their claims.

Role-Playing Drill:

• Partner with someone. One person pretends to be a Catfisher, creating a scenario where they request money. The other practices identifying red flags and refusing the request.

Key Takeaway

The Catfisher exploits emotional vulnerability to build trust and manipulate. Protect yourself by verifying online connections and remembering that true relationships don't involve financial pressure.

Chapter 48: The Deepfake Puppeteer

The Deceptive Face of AI

You receive a personalized voicemail from a well-known charity: **"This is Emma Jones, our outreach director. We're raising urgent funds for disaster relief. As one of our loyal donors, can we count on you for a $1,000 contribution today?"** The voice sounds warm and familiar, and they reference your past donation details. You quickly transfer the money. Days later, you learn the charity never contacted you. The voicemail was a deepfake designed to impersonate the outreach director and exploit your goodwill.

This is the **Deepfake Puppeteer**, where scammers use AI-generated voices, videos, or photos to impersonate trusted individuals or organizations. By mimicking real people with uncanny accuracy, they manipulate their targets into taking actions they wouldn't otherwise consider.

How It Works

1. **Collecting Data:** The manipulator gathers publicly available videos, photos, or recordings of the target.
2. **Creating the Deepfake:** Using AI tools, they generate convincing fake content that replicates the target's appearance or voice.
3. **Deploying the Manipulation:** The deepfake is used to make demands, spread misinformation, or impersonate someone in a position of trust.

The Deepfake Puppeteer is particularly dangerous because of the growing accessibility of AI tools, making it easier than ever to create convincing fake content.

Real-Life Examples

1. **Impersonation for Fraud:** Scammers use deepfake videos of executives to instruct employees to transfer funds or reveal sensitive information.
2. **Extortion Scams:** Fraudsters create fake compromising videos of victims and threaten to release them unless they're paid.
3. **Disinformation Campaigns:** Manipulators use deepfakes to spread false statements attributed to public figures, causing confusion or panic.

Why It Works

The Deepfake Puppeteer preys on three vulnerabilities:
1. **Trust in Visuals:** People are conditioned to believe what they see, making realistic deepfakes highly convincing.
2. **Reliance on Authority:** Victims often comply with requests from individuals they recognize or respect.
3. **Lack of Awareness:** Many people are unfamiliar with the capabilities of deepfake technology, making them more susceptible.

This tactic works because it combines advanced technology with psychological manipulation, creating a powerful illusion of authenticity.

How to Spot the Deepfake Puppeteer

1. **Unusual Requests:** Watch out for unexpected demands, even from familiar faces or voices.
2. **Minor Inconsistencies:** Deepfakes may show subtle visual glitches, such as unnatural lighting or awkward facial movements.
3. **Verify Through Other Channels:** Always confirm requests through a separate method, such as a phone call or email.

Exercise: Test for Deepfakes

1. Write down two ways to verify a video or audio message, such as:
   o   Asking follow-up questions only the real person would know.
   o   Checking for irregularities like unnatural speech patterns or mismatched visuals.
2. Practice verifying requests by using alternative communication channels before acting.

Role-Playing Drill:

- Partner with someone. One person creates a deepfake scenario (e.g. posing as a boss or colleague), while the other practices verifying the authenticity of the message before responding.

Key Takeaway

The Deepfake Puppeteer uses advanced AI to impersonate trusted individuals and manipulate victims. Always verify requests, and remember: even convincing visuals can be deceptive.

Chapter 49: The Privacy Blackmail Trap

How Fear and Privacy Collide

One morning, you open your inbox to a shocking message: **"We've accessed your webcam and recorded compromising footage of you. Unless you send $1,500 in Bitcoin within 48 hours, the video will be sent to your contacts."** Panicked, you check the email's details. It even includes a password you once used, making it feel credible. You debate paying to avoid the embarrassment, but the footage never existed. The email was a bluff designed to manipulate your fear.

This is the **Privacy Blackmail Trap**, a tactic where scammers use either fabricated claims or real stolen information to extort money. The threat of exposure, even if baseless, is often enough to drive victims to comply.

How It Works

1. **Stolen or Fake Data:** Manipulators use hacked passwords, email addresses, or vague personal details to appear credible.
2. **Fabricated Scenarios:** They create alarming but false claims, such as hacked webcams or private file access, to induce panic.
3. **Demanding Ransom:** Victims are instructed to pay a sum — usually in untraceable cryptocurrency — to prevent the fabricated "leak."

The Privacy Blackmail Trap works because it targets deeply personal fears, exploiting the human need to protect one's reputation and relationships.

Real-Life Examples

1. **Webcam Scams:** Fraudsters claim to have recorded compromising footage via the victim's device and demand payment to suppress it.
2. **Hacked Email Threats:** Scammers send emails containing passwords obtained from data breaches to convince victims they've been hacked.
3. **Fake Evidence Manipulation:** Manipulators create fake "evidence" such as doctored images or videos to pressure victims into compliance.

Why It Works

The Privacy Blackmail Trap manipulates three powerful fears:
1. **Fear of Exposure:** Victims often panic at the thought of their private lives being made public.
2. **Belief in Specific Details:** The inclusion of stolen passwords or personal data makes the threat feel real.
3. **Urgency Under Pressure:** Threats with deadlines ("48 hours to respond") drive rushed decisions.

This tactic is successful because victims often act out of fear rather than taking time to verify the scam.

How to Spot the Privacy Blackmail Trap

1. **Simplistic Language:** Scammers often use vague claims that don't specify any actual private details.
2. **Data From Old Breaches:** Check if the passwords they mention are outdated or from known data leaks.
3. **Unreasonable Requests:** Demands for cryptocurrency payments are a major red flag.

Exercise: Protect Your Privacy

1. Search online to see if your email address or passwords appear in any recent data breaches. Change compromised passwords immediately.
2. Write down three actions to safeguard your online privacy, such as:
    - Using a password manager to create unique passwords.
    - Enabling two-factor authentication for all accounts.
    - Covering your webcam when not in use.

Role-Playing Drill:

- Partner with someone. One person pretends to be a scammer using vague threats of exposure, while the other practices staying calm, verifying the claim, and refusing to engage.

Key Takeaway

The Privacy Blackmail Trap relies on fear and urgency to manipulate victims. Verify all claims, secure your accounts, and remember: real hackers don't send warnings.

Chapter 50: The Ransomware Ruse

How Ransomware Takes Control

You open an email from what appears to be your IT department: **"Please update your system with this security patch immediately."** Trusting the message, you download the attachment. Moments later, your computer locks up, and a terrifying message appears: **"Your files have been encrypted. Pay $5,000 in Bitcoin to recover them."** Panicked, you realize all your data — photos, work documents, and personal files — are inaccessible.

This is the **Ransomware Ruse**, where scammers infect a victim's device with malicious software that encrypts files, making them inaccessible. They demand payment in exchange for a decryption key, preying on the victim's desperation to regain control of their data.

How It Works

1. **Delivery of Harmful Files:** Ransomware is typically installed through email attachments, fake software updates, or malicious websites.
2. **Encrypting Files:** Once activated, critical files are locked, often including backups, rendering them unusable.
3. **Demanding Payment:** Victims receive instructions to pay a ransom — usually in cryptocurrency — in exchange for the decryption key.

The Ransomware Ruse succeeds because it targets both individual users and organizations, where the loss of critical data can have devastating consequences.

Real-Life Examples

1. **Hoax Emails:** Fraudsters disguise ransomware as email attachments, such as invoices or resumes, tricking victims into downloading it.
2. **Fake Software Updates:** Scammers create pop-ups urging users to install "updates" that deliver ransomware instead.
3. **Targeted Attacks on Businesses:** Cybercriminals target companies, locking entire networks and demanding large sums to restore operations.

Why It Works

The Ransomware Ruse exploits three core vulnerabilities:
1. **Dependence on Digital Data:** Victims fear losing irreplaceable files, such as business records or personal photos.
2. **Lack of Preparedness:** Many users and companies lack secure backups, making them more likely to comply with ransom demands.
3. **Panic-Induced Decisions:** The pressure of a ticking deadline drives victims to pay rather than explore alternatives.

This tactic works because it combines fear, urgency, and technical barriers, making victims feel helpless.

How to Spot the Ransomware Ruse

1. **Unsolicited Attachments:** Be wary of unexpected emails with attachments or links, especially from unknown senders.
2. **Pop-Up Urgency:** Avoid clicking on pop-ups claiming your system needs immediate updates.
3. **Encrypted Files Without Warning:** If your files suddenly become inaccessible, ransomware may be the cause.

Exercise: Build a Ransomware Defense

1. Write down three steps to protect against ransomware attacks, such as:
    o   Regularly backing up important files to an external device.
    o   Keeping all software and antivirus programs up to date.
    o   Avoiding suspicious links and attachments.

Role-Playing Drill:

- Partner with someone. One person plays the role of a scammer delivering ransomware through a fake email, while the other practices identifying red flags and safely handling the situation.

Key Takeaway

The Ransomware Ruse manipulates your dependency on digital files to demand payment. Protect yourself by maintaining secure backups, avoiding suspicious downloads, and staying vigilant against fake updates.

Chapter 51: The Subscription Steal

How Subscriptions Become Scams

You receive an email with the subject line: **"Action Required: Your Subscription Is About to Expire."** The sender appears to be a trusted streaming service such Spotify or Netflix, and the email includes a link to "renew" your subscription. Concerned about losing access, you click the link, enter your credit card information, and confirm payment. Later, you notice unauthorized charges on your card. The email wasn't from the service, and your details are now in the hands of a scammer.

This is the **Subscription Steal**, a tactic where fraudsters create fake renewal notifications to trick victims into sharing payment information. By preying on the fear of losing access to services, they exploit quick reactions to extract financial details.

How It Works

1. **Creating Fake Notifications:** The manipulator sends realistic-looking emails, texts, or app notifications mimicking trusted services.
2. **Pressuring Immediate Action:** Victims are urged to "renew" to avoid service disruption, often with phrases such as "urgent" or "final notice."
3. **Harvesting Financial Data:** Links lead to counterfeit payment pages where victims unknowingly submit their credit card information.

The Subscription Steal thrives on routine habits — most people don't think twice about renewing a service they use regularly.

Real-Life Examples

1. **Streaming Service Scams:** Fraudsters impersonate platforms such as Prime or Disney+, sending fake renewal emails to collect payment details.
2. **Software Licensing Fraud:** Emails claiming software licenses are expiring lead victims to phishing sites.
3. **App Store Renewal Hoaxes:** Scammers mimic app store notifications to trick users into updating billing information.

Why It Works

The Subscription Steal manipulates three key behaviors:
1. **Trust in Familiar Services:** Victims are less suspicious when messages appear to come from brands they use daily.
2. **Routine Compliance:** People are accustomed to renewing subscriptions, making fake requests feel normal.
3. **Fear of Losing Access:** The threat of losing a valued service drives victims to act quickly without verifying authenticity.

This tactic works because it blends seamlessly into the constant flow of legitimate subscription updates.

How to Spot the Subscription Steal

1. **Check the Sender's Details:** Scammers often use email addresses or domains that are close but not identical to official ones.
2. **Verify Links:** Hover over links to see where they lead — legitimate services will always use their official domain.
3. **Inspect the Message:** Look for typos, simplified greetings, or inconsistent branding, which are common in fake notifications.

Exercise: Review Subscription Emails

1. Find a recent subscription-related email in your inbox. Ask yourself:
   o "Is the sender's address authentic?"
   o "Does the email request action through a third-party link?"
2. Practice logging into the service directly instead of clicking links in the email to confirm its legitimacy.

Role-Playing Drill:

- Partner with someone. One person acts as the manipulator creating a fake renewal notice, while the other practices identifying inconsistencies and verifying through official channels.

Key Takeaway

The Subscription Steal exploits trust in everyday services to collect financial information. Always verify renewal notices by logging into your account directly and avoid acting on unsolicited messages.

Chapter 52: The Survey Snare

When a Survey Is More Than It Seems

You see a social media post: **"Complete our quick survey and win a $100 gift card!"** The link leads to a professional-looking questionnaire asking for your name, email, date of birth, and even partial credit card details to verify your "eligibility." Excited about the reward, you provide the information. Weeks later, you realize your identity has been stolen and used to open unauthorized accounts.

This is the **Survey Snare**, a tactic where scammers create fake polls or surveys to trick victims into willingly sharing personal and financial information. By disguising their schemes as harmless questionnaires, they make the scam appear legitimate and enticing.

(Speech bubble, left) I filled out a survey for a free $100 card — just needed to enter some info.

(Speech bubble, right) Did it ask for payment details? That could be a scam.

How It Works

1. **Crafting the Survey:** The manipulator designs a believable poll or questionnaire, often hosted on fake but professional-looking websites.
2. **Incentivizing Participation:** Victims are promised rewards like gift cards, discounts, or prizes for completing the survey.
3. **Harvesting Data:** The survey collects personal information under the guise of eligibility or verification requirements.

The Survey Snare works because people are accustomed to filling out surveys for promotions or feedback, lowering their guard.

Real-Life Examples

1. **Fake Gift Card Surveys:** Fraudsters offer gift cards for popular retailers in exchange for completing surveys that collect sensitive data.
2. **Social Media Poll Scams:** Manipulators share links to surveys claiming to support charities, using them to harvest personal information.
3. **Event Feedback Fraud:** Fake surveys about recent events or purchases trick victims into sharing unnecessary details.

Why It Works

The Survey Snare exploits three common tendencies:

1. **Appeal of Rewards:** The promise of free items or discounts encourages victims to participate without questioning the source.
2. **Normalization of Surveys:** Victims often associate surveys with legitimate feedback or promotions, making them more susceptible to being tricked.
3. **Assumption of Harmlessness:** Filling out forms feels routine, so people rarely consider the risks of sharing data.

This tactic works because it disguises exploitation as an everyday activity.

How to Spot the Survey Snare

1. **Too-Good-To-Be-True Rewards:** Be cautious of surveys promising unusually high-value rewards for minimal effort.
2. **Unfamiliar Links:** Verify the website hosting the survey to ensure it is associated with a legitimate organization.
3. **Excessive Data Requests:** Legitimate surveys rarely ask for sensitive information like credit card numbers or social security details.

Exercise: Evaluate a Survey

1. Find a survey online and ask yourself:
   - "Is this survey hosted on a trusted website?"
   - "Am I being asked for information beyond what's necessary?"
2. Practice researching the organization offering the survey to confirm its legitimacy.

Role-Playing Drill:

- Partner with someone. One person creates a fake survey scenario, while the other practices identifying red flags and verifying its authenticity before participating.

Key Takeaway

The Survey Snare uses fake polls to collect sensitive information. Always verify the source, question the reward's legitimacy, and avoid sharing unnecessary details.

Chapter 53: The Bogus Giveaway

When "Free" Comes at a Cost

You're scrolling through social media when you see a post: **"We're giving away 10 new laptops to celebrate our anniversary! Enter by clicking here!"** The link takes you to a sleek website with a form where you are required to fill in your personal details, including your address and payment information for a "small shipping fee." Days later, you notice unauthorized charges on your credit card — and realize the giveaway was a scam.

This is the **Bogus Giveaway**, a tactic where scammers lure victims with fake prize offers to steal their personal information or money. By combining excitement with a sense of urgency, they trick victims into taking quick, unverified actions.

How It Works

1. **Designing the Trap:** Manipulators create professional-looking ads or websites promising free prizes such as electronics, gift cards, or cash.
2. **Requiring Details to "Claim" the Prize:** Victims are asked to fill out forms with personal or financial information, often under the guise of verifying eligibility.
3. **Exploiting the Data:** The information is either sold, used for identity theft, or used to charge victims fraudulent fees.

The Bogus Giveaway thrives because it preys on people's excitement over winning something valuable for "free."

Real-Life Examples

1. **Fake Tech Giveaways:** Scammers promise free gadgets such as smartphones or tablets, requiring credit card details for shipping costs.
2. **Social Media Contests:** Fraudsters use fake brand pages to promote giveaways, harvesting data from participants.
3. **Email Sweepstakes Hoaxes:** Emails claim you've won a cash prize or luxury vacation, asking for bank details to "transfer the funds."

Why It Works

The Bogus Giveaway exploits three key tendencies:

1. **Excitement Over Rewards:** The allure of winning a high-value item creates emotional engagement, making people throw caution to the wind.
2. **Trust in Familiar Brands:** Fake giveaways often mimic reputable companies, making them seem legitimate.
3. **Time Pressure:** Countdown timers or limited-entry claims pressure victims into acting without verifying the offer.

This tactic works because it manipulates emotions, encouraging impulsive decisions that bypass logic.

How to Spot the Bogus Giveaway

1. **Verify the Source:** Check if the giveaway is hosted on the official website or social media page of the company.
2. **Excessive Information Requests:** Be cautious if the giveaway asks for sensitive details like your address, credit card, or social security number.
3. **Unrealistic Rewards:** High-value prizes for minimal effort (e.g. "Just click to win a car!") are often too good to be true.

Exercise: Evaluate a Giveaway Offer

1. Find an online giveaway and assess its legitimacy by asking:
   - "Is this hosted by the company's official website or page?"
   - "Am I being asked for unnecessary information or payment?"
2. Practice looking for reviews or warnings about the giveaway online to confirm whether it's legitimate.

Role-Playing Drill:

- Partner with someone. One person presents a fake giveaway scenario, while the other practices identifying red flags and verifying the offer before engaging.

Key Takeaway

The Bogus Giveaway manipulates excitement and urgency to extract personal details or money. Verify all offers, and remember: genuine giveaways never ask for sensitive information or payment to claim a prize.

Chapter 54: The Support Scam

You're working on your computer when your phone rings. The caller introduces themselves as a representative from your Internet provider: **"We've detected unusual activity on your network, which may have compromised your security. We need to fix it immediately."** They guide you through installing software, claiming it will resolve the issue. However, this program isn't protective — it grants them full access to your computer. Moments later, they demand a fee for "fixing" the problem, or worse, they start transferring your personal data.

This is the **Support Scam**, a tactic where fraudsters impersonate technical support to exploit trust. By using convincing jargon and creating urgency, they trick victims into granting access to devices or paying for non-existent repairs.

How It Works

1. **Creating the Alarm:** Scammers use pop-ups, fake error messages, or unsolicited calls to convince victims their devices are at risk.
2. **Establishing Credibility:** Posing as legitimate support staff, they use technical jargon to gain the victim's trust.
3. **Gaining Access or Payment:** Victims are persuaded to install remote access software or pay for unnecessary services.

The Support Scam succeeds because most people lack the technical knowledge to identify whether the issue is real.

Real-Life Examples

1. **Fake Microsoft Support:** Scammers cold-call victims, claiming to be from Microsoft and offering to "fix" non-existent issues.
2. **Pop-Up Warning Scams:** Fraudulent ads display warnings about supposed infections, directing victims to fake support hotlines.
3. **Payment for Useless Services:** Victims are charged for "repairs" that don't solve any actual problems.

Why It Works

The Support Scam relies on three main strategies:
1. **Creating Fear:** Alarming messages or calls make victims panic, prompting them to act quickly.
2. **Appearing Professional:** The use of technical terms and convincing scripts builds credibility.
3. **Exploiting Confusion:** Most people don't understand how to verify technical issues, making them vulnerable to manipulation.

This tactic works because it turns unfamiliarity with technology into a gateway for exploitation.

How to Spot the Support Scam

1. **Unsolicited Communication:** Be suspicious of unexpected pop-ups or calls claiming your device has issues.
2. **Pressure to Act Quickly:** Scammers often emphasize urgency to prevent victims from seeking a second opinion.
3. **Requests for Remote Access:** Legitimate support rarely requires you to install software or grant remote control without prior contact.

Exercise: Respond to a Fake Support Call

1. Write down two responses to unsolicited tech support claims, such as:
   o "I'll contact my device's official support team directly."
   o "Please provide documentation of the issue you're referring to."
2. Practice refusing remote access or payments when pressured by someone claiming to be from technical support.

Role-Playing Drill:

- Partner with someone. One person plays a fake support agent, while the other practices staying calm, verifying the claims, and refusing access or payment.

Key Takeaway

The Support Scam exploits fear and confusion about technology to gain access or money. Verify all technical issues through official channels and never allow unsolicited remote access.

Chapter 55: The Trojan Ad

When Ads Turn Dangerous

You're browsing your favorite news site when a colorful ad catches your eye: **"Win a Trip to Hawaii! Click Here to Claim!"** The ad looks legitimate, and the site hosting it is trusted, so you click. Instantly, your computer slows down, and pop-ups start appearing. Unbeknownst to you, clicking the ad installed malware designed to track your activities and extract sensitive data such as passwords and payment details.

This is the **Trojan Ad**, a tactic where scammers embed malicious code into online advertisements. By disguising malware within enticing banners or pop-ups, they exploit trust in websites and users' curiosity to infect devices.

How It Works

1. **Planting the Ad:** Fraudsters create ads with embedded malicious code, often using trusted ad networks to distribute them.
2. **Enticing the Victim:** Ads are designed to attract attention with appealing offers, such as prizes, discounts, or urgent warnings.
3. **Triggering Malware:** Clicking the ad activates hidden code, which downloads malware, such as spyware or ransomware, onto the victim's device.

The Trojan Ad succeeds because users often associate ads with promotions rather than threats, making them less cautious.

Real-Life Examples

1. **Fake Prize Ads:** Ads offering vacations, cash, or electronics lead to sites that install spyware or steal credentials.
2. **Malicious Pop-Ups:** Fraudsters design pop-ups claiming the victim's device has a virus, tricking them into clicking for "solutions."
3. **Infected Ad Networks:** Even legitimate websites sometimes unknowingly host Trojan Ads through compromised ad services.

Why It Works

The Trojan Ad relies on three key vulnerabilities:

1. **Trust in Websites:** Users assume ads on trusted sites are vetted, reducing their suspicion of malicious content.
2. **Attraction to Deals:** Promises of free rewards or exclusive offers prompt quick clicks.
3. **Technical Invisibility:** Embedded malware operates silently, often going undetected until it's too late.

This tactic works because it disguises danger as an opportunity, blending seamlessly into the digital landscape.

How to Spot the Trojan Ad

1. **Too-Good-To-Be-True Offers:** Be cautious of ads promising significant rewards for minimal effort.
2. **Unexpected Pop-Ups:** Ads claiming urgent action is required, such as fixing a virus, are often malicious.
3. **Unfamiliar Sources:** Hover over ad links to check the URL before clicking — legitimate ads lead to recognizable domains.

Exercise: Practice Safe Browsing

1. Visit a trusted site with ads. Hover over several ads without clicking, and ask yourself:
    o   "Does this offer seem realistic?"
    o   "Is the URL trustworthy?"
2. Write down two strategies to avoid Trojan Ads, such as using an ad blocker or avoiding ads entirely.

Role-Playing Drill:

- Partner with someone. One person creates a fake scenario involving a tempting ad, while the other practices identifying and avoiding it.

Key Takeaway

The Trojan Ad hides malicious intent within seemingly harmless promotions. Avoid clicking ads from unverified sources, and use security measures such as ad blockers and antivirus software to stay protected.

Chapter 56: The Public Wi-Fi Trap

You're at the airport and connect to the free public Wi-Fi to check your bank account. Everything seems normal until days later, when you notice unauthorized transactions. Unbeknownst to you, a hacker using the same network intercepted your login credentials using a technique called a "man-in-the-middle" attack.

This is the **Public Wi-Fi Trap**, where scammers exploit insecure networks to steal data. By eavesdropping on unencrypted traffic, they can intercept passwords, credit card numbers, and other sensitive information.

How It Works

1. **Setting the Trap:** Fraudsters connect to public Wi-Fi networks or create fake hotspots with similar names to legitimate ones.
2. **Monitoring Activity:** They use software to intercept unencrypted data transmitted over the network, such as login credentials or personal information.
3. **Exploiting the Data:** Stolen information is used for identity theft, account breaches, or financial fraud.

The Public Wi-Fi Trap succeeds because most users assume public networks are secure and don't take precautions.

Real-Life Examples

1. **Fake Hotspots:** Hackers create Wi-Fi networks with names like "Airport Free Wi-Fi" to trick users into connecting.
2. **Man-in-the-Middle Attacks:** Fraudsters intercept data on legitimate public networks, stealing passwords and other details.
3. **Session Hijacking:** Scammers take control of active sessions, such as email or social media accounts, by stealing cookies.

Why It Works

The Public Wi-Fi Trap exploits three common behaviors:

1. **Assumption of Security:** Many people assume public networks are safe because they're widely used.
2. **Lack of Encryption:** Unencrypted connections make it easy for hackers to intercept data.
3. **Convenience Over Caution:** Users prioritize quick access over secure browsing when connecting to public Wi-Fi.

This tactic works because it leverages routine actions, such as checking emails or making transactions, to extract sensitive information.

How to Spot the Public Wi-Fi Trap

1. **Unfamiliar Networks:** Be wary of networks with generic names or those that don't require a password.
2. **Unencrypted Connections:** Avoid websites without HTTPS (the padlock icon) when using public Wi-Fi.
3. **Suspicious Activity:** If a network suddenly disconnects and reconnects, it could be a sign of tampering.

Exercise: Practice Safe Wi-Fi Usage

1. Write down three strategies for secure browsing on public Wi-Fi, such as:
    o   Using a virtual private network (VPN) to encrypt your data.
    o   Avoiding financial transactions on public networks.
    o   Disconnecting from public Wi-Fi when not in use.
2. Check your device settings to ensure it doesn't automatically connect to unfamiliar networks.

Role-Playing Drill:

*   Partner with someone. One person plays a hacker setting up a fake hotspot, while the other practices identifying and avoiding insecure networks.

Key Takeaway

The Public Wi-Fi Trap manipulates the convenience of free networks to steal sensitive data. Always use encryption, verify networks, and limit sensitive activity when connected to public Wi-Fi.

Chapter 57: The QR Code Con

You're at a restaurant, and the menu includes a QR code for easy access to their online ordering system. Without thinking, you scan it and land on what looks like their website. It asks you to log in with your email and password, so you do. Later, you notice unauthorized activity in your accounts. The QR code wasn't placed by the restaurant — it was a fake notice applied by a scammer to harvest your credentials.

This is the **QR Code Con**, a tactic where fraudsters manipulate the trust and convenience of QR codes to misdirect users to malicious websites. By altering legitimate-looking codes or planting fake ones, they exploit your willingness to engage without verifying.

How It Works

1. **Planting the Code:** Scammers place fake QR code stickers on posters, menus, or advertisements. These codes redirect users to malicious sites or initiate unauthorized downloads.
2. **Exploiting Trust:** Victims assume the QR code is legitimate, especially if it's placed in trusted environments like restaurants or public transport.
3. **Stealing Data or Delivering Dangerous Software:** Once the victim scans the code, they're tricked into sharing credentials, financial details, or unknowingly downloading malware.

The QR Code Con thrives because QR codes are quick and easy to use, and most people rarely verify their source.

Real-Life Examples

1. **Fake Menu Codes:** Fraudsters replace QR codes on restaurant menus with their own, redirecting customers to phishing sites.
2. **Parking Payment Scams:** Fake QR codes placed on parking meters lead users to fraudulent payment portals.
3. **Event Ticketing Hoaxes:** QR codes on counterfeit tickets direct victims to infected sites.

Why It Works

The QR Code Con exploits three key behaviors:

1. **Assumption of Authenticity:** QR codes are seen as harmless, especially when used in professional settings.
2. **Speed Over Caution:** Scanning a code feels routine, making users less likely to pause and verify.
3. **Trust in Appearance:** Codes are easy to replicate, and fake ones often look identical to legitimate codes.

This tactic works because it leverages convenience and disguises itself within trusted environments.

How to Spot the QR Code Con

1. **Inspect the Code:** Check for signs of tampering, such as stickers placed over original codes.
2. **Be Wary of Shortened Links:** Scammers often use shortened URLs to hide the true destination of their fake QR codes.
3. **Verify the Source:** Confirm with the business or organization that the QR code is legitimate before scanning.

Exercise: Evaluate QR Code Safety

1. Locate a QR code you've recently scanned and ask:
   - "Was it placed in a secure location?"
   - "Did I verify the organization behind it?"
2. Practice using a QR scanner app that shows the URL before opening it, allowing you to verify the destination.

Role-Playing Drill:

- Partner with someone. One person sets up a fake QR code scenario, while the other practices identifying red flags and verifying legitimacy before scanning.

Key Takeaway

The QR Code Con turns convenience into a weapon for scams. Always inspect QR codes for authenticity, verify their sources, and be cautious of shortened or unfamiliar URLs.

Chapter 58: The Crypto Trap

How Promises of Wealth Become a Trap

A friend excitedly shares a new cryptocurrency platform, claiming, **"I made $5,000 in just two days — this is your chance to get in early!"** They show you a professional-looking website filled with testimonials and graphs of rising profits. You invest $1,000, and at first, your account shows rapid growth. But when you try to withdraw your earnings, you're told you need to deposit more money to "unlock" your funds. Days later, the website disappears, along with your investment.

This is the **Crypto Trap**, a scheme where scammers exploit the buzz around cryptocurrency to deceive victims. By promising high returns, leveraging fear of missing out, and creating fake platforms, they lure individuals into fraudulent investments.

My balance on this new crypto site doubled overnight!

That sounds too good to be true. Have you tried withdrawing?

How It Works

1. **Setting the Hook:** Scammers create professional-looking websites or social media accounts to advertise "once-in-a-lifetime" cryptocurrency opportunities.
2. **Building Trust:** They use fake testimonials, doctored screenshots of profits, and even paid influencers to make the scheme seem credible.
3. **Stealing Investments:** Victims deposit funds into the fake platform, which is then siphoned off by the scammers. Attempts to withdraw funds are blocked or require additional payments.

The Crypto Trap works because cryptocurrency is complex and poorly understood by many, making it easier to deceive victims with jargon and promises.

Real-Life Examples

1. **Ponzi Crypto Schemes:** Scammers use funds from new investors to pay "returns" to earlier ones, creating the illusion of success.
2. **Fake ICOs (Initial Coin Offerings):** Fraudsters create fake cryptocurrencies, convincing victims to buy tokens that are worthless.
3. **Phishing Wallet Scams:** Victims are tricked into entering their wallet credentials on fake platforms, allowing scammers to steal their funds.

Why It Works

The Crypto Trap leverages three main factors:
1. **Promise of High Returns:** Victims are drawn to the idea of making significant profits in a short time.
2. **Trust in Trends:** The popularity and complexity of cryptocurrency make scams appear legitimate.
3. **Fear of Missing Out:** Exclusive "early access" opportunities push victims to act without researching.

This tactic works because it combines confusion about cryptocurrency with psychological pressure to act quickly.

How to Spot the Crypto Trap

1. **Verify Platforms:** Check if the platform is registered or reviewed by credible financial authorities.
2. **Avoid Unrealistic Promises:** Be cautious of platforms guaranteeing massive profits or "risk-free" investments.
3. **Watch for Withdrawal Restrictions:** Legitimate platforms don't block access to your funds or require extra payments to withdraw.

Exercise: Research a Crypto Investment

1. Find a cryptocurrency platform and research its credibility by asking:
   - "Is this platform regulated by a recognized authority?"
   - "Are the testimonials and reviews consistent and verifiable?"
2. Practice searching for red flags like fake reviews or unreasonably high returns.

Role-Playing Drill:

- Partner with someone. One person pitches a fake crypto investment, while the other practices asking critical questions and verifying its legitimacy.

Key Takeaway

The Crypto Trap exploits the buzz and confusion around cryptocurrency to deceive victims. Avoid platforms with unrealistic promises, verify credibility, and never invest without thorough research.

Chapter 59: The Influencer Lie

How Influence Becomes Exploitation

You're scrolling through Instagram when a well-known influencer you admire shares a limited-time offer: **"Get luxury skincare products for 70% off using my special link!"** Eager to grab the deal, you follow the link and purchase the product. Days turn into weeks, and nothing arrives. You later discover the profile wasn't run by the influencer at all — it was a fraudster mimicking their account to promote scams.

This is the **Influencer Lie**, a tactic where scammers pose as influencers to exploit trust and social proof. By leveraging the perceived credibility and popularity of influencers, they trick victims into purchasing fake products, sharing personal details, or engaging with fraudulent services.

How It Works

1. **Impersonating an Influencer:** Fraudsters create fake profiles mimicking popular influencers or invent entirely new personas.
2. **Promoting Fake Deals:** They share posts or send direct messages offering exclusive discounts, giveaways, or investment opportunities.
3. **Exploiting Engagement:** Victims who follow the links are directed to fraudulent websites, where they lose money or share sensitive information.

The Influencer Lie succeeds because people associate influencers with trustworthiness and authentic recommendations.

Real-Life Examples

1. **Exclusive Collaboration Scams:** Fake influencers claim to launch limited-edition products, convincing followers to pre-order items that don't exist.
2. **Event Ticket Fraud:** Fraudsters impersonate influencers promoting "VIP access" to exclusive events, collecting payments for tickets that turn out to be fake.
3. **Personalized Advice Hoaxes:** Imposters offer one-on-one coaching or consultations for a fee, disappearing after receiving payment without providing the promised service.

Why It Works

The Influencer Lie preys on three psychological factors:

1. **Trust in Popularity:** People often trust influencers due to their large followings and perceived expertise.
2. **Desire for Deals:** Limited-time offers or exclusive discounts encourage impulsive decisions.
3. **Social Proof:** Comments and likes (often fake) make the promotion appear credible.

This tactic works because it combines the illusion of authenticity with urgency, prompting quick action.

How to Spot the Influencer Lie

1. **Check for Verification:** Genuine influencers often have verified accounts with a blue checkmark on platforms like Instagram or Twitter.
2. **Investigate Links:** Avoid clicking links from posts or profiles that seem suspicious or lack a clear connection to the influencer.
3. **Look for Interaction Patterns:** Fake influencer profiles often have inconsistent engagement, like lots of followers but very few likes or comments.

Exercise: Verify Influencer Promotions

1. Find a recent influencer post promoting a deal or product. Ask yourself:
   - "Is this post consistent with the influencer's usual content?"
   - "Does the link lead to the official website of the product or brand?"
2. Write down two ways to confirm the authenticity of influencer endorsements, such as cross-checking their website or contacting the brand directly.

Role-Playing Drill:

- Partner with someone. One person creates a fake influencer scenario, while the other practices identifying inconsistencies and verifying legitimacy.

Key Takeaway

The Influencer Lie manipulates trust in social media figures to promote scams. Always verify endorsements and check profiles for authenticity before engaging.

Chapter 60: The Phone App Fraud

When Convenience Comes at a Price

You're searching for a budgeting app and find one with excellent reviews and promises of easy-to-use features. You download it, enter your financial details to "track expenses," and think nothing of it. Weeks later, you notice unauthorized charges on your credit card. The app wasn't designed to help you manage money — it was created to steal it.

This is the **Phone App Fraud**, a tactic where scammers design fake apps that look legitimate but contain hidden malware or data-collection tools. By disguising malicious intent as helpful functionality, they gain access to sensitive information or exploit users financially.

> **Ever since I downloaded that budgeting app, I've seen strange charges on my card.**

> **It might be fake. Did you check who developed it?**

How It Works

1. **Developing the App:** Scammers create apps that mimic popular tools, such as fitness trackers, budgeting software, or games.
2. **Uploading to App Stores:** These apps are uploaded to app stores, sometimes slipping past security reviews, or are promoted through third-party websites.
3. **Exploiting Users:** Once installed, the app collects sensitive data, such as passwords, or charges hidden fees for fake services.

The Phone App Fraud thrives on the convenience and ubiquity of mobile apps, making it easy to reach unsuspecting victims.

Real-Life Examples

1. **Fake Language Learning Apps:** Apps promising quick fluency in new languages collect sensitive data, such as email logins, during the registration process.
2. **Health Tracking Hoaxes:** Malicious apps claim to track steps or monitor sleep but secretly sell users' private health metrics to third parties.
3. **Gaming Add-On Scams:** Apps offering exclusive in-game content or cheats for popular games charge hidden fees or embed malware that compromises user devices.

Why It Works

The Phone App Fraud exploits three common behaviors:
1. **Trust in App Stores:** Many users assume all apps on official platforms such as Google Play or Apple's App Store are safe.
2. **Lack of Vigilance:** Most people don't thoroughly research apps before downloading, especially free ones.
3. **Convenience Over Security:** Victims prioritize features and ease of use, often overlooking potential risks.

This tactic works because it blends seamlessly into the routine of downloading and using mobile apps.

How to Spot the Phone App Fraud

1. **Check the Developer:** Verify the app's developer and ensure it's associated with a reputable company.
2. **Read Reviews Carefully:** Be cautious of apps with only glowing, generic reviews or very few downloads.
3. **Monitor Permissions:** Avoid apps that request unnecessary permissions, like access to your contacts or financial data.

Exercise: Evaluate a New App

1. Find an app you recently downloaded and ask yourself:
   o "Does this app's developer have a legitimate website?"
   o "Do the reviews include specific details, or are they oversimplistic?"
2. Write down two ways to verify app safety, such as researching the developer or checking for news about similar scams.

Role-Playing Drill:

- Partner with someone. One person presents a fake app scenario, while the other practices verifying the app's legitimacy before downloading.

Key Takeaway

The Phone App Fraud disguises malicious intent as helpful tools to exploit users. Always research apps, monitor permissions, and stick to downloads from reputable developers and app stores.

Section IV: Exploiting Cognitive Biases

Cognitive biases are mental shortcuts humans use to make decisions, but these shortcuts are far from fool proof. Manipulators exploit these biases to influence your choices without you realizing it. From your tendency to trust authority figures to your aversion to losses, these biases can be turned into tools for deception, steering your decisions in ways that serve someone else's agenda.

In this section, we'll expose how cognitive biases can be used against you and teach you to recognize and resist these manipulative tactics. By understanding how your mind works, you can protect yourself from being misled and regain control of your decision-making.

Chapter 61: The Authority Bias

When Authority Masks Intent

You receive a phone call from someone claiming to be from the IRS. The stern voice on the line warns: **"Your account is under review for tax evasion. If you don't pay $2,000 today, we'll issue an arrest warrant."** Terrified, you comply without questioning the legitimacy of the claim. Later, you discover the caller wasn't from the IRS — they used the Authority Bias to exploit your trust in official figures.

The **Authority Bias** is a cognitive shortcut where people defer to those they perceive as authoritative. Scammers manipulate this bias by mimicking authority figures to make their demands appear legitimate and unquestionable.

How It Works

1. **Adopting an Authoritative Persona:** Manipulators impersonate professionals such as government officials, or doctors.
2. **Creating Pressure:** They use formal language, official jargon, or dire consequences to make victims feel compelled to act immediately.
3. **Minimizing Doubts:** The appearance of authority discourages critical thinking, making people less likely to question the manipulator's claims.

The Authority Bias thrives on trust and the natural human tendency to respect those in perceived positions of power.

Real-Life Examples

1. **Legal Aid Scams:** Fraudsters claim to be attorneys, pressuring victims to pay "legal fees" for non-existent court cases.
2. **Academic Authority Fraud:** Manipulators pose as university representatives, demanding payments for fabricated tuition or exam-related issues.
3. **Inspection Hoaxes:** Scammers impersonate safety inspectors, pressuring businesses to pay fines for fake violations or buy unnecessary services.

Why It Works

The Authority Bias relies on three psychological triggers:

1. **Deference to Expertise:** People assume that authority figures have superior knowledge and rarely challenge their directives.
2. **Fear of Consequences:** Threats of punishment, fines, or other negative outcomes create a sense of urgency and compliance.
3. **Credibility Through Appearance:** Uniforms, titles, and formal language make manipulative claims seem legitimate.

This tactic works because it plays on deep-seated instincts to obey perceived authority.

How to Spot the Authority Bias

1. **Verify Credentials:** Always ask for identification or credentials and independently confirm their legitimacy.
2. **Beware of Urgency:** Legitimate authorities rarely pressure you to act immediately without verification.
3. **Question Unusual Requests:** Authority figures should not demand sensitive information or payments over the phone or online.

1. Think of a recent situation where someone in authority influenced your decision. Reflect:
   - ○ "Did I verify their identity before complying?"
   - ○ "Did I feel pressured to act without questioning?"
2. Practice asking for credentials and taking time to verify claims in future interactions.

Role-Playing Drill:

- Partner with someone. One person acts as a manipulative authority figure, while the other practices questioning their legitimacy and verifying their claims.

Key Takeaway

The Authority Bias leverages trust in authority figures to manipulate decisions. Always verify credentials, question requests, and resist acting out of fear or urgency.

Chapter 62: The Recency Effect

How Recent Events Shape Choices

You're at a car dealership, debating whether to purchase the extended warranty. The salesperson leans in, saying: **"Just last week, a customer's transmission failed a month after their warranty expired — it cost them thousands to repair."** The story sticks in your mind, making you fear a similar fate. Convinced, you pay for the extended warranty, only to realize later that the decision was based on an isolated event rather than the actual reliability of the car.

This is the **Recency Effect**, a cognitive bias where recent information or events carry more weight in decision-making than they should. Manipulators exploit this bias by highlighting vivid, timely examples to sway choices, even when those examples don't represent the broader context.

How It Works

1. **Selecting the Example:** Manipulators choose a recent, memorable event or story that supports their agenda.
2. **Focusing Attention:** They emphasize the recency of the example, making it seem more relevant or probable than it actually is.
3. **Triggering Emotional Reactions:** The example is often framed to evoke strong emotions, like fear or urgency, to override rational thinking.

The Recency Effect succeeds because human memory is naturally biased toward recent events, making them seem more important than distant or less vivid examples.

Real-Life Examples

1. **Insurance Upselling:** Agents highlight recent accidents or disasters to convince customers to buy additional coverage, even when the risks are low.
2. **Media-Inspired Purchases:** After a news report about a food recall, customers may rush to buy organic or premium products, believing they're safer.
3. **Travel Fear Marketing:** Airlines or travel agencies promote "last-minute travel insurance" after a highly publicized travel mishap, using recent events to drive purchases.

Why It Works

The Recency Effect thrives on three factors:

1. **Emotional Impact:** Recent events feel more vivid and personal, especially if they evoke fear or loss.
2. **Ease of Recall:** Human memory prioritizes recent information, making it feel more relevant than older or abstract data.
3. **Sense of Urgency:** Recent examples create a perception that action must be taken immediately to avoid negative outcomes.

This tactic works because it avoids broader analysis, directing attention to one specific, timely detail.

How to Spot the Recency Effect

1. **Question the Context:** Ask whether the example reflects a broader trend or is an isolated incident.
2. **Look for Patterns:** Consider long-term data or historical information to balance recent anecdotes.
3. **Resist Emotional Triggers:** Be cautious when recent events are used to evoke fear, urgency, or other strong emotions.

1. Think of a recent decision influenced by a vivid story or event. Ask yourself:
   - "Was this example part of a pattern or a one-off occurrence?"
   - "What does the broader data suggest about this situation?"
2. Write down three questions to help evaluate future examples, such as:
   - "How representative is this event?"
   - "What are the odds of this happening to me?"

Role-Playing Drill:

- Partner with someone. One person presents a decision scenario based on a recent event, while the other practices identifying the Recency Effect and asking clarifying questions.

Key Takeaway

The Recency Effect uses recent events to distort decision-making. Balance timely examples with broader context and resist emotional responses to avoid being manipulated.

Chapter 63: The Commitment Trap

How Small Yeses Lead to Bigger Ones

At a mall, a fundraiser asks if you have a moment to discuss saving endangered animals. Feeling polite, you agree and listen to their pitch. Afterward, they ask if you'd like to make a small, one-time donation. You give $5, but before you leave, they suggest you sign up for a monthly donation plan. Because you've already said yes, it feels awkward to decline. Months later, you're still paying for a commitment you didn't intend to make.

This is the **Commitment Trap**, where manipulators use a series of escalating requests to exploit your desire for consistency. By securing a small initial agreement, they make it psychologically harder for you to say no to larger demands.

How It Works

1. **Starting Small:** Manipulators begin with a low-effort request, like signing a petition or answering a question, to build engagement.
2. **Escalating the Ask:** Once the victim agrees, they make a larger request that feels consistent with the initial commitment.
3. **Leveraging Cognitive Dissonance:** Saying no after an initial yes feels inconsistent, creating discomfort that leads victims to comply.

The Commitment Trap works because humans have a natural tendency to stay consistent with their previous actions and statements.

Real-Life Examples

1. **Sales Techniques:** Car dealers get customers to agree to small add-ons before suggesting costly upgrades or warranties.
2. **Fundraising Campaigns:** Charities ask for small donations first, later pushing for recurring contributions or larger gifts.
3. **Online Free Trials:** Free trials hook users into paid subscriptions by requiring small actions, like entering credit card details.

Why It Works

The Commitment Trap thrives on three psychological tendencies:
1. **Desire for Consistency:** People want to appear consistent in their actions and decisions.
2. **Escalation of Investment:** Each additional commitment makes backing out feel more difficult.
3. **Social Pressure:** Manipulators frame the larger request as a natural next step, making refusal seem unreasonable.

This tactic works because it turns politeness and small actions into gateways for larger obligations.

How to Spot the Commitment Trap

1. **Recognize the Pattern:** Be cautious when a small agreement is quickly followed by a larger request.
2. **Pause Before Escalating:** Reflect on whether the larger commitment aligns with your actual goals or intentions.
3. **Separate Decisions:** Treat each request as a standalone decision, not an extension of previous actions.

1. Think of a time you agreed to something small but felt pressured to escalate. Ask yourself:
   o "Did I feel obligated to say yes because of my earlier action?"
   o "Would I have agreed to the larger request if it came first?"
2. Write down two strategies to pause and evaluate larger requests in the future.

Role-Playing Drill:

- Partner with someone. One person presents a small, harmless request, escalating it into a larger one. The other practices recognizing the trap and declining without guilt.

Key Takeaway

The Commitment Trap turns small agreements into larger obligations. Stay mindful of escalating requests, and remember: you're not obligated to say yes just to stay consistent.

Chapter 64: The Consensus Effect

How Popularity Becomes Persuasion

You're browsing an online store and see a product with hundreds of five-star reviews and testimonials claiming, **"This is the best purchase I've ever made!"** Trusting the overwhelming positivity, you buy it. When it arrives, it's poorly made and doesn't match the description. Frustrated, you revisit the site and realize many of the reviews are suspiciously similar, and the reviewers don't seem legitimate.

This is the **Consensus Effect**, a tactic where manipulators create the illusion of widespread approval to sway decisions. By fabricating popularity, they make their product, service, or message seem trustworthy and desirable.

How It Works

1. **Generating Fake Support:** Manipulators write or pay for fake reviews, likes, or endorsements to create the appearance of popularity.
2. **Exploiting Social Proof:** People tend to trust and follow the crowd, assuming popular choices are the safest or best.
3. **Minimizing Doubts:** High ratings or glowing testimonials discourage critical thinking or further research.

The Consensus Effect thrives because humans often trust collective judgment, especially when making quick decisions.

Real-Life Examples

1. **Fake Product Reviews:** Online sellers inflate ratings and reviews to make low-quality items appear reliable.
2. **Social Media Endorsements:** Fraudsters buy fake followers and likes to appear influential, convincing people to trust them.
3. **Event Popularity Scams:** Manipulators falsely claim that events are "sold out" or highly attended to drive ticket sales.

Why It Works

The Consensus Effect relies on three psychological tendencies:

1. **Trust in Numbers:** People assume large groups can't be wrong, so popularity is equated with quality or legitimacy.
2. **Perceived Demand:** High popularity makes people believe the product or service is highly sought-after, prompting quick decisions to avoid losing an opportunity.
3. **Reduced Scrutiny:** Widespread approval discourages people from questioning the details.

This tactic works because it creates a false sense of security by leveraging social validation.

How to Spot the Consensus Effect

1. **Check Reviewer Patterns:** Look for signs of fake reviews, such as generic language, similar usernames, or identical posting times.
2. **Verify Social Proof:** Investigate whether endorsements or high ratings come from credible sources.
3. **Don't Be Fooled By Overwhelming Positivity:** Products or services with only glowing feedback may be too good to be true.

1. Choose a product or service with high ratings and ask yourself:
   o "Are these reviews specific and credible?"
   o "Do the reviewers have a history of authentic activity?"
2. Write down two methods to verify the legitimacy of popularity claims, such as cross-checking reviews on multiple platforms.

Role-Playing Drill:

- Partner with someone. One person creates a scenario involving fake social proof, while the other practices identifying red flags and verifying authenticity.

Key Takeaway

The Consensus Effect manipulates trust in popularity to influence decisions. Always investigate reviews, endorsements, and ratings to ensure they're legitimate before acting.

Chapter 65: The Rarity Mirage

When Scarcity Turns into Deception

You're browsing a travel website for vacation deals. One offer catches your attention: **"3 seats left at this price!"** Concerned about missing the deal, you immediately book your ticket. Days later, you revisit the same site, only to find the exact same deal with the same warning. You realize the scarcity message was fake, designed to rush you into making a decision.

This is the **Rarity Mirage**, a tactic where manipulators fabricate scarcity to make products or opportunities seem more valuable. By convincing you something is in short supply, they trigger an emotional response that overrides logical decision-making.

How It Works

1. **Creating False Limits:** Manipulators display fake low-stock warnings, like "Last Few in Stock" or "Exclusive Item."
2. **Inflating Urgency with Timers:** They use countdown clocks to suggest fleeting opportunities, pushing for rushed decisions.
3. **Amplifying Exclusivity:** The item is marketed as rare or unavailable elsewhere, increasing its perceived worth.

The Rarity Mirage is effective because humans are psychologically programmed to value things that appear scarce, associating rarity with importance or desirability.

Real-Life Examples

1. **Fake Hotel Bookings:** Travel websites display alerts like "3 people are looking at this room," even when no one else is browsing.
2. **Online Auctions:** Sellers create fake bidding wars to inflate prices, making buyers believe the item is highly sought after.
3. **Streaming Service Hype:** Limited-time access to shows or events prompts viewers to subscribe or renew memberships unnecessarily.

Why It Works

The Rarity Mirage capitalizes on three psychological triggers:
1. **Value Through Scarcity:** People associate rarity with higher value or exclusivity.
2. **Fear of Losing Out On a Deal:** The possibility of missing a "one-time" opportunity creates anxiety and urgency.
3. **Impulsive Decision-Making:** Scarcity disrupts logical evaluation, prompting immediate action.

This tactic works because it overrides careful consideration with emotional urgency.

How to Spot the Rarity Mirage

1. **Refresh the Website Page You Are Visiting:** Fake scarcity tactics often reset when you reload the website.
2. **Research Availability:** Check whether the same item is sold elsewhere or if similar deals are offered by competitors.
3. **Pause Before Acting:** Resist the urge to buy immediately — most "limited offers" don't truly expire.

1. Visit an online store with low-stock warnings. Ask yourself:
   o "Does the warning change if I refresh or return later?"
   o "Is this product available from other retailers?"
2. Write down two strategies to resist scarcity pressure, such as waiting 24 hours before making a purchase.

Role-Playing Drill:

- Partner with someone. One person creates a scarcity scenario, while the other practices identifying manipulation and staying calm under pressure.

Key Takeaway

The Rarity Mirage manipulates urgency and scarcity to pressure decisions. Always verify claims of limited availability and avoid rushing purchases driven by fear of missing out.

Chapter 66: The Extreme Evaluator

How Comparisons Shape Decisions

You're shopping for a new TV, and the salesperson shows you a $5,000 state-of-the-art model. Shocked at the price, you immediately decline. Then they show you another option, priced at $2,500, emphasizing it has most of the same features. Relieved by the contrast, you purchase it, even though it's still more expensive than you planned to spend.

This is the **Extreme Evaluator**, a tactic where manipulators use extreme comparisons to influence decisions. By presenting an exaggerated option first, they make the alternative seem more reasonable, even if it's still overpriced or unnecessary.

How It Works

1. **Introducing an Outlier:** Manipulators begin with an exaggerated or impractical option to make the next choice seem more appealing.
2. **Positioning a Preferred Choice:** They strategically highlight an alternative that appears balanced or favorable in comparison to the extreme option.
3. **Leveraging Relative Value:** The contrast between the options shifts focus away from the actual cost or relevance of the preferred choice.

The Extreme Evaluator is effective because human decision-making is heavily influenced by context, making comparisons a powerful tool for shaping perceptions.

Real-Life Examples

1. **Upselling at Restaurants:** Menus include a $150 steak to make the $75 steak seem affordable, even though both are overpriced.
2. **Gym Memberships:** Gyms show premium packages with high fees to make the mid-tier package look like better value.
3. **Tech Gadgets:** Retailers display overpriced flagship products to push customers toward mid-range models with higher profit margins.

How to Spot the Extreme Evaluator

1. **Revisit Your Original Needs:** Before comparing options, ask if the alternatives meet your initial goals or budget.
2. **Question the Context:** Be wary when the first option is excessively high or seems out of place — it may be there to influence your perception.
3. **Research Alternatives Independently:** Check if similar products or services are available at better prices elsewhere.

Exercise: Reflect on Past Purchases

1. Think of a time you chose an option because it seemed reasonable compared to a more expensive alternative. Reflect:
   o "Would I have chosen this if the first option hadn't been presented?"
   o "Did I spend more than I originally planned?"

Role-Playing Drill:

- Partner with someone. One person presents an exaggerated option, followed by a more "reasonable" one. The other practices identifying the tactic and focusing on their original budget or needs.

Key Takeaway

The Extreme Evaluator manipulates your choices by setting unrealistic comparisons to influence your perception of value. Always review options based on your needs, not on the contrast presented to you.

Chapter 67: The Availability Heuristic

How Recent Events Cloud Judgment

You're planning a vacation to a coastal city when a news report flashes: **"Shark Attack Claims Life of Swimmer."** The story sticks in your mind, and you cancel your trip, choosing a mountain destination instead. What you don't realize is that shark attacks are incredibly rare, but the vividness of the story made it feel like a likely risk.

This is the **Availability Heuristic**, a cognitive bias where recent or vivid examples dominate your decision-making. Manipulators use this bias by highlighting specific events or anecdotes that distort your perception of reality, making improbable risks seem imminent.

How It Works

1. **Highlighting Memorable Events:** Manipulators emphasize unusual, vivid examples to influence your choices.
2. **Skewing Risk Perception:** By focusing on a specific event, they make it seem more common or probable than it actually is.
3. **Triggering Emotional Reactions:** The vividness of the example clouds logical evaluation of actual risks.

The Availability Heuristic works because the human brain prioritizes information that is easy to recall, even if it's not representative of broader trends.

Real-Life Examples

1. **Travel Safety Concerns:** Highlighting a recent plane crash causes travelers to overestimate the danger of flying.
2. **Health Product Marketing:** Ads show dramatic testimonials of miraculous recoveries to sell supplements, even if such cases are rare.
3. **Home Security Sales:** Burglary anecdotes from neighboring towns are used to convince homeowners to install expensive security systems.

How to Spot the Availability Heuristic

1. **Question the Sample Size:** Ask if the example reflects a broader trend or is an isolated incident.
2. **Research the Actual Risk:** Look for statistics or data to validate the likelihood of the event influencing your decision.
3. **Resist Emotional Reactions:** Be cautious of decisions driven by fear, excitement, or other strong emotions tied to specific examples.

Exercise: Test Vivid Examples

1. Recall a recent decision influenced by a vivid example. Ask yourself:
   - "Was this event likely, or was it memorable because it was unusual?"
   - "Did I consider other possibilities or just focus on this one example?"

Role-Playing Drill:

- Partner with someone. One person presents a vivid anecdote to influence a decision, while the other practices questioning its relevance and considering broader context.

Key Takeaway

The Availability Heuristic uses vivid or recent examples to distort your judgment of likelihood or risk. Balance anecdotal examples with statistical data to make more informed decisions.

Chapter 68: The Familiarity Bias

When Familiarity Breeds Trust

You're planning a family vacation and searching for a travel agency. One agency catches your attention because you've seen their ads on Instagram, YouTube, and even in magazines. Their tagline, **"Trusted by millions,"** sticks in your mind. Without comparing alternatives, you book a package through them, assuming their widespread presence means reliability. After the trip, you realize you overpaid and that better deals were available through lesser-known providers.

This is the **Familiarity Bias**, where repeated exposure creates a sense of trust or credibility. Manipulators exploit this bias by flooding your attention with consistent messaging, making you believe their service or product is the best option without evidence to back it up.

How It Works

1. **Flooding the Audience:** Manipulators ensure their brand, product, or idea appears in multiple places — ads, emails, social media, or word-of-mouth.
2. **Creating a Sense of Comfort:** Familiar messages make people feel at ease, leading them to perceive them as safe or credible.
3. **Lowering Critical Evaluation:** Repeated exposure makes people less likely to question the validity of the product or idea, as familiarity creates an illusion of trustworthiness.

The Familiarity Bias works because humans instinctively trust what they recognize, associating these messages with safety and legitimacy.

Real-Life Examples

1. **Streaming Platforms:** A new series is repeatedly advertised across social media, email newsletters, and app notifications, making viewers assume it's a must-watch hit.
2. **Job Recruitment Services:** Career platforms constantly show the same companies in job recommendations, leading job seekers to perceive them as top employers without checking reviews.
3. **Charity Campaigns:** Non-profits bombard potential donors with the same message across mailers, emails, and ads, fostering trust through repeated exposure rather than transparent credibility.

Why It Works

The Familiarity Bias relies on three key tendencies:
1. **Comfort in Recognition:** People feel safer with things they've encountered multiple times, even if they're unfamiliar with the details.
2. **Shortcut to Credibility:** Familiarity creates the illusion of legitimacy, saving the brain from deeper analysis.
3. **Reduced Suspicion:** Overexposure dulls doubt, making the subject seem less like a risk.

This tactic works because it plays on the human tendency to associate repeating statements with trustworthiness.

How to Spot the Familiarity Bias

1. **Check the Source:** Ensure the subject's credibility by researching its background and legitimacy, not just its visibility.
2. **Look Beyond the Surface:** Compare alternatives before deciding.
3. **Notice Patterns:** Be wary when the same messages or claims appear frequently without substantive proof.

Exercise: Analyze Repeated Messages

1. Think of a brand or product you've seen advertised repeatedly. Ask yourself:
   - "What specific evidence supports their claims?"
   - "Have I considered other options, or am I choosing them because they're familiar?"
2. Write down two steps you can take to verify credibility beyond repeated exposure, such as checking reviews or independent sources.

Role-Playing Drill:

- Partner with someone. One person presents a product with repeated messaging, while the other practices asking questions to assess its legitimacy.

Key Takeaway

The Familiarity Bias manipulates trust through repeating messages, making something appear reliable without actual proof. Always verify credibility beyond repeated exposure and consider alternatives before committing.

It's only $45 a month — sounds like a deal!

That's $540 a year. The annual plan is actually cheaper.

"$500/year" and "$45/month — Unlimited Access!"

Chapter 69: The Framing Effect

How Presentation Changes Decisions

You're offered a payment plan for a subscription service. The representative presents two options: **"Pay $500 annually upfront"** or **"Only $45 a month for unlimited access!"** You choose the monthly option, feeling it's a better deal, even though it costs $540 over the year. The way the information was framed influenced your perception of value.

This is the **Framing Effect**, where the way information is presented shapes how it's perceived. Manipulators exploit this bias by emphasizing positive aspects or downplaying negatives, steering decisions toward their desired outcome.

How It Works

1. **Emphasizing Positives:** Manipulators highlight favorable details, such as discounts or bonuses, while minimizing drawbacks.
2. **Strategic Language Choices:** The use of words like "only" or "exclusive" influences how information is interpreted.
3. **Hiding True Costs:** Information is framed to make expenses or risks seem smaller or less significant.

The Framing Effect works because humans rely on context and presentation to evaluate choices, often making snap judgments based on surface impressions.

Real-Life Examples

1. **Medical Decisions:** A treatment is described as having a 90% success rate instead of a 10% failure rate, making it sound more appealing.
2. **Restaurant Menus:** Items are labeled as "Chef's Special" or "Locally Sourced" to frame them as premium, justifying higher prices.
3. **Retail Discounts:** Stores highlight **"You save $50!"** instead of simply listing the price, focusing attention on perceived value.

Why It Works

The Framing Effect thrives on three psychological factors:

1. **Context Drives Perception:** People interpret information differently depending on how it's presented.
2. **Positive Over Negative Framing:** Humans are naturally drawn to benefits and tend to avoid focusing on losses or risks.
3. **Reduced Analytical Thinking:** Framing shortcuts logical evaluation, making surface impressions more influential.

This tactic works because it leverages presentation to guide interpretation, often without the victim noticing.

How to Spot the Framing Effect

1. **Rephrase the Information:** Reframe the details yourself to see how the context changes your perception.
2. **Focus on the Facts:** Look beyond how something is presented and evaluate the core details objectively.
3. **Compare Alternatives:** Consider how similar options are described to detect manipulative framing.

Exercise: Reframe a Scenario

1. Think of a recent decision influenced by framing. Ask yourself:
   o "How would I perceive this if it were presented differently?"
   o "Does the framing align with the actual value or cost?"
2. Practice rephrasing offers or descriptions to uncover their true meaning.

Role-Playing Drill:

- Partner with someone. One person presents a framed scenario, while the other practices rephrasing it to evaluate the decision objectively.

Key Takeaway

The Framing Effect shapes decisions by manipulating how information is presented. Stay focused on the facts and reframe details to see the full picture before making choices.

Chapter 70: The Halo Effect

When Positivity Overshadows the Truth

You're shopping for a new smartphone and are drawn to a specific brand known for its sleek design. The salesperson praises the device's aesthetics, emphasizing its elegant build and premium look. Impressed, you purchase it without thoroughly comparing features or researching reviews. Later, you discover the phone's performance and battery life don't match its high price.

This is the **Halo Effect**, where a single positive trait, like appearance or reputation, leads to an inflated perception of overall quality. Manipulators exploit this bias by focusing on one standout feature to distract from flaws or shortcomings.

How It Works

1. **Highlighting Strengths:** Manipulators emphasize a single positive attribute, like visual appeal or past success, to influence perception.
2. **Creating Emotional Appeal:** They use that strength to evoke admiration, trust, or excitement, diverting attention from potential negatives.
3. **Leveraging Assumptions:** Victims assume that excellence in one area reflects the overall quality, even when there's no evidence to support it.

The Halo Effect works because humans often generalize, letting a single positive aspect dominate their evaluation.

Real-Life Examples

1. **Celebrity Endorsements:** A famous athlete promotes a sports drink, leading people to assume it's the healthiest option despite lacking nutritional proof.
2. **Corporate Reputation:** A company with a strong environmental record launches a product, and customers assume it's high-quality without further research.
3. **Luxury Branding:** A high-end clothing brand known for its stylish designs launches a line of accessories. Customers assume the accessories are equally high-quality, even though they haven't been reviewed or tested.

Why It Works

The Halo Effect relies on three cognitive tendencies:
1. **Attraction to Excellence:** People are drawn to outstanding traits and often associate them with overall quality.
2. **Mental Shortcuts:** The brain simplifies evaluations by generalizing from one positive aspect.
3. **Reduced Doubt:** Admiration for a standout trait lowers critical analysis of other factors.

This tactic works because it builds trust and credibility through partial impressions rather than complete assessments.

How to Spot the Halo Effect

1. **Look Beyond the Highlight:** Ask whether the emphasized trait truly reflects the overall quality of the product, person, or service.
2. **Research Details:** Investigate other features or aspects that may have been overshadowed.
3. **Question Assumptions:** Challenge whether the positive trait is relevant to your decision or merely a distraction.

Exercise: Identify a Halo Bias

1. Think of a recent purchase influenced by one standout feature. Reflect:
   o "Did this feature align with the overall quality?"
   o "Were there other factors I overlooked?"
2. Write down two ways to evaluate items holistically in the future, such as comparing multiple features or checking reviews.

Role-Playing Drill:

- Partner with someone. One person highlights a single exceptional trait of a product or service, while the other practices identifying and questioning potential shortcomings.

Key Takeaway

The Halo Effect leverages a single positive trait to create unwarranted trust. Always evaluate all aspects of a decision and avoid letting one strength overshadow critical thinking.

I totally get investing now. I bought their advanced toolset.

But that was just an intro talk. Maybe check expert reviews first?

Chapter 71: The Dunning-Kruger Effect Exploit

How Overconfidence Becomes a Tool for Manipulation

Imagine you're at a seminar on stock trading. The presenter teaches basic concepts like "buy low, sell high," praising the audience for their quick understanding. Feeling empowered, you purchase their advanced course and software tools, believing you're ready to become a professional trader. Weeks later, you realize you've spent hundreds of dollars but lack the deeper expertise needed for success.

This is the **Dunning-Kruger Effect Exploit**, where manipulators convince people they've mastered a topic after gaining minimal knowledge. By inflating confidence, they prompt individuals to make risky decisions, often to the manipulator's advantage.

How It Works

1. **Simplifying Concepts:** Manipulators present basic information as ground-breaking knowledge to make victims feel competent.
2. **Praising Quick Learners:** They exaggerate the victim's progress, building a false sense of expertise.
3. **Encouraging Overreach:** Once victims feel overconfident, manipulators push them to make larger commitments, like investments or purchases.

This tactic works because humans tend to overestimate their abilities after learning the basics of a subject, believing they're more skilled than they truly are.

Real-Life Examples

1. **Get-Rich-Quick Schemes:** Scammers teach simplistic financial strategies, convincing victims they can achieve wealth easily if they buy expensive resources.
2. **Fitness Plans:** Manipulators overpraise beginners for basic workouts, selling them advanced training programs they're not ready for.
3. **DIY Tutorials:** Minimal knowledge from tutorials is framed as sufficient expertise, encouraging people to buy expensive tools or materials for complex projects.

Why It Works

The Dunning-Kruger Effect Exploit thrives on three psychological tendencies:

1. **Overestimation of Knowledge:** People with limited knowledge often believe they know more than they actually do.
2. **Desire for Mastery:** Victims want to feel competent, making them receptive to flattery and praise.
3. **Ignoring Complexity:** Simplistic explanations create the illusion that a subject is easy to master, reducing caution.

This tactic works because it feeds overconfidence, pushing victims into decisions they're not prepared to make.

How to Spot the Dunning-Kruger Effect Exploit

1. **Assess the Complexity:** Ask yourself if the topic is being oversimplified or If there's more to learn.
2. **Seek Third-Party Validation:** Research whether the claims being made align with expert opinions or credible sources.
3. **Pause Before Committing:** Reflect on whether your confidence matches your actual level of understanding.

Exercise: Test Your Knowledge

1. Think of a subject where you feel confident after learning the basics. Ask yourself:
   o "How would an expert view my understanding?"
   o "What areas of this topic do I still need to explore?"
2. Write down two ways to assess your expertise more accurately, such as consulting a professional or diving deeper into advanced resources.

Role-Playing Drill:

- Partner with someone. One person presents a simplified scenario, while the other practices identifying gaps in their understanding and resisting overconfidence.

Key Takeaway

The Dunning-Kruger Effect Exploit inflates confidence to manipulate decisions. Recognize the limits of your knowledge, seek credible sources, and avoid acting on premature confidence.

Chapter 72: The Single Trait Trap

How One Trait Dominates the Decision

You're shopping for a new car, and the salesperson highlights its incredible fuel efficiency, claiming it will save you money in the long run. The advertisements also showcase glowing testimonials about the car's low gas consumption. Convinced, you make the purchase, but later you realize the car lacks important safety features and has expensive maintenance costs.

This is the **Single Trait Trap**, where one standout feature is exaggerated to divert attention from flaws or risks. Manipulators rely on this tactic to steer decisions, knowing that focusing on a single appealing trait will prevent a more thorough evaluation.

How It Works

1. **Highlighting the Strength:** Manipulators focus on a standout feature or benefit, ignoring potential downsides.
2. **Reinforcing the Message:** They repeat the positive trait in marketing, sales pitches, or reviews to make it the focal point.
3. **Downplaying Negatives:** Flaws are omitted, minimized, or hidden, ensuring the emphasis remains on the chosen characteristic.

The Single Trait Trap works because people naturally focus on memorable or impressive details, often neglecting a broader analysis.

Real-Life Examples

1. **Luxury Branding:** A watch brand markets its "Swiss craftsmanship" while concealing its high repair costs and lack of durability.
2. **Job Candidate Evaluations:** A candidate's prestigious university degree overshadows their lack of relevant experience.
3. **Real Estate Sales:** A house with a beautiful backyard is promoted heavily, while structural issues or poor location are downplayed.

Why It Works

The Single Trait Trap thrives on three psychological tendencies:

1. **Focus on Excellence:** People are drawn to standout qualities and often assume they indicate overall value.
2. **Limited Attention Span:** It's easier to focus on one striking feature than to evaluate a product or situation holistically.
3. **Emotional Anchoring:** A single positive trait creates a sense of trust or desire, reducing doubt about other aspects.

This tactic works because it narrows attention to one appealing characteristic, making it harder to consider other factors.

How to Spot the Single Trait Trap

1. **Identify Missing Information:** Ask whether other important details are being ignored or hidden.
2. **Balance Features:** Evaluate how the standout trait compares to other essential factors for your decision.
3. **Seek Unbiased Reviews:** Look for feedback that considers both strengths and weaknesses.

Exercise: Evaluate a Single Trait

1. Think of a product or service you were drawn to because of one specific feature. Ask yourself:
   o "Did I overlook other factors?"
   o "Would I make the same decision if I focused on the full picture?"
2. Practice identifying other critical traits or areas for future evaluations.

Role-Playing Drill:

- Partner with someone. One person emphasizes a single positive trait in a product or scenario, while the other practices asking about additional details and potential downsides.

Key Takeaway

The Single Trait Trap manipulates focus by emphasizing one positive characteristic while hiding flaws. Always evaluate the full picture and question whether other factors are being intentionally downplayed.

Chapter 73: The Loss Aversion Conundrum

When Fear of Loss Drives Decisions

You're considering joining a fitness program but feel unsure about the cost. The trainer emails you, saying, **"If you don't sign up by midnight, you'll miss out on this $150 discount."** The thought of losing the deal pushes you to enroll immediately, even though you're not completely confident it's the right fit.

This is the **Loss Aversion Conundrum**, a tactic where manipulators highlight what you'll lose by not acting rather than what you might gain. By focusing on potential losses, they trigger a psychological response that prioritizes avoiding regret over logical decision-making.

How It Works

1. **Highlighting Missed Opportunities:** Manipulators frame decisions around what victims could lose rather than potential benefits.
2. **Creating Emotional Pressure:** The fear of missing out on value or opportunity drives impulsive actions.
3. **Minimizing Rational Analysis:** Victims focus on avoiding immediate loss, often neglecting to evaluate long-term outcomes.

The Loss Aversion Conundrum works because humans feel the pain of loss more acutely than the pleasure of gain, making loss avoidance a powerful motivator.

Real-Life Examples

1. **Exclusive Event Invitations:** Organizers claim tickets are selling out quickly, pressuring attendees to book immediately, even though plenty of seats remain available.
2. **Auto Warranty Notices:** Car warranty companies send letters stating coverage will "end soon," encouraging unnecessary renewals or upgrades.
3. **Loyalty Program Alerts:** Retailers warn customers that accumulated rewards points will expire shortly, prompting rushed purchases to redeem them.

Why It Works

The Loss Aversion Conundrum leverages three psychological tendencies:

1. **Pain of Loss:** People often feel more motivated to avoid losing something they already have than to gain something new.
2. **Urgency to Act:** The thought of losing out creates a sense of immediate pressure, leading to snap decisions.
3. **Emotional Weight:** Loss carries a heavier emotional impact than equivalent gains, making it a stronger motivator.

This tactic works because it turns potential loss into a priority, often overriding logical evaluation.

How to Spot the Loss Aversion Conundrum

1. **Identify the Framing:** Ask whether the offer focuses on what you're losing instead of what you're gaining.
2. **Pause to Evaluate:** Step back and consider if the urgency is genuine or manufactured.
3. **Compare Long-Term Impact:** Reflect on whether acting quickly aligns with your overall goals or priorities.

Exercise: Reflect on Loss Framing

1. Think of a recent decision driven by a fear of loss. Ask yourself:
   - "Was the urgency real, or was it created to pressure me?"
   - "Did I consider the benefits and risks equally?"
2. Write down two strategies to avoid being pressured by loss-focused messaging, such as setting a 24-hour pause rule.

Role-Playing Drill:

- Partner with someone. One person uses loss aversion messaging to create urgency, while the other practices identifying the tactic and evaluating the decision objectively.

Key Takeaway

The Loss Aversion Conundrum manipulates decisions by focusing on potential losses. Avoid rushing into actions — evaluate both risks and rewards before deciding.

Chapter 74: The Status Quo Bias Manipulation

When Comfort Leads to Missed Opportunities

You've had the same Internet provider for years, despite frequent outages and rising costs. Every time you consider switching, the thought of researching alternatives and going through the process feels overwhelming. The provider sends you a loyalty discount to encourage you to stay, and you renew your plan without exploring better options.

This is the **Status Quo Bias Manipulation**, where manipulators rely on the human tendency to stick with familiar choices rather than explore new ones. By making change seem inconvenient or unnecessary, they maintain control over your decisions.

How It Works

1. **Reinforcing Familiarity:** Manipulators emphasize the comfort and reliability of the current option.
2. **Highlighting Effort:** They exaggerate the effort or risk involved in making a change.
3. **Framing Alternatives as Uncertain:** New options are portrayed as risky or unreliable, discouraging exploration.

The Status Quo Bias Manipulation works because humans naturally prefer stability and consistency, even when change could lead to better outcomes.

Real-Life Examples

1. **Utility Providers:** Electricity or cable companies offer small loyalty discounts to keep customers from switching to cheaper competitors.
2. **Banking Services:** Banks stress the "seamlessness" of staying with their accounts while downplaying the benefits of moving to another institution.
3. **Corporate Software:** Businesses discourage switching platforms by emphasizing the costs of training employees on new systems.

Why It Works

This manipulation relies on three psychological tendencies:

1. **Comfort in Familiarity:** People prefer sticking with what they know rather than taking risks with the unknown.
2. **Avoidance of Effort:** Change often requires time, research, and adjustments, which many people instinctively avoid.
3. **Perception of Stability:** Familiar options are perceived as safer and less likely to disrupt existing routines.

This tactic works because it keeps people locked into decisions by making alternatives seem unappealing or overly complex.

How to Spot the Status Quo Bias Manipulation

1. **Evaluate Alternatives:** Take the time to explore and compare other options, even if they require effort.
2. **Recognize Emotional Barriers:** Identify whether hesitation comes from fear of disruption or actual risks.
3. **Weigh Long-Term Benefits:** Consider whether staying with the familiar truly serves your best interests.

Exercise: Challenge Your Comfort Zone

1. Think of a service, subscription, or routine you've stuck with for years. Reflect:
    o "Have I actively compared alternatives?"
    o "What benefits might I gain from exploring new options?"
2. Write down two steps you can take to evaluate alternatives, such as researching reviews or seeking recommendations.

Role-Playing Drill:

- Partner with someone. One person plays the role of a service provider emphasizing the ease of staying, while the other practices weighing pros and cons of switching.

Key Takeaway

The Status Quo Bias Manipulation uses comfort and familiarity to maintain control over your decisions. Take the time to evaluate whether staying in your current situation truly aligns with your goals or if change could benefit you.

Chapter 75: The Optimism Bias Trick

When Optimism Clouds Judgment

You're offered a discounted extended warranty for a laptop. Confident in its brand reputation and your careful handling, you decline, thinking, **"I've never needed a warranty before."** A few months later, the laptop unexpectedly malfunctions, and the repair costs outweigh the original price of the warranty.

This is the **Optimism Bias Trick**, where manipulators exploit the assumption that bad outcomes are unlikely to happen to you. By reinforcing overconfidence and minimizing risks, they prompt decisions that ignore potential downsides.

How It Works

1. **Minimizing Risk Perception:** Manipulators reassure you that the likelihood of problems is slim or irrelevant.
2. **Encouraging Overconfidence:** They appeal to your belief in your own good luck, skills, or judgment to downplay caution.
3. **Redirecting Focus:** By emphasizing benefits or positive possibilities, they shift attention away from safeguards or contingencies.

The Optimism Bias Trick works because humans often overestimate their immunity to negative outcomes, leading to riskier choices.

Real-Life Examples

1. **Travel Insurance Declines:** Agents subtly encourage travelers to skip insurance, framing it as unnecessary for their "safe" plans.
2. **Loan Agreements:** Borrowers are encouraged to take on high-interest loans, assuming they'll repay quickly without considering financial challenges.
3. **Event Deposits:** Companies emphasize non-refundable terms after assuring customers that cancellations are unlikely.

Why It Works

This manipulation relies on three cognitive tendencies:

1. **Overestimation of Personal Control:** People believe their actions or decisions will prevent bad outcomes.
2. **Focus on Positive Scenarios:** Optimism narrows attention to best-case outcomes, ignoring potential risks.
3. **Aversion to Planning for Problems:** Preparing for potential setbacks feels unnecessary when outcomes seem assured.

This tactic works because it reinforces confidence, reducing precautionary measures or thorough evaluation.

How to Spot the Optimism Bias Trick

1. **Consider Past Experiences:** Reflect on whether previous decisions turned out differently than expected.
2. **Anticipate Worst-Case Scenarios:** Ask, "What would I do if things didn't go as planned?"
3. **Research Alternatives:** Look for unbiased opinions or data that highlight risks or precautions.

Exercise: Reflect on Missed Precautions

1. Think of a recent decision where optimism influenced your choice. Reflect:
   - "What risks did I overlook?"
   - "How could I have prepared better?"
2. Write down two steps to ensure balanced decision-making, such as researching risks or consulting experts.

Role-Playing Drill:

- Partner with someone. One person presents an overly optimistic scenario, while the other practices identifying potential risks and countermeasures.

Key Takeaway

The Optimism Bias Trick manipulates your confidence, making you overlook risks and safeguards. Balance positive expectations with realistic preparation to avoid unexpected setbacks.

Chapter 76: The Confirmation Bias Bait

How Familiar Ideas Build Trust

You're considering a new fitness program and come across an ad that says, **"Scientific evidence proves that high-intensity workouts burn more calories."** Since you already believe high-intensity workouts are effective, you quickly sign up for the program without exploring other options. Later, you discover the plan doesn't align with your fitness goals or health needs.

This is the **Confirmation Bias Bait**, a tactic where manipulators provide information that aligns with your existing beliefs to gain trust and steer your decisions. By confirming what you already think is true, they bypass critical analysis and guide you into their desired outcome.

How It Works

1. **Identifying Beliefs:** Manipulators study your preferences, opinions, or biases to craft targeted messages.
2. **Reinforcing Comfort Zones:** They provide data, testimonials, or stories that align with your existing worldview, making their offer seem trustworthy.
3. **Suppressing Contradictory Evidence:** Dissenting information is omitted, keeping you focused on their carefully curated narrative.

The Confirmation Bias Bait works because humans naturally seek information that supports their beliefs and avoid details that challenge them.

Real-Life Examples

1. **Eco-Friendly Branding:** A cleaning product advertises its use of natural ingredients to appeal to environmentally conscious consumers, while omitting its high plastic packaging usage.
2. **Streaming Recommendations:** A platform promotes shows or movies that match a user's viewing history, encouraging continued subscriptions without showcasing diverse options.
3. **Education Programs:** Online courses emphasize how their teaching aligns with widely accepted study methods but neglect to mention the lack of accreditation or credentials.

Why It Works

This manipulation leverages three psychological tendencies:
1. **Comfort in Agreement:** People are more likely to trust information that aligns with their pre-existing beliefs.
2. **Selective Attention:** Victims focus on supportive details, ignoring gaps or alternative perspectives.
3. **Resistance to Contradiction:** Contradictory information feels uncomfortable, reducing motivation to seek it out.

This tactic works because it creates a false sense of validation, leading people to lower their guard.

How to Spot the Confirmation Bias Bait

1. **Seek Contrasting Perspectives:** Explore alternative viewpoints or information that challenges your assumptions.
2. **Check for Missing Details:** Ask whether important facts or counterarguments are being excluded.
3. **Verify Claims Independently:** Research the sources or data supporting the message to ensure accuracy.

Exercise: Test Your Assumptions

1. Identify a recent decision that aligned with your beliefs. Ask yourself:
   - "Did I actively seek out alternative viewpoints?"
   - "Was I presented with all the relevant information?"
2. Write down two strategies to challenge your assumptions, such as asking questions or consulting impartial sources.

Role-Playing Drill:

- Partner with someone. One person presents an argument that aligns with the other's beliefs, while the other practices questioning its validity and seeking alternative perspectives.

Key Takeaway

The Confirmation Bias Bait manipulates trust by aligning with existing beliefs. Balance your comfort zone with a willingness to explore alternative views and verify information.

Chapter 77: The Anchoring Trap

When the First Number Sticks

You're shopping for a new sofa, and the salesperson shows you a high-end model priced at $4,000. It's beautiful but out of your budget. Then they show you another sofa for $2,000, emphasizing its "significant savings" compared to the first option. Relieved, you buy it, even though it's more expensive than you planned to spend.

This is the **Anchoring Trap**, where an initial value is presented to shape your perception of subsequent options. By anchoring your expectations to an exaggerated baseline, manipulators make alternatives seem more appealing, even when they're not ideal.

How It Works

1. **Establishing the Anchor:** Manipulators present an initial number, price, or value to create a reference point.
2. **Shaping Comparisons:** Future options are framed relative to the anchor, making them seem better or more reasonable.
3. **Fostering Quick Decisions:** Anchoring discourages deeper analysis, as people focus on the initial value rather than the broader context.

The Anchoring Trap works because humans are influenced by the first piece of information they encounter, even when it's irrelevant or exaggerated.

Real-Life Examples

1. **Retail Discounts:** Stores advertise inflated "original prices" to make standard discounts seem extraordinary.
2. **Salary Negotiations:** Employers start with a low offer, making slightly higher amounts seem generous, even if they're below market value.
3. **Luxury Comparisons:** Car dealerships show premium models first, making mid-range options seem affordable by comparison.

Why It Works

The Anchoring Trap thrives on three cognitive tendencies:
1. **Focus on Initial Values:** People instinctively reference the first number they encounter, even when irrelevant.
2. **Ease of Comparison:** Anchors simplify decisions by creating clear contrasts, even if they're misleading.
3. **Emotional Influence:** High anchors create relief when subsequent options feel like savings or compromises.

This tactic works because it shapes perceptions, steering decisions toward alternatives that may not truly align with your needs.

How to Spot the Anchoring Trap

1. **Ignore the Anchor:** Focus on whether the option meets your needs rather than comparing it to the initial value.
2. **Research Actual Costs:** Investigate average prices or values to establish an independent baseline.
3. **Evaluate Alternatives:** Consider options without referencing the anchor to assess their standalone value.

Exercise: Identify an Anchor

1. Think of a recent purchase influenced by an initial price or value. Reflect:
    o "Did I evaluate the option independently of the anchor?"
    o "Was the anchor relevant to my decision?"
2. Write down two ways to avoid anchoring in future decisions, such as comparing multiple sources or setting your own baseline.

Role-Playing Drill:

- Partner with someone. One person presents an anchored scenario, while the other practices identifying and ignoring the anchor to make an objective choice.

Key Takeaway

The Anchoring Trap steers decisions by presenting an initial value to shape perceptions. Focus on your own priorities and research independently to avoid being influenced by artificial benchmarks.

Chapter 78: The Illusory Truth Effect

When Illusion Becomes Belief

You hear a friend mention a popular diet plan claiming, **"You can lose 10 pounds in a week!"** Later, you see the same message in social media ads and hear it on a podcast. You decide to try the diet, only to find it unsustainable and potentially harmful.

This is the **Illusory Truth Effect**, where statements that are broadcasted on several platforms begin to feel accurate. Manipulators exploit this, building trust and confidence in false or misleading claims.

How It Works

1. **Message Frequency Reinforces Familiarity:** The more often a statement is heard or seen, the more familiar it feels, leading to perceived accuracy.
2. **Reducing Effortful Thinking:** Familiar statements are processed more easily by the brain, creating a shortcut to perceived truth.
3. **Widespread Messaging:** Manipulators amplify their claims across multiple platforms to ensure consistent exposure.

The Illusory Truth Effect works because humans equate familiarity with reliability, making some falsehoods feel convincing over time.

Real-Life Examples

1. **Health Myths:** Claims such as **"Detox teas cleanse your system"** are repeated in ads, despite lacking scientific support.
2. **Political Narratives:** Politicians repeat misleading statistics or slogans to shape public opinion.
3. **Product Superiority Claims:** Brands repeatedly declare themselves as **"#1 in customer satisfaction"** without providing evidence.

Why It Works

This manipulation thrives on three psychological tendencies:

1. **Ease of Processing:** Familiar statements are easier to process, making them feel true.
2. **Trust in The Illusion:** Consistent exposure lowers resistance to the message, especially if it's unchallenged.
3. **Social Validation:** Hearing the same message from multiple sources creates the fake assurance of consensus.

This tactic works because it removes doubt by serving the same messaging frequently to individuals.

How to Spot the Illusory Truth Effect

1. **Seek Evidence:** Look for independent verification of repeated claims.
2. **Question the Source:** Identify whether the message originates from credible, unbiased sources.
3. **Recognize Patterns:** Watch out for messages that lack substance.

Exercise: Analyze Illusory Claims

1. Identify a belief or statement you've encountered multiple times. Reflect:
   o "Is this claim supported by evidence?"
   o "Where have I seen or heard it before?"
2. Write down two ways to verify information, such as consulting expert opinions or checking reliable sources.

Role-Playing Drill:

- Partner with someone. One person repeats a false claim, while the other practices identifying repetition and questioning its validity.

Key Takeaway

The Illusory Truth Effect aims to transform falsehoods into perceived truths. Always verify claims and avoid assuming accuracy based on familiarity alone.

This course isn't helping me, but I paid for it—so I have to finish.

But if it's not useful anymore, why keep going?

Chapter 79: The Sunk Cost Fallacy Lever

When Past Investments Cloud Judgment

You've subscribed to an online course but find it unhelpful after the first few weeks. Despite this, you continue attending, thinking, **"I've already paid for it, so I need to finish."** The time and money you've spent keep you committed, even though the course isn't benefiting you.

This is the **Sunk Cost Fallacy Lever**, where manipulators exploit your reluctance to abandon past investments, prompting continued commitment to bad decisions.

How It Works

1. **Highlighting Past Investments:** Manipulators remind you of the time, money, or effort you've already spent to keep you engaged.

2. **Triggering Emotional Attachments:** They use guilt or pride to tie your identity to the decision, making withdrawal feel like failure.

3. **Downplaying Future Costs:** The emphasis stays on what's been invested, diverting attention from the ongoing toll.

The Sunk Cost Fallacy Lever works because humans dislike the feeling of waste and prefer to justify previous decisions, even at a continued cost.

Real-Life Examples

1. **Subscription Renewals:** Services highlight your years of membership to encourage renewals, even if you no longer find value.

2. **Expensive Repairs:** Mechanics emphasize previous repair costs to justify further investment in a failing vehicle.

3. **Event Attendance:** People attend an event they don't enjoy simply because they paid for the tickets.

Why It Works

This manipulation leverages three cognitive tendencies:

1. **Aversion to Waste:** People feel compelled to "make the most" of past investments.

2. **Emotional Commitment:** Time and effort create a sense of personal attachment, discouraging change.

3. **Rationalization of Effort:** Victims justify poor decisions by focusing on what they've already given, rather than what they stand to lose.

This tactic works because it keeps people locked into cycles of diminishing returns.

How to Spot the Sunk Cost Fallacy Lever

1. **Focus on the Future:** Ask yourself, "What will continuing cost me, and is it worth it?"

2. **Separate Emotions from Logic:** Recognize when guilt or pride is influencing your decision.

3. **Evaluate Alternatives:** Consider whether walking away could open better opportunities.

Exercise: Reassess a Past Investment

1. Think of a recent situation where you felt stuck because of past investments. Reflect:
   o "Did continuing truly benefit me?"
   o "What alternatives could I have explored?"

2. Write down two steps to prioritize future value over past costs, such as setting clear limits on additional investments.

Role-Playing Drill:

- Partner with someone. One person highlights sunk costs, while the other practices focusing on future benefits and rational decision-making.

Key Takeaway

The Sunk Cost Fallacy Lever keeps people committed to poor decisions by emphasizing past investments. Shift your focus to future outcomes and recognize when it's better to let go.

Chapter 80: The Framing Effect Twist

When Presentation Changes Perception

You're shopping for health insurance and see two plans. One is described as covering **"90% of medical expenses,"** while the other highlights that **"you'll pay only 10% out-of-pocket."** Both plans offer the same coverage, but the first feels more generous, so you choose it without comparing the details further.

This is the **Framing Effect Twist**, where manipulators shape how you perceive choices by altering the way information is presented. By emphasizing positives or reframing negatives, they nudge you toward decisions that serve their interests, even when the underlying facts remain unchanged.

How It Works

1. **Highlighting the Positive Frame:** Manipulators emphasize benefits or favorable aspects of an option to make it seem more appealing.
2. **Minimizing the Negative Frame:** They present drawbacks in a way that makes them feel insignificant or even acceptable.
3. **Redirecting Focus:** By controlling the language or structure of information, manipulators guide your attention to what they want you to see.

The Framing Effect Twist works because humans rely on context to interpret information, often reacting emotionally to the way it's presented rather than evaluating the facts.

Real-Life Examples

1. **Hotel Rates:** A hotel advertises "Stay for just $150 per night" instead of the total cost of a week-long stay, making the expense seem less intimidating.
2. **Warranty Offers:** Electronics retailers promote "Peace of mind for just 50 cents a day" rather than stating the full yearly cost of the warranty.
3. **Insurance Plans:** Health insurers highlight "90% of claims paid on time" instead of mentioning that 10% are delayed, framing their service as reliable.

Why It Works

This tactic thrives on three psychological tendencies:
1. **Emotional Reactions to Words:** Positive language evokes trust or excitement, while negatives provoke caution.
2. **Simplified Decision-Making:** Framing reduces the need for deeper analysis, making quick choices more likely.
3. **Context-Driven Judgment:** People interpret information based on how it's framed, not its actual content.

The Framing Effect Twist works because it capitalizes on human reliance on context, nudging decisions toward what feels more appealing.

How to Spot the Framing Effect Twist

1. **Rephrase the Information:** Rewrite statements in different ways to see if the underlying meaning changes.
2. **Compare Options Objectively:** Focus on the actual data or facts, rather than the language used to describe them.
3. **Recognize Emotional Triggers:** Be wary of words or phrases designed to elicit strong feelings.

Exercise: Reframe a Decision

1. Think of a recent decision influenced by how it was framed. Reflect:
   o "Would I feel differently if the wording were changed?"
   o "Did the framing emphasize benefits or minimize drawbacks?"
2. Write down two strategies to evaluate options based on facts, such as creating a pros-and-cons list.

Role-Playing Drill:

• Partner with someone. One person presents the same information with different framing (positive vs. negative), while the other practices identifying the true meaning behind the language.

Key Takeaway

The Framing Effect Twist manipulates decisions by shaping how information is presented. To counter this, focus on the underlying facts and avoid being swayed by emotional or persuasive language.

Section V: Defensive Mastery

This final section equips you with the tools to defend against some of the most insidious and subtle manipulation tactics. Each chapter dissects a specific technique, revealing how manipulators operate and offering actionable strategies to protect yourself. Whether the attack comes through emotional appeals, digital deception, or psychological pressure, you'll learn to recognize the signs, respond with confidence, and stay in control.

Chapter 81: The Psychological Takeover

How Emotional Intensity Undermines Logic

You're negotiating a refund for a defective product, and the representative becomes increasingly agitated, raising their voice and flooding the conversation with emotional outbursts. Overwhelmed, you relent and accept store credit instead of insisting on a full refund.

This is the **Psychological Takeover**, where manipulators use intense emotions — such as anger, despair, or excitement — to hijack logical reasoning. By creating an emotionally charged environment, they overwhelm your ability to think clearly, pressuring you into compliance.

How It Works

1. **Escalating Emotions:** Manipulators amplify feelings of fear, anger, or urgency to create mental overwhelm.
2. **Diverting Focus:** Emotional intensity distracts you from evaluating the situation critically or questioning their intentions.
3. **Demanding Immediate Action:** Once logic is disrupted, manipulators push for decisions before emotions settle.

The Psychological Takeover works because humans prioritize emotional responses over rational thinking in high-stress situations.

Real-Life Examples

1. **Aggressive Sales Tactics:** High-pressure salespeople use excitement and urgency to rush buyers into expensive purchases.
2. **Personal Conflicts:** Manipulators in relationships escalate arguments to guilt or pressure their partners into giving in.
3. **Workplace Demands:** A manager raises their voice and emphasizes tight deadlines to pressure employees into taking on extra tasks without question.

Why It Works

This tactic exploits three key psychological tendencies:

1. **Emotional Overload:** High-intensity emotions block rational thought, creating a reactive mindset.
2. **Desire to De-escalate:** Targets comply to reduce emotional tension or avoid further conflict.
3. **Rushed Decisions:** Emotional urgency prompts snap judgments, leaving little time for reflection.

This tactic works because it capitalizes on heightened emotions to cloud judgment and force hasty actions.

How to Spot the Psychological Takeover

1. **Recognize Emotional Shifts:** Notice when a conversation becomes overly heated or dramatic.
2. **Pause and Reflect:** Take a step back to let emotions subside before responding.
3. **Ask for Time:** Request a break to assess the situation calmly and regain focus.

Exercise: Practice Emotional Detachment

1. Recall a situation where you felt pressured during an emotional conversation. Reflect:
   o "How could I have paused to regain control?"
   o "What questions could I have asked to slow things down?"
2. Write down two strategies to use when facing emotional pressure, such as taking deep breaths or stepping away momentarily.

Role-Playing Drill:

- Partner with someone. One person practices escalating emotions, while the other works on staying calm and responding logically.

Key Takeaway

The Psychological Takeover relies on emotional intensity to overpower logical reasoning. Stay calm, pause for reflection, and avoid rushing into decisions under emotional pressure.

Chapter 82: The False Helper

When Someone Has Hidden Motives

You're at a crowded train station, struggling to carry your luggage up the stairs. A stranger offers assistance, smiling and insisting they only want to help. While they carry your bag, you notice later that your wallet is missing.

This is the **False Helper**, where manipulators use the guise of goodwill to lower your defenses. By appearing generous and selfless, they gain trust and access, paving the way for exploitation.

How It Works

1. **Establishing Trust Through Kindness:** Manipulators perform helpful gestures to appear trustworthy and approachable.
2. **Identifying Vulnerabilities:** They target moments when victims are distracted, overwhelmed, or in need of assistance.
3. **Capitalizing on Gratitude:** By earning appreciation, manipulators create a sense of obligation or lower the target's suspicion.

The False Helper works because humans are conditioned to trust and appreciate acts of kindness, making them less likely to question the helper's motives.

Real-Life Examples

1. **Online Scams:** Fraudsters offer free advice or tech support, then request sensitive information or payment for unnecessary services.
2. **In-Person Theft:** Pickpockets distract their targets by offering to help with directions or heavy bags while stealing from them.
3. **Professional Settings:** Colleagues offer to "help" with a project to gain access to confidential documents or ideas they can claim as their own.

Why It Works

This manipulation thrives on three psychological tendencies:
1. **Reciprocity Instinct:** People feel compelled to trust and repay acts of kindness.
2. **Lowered Defenses:** Acts of goodwill create an emotional barrier against suspicion.
3. **Gratitude Blindness:** Targets focus on the apparent kindness, missing potential red flags.

This tactic works because it combines trust-building with strategic exploitation, taking advantage of moments when victims are most vulnerable.

How to Spot the False Helper

1. **Question the Motive:** Ask yourself, "Is this act of kindness necessary, or could it serve a hidden purpose?"
2. **Stay Vigilant in Vulnerable Moments:** Be cautious when receiving help in high-stress or crowded environments.
3. **Set Boundaries:** Politely decline assistance if something feels off, and observe how the person reacts.

Exercise: Recognize Genuine Help

1. Reflect on a situation where you received unexpected help. Ask yourself:
   o "Did the person's behavior seem overly insistent or calculated?"
   o "Were there any hidden consequences of accepting the help?"
2. Write down two strategies to evaluate goodwill, such as staying alert to motives or maintaining control over personal belongings.

Role-Playing Drill:

- Partner with someone. One person offers unsolicited help in a simulated scenario, while the other practices politely setting boundaries and identifying suspicious behavior.

Key Takeaway

The False Helper manipulates trust by disguising exploitation as kindness. Stay alert and evaluate acts of goodwill, especially in vulnerable moments, to protect yourself from hidden motives.

Chapter 83: The Deceptive Question

You're chatting with someone new at a networking event. They ask, **"What's your role at the company?"** followed by **"Do you handle client accounts or payments?"** The questions feel friendly and engaging, so you answer openly. Days later, you realize they've used the information to pose as you in an email sent to your clients.

This is the **Deceptive Question**, where manipulators mask their motives with casual or polite inquiries to gather personal, financial, or sensitive information. By disguising their true intent, they lure targets into revealing more than they realize.

How It Works

1. **Building Rapport:** Manipulators establish a friendly or professional connection to create a sense of safety.
2. **Using Open-Ended Questions:** They ask broad or seemingly innocent questions to encourage detailed responses.
3. **Extracting Key Details:** They steer the conversation toward information that can be exploited, such as passwords, schedules, or sensitive access points.

The Deceptive Question works because humans are naturally inclined to answer questions in social or professional settings without suspicion, especially when rapport has been established.

Real-Life Examples

1. **Charity Fundraisers:** Individuals posing as charitable organizations ask questions about your income or spending habits under the guise of assessing how much you can donate.
2. **Event Invitations:** Someone asks about your availability, workplace location, or routine under the pretense of inviting you to an exclusive networking event.
3. **Neighborly Conversations:** A new neighbor casually inquires about your home's security features or the schedules of others in the community, masking intentions to gather exploitable details.

Why It Works

This tactic relies on three key psychological tendencies:

1. **Trust in Familiarity:** People are more likely to open up to someone who seems approachable or relatable.
2. **Desire to Be Polite:** Answering questions feels natural in social or professional interactions.
3. **Subtlety of Questions:** The manipulator's inquiries often feel harmless, lowering the target's guard.

The Deceptive Question works because it disguises exploitation as casual curiosity, encouraging targets to share sensitive details without realizing the risk.

How to Spot the Deceptive Question

1. **Evaluate the Context:** Ask yourself if the question is appropriate for the situation or if it feels out of place.
2. **Avoid Oversharing:** Stick to general answers and avoid giving unnecessary personal or sensitive details.
3. **Question the Questioner:** Politely inquire why they need specific information and observe their response.

Exercise: Filter Your Answers

1. Reflect on a recent conversation where someone asked personal questions. Ask yourself:
   o "Was the information I shared necessary?"
   o "Could they use any details I shared against me?"
2. Write down two strategies to limit your responses, such as giving broad answers or redirecting the conversation.

Role-Playing Drill:

- Partner with someone. One person asks open-ended questions, while the other practices identifying and avoiding over-disclosure.

Key Takeaway

The Deceptive Question uses subtle inquiries to extract critical information under the guise of casual conversation. Protect yourself by staying alert, questioning motives, and limiting the details you share.

Chapter 84: The "Too Good to Be True" Trap

How Temptation Overrides Caution

You receive an email that says, **"You've been selected for an all-expenses-paid vacation!"** Excited, you click the link and follow instructions to claim your prize. Only later do you realize the catch: you've shared your personal information, fallen for a scam, or been charged "processing fees" for a trip that doesn't exist.

This is the **"Too Good to Be True" Trap**, where manipulators exploit irresistible offers to lure people into making hasty decisions. These offers are designed to appeal to emotions like excitement or greed, distracting targets from asking critical questions.

How It Works

1. **Creating an Irresistible Offer:** Manipulators promise unbelievable rewards, such as huge discounts, free prizes, or exclusive opportunities.
2. **Building Urgency:** Victims are pressured to act quickly before the offer "expires," leaving no time to verify its authenticity.
3. **Masking Hidden Costs:** The full terms and consequences of the offer are obscured, ensuring that victims only realize the risks after they've taken the bait.

The "Too Good to Be True" Trap works because the promise of a reward overrides critical thinking, leading people to act recklessly.

Real-Life Examples

1. **Lottery Scams:** Emails claim you've won a foreign lottery but require an upfront fee to process your "winnings."
2. **Unbelievable Discounts:** Ads promise high-value items like smartphones or luxury handbags at impossibly low prices, leading to non-existent or counterfeit products.
3. **Job Offers:** Scammers offer "work-from-home" jobs with high pay but request upfront fees for training or equipment.

Why It Works

This manipulation thrives on three psychological tendencies:

1. **Excitement Over Caution:** The allure of a reward clouds judgment and reduces doubt.
2. **Desire for Exclusivity:** Offers make targets feel special, encouraging quick action.
3. **Trust in Appearances:** Professional-looking websites give a false sense of legitimacy.

This tactic works because it appeals to emotional desires while minimizing the opportunity for rational evaluation.

How to Spot the "Too Good to Be True" Trap

1. **Question the Offer:** Ask, "Is this offer realistic? Why would they give away such a large reward?"
2. **Research the Source:** Verify the sender or company offering the deal through independent channels.
3. **Look for Hidden Terms:** Check for vague conditions, hidden fees, or requests for personal or financial information.

Exercise: Evaluate Tempting Offers

1. Think of a time when you were tempted by an unbelievable deal or prize. Reflect:
   - "Did I verify the offer's authenticity?"
   - "What questions should I have asked before acting?"
2. Write down two steps to assess future offers, such as researching the source or comparing similar deals.

Role-Playing Drill:

- Partner with someone. One person presents an enticing but unrealistic offer, while the other practices identifying red flags and asking clarifying questions.

Key Takeaway

The "Too Good to Be True" Trap manipulates emotions with tempting offers. Always verify the details and question offers that seem overly generous or unrealistic.

Chapter 85: The False Urgency Alarm

When Pressure Overrides Caution

You're booking tickets for a concert, and a banner on the website says, **"Only 5 seats left!"** Feeling the rush, you complete the purchase without checking the seating arrangement or refund policy. Later, you find better seats on a different platform — still available at a lower price. The "limited seats" message wasn't true.

This is the **False Urgency Alarm**, a manipulation tactic that fabricates pressure to force quick decisions. By making opportunities seem fleeting, manipulators prevent targets from fully analyzing their options, increasing the chances of impulsive actions.

How It Works

1. **Simulating Restrictions:** Manipulators create fake limited stock or exclusive deadlines to make offers seem rare.
2. **Triggering Decision Fatigue:** The rush to act overwhelms logical thinking and encourages emotional responses.
3. **Hiding Flaws or Risks:** Urgency makes people overlook essential details, like hidden fees or poor quality.

The False Urgency Alarm works because humans instinctively prioritize immediate action when faced with perceived scarcity or pressure, often neglecting thorough evaluation.

Real-Life Examples

1. **Limited-Edition Drops:** Online stores claim items are part of an exclusive release, but restock the same products regularly.
2. **Travel Deals:** Airline websites display messages like **"Only 2 seats left at this price!"** even when more seats are available, creating unnecessary pressure to book quickly.
3. **Real Estate Listings:** Agents emphasize phrases like, **"This property won't stay on the market long!"** to prevent buyers from exploring alternatives.

Why It Works

This tactic preys on three psychological tendencies:
1. **Response to False Alarms:** People make faster, less considered decisions when they feel rushed.
2. **Focus on "Unique Offers":** Limited availability creates a sense of value and importance.
3. **Not Wanting to Miss Out:** The possibility losing out on a deal or opportunity amplifies urgency.

The False Urgency Alarm works because it creates artificial constraints that drive hasty decisions.

How to Spot the False Urgency Alarm

1. **Check for Consistency:** Look for evidence that the urgency is genuine, such as product availability across multiple platforms.
2. **Don't Act Immediately:** Take a moment to evaluate the offer, even if the deadline seems short.
3. **Investigate the Source:** Research the sender or company to confirm the legitimacy of their claims.

Exercise: Practice Pausing Under Pressure

1. Recall a recent situation where you felt rushed to act. Reflect:
   o "What would I have done differently with more time?"
   o "Was the urgency real or manufactured?"
2. Write down two strategies to create space for evaluation, such as setting a personal time limit before responding.

Role-Playing Drill:

- Partner with someone. One person creates an artificial sense of urgency, while the other practices pausing and asking clarifying questions before deciding.

Key Takeaway

The False Urgency Alarm pressures decisions by fabricating time constraints. Slow down, verify the claims, and ensure your actions align with your priorities.

Chapter 86: The Trust Shortcut

When Familiarity Opens the Door

You're on vacation in a foreign city when someone approaches you and says, **"Aren't you from Chicago? I used to live there!"** Excited by the connection, you chat freely, sharing details about your plans and hotel. Hours later, you realize your room was broken into—and you suspect the person used your shared details to target you.

This is the **Trust Shortcut**, where manipulators create instant familiarity to lower defenses. By mimicking social cues, finding common ground, or appearing knowledgeable, they establish trust without earning it, leaving their targets vulnerable to exploitation.

How It Works

1. **Creating a Connection:** Manipulators identify or invent similarities — such as shared hometowns, schools, or hobbies — to build a sense of rapport.
2. **Mimicking Behavior:** They mirror body language, tone, or speech patterns to make interactions feel comfortable and natural.
3. **Leveraging the Bond:** Once trust is established, they subtly introduce requests, extract information, or exploit the relationship.

The Trust Shortcut works because humans tend to trust those who seem similar or relatable, often overlooking inconsistencies.

Real-Life Examples

1. **Job Scams:** Fraudsters pose as former employees of a company, claiming insider knowledge to build trust during recruitment or investment schemes.
2. **Tourist Cons:** Manipulators pose as fellow travelers, sharing fabricated experiences to gain trust and steal belongings.
3. **Neighborhood Scams:** Fraudsters pose as new neighbors, mentioning nearby landmarks or community events to seem credible. They then exploit this trust to borrow money, gain access to homes, or gather sensitive information.

Why It Works

This manipulation tactic succeeds because of three key psychological tendencies:
1. **Bias Toward Similarity:** People trust those they perceive as being like themselves.
2. **Desire for Belonging:** Establishing common ground makes interactions feel meaningful and safe.
3. **Assumed Credibility:** Targets are less likely to question someone who seems relatable or familiar.

The Trust Shortcut works because it creates the illusion of authenticity, allowing manipulators to remove doubt.

How to Spot the Trust Shortcut

1. **Verify Claims of Familiarity:** Ask follow-up questions to confirm shared details or connections.
2. **Be Cautious of Over-Friendliness:** Stay alert if someone seems overly eager to bond or establish trust.
3. **Trust Your Instincts:** If something feels too convenient or "perfect," take a step back to reassess.

Exercise: Practice Verifying Connections

1. Recall a situation where someone quickly earned your trust by mentioning a shared connection. Reflect:
   o "Did I ask questions to confirm their story?"
   o "Could I have been more cautious?"
2. Write down two strategies for verifying shared connections, such as asking for specific details or consulting mutual acquaintances.

Role-Playing Drill:

- Partner with someone. One person pretends to establish a quick connection based on a shared interest or background, while the other practices asking follow-up questions to verify the claim.

Key Takeaway

The Trust Shortcut manipulates social cues and similarities to create false trust. Always verify claims of familiarity and be mindful of overly friendly interactions to avoid being exploited.

Chapter 87: The Credential Snatch

When Security Is an Illusion

You receive an email from what appears to be your streaming service: **"Your subscription payment failed. Log in now to avoid account suspension."** The email includes a link to a login page that looks identical to the official site. Without hesitation, you enter your username and password, only to discover later that your account was hacked, and someone made unauthorized purchases using your payment details.

This is the **Credential Snatch**, where manipulators replicate trusted systems or platforms to steal login information. By creating authentic-looking interfaces and presenting fabricated scenarios, they exploit trust and gain unauthorized access to sensitive accounts or personal data.

How It Works

1. **Imitating Legitimate Interfaces:** Manipulators replicate login pages, emails, or apps to collect credentials.
2. **Preying on Confidence:** They design their traps to look as authentic as possible, relying on visual and contextual familiarity.
3. **Creating a False Narrative:** Scammers fabricate stories like "suspicious activity" or "account upgrades" to compel action.

The Credential Snatch works because people trust familiar platforms and often act quickly in response to perceived threats.

Real-Life Examples

1. **Gaming Account Theft:** Fraudsters create fake promotions for in-game rewards, directing players to login pages that steal their gaming credentials.
2. **E-Learning Platform Hoaxes:** Students are tricked into logging into counterfeit online learning portals, compromising their account details and grades.
3. **Fake Charity Websites:** During donation drives, scammers replicate legitimate charity sites, urging users to log in and provide payment information.

Why It Works

This tactic succeeds because of three key factors:

1. **Visual Authenticity:** Replicating trusted interfaces lowers suspicion.
2. **Urgency to Act:** Fabricated threats encourage immediate responses.
3. **Blind Trust:** People assume familiar communication is legitimate and act without verifying.

How to Spot the Credential Snatch

1. **Carefully Review URLs:** Check for inconsistencies or slight alterations in web addresses.
2. **Avoid Clicking Links:** Navigate directly to official websites rather than using links in emails or texts.
3. **Confirm Requests:** Contact the organization directly to verify any urgent claims.

Exercise: Test Credential Awareness

1. Review a recent email or text asking for login details. Ask:
   o "Did I check the sender's authenticity?"
   o "Was the request urgent or unusual?"
2. Write down two steps to evaluate login pages, such as checking URLs or using official apps.

Role-Playing Drill:

- Partner with someone. One person creates a fake login scenario, while the other practices identifying red flags and verifying legitimacy.

Key Takeaway

The Credential Snatch manipulates trust to extract sensitive login details. Stay vigilant, verify sources, and avoid entering credentials without double-checking authenticity.

Chapter 88: The Power Pose

When Authority Is Faked

A man in a suit approaches you at a train station, flashing a badge and claiming to be from transportation services. He demands your ticket and ID for verification. You comply, only to later find out he wasn't an official employee — he was gathering personal data for identity theft.

This is the **Power Pose**, where manipulators adopt the appearance or behavior of authority figures to intimidate and coerce compliance. By leveraging symbols of authority, such as uniforms, badges, or professional language, they exploit the natural tendency to defer to those in power.

How It Works

1. **Mimicking Authority:** Manipulators dress, speak, or act in ways that align with trusted authority figures.
2. **Creating Pressure:** They use commanding tones or intimidating stances to discourage questioning.
3. **Demanding Compliance:** Targets are conditioned to follow authority, making them less likely to resist.

The Power Pose works because humans are taught to respect and obey perceived authority, even when the legitimacy is questionable.

Real-Life Examples

1. **Fake Inspectors:** Scammers pose as safety inspectors, demanding access to homes or businesses under false pretenses.
2. **Impostor Officials:** Fraudsters pretend to be law enforcement officers to extract personal information or payments.
3. **Corporate Impostors:** Manipulators pose as senior executives, pressuring employees to share confidential data.

Why It Works

This tactic relies on three psychological principles:

1. **Respect for Authority:** People are conditioned to trust those who appear to hold power.
2. **Fear of Repercussions:** The risk of disobeying authority discourages resistance.
3. **Lack of Verification:** Targets rarely question authority figures, assuming legitimacy.

How to Spot the Power Pose

1. **Ask for Verification:** Request credentials or contact the organization they claim to represent.
2. **Question the Context:** Assess whether the person's behavior aligns with their supposed authority.
3. **Trust Your Instincts:** If something feels off, take time to verify before complying.

Exercise: Practice Questioning Authority

1. Reflect on a situation where you complied with an authority figure. Ask yourself:
   o "Did I verify their legitimacy?"
   o "Was their request reasonable for the situation?"
2. Write down two steps to assess authority, such as checking credentials or consulting a second opinion.

Role-Playing Drill:

- Partner with someone. One person pretends to be an authority figure, while the other practices asking for verification and maintaining composure.

Key Takeaway

The Power Pose uses symbols of authority to manipulate and intimidate. Always verify claims of authority before complying, and don't hesitate to ask questions.

"Your child has been in an accident! Send $2,000 for immediate medical attention."

Chapter 89: The Unverified Crisis

You receive a phone call late at night. The voice on the other end says, **"Your cousin has been arrested while traveling abroad. We need $3,000 immediately to post bail."** Without verifying, you wire the money, only to discover later that your cousin was never in trouble, and the caller was a scammer.

This is the **Unverified Crisis**, where manipulators fabricate emergencies to evoke fear and urgency. The target's emotional response overrides logic, leading to ill-considered actions such as transferring money or sharing sensitive information.

How It Works

1. **Choosing a Vulnerable Target:** Scammers target individuals who are likely to respond emotionally, such as family members or business owners.
2. **Crafting a Plausible Crisis:** They create situations that feel urgent and realistic, like accidents, legal trouble, or compromised accounts.
3. **Demanding Immediate Action:** Victims are pressured to act quickly, giving them little time to question or verify the situation.

The Unverified Crisis works because fear and urgency cloud rational thinking, making people act without considering alternatives.

Real-Life Examples

1. **Grandparent Scams:** Fraudsters pretend to be a grandchild in trouble, asking for money to handle an emergency.
2. **Disaster Relief Hoaxes:** Criminals pretend to represent aid organizations, claiming a family member has been affected by a natural disaster and urgently needs financial assistance.
3. **Ransom Scams:** Targets are told a loved one has been kidnapped, with demands for immediate payment to ensure their safety.

Why It Works

This manipulation succeeds due to three psychological factors:

1. **Emotional Overload:** Fear and concern for loved ones overshadow logic and reduce doubt.
2. **Authority in Crisis:** The caller often claims to be a figure of authority (a police officer or doctor), adding credibility.
3. **Time Pressure:** The urgency of the crisis discourages verification, forcing thoughtless decisions.

How to Spot the Unverified Crisis

1. **Pause and Assess:** Ask yourself if the situation makes sense before taking action.
2. **Verify the Claim:** Contact the supposed authority figure or individual involved using official channels.
3. **Be Wary of Payments:** Avoid sending money or sharing information until the situation is confirmed.

Exercise: Prepare for Crisis Scenarios

1. Think of a time you felt rushed to act in an emergency. Reflect:
    o   "What steps did I take to verify the situation?"
    o   "How could I have handled it better?"
2. Write down two strategies to verify emergencies, such as contacting the person directly or consulting a trusted source.

Role-Playing Drill:

*   Partner with someone. One person creates a fake crisis scenario, while the other practices asking questions and verifying details before acting.

Key Takeaway

The Unverified Crisis manipulates emotions by fabricating emergencies. Stay calm, verify claims, and never act impulsively in high-pressure situations.

Chapter 90: The Oversharing Setup

When Friendly Chats Turn Dangerous

You're sitting at a café when a stranger strikes up a conversation. They ask, **"Do you work nearby? What's your favorite thing about your office?"** Flattered by their interest, you share details about your job and schedule. Later, you realize your office experienced a break-in, and the stranger may have used your answers to plan it.

This is the **Oversharing Setup**, where manipulators use casual conversation to subtly extract useful information. By appearing friendly and non-threatening, they trick targets into divulging sensitive details.

How It Works

1. **Starting Small:** Manipulators begin with harmless questions to establish rapport.
2. **Earning Trust:** They act interested and supportive, encouraging the target to open up.
3. **Extracting Key Details:** They steer the conversation toward information that can be exploited, like routines, job details, or personal preferences.

The Oversharing Setup works because people are naturally inclined to talk about themselves, especially when prompted by a seemingly friendly person.

Real-Life Examples

1. **Workplace Espionage:** A competitor poses as a friendly stranger, asking employees about company operations or upcoming projects.
2. **Burglar Planning:** Manipulators ask about vacation plans or daily schedules to identify when a home will be empty.
3. **Networking Event Manipulation:** Scammers attend professional networking events, posing as industry insiders. They ask detailed questions about business strategies or personal finances, later using the information for fraudulent schemes.

Why It Works

This tactic thrives on three psychological tendencies:

1. **Desire to Connect:** People enjoy talking about themselves and sharing experiences.
2. **Lowered Defenses:** Casual conversation feels safe, making targets less cautious.
3. **Unaware Risks:** Most people don't realize how seemingly minor details can be exploited.

How to Spot the Oversharing Setup

1. **Watch Out For Probing Questions:** Notice if the other person consistently steers the conversation toward personal details.
2. **Limit Information:** Share only general answers, especially with strangers or new acquaintances.
3. **Redirect the Conversation:** Politely shift topics if the questions feel too specific or invasive.

Exercise: Practice Limiting Information

1. Think of a recent casual conversation where you shared personal details. Reflect:
   - "Did I reveal more than necessary?"
   - "Could this information be used against me?"
2. Write down two strategies to manage oversharing, such as keeping answers vague or steering conversations to neutral topics.

Role-Playing Drill:

- Partner with someone. One person asks friendly but probing questions, while the other practices identifying and limiting oversharing.

Key Takeaway

The Oversharing Setup uses casual conversation to extract sensitive details. Stay mindful of what you share, especially with people you don't know well.

Chapter 91: The False Confirmation Request

When Confirming Leads to Compromising

You receive a text that says, **"Your bank account has been temporarily locked. Reply with your account PIN to unlock it."** Concerned about accessing your funds, you respond immediately. Moments later, you notice unauthorized transactions in your account.

This is the **False Confirmation Request**, where manipulators send fake prompts to trick people into sharing sensitive details. By appearing legitimate and urgent, these requests exploit the target's instinct to resolve issues quickly.

How It Works

1. **Mimicking Official Communication:** Scammers craft messages that look like they're from trusted organizations.
2. **Creating a Sense of Necessity:** Victims are prompted to act immediately to avoid consequences such as account suspension.
3. **Extracting Information:** Once the target provides the requested details, scammers use them for unauthorized access.

The False Confirmation Request works because people often prioritize solving problems over verifying authenticity.

Real-Life Examples

1. **Fake Password Resets:** Emails ask users to "confirm" their passwords, leading to compromised accounts.
2. **Banking Scams:** Fraudsters pose as bank representatives, requesting account or card details to resolve non-existent issues.
3. **Job Application Scams:** Fraudsters send emails claiming to be recruiters, asking applicants to confirm personal information such as Social Security numbers or banking details to "finalize" a job offer.

Why It Works

This tactic thrives on three key factors:

1. **Trust in Familiarity:** Messages mimic real companies or services.
2. **Desire for Resolution:** People act quickly to avoid perceived problems or interruptions.
3. **Lack of Verification:** The sense of urgency overrides careful scrutiny.

How to Spot the False Confirmation Request

1. **Avoid Sharing Sensitive Details:** Legitimate companies rarely ask for passwords or account numbers via email or text.
2. **Verify the Source:** Contact the organization directly using official contact information.
3. **Look for Red Flags:** Check for generic greetings, spelling errors, or unusual requests.

Exercise: Recognize Legitimate Requests

1. Review recent emails or texts asking for account confirmations. Ask:
    o   "Did the request seem unusual or urgent?"
    o   "Was it from a verified source?"
2. Write down two steps to confirm legitimacy, such as contacting the company directly or reviewing account activity.

Role-Playing Drill:

*   Partner with someone. One person creates a false confirmation scenario, while the other practices identifying and verifying legitimate requests.

Key Takeaway

The False Confirmation Request uses fake prompts to extract sensitive details. Always verify requests independently and avoid acting spur-of-the-moment to protect your information.

Chapter 92: The Hidden Link Trick

When Links Become Deceptive

You receive a text from a popular online retailer: **"Your recent order couldn't be processed. Click here to update your payment details."** The link appears to take you to the retailer's official site, complete with the same layout and branding. Trusting it, you enter your payment information. Hours later, you discover fraudulent charges on your credit card — the message was a scam.

This is the **Hidden Link Trick**, where attackers conceal harmful links under legitimate-looking text or buttons. By mimicking trusted platforms, they trick targets into unknowingly providing sensitive details, installing malware, or making unauthorized payments.

How It Works

1. **Crafting Convincing Messages:** Manipulators design messages that appear to come from trusted organizations, complete with logos and official wording.
2. **Hiding the URL:** The visible link text or button disguises the destination, making it look legitimate while redirecting to malicious sites.
3. **Prompting Urgent Action:** Messages often emphasize urgency, pressuring the recipient to act without checking the link.

The Hidden Link Trick works because it exploits the assumption that familiar-looking emails or texts are trustworthy, especially when the links appear authentic.

Real-Life Examples

1. **Package Delivery Scams:** Victims receive messages claiming, **"Your package couldn't be delivered. Click here to reschedule,"** directing them to a fake website that collects payment details.
2. **Social Media Messages:** Fraudsters use hacked accounts to send messages like, **"Check out this video!"** with malicious links.
3. **Contest Winner Hoaxes:** Scammers send links claiming the recipient has won a prize. Clicking the link directs the target to a malicious site requesting personal or financial details to "claim" the prize.

Why It Works

This tactic thrives due to three psychological tendencies:

1. **Assumed Legitimacy:** Targets believe messages are from trusted sources.
2. **Overlooking the Details:** Many people don't check URLs before clicking, especially on mobile devices.
3. **Emotional Triggers:** Urgency or sympathy distracts from verifying the link's authenticity.

How to Spot the Hidden Link Trick

1. **Hover Over Links:** Check the URL that appears when hovering over a link to ensure it matches the expected destination.
2. **Inspect the Sender:** Verify the email address or phone number to confirm it matches the official source.
3. **Use Official Websites:** Instead of clicking links, manually navigate to the organization's website.

Exercise: Test Your Link Awareness

1. Review recent emails with links. Reflect:
   o "Did I check the URLs before clicking?"
   o "Did the link's destination match its appearance?"
2. Write down two strategies to verify links, such as hovering over the URL or avoiding clicking links in unsolicited messages.

Role-Playing Drill:

- Partner with someone. One person creates a fake email with a disguised link, while the other practices identifying and verifying the destination before clicking.

Key Takeaway

The Hidden Link Trick masks malicious URLs to steal information or install malware. Always check links before clicking, and rely on official sources for sensitive tasks.

Chapter 93: The Overload Maneuver

You receive a phone call from someone claiming to be tech support. They instruct you to open your computer settings and begin describing complicated technical steps.

Overwhelmed, you feel compelled to follow their instructions, even when they ask you to download a file you don't recognize. After the call, your computer is infected with malware, and the "support agent" vanishes.

This is the **Overload Maneuver**, where manipulators intentionally create a flood of information to confuse and distract their targets. By overwhelming victims, they make it harder to analyze the situation or recognize malicious intentions.

How It Works

1. **Generating Confusion:** Manipulators provide excessive or contradictory information to overwhelm the target.
2. **Creating a Sense of Expertise:** They appear knowledgeable, making victims feel pressured to comply.
3. **Distracting from Red Flags:** The complexity prevents targets from noticing inconsistencies or potential risks.

The Overload Maneuver works because people often defer to authority figures or "experts" when faced with confusing situations.

Real-Life Examples

1. **Tech Support Scams:** Fraudsters pose as IT experts, bombarding victims with technical jargon to trick them into installing malware.
2. **Fake Healthcare Hoaxes:** Scammers provide lengthy, detailed explanations of fake medical treatments or insurance policies, confusing victims into purchasing fraudulent services or sharing sensitive information.
3. **Online Terms and Conditions:** Some malicious apps or websites bury harmful clauses in lengthy terms to confuse users into agreeing.

Why It Works

This tactic succeeds due to three psychological factors:

1. **Cognitive Overload:** Too much information reduces the ability to think critically.
2. **Reliance on Authority:** Targets assume the manipulator's expertise is genuine.
3. **Urgency to Comply:** The overwhelming nature of the situation pushes people to act quickly.

How to Spot the Overload Maneuver

1. **Pause and Simplify:** Take a moment to break down the information and assess it step by step.
2. **Verify Claims:** Cross-check any advice or instructions with a trusted source before acting.
3. **Trust Your Instincts:** If something feels unnecessarily complex, it may be intentional.

Exercise: Manage Overload Scenarios

1. Recall a time when you felt overwhelmed by excessive information. Reflect:
   o "How did I react to the situation?"
   o "Could I have taken steps to simplify it?"
2. Write down two strategies for managing overload, such as asking for clarification or consulting a second opinion.

Role-Playing Drill:

• Partner with someone. One person plays a manipulator flooding the other with information, while the second practices identifying key points and resisting pressure to act.

Key Takeaway

The Overload Maneuver uses excessive information to confuse and distract. Slow down, simplify the situation, and check claims before taking action.

Chapter 94: The Emotional Leverage

When Emotions Become Tools of Manipulation

Imagine you get a frantic call from someone claiming to be a relative: **"I got arrested, and I need you to send money immediately for bail!"** The voice sounds convincing, and the panic in their tone feels real. Distraught, you wire the money without asking questions. Later, you realize it wasn't your loved one — it was a scammer exploiting your emotions to steal from you.

This is **Emotional Leverage**, where manipulators weaponize trust, guilt, fear, or love to cloud judgment. By targeting deep-seated feelings, they bypass critical thinking, making it easier to gain compliance.

How It Works

1. **Establishing Trust:** The manipulator pretends to be someone you know or a trusted figure, like a friend or family member.
2. **Triggering an Emotional Reaction:** They use scenarios that evoke strong emotions, such as fear, guilt, or urgency.
3. **Exploiting Vulnerability:** Once you're emotionally invested, they push for immediate action, like transferring money or sharing sensitive information.

Emotional Leverage works because feelings like love, guilt, and fear often override logic, especially in high-pressure situations.

Real-Life Examples

1. **Adoption Fraud:** Manipulators claim to be raising funds for a child's adoption, sharing emotional stories and fabricated photos to solicit donations.
2. **Fake Medical Fundraisers:** Fraudsters create campaigns for non-existent surgeries or treatments, exploiting people's compassion to raise money.
3. **Animal Rescue Cons:** Scammers post heart-wrenching stories of abused animals needing urgent care, asking for financial support to cover "veterinary costs."

Why It Works

This tactic thrives on three key psychological factors:
1. **Emotional Intensity:** Strong feelings cloud judgment, making targets more susceptible.
2. **Urgency of Connection:** Personal bonds or the appearance of trust encourage swift action.
3. **Fear of Consequences:** The perceived cost of inaction (e.g., harm to a loved one) overrides caution.

How to Spot Emotional Leverage

1. **Verify the Situation:** Contact the person or organization directly using official channels.
2. **Pause and Reflect:** Take time to process the emotions before acting.
3. **Look for Manipulative Patterns:** Be wary of messages that evoke panic or guilt to compel action.

Exercise: Reflect on Emotional Decisions

1. Think of a time when an emotional appeal influenced a decision. Reflect:
   o "What emotions drove my choice?"
   o "Would I have acted differently with more time?"
2. Write down two strategies to manage emotional situations, like verifying claims or seeking a second opinion.

Role-Playing Drill:

• Partner with someone. One person pretends to be a manipulator using emotional appeals, while the other practices staying calm and verifying the situation.

Key Takeaway

Emotional Leverage preys on strong feelings to manipulate decisions. Pause, verify, and think critically to protect yourself from these tactics.

Chapter 95: The Insider Ploy

When Familiarity Breeds Deception

A person walks into your workplace wearing a uniform and holding a clipboard. They greet you warmly, saying, **"I'm here to check the office equipment for updates. Can you let me into the server room?"** Believing they're an employee from another branch, you grant access. Hours later, IT discovers a data breach — this person wasn't from your company at all.

This is the **Insider Ploy**, where manipulators pose as trusted insiders to exploit systems or gain access to sensitive information. By appearing familiar, they lower defenses and create opportunities to carry out their schemes.

How It Works

1. **Establishing Familiarity:** The manipulator pretends to be part of a group the target trusts, like co-workers or community members.
2. **Blending In:** They use uniforms, jargon, or insider knowledge to appear legitimate.
3. **Requesting Access:** Once trust is established, they ask for favors, access, or information that aids their agenda.

The Insider Ploy works because people naturally trust those they perceive as part of their in-group or organization.

Real-Life Examples

1. **Workplace Impersonation:** A fraudster claims to be an IT technician and asks employees for passwords to "fix" issues.
2. **Community Scams:** Someone poses as a neighbor or local service provider to gain entry to homes.
3. **Event Infiltration:** Scammers pretend to be event staff to steal personal belongings or gather information.

Why It Works

This tactic thrives on three psychological factors:

1. **Trust in Familiarity:** Targets are less likely to question someone who seems to belong.
2. **Deference to Authority:** Uniforms or professional language create a sense of legitimacy.
3. **Desire to Help:** People naturally want to assist those who appear to be part of their group.

How to Spot the Insider Ploy

1. **Verify Credentials:** Ask for identification or confirm their story with a trusted source.
2. **Be Cautious with Access:** Avoid granting entry or sharing information without proper verification.
3. **Look for Inconsistencies:** Watch for behavior or knowledge that doesn't align with their claimed role.

Exercise: Practice Verifying Insiders

1. Reflect on a time when someone claimed to be an insider. Ask:
    o "Did I confirm their credentials?"
    o "What steps could I have taken to verify their identity?"
2. Write down two strategies to verify insiders, such as requesting official IDs or consulting a manager.

Role-Playing Drill:

- Partner with someone. One person acts as an insider requesting access, while the other practices asking questions and verifying credentials.

Key Takeaway

The Insider Ploy leverages familiarity to gain trust and access. Always check identities, even when someone appears to belong.

Chapter 96: The Phony Transaction

When Payments Go to Scammers

You receive a text message claiming to be from your utility provider: **"Your electricity bill is overdue. Click here to avoid disconnection."** The link takes you to a page that looks just like the provider's payment portal. Panicking at the thought of losing power, you quickly enter your payment information and submit it. Hours later, you realize the payment never went to your utility company — it was a scammer's account.

This is the **Phony Transaction**, where fraudsters create fake payment requests to trick individuals into handing over money or sensitive financial information. By mimicking trusted sources and creating a sense of urgency, they exploit trust and fear to succeed.

"Wait — did you check if that message was really from the utility company?"

It looked official. But... maybe I should double-check.

How It Works

1. **Researching Targets:** Scammers identify individuals or businesses likely to receive similar invoices.
2. **Creating Plausible Requests:** They design invoices or emails that look official and legitimate.
3. **Demanding Urgency:** Messages often emphasize overdue payments or immediate action to pressure compliance.

The Phony Transaction works because people often process payments quickly, especially in busy environments.

Real-Life Examples

1. **Vendor Fraud:** Fraudsters send fake invoices to businesses, claiming to represent a legitimate supplier.
2. **Subscription Payment Scams:** Fake notices trick individuals into "paying" for service payments that apparently didn't go through.
3. **Fake Tax Payments:** Scammers pose as tax agencies, sending false notices about unpaid taxes.

Why It Works

This tactic thrives due to three psychological tendencies:
1. **Trust in Professional Design:** Fake invoices mimic legitimate formats.
2. **Fear of Consequences:** Targets worry about penalties for non-payment.
3. **Lack of Verification:** Busy environments reduce time to check requests.

How to Spot the Phony Transaction

1. **Check the Source:** Confirm the sender's identity before processing payments.
2. **Review Invoice Details:** Look for inconsistencies, like unusual account numbers or vague descriptions.
3. **Contact the Vendor:** Call or email the organization directly using official contact information.

Exercise: Audit Recent Invoices

1. Review your last five payment requests. Ask:
   - "Did I verify the source before processing the payment?"
   - "Were there any red flags I overlooked?"
2. Write down two steps to verify future invoices, such as cross-checking with known vendor records.

Role-Playing Drill:

- Partner with someone. One person creates a fake invoice scenario, while the other practices identifying red flags and checking the authenticity of the request.

Key Takeaway

The Phony Transaction exploits the trust and speed of payment processing. Always cross-check invoices and payment requests to prevent financial loss.

Chapter 97: The Digital Impersonator

You receive a message on a social media platform from someone claiming to be an old friend: **"Hey! It's been ages. I need a small favor—can you send me your phone number and email so we can reconnect?"** The request seems innocent, so you comply. Later, you discover the account was hacked, and your information is being used in other scams.

This is the **Digital Impersonator**, where scammers pose as trusted individuals or institutions online to extract personal or financial information. By assuming the identity of someone the victim knows or respects, they bypass doubt and gain compliance.

How It Works

1. **Creating Credibility:** Impersonators hack existing accounts or create fake profiles to appear authentic.
2. **Establishing Urgency:** They craft messages that encourage quick responses, such as needing help or resolving urgent issues.
3. **Extracting Information:** Once trust is gained, they request personal details, financial information, or even payments.

The Digital Impersonator works because it preys on the inherent trust people place in familiar identities and platforms.

Real-Life Examples

1. **Hacked Social Media Accounts:** Scammers use compromised profiles to send messages asking for money or personal information.
2. **Email Spoofing:** Fraudsters send emails from fake domains resembling legitimate companies, requesting sensitive data.
3. **Fake Customer Service Accounts:** Impersonators create accounts on social platforms, offering "help" to users and stealing their information.

Why It Works

This tactic thrives due to three psychological factors:

1. **Trust in Familiarity:** Victims are less likely to question requests from people or institutions they know.
2. **Speed Over Scrutiny:** Urgent requests prevent thorough checks.
3. **Emotional Connections:** Impersonators exploit personal bonds to compel action.

How to Spot the Digital Impersonator

1. **Verify Requests:** Contact the person or organization directly using official channels.
2. **Check for Inconsistencies:** Look for unusual grammar, tone, or behavior in messages.
3. **Be Cautious With Links:** Avoid clicking links from unexpected messages without confirming their authenticity.

Exercise: Analyze Recent Messages

1. Review the last three unexpected messages you received.
   - Were they consistent with the sender's usual tone?
   - Did they include suspicious requests or links?
2. Write down steps you'll take to verify future communications, such as calling the sender directly.

Role-Playing Drill:

- Partner with someone. One person acts as a scammer impersonating someone you know, while the other practices identifying red flags.

Key Takeaway

The Digital Impersonator exploits trust in familiar identities to gain sensitive information. Always confirm details to protect yourself.

Chapter 98: The Recurring Roulette

When Persistence Becomes Manipulation

You receive frequent texts from someone claiming to represent a charity. Each message starts friendly, like **"Hope you're doing well!"**, but over time, they become more insistent: **"Have you had a chance to donate yet? We're counting on you!"** Feeling guilty and worn down, you eventually send money—only to realize later the charity doesn't exist.

This is the **Recurring Roulette**, where manipulators use repeated attempts to wear down resistance, establish trust, or create guilt. By presenting themselves as consistent and reliable, they build a façade of credibility.

How It Works

1. **Establishing Presence:** The manipulator repeatedly contacts the target to stay on their radar.
2. **Building Trust:** Frequent interactions create the illusion of familiarity and credibility.
3. **Wearing Down Defenses:** Over time, the persistence erodes doubt and leads to compliance.

The Recurring Roulette works because repetition builds trust and makes targets feel obligated to respond.

Real-Life Examples

1. **Persistent Telemarketing Scams:** Fraudsters call repeatedly, using familiarity to gain trust and sell fraudulent products.
2. **Email Drip Scams:** Scammers send a series of emails with escalating urgency to pressure recipients into compliance.
3. **Subscription Fraud:** Fake services send recurring payment reminders, hoping the victim will pay without questioning.

Why It Works

This tactic thrives due to three psychological factors:

1. **Familiarity Through Repetition:** Frequent contact creates a false sense of trust.
2. **Emotional Fatigue:** Targets give in to stop the persistence.
3. **Perceived Obligation:** Consistent communication makes victims feel indebted to respond.

How to Spot the Recurring Roulette

1. **Set Boundaries:** Avoid responding to unsolicited messages or calls.
2. **Verify Identities:** Confirm the sender's legitimacy through official channels.
3. **Watch for Escalation:** Be cautious if messages become increasingly urgent or demanding.

Exercise: Identify Persistent Tactics

1. Reflect on a time you experienced persistent communication. Ask:
   o "Did their repeated attempts make me feel obligated?"
   o "What steps could I have taken to stop the manipulation?"
2. Write down two ways to handle repeated attempts, like blocking numbers or reporting spam.

Role-Playing Drill:

- Partner with someone. One person acts as a persistent scammer, while the other practices setting boundaries and ignoring pressure.

Key Takeaway

The Recurring Roulette relies on persistence to wear down resistance and build false trust. Stay firm, set boundaries, and double check all claims.

Chapter 99: The Open Door Trap

When Vulnerabilities Are Left Unchecked

You're at a coffee shop, and after finishing your drink, you head to the restroom, leaving your laptop unlocked. A passer-by takes advantage of the moment, quickly accessing your open emails to gather sensitive information. By the time you return, nothing seems amiss, but your data has been compromised.

This is the **Open Door Trap**, where manipulators exploit unsecured physical or digital spaces to access sensitive information or systems. A single lapse in vigilance is all they need to take advantage.

How It Works

1. **Identifying Vulnerabilities:** Scammers look for unattended devices or poorly secured accounts.
2. **Gaining Access:** They exploit physical proximity or unprotected networks to retrieve data.
3. **Executing Their Plan:** Once inside, they steal information or install malicious software.

The Open Door Trap works because even brief lapses in security create opportunities for exploitation.

Real-Life Examples

1. **Unattended Devices:** Laptops, phones, or tablets left unlocked in public spaces become targets for thieves.
2. **Public Wi-Fi Risks:** Unsecured connections allow attackers to intercept sensitive data.
3. **Open Accounts:** Forgotten logins on shared computers can be exploited for malicious purposes.

Why It Works

This tactic thrives on three psychological factors:

1. **Overconfidence in Safety:** Targets underestimate risks in familiar environments.
2. **Human Error:** Simple oversights, like forgetting to lock devices, create vulnerabilities.
3. **Speed of Exploitation:** Scammers act quickly to exploit brief moments of inattention.

How to Spot the Open Door Trap

1. **Secure Your Devices:** Always lock screens when stepping away.
2. **Avoid Public Wi-Fi:** Use a VPN or avoid transmitting sensitive data over unsecured networks.
3. **Log Out:** Ensure accounts are logged out when using shared devices.

Exercise: Secure Your Devices

1. List three physical or digital spaces where you often leave things unsecured.
   - Example: Laptops in public places, Wi-Fi networks, shared computers.
2. Write two steps to secure these spaces, like enabling auto-lock or using encrypted connections.

Role-Playing Drill:

- Practice identifying security vulnerabilities in a shared environment with a partner.

Key Takeaway

The Open Door Trap exploits unsecured spaces and devices. Vigilance and secure habits are key to avoiding these breaches.

Chapter 100: The Confidence Con

When Charm Masks Deception

You meet someone who introduces themselves as a successful entrepreneur. They speak with charisma, sharing tales of their past achievements and emphasizing their bold vision for the future. Excited by their energy and confidence, you agree to invest in their venture without conducting much research. Weeks later, you discover the entire project was a façade — they disappeared with your money.

This is the **Confidence Con**, where manipulators use charm, assertiveness, and persuasive storytelling to distract targets from potential risks. By projecting authority and certainty, they compel trust and compliance, often overriding logic.

How It Works

1. **Projecting Authority:** Manipulators use their demeanor, attire, and communication style to appear credible and trustworthy.
2. **Telling Convincing Stories:** They craft narratives designed to resonate emotionally, weaving in details that seem plausible.
3. **Suppressing Doubts:** Their boldness makes questioning them feel awkward or unnecessary, silencing doubt.

The Confidence Con succeeds because humans are naturally drawn to assertive individuals who seem to "know what they're doing."

Real-Life Examples

1. **Fraudulent Start-ups:** Scammers pitch fake investment opportunities with polished presentations and rehearsed pitches.
2. **Online Fibs:** Social media users exaggerate their credentials or success stories to promote dubious products or services, earning trust through their confident personas.
3. **Fake Experts:** Fraudsters pose as skilled professionals, confidently offering services they aren't qualified to perform.

Why It Works

This tactic thrives on three key psychological elements:

1. **Appeal to Authority:** People instinctively trust individuals who appear confident and self-assured.
2. **Emotional Connection:** Charm disarms defenses, making targets more likely to believe in the manipulator's intentions.
3. **Pressure to Trust:** Doubting someone so confident can feel socially uncomfortable, especially in public or professional settings.

How to Spot the Confidence Con

1. **Verify Claims:** Ask for tangible proof of credentials, achievements, or plans.
2. **Pause and Reflect:** Avoid being swept up in someone's enthusiasm; take time to evaluate.
3. **Trust Your Instincts:** If something feels off, don't ignore your gut. Confidence isn't proof of honesty.

Exercise: Challenge Bold Claims

1. Think of a time you were impressed by someone's confidence. Reflect on:
   o Did they provide evidence for their claims?
   o Were there any red flags you ignored?
2. Write down two questions you'll ask in the future when someone pitches an idea confidently.

Role-Playing Drill:

• Partner with someone to simulate a confident pitch. Practice asking critical questions to assess their claims.

Key Takeaway

The Confidence Con relies on charm and assertiveness to obscure doubts and risks. Stay grounded, ask questions, and always seek evidence.

Conclusion

You've now explored 100 human hacking strategies — manipulation tactics that range from exploiting emotions to leveraging cognitive biases and digital vulnerabilities. While the tactics may vary, their common goal is to influence decisions, often at the expense of logic, trust, or security. This knowledge is your armor, equipping you to recognize, resist, and neutralize manipulation in everyday situations.

Awareness Is Your First Line of Defense

Awareness is the cornerstone of protection. Whether it's spotting a suspicious email, questioning a too-good-to-be-true offer, or recognizing emotional triggers during negotiations, being vigilant allows you to pause and evaluate before acting. Manipulators rely on automatic, unthinking responses. By slowing down and applying critical thinking, you disrupt their strategy.

Practical Tip: Make it a habit to ask yourself, **"What's the motive behind this request?"** This single question can uncover hidden agendas.

Trust, But Verify

Trust is essential in human interactions, but blind trust can be a vulnerability. This book has highlighted countless examples where scammers exploited trust to achieve their goals. Moving forward, adopt a mindset of cautious curiosity—trusting others while verifying their claims. This balance ensures you remain open to genuine connections while protecting yourself from deceit.

Practical Tip: Always check the source of communication, whether it's an email, phone call, or social media message. If in doubt, contact the organization or person directly using official channels.

Embrace Critical Thinking

Manipulators thrive when emotions override logic. From false urgency to fabricated authority, they create scenarios that cloud judgment. Counter this by adopting a problem-solving mindset. Break down situations into facts, evaluate evidence, and assess potential outcomes.

Practical Tip: When faced with a high-pressure decision, take a moment to breathe and ask, **"What are the risks if I wait or say no?"** Most genuine opportunities will withstand scrutiny.

Practice Digital Hygiene

In today's interconnected world, many manipulation tactics are digital. Protecting yourself online is no longer optional—it's essential. Be wary of unsolicited links, create strong passwords, and avoid sharing personal information on unsecured platforms.

Practical Tip: Use tools such as two-factor authentication (2FA) and password managers to add layers of security to your accounts.

Resist Emotional Manipulation

Whether it's guilt, fear, or flattery, manipulators often target emotions to influence decisions. Recognizing these triggers is the key to neutralizing their power.

Practical Tip: When you feel an emotional reaction, pause and ask yourself, **"Is this emotion clouding my judgment?"** If so, take time to regain perspective before acting.

Build a Cautious Yet Open Mindset

This book has provided countless examples of how manipulators exploit assumptions. Going forward, question the surface and seek the deeper truth.

Practical Tip: Develop a mantra like, **"Is there more to this story?"** Use it whenever you encounter decisions that feel rushed or one-sided.

Share Your Knowledge

Knowledge is most powerful when shared. By teaching friends, family, and colleagues about the tactics you've learned, you create a ripple effect of awareness. Manipulators thrive in ignorance; your awareness can inspire others to protect themselves.

Practical Tip: Share examples of manipulation you've encountered and how you resisted. Real-life stories resonate and educate effectively.

A Final Word

The manipulation tactics outlined in this book are not just theoretical — they exist in daily life, from the workplace to online interactions. By mastering these insights, you've gained the power to recognize deception, protect your interests, and make confident decisions.

Remember: Awareness is your shield, critical thinking is your sword, and caution is your ally. Armed with these tools, you can navigate the complexities of human interaction with clarity and control. The world may be full of manipulative tactics, but you now have the strategies to stay one step ahead.

Appendix A: Your Quick Reference Guide

This appendix is your roadmap to navigating the strategies covered in this book. Each chapter is summarized in a single line, providing you with a quick refresher on the manipulation tactics and how to spot them. Use it as your go-to guide for recognizing, understanding, and countering manipulative behaviors in everyday life.

Section I: Trust and Authority Exploits (Chapters 1–20)

Chapter 1: The Imposter Gambit
Pretend to be someone trustworthy to gain access or information.

Chapter 2: The Fake Badge
Exploit authority symbols like uniforms or titles to demand compliance.

Chapter 3: The Friendly Stranger
Build rapport to lower your defenses.

Chapter 4: The Expert Trap
Use technical language or complex jargon to confuse and intimidate.

Chapter 5: The Scarcity Hook
Claim resources are limited to create urgency and compel action.

Chapter 6: The Urgent Boss
Fake being a superior giving time-sensitive orders.

Chapter 7: The Insider Illusion
Pretend to be part of your team or company to build trust.

Chapter 8: The Overconfidence Play
Act so self-assured that others don't question your legitimacy.

Chapter 9: The Trust Triangle
Use a mutual connection or non-existing intermediary to gain trust.

Chapter 10: The Chain of Command
Exploit hierarchies by pressuring people to defer decisions to "superiors."

Chapter 11: The Name Drop
Mention known figures or organizations to establish credibility.

Chapter 12: The Call from the Top
Claim directives are coming from a higher authority to force compliance.

Chapter 13: The Financial Fraudster
Pose as a financial professional to steal money or access accounts.

Chapter 14: The Benevolent Guide
Pretend to help victims while secretly exploiting them.

Chapter 15: The Legal Threat
Use fake legal warnings to scare people into cooperation.

Chapter 16: The Medical Manipulator
Exploit trust in medical professionals to extract information or create panic.

Chapter 17: The Social Media Savior
Pose as a helpful social media contact to phish for details.

Chapter 18: The Customer Service Con
Mimic support agents to gain access to personal data or accounts.

Chapter 19: The Policeman's Bluff
Impersonate law enforcement to coerce or intimidate.

Chapter 20: The Religious Mask
Exploit faith or spiritual trust for manipulation.

Section II: Emotional Manipulation Tactics (Chapters 21–40)

Chapter 21: The Fear Trigger
Incite fear to make people act without thinking.

Chapter 22: The Sympathy Card
Play on emotions of pity or compassion.

Chapter 23: The Guilt Lever
Exploit guilt to make someone comply.

Chapter 24: The Flattery Trap
Use excessive compliments to disarm scepticism.

Chapter 25: The Greed Ploy
Promise riches or rewards to lure people into a trap.
Chapter 26: The Pride Bull's Eye
Appeal to ego to make targets feel special or chosen.
Chapter 27: The Hope Hoax
Dangle false hope, like job offers.
Chapter 28: The Panic Button
Create a crisis to demand immediate action.
Chapter 29: The Shame Shove
Use shame to push compliance.
Chapter 30: The Empathy Bomb
Overload someone with emotional stories to cloud their judgment.
Chapter 31: The Anger Catalyst
Provoke anger to distract from logical thinking.
Chapter 32: The Nostalgia Smokescreen
Invoke fond memories to lower defenses.
Chapter 33: The Curiosity Click
Exploit curiosity to make someone click, open, or engage.
Chapter 34: The Imaginary Acquittance
Pretend to share interests to forge a connection.
Chapter 35: The Relationship Hijack
Use familial or romantic ties to manipulate trust.
Chapter 36: The Gratitude Debt
Offer a small favor to create a sense of obligation.
Chapter 37: The Exclusive Offer
Make someone feel special by offering "privileged" information or deals.
Chapter 38: The Ticking Timer
Create urgency with manufactured deadlines to force snap decisions.
Chapter 39: The Isolation Tactic
Separate targets from others to make them easier to manipulate.
Chapter 40: The Distraction Game
Overload someone's attention to sneak past defenses.

Section III: Digital Manipulation and Online Scams (Chapters 41-60)

Chapter 41: The Clickbait Lure
Create irresistible headlines to drive action.
Chapter 42: The Baited Email
Send convincing emails designed to steal personal or financial information.
Chapter 43: The Digital Spy
Use social media to gather intelligence and exploit personal data.
Chapter 44: The Untrue Profile
Create personas to infiltrate social networks.
Chapter 45: The Malware Messenger
Send links that install malicious software.
Chapter 46: The Passcode Pilfer
Steal passwords, logins, and secure credentials through deception.
Chapter 47: The Catfisher
Pretend to be a romantic partner online to gain trust.
Chapter 48: The Deepfake Puppeteer
Use AI-generated content to impersonate real people.
Chapter 49: The Privacy Blackmail Trap
Blackmail someone using fabricated or stolen private data.
Chapter 50: The Ransomware Ruse
Encrypt someone's files and demand payment to unlock them.
Chapter 51: The Subscription Steal
Fake renewal notices that steal credit card details.

Chapter 52: The Survey Snare
Use fake polls to gather sensitive information.
Chapter 53: The Bogus Giveaway
Promise non-existing prizes in exchange for personal details.
Chapter 54: The Support Scam
Imitate tech support to gain remote control of devices.
Chapter 55: The Trojan Ad
Embed malicious code in seemingly harmless advertisements.
Chapter 56: The Public Wi-Fi Trap
Intercept data over insecure networks.
Chapter 57: The QR Code Con
Use fake QR codes to direct users to malicious sites.
Chapter 58: The Crypto Trap
Scam people through fraudulent cryptocurrency investments.
Chapter 59: The Influencer Lie
Pretend to be an influencer to promote scams.
Chapter 60: The Phone App Fraud
Create malicious apps disguised as useful tools.

Section IV: Exploiting Cognitive Biases (Chapters 61–80)

Chapter 61: The Authority Bias
Manipulate deference to perceived authority.
Chapter 62: The Recency Effect
Exploit recent events to sway decisions.
Chapter 63: The Commitment Trap
Secure a small agreement to trigger larger commitments.
Chapter 64: The Consensus Effect
Use fake popularity or testimonials to create trust.
Chapter 65: The Rarity Mirage
Make things appear more valuable by faking scarcity.
Chapter 66: The Extreme Evaluator
Present extreme comparisons to sway choices.
Chapter 67: The Availability Heuristic
Exploit what's top of mind to skew decisions.
Chapter 68: The Familiarity Bias
Use repetition to build misplaced trust.
Chapter 69: The Framing Effect
Manipulate perception by changing how information is presented.
Chapter 70: The Halo Effect
Exploit positive traits to create unwarranted trust.
Chapter 71: The Dunning-Kruger Effect Exploit
Convince people they know more than they actually do, prompting overconfidence.
Chapter 72: The Single Trait Trap
Use one positive characteristic to overshadow flaws or risks.
Chapter 73: The Loss Aversion Conundrum
Emphasize potential losses to pressure fast decision-making.
Chapter 74: The Status Quo Bias Manipulation
Exploit people's tendency to resist change, keeping them locked into a decision.
Chapter 75: The Optimism Bias Trick
Exploit the belief that "it won't happen to me" to lower caution.
Chapter 76: The Confirmation Bias Bait
Present information that aligns with existing beliefs to gain trust.
Chapter 77: The Anchoring Trap
Present an initial (often extreme) value to influence future decisions.
Chapter 78: The Illusory Truth Effect
Repeat falsehoods often enough that they feel true.

Chapter 79: The Sunk Cost Fallacy Lever

Keep people invested by reminding them how much they've already "spent" (time, money, effort).

Chapter 80: The Framing Effect Twist

Shape how choices are perceived by altering how they're presented.

Section V: Defensive Mastery (Chapters 81–100)

Chapter 81: The Psychological Takeover

Manipulators create emotional intensity to override logical thinking.

Chapter 82: The False Helper

Disguise manipulation as acts of kindness or goodwill.

Chapter 83: The Deceptive Question

Seemingly innocent questions are designed to extract key information.

Chapter 84: The "Too Good to Be True" Trap

Attractive offers lure people into lowering their guard.

Chapter 85: The False Urgency Alarm

Creating a false sense of urgency pressures people into hasty decisions.

Chapter 86: The Trust Shortcut

Exploit recognizable details or patterns to quickly gain false trust.

Chapter 87: The Credential Snatch

Directly or indirectly manipulating people to reveal their login credentials.

Chapter 88: The Power Pose

Pretend to be an authority figure to intimidate or persuade.

Chapter 89: The Unverified Crisis

Inventing emergencies to force quick, unquestioned actions.

Chapter 90: The Oversharing Setup

Engaging people in conversation to casually extract sensitive information.

Chapter 91: The False Confirmation Request

Sending false prompts to confirm sensitive details like passwords or bank accounts.

Chapter 92: The Hidden Link Trick

Masking malicious links with legitimate-looking text or buttons.

Chapter 93: The Overload Maneuver

Flooding a target with complex or excessive information to confuse and distract.

Chapter 94: The Emotional Leverage

Exploit personal bonds and feelings to influence decisions.

Chapter 95: The Insider Ploy

Pretending to be part of a familiar group or organization to bypass suspicion.

Chapter 96: The Phony Transaction

Sending fake invoices or payment requests to extract money or financial details.

Chapter 97: The Digital Impersonator

Dupes unsuspecting individuals to divulge sensitive information.

Chapter 98: The Recurring Roulette

Persistent attempts at manipulation that build over time to gain trust.

Chapter 99: The Open Door Trap

Exploiting physical or digital spaces left unsecured by human oversight.

Chapter 100: The Confidence Con

Using boldness and charm to manipulate targets into ignoring red flags.

Appendix B: Chapter Overview by Section

This appendix provides a clear breakdown of this book's sections and chapters. Make it your quick reference guide to explore specific manipulation tactics or defensive strategies grouped by theme.

Section I: Trust and Authority Exploits

- The Imposter Gambit
- The Fake Badge
- The Friendly Stranger
- The Expert Trap
- The Scarcity Hook
- The Urgent Boss
- The Insider Illusion
- The Overconfidence Play
- The Trust Triangle
- The Chain of Command
- The Name Drop
- The Call from the Top
- The Financial Fraudster
- The Benevolent Guide
- The Legal Threat
- The Medical Manipulator
- The Social Media Savior
- The Customer Service Con
- The Policeman's Bluff
- The Religious Mask

Section II: Emotional Manipulation Tactics

- The Fear Trigger
- The Sympathy Card
- The Guilt Lever
- The Flattery Trap
- The Greed Ploy
- The Pride Bull's Eye
- The Hope Hoax
- The Panic Button
- The Shame Shove
- The Empathy Bomb
- The Anger Catalyst
- The Nostalgia Smokescreen
- The Curiosity Click
- The Imaginary Acquittance
- The Relationship Hijack
- The Gratitude Debt
- The Exclusive Offer
- The Ticking Timer
- The Isolation Tactic
- The Distraction Game

Section III: Digital Manipulation and Online Scams

- The Clickbait Lure
- The Baited Email
- The Digital Spy
- The Untrue Profile
- The Malware Messenger
- The Passcode Pilfer
- The Catfisher
- The Deepfake Puppeteer
- The Privacy Blackmail Trap
- The Ransomware Ruse
- The Subscription Steal
- The Survey Snare
- The Bogus Giveaway
- The Support Scam
- The Trojan Ad
- The Public Wi-Fi Trap
- The QR Code Con
- The Crypto Trap
- The Influencer Lie
- The Phone App Fraud

Section IV: Exploiting Cognitive Biases

- The Authority Bias
- The Recency Effect
- The Commitment Trap
- The Consensus Effect
- The Rarity Mirage
- The Extreme Evaluator
- The Availability Heuristic
- The Familiarity Bias
- The Framing Effect
- The Halo Effect
- The Dunning-Kruger Effect Exploit
- The Single Trait Trap
- The Loss Aversion Conundrum
- The Status Quo Bias Manipulation
- The Optimism Bias Trick
- The Confirmation Bias Bait
- The Anchoring Trap
- The Illusory Truth Effect
- The Sunk Cost Fallacy Lever
- The Framing Effect Twist

- The Psychological Takeover
- The False Helper
- The Deceptive Question
- The "Too Good to Be True" Trap
- The False Urgency Alarm
- The Trust Shortcut
- The Credential Snatch
- The Power Pose
- The Unverified Crisis
- The Oversharing Setup

- The False Confirmation Request
- The Hidden Link Trick
- The Overload Maneuver
- The Emotional Leverage
- The Insider Ploy
- The Phony Transaction
- The Digital Impersonator
- The Recurring Roulette
- The Open Door Trap
- The Confidence Con

Appendix C: Practice Scenarios

This appendix is designed to help you apply the insights from the book to real-world situations. Each scenario highlights manipulative tactics, while the challenge section provides actionable steps to identify and counter them. These exercises will build your confidence in spotting manipulation and responding effectively.

Scenario 1: The Pressure Sale

Problem: You're at a car dealership, and the salesperson says, "This deal is only good for today. If you leave, someone else will take the car."

Challenge: Recognize this as a false urgency tactic designed to rush your decision. Step back, leave the dealership, and research other options. Remember, a legitimate deal will not require immediate action without time to think.

Scenario 2: The Fake Charity Call

Problem: A phone call claims to be from a disaster relief fund. The caller shares a heart-breaking story and pressures you to donate immediately.

Challenge: Never donate under pressure. Politely end the call, research the charity independently, and donate through official channels if it's legitimate. Look for registered charity numbers and verified websites.

Scenario 3: The Inflated Anchor

Problem: A subscription service offers a "discount" of $100 off their "regular price" of $300, but you later find the regular price is always $200.

Challenge: Identify this as an anchoring tactic. Compare the offer to other subscriptions, focusing on actual value instead of arbitrary discounts. Ignore inflated "original prices" and assess the deal rationally.

Scenario 4: The Phony Invoice

Problem: You receive an email claiming you owe $500 for a service you never ordered, with a link to "review the details."

Challenge: Avoid clicking the link. Verify the claim by contacting the service provider directly using official contact details, not the ones in the email. Use secure systems to check your account for discrepancies.

Scenario 5: The Fake Authority

Problem: Someone claiming to be an IT technician says they've detected malware on your device and requests your login credentials to "fix it."

Challenge: Refuse to share credentials over the phone or email. Contact your IT department or service provider directly to confirm the issue. If the request was fraudulent, report it immediately.

Scenario 6: The Limited-Time Investment

Problem: A friend forwards you an investment opportunity promising 20% returns, but you must act "within 24 hours."

Challenge: Decline to act hastily. Research the investment independently and consult a trusted financial advisor. Genuine opportunities will withstand scrutiny and allow time for due diligence.

Scenario 7: The Emotional Appeal

Problem: A co-worker asks you to cover for them, saying, "I've had such a rough week. Please, just this once!"

Challenge: Set clear boundaries. Offer assistance that doesn't compromise your priorities, such as sharing helpful resources or suggesting alternative solutions.

Scenario 8: The Overloaded Terms

Problem: An app's terms and conditions are pages long, with hidden clauses about data collection that you're tempted to skip reading.

Challenge: Use tools like contract summarizers to identify key clauses quickly. Avoid installing apps or agreeing to terms that demand excessive data permissions.

Problem: Everyone in your office is investing in a trendy new stock, and they encourage you to do the same, calling it "a sure thing."

Challenge: Resist peer pressure by consulting independent financial data and experts. Base your decision on objective analysis, not group behavior.

Scenario 10: The Crisis Hoax

Problem: A colleague says the company network has been hacked and urgently asks for your password to fix the issue.

Challenge: Do not share sensitive information under pressure. Contact your IT department directly to confirm the issue. Report suspicious activity to ensure others are aware.

Scenario 11: The Flattering Pitch

Problem: A recruiter reaches out, saying you're the "perfect candidate" for an exclusive position—but it requires a costly training program first.

Challenge: Recognize flattery as a tactic to lower your guard. Research the recruiter and training program independently before committing any money.

Scenario 12: The Deepfake Distortion

Problem: You receive a video message from your manager asking for an immediate transfer of funds. Something feels off, but it looks and sounds like them.

Challenge: Verify the request by calling your manager directly using a trusted number. Avoid acting solely on digital messages, especially when financial transactions are involved.

Scenario 13: The Nostalgia Trap

Problem: An ad for a product you loved as a child promises to bring back "the good old days," but the price is significantly inflated.

Challenge: Separate sentiment from value. Research alternative products that evoke the same nostalgia but offer better quality or pricing.

Scenario 14: The Fake Confirmation Email

Problem: An email asks you to "confirm your account details" to prevent it from being deactivated, with a link that looks like your bank's website.

Challenge: Do not click the link. Contact your bank directly using their official website or phone number to verify the email's authenticity.

Scenario 15: The Loyalty Trap

Problem: A subscription service you rarely use offers you a "special deal" to renew at a discount, reminding you of how long you've been a customer.

Challenge: Assess whether the service still provides value. Avoid renewing based solely on past investment (sunk cost fallacy) and evaluate current utility instead.

Appendix D: Your Checklist for Mastering Manipulation

This checklist consolidates the essential lessons from the book into actionable steps. Each point provides a simple practice to help you identify, resist, and overcome manipulation tactics in everyday life. Use this as a reference guide to stay vigilant and empowered against manipulative tactics.

1. Pause Before Reacting

- Take a breath and assess the situation before acting.
- Don't let urgency or emotions cloud your judgment.
- A pause is often enough to disrupt manipulation.

2. Verify Credibility

- Always double-check authority figures, credentials, or sources.
- Contact organizations directly to confirm any claims.
- Trust actions over appearances or titles.

3. Be Wary of Emotional Hooks

- Recognize when guilt, fear, or sympathy is being leveraged.
- Ask yourself: "Is this emotion clouding my logical thinking?"
- Focus on facts rather than emotional appeals.

4. Question Scarcity Claims

- Don't let phrases such as "limited time only" rush you into action.
- Research whether the scarcity is genuine or fabricated.
- Remember: real opportunities don't require panic.

5. Strengthen Your Digital Hygiene
- Use strong, unique passwords for every account.
- Avoid clicking on unsolicited links or downloading unknown files.
- Regularly update software to reduce vulnerabilities.

6. Spot Repetition Tactics
- Be cautious of brands or ideas you trust solely because you've seen them repeatedly.
- Ask: "Do I trust this based on facts or familiarity?"
- Research alternatives to broaden your perspective.

7. Focus on the Big Picture
- Don't let one impressive trait overshadow flaws (e.g., a product with a great feature but poor reliability).
- Evaluate all aspects of a decision before committing.
- Balance logic with instinct.

8. Separate Facts from Opinions
- When presented with information, identify what's factual versus speculative.
- Prioritize evidence-backed claims over assumptions or promises.
- Seek multiple sources to confirm the truth.

9. Be Comfortable Saying No
- Decline requests or offers that pressure you into immediate action.
- Practice polite ways to say no without over-explaining.
- Saying no is your right—not an invitation for negotiation.

10. Watch for Authority Traps
- Question claims of superiority, like "I'm an expert," without proof.
- Avoid deferring to someone just because of a title or uniform.
- Seek second opinions before complying with authority-based requests.

11. Recognize Patterns in Manipulation
- Pay attention to recurring tactics, like fake crises or exaggerated claims.
- Track previous experiences where you felt pressured or misled.
- Reflect on what worked to resist them.

12. Protect Personal Data
- Avoid sharing unnecessary details about yourself online or in person.
- Think carefully about how much information you provide during casual conversations.
- Remember: manipulators use small details to build trust or exploit vulnerabilities.

13. Evaluate Before Clicking
- Hover over links to check their destination before clicking.
- Verify the sender of emails and messages, especially if they include attachments.
- Trust your instincts if something feels "off" online.

14. Balance Logic with Emotion
- Let emotions guide, but not dominate, your decisions.
- Use critical thinking to evaluate whether a situation aligns with your goals.
- Keep a logical checklist to stay grounded.

15. Practice Self-Awareness
- Regularly reflect on past situations where manipulation might have occurred.
- Ask: "What made me trust this person or offer?"
- Build awareness of your own biases to reduce vulnerability.

Pro Tip:

Remember, manipulation thrives on complacency and haste. The insights in this book aren't just tools for defense — they're habits to sharpen your critical thinking and self-awareness. By practicing these steps, you'll build an automatic resistance to manipulation, empowering you to make confident, informed decisions in every aspect of your life.

Part 3: Systems Thinking

An AI's Guide to 100 Ways to Spot Connections Humans Often Overlook

Introduction:
Seeing What Others Miss

Imagine a web stretched out before you. Some threads are easy to see — clear, bold, and obvious. But others fade into the background, quietly shaping everything around them. Most people focus only on the visible threads, missing the deeper interconnections that truly define the system. Systems thinking is about stepping back to see the whole web — how everything interacts, influences, and evolves together.

This book is your guide to systems thinking, a mindset and a skillset that will forever change the way you approach problems. With it, you'll learn to think beyond isolated parts and surface-level causes, uncovering the structures, flows, and forces that drive the bigger picture. By mastering these insights, you'll discover how to make smarter decisions, anticipate ripple effects, and design solutions that truly last.

Who This Book Is For

This book is for problem-solvers, innovators, leaders, and lifelong learners. It's for anyone who looks at the world and knows there's more going on than meets the eye. Whether you're leading a team, analyzing complex challenges, or simply trying to make better decisions in your own life, systems thinking will unlock a new level of understanding.

From business professionals navigating intricate organizations to environmentalists tackling global challenges, systems thinking is the missing tool for seeing clearly in a complex world. Even if you've never thought of yourself as "analytical" or "technical," this book will guide you step-by-step in discovering how to see the unseen and connect the dots others miss.

Why Systems Thinking Matters

The challenges of society are systemic by nature. They aren't caused by one single thing, nor can they be solved by simple fixes. Whether it's an environmental issue, an organizational bottleneck, or a personal challenge, problems exist in interconnected webs.

Systems thinking offers clarity in this chaos. It equips you to see the underlying structures that drive behavior and outcomes. Once you can do that, you'll find opportunities for change that others overlook. This isn't just about solving problems; it's about transforming how you think, act, and create.

What You'll Gain

With this book, you'll learn how to:

- Recognize the unseen interconnections that influence your world.
- Uncover root causes instead of reacting to surface-level symptoms.
- Design solutions that work sustainably, not just temporarily.
- Make smarter, faster decisions by focusing on the right leverage points.

More importantly, you'll gain a mindset that shifts the way you see everything — from the systems in nature and society to the systems in your own daily life. It's a new lens for understanding the world.

Section I: The Basics of Seeing Systems

Understanding systems starts with how you see them. In this section, you'll learn to step back, identify relationships, and recognize the structures that shape the world around you. These foundational skills will open your eyes to connections and influences you may never have noticed before, giving you the clarity to analyze problems and opportunities in a whole new way.

Chapter 1: Zoom Out to See the Big Picture

The Power of Perspective

To solve any problem effectively, you need to resist the urge to focus solely on what's immediately in front of you. Zooming out allows you to see how smaller pieces fit into a larger whole, revealing connections and influences that would otherwise remain invisible. Without this broader perspective, you risk treating symptoms instead of addressing root causes.

How to Zoom Out

1. **Start with Context:** Ask yourself, "What system is this problem a part of?" Instead of isolating an issue, consider how it fits into a larger environment or network.
2. **Use Visual Tools:** Sketch diagrams or maps of how various components interact within the system. This can help highlight overlooked connections.
3. **Shift Between Levels:** Alternate between granular details and the broader picture, asking, "How does this piece contribute to the system as a whole?"
4. **Ask Systemic Questions:** Replace "What's wrong?" with "What external factors influence this situation?" and "What ripple effects might this create?"

Real-World Example

Imagine a city facing frequent power outages. A narrow view might blame aging infrastructure. However, zooming out reveals a more complex web of factors: population growth, poor urban planning, and resource mismanagement. Addressing the infrastructure alone would miss the broader, systemic causes. By zooming out, city planners can tackle root issues, such as demand forecasting or improving resource allocation.

Why It Matters

Zooming out empowers you to see the world as an interconnected whole. It prevents you from getting stuck on immediate symptoms and instead focuses your attention on systemic drivers of change. This shift in perspective is the first and most essential step toward becoming a systems thinker.

Exercises

1. **Map the Bigger Picture:** Think of a current challenge in your life — personal, professional, or societal. Sketch a diagram showing how it connects to other areas, such as people, resources, or external forces. Reflect on what might be influencing the problem beyond its immediate context.
2. **Zoom Out Physically:** Go to a high point in your neighborhood — a hill, a tall building, or even an aerial photo online. Observe the broader environment and think about how what you see (roads, traffic, green spaces) might influence specific events, like traffic jams or neighborhood dynamics.
3. **Ask Three Why's:** For any problem, ask yourself, "Why is this happening?" three times, each time moving further away from the surface issue. For example: "Why is my team missing deadlines? Because tasks aren't clear. Why aren't tasks clear? Because we lack a process for assigning roles. Why do we lack a process? Because we haven't discussed priorities as a group."

Key Takeaway

The bigger picture often holds the true solution. Zooming out helps you see it.

Chapter 2: Identify Key Stakeholders

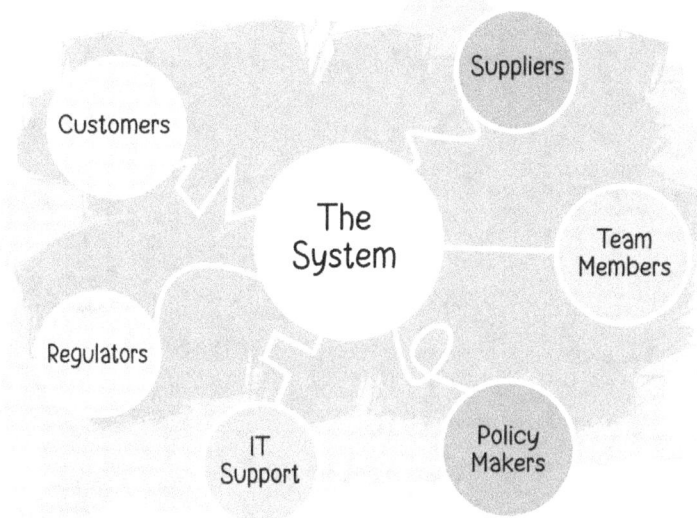

The Stakeholders Difference

In every system, there are individuals, groups, or entities that influence or are influenced by its behavior. These are the stakeholders, and understanding their roles is critical for grasping how the system functions. Stakeholders are the threads that hold the system together. Missing even one important stakeholder can cause you to misinterpret a system's problems, overlook potential solutions, or make changes that backfire.

Take a workplace environment as an example. If you're trying to boost team productivity, the obvious stakeholders might seem to be just the team members themselves. But by looking deeper, you'll uncover other crucial players: managers who set expectations, clients whose demands affect workloads, and even the IT team maintaining the tools your staff relies on. Identifying all stakeholders ensures your approach is grounded in the full complexity of the system.

How to Identify Key Stakeholders

1. **Outline Influencers and Impacted Parties:** Start by asking two questions:
   o Who has the power to affect the system?
   o Who is affected by the system's outcomes?
   Use this to create a simple map or list.
2. **Classify Relationships:** Not all stakeholders play the same role. Some actively shape the system (e.g. leaders, regulators), while others are recipients of its outputs (e.g. customers, employees). Distinguish between decision-makers, participants, and bystanders.
3. **Trace Connections:** Explore how stakeholders interact with each other. For example, how do employee needs align – or conflict – with organizational goals? Are suppliers working in harmony with logistical systems? This reveals the system's dynamics.
4. **Listen and Learn:** Engage with stakeholders directly. What are their needs, concerns, and priorities? Their perspectives may reveal blind spots in your understanding.

Real-World Example

Consider the development of a new public park. At first glance, the stakeholders might seem obvious: the local government funding it and the residents who will use it. But with a deeper dive, additional players emerge: environmental organizations concerned about preserving green spaces, businesses that could benefit from increased foot traffic, and construction teams tasked with building the park.

By identifying and understanding these diverse stakeholders, planners can anticipate challenges, balance competing interests, and ensure long-term success.

Why It Matters

Ignoring key stakeholders leads to incomplete solutions. Imagine redesigning a public transportation system while overlooking the needs of low-income communities who rely on it most. Or implementing a workplace policy without consulting the very employees it affects. Recognizing stakeholders ensures your decisions account for the system's complexity, making them more effective and sustainable.

Exercises

1. **Stakeholder Structure:** Choose a challenge you're working on and make a list of everyone it impacts or involves. Next, draw a diagram showing how these stakeholders interact with one another and the system itself.
2. **Role Reversal Exercise:** Pick one stakeholder and write down the problem from their perspective. What do they want? What challenges do they face? Reflect on how this changes your understanding of the issue.
3. **Interview a Stakeholder:** Identify one key player in a system you're studying (e.g. a colleague, customer, or community member). Ask them about their priorities and challenges related to the issue. Take notes on what new insights emerge.

Key Takeaway

Systems are shaped by the people and groups within them. Identifying key stakeholders ensures you see the whole picture.

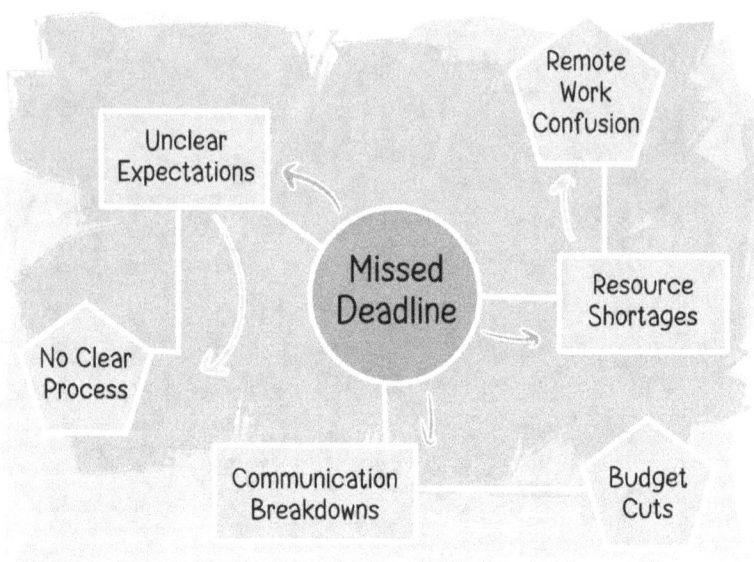

Chapter 3: Trace Causal Links

Every system behaves the way it does because of an intricate web of consequences. Tracing causal links means following the chain of events and influences to understand why things happen the way they do. It's about moving beyond symptoms and uncovering the forces driving behavior within a system.

Consider a spike in employee turnover at a company. A superficial glance might blame low morale, but tracing the causal links reveals a deeper story: Morale declined because of high workloads, which were caused by understaffing, which stemmed from a budget freeze, which, in turn, resulted from declining profits. Understanding these links allows you to address the root causes instead of just firefighting the symptoms.

How to Trace Causal Links

1. **Start with the Event:** Identify the problem or behavior you want to analyze. Be specific — this is your starting point.
2. **Ask "Why?" Repeatedly:** For each identified cause, ask, "Why is this happening?" Follow the chain until you reach the most fundamental root cause. This is often called the "Five Whys" technique, though it may take more or fewer questions.
3. **Distinguish Direct Causes from Indirect Ones:** Not all links are equally influential. Direct causes have an immediate impact, while indirect ones often create ripple effects over time.
4. **Create a Causal Chart:** Visualize the relationships between causes and effects. This makes it easier to spot interconnections you might have missed.

Real-World Example

Imagine a school facing a sudden decline in test scores. Tracing the causal links might uncover the following:

- Decline in scores is linked to reduced classroom time.
- Reduced classroom time stems from teacher absences.
- Teacher absences are tied to burnout.
- Burnout is linked to increased administrative workloads.

By addressing the root cause — burnout — administrators could significantly improve scores without focusing solely on test preparation.

Why It Matters

Tracing causal links prevents you from wasting time on superficial fixes. It allows you to pinpoint what's truly driving system behavior so you can focus your energy where it matters most. Without this skill, you risk treating symptoms while the underlying issues continue to fester.

Exercises

1. **Causal Chain Analysis:** Pick a recent problem you've encountered. Write it down, then repeatedly ask, "Why is this happening?" until you reach the root cause. Reflect on whether your initial understanding missed anything.
2. **Visualize a Cause Outline:** For a chosen issue, draw a diagram showing all contributing factors and their relationships. Highlight direct causes in one color and indirect ones in another.
3. **Apply in Everyday Life:** The next time you encounter a personal or professional challenge, pause before reacting. Ask yourself, "What caused this situation, and what might have caused that?" Practice tracing causal links to develop this habit.

Key Takeaway

Systems behave the way they do for a reason. Tracing causal links helps you understand why.

Chapter 4: Spot Feedback Loops

Feedback loops are the beating heart of any system. They explain why some systems spiral out of control while others stabilize themselves. A feedback loop occurs when a system's output influences its input, creating a cycle. Recognizing these loops is key to understanding system behavior and designing effective interventions.

There are two main types of feedback loops:

1. **Reinforcing Loops** amplify changes. For example, a social media post that gains likes encourages more people to view it, leading to even more likes — a self-reinforcing cycle.

2. **Balancing Loops** counteract changes to maintain stability. For instance, a thermostat balances room temperature by activating heating or cooling as needed.

Spotting recursive patterns in a system lets you anticipate behaviors, whether it's exponential growth, collapse, or equilibrium.

How to Spot Feedback Loops

1. **Look for Recurring Cycles:** Identify situations where outputs loop back into the system to influence future behavior.
2. **Chart the Flow:** Diagram the relationships between elements, showing how one affects another. Pay attention to where the process forms a closed loop.
3. **Distinguish Between Reinforcing and Balancing Loops:**
   - Reinforcing loops escalate or amplify changes.
   - Balancing loops regulate or stabilize the system.
4. **Identify Delays:** Many feedback loops involve time lags, where the effects of an action aren't immediately visible. Recognizing these delays helps predict outcomes more accurately.

Real-World Example

Take urban traffic congestion. A reinforcing feedback loop occurs when increased car use leads to longer commute times, prompting even more people to rely on cars instead of public transport. A balancing loop could involve toll charges that discourage excessive driving, stabilizing traffic levels. Recognizing these loops allows city planners to design interventions that break harmful cycles and strengthen stabilizing ones.

Why It Matters

Feedback loops are the underlying drivers of many systemic behaviors. Without recognizing them, you may misinterpret patterns, waste effort addressing symptoms, or unintentionally make problems worse. Understanding these loops allows you to predict outcomes and intervene effectively.

Exercises

1. **Feedback Mapping:** Choose a recurring issue you've observed (e.g. productivity cycles at work, mood swings, or resource shortages). Create a simple diagram showing the feedback loop that drives it.
2. **Identify Reinforcing vs. Balancing Loops:** Look at a system you interact with daily (e.g. a budgeting process or exercise routine) and identify whether the cycles involved are reinforcing or balancing.
3. **Test for Delays:** Reflect on a situation where you noticed delayed consequences (e.g. implementing a new policy or adopting a new habit). Lay out how the delay affected the feedback loop.

Key Takeaway:

Feedback loops are the engines of system behavior — spotting them lets you predict and shape outcomes.

Chapter 5: Unpack Delay Dynamics

The Waiting Game of Systems

Delays are the hidden time bombs in every system. They occur when there's a gap between cause and effect, often making it difficult to see how actions influence outcomes. This can lead to impatience, poor decisions, or unintended consequences.

For example, consider starting a new workout routine. You won't see results immediately; the benefits come after weeks of consistent effort. Without understanding this delay, you might assume the routine isn't working and give up prematurely. Similarly, in larger systems, ignoring delays can lead to overcorrections or destabilization.

How to Recognize Delays

1. **Identify Where Action Meets Response:** Look for areas where the system takes time to react. These could be physical delays (e.g. shipping times), human delays (e.g. decision-making processes), or environmental delays (e.g. climate response to emissions).
2. **Separate Immediate from Long-Term Effects:** Distinguish between outcomes that occur right away and those that emerge later.
3. **Analyze the Gap:** Estimate the time lag between action and result. This helps you predict when effects will appear and avoid overreacting in the meantime.
4. **Account for Compounding Effects:** Recognize how delays can amplify or obscure the system's behavior over time.

Real-World Example

In agriculture, overusing fertilizer might initially boost crop yields, leading farmers to assume the strategy is working. However, the delayed effect of soil degradation could cause long-term productivity losses. Recognizing these dynamics allows for sustainable practices that balance short-term gains with long-term health.

Why It Matters

Delays make systems tricky to manage. Reacting too soon may cause overcorrections, while acting too late risks irreversible damage. By understanding delay dynamics, you can better predict outcomes, avoid hasty decisions, and design strategies that account for the system's natural pace.

Exercises

1. **Identify a Delay:** Think of a situation where you experienced a delay between action and result (e.g. a project rollout or personal habit change). Write down the immediate and delayed effects and reflect on how the delay influenced your response.
2. **Analyze a System with Delays:** Choose a system (e.g. a supply chain, education process, or health goal). Pinpoint where delays occur and how they affect the system's overall behavior.
3. **Set a Patience Strategy:** For a goal you're currently working toward, list potential delays you might encounter and plan how to stay consistent during the waiting period.

Key Takeaway

Delays obscure cause-and-effect relationships. Understanding them helps you predict and manage outcomes effectively.

Chapter 6: Look for System Boundaries

Defining the Edges of a System

Systems can also be defined as ecosystems — they operate within boundaries that define what is part of the system and what lies outside it. But unlike physical fences, these boundaries are often conceptual and shaped by the observer's perspective. The boundaries you choose to define will impact how you understand a system and the solutions you propose.

Systems can also overlap. For instance: A public school system intersects with community organizations, local businesses, and even state policies. If you ignore these overlaps, you might overlook critical influences that shape the system's behavior.

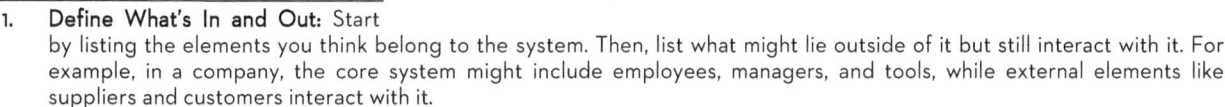

How to Identify System Boundaries

1. **Define What's In and Out:** Start by listing the elements you think belong to the system. Then, list what might lie outside of it but still interact with it. For example, in a company, the core system might include employees, managers, and tools, while external elements like suppliers and customers interact with it.

2. **Look for Overlaps:** Most systems don't operate in isolation. Think about where your system might intersect with others. For instance, a healthcare system overlaps with public transportation when patients need to reach hospitals.

3. **Acknowledge Flexibility:** Remember that boundaries are often artificial. For example, a marketing campaign might seem internal to a business, but it extends into the customer's world, influencing their behavior. Boundaries should evolve as your understanding of the system deepens.

4. **Watch for Boundary Changes:** Systems are dynamic, and their boundaries can shift over time. A small start-up might initially include only a handful of employees but later expand to contractors, suppliers, and global teams.

Real-World Example

Take climate change as an example. Initially, people viewed it as a system limited to environmental science. But over time, we've expanded the boundary to include energy policies, economic systems, and even social behaviors. Ignoring these broader boundaries would lead to ineffective solutions, such as addressing emissions from power plants but overlooking consumer behavior or global trade policies.

Why It Matters

Where you draw the line around a system shapes your understanding of it. If your boundary is too narrow, you may overlook critical influences or connections. If it's too broad, you risk becoming overwhelmed by irrelevant details. The key is to define boundaries that help you focus on what's important while staying aware of external forces.

Exercises

1. **Boundary Layout:** Think of a system you interact with daily, like your household budget. Write down what you include as part of the system (income, expenses, savings) and what you exclude. Then ask: Are there external factors (e.g. market trends) that influence it? Reflect on how adjusting the boundary changes your understanding.

2. **Analyze Overlapping Systems:** Pick two systems that interact in your life, such as your workplace and your family life. Create a diagram that shows where their boundaries overlap and how that interaction affects your decisions.

3. **Reassess a System Boundary:** Look at a problem you've analyzed before. Redraw the system's boundaries to include elements you initially excluded. What new insights or opportunities emerge?

Key Takeaway

Understanding and adjusting system boundaries lets you see the system more clearly, ensuring you include all relevant factors while avoiding unnecessary complexity.

Chapter 7: Observe Resource Flows

Every system relies on the movement of resources. These could be tangible resources, such as water or materials, or intangible ones, like knowledge or influence. Observing resource flows helps you understand how the system sustains itself, identifies inefficiencies, and reveals points of accumulation or loss.

Consider a supply chain. Resources like raw materials flow from suppliers to manufacturers, then to distributors, and finally to customers. At each stage, there may be delays, bottlenecks, or losses. By observing the flow of these resources, businesses can pinpoint inefficiencies, reduce waste, and improve performance.

Resource flows also exist in non-physical systems. For instance, in a workplace, knowledge flows from leadership to employees, while feedback flows in the opposite direction. Understanding these flows can improve communication and decision-making.

How to Observe Resource Flows

1. **Identify Inputs and Outputs:** Start by listing what enters the system (e.g. money, energy, or ideas) and what leaves it.
2. **Trace the Path:** Visualize how resources move between different parts of the system. Look for areas where they accumulate (stocks) or where the flow slows down (bottlenecks).
3. **Spot Inefficiencies:** Identify points where resources are wasted, mismanaged, or delayed. For example, excessive paperwork might slow down the flow of approvals in an organization.
4. **Analyze Reinforcing Cycles:** Some resource flows return to the system as feedback. For instance, customer reviews flow back into the business as insights for improvement.

Real-World Example

Think about energy use in a household. Electricity flows into the home, powering appliances and lighting. Along the way, inefficiencies like poor insulation or outdated devices cause energy loss. Observing this flow allows homeowners to make targeted improvements, like installing energy-efficient windows or upgrading appliances, to reduce waste and costs.

Why It Matters

Resource flows are the lifeblood of a system. Mismanaging them leads to inefficiencies, shortages, or even system failure. By understanding these flows, you can identify opportunities to improve performance, reduce waste, and make the system more sustainable.

Exercises

1. **Track a Resource:** Choose a resource you use daily (e.g. water, time, or money). Map its flow from input to output, noting where it accumulates or is wasted.
2. **Flow Diagram:** Pick a system you interact with, like your office workflow. Create a diagram showing the flow of information or tasks and highlight where delays or bottlenecks occur.
3. **Improve a Flow:** Identify a flow you want to optimize — like your daily schedule. Look for points where time or energy is wasted and brainstorm ways to streamline the process.

Key Takeaway

Understanding how resources flow through a system helps you spot inefficiencies, optimize performance, and ensure sustainability.

Chapter 8: Notice Points of Tension

Systems are rarely in perfect harmony. Instead, they are shaped by competing forces pulling in different directions. These points of tension often highlight areas of instability or inefficiency within the system. Recognizing them allows you to diagnose challenges, resolve conflicts, and design solutions that balance competing priorities.

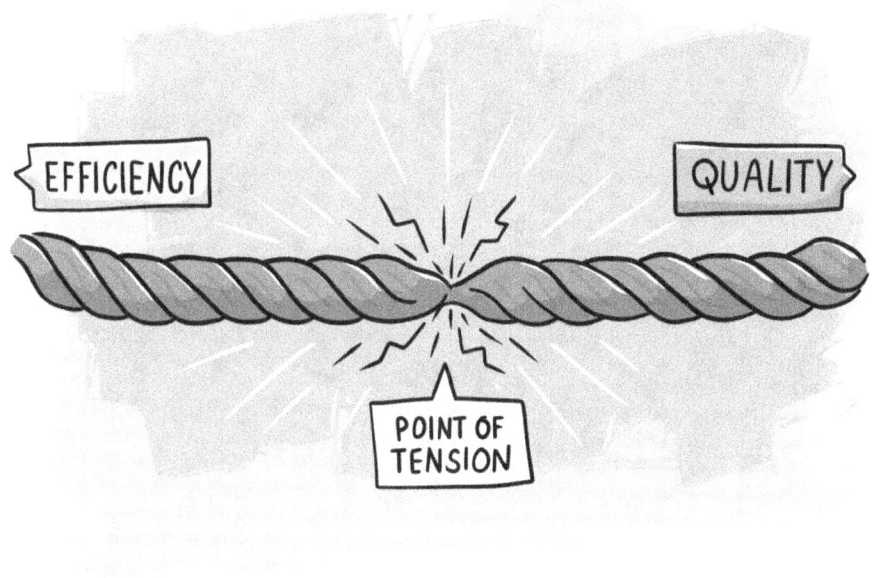

For example, a company might face tension between its need for innovation (which requires risk-taking) and its need for stability (which requires adherence to proven processes). If this tension goes unmanaged, it could lead to burnout, conflict, or stagnation. However, by identifying and addressing the tension, the company can find ways to encourage innovation without sacrificing stability.

How to Identify Points of Tension

1. **Look for Symptoms:** Tensions often manifest as recurring problems, such as delays, conflicts, or inefficiencies. Ask yourself what forces might be pulling against each other.
2. **Identify Trade-Offs:** Consider where the system forces you to choose between competing goals, such as speed vs. accuracy or cost vs. quality.
3. **Pinpoint Hotspots:** Focus on areas where these tensions are most visible, such as team disagreements, overused resources, or missed deadlines.
4. **Ask Why the Tension Exists:** Trace the root causes of the tension. For example, is it due to external pressures, conflicting priorities, or misaligned incentives?

Real-World Example

Consider a non-profit organization working to expand its reach. The tension lies between fundraising efforts (to support growth) and program delivery (to meet current needs). Ignoring this tension could stretch resources too thin, compromising both goals. Recognizing the tension allows the organization to strategically allocate resources, balancing immediate impact with future sustainability.

Why It Matters

Points of tension reveal where systems are under stress. Ignoring these areas risks escalation and failure, while addressing them creates opportunities for growth, resolution, and balance.

Exercises

1. **Tension Diagram:** Identify a system in your life with recurring challenges (e.g. work-life balance). List the forces pulling in opposite directions and reflect on how they influence each other.
2. **Visualize a Trade-Off:** Draw a simple chart with two competing priorities (e.g. cost vs. quality). Plot current and desired states to see where adjustments are needed.
3. **Explore Root Causes:** Pick a recurring tension in your workplace or personal life. Ask why it exists and what changes could ease the strain.

Key Takeaway

Tensions highlight the competing forces shaping a system. Addressing them leads to better balance and long-term success.

Chapter 9: Uncover Emergent Behavior

The Power of Emergence

Some of the most fascinating aspects of systems are behaviors that arise spontaneously from interactions between parts. These are called emergent behaviors. Unlike predictable outputs of simple systems, emergent behaviors are often surprising and cannot be easily traced to a single cause. They occur when individual components of a system interact in ways that produce something greater than the sum of its parts.

Consider a traffic system. The collective movement of traffic jams emerges not from individual drivers but from how their decisions interact — accelerating, braking, merging — all within the broader constraints of road design and traffic laws. Similarly, in nature, a beehive's intricate organization emerges from the actions of individual bees following simple rules.

Emergent behavior can be constructive or destructive. In business, for instance, creativity can emerge from collaboration, while chaos might emerge from poor communication. Understanding how and why emergence occurs allows you to harness it for positive outcomes and mitigate its downsides.

How to Recognize Emergent Behavior

1. **Look Beyond Individual Actions:** Focus on how the collective behavior of a system differs from the behavior of its parts. For example, a single employee working overtime won't affect much, but a culture of overwork across an organization could lead to widespread burnout.
2. **Identify Simple Rules or Interactions:** Emergence often stems from simple behaviors. In an ant colony, ants don't "plan" their foraging routes; they leave pheromone trails that others follow, creating complex, efficient networks.
3. **Analyze Unexpected Outcomes:** If the system produces outcomes that can't be explained by its individual components, emergence is likely at play.
4. **Trace Recursive Patterns:** Emergent behaviors often reinforce themselves through dynamic interconnections. For example, viral trends on social media arise when user interactions (likes, shares, comments) amplify visibility, creating a self-reinforcing cycle.

Real-World Example

In financial markets, stock prices are influenced by countless individual investors making decisions based on available information. The emergent behavior of the market — such as bubbles or crashes — results not from any single investor but from how their actions collectively interact within the system. Recognizing this can help analysts predict and prepare for these large-scale events.

Why It Matters

Emergent behaviors are often unpredictable and can either be a system's greatest strength or its Achilles' heel. Failing to account for emergence can lead to surprises, such as unintended consequences of policies or plans. However, when understood, emergence can be used to foster creativity, innovation, and resilience within a system.

Exercises

1. **Observe Emergence in Nature:** Spend time observing natural systems like bird flocks, schools of fish, or ant colonies. Reflect on how their behaviors result from interactions rather than centralized control.
2. **Analyze a Group Dynamic:** Think about a group you belong to (e.g. your workplace or a community). Identify behaviors or outcomes that emerge from the group's interactions, such as shared values or recurring conflicts.
3. **Harness Positive Emergence:** Choose a project or team you're part of and brainstorm ways to encourage interactions that lead to constructive outcomes, like fostering collaboration or open communication.

Key Takeaway

Emergent behavior arises from interactions between parts of a system — understanding it helps you harness its potential and anticipate its challenges.

Chapter 10: Understand System History

To understand why a system behaves the way it does today, you need to look at where it came from. Systems are shaped by their histories, with past decisions, events, and interactions creating the conditions you see now. Whether it's a company's organizational structure, a city's infrastructure, or a natural ecosystem, its history holds the clues to understanding its present and shaping its future.

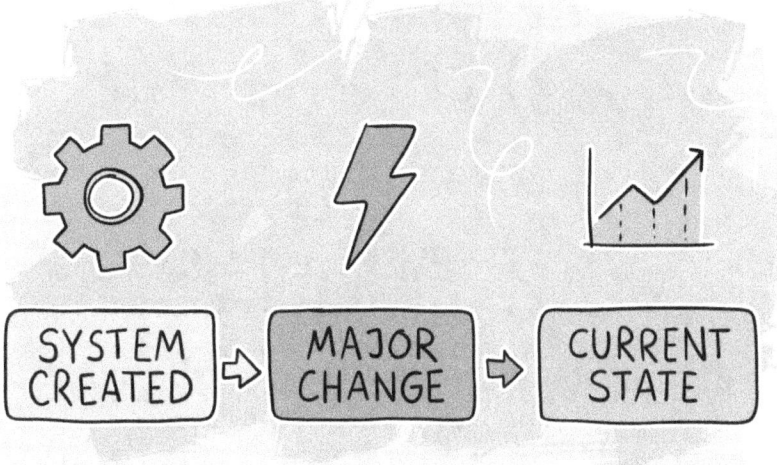

For example, consider a company struggling with low employee morale. A superficial analysis might point to current leadership. But digging into the company's history might reveal a deeper story: years of layoffs, missed opportunities for innovation, and a legacy of poor communication. These historical factors contribute to the current state and provide insight into how to address the root issues.

How to Analyze System History

1. **Trace the Origin:** Start by asking, "Where did this system come from?" Identify its purpose at creation and how it has evolved.
2. **Identify Key Events:** Look for major turning points, such as leadership changes, policy shifts, or external disruptions. These events often create lasting impacts.
3. **Follow the Chain of Decisions:** Systems are shaped by decisions over time. Understanding the rationale behind these decisions – whether good or bad – helps you identify where the system succeeded or went off track.
4. **Assess Path Dependencies:** Many systems become "locked in" by past choices, making certain paths easier to follow and others harder. For example, a city built around cars may struggle to pivot to public transportation due to existing infrastructure investments.

Real-World Example

Consider the U.S. healthcare system. Its complexity and challenges are deeply rooted in historical events, such as the employer-based insurance model introduced during World War II, the introduction of Medicare and Medicaid in the 1960s, and subsequent policy changes. Without understanding this history, reform efforts often miss the systemic constraints and opportunities for meaningful change.

Why It Matters

Understanding a system's history prevents you from making superficial judgments or misdiagnosing problems. It also helps you avoid repeating past mistakes. By seeing how the present has been shaped by the past, you can make more informed decisions about the future.

Exercises

1. **Create a System Timeline:** Choose a system you're part of (e.g. your workplace or community) and define its key events. Reflect on how these events shaped the current state.
2. **Analyze Path Dependencies:** Identify a decision in your life or work that's been constrained by past choices (e.g. choosing a tool because it's already in use). Reflect on whether these constraints are still valid.
3. **Ask "What if?":** Imagine how the system might look today if a key event in its history had unfolded differently. Consider what lessons this alternate history might offer for the future.

Key Takeaway

A system's present behavior is rooted in its past. Understanding its history gives you the insights needed to shape its future.

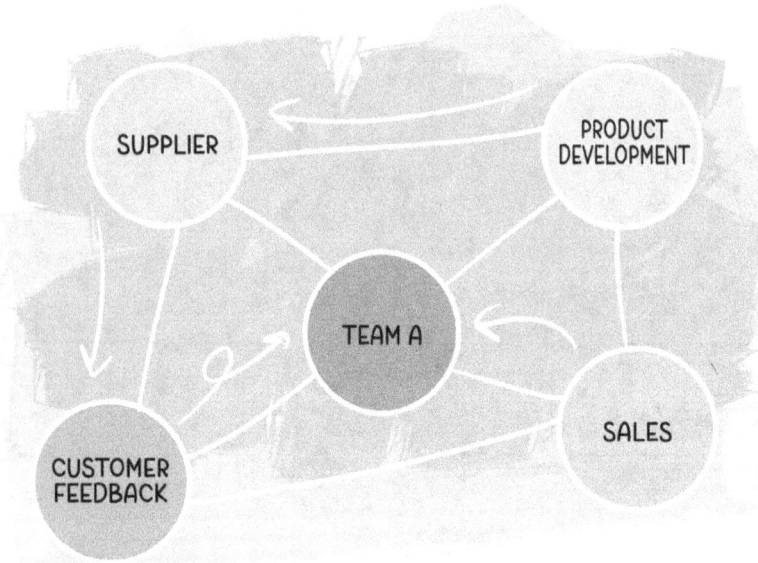

Chapter 11: Visualize Interconnections

Systems are made up of interconnected parts, and those connections often determine how the system behaves. Visualizing interconnections allows you to understand the relationships between components and understand the flow of influence. Without this visualization, connections may remain invisible, leaving you unaware of key dynamics.

For example, imagine a small business facing declining sales. A surface-level analysis might focus on marketing strategies. But a visual guide could reveal connections to other factors, such as product quality, supply chain delays, or customer service issues. Seeing the entire web of influences enables a more holistic understanding of the problem.

How to Visualize Interconnections

1. **Identify the Key Elements:** Start by listing all the major parts of the system. This could include people, processes, resources, or external influences.
2. **Draw Connections:** Use arrows or lines to indicate relationships between the elements. For example, draw a line from "Customer Feedback" to "Product Development" to show how feedback influences product design.
3. **Distinguish Connection Types:** Use different styles (e.g. dashed vs. solid lines) or colors to represent the nature of the connection, such as direct vs. indirect or positive vs. negative influence.
4. **Focus on Feedback Loops:** Highlight areas where connections form closed loops, as these are often the drivers of system behavior.

Real-World Example

In public health, visualizing interconnections is essential for understanding disease outbreaks. A map might show how factors like population density, access to healthcare, and vaccination rates interact. This helps policymakers see the big picture, identify weak points in the system, and design targeted interventions.

Why It Matters

When you visualize interconnections, you make the system's complexity visible. This prevents you from focusing too narrowly on individual components and instead encourages you to see how the whole system operates. Understanding these relationships helps you identify leverage points, anticipate ripple effects, and design more effective solutions.

Exercises

1. **Create a System Structure:** Choose a system you interact with (e.g. your workplace or community) and list its key components. Draw a diagram showing how they influence one another, using arrows to represent connections.
2. **Focus on One Connection:** Pick a single connection from your map (e.g. between two teams or departments). Analyze how strengthening or weakening this connection might affect the system.
3. **Look for Overlooked Links:** Review your plan and ask, "Are there any connections I missed?" Add these and reflect on how they change your understanding of the system.

Key Takeaway

Visualizing interconnections helps you understand how the parts of a system interact, revealing opportunities to improve its behavior.

Chapter 12: Distinguish Stocks from Flows

The Building Blocks of Systems

To truly understand how systems function, you need to grasp the distinction between stocks and flows. Stocks are accumulations within a system — resources, people, energy, or information that build up over time. Flows, on the other hand, are the movement of those resources into or out of the system.

Consider a savings account. The account balance is a stock, while deposits and withdrawals are flows. The balance only changes when the inflow (deposits) exceeds the outflow (withdrawals), or vice versa. Understanding these dynamics is key to managing systems effectively.

How to Distinguish Stocks from Flows

1. **Identify What's Being Accumulated:** Look for quantities that build up over time, such as money, energy, or people. These are the stocks.
2. **Trace Inflows and Outflows:** Determine what adds to or depletes the stock. For example, a population's stock grows through births (inflows) and shrinks through deaths and migration (outflows).
3. **Consider Time Lags:** Stocks often act as buffers, absorbing changes in inflows and outflows. Recognizing these delays helps you predict how the system will respond to interventions.
4. **Visualize the Relationship:** Use a diagram to define the stocks and flows in the system. This makes it easier to see how changes in flows affect the stock over time.

Real-World Example

In environmental systems, forests act as a stock of carbon, storing CO_2 over decades. The flows include carbon absorption (via tree growth) and carbon release (via deforestation or wildfires). Policies aimed at reducing atmospheric CO_2 must address both inflows and outflows to manage this stock effectively.

Why It Matters

Confusing stocks and flows leads to poor decision-making. For example, in managing budgets, focusing only on monthly income (a flow) while ignoring savings (a stock) could result in financial instability. By distinguishing between the two, you gain clarity on how systems accumulate, deplete, and stabilize over time.

Exercises

1. **Analyze a Stock and Flow:** Choose a system in your life (e.g. household expenses). Identify one stock (e.g. your savings) and its inflows (income) and outflows (expenses). Reflect on how changing the flows would affect the stock.
2. **Track a Stock Over Time:** Pick a stock (e.g. your energy levels) and observe how it changes throughout the day. Identify the inflows (rest, food) and outflows (work, exercise) affecting it.
3. **Create a Stock-Flow Diagram:** Choose a system, such as a water supply or project timeline. Use a simple diagram to illustrate its stocks and flows, noting how they influence one another.

Key Takeaway

Distinguishing stocks from flows helps you understand how resources accumulate, deplete, and stabilize within a system.

Chapter 13: Notice Self-Organization

The Magic of Systems That Organize Themselves

Not all systems require a leader to function effectively. Some systems have the remarkable ability to organize themselves without external control. This phenomenon, called self-organization, occurs when the components of a system interact in ways that lead to structure, order, or patterns — often spontaneously.

Consider a flock of birds flying in perfect unison. There's no single leader directing their movements; instead, each bird follows simple rules, such as maintaining a certain distance and mirroring the direction of its neighbors. Together, their interactions create the stunning, cohesive behavior that can often be seen.

Self-organization isn't limited to nature. Social systems, markets, and even certain technologies exhibit self-organizing behavior. Recognizing this phenomenon allows you to understand how systems adapt, evolve, and maintain stability on their own—and how you can work with, rather than against, this natural order.

How to Recognize Self-Organization

1. **Look for Patterns Without Central Control:** Identify systems where order emerges from individual actions rather than top-down planning. For example, in a marketplace, prices adjust dynamically based on the actions of buyers and sellers, not a central authority.
2. **Find the Simple Rules:** Self-organization often arises from simple, localized interactions. In an ant colony, ants leave pheromone trails that others follow, collectively creating efficient foraging paths.
3. **Observe Adaptation:** Self-organizing systems can adjust to changes in their environment. For example, ecosystems adapt to disturbances by reorganizing themselves around available resources.
4. **Spot Decentralized Feedback Loops:** These systems rely on feedback from their components to maintain order. For instance, traffic flow adjusts as individual drivers respond to road conditions, creating an overall pattern.

Real-World Example

Online platforms often exhibit self-organization. Consider Wikipedia: its articles are created, edited, and refined by individual contributors following a few simple rules, such as providing citations and adhering to neutral language. The result is a comprehensive and dynamic knowledge base with no single editor in charge.

Why It Matters

Understanding self-organization helps you see that not all systems require micromanagement. Intervening too heavily in a self-organizing system can disrupt its natural balance. For example, imposing rigid rules on a creative team might stifle the organic collaboration that leads to innovation. By recognizing and respecting self-organization, you can design systems that foster resilience, adaptability, and creativity.

Exercises

1. **Observe a Self-Organizing System:** Spend time watching a system that organizes itself, such as a group of people queuing in a crowded space or a school of fish swimming together. Reflect on what simple rules or interactions drive the system's order.
2. **Analyze Your Workplace:** Identify areas where your team or organization exhibits self-organization. What rules allow this to happen? How can you support these natural dynamics?
3. **Design for Self-Organization:** Choose a project or task and create conditions that allow the system to organize itself. For example, instead of assigning tasks directly, provide general goals and let the team decide how to achieve them.

Key Takeaway

Self-organizing systems create structure and order without external control. Understanding this dynamic allows you to design systems that harness natural adaptability and creativity.

Chapter 14: Focus on Tipping Points

Every system has thresholds — moments when a small change can cause a dramatic shift. These are called tipping points. At these critical moments, a system transitions from one state to another, often irreversibly.

Think of a snow-covered mountainside. For hours, snow piles up harmlessly. Then, one final snowflake lands, and an avalanche is triggered. It wasn't the size of the snowflake that mattered, but the fact that the system had reached its tipping point.

Tipping points can lead to both positive and negative outcomes. In social movements, a single event can galvanize mass participation, transforming the movement overnight. In environmental systems, crossing a tipping point might result in irreversible damage, such as the melting of polar ice caps. Recognizing tipping points helps you anticipate change and identify where small actions can have the greatest impact.

How to Identify Tipping Points

1. **Understand System Thresholds:** Identify the conditions under which the system might shift states. For example, in a workplace, morale may reach a tipping point where even one more unresolved issue triggers widespread dissatisfaction.
2. **Track Early Warning Signs:** Tipping points are often preceded by small, incremental changes. For instance, a rising temperature in a server room might lead to sudden system failure once a critical heat threshold is crossed.
3. **Recognize Nonlinear Behavior:** In many systems, change is not gradual — it accelerates suddenly as the tipping point approaches. Monitor patterns for signs of such rapid escalation.
4. **Focus on Leverage Points:** Tipping points are often influenced by specific areas of the system where small interventions can create outsized effects.

Real-World Example

In public health, tipping points play a key role in epidemic outbreaks. Initially, a few isolated cases of a disease may seem manageable. But once the infection rate crosses a critical threshold, the disease can spread exponentially, overwhelming healthcare systems. Identifying and addressing this tipping point early — through measures such as vaccination campaigns — can prevent catastrophe.

Why It Matters

Tipping points represent moments of opportunity and risk. If you act too late, you may face consequences that are difficult or impossible to reverse. But if you recognize a tipping point early, you can take targeted actions to steer the system in a desired direction.

Exercises

1. **Reflect on Personal Tipping Points:** Think of a time in your life when a small decision or event caused a major change (e.g. choosing a career path or joining a new social group). What conditions made that tipping point possible?
2. **Analyze a System at Risk:** Choose a system you're part of and identify any thresholds it may be approaching (e.g. team burnout or financial instability). What small actions could prevent a negative tipping point or encourage a positive one?
3. **Create a Tipping Point Strategy:** For a goal you're working toward, identify the leverage points where small efforts could create significant progress. Plan how to focus your energy on these critical areas.

Key Takeaway

Tipping points are moments when small changes create big shifts — understanding them allows you to anticipate risks and seize opportunities.

Chapter 15: See Patterns Across Scales

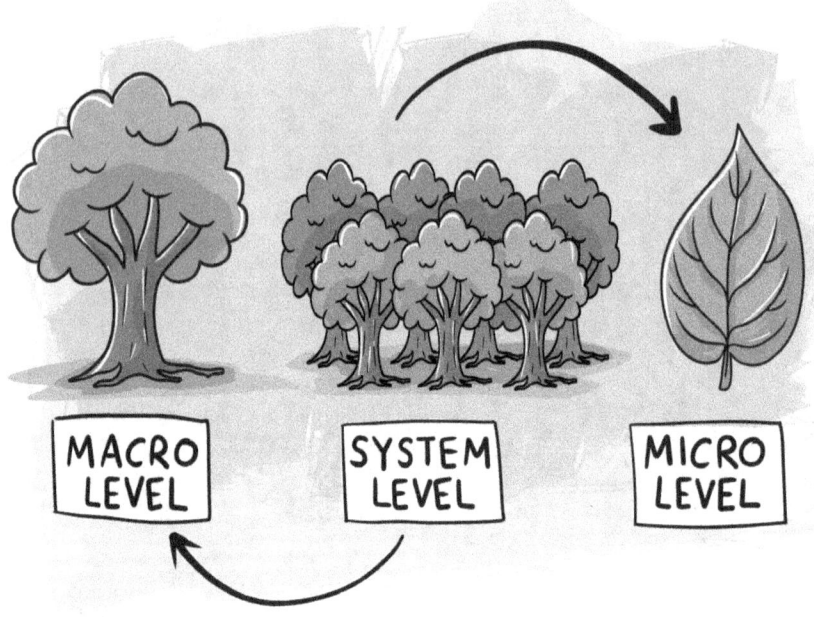

MACRO LEVEL **SYSTEM LEVEL** **MICRO LEVEL**

Patterns at Every Level

Systems often exhibit patterns that repeat across different scales. This concept, called scale invariance, is key to understanding how systems behave in both the smallest details and the biggest structures. By recognizing patterns across scales, you gain insight into how small actions influence larger systems — and vice versa.

For example, in a business, the communication patterns within a small team may mirror those of the entire organization. A team prone to silos might reflect a larger organizational culture of fragmented departments. Conversely, changes at the macro scale — such as company-wide policy shifts — often trickle down and reshape the micro scale.

The ability to see patterns across scales is like having a zoom lens for systems. It allows you to connect the dots between what happens at different levels, making your understanding of the system far more robust.

How to Spot Patterns Across Scales

1. **Zoom In and Out:** Start at one level — micro, macro, or in between — and observe how patterns repeat or shift as you zoom in or out. For example, notice how social trends emerge in both individual behaviors and community-wide dynamics.
2. **Look for Fractals:** Fractals are self-repeating structures found in systems, such as the branching patterns of trees or river networks. Spotting these can reveal universal rules governing the system.
3. **Compare Across Levels:** Identify a pattern at one scale and ask whether it exists at other levels. For example, a school system's allocation of resources might mirror national educational funding trends.
4. **Analyze Scale-Specific Behaviors:** Some patterns may only emerge at certain scales. For instance, individual decision-making in traffic differs from city-wide traffic flow patterns.

Real-World Example

Climate systems offer a striking example of patterns across scales. At the smallest scale, changes in plant respiration influence local carbon dioxide levels. Zooming out, these changes aggregate to affect regional weather patterns, which in turn influence global climate. Recognizing this interconnectedness helps scientists predict and address climate change at all levels.

Why It Matters

Failing to see patterns across scales can lead to blind spots. A solution that works at the micro level may not address larger issues, while focusing solely on the macro level risks missing key details. By analyzing multiple scales, you can design solutions that are effective and aligned with the system's dynamics as a whole.

Exercises

1. **Zoom In and Out on a System:** Pick a system you're familiar with, such as your workplace. Observe how patterns at the team level reflect or differ from those at the organizational level. Write down your observations.
2. **Identify Fractals in Nature or Life:** Spend time observing systems like trees, rivers, or family structures. Look for self-repeating patterns that appear across different scales. Reflect on what these patterns reveal about the system.
3. **Compare Solutions Across Scales:** Think about a recent problem you solved (e.g. improving your daily schedule). Consider how that solution might work at a larger scale (e.g. managing a team) or smaller scale (e.g. personal habits).

Key Takeaway

Recognizing patterns across scales helps you understand how systems behave at every level, from the micro to the macro.

Chapter 16: Look for Missing Connections

When analyzing a system, it's tempting to focus solely on what's present: the visible people, processes, and interactions driving its behavior. However, just as important are the connections that *should* exist but don't. Missing connections act like broken links in a chain, interrupting the flow of resources, information, or influence, and leaving the system vulnerable to inefficiencies, delays, or even collapse.

Consider a workplace where departments operate in silos. Each team focuses on its tasks without communicating with others. The absence of collaboration means missed opportunities to share insights, align goals, or avoid redundant efforts. Similarly, in urban planning, a lack of coordination between transportation and housing developers can lead to neighborhoods poorly served by public transit.

Identifying these gaps is like finding the missing pieces of a puzzle. Once they are acknowledged and addressed, the system becomes more cohesive and efficient.

How to Identify Missing Connections

1. **Outline the System:** Start by sketching out the system's components and the connections between them. Focus on how resources, information, or influence flow from one part to another.
2. **Spot the Breaks:** Look for interruptions in the flow—places where resources should move seamlessly but don't. For instance, is a lack of communication between teams causing project delays?
3. **Ask "What's Missing?":** Step back and ask whether new connections could improve the system. For example, would connecting two previously isolated departments foster collaboration?
4. **Test New Connections:** Experiment with bridging the gaps. Introduce a feedback mechanism or communication channel between disconnected components and observe how it changes the system's behavior.

Real-World Example

Consider healthcare systems, where missing connections often lead to inefficiencies. A patient might visit multiple specialists, but without a shared medical record, doctors lack access to the full picture of the patient's condition. This gap increases the risk of misdiagnosis or redundant tests. Implementing electronic health records bridges this connection, enabling doctors, pharmacists, and patients to collaborate effectively.

Why It Matters

Missing connections create inefficiencies, waste, and vulnerabilities within a system. Ignoring these gaps can perpetuate problems or even cause systemic failures. Conversely, identifying and addressing them unlocks opportunities for improvement, creating stronger and more efficient systems.

For instance, adding a simple communication channel between two teams can transform how they collaborate. Similarly, connecting isolated parts of a supply chain can streamline operations, reduce costs, and improve customer satisfaction.

Exercises

1. **Identify Missing Links:** Choose a system you interact with regularly, such as a workplace process or community project. Sketch its components and connections. Highlight areas where connections are missing and reflect on how those gaps affect the system.
2. **Spot a Missed Opportunity:** Think of a situation where poor communication or coordination caused a problem. Identify which connection was missing and how bridging it might have changed the outcome.
3. **Create a New Connection:** In your personal or professional life, find a missing connection (e.g. between two colleagues or departments). Introduce a way to link them, such as regular meetings or a shared tool, and observe how the system improves.

Key Takeaway

Missing connections weaken systems by disrupting the flow of resources or information — bridging these gaps strengthens the system and creates new opportunities for efficiency.

Chapter 17: Assess System Resilience

Resilience is the ability of a system to withstand shocks, recover from disruptions, and continue functioning. It's a defining characteristic of systems that survive and thrive over time. In a resilient system, stressors may cause temporary setbacks, but the system adapts and stabilizes without breaking.

Imagine a resilient community facing a natural disaster. Strong emergency services, clear communication, and well-coordinated recovery efforts allow the community to bounce back quickly. In contrast, a community lacking these features might take years to recover — or never fully regain stability. The difference lies in the system's ability to absorb challenges and adapt to new conditions.

Assessing resilience allows you to pinpoint strengths, vulnerabilities, and areas where the system might fail under pressure. This understanding helps you build systems that are better equipped to handle change and disruption.

How to Unpack System Resilience

1. **Identify Vulnerabilities:** Look for areas where the system is most likely to break down under stress. For example, does a workplace rely too heavily on one key employee?
2. **Evaluate Redundancies:** Resilient systems often have backups or alternative pathways. For instance, a resilient transportation system includes multiple modes of travel, such as buses, trains, and bike lanes.
3. **Assess Flexibility:** Resilient systems can adapt to new conditions. For example, a company that quickly shifts to remote work during a crisis demonstrates flexibility.
4. **Test Recovery Capacity:** Consider how well the system can recover after a disruption. Does it bounce back quickly, or does it take too long to regain stability?

Real-World Example

The COVID-19 pandemic revealed stark differences in resilience across industries. Companies with strong digital infrastructures and flexible work policies adapted quickly to remote work, maintaining productivity. In contrast, businesses without these features faced significant disruptions. Assessing and improving resilience in advance could have minimized these impacts.

Why It Matters

Without resilience, systems are fragile and prone to collapse under pressure. A resilient system, however, can endure shocks, adapt to change, and emerge stronger. For example, a resilient organization with cross-trained employees can maintain operations even if key staff are unavailable. Similarly, a resilient personal schedule with built-in flexibility allows you to adapt to unexpected events without stress.

Strengthening resilience isn't just about preparing for worst-case scenarios; it's about building systems that thrive in uncertain and dynamic environments.

Exercises

1. **Reflect on a Past Disruption:** Think of a time when a system you relied on faced a disruption (e.g. a delayed project or personal setback). What made the system resilient — or why did it struggle to recover?
2. **Analyze Redundancies:** Choose a system in your life, such as a financial plan or a team workflow. Identify areas where you have backups or alternative options — and areas where you don't.
3. **Strengthen Your Resilience:** Identify one area of your life or work where resilience could be improved. For example, create a contingency plan for a critical project or cross-train team members to handle multiple roles.

Key Takeaway

Resilient systems can endure shocks, adapt to change, and recover quickly — assessing and building resilience ensures long-term stability and success.

Chapter 18: Find Balancing Forces

Every system operates within a delicate balance. This balance is maintained by forces that push the system in different directions. These forces act as stabilizers, preventing a system from spiraling out of control or veering into chaos.

Think about your body's internal temperature. When you're too hot, your body sweats to cool down. When you're too cold, you shiver to generate heat. These opposing forces work together to maintain a stable internal temperature — a classic example of a balancing force in action.

Balancing forces are essential for stability, but they can also create resistance to change. For example, in an organization, efforts to introduce innovation might meet balancing forces like established traditions or doubt from employees. Recognizing these forces helps you understand how systems maintain stability and how to work with, rather than against, them.

How to Identify Balancing Forces

1. **Look for Stabilizing Patterns:** Observe areas where the system consistently resists change. For example, are productivity levels in a workplace relatively steady despite fluctuations in workload?
2. **Trace Opposing Forces:** Identify the forces pushing the system in opposite directions. For instance, growth might be balanced by resource limitations or regulatory constraints.
3. **Distinguish Positive and Negative Balancing Forces:** Some balancing forces are beneficial (e.g. quality control processes), while others can stifle progress (e.g. excessive bureaucracy).
4. **Monitor Feedback Loops:** Balancing forces often operate through recursive patterns that self-correct the system, like a thermostat regulating temperature.

Real-World Example

In an economy, inflation is a balancing force for consumer demand. When demand rises too quickly, inflation makes goods more expensive, reducing spending and stabilizing the system. Conversely, when demand falls, prices drop, encouraging spending and boosting the economy. This dynamic helps maintain a balance, preventing extreme booms or busts.

Why It Matters

Balancing forces are the "brakes" that keep systems from going off track. Ignoring them can lead to frustration when efforts to create change meet resistance. But understanding these forces allows you to anticipate challenges, adapt your strategies, and even leverage balancing forces to your advantage. For example, by aligning new initiatives with existing traditions, you can introduce change without disrupting stability.

Exercises

1. **Identify Balancing Forces in Your Life:** Think of a situation where stability is maintained despite external pressures (e.g. a family dynamic or workplace culture). Reflect on what forces are keeping the system balanced.
2. **Outline Opposing Forces:** Choose a project or goal and list the forces pushing for progress and those resisting change. Identify which balancing forces are helpful and which are hindrances.
3. **Work with Balancing Forces:** For a challenge you're facing, brainstorm ways to align your efforts with the system's stabilizing forces instead of working against them.

Key Takeaway

Balancing forces stabilize systems by counteracting change — understanding them helps you work with the system to achieve your goals.

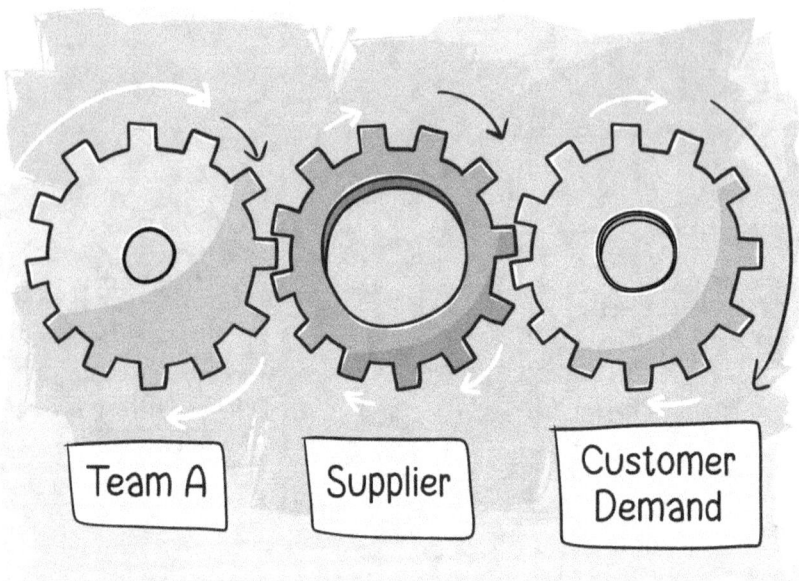

Chapter 19: See Dependencies

How Systems Rely on Each Other

Systems are built on dependencies. Each part of a system relies on others to function, creating a web of interconnected relationships. Understanding these dependencies is crucial for identifying where a system is strong, where it is vulnerable, and how changes to one part might ripple through the entire system.

Imagine a manufacturing process. The production line depends on a steady supply of materials, skilled workers, and functional machinery. If any of these dependencies fail — say, a supplier misses a delivery — the entire system can grind to a halt. Similarly, in social systems, communities depend on resources like clean water, transportation, and education to thrive.

Dependencies create both opportunities and risks. They enable collaboration and efficiency, but they also make systems fragile if critical dependencies are overlooked or disrupted.

How to Identify Dependencies

1. **Map the System:** Create a diagram of the system's components and connections. Identify where one part relies on another to function.
2. **Trace Critical Pathways:** Focus on dependencies that are essential for the system to operate. For example, a hospital's dependency on electricity is more critical than its dependency on cafeteria services.
3. **Look for Single Points of Failure:** Identify areas where the system relies too heavily on one component. For example, if a business depends on a single supplier, it's vulnerable to disruptions in that supply chain.
4. **Analyze the Ripple Effect:** Consider how changes to one dependency might impact the rest of the system.

Real-World Example

In the global supply chain, dependencies are especially pronounced. A delay at a major shipping port can disrupt production schedules, inventory levels, and retail availability worldwide. Recognizing these dependencies allows businesses to diversify suppliers, build buffer stocks, or improve logistics to reduce vulnerability.

Why It Matters

Dependencies reveal the interdependence of systems. Ignoring them risks overlooking vulnerabilities or underestimating the impact of changes. By identifying dependencies, you can strengthen critical connections, reduce risks, and design systems that are more robust and reliable.

Exercises

1. **Identify Your Dependencies:** Choose a system you rely on (e.g. your work schedule or a household routine). Create a diagram showing how its parts depend on one another. Reflect on which dependencies are most critical.
2. **Spot a Weak Link:** Identify one dependency in your personal or professional life that feels fragile or unreliable. Brainstorm ways to strengthen or replace it.
3. **Assess Ripple Effects:** Think of a recent change in a system you're part of. Trace how that change impacted other components and what this reveals about the system's dependencies.

Key Takeaway

Dependencies are the glue that holds systems together. Understanding them helps you identify strengths, vulnerabilities, and opportunities for improvement.

Chapter 20: Recognize How Systems Change

No system stays the same forever. Whether it's a natural ecosystem, a business, or a community, systems constantly evolve in response to internal and external pressures. Recognizing how systems change helps you anticipate shifts, adapt to new conditions, and guide systems toward desired outcomes.

System change can occur gradually or suddenly. A forest, for instance, evolves slowly as plants and animals adapt to changing conditions. But a sudden wildfire can trigger rapid transformation, creating opportunities for new species to thrive. Similarly, in organizations, gradual shifts in culture might build over years, while a merger or leadership change can create immediate upheaval.

Understanding how systems change allows you to work with the forces of evolution rather than resisting them.

How to Recognize System Change

1. **Identify Driving Forces:** Look for factors influencing change, such as technology, regulations, or shifting consumer preferences.
2. **Distinguish Gradual from Sudden Change:** Recognize whether the system is evolving incrementally or undergoing a rapid transformation. For example, climate change involves both slow temperature increases and sudden extreme weather events.
3. **Monitor Recursive Patterns:** For example, a growing population creates demand for housing, which drives urban expansion, creating further population growth.
4. **Observe Tipping Points:** Many changes occur when systems cross critical thresholds, leading to rapid shifts in behavior.

Real-World Example

In technology, the adoption of smartphones is a clear example of system change. Gradual improvements in connectivity and affordability prepared the market, but the introduction of app ecosystems caused a tipping point, rapidly transforming industries like communication, entertainment, and commerce.

Why It Matters

Ignoring system change can leave you unprepared for challenges or opportunities. By recognizing how systems evolve, you can anticipate shifts, adapt strategies, and influence outcomes. For example, understanding how consumer habits are changing allows businesses to innovate and stay ahead of competitors.

Exercises

1. **Track Changes in a System:** Choose a system you're part of (e.g. your workplace or a social group). Reflect on how it has changed over the past five years. What forces drove those changes?
2. **Predict Future Changes:** Think of a system you rely on and list factors that might drive change in the next five years. Consider how you could adapt to or influence these shifts.
3. **Analyze a Sudden Change:** Reflect on a recent event that caused rapid change in your life or work. Identify the tipping point and what enabled the transformation.

Key Takeaway

Systems evolve in response to internal and external forces — recognizing how they change allows you to anticipate, adapt to, and shape their evolution.

Section II: Analyzing Human-Created Systems

Human-created systems — organizations, economies, communities, and more — are some of the most complex yet familiar systems humans interact with daily. Unlike natural systems, they are influenced by rules, norms, hierarchies, and human behaviors. This section dives into the structures and dynamics that define these systems, equipping you with tools to uncover the forces shaping them, identify their weaknesses, and harness their potential. By mastering these chapters, you'll gain insight into how human systems operate and learn to analyze them with precision and purpose.

Chapter 21: Study Incentive Structures

The Power of Rewards and Penalties

Incentive structures are like the operating system of human-created systems. They're the subtle, often invisible forces that guide how individuals and organizations behave. Incentives come in many forms: financial rewards, social recognition, penalties, or even the promise of autonomy. By understanding these structures, you can decode why people act the way they do and make adjustments to drive desired outcomes.

Consider a workplace environment where employees receive bonuses for meeting sales targets. This incentive motivates employees to focus on closing deals. But what if those deals come at the expense of long-term client satisfaction? Or what if the reward structure inadvertently encourages competition over teamwork? Incentive structures aren't inherently good or bad— they simply drive behavior in whatever direction they're designed to. The challenge lies in ensuring those directions align with the broader goals of the system.

Incentives aren't limited to financial rewards. Social incentives, like public recognition or inclusion in decision-making, can be just as powerful. Negative incentives, such as fines or warnings, also play a role. Together, rewards and penalties create a framework that influences decision-making.

How to Analyze Incentive Structures

1. **Identify Explicit and Implicit Incentives:** Start by listing the formal incentives in the system, such as pay bonuses or performance reviews. Then, dig deeper to uncover implicit ones. For example, does a culture of overworking subtly reward employees who sacrifice personal time?

2. **Trace Behavior Back to Incentives:** Observe how the system's incentives shape specific behaviors. Are employees prioritizing speed over quality? Are citizens complying with recycling programs because of fines or because of social pressure?

3. **Check for Alignment:** Compare the incentives to the system's overarching goals. Are they driving behavior that contributes to long-term success, or do they focus narrowly on short-term gains?

4. **Consider Feedback Loops:** Incentives often create self-reinforcing cycles. For example, rewarding innovation might lead to a culture of experimentation, which in turn produces more innovation.

Real-World Example

In urban transportation, toll roads are designed as a negative incentive to discourage congestion and encourage alternative routes or public transport. But if public transit is unreliable or inaccessible, the toll system can disproportionately affect low-income commuters without achieving its goal. Adjusting the incentive structure — such as reinvesting toll revenue into improving public transport — could better align individual behavior with the system's objectives.

Why It Matters

Incentive structures influence nearly every decision within a system. Ignoring them risks misinterpreting why people behave as they do—or worse, designing systems that unintentionally reward counterproductive actions. By studying incentives, you can align individual motivations with the system's goals, ensuring smoother operations and more sustainable outcomes.

Exercises

1. **List Incentives in Your Life:** Identify explicit incentives (e.g. salary bonuses) and implicit ones (e.g. praise from peers) in your workplace, school, or community. Reflect on how they shape behavior.

2. **Evaluate a Policy's Incentives:** Choose a policy or program, such as recycling incentives or tax credits for electric vehicles. Analyze how its rewards and penalties influence public behavior and whether they achieve the desired outcomes.

3. **Redesign a System's Incentives:** Think of a system you're part of, like a workplace or a team project. Identify a misaligned incentive and propose a way to better align it with the system's objectives.

Key Takeaway

Incentive structures drive behavior in systems — aligning them helps achieve better, long-term outcomes.

Chapter 22: Watch Out for Backfiring Motivators

When Good Intentions Backfire

Not all incentives produce the outcomes you expect. Sometimes, a reward or penalty designed to encourage productive behavior has the opposite effect, creating unintended consequences that harm the system. These backfiring motivators are common in human-created systems where complexity often masks how people will react to incentives.

For example, a company that offers bonuses for resolving customer complaints quickly might see employees prioritizing speed over quality. While the intent is to improve customer satisfaction, the actual outcome could be rushed solutions that leave customers dissatisfied. These unintended consequences occur because the incentive focuses on a narrow metric — speed —without accounting for broader goals such as quality or customer trust.

Similarly, fines or penalties can backfire if they unintentionally reinforce undesirable behaviors. A famous example is day-care centers that introduced fines for parents who picked up their children late. Instead of reducing late pickups, the fines made parents feel they were paying for extra time, causing lateness to increase.

How to Identify Backfiring Motivators

1. **Examine Behavioral Side Effects:** Look for unintended behaviors that arise from the incentive. Are people cutting corners, exploiting loopholes, or prioritizing short-term gains over long-term benefits?
2. **Analyze Mismatched Goals:** Consider whether the incentive rewards specific outcomes at the expense of broader system objectives.
3. **Evaluate Feedback Loops:** Some backfiring motivators create patterns that amplify the problem. For example, rewarding individual performance might increase competition while eroding team collaboration.
4. **Test for Perverse Outcomes:** Ask whether the incentive unintentionally encourages the very behavior it's trying to prevent.

Real-World Example

In environmental policy, programs offering subsidies for renewable energy installations often attract companies that prioritize the subsidy over quality. For instance, some solar companies focus on meeting minimum installation criteria to claim subsidies rather than ensuring long-term efficiency. This undermines the program's goal of reducing carbon emissions.

Why It Matters

Backfiring motivators can derail even the best-intentioned systems. Recognizing them allows you to refine incentives and minimize harm. By thinking critically about how people respond to rewards and penalties, you can design systems that encourage desired outcomes without unintended side effects.

Exercises

1. **Reflect on Personal Experience:** Think of a situation where a reward or penalty produced unintended consequences (e.g. rushing to complete a task for a bonus). Analyze what caused the backfire and how it could be corrected.
2. **Evaluate a Policy:** Choose a policy or rule with incentives attached. Identify whether it has backfired and what unintended behaviors it encouraged.
3. **Redesign a Backfiring Incentive:** Identify an incentive in your workplace or community that could backfire. Propose changes to ensure it aligns with long-term goals.

Key Takeaway

Poorly designed incentives can backfire, causing harm instead of progress — analyzing motivators helps you design systems that encourage productive behavior without unintended consequences.

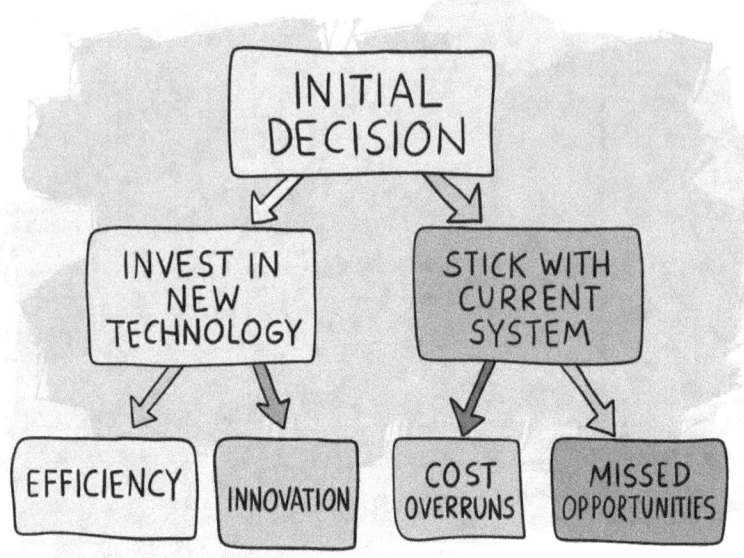

Chapter 23: Track Decision Pathways

Every decision within a system creates a ripple effect, influencing outcomes in ways that aren't always obvious. Decision pathways are the chains of choices that propagate through a system, creating feedback loops, bottlenecks, or opportunities for change. By tracking these pathways, you gain a deeper understanding of how individual choices shape the overall system.

Consider a city deciding whether to invest in public transport or road expansion. Choosing public transport might reduce traffic congestion and emissions, while road expansion could encourage more cars, worsening air quality in the long term. Each decision sets off a cascade of consequences that interact with other parts of the system. Tracking these pathways ensures that decision-makers anticipate both immediate outcomes and downstream effects.

How to Track Decision Pathways

1. **Start with the Initial Decision:** Identify a key decision within the system. What factors influenced it, and who made it?
2. **Determine Subsequent Steps:** Follow how this decision propagated through the system. Did it lead to changes in resources, behaviors, or structures?
3. **Spot Feedback Loops:** Look for pathways where decisions influence future choices. For instance, a decision to automate a process might free up resources, enabling further automation.
4. **Analyze Missed Pathways:** Consider what alternatives weren't chosen and how they might have influenced the system differently.

Real-World Example

In software development, choosing a particular coding framework can shape future decisions about compatibility, scalability, and updates. A poorly chosen framework might lead to long-term technical debt, limiting the system's ability to adapt. Tracking the decision pathway highlights where missteps occurred and how they could have been avoided.

Why It Matters

Understanding decision pathways prevents you from making short-sighted choices. By tracking how decisions ripple through a system, you can anticipate unintended consequences, identify leverage points, and refine future decision-making processes.

Exercises

1. **Track a Personal Decision Pathway:** Reflect on a major decision you made (e.g. pursuing a career path). Outline how that choice influenced subsequent events and opportunities.
2. **Analyze a Group Decision:** Choose a recent team or organizational decision. Trace its pathway and reflect on whether the outcomes aligned with the original intent.
3. **Simulate an Alternative Pathway:** Pick a decision in your workplace or community and imagine an alternative choice. Reflect on how this hypothetical pathway would have changed the system's behavior.

Key Takeaway

Decision pathways reveal how choices shape outcomes — tracking them ensures better decisions and system-wide improvements.

Chapter 24: Examine Rules and Norms

The Frameworks That Shape Systems

Every human-created system is governed by a mix of rules and norms. Rules are the formal, explicit guidelines — laws, policies, or procedures — that define what is allowed and what isn't. Norms, on the other hand, are the informal, often unwritten expectations that emerge from shared behavior, culture, or tradition. Both play critical roles in shaping how systems function, and understanding them is essential for analyzing and improving those systems.

Consider a workplace. Official rules might dictate policies like working hours or performance reviews, but informal norms — such as the expectation to reply to emails after hours — often have just as much influence, if not more. Ignoring these norms can lead to misunderstandings, inefficiencies, or even systemic breakdowns.

Rules and norms interact in powerful ways. Sometimes, they reinforce each other: for example, safety regulations (rules) and a culture of accountability (norms) can together create a strong emphasis on workplace safety. Other times, they conflict: a rule might ban overtime, but a norm of working late could pressure employees to stay after hours anyway. Understanding both frameworks is crucial for diagnosing problems and designing solutions that align with how the system truly operates.

How to Examine Rules and Norms

1. **Distinguish Between Rules and Norms:** Identify which guidelines are formal (e.g. written policies) and which are informal (e.g. social expectations).
2. **Observe Behavior:** Pay attention to how people actually act within the system. Are they following the rules, ignoring them, or adhering more closely to norms?
3. **Look for Conflicts:** Identify where rules and norms might clash. For instance, do policies about collaboration conflict with an individualistic office culture?
4. **Assess Effectiveness:** Consider whether the existing rules and norms are helping or hindering the system's goals. Are outdated rules causing inefficiencies? Are harmful norms holding people back?

Real-World Example

In the education system, official rules might require schools to adhere to strict curricula. However, norms among teachers might emphasize creative, flexible lesson plans. When these norms conflict with rigid rules, it can lead to frustration and burnout for teachers. Resolving such conflicts — perhaps by introducing more flexible policies — can create a better balance between innovation and accountability.

Why It Matters

Rules and norms shape behavior in powerful ways, but they're often misunderstood or overlooked. Ignoring norms can lead to blind spots in how a system operates, while blindly enforcing rules without understanding their effects can create resentment or inefficiency. Examining these frameworks allows you to identify misalignments, resolve conflicts, and design systems that work more effectively.

Exercises

1. **Identify Rules and Norms in Your Life:** Pick a system you're part of, such as your workplace or a community group. List its formal rules and unwritten norms. Reflect on how they interact.
2. **Spot Conflicts:** Think of a time when a rule conflicted with a norm in your life. How did this tension impact the system, and how might it have been resolved?
3. **Redesign a Rule or Norm:** Identify a rule or norm in a system that feels outdated or ineffective. Propose changes that would better align with the system's goals.

Key Takeaway

Rules and norms define how systems function — analyzing both helps you identify misalignments and improve outcomes.

Chapter 25: Map Communication Channels

The Lifeblood of Human Systems

Communication is the lifeblood of any human-created system. It's how information flows, decisions are made, and actions are coordinated. But not all communication is created equal. Some channels are strong, consistent, and effective, while others are weak, sporadic, or prone to misinterpretation. Mapping these channels allows you to visualize how information travels through the system, where breakdowns occur, and how communication could be improved.

Imagine a company launching a new product. If communication between marketing and production teams is clear and consistent, the launch is likely to go smoothly. But if communication is sporadic or siloed — if marketing doesn't know production timelines, for example — delays, confusion, and missed opportunities can result.

Communication channels can be formal (e.g. weekly reports or scheduled meetings) or informal (e.g. hallway chats or Slack messages). Both types play important roles, and both need to be understood to improve the flow of information.

How to Map Communication Channels

1. **Identify the Nodes:** Start by listing the individuals, teams, or departments involved in the system. These will serve as the nodes in your map.
2. **Trace the Channels:** Identify how information flows between nodes. Do teams communicate via email, meetings, or informal conversations?
3. **Assess Strength and Quality:** Evaluate each channel for reliability, clarity, and frequency. Are some channels overloaded with noise? Are others underutilized?
4. **Spot Bottlenecks and Gaps:** Look for areas where communication breaks down. For example, does important information get stuck at a managerial level instead of reaching the broader team?

Real-World Example

In large hospitals, effective communication between doctors, nurses, and administrative staff is essential for patient care. Mapping communication channels can reveal inefficiencies, such as a lack of direct communication between doctors and nurses, which might delay critical decisions. Improving these channels—like introducing shared digital records or cross-functional meetings — can streamline care and reduce errors.

Why It Matters

Poor communication is one of the most common reasons systems fail. Information bottlenecks, misinterpretations, or missing channels can lead to wasted time, costly mistakes, or even systemic breakdowns. By mapping and improving communication channels, you can ensure that information flows smoothly and the system operates more efficiently.

Exercises

1. **Map Your Communication Network:** Choose a system you're part of, like a workplace or a social group. Create a diagram showing how information flows between its components. Reflect on where communication is strong and where it's weak.
2. **Spot Bottlenecks:** Think of a time when poor communication caused problems. What channel broke down, and how could it have been improved?
3. **Redesign a Communication Channel:** Identify a weak communication channel in a system you're part of. Propose a way to strengthen it, such as introducing clearer protocols or using better tools.

Key Takeaway

Communication channels are essential for the smooth operation of systems. Mapping and improving them prevents breakdowns and enhances outcomes.

Chapter 26: Notice Bottlenecks

In any system, bottlenecks are points where flows — whether of resources, information, or work — get stuck or slowed. They act like a clogged artery in a circulatory system, disrupting the entire system's efficiency and capacity. Identifying and addressing bottlenecks is one of the most effective ways to improve performance and ensure smooth operation.

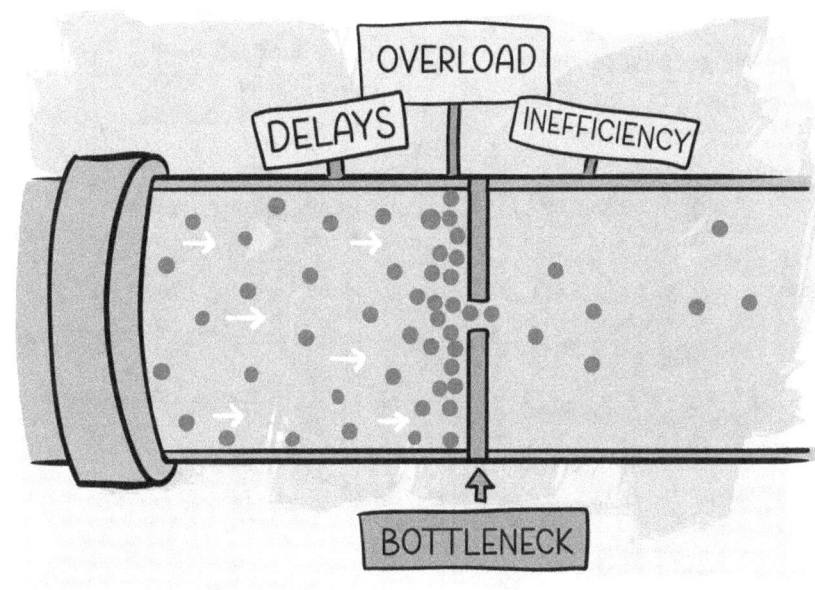

For example, in a supply chain, a bottleneck might occur at a manufacturing plant that can't meet demand. The delay at this point affects the entire chain, leading to late deliveries, frustrated customers, and lost revenue. Similarly, in a team project, a bottleneck might be a single overworked individual responsible for approving every decision.

Bottlenecks aren't always obvious. They often hide within layers of processes or routines, their effects rippling outward in ways that mask the root cause. By pinpointing these constrictions, you can unlock greater efficiency and improve outcomes across the system.

How to Identify Bottlenecks

1. **Track the Flow:** Start by visualizing how resources, tasks, or information move through the system. Look for stages where progress slows or stops.
2. **Measure Wait Times:** Bottlenecks often create delays. Identify areas where tasks or resources spend the most time waiting to move forward.
3. **Analyze Overloaded Points:** Look for components of the system that consistently operate at or beyond their capacity. For instance, is one team overwhelmed while others are underutilized?
4. **Observe Downstream Effects:** Bottlenecks often cause ripple effects, such as missed deadlines or errors in later stages. Trace these problems back to their source.

Real-World Example

In healthcare, emergency rooms are often bottlenecks in hospital systems. Patients may wait hours for a doctor because beds are full, diagnostics are delayed, or specialists are unavailable. These bottlenecks affect the entire hospital, reducing overall efficiency and patient satisfaction. Addressing them — by streamlining patient triage, increasing staff capacity, or improving communication — can transform the system.

Why It Matters

Bottlenecks reduce the capacity of the entire system. Even if every other part of the system operates efficiently, a single bottleneck can limit output, create frustration, and inflate costs. By identifying and addressing these constrictions, you can unlock the system's full potential and create more reliable, scalable processes.

Exercises

1. **Identify a Bottleneck in Your Life:** Think of a recurring task or process (e.g. preparing for meetings or completing a household chore). Pinpoint where progress consistently slows down and why.
2. **Map a Workflow:** Choose a system you interact with, such as a workplace process. Sketch out the flow of tasks and identify where delays or backlogs occur.
3. **Brainstorm Solutions:** For a bottleneck you've identified, list potential solutions, such as redistributing work, automating tasks, or simplifying approvals.

Key Takeaway

Bottlenecks slow down systems and limit their potential — identifying and addressing them improves efficiency and unlocks new capacity.

Chapter 27: Identify System Archetypes

The Blueprint of Systems

Systems, despite their complexity, often follow familiar patterns. These recurring structures, called system archetypes, help explain why systems behave the way they do. Identifying these archetypes allows you to anticipate outcomes, diagnose problems, and design smarter interventions.

One classic archetype is "Success to the Successful." In this structure, resources flow disproportionately to those already succeeding, creating a feedback loop that reinforces their advantage. Think of educational funding: well-funded schools produce better results, attracting more funding, while underfunded schools struggle to improve. Another common archetype is "Shifting the Burden," where short-term fixes address symptoms but ignore root causes. For example, relying on overtime to meet deadlines instead of improving workflow efficiency.

By recognizing archetypes, you can simplify complex systems and identify leverage points where small changes have big impacts.

How to Identify System Archetypes

1. **Look for Feedback Loops:** Many archetypes involve reinforcing or balancing loops. For instance, a loop might reinforce growth (e.g. word-of-mouth promotion) or maintain stability (e.g. thermostat regulation).
2. **Analyze Recurring Problems:** Patterns of recurring challenges — like resource inequalities or declining performance— often signal an underlying archetype.
3. **Match Behaviors to Archetypes:** Compare the system's behavior to common archetypes, such as "Limits to Growth," where expansion eventually hits a constraint, or "Fixes That Fail," where solutions create new problems.
4. **Identify Root Causes:** Archetypes often reveal deeper issues driving system behavior. For example, in "Escalation," competition between two actors leads to mutually destructive behavior.

Real-World Example

A company experiencing high turnover might fall into the "Fixes That Fail" archetype. To address staff departures, it increases recruitment efforts rather than addressing the root cause of dissatisfaction. Over time, turnover continues, and recruitment costs escalate. Recognizing this archetype enables leaders to focus on improving workplace culture instead of relying on short-term fixes.

Why It Matters

System archetypes simplify complexity, revealing the recurring structures that drive system behavior. By identifying these patterns, you can anticipate problems, avoid ineffective solutions, and target interventions where they will have the most impact.

Exercises

1. **Spot an Archetype in Your Life:** Think of a recurring problem in a system you interact with (e.g. a work process or family routine). Identify whether it matches an archetype, such as "Shifting the Burden" or "Escalation."
2. **Outline a Feedback Loop:** Choose a system and map its feedback loops. Determine whether they are reinforcing (driving growth or decline) or balancing (maintaining stability).
3. **Break the Pattern:** For a system archetype you've identified, brainstorm ways to intervene and disrupt the pattern. For example, how can you address the root cause in a "Fixes That Fail" structure?

Key Takeaway

System archetypes reveal recurring patterns of behavior — understanding them allows you to diagnose problems and design effective solutions.

Chapter 28: Explore Power Bases

Power is the force that drives decisions, shapes relationships, and determines resource allocation within human-created systems. But power is not always where it seems to be. While formal authority represents one kind of power, informal power bases often have equal or greater influence. These hidden forces can include subject-matter expertise, control over critical resources, social connections, or even sheer charisma.

Exploring power bases allows you to identify where influence truly lies, how decisions are shaped, and how to build strategies that align with these dynamics. Whether you're working to implement change, resolve conflicts, or simply understand a system, recognizing power bases ensures you can act effectively and with foresight.

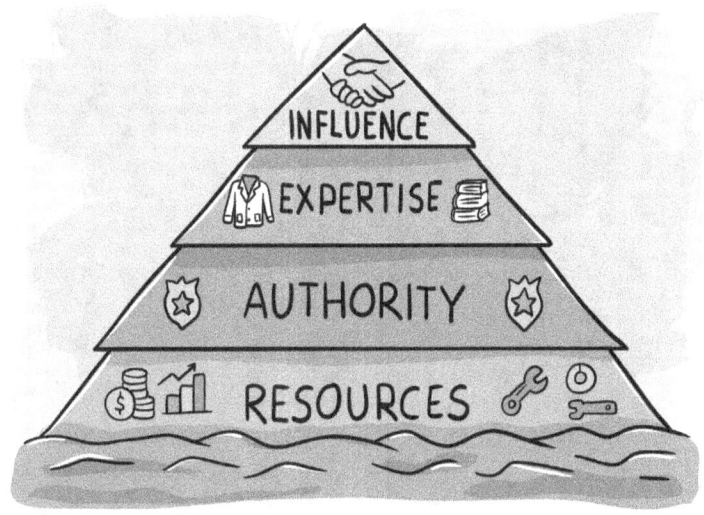

How to Explore Power Bases

1. **Identify Formal Power:** Start by visualizing explicit authority in the system — individuals or groups with official titles or positions. This could include CEOs, policymakers, or project managers who are empowered by organizational structures to make decisions.
2. **Uncover Informal Power:** Look for people who, despite lacking formal authority, influence outcomes through expertise, social connections, or credibility. Informal power often lies with individuals who others seek out for advice, support, or resources.
3. **Trace Resource Control:** Power is closely tied to control over key resources — money, knowledge, tools, or networks. For example, a department controlling a critical budget might have outsized influence even if its official rank is lower in the hierarchy.
4. **Analyze Relationships:** Power flows through relationships. Observe alliances, rivalries, and networks to see how influence is distributed. For example, in a team project, an unofficial leader might emerge due to their ability to mediate conflicts and rally others.

Real-World Example

Consider a local government planning a community development project. The mayor holds formal power to approve the budget and make high-level decisions. However, a long-standing community leader with no official role might wield more influence because of their relationships with residents and their deep understanding of local needs. Ignoring this informal power base could lead to public resistance, even if the mayor's plan is sound. Recognizing the leader's influence allows for collaboration and greater alignment with community priorities.

Why It Matters

Power bases dictate how systems operate, who gets heard, and how change happens. Failing to recognize informal power can derail well-intentioned plans, create unnecessary conflict, or limit the system's ability to adapt. Conversely, understanding both formal and informal power enables you to anticipate resistance, build coalitions, and ensure solutions are accepted and implemented.

For example, if you're leading a project and focus solely on the formal hierarchy, you might miss the opportunity to engage informal influencers who can help rally the team. Similarly, in a negotiation, understanding who controls key resources allows you to target your efforts where they will have the most impact.

Exercises

1. **Map Power in a System You Know:** Think of a system you're part of, such as your workplace or a community group. Identify the individuals or groups with formal authority and those with informal influence. Reflect on how their power shapes decisions and outcomes.
2. **Trace Resource Control:** Pick a system and analyze who controls its key resources, such as budgets, information, or tools. How does resource control affect the flow of power?
3. **Navigate Power Dynamics:** For a challenge you're facing, consider how power is distributed. Who do you need to engage or influence to achieve your goal? How can you align your approach with the system's power dynamics?

Key Takeaway

Power is a combination of formal authority, resource control, and informal influence. Understanding these dynamics allows you to navigate systems more effectively and achieve lasting results.

Chapter 29: Find Leverage Points

In complex systems, not all actions have equal weight. Some points within the system — known as leverage points — hold disproportionate influence over its behavior. Identifying and acting on these points allows you to create meaningful change with minimal effort, avoiding wasted energy on areas that yield little impact.

For example, consider a city trying to reduce traffic congestion. Building more roads might seem like a logical solution, but it often encourages more car usage, worsening the problem over time. A better leverage point might be investing in affordable public transit. By changing how people move through the system, this single intervention can alleviate congestion, reduce emissions, and improve urban mobility.

Leverage points are not always obvious. They often exist at deeper levels of the system, such as the underlying rules, goals, or feedback loops, rather than at surface-level processes. Finding these points requires a deep understanding of how the system operates and where small changes can trigger larger, cascading effects.

How to Identify Leverage Points

1. **Define the System:** Start by visualizing the system's components and connections. Identify areas where influence flows through multiple parts of the system.
2. **Analyze Feedback Loops:** Feedback loops—whether reinforcing or balancing—are often powerful leverage points. For example, amplifying a positive feedback loop can drive growth, while interrupting a negative loop can stabilize the system.
3. **Focus on Underlying Structures:** Leverage points are often found in the system's foundational rules, norms, or goals. Ask: What structural changes could shift the system's behavior?
4. **Test Small Changes:** Experiment with small interventions in different parts of the system. Observe which ones create the greatest ripple effects.

Real-World Example

In public health, childhood vaccination programs serve as a critical leverage point. By immunizing children against preventable diseases, these programs reduce illness, decrease healthcare costs, and improve long-term societal health. This single intervention has a far-reaching impact, benefiting both individuals and the broader system.

Why It Matters

Without understanding leverage points, efforts to improve systems often focus on surface-level symptoms rather than root causes. This can lead to wasted resources or unintended consequences. By targeting leverage points, you maximize impact while minimizing effort, making your interventions more efficient and effective.

For instance, a company struggling with low employee morale might initially focus on superficial fixes like team-building activities. However, identifying a deeper leverage point — such as improving leadership communication — can create a lasting cultural shift that boosts morale across the organization.

Exercises

1. **Identify a Leverage Point in Your Life:** Think of a recurring issue, such as managing your time or improving teamwork. What small change could have a large, positive impact?
2. **Map a System for Leverage Points:** Choose a system you interact with (e.g. a work process or a family routine). Identify areas where small interventions could create significant improvements.
3. **Experiment with Leverage:** Test a small change in a system, such as streamlining a single step in a workflow. Observe how this impacts the larger system.

Key Takeaway

Leverage points are areas where small actions create big changes — identifying and targeting these points allows you to maximize impact and efficiency.

Chapter 30: Trace Resource Inequalities

In human-created systems, resources are rarely distributed evenly. Whether it's wealth, access to education, or even time, these inequalities shape how systems function, often creating imbalances that perpetuate themselves over time. Tracing resource inequalities allows you to understand where these imbalances exist, how they affect the system, and what changes could create more equitable outcomes.

Take the example of a school system. Schools in wealthy neighborhoods often have better funding, smaller class sizes, and more extracurricular programs. Meanwhile, schools in underprivileged areas struggle with larger class sizes, fewer resources, and less experienced teachers. These inequalities create feedback loops: better-funded schools produce higher-achieving students, attracting more funding, while underfunded schools fall further behind.

Understanding resource inequalities isn't just about identifying disparities — it's about recognizing how those disparities shape the system's behavior and finding ways to address them.

How to Trace Resource Inequalities

1. **Identify Key Resources:** Start by listing the critical resources within the system, such as money, time, information, or access to services.
2. **Structure Distribution:** Visualize how these resources are distributed among different parts of the system. Are some groups, departments, or individuals receiving significantly more or less than others?
3. **Trace Causes:** Investigate why these inequalities exist. Are they the result of historical decisions, structural biases, or external constraints?
4. **Analyze Impacts:** Consider how resource inequalities affect system behavior. For instance, do they create bottlenecks, reinforce negative feedback loops, or limit opportunities for growth?

Real-World Example

In global development, resource inequalities are starkly visible. Wealthy countries have access to advanced healthcare, infrastructure, and education, while poorer nations struggle with basic necessities. These disparities perpetuate cycles of poverty and hinder global progress. Addressing these inequalities through targeted interventions — such as international aid or fair trade agreements — can create more balanced and sustainable systems.

Why It Matters

Resource inequalities create inefficiencies, limit opportunities, and reinforce systemic disadvantages. Ignoring these disparities can lead to short-term fixes that fail to address underlying problems. By tracing resource inequalities, you can design interventions that redistribute resources more equitably, improving outcomes for the entire system.

For example, in a workplace, an overworked team might struggle to meet deadlines while other teams have excess capacity. Redistributing workloads and resources not only improves team performance but also enhances overall productivity.

Exercises

1. **Identify Inequalities in Your Life:** Think of a system you're part of, such as your workplace or community. Where do you see disparities in resources like time, information, or support?
2. **Pinpoint a Resource Gap:** Choose a system and create a visual map of its resource distribution. Highlight areas of abundance and scarcity.
3. **Propose a Redistribution Strategy:** For a resource inequality you've identified, brainstorm ways to redistribute resources more equitably. What steps could you take to make the system fairer?

Key Takeaway

Resource inequalities shape how systems function. Addressing these disparities can create more equitable and effective outcomes.

Chapter 31: Spot Structural Biases

The Invisible Tilt of Systems

Every human-created system has built-in structures — rules, policies, cultural norms, and historical contexts — that shape its behavior. Sometimes, these structures create biases that advantage some groups while disadvantaging others. Unlike personal bias, structural bias is embedded within the system itself, influencing outcomes regardless of individual intentions.

For example, consider hiring practices. A company might genuinely want a diverse workforce, but if its job advertisements use jargon that appeals to a narrow demographic, or if its recruitment relies on referrals from current employees (who are demographically similar), structural biases limit who applies and gets hired. These biases don't stem from deliberate exclusion but from how the system is designed.

Spotting structural biases requires looking at how the system operates beneath the surface. It's not about blaming individuals but understanding the frameworks that perpetuate inequality, inefficiency, or unfairness — and finding ways to make the system more equitable.

How to Spot Structural Biases

1. **Examine Outcomes:** Start by analyzing who benefits and who doesn't from the system. For example, do certain groups consistently have better access to resources or opportunities?
2. **Trace the Rules:** Look at the formal policies or informal norms that guide decision-making. Are there policies that unintentionally exclude or disadvantage certain groups?
3. **Consider Historical Contexts:** Many structural biases are rooted in historical inequalities. For instance, systemic disparities in education or housing can stem from policies enacted decades ago.
4. **Analyze Access Points:** Determine whether all participants have equal access to the system's benefits. Are there barriers—such as costs, language, or geography—that prevent equitable participation?

Real-World Example

In healthcare, structural biases often manifest in unequal access to services. Rural communities, for instance, might lack nearby hospitals, forcing residents to travel long distances for care. This geographic bias creates disparities in health outcomes, even though the healthcare system itself may aim to serve everyone equally. Addressing this bias requires systemic changes, such as investing in telemedicine or rural health facilities.

Why It Matters

Structural biases create systemic inefficiencies and inequities. They prevent the system from reaching its full potential by limiting participation or concentrating benefits among a few. Ignoring these biases perpetuates inequality, while addressing them can unlock new opportunities and make the system more inclusive and effective.

For instance, a workplace that actively identifies and reduces structural biases — by standardizing interviews or offering remote work options — can attract a more diverse talent pool, leading to innovation and better team performance.

Exercises

1. **Spot Structural Biases in Your Life:** Identify a system you interact with (e.g. a workplace or educational program). Look for disparities in outcomes and consider what structural factors might contribute.
2. **Analyze a Policy or Rule:** Choose a formal policy or rule in a system you know. Reflect on whether it unintentionally creates barriers or advantages for certain groups.
3. **Propose a Systemic Change:** For a structural bias you've identified, brainstorm ways to redesign the system to make it more equitable, such as revising eligibility criteria or creating new access points.

Key Takeaway

Structural biases are ingrained in systems. Identifying and addressing them leads to fairer and more effective results.

Chapter 32: Understand The Snowball Effect

How Small Changes Become Big Shifts

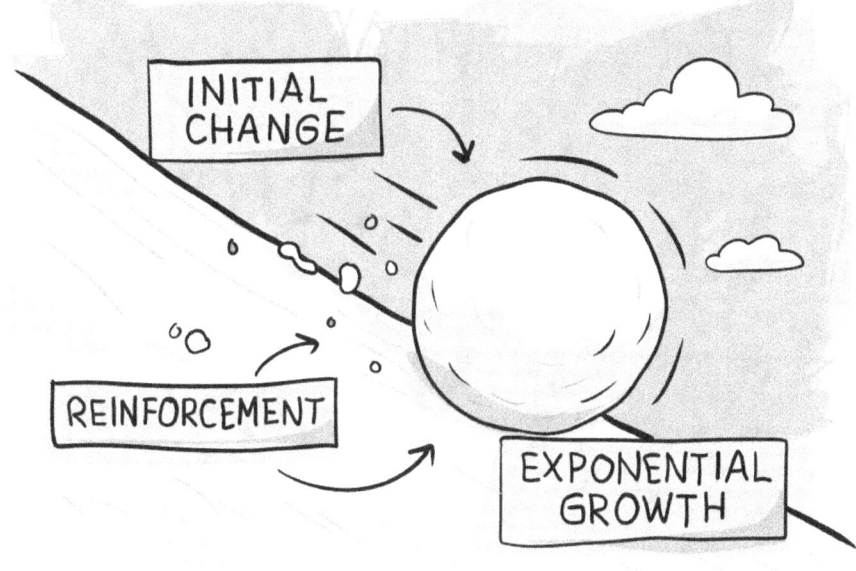

In many systems, a small change can set off a chain reaction that grows in scale and impact. This is called the snowball effect. Understanding this dynamic helps you anticipate exponential growth or decline and design interventions that harness or counteract it.

For example, in personal finance, saving a small amount of money each month can snowball into substantial savings over years due to compound interest. Conversely, in social media, a single post can go viral if enough people share it early, triggering a cascade of visibility and engagement. The snowball effect can drive growth, innovation, or progress, but it can also amplify problems if left unchecked.

Recognizing when and where snowball effects occur allows you to influence systems more strategically, either by nurturing positive changes or intervening before negative dynamics spiral out of control.

How to Understand The Snowball Effect

1. **Identify Reinforcing Loops:** Look for areas where a small input amplifies itself through feedback, such as word-of-mouth promotion or recurring customer loyalty.
2. **Trace the Starting Point:** Pinpoint the initial change or trigger that sets the snowball in motion. For instance, what prompted a sudden spike in product demand?
3. **Monitor Acceleration:** Snowball effects often begin slowly but grow exponentially. Observe where growth or change accelerates, and identify whether it's beneficial or harmful.
4. **Intervene Early:** If a snowball effect is creating negative outcomes, the best time to intervene is in the early stages, before it gains momentum.

Real-World Example

In environmental systems, deforestation can create a snowball effect. Cutting down trees reduces carbon absorption, contributing to climate change, which in turn accelerates deforestation through droughts or wildfires. Addressing this cycle requires interventions like reforestation programs to slow or reverse the snowball effect before it causes irreversible damage.

Why It Matters

The snowball effect explains why systems can change so rapidly and dramatically. Ignoring these dynamics can leave you unprepared for exponential growth or decline. By understanding and leveraging the snowball effect, you can design systems that amplify positive outcomes, mitigate risks, and create long-lasting impacts.

For example, a company launching a new product might focus on creating early momentum through targeted marketing, knowing that an initial burst of adoption can snowball into widespread popularity. Similarly, addressing small problems early — like a minor error in a workflow — prevents them from escalating into larger crises.

Exercises

1. **Identify a Snowball Effect:** Think of a system where small changes have grown into significant outcomes (e.g. a viral trend or a growing habit). Reflect on what caused the snowball effect.
2. **Create a Feedback Pattern:** Choose a system and identify a reinforcing loop that creates a snowball effect. Consider how this loop could be nurtured or disrupted.
3. **Design a Snowball Strategy:** For a project or goal you're working on, brainstorm ways to create a snowball effect. What small actions could trigger exponential growth or progress?

Key Takeaway

The snowball effect demonstrates how small actions can rapidly escalate — recognizing this process helps you magnify positive changes and tackle issues before they grow.

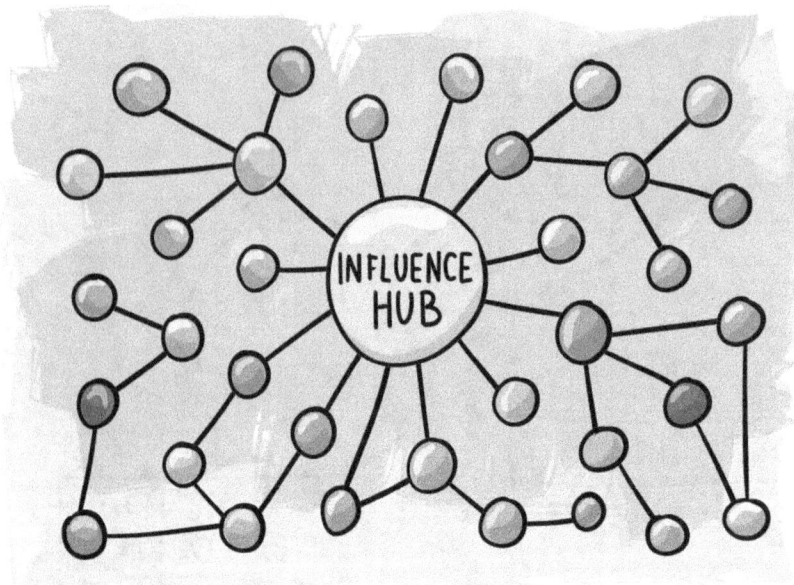

Chapter 33:
Analyze Network Centrality

In any system, some parts are more connected and influential than others. These highly connected nodes are referred to as "central nodes," and their position in the network makes them critical to the system's operation. Understanding network centrality helps you identify which nodes are essential for maintaining the system's structure, which ones facilitate communication, and which ones could cause major disruption if removed.

Think of a social network: a central influencer with a large number of connections can amplify information quickly, whereas a less connected individual has limited reach. Similarly, in an organizational structure, a department that serves as the hub for communication between other teams holds significant influence over workflows and outcomes.

Central nodes aren't always obvious. They might not hold formal authority or dominate resources, but their position in the network makes them pivotal. By analyzing network centrality, you can uncover hidden influencers, anticipate vulnerabilities, and strategically target interventions.

How to Analyze Network Centrality

1. **Define the Network:** Start by creating a diagram of the system's nodes (e.g. individuals, teams, or departments) and their connections. Include both direct and indirect relationships.
2. **Identify Highly Connected Nodes:** Look for nodes with the most connections. These are often the central hubs that facilitate information flow and decision-making.
3. **Evaluate Dependency:** Consider how dependent the system is on these central nodes. What happens if they are removed or disrupted?
4. **Look for Bottlenecks:** Sometimes, overly central nodes can become bottlenecks, slowing down the system due to their outsized influence.

Real-World Example

In supply chains, distribution hubs often serve as central nodes. For instance, a major shipping port connects suppliers, manufacturers, and distributors worldwide. Disruptions at these central nodes — like a port strike or a natural disaster — can ripple across the entire supply chain, causing delays and shortages.

Why It Matters

Central nodes are both strengths and vulnerabilities in a system. Their connectivity makes them indispensable for efficiency and coordination, but it also means that disruptions at these points can have outsized effects. By analyzing network centrality, you can protect critical nodes, improve their functionality, or design systems that are less reliant on single points of failure.

For example, in an organization, central nodes like project managers can facilitate communication across teams. However, if all information flows through one individual, their absence (e.g. due to illness) can create delays. Building redundancy — such as empowering multiple people to handle communication — reduces this vulnerability.

Exercises

1. **Map a Network You Know:** Choose a network you interact with, like your workplace or a social group. Identify the central nodes and reflect on their role in the system.
2. **Analyze Dependency:** For a system you're part of, consider how dependent it is on its central nodes. What would happen if one of these nodes failed?
3. **Strengthen a Network:** Identify a central node in a system you know. Brainstorm ways to either reduce dependency on this node or enhance its functionality.

Key Takeaway

Network centrality reveals the critical nodes that influence system behavior — analyzing these hubs helps you strengthen systems and reduce vulnerabilities.

Chapter 34: Look for Cross-System Overlaps

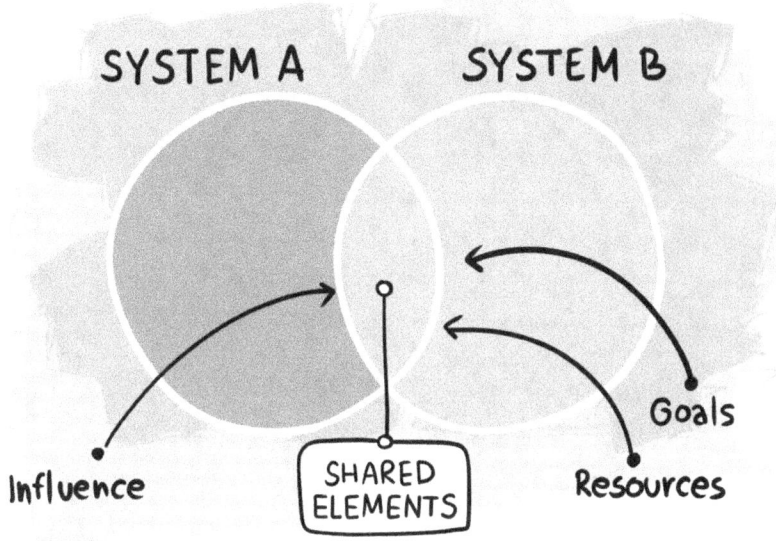

When Systems Intersect

No system exists in isolation. Human-created systems often overlap with or depend on other systems, sharing resources, goals, or elements that influence one another. Recognizing these cross-system overlaps allows you to see how interconnected systems shape behavior, create dependencies, and amplify outcomes.

Consider urban transportation systems and housing policies. The two might seem separate, but they're deeply interconnected. Affordable housing near public transit hubs reduces commute times, improves access to jobs, and reduces congestion. Ignoring this overlap can lead to poorly integrated systems that fail to meet the needs of the people they serve.

Cross-system overlaps often create opportunities for synergy but can also introduce risks. Identifying and understanding these overlaps ensures that you can leverage their strengths and mitigate potential conflicts.

How to Identify Cross-System Overlaps

1. **Map the Systems:** Start by outlining the individual systems you're analyzing. Look for areas where they share resources, influence each other, or have overlapping goals.
2. **Analyze Shared Elements:** Focus on the areas of overlap. Are the systems competing for the same resources, or are they working together to achieve complementary objectives?
3. **Consider Cascading Effects:** Changes in one system often impact the other. For example, how do changes in an education system affect the local labor market?
4. **Leverage Synergies:** Look for ways the systems can support each other. For example, aligning health programs with community centers can improve access to care.

Real-World Example

In disaster response, emergency management systems overlap with healthcare, transportation, and communication networks. A well-coordinated response relies on understanding how these systems interact—for example, ensuring that roads are clear for ambulances and that hospitals have the resources they need to handle surges of patients.

Why It Matters

Ignoring cross-system overlaps can lead to inefficiencies, conflicts, or missed opportunities. By recognizing these intersections, you can design solutions that work across systems, achieving better outcomes with fewer resources. For example, integrating public health initiatives with education systems can improve awareness and outcomes in both areas.

Conversely, poorly managed overlaps can create cascading failures. If an energy grid and transportation network are poorly integrated, a blackout could disrupt public transit, creating widespread chaos. Identifying and addressing these vulnerabilities ensures greater system resilience.

Exercises

1. **Identify an Overlap:** Think of two systems you interact with (e.g. work processes and team communication). Where do they overlap, and how does this affect outcomes?
2. **Lay Out Shared Elements:** Choose two overlapping systems and list the resources, goals, or dependencies they share. Reflect on whether these overlaps create opportunities or risks.
3. **Leverage Synergies:** For a pair of systems you know, brainstorm ways to improve their integration. How can better alignment enhance outcomes for both?

Key Takeaway

Cross-system overlaps reveal shared elements and dependencies. Understanding them allows you to design more integrated, efficient, and resilient solutions.

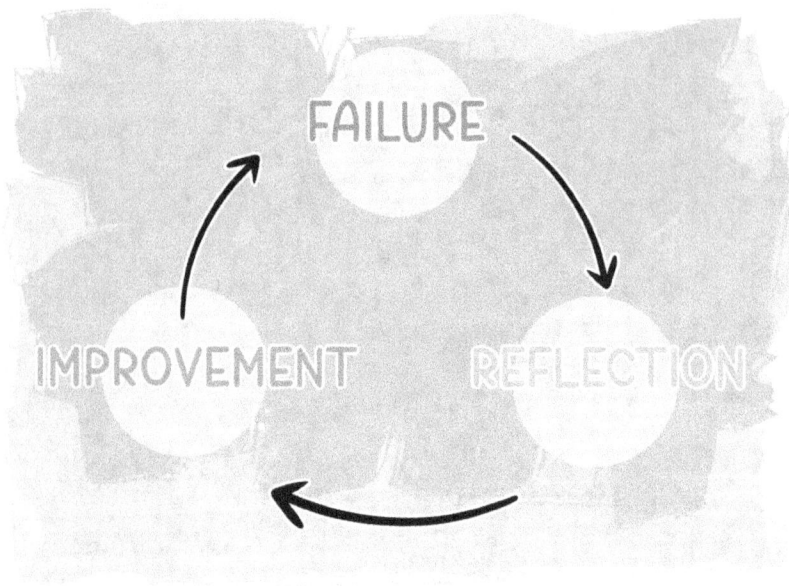

FAILURE

IMPROVEMENT REFLECTION

Chapter 35: Track Failures to Learn

The Value of Failure

Failures are inevitable in any human-created system. However, what distinguishes high-performing systems from struggling ones is their ability to learn from these failures. When systems fail to reflect on mistakes, they're doomed to repeat them. Tracking failures to learn ensures that each setback becomes a stepping stone toward improvement, not a permanent obstacle.

Consider product recalls in manufacturing. A company that identifies the root cause—such as a flaw in the production line—can redesign its processes to prevent future issues. A company that ignores the failure might face repeated recalls, damaging its reputation and profitability.

Failures aren't just opportunities to fix mistakes; they're windows into the system's vulnerabilities. By analyzing these moments, you can uncover deeper issues, anticipate future risks, and strengthen the system as a whole.

How to Track Failures to Learn

1. **Document Failures:** Keep a record of failures, including what happened, why it happened, and what the outcomes were.
2. **Analyze Root Causes:** Look beyond surface-level symptoms to identify the underlying causes of the failure. Was it due to poor communication, resource constraints, or flawed processes?
3. **Create Feedback Loops:** Build mechanisms that ensure lessons from failures are incorporated into future decisions. For example, implement after-action reviews or post-mortems.
4. **Encourage a Growth Mindset:** Foster a culture where failures are seen as opportunities to learn, not punishable offenses. This encourages openness and innovation.

Real-World Example

In aviation, the industry's exceptional safety record is due to its rigorous approach to learning from failures. Every accident or near-miss is thoroughly investigated, with findings shared across airlines and manufacturers. This culture of learning has led to continuous improvements in technology, training, and safety protocols.

Why It Matters

Failures are some of the most valuable data points in a system. Ignoring them leads to repeated mistakes, wasted resources, and unnecessary risks. Tracking failures to learn ensures that each misstep drives growth and resilience, transforming short-term setbacks into long-term progress.

For instance, a software development team that regularly reviews project failures can improve workflows, prevent bugs, and deliver better products. In contrast, a team that avoids addressing failures risks creating technical debt and missed deadlines.

Exercises

1. **Reflect on a Recent Failure:** Think of a failure you experienced in a system (e.g. a missed deadline or a flawed project). What lessons did you take from it, and how could the system improve?
2. **Conduct a Root Cause Analysis:** Choose a failure in your workplace or community and dig into its root causes. What underlying issues contributed, and how can they be addressed?
3. **Design a Feedback Loop:** For a system you're part of, propose a way to ensure failures are regularly analyzed and their lessons implemented.

Key Takeaway

Failures are opportunities for learning. Tracking them allows systems to grow, adapt, and become more resilient over time.

Chapter 36: Identify Siloed Thinking

The Isolation Problem

Siloed thinking occurs when parts of a system operate in isolation, focusing narrowly on their own goals without considering how their actions affect the broader system. This mindset can emerge in teams, departments, or even entire organizations, creating inefficiencies, redundancies, and missed opportunities for collaboration.

Imagine a large organization where the marketing, sales, and product teams work independently. The marketing team launches campaigns without consulting the product team, leading to an influx of customers for a feature still in development. Meanwhile, the sales team, unaware of these efforts, misses opportunities to align their pitch. Each team might feel it's doing its job well, but the lack of coordination creates chaos at the system level.

Siloed thinking is one of the most common barriers to system-wide efficiency. Identifying and addressing it is crucial for unlocking the system's full potential.

How to Identify Siloed Thinking

1. **Look for Isolated Goals:** Check whether different parts of the system have conflicting or disconnected objectives. Are teams pursuing their own KPIs without aligning with broader goals?
2. **Trace Information Flows:** Siloed systems often have poor communication channels. Identify where information gets stuck or fails to reach key stakeholders.
3. **Analyze Duplication of Effort:** Siloed thinking often leads to redundant work. For example, are two teams solving the same problem independently without realizing it?
4. **Watch for Blame Shifting:** In siloed systems, problems are often passed between teams, with little ownership or collaboration to resolve them.

Real-World Example

In healthcare, siloed thinking often occurs between different departments in a hospital. A patient might receive care from several specialists who don't coordinate, leading to redundant tests, conflicting advice, and delayed treatment. Integrated care models address this issue by fostering collaboration and information sharing across departments, improving outcomes and efficiency.

Why It Matters

Siloed thinking prevents systems from functioning as cohesive units. It wastes resources, creates delays, and leads to suboptimal outcomes. Addressing this mindset promotes collaboration, increases efficiency, and ensures that all parts of the system work toward shared goals.

For instance, an organization that breaks down silos between its marketing and product teams can align campaigns with actual product availability, boosting customer satisfaction and revenue. Similarly, in government, breaking down silos between agencies enables more coordinated and effective policy implementation.

Exercises

1. **Spot Silos in Your Life:** Think of a system you're part of (e.g. your workplace or a community group). Identify where siloed thinking might exist and how it affects outcomes.
2. **Trace Communication Gaps:** Choose a system and sketch out its communication flows. Highlight areas where information doesn't travel freely and consider how to improve these connections.
3. **Propose a Collaboration Strategy:** For a siloed system you've identified, suggest ways to improve collaboration. For example, introduce cross-functional meetings or shared goals.

Key Takeaway

Siloed thinking isolates parts of a system. Breaking down these barriers fosters collaboration and improves outcomes.

Chapter 37: Evaluate the Role of Middle Actors

The Connectors in the System

Middle actors, or intermediaries, are the connectors in a system. They bridge gaps between different components, ensuring resources, information, or influence flow smoothly. While often overlooked, these actors are essential for keeping the system functional.

Consider a supply chain: distributors act as middle actors, linking manufacturers to retailers. Without their role, products would have no efficient path to market. Similarly, in social systems, middle actors might include community leaders who translate government policies into actionable programs for local residents.

Middle actors are not just conduits — they often shape how the system operates. They can act as gatekeepers, amplifiers, or even bottlenecks. Understanding their role allows you to identify opportunities for optimization and ensure the system runs smoothly.

How to Evaluate the Role of Middle Actors

1. **Identify Key Intermediaries:** Map the system and highlight the individuals, teams, or entities that connect different parts.
2. **Analyze Their Functions:** What role do these middle actors play? Are they facilitators, decision-makers, or gatekeepers?
3. **Assess Their Impact:** Consider how effectively the middle actors perform their role. Do they accelerate workflows, or do they create bottlenecks?
4. **Examine Power Dynamics:** Middle actors often have significant influence over the system. Evaluate whether they use this influence to support or hinder the system's goals.

Real-World Example

In energy systems, utilities serve as middle actors between power generators and consumers. Their role goes beyond simple distribution—they manage demand, maintain infrastructure, and regulate pricing. When utilities fail to perform effectively, the entire energy system suffers, leading to outages, inefficiencies, or rising costs.

Why It Matters

Middle actors are the glue that holds systems together. When they perform well, they enable efficiency, coordination, and resilience. But if they become bottlenecks or misuse their influence, they can disrupt the system's flow. Understanding their role allows you to optimize these critical connections and improve overall performance.

For instance, in a workplace, a manager who effectively coordinates between executives and employees ensures clear communication and smooth operations. Conversely, a manager who withholds information or creates unnecessary bureaucracy can slow progress and frustrate team members.

Exercises

1. **Identify Middle Actors:** Choose a system you interact with, such as a supply chain or a project team. Visualize the intermediaries and consider how they impact the system's flow.
2. **Analyze a Bottleneck:** Think of a middle actor who slows down the system. What causes the bottleneck, and how could it be addressed?
3. **Redesign a Middle Actor's Role:** For a system you're part of, propose ways to optimize the role of an intermediary. Could they take on new responsibilities or use better tools?

Key Takeaway

Middle actors link and shape systems — grasping their role enables you to enhance their impact and boost system performance.

Chapter 38: See Intermediary Goals

The Balancing Act

Intermediaries within a system often serve as bridges between different components, but they aren't neutral players. They have their own goals, which might align with, complement, or conflict with the system's overall objectives. Recognizing these intermediary goals is critical for understanding how systems operate and where friction or inefficiencies may arise.

For instance, in a supply chain, a logistics company may aim to maximize profit, while the retailer it serves prioritizes cost reduction. If their goals aren't aligned, the logistics company might cut corners on delivery quality, creating dissatisfaction for the retailer's customers.

Intermediary goals often influence how resources are allocated, how decisions are made, and how effectively the system functions. By understanding these goals, you can address conflicts, build alignment, and improve system-wide outcomes.

How to See Intermediary Goals

1. **Identify the Intermediaries:** Map the system and locate the players who connect different parts, such as managers, contractors, or distributors.
2. **Understand Their Objectives:** Ask what these intermediaries aim to achieve. Are their goals purely financial, or do they include other priorities like efficiency, reputation, or growth?
3. **Assess Goal Alignment:** Compare the intermediary's goals with the system's overall objectives. Are they working toward the same outcomes, or are their priorities misaligned?
4. **Monitor Trade-offs:** Intermediaries often balance competing demands. Consider whether their decisions create value for the entire system or just for their own role.

Real-World Example

In financial systems, investment brokers act as intermediaries between investors and markets. While their goal is to facilitate trades, they might also prioritize earning commissions, leading to conflicts of interest. This misalignment can result in brokers recommending frequent trades that benefit them but harm their clients' portfolios.

Why It Matters

Intermediary goals shape how systems function. Misaligned goals can create inefficiencies, conflicts, or poor outcomes, while well-aligned goals foster collaboration and system-wide success. Recognizing and addressing these dynamics ensures that intermediaries contribute to, rather than detract from, the system's objectives.

For example, in a non-profit organization, aligning the goals of fundraisers (securing donations) with program teams (delivering impact) ensures that resources are allocated effectively and mission objectives are met.

Exercises

1. **Identify Intermediary Goals:** Choose an intermediary in a system you know, such as a manager or contractor. Reflect on their goals and how they align with the broader system.
2. **Analyze a Conflict:** Think of a situation where intermediary goals created friction. How did this affect the system, and what changes could improve alignment?
3. **Propose a Realignment:** For a misaligned intermediary in a system you interact with, brainstorm ways to align their goals with the system's overall objectives.

Key Takeaway

Intermediaries have their own goals — understanding and aligning these goals with the system's objectives creates smoother, more effective operations.

Chapter 39: Spot the Pace of Change

Why Speed Matters

Systems don't change at a uniform pace. Some evolve rapidly, driven by innovation, crises, or competition, while others shift slowly due to entrenched norms, resource constraints, or bureaucratic inertia. The pace of change in a system significantly affects its outcomes, adaptability, and long-term stability. Recognizing the speed at which a system operates allows you to anticipate challenges, plan interventions, and ensure the system's evolution aligns with its goals.

For example, the technology industry moves quickly, with constant innovations reshaping markets and consumer behavior. In contrast, public education systems often evolve slowly, requiring years to implement new policies or teaching methods. Each pace has its pros and cons: rapid change can foster innovation but risks instability, while slow change allows for careful deliberation but may struggle to adapt to urgent needs.

By spotting the pace of change, you can align your actions with the system's natural rhythm or introduce mechanisms to accelerate or decelerate its evolution as needed.

How to Spot the Pace of Change

1. **Observe the System's History:** Study past changes to understand how quickly the system has evolved over time. Does it adapt frequently, or are shifts rare and significant?
2. **Analyze External Pressures:** Systems often respond to external forces like market demands, technological advances, or societal expectations. Faster systems are often subject to intense competition or innovation, while slower systems may operate in stable or regulated environments.
3. **Identify Internal Constraints:** Look for structural factors that limit the pace of change, such as rigid hierarchies, resource shortages, or deeply embedded traditions.
4. **Assess Feedback Loops:** Rapid systems tend to have tight, short-term feedback loops, while slower systems may rely on longer cycles of evaluation and response.

Real-World Example

Consider urban planning. Large infrastructure projects like building highways or public transit systems often unfold over decades due to funding challenges, political debates, and community involvement. In contrast, temporary solutions like bike lanes or ride-sharing services can emerge quickly, addressing immediate transportation needs while larger projects progress.

Why It Matters

The pace of change determines how effectively a system can respond to opportunities or challenges. Ignoring the system's speed risks misaligned strategies — pushing too fast may lead to instability, while moving too slowly can result in missed opportunities.

For instance, a business trying to implement a fast-paced digital transformation in a traditionally slow-moving organization may face resistance and burnout. Conversely, a company that waits too long to adapt to industry changes risks losing market relevance. Aligning with the system's natural pace — or strategically modifying it — ensures smoother, more effective transitions.

Exercises

1. **Analyze a System's Speed:** Choose a system you interact with, such as your workplace or a local community project. Reflect on whether it changes quickly or slowly and why.
2. **Plan a Change Strategy:** For a system with a defined pace of change, brainstorm how you might align your goals with its rhythm. For example, should you accelerate or slow down your efforts?
3. **Simulate a Different Pace:** Imagine speeding up or slowing down a system's change process. What benefits and risks would this create?

Key Takeaway:

Systems evolve at different speeds — recognizing their pace of change allows you to align strategies and ensure sustainable evolution.

Chapter 40: Detect Systemic Fragility

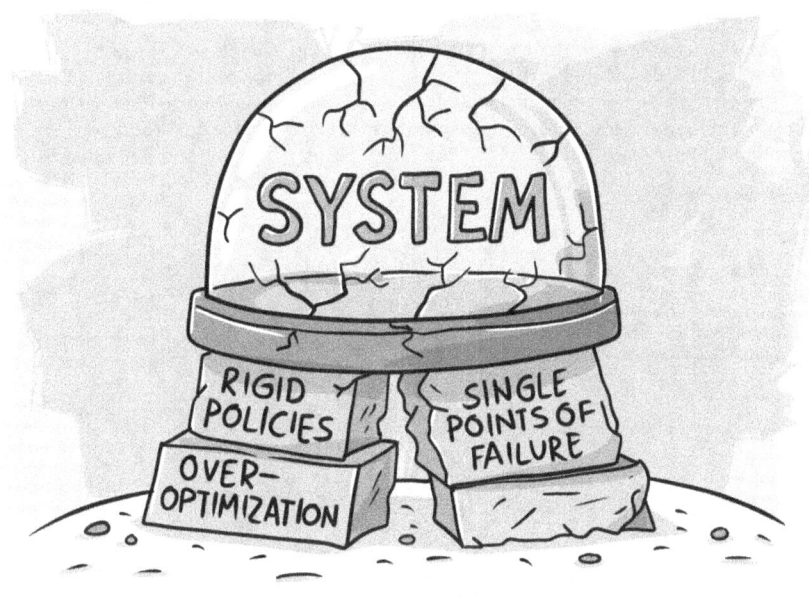

Fragile systems are those that cannot adapt to stress or disruption. Unlike resilient systems, which bend and recover, fragile systems break when faced with unexpected challenges. Detecting systemic fragility allows you to identify vulnerabilities and build strategies to make the system more robust and adaptable.

Fragility often arises from rigidity — overly strict rules, reliance on single points of failure, or excessive focus on efficiency at the expense of flexibility. For instance, a company that relies on one supplier for critical materials is fragile; any disruption to that supplier can halt operations. Similarly, a financial system optimized for short-term gains but unprepared for economic shocks can collapse during crises.

Fragility isn't always obvious. Systems may appear stable under normal conditions, only to fail dramatically when faced with sudden changes. Detecting these vulnerabilities before they cause failure is essential for long-term sustainability.

How to Detect Systemic Fragility

1. **Look for Single Points of Failure:** Identify components that, if disrupted, would collapse the entire system. Examples include sole suppliers, critical infrastructure, or over-reliance on specific individuals.
2. **Evaluate Adaptability:** Test whether the system can adjust to changing conditions. Rigid systems often resist adaptation, leading to fragility.
3. **Analyze Stress Scenarios:** Consider how the system would respond to extreme events, such as economic downturns, natural disasters, or sudden market shifts.
4. **Watch for Over-Optimization:** Systems focused solely on efficiency often lack the redundancy or slack needed to handle disruptions.

Real-World Example

The COVID-19 pandemic exposed fragility in global supply chains. Many industries relied on "just-in-time" manufacturing, which minimized inventory to cut costs. When production disruptions occurred, these supply chains collapsed, leaving companies unable to meet demand. Introducing redundancies — such as multiple suppliers or inventory buffers — could have mitigated this fragility.

Why It Matters

Fragile systems are prone to catastrophic failure, often without warning. By detecting fragility early, you can redesign systems to handle stress, adapt to change, and recover from disruptions. Resilient systems aren't just stronger—they're also more sustainable and better equipped to seize opportunities in uncertain environments.

For example, a community with diverse sources of energy — solar, wind, and backup generators—is more resilient than one relying solely on a centralized power grid. Similarly, a workplace that cross-trains employees ensures continuity if key team members are unavailable.

Exercises

1. **Identify a Single Point of Failure:** Think of a system you interact with, such as a workflow or a household routine. Pinpoint a dependency that could disrupt the entire system if it fails.
2. **Analyze a Past Disruption:** Reflect on a time when a system you relied on failed. What made it fragile, and how could it have been strengthened?
3. **Design for Resilience:** Choose a system and propose ways to make it less fragile, such as adding redundancies, increasing flexibility, or planning for disruptions.

Key Takeaway

Fragile systems break under stress — detecting vulnerabilities early allows you to build resilience and ensure long-term stability.

Section III: Spotting Patterns in Natural Systems

Natural systems are rich with lessons for understanding complexity. From the rhythmic cycles of seasons to the dynamic flow of energy through ecosystems, nature provides a blueprint for how interconnected systems operate. These systems evolve, adapt, and self-correct in ways that humans often overlook but can learn from to design better solutions. This section explores the recurring patterns, interactions, and adaptations that make natural systems resilient and sustainable. By recognizing these patterns, you can apply their principles to solve problems, optimize designs, and build systems that thrive in harmony with their environment.

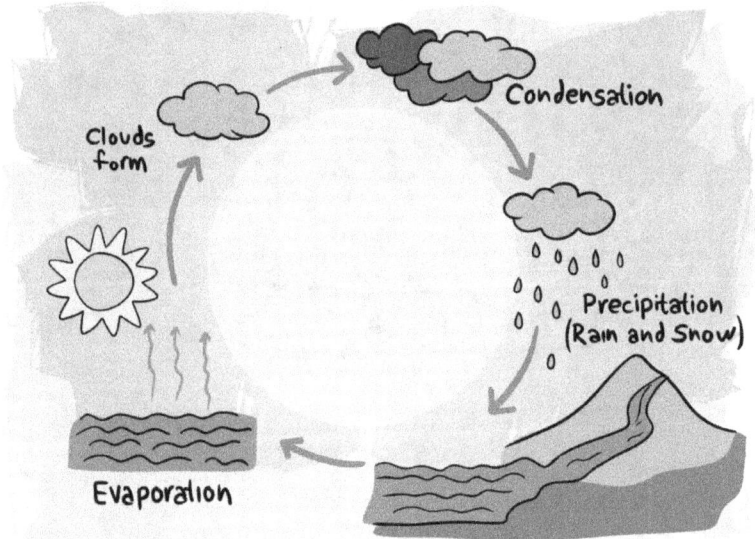

Chapter 41: See Cycles Everywhere

The Rhythm of Nature

Cycles are one of the most defining features of natural systems. They are the recurring processes that shape ecosystems, regulate resources, and sustain life. From the orbit of planets creating seasons to the daily rise and fall of tides, cycles bring predictability and balance to nature's complexity.

Consider the water cycle. Rain falls, fills rivers, and eventually evaporates, returning to the atmosphere. This cycle ensures that water — a finite resource — is continuously redistributed and made available to support life. Similarly, seasonal cycles dictate when animals migrate, plants flower, and farmers plant crops. Without these predictable rhythms, life would struggle to adapt and thrive.

Recognizing cycles allows you to anticipate changes, manage resources wisely, and align your actions with the system's natural rhythm.

How to Spot Cycles

1. **Look for Repetition:** Observe processes or behaviors that occur repeatedly over time, such as migrations, breeding seasons, or nutrient renewal.
2. **Outline Inputs and Outputs:** Cycles often involve the movement of resources (e.g. water, energy, nutrients). Identify where these flows begin, where they end, and how they repeat.
3. **Track Timing:** Many cycles are tied to specific timeframes, like the lunar month or annual growing seasons. Understanding timing helps you predict and plan for changes.
4. **Distinguish Between Small and Large Cycles:** Some cycles are quick and local (e.g. day-night), while others are slow and global (e.g. glacial periods). Identify how they interact.

Real-World Example

Forests rely on the carbon cycle to grow and sustain life. Trees absorb carbon dioxide from the atmosphere during photosynthesis, storing it as biomass. When trees die and decompose, this carbon returns to the soil or the air, completing the cycle. Interrupting this rhythm — such as through deforestation — can disrupt entire ecosystems and contribute to climate change.

Why It Matters

Understanding cycles helps you manage resources sustainably and predict system behavior. For example, farmers who align planting schedules with seasonal cycles maximize crop yields while conserving water and soil health. Similarly, businesses that anticipate economic cycles can make smarter decisions about expansion or investment.

Ignoring cycles, on the other hand, risks inefficiency, waste, or disaster. For instance, overharvesting during a population's reproductive cycle can lead to species collapse, disrupting the broader ecosystem.

Exercises

1. **Identify Cycles in Your Life:** Reflect on cycles you rely on, such as meal preparation, work schedules, or sleep patterns. How do these rhythms affect your daily life?
2. **Observe a Natural Cycle:** Spend time observing a natural process, like the phases of the moon or the growth of a plant. Reflect on how it repeats and supports other systems.
3. **Map a System's Cycle:** Choose a system you interact with (e.g. water usage or food production). Visualize its inputs, outputs, and how they repeat over time.

Key Takeaway

Cycles bring rhythm and balance to systems. Recognizing and aligning with them creates harmony and sustainability.

Chapter 42:
Understand Energy Flows

Energy is the driving force of all natural systems. It flows from one part of an ecosystem to another, enabling growth, movement, reproduction, and renewal. Understanding energy flows reveals how systems function, where inefficiencies arise, and how to optimize processes.

In most ecosystems, the sun is the primary energy source. Plants capture solar energy through photosynthesis, converting it into food that fuels other organisms. Herbivores consume plants, transferring energy to the next level of the food chain, while predators continue the flow. Decomposers, like fungi and bacteria, break down dead organisms, returning energy and nutrients to the soil. This cycle ensures that energy flows continuously through the system, sustaining life.

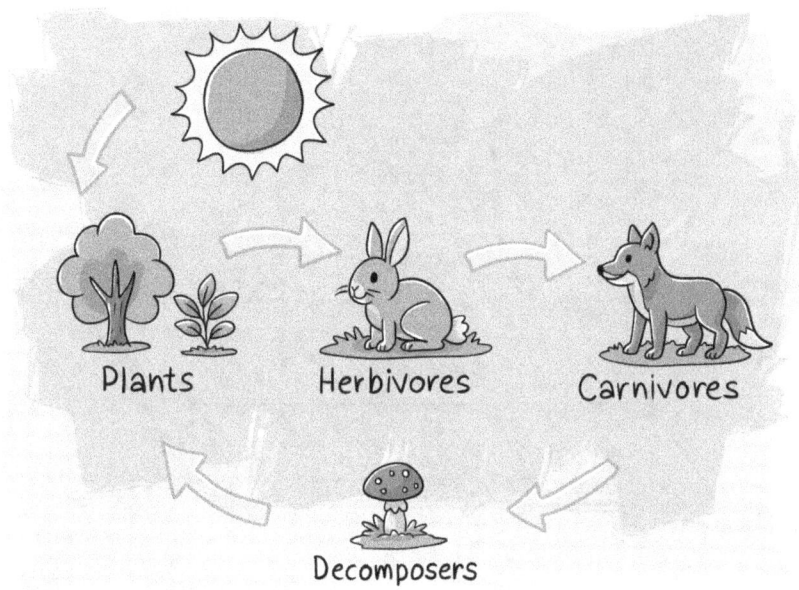

Plants   Herbivores   Carnivores

Decomposers

How to Understand Energy Flows

1. **Follow the Energy Source:** Identify the primary energy input (e.g. sunlight, food, fuel) and trace how it moves through the system.
2. **Track Transformations:** Energy changes form as it flows—solar energy becomes chemical energy in plants, which becomes kinetic energy in animals. Map these transformations.
3. **Identify Losses:** No system is perfectly efficient. Look for where energy is lost (e.g. as heat or waste) and consider how these losses affect the system.
4. **Observe Recursive Patterns:** Some energy flows create self-perpetuating cycles, such as a population explosion of herbivores leading to overgrazing and ecosystem collapse.

Real-World Example

In agriculture, energy flows directly impact productivity. Crops capture solar energy, which humans and livestock consume. Excessive tilling or overuse of fertilizers can disrupt this flow, depleting soil energy and reducing long-term yields. Sustainable practices like crop rotation or organic farming help maintain energy balance.

Why It Matters

Energy flows determine the efficiency and resilience of a system. Systems that manage energy poorly — whether through waste, overuse, or misallocation — become unsustainable and prone to failure. Understanding energy flows allows you to optimize processes, reduce inefficiencies, and design systems that last.

For instance, renewable energy systems like solar or wind power mimic natural energy flows, harnessing and converting energy sustainably. Businesses or cities that adopt these systems reduce reliance on finite resources while maintaining energy security.

Exercises

1. **Trace Energy in Your Life:** Consider how energy flows through your daily routine. What fuels your food, transportation, or electricity use?
2. **Visualize an Ecosystem's Energy Flow:** Choose an ecosystem (e.g. a garden or forest) and outline how energy flows between its components. Reflect on where energy is gained or lost.
3. **Optimize an Energy System:** Identify an energy flow you rely on, like home heating or food storage. Brainstorm ways to reduce waste or increase efficiency.

Key Takeaway

Energy flows are the lifeblood of natural systems. Tracking and optimizing them ensures sustainability and efficiency.

Chapter 43: Uncover Predator-Prey Dynamics

The Balance of Nature

Predator-prey dynamics are one of the most fascinating and critical aspects of natural systems. These relationships shape ecosystems by regulating populations, controlling resources, and maintaining balance. Predators keep prey populations in check, preventing overgrazing or resource depletion, while prey availability determines predator survival.

For instance, wolves in Yellowstone National Park play a vital role in controlling deer and elk populations. Without wolves, these herbivores overgraze vegetation, leading to ecosystem degradation. Reintroducing wolves restored balance, allowing plant life to recover, which in turn benefited birds, insects, and even rivers that were less impacted by erosion.

Predator-prey dynamics are not just about direct interactions. They ripple throughout ecosystems. A single predator's actions can affect everything from vegetation growth to the behavior of other species. Understanding these dynamics reveals the interconnectedness of natural systems and the importance of every component.

How to Uncover Predator-Prey Dynamics

1. **Identify the Players:** Start by mapping the predators and prey within the system. What species interact, and how do their populations fluctuate?
2. **Analyze Population Cycles:** Predator and prey populations often rise and fall in cycles, with one influencing the other. Look for patterns over time.
3. **Observe Ripple Effects:** Predator-prey dynamics extend beyond direct relationships. How do changes in these populations affect plants, competitors, or other species?
4. **Consider Human Influence:** Humans often disrupt predator-prey dynamics through activities like hunting, farming, or habitat destruction. Assess how these changes impact the broader system.

Real-World Example

Shark populations in marine ecosystems regulate fish species. Overfishing of sharks can lead to a boom in mid-level predators, which then overconsume smaller fish or marine plants, destabilizing the entire food web. Protecting sharks restores this balance, ensuring the health of coral reefs and other marine ecosystems.

Why It Matters

Predator-prey dynamics highlight the balance required for ecosystems to thrive. Disrupting these relationships—such as removing predators or overexploiting prey—can lead to cascading failures that destabilize entire systems. Recognizing and respecting these dynamics is essential for conservation, resource management, and ecosystem restoration.

For example, when humans hunt top predators to near extinction, it often creates unintended consequences, like the spread of invasive species or crop destruction by unchecked herbivores. Protecting these predators preserves the equilibrium and health of the broader system.

Exercises

1. **Define a Predator-Prey Relationship:** Choose an ecosystem (e.g. a forest or ocean) and map its predator-prey dynamics. Reflect on how these interactions shape the environment.
2. **Analyze Human Impact:** Think of a predator-prey system affected by human activity, such as urban expansion or fishing. What changes have occurred, and how could they be addressed?
3. **Simulate a Disruption:** Imagine removing a predator or prey species from a system you've studied. Predict how this would affect the ecosystem's balance.

Key Takeaway

Predator-prey dynamics regulate ecosystems. Understanding these relationships ensures balance and prevents cascading failures.

Chapter 44: Trace Nutrient Paths

The Circulation of Life's Building Blocks

Nutrients like carbon, nitrogen, and phosphorus move through ecosystems in complex but predictable pathways. These nutrient cycles sustain life by ensuring essential elements are continually recycled and made available to living organisms. Understanding these paths allows you to see how ecosystems maintain balance and where disruptions can cause systemic problems.

For instance, in the carbon cycle, plants absorb carbon dioxide from the atmosphere during photosynthesis, storing it in their tissues. When plants die, decomposers break down the organic material, releasing carbon back into the soil and air. This continuous flow supports life while maintaining the planet's carbon balance.

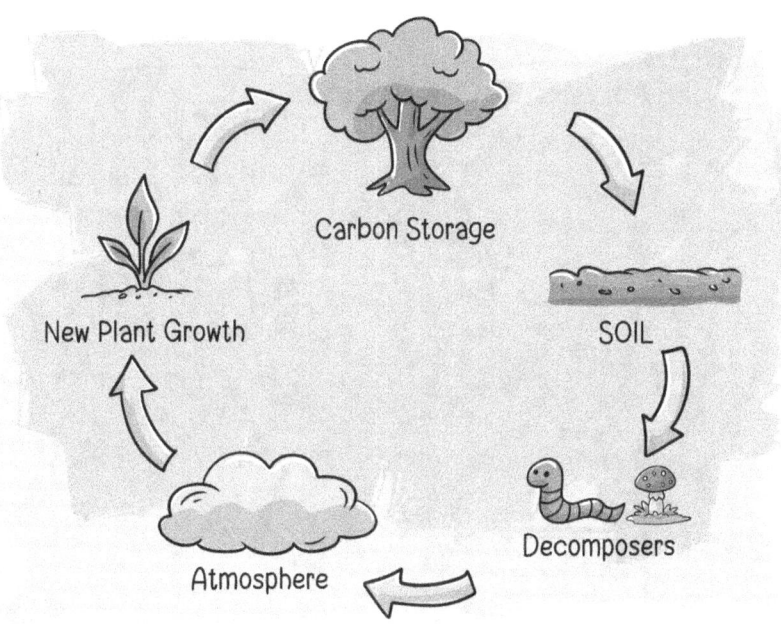

Nutrient paths don't just sustain individual species — they link entire ecosystems. When one part of the cycle is disrupted, such as through excessive carbon emissions or deforestation, the ripple effects can destabilize the system.

How to Trace Nutrient Paths

1. **Identify the Elements:** Focus on one nutrient, like nitrogen or phosphorus. Where does it come from, and how does it move through the system?
2. **Trace the Flow:** Create a diagram showing how the nutrient cycles between the atmosphere, soil, plants, animals, and decomposers.
3. **Look for Bottlenecks:** Disruptions in nutrient paths — like soil depletion or pollution — can create bottlenecks that limit the system's efficiency.
4. **Consider External Inputs:** Human activities like agriculture or industry often introduce excess nutrients, causing imbalances like algal blooms or soil degradation.

Real-World Example

The nitrogen cycle is essential for agriculture, but excessive fertilizer use disrupts it. Runoff from farms introduces excess nitrogen into rivers, causing algal blooms that deplete oxygen and harm aquatic life. Sustainable farming practices, like crop rotation and controlled fertilizer use, help restore balance.

Why It Matters

Tracing nutrient paths reveals how ecosystems sustain life and adapt to change. Ignoring these cycles leads to inefficiencies, waste, or even ecological collapse. For example, deforestation interrupts the water and carbon cycles, reducing soil fertility and accelerating climate change. Restoring these cycles improves ecosystem health and resilience.

Understanding nutrient paths also provides insights for sustainable practices. Composting, for instance, mimics natural nutrient recycling, turning organic waste into valuable resources that enrich the soil and reduce landfill waste.

Exercises

1. **Map a Nutrient Cycle:** Choose a nutrient like carbon or phosphorus and sketch out its flow through a local ecosystem. Reflect on how it supports life.
2. **Identify a Disruption:** Think of a nutrient cycle affected by human activity (e.g. industrial emissions or deforestation). How has this disruption impacted the ecosystem?
3. **Design a Restoration Plan:** Propose ways to restore balance to a disrupted nutrient cycle, such as reforestation, composting, or reducing pollution.

Key Takeaway

Nutrient paths sustain ecosystems. Tracing these cycles reveals opportunities to restore balance and improve sustainability.

Chapter 45: Find Anchor Points

Anchor points are the critical species, processes, or elements that hold ecosystems together. Without them, the entire system can collapse or become unbalanced. These elements often have a disproportionate impact relative to their size or visibility, making them essential for the system's health and resilience.

For example, consider coral reefs. Though they occupy less than 1% of the ocean floor, they support approximately 25% of all marine species by providing habitat, food, and shelter. Coral itself acts as an anchor point for the reef ecosystem — without healthy coral, the entire network of species it supports would decline.

Anchor points aren't always obvious. They can range from a keystone species like wolves in Yellowstone to physical elements like soil in a forest. Identifying these critical components allows you to focus conservation or intervention efforts where they matter most.

How to Find Anchor Points

1. **Identify Disproportionate Impacts:** Look for species or elements that have an outsized effect on the system compared to their size or population. For instance, a small predator might regulate prey populations that would otherwise overconsume resources.
2. **Observe System Dependencies:** Analyze which parts of the system rely heavily on a specific element or species. This might include plants that provide the primary food source for herbivores or water sources that sustain entire ecosystems.
3. **Monitor Changes:** Pay attention to what happens when an element is removed or disrupted. A significant system-wide response often indicates an anchor point.
4. **Consider Indirect Effects:** Anchor points often stabilize systems indirectly, such as by maintaining a balance between competing species or supporting key nutrient flows.

Real-World Example

In tropical rainforests, large fruit-bearing trees are anchor points that sustain biodiversity. These trees provide food for a wide range of animals, from insects to birds to larger mammals like monkeys. When these trees are cut down, the ripple effects disrupt food availability, pollination, and habitat, destabilizing the entire ecosystem.

Why It Matters

Anchor points are the foundation of ecosystem stability. Protecting them ensures the long-term health and resilience of the system, while ignoring or removing them can lead to cascading failures. For instance, overfishing keystone species like sharks or tuna can destabilize entire marine food webs, allowing smaller prey populations to explode and overconsume resources.

By identifying anchor points, you can target conservation and resource management efforts more effectively. For example, protecting pollinators like bees helps stabilize agricultural systems, ensuring food security and biodiversity.

Exercises

1. **Identify Anchor Points in an Ecosystem:** Choose an ecosystem you know (e.g. a local park or a coral reef). Identify one or two anchor points and reflect on how they stabilize the system.
2. **Analyze a Loss of Stability:** Think of a time when an anchor point in a system you know was disrupted (e.g. a tree being cut down or a species going extinct). What were the ripple effects?
3. **Develop a Protection Strategy:** For a critical anchor point you've identified, brainstorm ways to protect or restore it. This might include replanting trees, regulating fishing, or reducing pollution.

Key Takeaway

Anchor points are essential for stability. Protecting them prevents system collapse and ensures resilience.

Chapter 46:
Notice Niche
Functions

In every ecosystem, species or processes perform unique roles that contribute to the system's overall success. These are called niche functions, and they often fill critical gaps that other elements cannot. Without them, the system may lose balance, become less efficient, or struggle to recover from disruptions.

Consider dung beetles, which may seem unimportant at first glance. Their niche function involves breaking down animal waste, recycling nutrients back into the soil, and reducing parasites. Without dung beetles, ecosystems would struggle with waste accumulation, nutrient depletion, and disease outbreaks.

Niche functions aren't limited to species. They can include unique processes, like the way fungi decompose dead material and make nutrients available to plants. Recognizing and valuing these roles allows you to appreciate how every part of an ecosystem contributes to its overall health.

How to Notice Niche Functions

1. **Look for Specialists:** Identify species or processes that perform highly specific roles, such as certain insects that pollinate only one type of flower.
2. **Trace Dependencies:** Consider what other parts of the system rely on this function. For instance, a plant that depends on a specific pollinator is an indicator of a niche relationship.
3. **Observe Redundancy or Lack of It:** Some niche functions are irreplaceable, while others may have backups. For example, multiple species might perform similar roles in diverse ecosystems, increasing resilience.
4. **Monitor System Disruptions:** Niche functions often become apparent when they're missing — what happens if a specific species disappears?

Real-World Example

In forests, woodpeckers perform a niche function by creating cavities in trees that later serve as nesting sites for birds, bats, and insects. If woodpeckers are absent, species that depend on these cavities struggle to find shelter, reducing biodiversity and ecosystem resilience.

Why It Matters

Niche functions ensure that ecosystems operate efficiently and adapt to change. Losing these functions can create bottlenecks or gaps that weaken the system. For example, the decline of a pollinator species can disrupt entire food webs, affecting crops, wild plants, and the animals that depend on them.

Protecting niche functions is often a cost-effective way to maintain ecosystem health. For instance, promoting the conservation of soil microbes improves nutrient cycling, reducing the need for chemical fertilizers and enhancing agricultural productivity.

Exercises

1. **Identify a Niche Function:** Think of a specific species or process in a system you know (e.g. a scavenger or a decomposer). Reflect on its unique role and how it supports the ecosystem.
2. **Observe Dependencies:** Choose an ecosystem and identify which parts depend on a specific niche function. How would its loss affect the system?
3. **Propose a Protection Plan:** For a niche function you've identified, brainstorm ways to safeguard or enhance it, such as habitat preservation or species reintroduction.

Key Takeaway

Niche functions are vital for ecosystem efficiency. Recognizing and protecting them ensures that systems remain balanced and resilient.

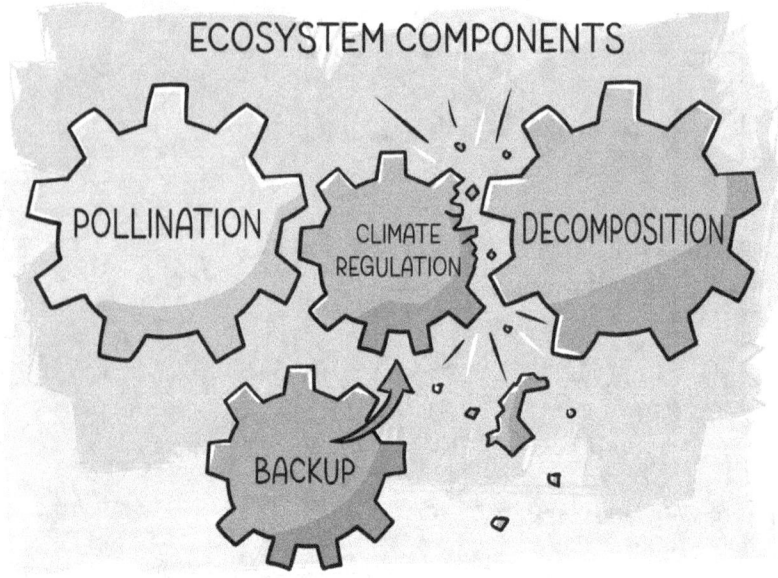

ECOSYSTEM COMPONENTS

POLLINATION

CLIMATE REGULATION

DECOMPOSITION

BACKUP

Chapter 47: Evaluate Mechanisms

Nature's Tools for Resilience

Ecosystems are remarkably adept at recovering from disruptions, whether it's a forest regrowing after a wildfire or a river cleansing itself after pollution. These recovery processes depend on mechanisms—natural tools and processes that allow systems to restore balance, adapt, and thrive. By evaluating these mechanisms, you can better understand what makes ecosystems resilient and how to support their recovery when stressed.

For example, after a volcanic eruption devastates a landscape, pioneer species like mosses and lichens play a crucial role in recolonizing the area. These species prepare the environment for more complex plants, gradually rebuilding the ecosystem over time. This mechanism of ecological succession ensures that life can bounce back, even after severe disruptions.

Evaluating mechanisms involves looking at both how ecosystems respond to stress and how they maintain equilibrium under normal conditions. Understanding these tools not only reveals the inner workings of natural systems but also offers valuable lessons for designing human systems that are more adaptable and sustainable.

How to Evaluate Mechanisms

1. **Identify Recovery Processes:** Look at how ecosystems bounce back from disruptions. What processes or species initiate recovery, and how do they interact?
2. **Analyze Stability Mechanisms:** Consider how ecosystems maintain balance in the absence of major disruptions. For example, what keeps predator-prey relationships in check or prevents soil erosion?
3. **Look for Redundancies:** Resilient systems often have multiple mechanisms performing similar functions, like several pollinator species that ensure plants reproduce even if one species declines.
4. **Assess Human Impact:** Many natural mechanisms are disrupted by human activity, such as deforestation or pollution. Evaluate how these impacts weaken the system's ability to recover.

Real-World Example

Wetlands act as natural water filtration mechanisms, trapping pollutants and sediments while maintaining water quality. When wetlands are destroyed for development, this mechanism is lost, leading to water contamination and increased flood risks. Restoring wetlands reactivates this natural tool, improving both ecosystem and human resilience.

Why It Matters

Mechanisms are the building blocks of resilience. Without them, ecosystems become fragile and less capable of adapting to stress. By evaluating these processes, you can identify where systems are vulnerable and how to strengthen them.

For instance, rewilding initiatives, which reintroduce species like wolves or beavers, aim to restore lost mechanisms that stabilize ecosystems. Beavers, for example, create dams that regulate water flow, prevent flooding, and create habitats for other species. These mechanisms benefit not just the ecosystem but also human communities nearby.

Exercises

1. **Observe a Recovery Mechanism:** Spend time in a natural area that has experienced disruption (e.g. a burned forest or a polluted river). Note how the ecosystem is recovering and which processes are involved.
2. **Map Stability Mechanisms:** Choose an ecosystem and identify the mechanisms that maintain its balance, such as nutrient cycling or predator-prey dynamics.
3. **Propose a Restoration Plan:** For a disrupted ecosystem, brainstorm ways to restore its natural mechanisms, like reintroducing species or reducing human impact.

Key Takeaway

Natural mechanisms drive resilience. Evaluating them helps you understand how ecosystems recover and how to support their stability.

Chapter 48: Find Cascading Effects

The Domino Effect in Ecosystems

Ecosystems are networks of interdependent relationships, where changes in one part can trigger a series of effects throughout the system. These cascading effects can amplify problems or create unexpected consequences, often far removed from the initial change. Recognizing these ripple effects is essential for understanding how ecosystems respond to disturbances and how to predict long-term impacts.

For example, when sea otter populations decline, sea urchins — one of their main prey — can proliferate unchecked. These urchins overgraze kelp forests, reducing habitat for fish and other marine life. This single disruption affects not only biodiversity but also fisheries that depend on healthy kelp ecosystems.

Cascading effects aren't always negative. Reintroducing wolves to Yellowstone National Park reduced deer overpopulation, allowing vegetation to recover and stabilizing riverbanks. Understanding these effects reveals how small interventions can create significant and sometimes surprising outcomes.

How to Find Cascading Effects

1. **Map Interdependencies:** Identify the connections between species, resources, and processes within the ecosystem. Look for elements that influence multiple others.
2. **Trace the Initial Change:** Examine what caused the initial disturbance, such as the removal of a predator or the introduction of an invasive species.
3. **Follow the Ripple Effects:** Analyze how the change impacts other components, both directly and indirectly. These effects often move through multiple levels of the system.
4. **Anticipate Long-Term Outcomes:** Cascading effects can take time to fully manifest. Consider how current changes might evolve and influence future conditions.

Real-World Example

The introduction of non-native zebra mussels into freshwater ecosystems is a classic example of cascading effects. These mussels filter plankton from the water, reducing food availability for native species and altering nutrient cycles. Their proliferation can also clog water intake systems, creating economic costs for humans.

Why It Matters

Cascading effects demonstrate the interconnectedness of ecosystems. Ignoring these ripple effects can lead to unintended consequences, like resource depletion or ecosystem collapse. Recognizing them allows for more informed decisions and interventions that account for both immediate and long-term impacts.

For example, in agriculture, excessive pesticide use may control pests initially but can also harm pollinators, reduce soil health, and create resistance in pest populations. Understanding these cascades helps farmers adopt practices like integrated pest management that minimize negative outcomes.

Exercises

1. **Sketch a Cascade:** Choose an ecosystem change (e.g. deforestation or overfishing) and map its direct and indirect effects on the system.
2. **Analyze a Positive Cascade:** Reflect on a time when a small intervention created widespread benefits, such as planting native vegetation to restore habitats.
3. **Design a Controlled Intervention:** For a system you know, propose an intervention and predict its cascading effects. Consider both positive and negative outcomes.

Key Takeaway

Cascading effects reveal how interconnected systems are. Understanding them helps you predict outcomes and design smarter interventions.

Chapter 49: Detect Resource Competition

The Struggle for Survival

In natural systems, resources like water, sunlight, nutrients, and space are finite. When multiple organisms or groups depend on the same limited resource, competition arises. This competition shapes how ecosystems evolve, which species thrive, and which ones decline. Detecting resource competition is essential for understanding the dynamics of any system, as it reveals where tensions exist and where interventions might stabilize the balance.

For example, in forests, tall trees compete for sunlight by growing higher, shading out smaller plants that cannot reach the canopy. In grasslands, plants with extensive root systems compete for water, often leaving shallow-rooted species at a disadvantage during droughts. These competitive interactions determine the structure, diversity, and resilience of ecosystems.

Resource competition doesn't just happen between species. It can also occur within a single population, as individuals compete for mates, food, or territory. Understanding these dynamics sheds light on how ecosystems self-regulate and how external factors, such as human activity, can disrupt this balance.

How to Detect Resource Competition

1. **Identify Shared Resources:** Determine which resources (e.g. water, sunlight, nutrients) are critical to the organisms or groups in the system.
2. **Observe Overlaps:** Look for instances where multiple species or groups depend on the same resource. Are there visible signs of competition, like slower growth or reduced diversity?
3. **Analyze Outcomes:** Study which species or groups are thriving and which are struggling. Competition often results in winners and losers, with weaker competitors being displaced or eliminated.
4. **Monitor External Pressures:** Human activities like deforestation or overfishing often intensify resource competition, pushing ecosystems beyond their limits.

Real-World Example

Overfishing in marine ecosystems creates intense resource competition among remaining species. For instance, when large fish are removed from a food web, smaller species may compete aggressively for the same prey, leading to imbalances and declines in biodiversity. This overexploitation also forces human communities dependent on fishing into direct competition for dwindling resources.

Why It Matters

Resource competition is a driving force in shaping ecosystems. It determines which species coexist, which adapt, and which disappear. Detecting these dynamics helps you understand why systems behave the way they do and what changes might tip the balance.

For instance, in agriculture, understanding resource competition between crops and weeds allows farmers to manage fields more effectively, minimizing losses without over-relying on chemical solutions. Similarly, urban planners can study competition for space and resources to design cities that reduce stress on natural and human systems.

Ignoring resource competition can lead to overexploitation, system collapse, or conflict. By recognizing these tensions early, you can design interventions that reduce competition and promote coexistence, such as restoring degraded habitats or redistributing resources.

Exercises

1. **Map Resource Competition:** Choose an ecosystem (e.g. a forest or ocean) and identify which species compete for critical resources. Reflect on how this competition shapes the ecosystem.
2. **Analyze Human Impact:** Think of a system where human activity has intensified resource competition, such as water use in agriculture. What consequences have emerged, and how could they be mitigated?
3. **Propose a Coexistence Strategy:** For a competitive system you've studied, brainstorm ways to reduce conflict and promote resource sharing, such as introducing buffer zones or optimizing resource use.

Key Takeaway

Resource competition shapes ecosystems. Detecting and managing it ensures balance, biodiversity, and long-term sustainability.

Chapter 50: Observe Natural "Evolution"

ADAPTATION OVER TIME

Evolution is nature's way of adapting to change. Over generations, species develop traits that help them survive and thrive in their environments. This process, driven by natural selection, shapes ecosystems, determines biodiversity, and creates systems that are dynamic and resilient. Observing natural evolution provides insight into how systems respond to pressures, adapt to new conditions, and maintain balance over time.

For instance, the beaks of Darwin's finches evolved to suit the types of food available on their islands. On islands with hard seeds, finches developed stronger, thicker beaks. On islands with flowers, their beaks became longer and more delicate to reach nectar. These adaptations illustrate how species evolve to fill ecological niches and maintain the system's diversity.

Natural evolution isn't limited to biology. Processes like rivers carving landscapes or plants adapting to urban environments also demonstrate how systems evolve in response to change. Recognizing these shifts helps you understand how systems self-correct and find new equilibrium points.

How to Observe Natural Evolution

1. **Identify Adaptations:** Look for traits in organisms or systems that seem uniquely suited to their environments. What pressures might have driven these adaptations?
2. **Trace Changes Over Time:** Study how species or systems have evolved in response to environmental changes. Are there visible shifts in behavior, structure, or function?
3. **Look for Unintended Consequences:** Evolution often produces trade-offs, where adaptations benefit survival in one way but create vulnerabilities in others.
4. **Consider External Influences:** Human activity can accelerate or disrupt natural evolution, as seen in antibiotic resistance or urban wildlife adapting to new environments.

Real-World Example

Peppered moths in industrial England evolved darker coloration to blend into soot-covered trees, avoiding predation. When pollution was reduced, lighter-colored moths regained dominance, showing how evolution reflects environmental conditions.

Why It Matters

Observing natural evolution reveals how systems adapt and innovate in response to challenges. This understanding is vital for managing ecosystems, predicting future changes, and designing human systems that mimic nature's adaptability.

For example, sustainable agriculture draws inspiration from evolution by developing crops resistant to drought or pests, reducing reliance on chemical interventions. Similarly, urban planners can study how plants and animals adapt to city life, using this knowledge to design greener, more resilient spaces.

Ignoring evolutionary processes can lead to unintended consequences. For instance, overusing pesticides accelerates the evolution of resistant pests, creating new challenges for farmers. Understanding and working with natural evolution helps systems stay balanced and sustainable.

Exercises

1. **Identify an Evolutionary Trait:** Choose a species or system and identify one of its adaptations. Reflect on how this trait benefits its survival and any trade-offs it creates.
2. **Trace Evolutionary Change:** Study a species or system that has visibly evolved over time (e.g. antibiotic resistance or urban wildlife). What pressures drove this change?
3. **Apply Evolutionary Lessons:** For a challenge in your life or work, think of ways to mimic evolutionary processes. How can you adapt to changes and build resilience?

Key Takeaway

Evolution is nature's way of adapting to change. Observing these processes reveals how systems innovate, balance, and thrive over time.

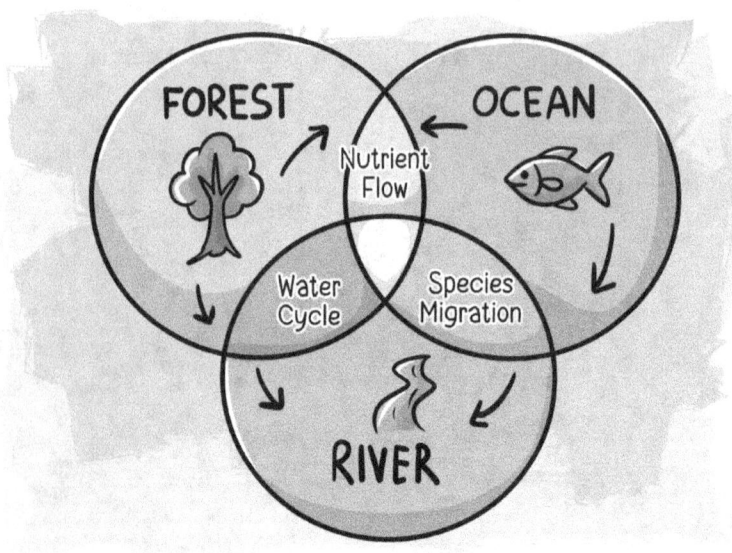

Chapter 51: Recognize Interconnected Ecosystems

Nothing Exists in Isolation

Ecosystems are not isolated entities. They're part of a larger network of interconnected systems that influence and depend on one another. What happens in one ecosystem often ripples into others, creating a web of interactions that sustain life on Earth. Recognizing these interconnections allows you to see the broader picture, where changes in one system can have cascading effects on others.

For example, forests play a critical role in regulating the water cycle by absorbing rainfall and releasing moisture into the atmosphere. This process influences nearby rivers, which depend on consistent water flow, and even oceans, where the rivers eventually drain. Similarly, nutrients washed from forests into rivers provide food for aquatic life, which in turn supports marine ecosystems. Disrupting one part of this chain — such as by deforesting a watershed—can destabilize the entire network.

Interconnected ecosystems teach us an essential lesson: everything is connected. By understanding these links, you can predict and mitigate unintended consequences, fostering a more holistic approach to conservation and resource management.

How to Recognize Interconnected Ecosystems

1. **Map Resource Flows:** Trace how water, nutrients, energy, or species move between ecosystems. For example, how does a river connect a mountain forest to the ocean?
2. **Look for Shared Species:** Many species rely on multiple ecosystems, such as migratory birds that nest in wetlands and feed in forests.
3. **Consider External Impacts:** Human activities like agriculture, urbanization, or deforestation often disrupt ecosystem connections. Identify where these activities create stress.
4. **Study Ecosystem Feedbacks:** Interconnected ecosystems often regulate each other, such as forests influencing rainfall patterns that sustain agriculture.

Real-World Example

Mangrove forests are a vital connection point between land and sea. They stabilize coastlines, filter pollutants from rivers, and provide nurseries for fish species that support both marine ecosystems and local fisheries. When mangroves are removed for development, these benefits are lost, leading to erosion, declining fish populations, and degraded water quality downstream.

Why It Matters

Recognizing interconnected ecosystems helps you see the full picture of how natural systems sustain life. Ignoring these links can lead to decisions that solve problems in one area but create new ones elsewhere. For instance, diverting rivers for irrigation might boost crop yields in the short term but deplete water supplies for downstream communities and ecosystems.

By understanding these connections, you can design solutions that benefit multiple ecosystems simultaneously. For example, restoring wetlands not only improves local biodiversity but also filters water, reduces flooding, and supports neighboring ecosystems like rivers and oceans.

Exercises

1. **Trace an Ecosystem Connection:** Choose two ecosystems near you, such as a forest and a river. Define how they influence and depend on each other.
2. **Analyze a Human Impact:** Think of a human activity, like farming or deforestation, that affects multiple ecosystems. What are the ripple effects, and how could they be mitigated?
3. **Design a Holistic Solution:** For a problem affecting one ecosystem, brainstorm ways to address it without harming connected systems. Could your solution benefit multiple ecosystems?

Key Takeaway

Ecosystems are deeply interconnected. Recognizing these links allows you to design solutions that support the health of entire networks.

Chapter 52: Spot Self-Healing Solutions

Nature's Built-In Repairs

Nature is a master of resilience. Many ecosystems have built-in mechanisms that allow them to heal themselves after disruptions, from storms to human intervention. These self-healing solutions rely on natural processes like regrowth, nutrient cycling, and species reintroduction to restore balance and functionality. Recognizing and supporting these processes can lead to sustainable, low-cost solutions for environmental challenges.

For instance, prairies and grasslands are adapted to recover from wildfires. Fire clears dead vegetation, releases nutrients into the soil, and encourages the growth of fire-resistant plants. Rather than preventing all fires, allowing controlled burns can activate these self-healing processes, improving the ecosystem's health.

How to Spot Self-Healing Solutions

1. **Identify Resilient Species:** Look for plants, animals, or processes that thrive in disrupted environments. These often play key roles in recovery.
2. **Observe Natural Recovery:** Study how ecosystems bounce back after disturbances like storms, droughts, or fires. What processes drive this recovery?
3. **Minimize Interference:** Self-healing processes often require minimal human intervention. Consider whether your actions support or hinder these natural mechanisms.
4. **Analyze Ecosystem Design:** Ecosystems with diverse species and redundant processes are often better equipped for self-healing.

Real-World Example

Coral reefs can recover from bleaching events if water conditions improve and stressors like overfishing or pollution are reduced. Left undisturbed, resilient coral species repopulate the reef, rebuilding habitats for marine life. Protecting reefs through marine reserves and pollution control gives these self-healing mechanisms a chance to work.

Why It Matters

Self-healing solutions are efficient, sustainable, and often require fewer resources than human interventions. Ignoring these processes can lead to unnecessary costs and disruptions, while working with them enhances recovery and resilience.

For example, reforesting degraded land with native plants supports self-healing by encouraging soil regeneration, water retention, and biodiversity recovery. In contrast, planting non-native species might slow these processes and create new challenges.

Understanding self-healing solutions also helps us design systems that mimic nature. Green infrastructure projects, like rain gardens, replicate natural water filtration processes, reducing the need for costly artificial solutions.

Exercises

1. **Observe Natural Recovery:** Visit an area recovering from disruption, like a cleared field or burned forest. Note the signs of self-healing, such as plant regrowth or animal return.
2. **Support a Self-Healing Process:** Think of a system you interact with that could recover naturally, like a garden or pond. How can you minimize interference and support its recovery?
3. **Design a Self-Healing System:** Apply the concept to a human system, like a workplace or community project. How could you build in processes that allow it to recover from setbacks?

Key Takeaway

Nature is inherently resilient. Spotting and supporting self-healing solutions ensures efficient, sustainable recovery from disruptions.

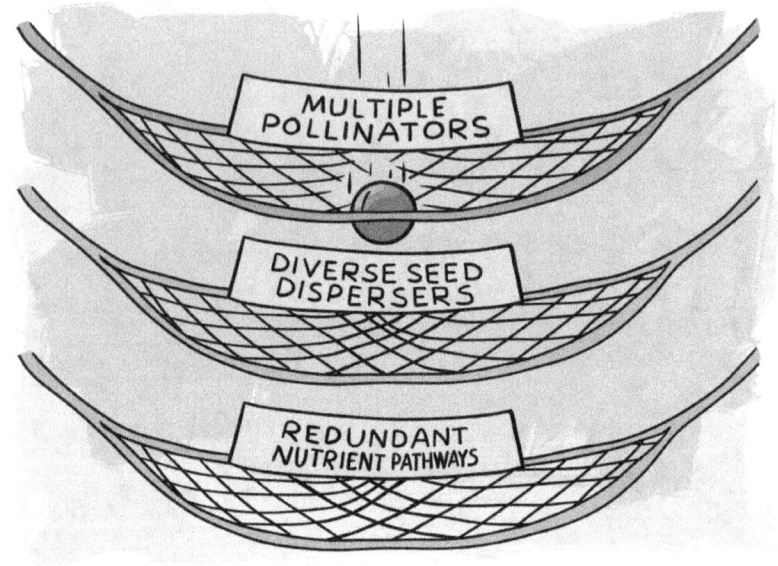

Chapter 53: See Nature's Redundancies

Built-In Backups for Survival

Redundancy is nature's way of ensuring resilience. In ecosystems, multiple species or processes often perform the same function, providing backups when one element is disrupted. This redundancy allows systems to maintain stability even under stress, ensuring continuity despite challenges like environmental changes or species loss.

For instance, tropical rainforests have numerous species of pollinators — bees, bats, birds, and butterflies — all contributing to the reproduction of plants. If one pollinator species declines due to disease or habitat loss, others can step in, preventing widespread disruption to the ecosystem. This overlap of functions creates a buffer that helps ecosystems adapt and thrive.

Seeing nature's redundancies highlights the importance of diversity. While efficiency may seem appealing, systems that rely too heavily on a single species, resource, or process become fragile and vulnerable to collapse. Nature shows us that redundancy is not waste, it's insurance.

How to See Nature's Redundancies

1. **Identify Overlapping Functions:** Look for processes or species that perform similar roles, such as multiple predators controlling prey populations or different plants stabilizing soil.
2. **Analyze Diversity:** Diverse ecosystems tend to have more redundancies, with multiple species providing the same ecosystem services (e.g. pollination, decomposition).
3. **Trace Responses to Stress:** Observe how the system behaves under disruption. Redundancy often becomes visible when one component fails but others continue the function.
4. **Watch for Lack of Redundancy:** Systems with low redundancy — such as monoculture farms or highly specialized industries — are more fragile.

Real-World Example

Mangroves provide multiple layers of redundancy in coastal protection. They reduce storm surges, trap sediment, and stabilize shorelines. If one mangrove species declines, others can perform similar roles, ensuring continued protection for coastal ecosystems and human communities. In contrast, engineered solutions like seawalls lack this redundancy and fail if damaged.

Why It Matters

Redundancy is critical for resilience. Systems that lack backups are prone to failure when their single point of reliance breaks down. For example, monoculture farming, which relies on one crop species, is vulnerable to pests or diseases, while polyculture farming creates redundancy by incorporating multiple crops that support each other.

Recognizing nature's redundancies also helps inform better system design. From urban planning to supply chains, building in overlapping functions ensures flexibility and adaptability. For example, decentralized energy grids with multiple renewable sources mimic the resilience of ecosystems, reducing the risk of widespread blackouts.

Exercises

1. **Spot Redundancies in Nature:** Choose an ecosystem (e.g. a forest or wetland) and identify overlapping functions or species that provide backups. Reflect on how these redundancies improve resilience.
2. **Analyze a Fragile System:** Think of a human system that lacks redundancy, such as a single-source supply chain or an over-reliance on one service. What risks does this create?
3. **Design for Redundancy:** Apply nature's principle of redundancy to a project or system you're part of. How can you build in backups to ensure continuity under stress?

Key Takeaway

Nature's redundancies ensure resilience. Incorporating overlapping functions in systems reduces fragility and prepares them for disruptions.

Chapter 54: Trace Habitat Fragmentation

Breaking the Web of Life

Habitat fragmentation occurs when large, continuous ecosystems are broken into smaller, disconnected patches. This fragmentation disrupts species movement, reduces biodiversity, and makes ecosystems less resilient to change. Tracing habitat fragmentation reveals how human activities like deforestation, road construction, and urban sprawl impact natural systems — and what can be done to restore connectivity.

For example, when forests are cleared for agriculture, wildlife corridors are severed, preventing species from migrating to find food, mates, or shelter. Over time, isolated populations become genetically weaker, reducing their ability to adapt to environmental changes. Fragmentation also impacts ecological processes like pollination and seed dispersal, as the animals responsible for these tasks can no longer move freely.

Understanding habitat fragmentation helps you see the bigger picture of ecosystem health. It highlights the need for strategies like wildlife corridors, reforestation, and land-use planning to restore connections and support biodiversity.

How to Trace Habitat Fragmentation

1. **Map Ecosystem Breaks:** Identify areas where natural habitats have been divided by roads, farmland, or urbanization. Focus on regions where connectivity is essential for wildlife.
2. **Analyze Impacts on Movement:** Study how fragmentation affects species' ability to move. Are populations becoming isolated, or are migration patterns disrupted?
3. **Look for Edge Effects:** Fragmentation creates edges—areas where habitat meets human-altered land. These edges often have different conditions, such as increased light or invasive species, which can harm native ecosystems.
4. **Assess Long-Term Risks:** Consider how fragmentation affects ecosystem resilience. Are species more vulnerable to extinction, or are ecosystems losing key functions like pollination?

Real-World Example

The Amazon rainforest is heavily fragmented by logging and agriculture, creating isolated patches of forest. This limits the movement of species like jaguars and toucans, disrupting food webs and reducing genetic diversity. Efforts to reconnect these fragments through wildlife corridors and protected reserves are critical for restoring balance.

Why It Matters

Habitat fragmentation weakens ecosystems by reducing biodiversity, disrupting ecological processes, and increasing vulnerability to climate change. Left unchecked, it can lead to species extinction and collapse of vital ecosystem services.

Tracing fragmentation highlights opportunities for restoration. For instance, reconnecting fragmented forests with wildlife corridors allows species to move freely, restoring migration patterns and genetic diversity. Similarly, urban green spaces and rooftop gardens create pockets of habitat in cities, supporting pollinators and other wildlife.

Exercises

1. **Outline Fragmentation Near You:** Choose a natural area and identify how human development has fragmented the habitat. Reflect on how this impacts species and ecosystem health.
2. **Analyze Edge Effects:** Visit a fragmented habitat and observe the edges. How do they differ from the interior, and how might they affect native species?
3. **Propose a Connectivity Plan:** For a fragmented system, brainstorm ways to restore connections, such as wildlife corridors, reforestation, or changes in land-use policies.

Key Takeaway

Habitat fragmentation disrupts ecosystems. Tracing and addressing these breaks restores connectivity and supports biodiversity.

Chapter 55: Watch Energy Minimization Strategies

The Efficiency of Nature

In natural systems, energy is a limited resource, and organisms have evolved strategies to use it as efficiently as possible. Energy minimization strategies allow species to conserve resources, reduce effort, and maximize survival. From the way birds fly in formation to the way plants grow toward sunlight, nature constantly finds ways to do more with less.

For example, geese flying in a V-formation take advantage of aerodynamic efficiency. The lead bird works hardest, creating a slipstream that reduces air resistance for the trailing birds. As the lead bird tires, another bird takes its place, ensuring the flock can travel long distances without exhausting any one member. This cooperative energy-sharing strategy exemplifies nature's focus on efficiency.

By watching these energy-saving methods, you can uncover lessons for designing human systems that optimize resource use and minimize waste. These principles apply everywhere — from engineering to team management to sustainable agriculture.

How to Watch Energy Minimization Strategies

1. **Observe Natural Movements:** Study how animals move in groups, like fish schools or bird flocks, to identify cooperative strategies that save energy.
2. **Track Resource Allocation:** Look for how organisms prioritize energy use, such as plants directing resources toward growth in sunlight-rich areas.
3. **Analyze Adaptations:** Many adaptations, like streamlined shapes in aquatic animals or hibernation in mammals, are designed to reduce energy expenditure.
4. **Find Examples in Human Systems:** Notice where energy minimization strategies already appear in human systems, such as shared transportation or optimized workflows.

Real-World Example

Ant colonies exemplify energy efficiency. Worker ants divide tasks like foraging, building, and defending the colony to minimize overlap and maximize productivity. Pheromone trails direct ants to the most efficient routes, ensuring that resources like food are gathered quickly and with minimal energy waste.

Why It Matters

Energy minimization strategies create resilience by allowing organisms and systems to thrive with limited resources. Ignoring these strategies can lead to inefficiency, waste, and unsustainable practices. For instance, industries that fail to optimize energy use may incur higher costs and environmental impacts.

By learning from nature, you can design systems that mimic these strategies. For example, businesses can adopt energy-efficient logistics, such as grouping deliveries to reduce fuel consumption. Similarly, urban planners can design cities that minimize commuting distances, reducing energy use for transportation.

Recognizing energy minimization also helps identify areas for improvement in existing systems. If a workflow or ecosystem is expending unnecessary energy, redesigning it with efficiency in mind can lead to better outcomes with fewer resources.

Exercises

1. **Observe Natural Efficiency:** Choose a natural process (e.g. animal migration or plant growth) and identify how energy is minimized. Reflect on what makes the process efficient.
2. **Analyze Human Efficiency:** Think of a system you interact with, like transportation or food production. Where is energy wasted, and how could it be conserved?
3. **Design an Energy-Saving System:** Apply an energy minimization strategy you've observed in nature to a human system, such as a workplace or community project.

Key Takeaway

Nature thrives by minimizing energy use. Observing these strategies can inspire more efficient and sustainable human systems.

Chapter 56: Look for Mutualism

Win-Win Relationships

Mutualism is one of nature's most fascinating strategies for success. It occurs when two or more species interact in ways that benefit all parties involved. These win-win relationships enhance survival, efficiency, and resilience, creating partnerships that strengthen entire ecosystems.

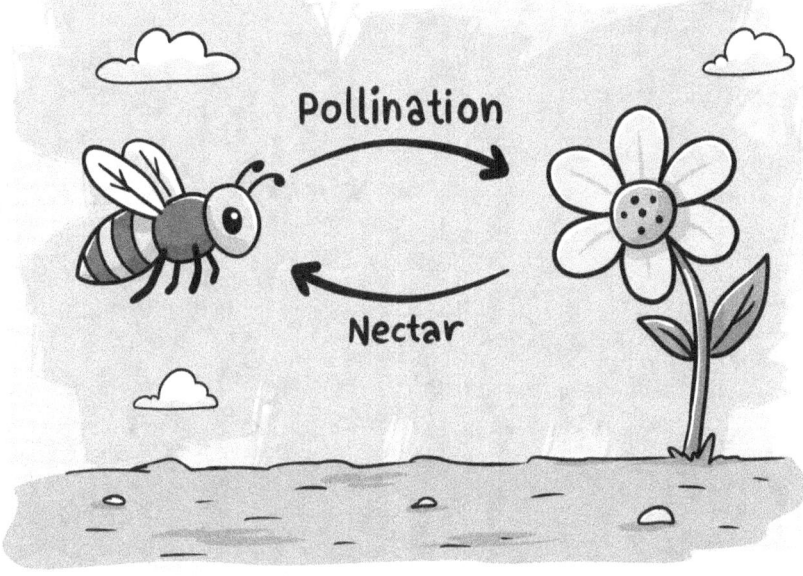

Consider bees and flowering plants. Bees collect nectar to feed their colonies, while flowers rely on bees to transfer pollen, enabling reproduction. This mutualistic relationship ensures the survival of both species and benefits broader systems like agriculture and biodiversity.

Mutualism isn't limited to species — it can involve entire ecosystems working together. For example, coral reefs host diverse marine species that depend on each other for shelter, food, and protection. Recognizing mutualism reveals how cooperation, not just competition, drives natural systems.

How to Look for Mutualism

1. **Identify Interactions:** Observe species that regularly interact, such as plants and pollinators or predators and scavengers. Consider how both parties benefit.
2. **Trace Dependencies:** Study how these relationships impact the broader system. For example, how does pollination benefit not just plants but also herbivores and predators?
3. **Observe Human-Nature Mutualism:** Look for ways humans benefit from and support ecosystems, such as through sustainable farming practices.
4. **Note Breakdowns:** Mutualism can fail under stress, such as when habitat loss disrupts pollinator-plant relationships. Analyze how to restore these partnerships.

Real-World Example

Sea anemones and clownfish have a classic mutualistic relationship. Clownfish live among anemone tentacles for protection from predators, while the anemone benefits from the clownfish removing debris and deterring potential threats. This partnership enhances survival for both species.

Why It Matters

Mutualism highlights the power of cooperation. Systems that foster mutual benefit are more resilient, sustainable, and efficient than those driven solely by competition. Ignoring mutualism can lead to imbalances, such as declines in crop yields when pollinator populations drop.

Understanding mutualism also inspires human systems. For example, partnerships between businesses and communities — such as companies supporting local farmers — create shared benefits that promote long-term success. Similarly, urban green spaces foster mutualism by improving residents' quality of life while supporting biodiversity.

Recognizing and supporting mutualistic relationships ensures stability and sustainability. When mutualism thrives, so does the system.

Exercises

1. **Identify a Mutualistic Pair:** Choose a species pair (e.g. bees and flowers) and reflect on how their relationship benefits both. How does this partnership impact the broader system?
2. **Analyze a Mutualism Breakdown:** Think of a mutualistic relationship disrupted by human activity (e.g. habitat loss or pollution). How might it be restored?
3. **Design a Mutualistic System:** Apply mutualism to a human system, such as a workplace or community. How can cooperation create shared benefits?

Key Takeaway

Mutualism drives resilience in nature. Fostering win-win relationships builds stronger, more sustainable systems.

Chapter 57: Detect Adaptive Behaviors

Adaptation is the hallmark of resilience in natural systems. Ecosystems and species continually adjust their behaviors, structures, or functions in response to changes in their environment. These adaptive behaviors help maintain balance, survive disruptions, and evolve over time. Detecting adaptive behaviors reveals how systems respond to stress and offers clues for designing systems that thrive in dynamic conditions.

For example, desert plants like cacti adapt to arid conditions by storing water in their tissues and developing spines to minimize evaporation. Similarly, animals like Arctic foxes change their fur color with the seasons — white in winter for camouflage in snow and brown in summer to blend with the tundra. These adaptations allow species to succeed in challenging and changing environments.

Understanding adaptive behaviors isn't just about marveling at nature's ingenuity — it's about learning from it. Observing these behaviors provides insights into how human systems can become more flexible, innovative, and sustainable.

How to Detect Adaptive Behaviors

1. **Observe Changes Over Time:** Look for shifts in how species or systems behave in response to environmental changes, such as migration patterns or feeding habits.
2. **Analyze Behavioral Triggers:** Identify what factors prompt adaptive behaviors, such as resource scarcity, predators, or climate fluctuations.
3. **Look for Structural Changes:** Adaptation isn't always about behavior—sometimes it involves physical changes, like thicker fur or deeper roots.
4. **Trace Feedback Cycles:** Adaptive behaviors often arise from dynamic interconnections in systems, where stress or disruption prompts self-correction.

Real-World Example

Coral reefs adapt to water conditions by building structures that support symbiotic relationships with algae. However, when water temperatures rise, corals expel algae in a process called bleaching, an adaptive behavior aimed at surviving stress. If conditions improve, the algae return, restoring the reef's balance.

Why It Matters

Adaptive behaviors are essential for survival and resilience. Systems that fail to adapt risk collapse when conditions change, while those that adjust can thrive in the face of uncertainty. For example, businesses that adapt to market trends—like shifting to online sales during a pandemic—are more likely to succeed than those that resist change.

Detecting adaptive behaviors in natural systems also inspires solutions for human challenges. Urban planners can learn from floodplain ecosystems that adapt to seasonal changes, designing cities that flex with water levels instead of resisting them. Similarly, organizations can adopt adaptive leadership models that respond dynamically to challenges.

Understanding adaptation allows you to anticipate change and design systems that align with it, rather than working against it.

Exercises

1. **Observe Adaptive Behavior:** Choose a species or ecosystem and identify how it adjusts to environmental changes, such as seasonal shifts or resource scarcity.
2. **Analyze a Human System:** Think of a system (e.g. a workplace or community) that successfully adapted to a challenge. What made this adaptation effective?
3. **Design an Adaptive System:** Apply principles of adaptation to a project or goal you're working on. How can you build flexibility into the system to handle future changes?

Key Takeaway

Adaptive behaviors help systems thrive in changing conditions. Detecting and learning from them builds resilience and flexibility in human systems.

Chapter 58:
Understand Biotic-Abiotic Interactions

Where Life Meets the Elements

Ecosystems are shaped by interactions between living (biotic) and non-living (abiotic) components. Plants, animals, fungi, and microbes rely on water, sunlight, air, and soil to survive, while these abiotic factors are in turn influenced by the activities of organisms. Understanding these interactions reveals how ecosystems function, adapt, and evolve.

For example, plants absorb sunlight and carbon dioxide to produce energy through photosynthesis, creating oxygen as a by-product. This oxygen supports animals and microbes, which in turn produce carbon dioxide through respiration, completing a cycle that balances gases in the atmosphere. Abiotic factors like temperature and precipitation also regulate where certain plants and animals can thrive, shaping biodiversity in different regions.

Recognizing biotic-abiotic interactions highlights the deep interconnectedness of life and environment. It shows how changes in one domain — such as pollution or deforestation — can ripple across both living organisms and non-living systems.

How to Understand Biotic-Abiotic Interactions

1. **Map Resource Flows:** Trace how abiotic resources like sunlight, water, and nutrients move through a system and support biotic components.
2. **Identify Feedback Mechanisms:** Look for cycles where living organisms influence abiotic factors, such as plants regulating soil nutrients or animals aerating the soil.
3. **Observe Environmental Limits:** Analyze how abiotic factors like temperature or pH set boundaries for where species can survive.
4. **Consider Disruptions:** Study how human activities like pollution or urbanization alter biotic-abiotic relationships, creating imbalances.

Real-World Example

Mangroves demonstrate the profound interplay between biotic and abiotic factors. Their roots stabilize soil, reducing erosion, while also filtering saltwater and improving water quality. In turn, this abiotic support enables a rich ecosystem of fish, birds, and other species to thrive. When mangroves are destroyed, these interactions collapse, leading to habitat loss and water degradation.

Why It Matters

Biotic-abiotic interactions are the foundation of ecosystem health. Ignoring these relationships can lead to environmental degradation, resource scarcity, and biodiversity loss. For example, over-extraction of water (an abiotic resource) for agriculture can dry up wetlands, disrupting the habitats of countless species.

Understanding these interactions also informs sustainable practices. For instance, farmers who maintain healthy soil biota (biotic) improve nutrient cycling and water retention (abiotic), boosting crop yields while reducing the need for chemical inputs. Similarly, urban designers can use green infrastructure to harmonize biotic and abiotic systems, like planting trees to regulate urban temperatures.

Exercises

1. **Map an Interaction:** Choose a local ecosystem and trace one biotic-abiotic interaction, such as how plants influence soil quality or how water availability affects animal populations.
2. **Analyze a Disruption:** Think of a system where human activity has disrupted biotic-abiotic interactions (e.g. deforestation or mining). What are the consequences, and how could they be mitigated?
3. **Propose a Balance:** Design a project or practice that restores harmony between biotic and abiotic factors, such as reforestation to improve water quality.

Key Takeaway

Biotic-abiotic interactions sustain ecosystems. Recognizing these connections promotes stronger environmental stewardship and smarter system design.

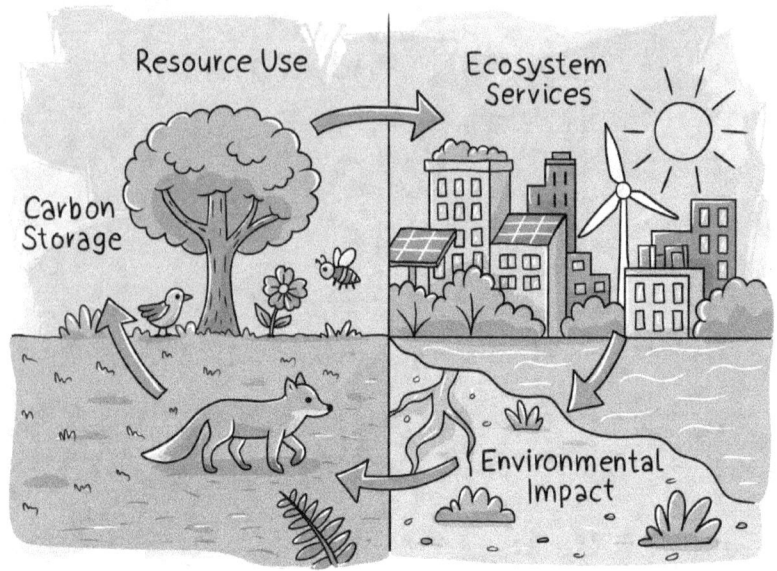

Chapter 59: See Human-Nature Interactions

A Two-Way Relationship

Humans and nature are deeply intertwined, each shaping the other over time. Human activities, from farming to urbanization, impact natural systems, while ecosystems provide essential resources and services that sustain human life. Recognizing these interactions helps uncover both the benefits humans derive from nature and the challenges they impose on it.

For example, forests act as carbon sinks, absorbing carbon dioxide and regulating the climate — services that benefit human health and agriculture. In return, deforestation disrupts these functions, contributing to climate change and reducing biodiversity. This two-way relationship underscores the need for balance.

By understanding these interactions, you can identify opportunities to align human activities with natural processes, fostering sustainable coexistence rather than conflict.

How to See Human-Nature Interactions

1. **Map Resource Dependencies:** Identify how human systems — such as agriculture, water supply, or energy—depend on natural resources and ecosystem services.
2. **Trace Environmental Impacts:** Study how human activities like construction, transportation, or industry affect natural systems.
3. **Look for Positive Feedback:** Observe where humans actively support nature, such as through reforestation, habitat restoration, or sustainable farming practices.
4. **Assess Long-Term Trade-Offs:** Evaluate whether current human activities are sustainable or if they risk depleting the ecosystems they depend on.

Real-World Example

Urban gardens represent a positive interaction between humans and nature. They provide fresh food, reduce urban heat, and support pollinators like bees and butterflies. In return, humans tend to these spaces, ensuring their health and productivity while reconnecting with the natural world.

Why It Matters

Human-nature interactions shape the planet's future. Mismanaged interactions lead to environmental degradation, resource scarcity, and declining quality of life, as seen in deforestation or pollution. Conversely, fostering harmonious interactions creates resilient systems that benefit both people and the environment.

For example, sustainable fisheries align human needs with ecological health by setting quotas and protecting breeding grounds, ensuring fish populations remain robust. Similarly, renewable energy sources like wind and solar reduce environmental impact while meeting human energy demands.

Understanding these dynamics also shifts the focus from short-term exploitation to long-term stewardship. By recognizing the mutual benefits of supporting nature, humans can create systems that thrive alongside the environment.

Exercises

1. **Map a Human-Nature Interaction:** Choose a local system, such as a park or a water source, and identify how humans use and impact it. What benefits flow in each direction?
2. **Analyze an Unsustainable Practice:** Think of a human activity that harms nature (e.g. overfishing or deforestation). What changes could make it more sustainable?
3. **Propose a Positive Interaction:** Design a project or practice that enhances human-nature interactions, like planting native species in urban areas or protecting local wetlands.

Key Takeaway

Human and natural systems are deeply connected. Recognizing these interactions creates opportunities for sustainable coexistence.

Chapter 60: Track Species Migration Networks

Species migration is one of nature's most dynamic and intricate processes. Birds, fish, mammals, and even insects travel vast distances, often crossing continents or oceans, to find food, reproduce, or escape changing seasons. These migration networks connect ecosystems across the globe, making them vital to biodiversity and ecosystem health.

For instance, monarch butterflies migrate thousands of miles between North America and Mexico, relying on specific habitats along the way for rest and refueling. If these habitats are disrupted — such as by deforestation or agriculture — the entire migration cycle is jeopardized, threatening the species' survival.

Tracking species migration networks reveals the interconnectedness of ecosystems and highlights the importance of preserving critical habitats along migration routes. It also underscores how changes in one location can ripple across entire regions, affecting biodiversity and ecological balance.

How to Track Species Migration Networks

1. **Identify Migratory Species:** Focus on species known for long-distance migrations, such as birds, whales, or butterflies. Study their life cycles and movement patterns.
2. **Define Critical Stopovers:** Highlight the key habitats these species rely on during migration, such as wetlands, breeding grounds, or feeding areas.
3. **Trace Threats Along Routes:** Analyze how human activities, like urbanization or climate change, disrupt these networks and what impacts result.
4. **Consider Broader Connections:** Migration networks link distant ecosystems. Study how changes in one region affect other parts of the network.

Real-World Example

The East Atlantic Flyway is a major migration route for millions of birds traveling between Europe and Africa. Along this route, wetlands like the Wadden Sea in northern Europe provide critical feeding grounds. Protecting these stopovers ensures that birds have the resources they need to complete their journeys and maintain healthy populations.

Why It Matters

Migration networks sustain ecosystems by distributing species, nutrients, and energy across regions. Disrupting these networks — such as through habitat loss or climate change — can collapse entire ecological systems and harm human communities that depend on them. For instance, the decline of migratory fish species like salmon impacts both aquatic ecosystems and the livelihoods of fishing communities.

Tracking migration networks also informs conservation efforts. By identifying and protecting key habitats, such as breeding grounds or stopover sites, you can ensure the survival of migratory species and the ecosystems they support.

Additionally, migration teaches us about adaptability and resilience. Understanding these networks inspires better design of human systems, such as transportation networks or global supply chains, to create efficient and sustainable connections.

Exercises

1. **Map a Migration Route:** Choose a migratory species and trace its route, including key habitats and stopover points. Reflect on what supports or threatens its journey.
2. **Analyze a Disrupted Network:** Think of a migration network affected by human activity, such as habitat loss or climate change. What consequences have emerged, and how could they be addressed?
3. **Design a Support Plan:** Propose ways to protect a migration network, such as creating wildlife corridors, conserving key habitats, or reducing pollution.

Key Takeaway

Migration networks connect ecosystems across the globe. Tracking and protecting these pathways ensures biodiversity and ecological balance.

Section IV: Applying Systems Thinking to Solve Problems

This final section bridges the gap between understanding systems and using that understanding to drive meaningful action. By applying systems thinking, you can tackle complex challenges, design solutions that adapt to change, and create systems that are resilient, efficient, and inclusive. From breaking problems into manageable subsystems to fostering collaboration and long-term sustainability, this section provides actionable strategies to solve real-world issues. Whether you're leading a team, managing a project, or addressing societal challenges, these tools empower you to think holistically and act decisively.

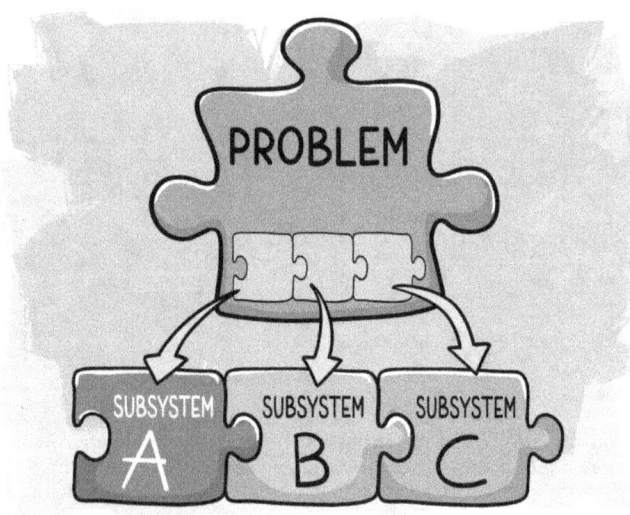

Chapter 61: Break Down the Problem into Subsystems

Dissecting Complexity

Large problems often feel overwhelming, but systems thinking offers a way to make them manageable: breaking them down into subsystems. These smaller, interrelated parts allow you to understand the root causes, identify connections, and develop targeted interventions without losing sight of the bigger picture.

For example, consider traffic congestion in a city. Instead of treating it as one massive issue, breaking it into subsystems—public transportation, road infrastructure, traffic laws, and driver behavior — reveals specific areas to address. Improving bus routes, optimizing traffic signals, and promoting carpooling all contribute to solving the larger problem.

This approach ensures that solutions are both effective and holistic, avoiding quick fixes that might inadvertently create new issues.

How to Break Down Problems

1. **Define the System:** Identify the overall problem and map the components that contribute to it.
2. **Isolate Subsystems:** Divide the problem into smaller, manageable parts based on function or influence, such as resources, stakeholders, or processes.
3. **Analyze Interconnections:** Study how each subsystem interacts with the others. Changes in one part may ripple through the system.
4. **Prioritize Actionable Parts:** Focus on subsystems where interventions are most likely to create meaningful impact.

Real-World Example

In healthcare, addressing patient wait times involves breaking the system into subsystems like staffing, scheduling, facility capacity, and patient flow. By improving appointment scheduling or optimizing resource allocation, wait times can be reduced without compromising care quality.

Why It Matters

Breaking down problems into subsystems makes complex challenges less intimidating and more actionable. It allows for focused, systematic interventions that address root causes rather than symptoms. For example, tackling climate change requires addressing subsystems like energy production, transportation, agriculture, and policy. Focusing solely on one aspect without considering others might lead to incomplete or counterproductive solutions.

This approach also encourages collaboration across disciplines. By identifying the components of a problem, you can involve relevant experts and stakeholders in each area, ensuring more comprehensive solutions.

Exercises

1. **Dissect a Personal Problem:** Choose a challenge you face, like time management or budgeting, and break it into subsystems. What parts can you tackle first?
2. **Analyze a Global Issue:** Select a complex issue like poverty or deforestation. Do a layout of its subsystems and think about how changes in one part might influence others.
3. **Design an Intervention:** For a subsystem you've identified, propose a targeted intervention. How would this change affect the larger system?

Key Takeaway

Breaking problems into subsystems makes them manageable and actionable. This approach ensures focused solutions without losing sight of the bigger picture.

Chapter 62: Use Feedback for Continuous Improvement

The Power of Iteration

Feedback is the cornerstone of systems thinking. By observing how actions produce results and adjusting based on what you learn, you create a continuous improvement cycle that makes systems more effective over time. Feedback allows you to identify what works, correct mistakes, and refine your approach, ensuring that solutions evolve alongside changing conditions.

For example, software development relies heavily on feedback. Developers release a product, collect user input on bugs and usability, and then update the software to better meet user needs. This iterative process ensures the product improves with each version, aligning more closely with its goals.

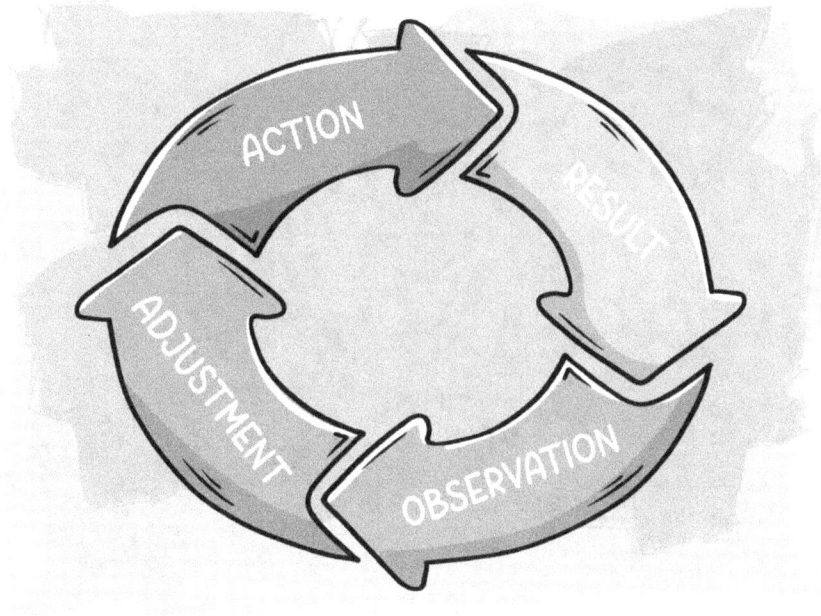

How to Use Feedback

1. **Set Clear Goals:** Define what success looks like so you can measure progress accurately.
2. **Collect Data:** Monitor results from actions, whether through surveys, metrics, or observations.
3. **Analyze Patterns:** Look for trends in the data that reveal what's working and what isn't.
4. **Make Adjustments:** Use what you've learned to refine your approach, and repeat the cycle for continuous improvement.

Real-World Example

In agriculture, feedback from crop yields informs farmers about the effectiveness of their practices. By testing different fertilizers or irrigation methods and monitoring results, farmers refine their strategies to maximize productivity while minimizing waste.

Why It Matters

Without feedback, systems stagnate, relying on outdated assumptions or guesswork. Continuous feedback ensures that actions remain aligned with goals, improving efficiency and effectiveness over time. For example, a company that regularly collects customer feedback can adapt its products to meet changing preferences, staying competitive in the market.

Feedback also reduces the risk of unintended consequences. By monitoring results in real-time, you can catch problems early and make course corrections before they escalate. This proactive approach saves time, money, and effort in the long run.

Exercises

1. **Apply Feedback in Your Life:** Choose a goal, like improving your diet or learning a skill. Create a feedback loop by tracking progress, reflecting on results, and adjusting your approach.
2. **Analyze a Feedback System:** Think of a system you interact with, like a workplace or school. How does it use feedback to improve? What could be done better?
3. **Design a Feedback System:** For a project or challenge, design a process that includes clear metrics, regular check-ins, and adjustment phases.

Key Takeaway

Feedback is essential for continuous improvement. Using it effectively ensures systems stay aligned with goals and adapt to changing conditions.

Chapter 63: Test Small Interventions

Why Small Steps Lead to Big Insights

When solving complex problems, starting with small, controlled interventions allows you to test ideas, observe results, and minimize risks. This approach helps uncover potential outcomes without committing significant resources or disrupting the entire system. Testing small interventions is especially valuable when working with systems that are unpredictable or have many interdependencies.

Consider urban planning. Instead of completely redesigning a city's public transit system, planners might test a single bike lane in a high-traffic area. By observing how the new lane affects traffic flow, safety, and public usage, they can refine their strategy before expanding citywide.

Small interventions act as experiments, providing insights that inform larger decisions. They reveal what works, what doesn't, and what might produce unintended consequences, making them a key tool for systems thinking.

How to Test Small Interventions

1. **Define Your Hypothesis:** Clearly state what you expect the intervention to achieve. This gives you a baseline for evaluating success or failure.
2. **Start Small:** Choose a manageable part of the system to test your idea. Look for areas where the risks are minimal but the potential insights are valuable.
3. **Observe and Measure:** Track changes carefully, using metrics or qualitative observations to understand how the system responds.
4. **Refine and Expand:** Use the results to refine your approach, then decide whether to scale the intervention or pivot to a new strategy.

Real-World Example

In public health, pilot programs are a common example of small interventions. A city might test a vaccination drive in one neighborhood before rolling it out to the entire population. By analyzing participation rates, challenges, and outcomes, officials can adjust their approach to maximize effectiveness and minimize resistance.

Why It Matters

Testing small interventions reduces risks and avoids costly mistakes. Instead of overhauling an entire system based on assumptions, you gather real-world data that informs smarter decisions. This approach also builds confidence in stakeholders, who can see tangible results before committing to larger-scale changes.

For instance, a company introducing a new product might test it in a single market before launching it globally. This trial period reveals customer reactions, potential flaws, and areas for improvement, increasing the likelihood of success at scale.

Small interventions also align with adaptive thinking. Systems are often too complex to predict all outcomes in advance, but iterative experimentation allows for ongoing learning and adjustment.

Exercises

1. **Design a Small Experiment:** Identify a problem you want to solve, such as improving a team workflow or reducing household waste. Propose a small-scale intervention to test your idea.
2. **Analyze a Past Intervention:** Think of a time when you or your organization tested a small change. What worked, what didn't, and what could have been improved?
3. **Plan a Scale-Up:** For a successful small intervention, outline the steps needed to expand it while minimizing risks.

Key Takeaway

Testing small interventions uncovers insights, minimizes risks, and builds confidence — an essential strategy for addressing complex systems.

Chapter 64: Activate Unused Resources

Finding the Hidden Gems in Your System

Many systems have untapped resources, whether they're underused materials, overlooked skills, or unrecognized opportunities. Activating these resources can improve efficiency, drive innovation, and unlock solutions to persistent problems. Recognizing and leveraging these hidden assets often requires a fresh perspective and creative thinking.

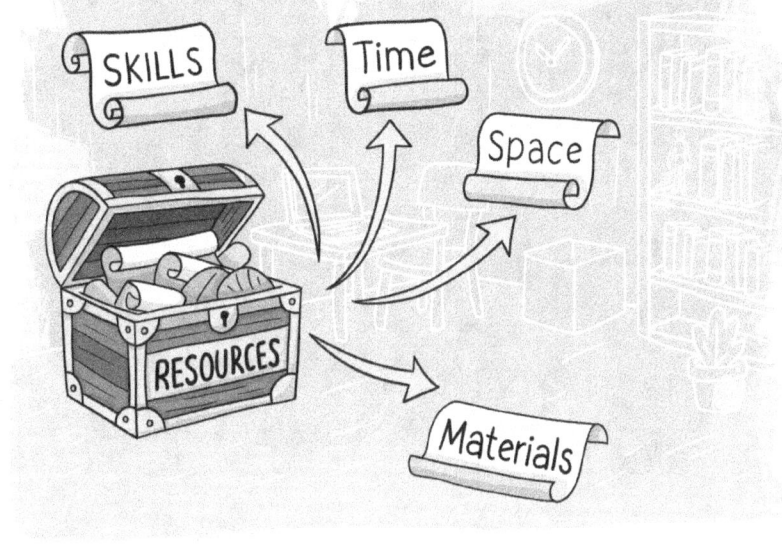

For example, during the COVID-19 pandemic, underutilized manufacturing facilities were retooled to produce masks, ventilators, and other critical supplies. By identifying these unused resources and repurposing them, governments and industries quickly addressed urgent needs without building new infrastructure.

Unused resources aren't always physical. They can include people's time, knowledge, or connections within a community. Identifying and activating these assets strengthens the system as a whole.

How to Activate Unused Resources

1. **Audit the System:** Look for resources that aren't being fully utilized, such as equipment sitting idle, team members with untapped skills, or vacant spaces.
2. **Rethink Purpose:** Consider how resources could be repurposed or reallocated to add value. What new roles could they play within the system?
3. **Engage Stakeholders:** Often, those within the system are aware of overlooked resources or potential opportunities. Involve them in brainstorming solutions.
4. **Test New Uses:** Experiment with how unused resources can be applied, ensuring that the new use aligns with the system's goals.

Real-World Example

Libraries, traditionally seen as book-lending facilities, have activated unused resources to serve broader community needs. Many now provide free Internet access, meeting spaces, and job training programs, making better use of their space and infrastructure while increasing their relevance and impact.

Why It Matters

Activating unused resources is a low-cost, high-impact way to enhance system performance. It reduces waste, maximizes efficiency, and often leads to creative problem-solving. For example, businesses that repurpose leftover materials can save money while reducing environmental impact.

Unused resources are also opportunities for resilience. In times of crisis, having access to untapped assets provides flexibility and adaptability. For instance, during natural disasters, schools are often converted into emergency shelters, repurposing their space to meet urgent community needs.

Recognizing these opportunities fosters a mindset of abundance rather than scarcity. Instead of focusing on limitations, you learn to see potential in what's already available.

Exercises

1. **Identify Unused Resources:** Audit your environment — home, workplace, or community — and list resources that are underutilized. How could they be put to better use?
2. **Rethink a Current Resource:** Choose a resource you already use, such as a skill or material, and brainstorm additional ways to leverage it.
3. **Implement a New Use:** Activate one unused resource in your system. Track its impact and reflect on how it enhances efficiency or solves a problem.

Key Takeaway

Unused resources are opportunities waiting to be unlocked. Activating them strengthens systems and drives innovation.

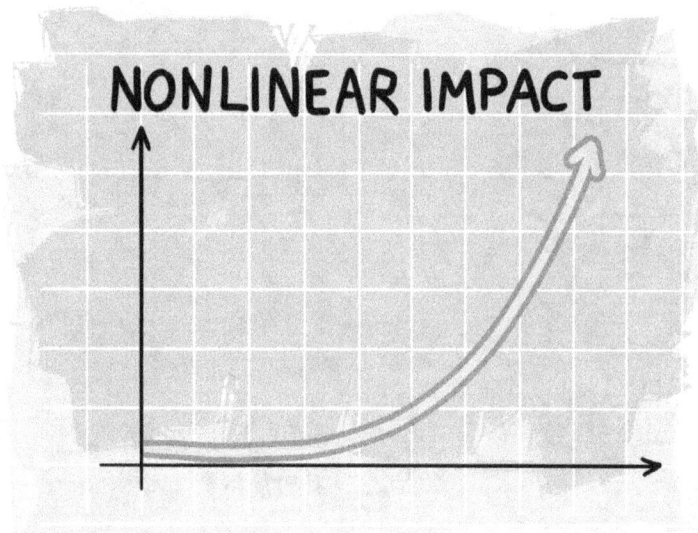

Chapter 65: Find Nonlinear Influences

When Small Actions Create Big Waves

Not all influences in a system are proportional. Some small changes can lead to disproportionately large effects, while seemingly significant actions might barely make a dent. These nonlinear influences are critical to understanding how systems behave, and identifying them allows you to leverage small efforts for maximum impact—or prevent minor missteps from spiraling into major problems.

For example, reintroducing wolves to Yellowstone National Park is a classic case of nonlinear influence. Though the wolf population was small, their presence triggered a cascade of changes: controlling deer populations, allowing vegetation to recover, stabilizing riverbanks, and improving ecosystem health. This single intervention produced benefits far beyond its immediate scope.

Nonlinear influences often appear in tipping points, feedback cycles, or compounding effects. Finding these areas allows you to act with precision and efficiency, targeting changes that produce outsized results.

How to Find Nonlinear Influences

1. **Map Cause-and-Effect Chains:** Trace how a small input propagates through the system. Look for points where a small action creates amplified effects.
2. **Identify Tipping Points:** Study thresholds where minor changes can trigger major shifts, such as critical mass in social movements or ecological balance.
3. **Analyze Delayed Effects:** Nonlinear influences often emerge over time, as small changes accumulate. Consider how short-term actions might produce long-term impacts.
4. **Focus on Leverage Points:** Look for places in the system where a small change can create a ripple effect, producing system-wide benefits.

Real-World Example

Vaccination programs exemplify nonlinear influence. A small increase in vaccination rates can lead to herd immunity, preventing outbreaks and protecting even those who aren't vaccinated. This ripple effect magnifies the impact of individual actions, creating widespread health benefits.

Why It Matters

Nonlinear influences reveal where effort is best spent. Instead of spreading resources thinly across the system, you can focus on high-leverage areas that create significant outcomes. For example, addressing bottlenecks in supply chains often yields far-reaching improvements in efficiency and reliability.

Ignoring nonlinear dynamics risks overlooking critical points of influence or underestimating the consequences of small actions. For instance, neglecting early signs of climate change can lead to catastrophic consequences later.

Understanding nonlinear influences fosters smarter problem-solving. It helps you design interventions that align with the system's natural dynamics, maximizing results while minimizing effort.

Exercises

1. **Identify a Nonlinear Influence:** Think of a system you interact with, such as a workplace or community. What small actions have had an outsized impact?
2. **Plan a Cause-and-Effect Chain:** Choose a change you'd like to make and trace its potential ripple effects through the system. Where might nonlinear influences emerge?
3. **Design a High-Leverage Intervention:** Propose an action that targets a nonlinear influence in a system you're working on. How could this small change create widespread benefits?

Key Takeaway

Nonlinear influences amplify small actions. Finding these points allows you to focus efforts where they create the greatest impact.

Chapter 66: Build Strong Systems

The Foundation of Resilience

Strong systems are those that endure shocks, adapt to change, and continue to function under pressure. Building such systems requires careful design, incorporating flexibility, redundancy, and diversity to withstand disruptions and recover quickly. Whether you're managing a team, designing infrastructure, or maintaining an ecosystem, building a strong system ensures long-term success.

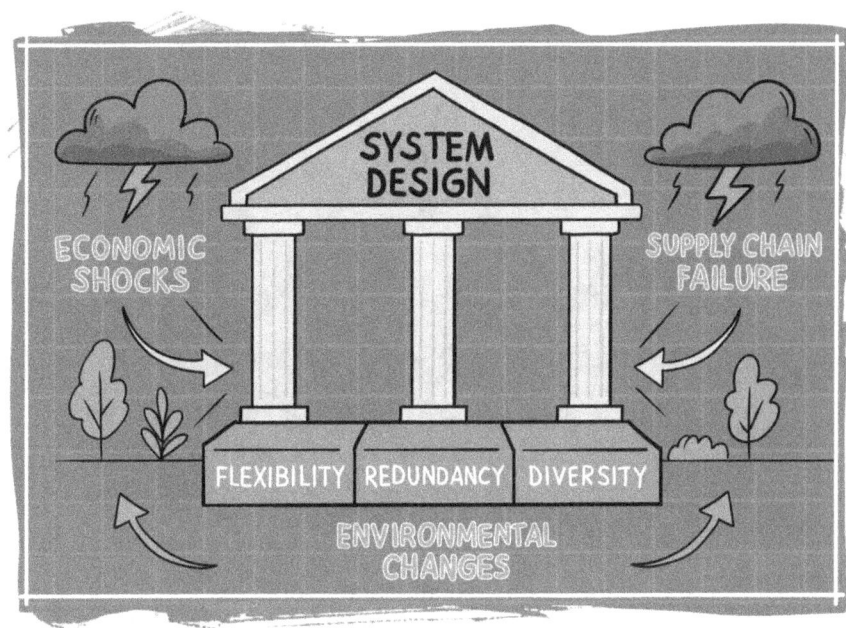

For example, natural ecosystems like wetlands are inherently strong because they combine diverse species, self-healing mechanisms, and flexible responses to environmental changes. When a flood occurs, wetlands absorb excess water, reducing damage to nearby areas. If one species is affected, others fill its role, maintaining balance.

Strong systems aren't rigid. They're adaptable. By balancing stability with the ability to evolve, these systems navigate uncertainty while maintaining their core functions.

How to Build Strong Systems

1. **Incorporate Redundancy:** Design systems with backups for critical functions, such as alternate supply chains or multiple communication channels.
2. **Foster Flexibility:** Ensure the system can adjust to new conditions, like adaptive workflows or modular designs.
3. **Enhance Diversity:** Include a variety of components — whether species, ideas, or stakeholders — to reduce reliance on a single element.
4. **Prepare for Stress:** Identify potential disruptions and design safeguards, such as risk management plans or emergency reserves.

Real-World Example

The Internet is a strong system due to its decentralized structure. Unlike traditional communication networks with single points of failure, the internet routes data through multiple pathways. If one connection is disrupted, others ensure the system continues to function, demonstrating redundancy and adaptability.

Why It Matters

Weak systems fail under stress, while strong systems persist and evolve. For example, businesses with rigid hierarchies often struggle to adapt to market changes, while those with decentralized decision-making thrive in dynamic environments.

Building strong systems also mitigates risk. Whether in natural disasters, economic downturns, or global crises, robust systems maintain stability and provide a foundation for recovery. For instance, resilient agricultural practices — like crop diversification — reduce vulnerability to pests, weather, or market fluctuations.

Strong systems inspire confidence and collaboration. When stakeholders trust a system's durability, they're more likely to invest, innovate, and engage, creating a virtuous cycle of growth and resilience.

Exercises

1. **Assess a System's Strength:** Choose a system you rely on, such as a workplace or community. Identify its strengths and weaknesses in handling stress.
2. **Design a Stronger System:** Apply principles of redundancy, flexibility, and diversity to improve a system you're part of. How can it better withstand disruptions?
3. **Simulate a Stress Test:** Imagine a scenario that challenges a system you know. How would it respond, and what changes could make it more resilient?

Key Takeaway

Strong systems balance stability with adaptability. Building them ensures resilience in the face of uncertainty.

Chapter 67: Eliminate Obstructions

Freeing the Flow

Obstructions — whether they are physical, procedural, or systemic — disrupt the flow of energy, information, or resources in a system. These bottlenecks slow progress, create inefficiencies, and reduce overall system performance. Eliminating obstructions is critical for restoring balance, improving efficiency, and unlocking the system's full potential.

For example, in supply chains, a single overloaded warehouse can delay shipments across an entire network. By identifying and addressing this bottleneck — perhaps by redistributing inventory or improving logistics — the system regains its flow, reducing delays and improving customer satisfaction.

Obstructions can be subtle, such as outdated processes or unproductive meetings, or obvious, like a failing component in a machine. Recognizing and removing them ensures that systems operate smoothly and adapt to changing demands.

How to Eliminate Obstructions

1. **Identify Bottlenecks:** Observe where flows slow down or stop, whether it's in communication, resource distribution, or decision-making.
2. **Analyze Root Causes:** Determine what's causing the obstruction. Is it a structural issue, a process inefficiency, or a lack of resources?
3. **Engage Stakeholders:** Involve those affected by the obstruction to gather insights and ideas for resolving it.
4. **Implement and Monitor Solutions:** Apply targeted interventions to remove the bottleneck, then monitor the system to ensure the obstruction doesn't return.

Real-World Example

In software development, teams often encounter bottlenecks during code reviews, where a single reviewer is overwhelmed with tasks. To address this, companies can train additional reviewers or automate parts of the process, freeing up the flow of work and speeding up project timelines.

Why It Matters

Obstructions reduce efficiency, waste resources, and frustrate stakeholders. Eliminating them unlocks the system's potential and creates opportunities for growth and innovation. For example, streamlining approval processes in an organization can reduce delays, empowering teams to act more decisively and achieve goals faster.

Addressing obstructions also fosters resilience. Systems with fewer bottlenecks are better equipped to handle stress, adapt to change, and recover from disruptions. For instance, decentralizing decision-making in disaster response ensures that critical actions aren't delayed by a single overwhelmed authority.

Beyond practical benefits, removing obstructions improves morale and engagement. When people see their efforts flowing smoothly, they're more motivated to contribute, creating a positive cycle of productivity and collaboration.

Exercises

1. **Map a Bottleneck:** Choose a system you're part of, such as a team workflow or a household routine. Identify one bottleneck that slows progress or creates frustration.
2. **Analyze the Obstruction:** Reflect on the root causes of the bottleneck. What factors contribute to the slowdown, and how might they be addressed?
3. **Propose a Solution:** Design and implement a change to remove the bottleneck. Monitor the results and consider whether further adjustments are needed.

Key Takeaway

Eliminating obstructions restores flow and efficiency. Targeting bottlenecks unleashes the full potential of any system.

Chapter 68:
Encourage Cross-System Collaboration

No system exists in isolation. Education, healthcare, transportation, the environment – all these systems interact and influence one another. Encouraging collaboration across systems reveals shared challenges, aligns goals, and creates solutions that benefit multiple areas simultaneously. Cross-system collaboration is essential for tackling complex problems and maximizing collective impact.

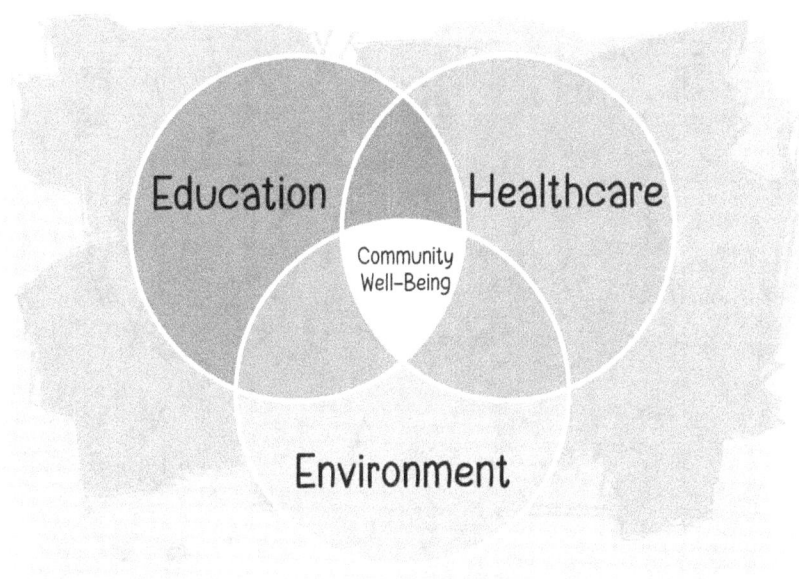

For example, addressing childhood obesity requires collaboration between education (to teach nutrition), healthcare (to monitor and manage health), and urban planning (to design safe spaces for exercise). When these systems work together, their combined efforts are far more effective than isolated actions.

Collaboration often uncovers synergies and opportunities that would otherwise remain hidden. It builds a culture of partnership, breaking down silos and fostering innovation that benefits the entire ecosystem.

How to Encourage Cross-System Collaboration

1. **Identify Shared Goals:** Look for areas where systems overlap or have mutual interests, such as improving public health or reducing resource waste.
2. **Engage Stakeholders:** Bring together representatives from different systems to share perspectives, identify connections, and brainstorm solutions.
3. **Align Efforts:** Coordinate actions to ensure that interventions in one system support or amplify efforts in another.
4. **Monitor Collective Impact:** Track how collaborative efforts influence all systems involved, refining the approach as needed.

Real-World Example

During the COVID-19 pandemic, governments coordinated between public health systems, educational institutions, and technology providers to facilitate remote learning. This collaboration ensured that students could continue their education while minimizing health risks, showcasing the power of cross-system partnership.

Why It Matters

Cross-system collaboration addresses challenges more effectively than isolated efforts. For example, integrating healthcare and social services ensures that patients receive holistic care, addressing both medical needs and underlying social determinants like housing or nutrition.

Collaboration also builds resilience. Systems that communicate and support one another adapt more effectively to disruptions, ensuring continuity of services. For instance, during natural disasters, partnerships between transportation, emergency response, and local governments enable faster recovery and resource distribution.

Encouraging collaboration fosters innovation by bringing diverse perspectives and expertise to the table. It breaks down barriers, aligns resources, and creates solutions that benefit multiple stakeholders.

Exercises

1. **Identify Overlaps:** Choose two systems you interact with, such as education and healthcare. Map areas where their goals or challenges overlap.
2. **Analyze a Collaboration:** Think of an example where systems worked together successfully. What made the collaboration effective, and what lessons can be applied elsewhere?
3. **Propose a Partnership:** For a problem you want to solve, suggest a collaboration between two or more systems. Outline how they could work together and what benefits might emerge.

Key Takeaway

Cross-system collaboration amplifies impact. Breaking silos and aligning efforts creates solutions that benefit multiple systems.

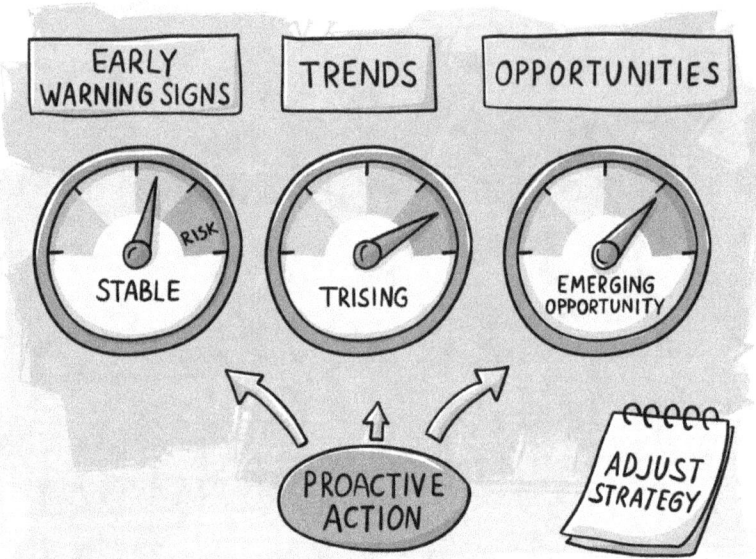

Chapter 69: Monitor Leading Indicators

The Early Signals of Change

Leading indicators are the early warning signs that give insight into how a system is likely to behave in the future. Unlike lagging indicators, which measure past performance, leading indicators point to emerging trends, risks, or opportunities. Monitoring these signals allows you to act proactively rather than reactively, making timely adjustments that can prevent problems or capitalize on advantages.

For example, in environmental conservation, declining pollinator populations are a leading indicator of broader ecosystem stress. Acting on this early signal—by addressing habitat loss or pesticide use—can prevent cascading failures that affect food systems and biodiversity.

Leading indicators are crucial in dynamic systems where change happens quickly. By focusing on these signals, you can better predict outcomes, adapt strategies, and build resilience against potential disruptions.

How to Monitor Leading Indicators

1. **Define Key Metrics:** Identify the specific indicators that provide early insight into system performance or health, such as resource levels, engagement rates, or behavior shifts.
2. **Track Regularly:** Set up systems to monitor these indicators consistently, ensuring that you capture trends as they emerge.
3. **Analyze Context:** Interpret leading indicators within the broader context of the system. What do changes in one area imply for the overall system?
4. **Act Promptly:** Use insights from leading indicators to adjust strategies, mitigate risks, or seize opportunities before they escalate or disappear.

Real-World Example

In finance, rising consumer debt levels often act as a leading indicator of economic downturns. By monitoring these levels, policymakers and businesses can adjust lending practices or prepare for potential slowdowns, reducing the impact of future crises.

Why It Matters

Monitoring leading indicators helps you stay ahead of change. Waiting for lagging indicators to confirm problems often means it's too late to prevent or minimize damage. For example, monitoring hospital admission trends during a disease outbreak allows health systems to prepare resources before cases peak, saving lives.

Leading indicators also uncover opportunities for innovation or growth. For instance, tracking user engagement on a new platform can reveal trends that guide future development, ensuring the system evolves in line with user needs.

This proactive approach reduces uncertainty and builds confidence in decision-making. It enables systems to adapt dynamically, responding to emerging signals instead of being blindsided by unexpected changes.

Exercises

1. **Identify a Leading Indicator:** Think of a system you're part of, such as a workplace or community project. What early signals could predict future success or challenges?
2. **Track a Trend:** Choose a metric to monitor over time, such as customer feedback or resource usage. Reflect on what changes in this indicator reveal about the system.
3. **Design a Monitoring Plan:** For a goal or system you're managing, outline a strategy to track and act on leading indicators. How will this plan keep you ahead of change?

Key Takeaway

Leading indicators are your early-warning system. Monitoring them enables proactive adjustments and better decision-making.

Chapter 70: Avoid Over-Optimization

Optimizing systems for maximum efficiency often seems like the ultimate goal. However, over-optimization can make systems brittle and vulnerable to disruptions. When every resource is used to its fullest capacity, there's no room for error, adaptation, or recovery, creating a system that's efficient but fragile.

Consider a factory operating with just-in-time inventory systems. While this reduces storage costs and improves efficiency, it leaves no buffer for supply chain delays. When a disruption occurs, such as a shipping delay or resource shortage, production grinds to a halt, revealing the hidden cost of over-optimization.

Striking a balance between efficiency and resilience is critical for building systems that are both high-performing and adaptable. Flexibility, redundancy, and safety margins may seem inefficient in the short term, but they are essential for long-term stability.

How to Avoid Over-Optimization

1. **Build Buffers:** Include safety margins in your system, such as backup resources, extra time, or redundant processes.
2. **Prioritize Resilience:** Balance efficiency with the ability to absorb shocks, adapt to change, and recover from setbacks.
3. **Test System Limits:** Regularly evaluate how the system performs under stress. Are there points where it becomes fragile?
4. **Plan for Uncertainty:** Design systems that can handle variability, whether it's fluctuating demand, environmental changes, or unexpected disruptions.

Real-World Example

In agriculture, monoculture farming is often optimized for maximum yield, focusing on a single crop. However, this approach makes farms highly vulnerable to pests, diseases, and climate fluctuations. By incorporating crop rotation and biodiversity — practices seen as less "efficient" — farmers build resilience, ensuring long-term productivity.

Why It Matters

Over-optimization sacrifices adaptability for short-term gains. While streamlined processes may work well in stable conditions, they fail under stress, leading to costly disruptions or even system collapse. For instance, power grids optimized without redundancy are more likely to experience widespread blackouts during high demand or equipment failures.

Balancing efficiency with resilience creates systems that perform well without compromising their ability to adapt. For example, businesses that maintain reserve funds or diversified supply chains are better equipped to weather economic downturns or market changes.

Recognizing the hidden costs of over-optimization helps you design systems that prioritize long-term sustainability over short-term perfection.

Exercises

1. **Assess a System's Flexibility:** Choose a system you know and evaluate whether it has room for adaptation or recovery. What changes could make it less fragile?
2. **Analyze Over-Optimization:** Reflect on a time when efficiency was prioritized over resilience. What were the consequences, and how could they have been mitigated?
3. **Design for Balance:** For a project or system, propose ways to balance efficiency with flexibility, ensuring it can handle uncertainty.

Key Takeaway

Over-optimization sacrifices resilience for short-term gains. Balancing efficiency with flexibility ensures long-term system stability.

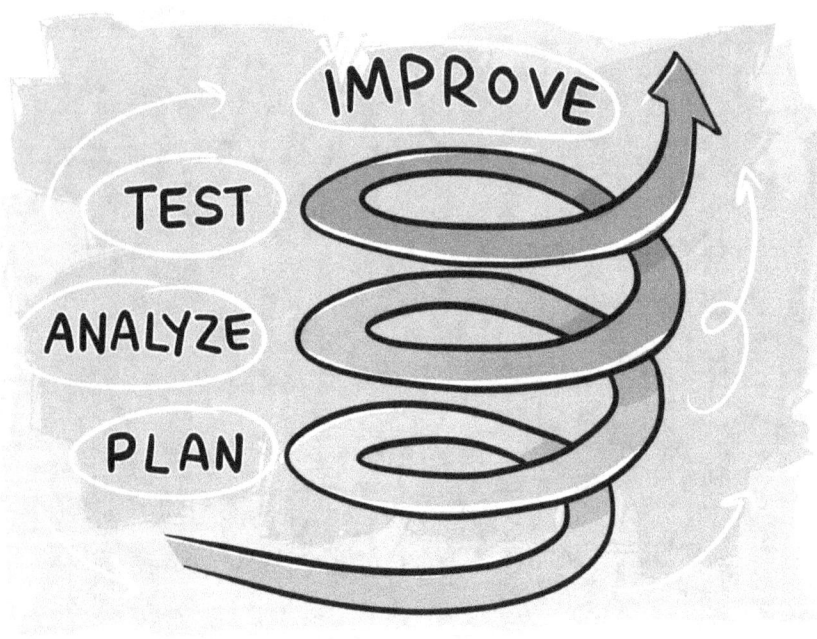

Chapter 71: Develop Iterative Solutions

Progress Through Iteration

In complex systems, solutions are rarely perfect on the first try. Iterative solutions embrace the idea of continuous refinement: starting with an initial idea, testing it, learning from results, and improving the approach in cycles. This method is particularly useful in dynamic or unpredictable systems, where conditions evolve and new challenges emerge.

Consider the development of mobile apps. Developers release a basic version (the minimum viable product), gather user feedback, and release updates to address bugs, add features, and enhance usability. Over time, the app evolves into a polished product that aligns with user needs, all thanks to iterative improvement.

Iteration fosters adaptability. Instead of waiting for a perfect plan, it allows you to act, learn, and adjust in real-time, ensuring that solutions remain relevant and effective.

How to Develop Iterative Solutions

1. **Start Small:** Begin with a basic version of your solution that addresses core needs without overcomplicating the design.
2. **Test and Gather Feedback:** Implement your solution on a small scale and monitor how the system responds. Collect feedback from stakeholders or users.
3. **Analyze Results:** Reflect on what worked, what didn't, and what unexpected outcomes emerged. Use these insights to refine your approach.
4. **Repeat and Scale:** Apply improvements in the next iteration, gradually expanding the solution's scope as it becomes more effective.

Real-World Example

Urban planners often use iterative approaches when introducing new infrastructure. For instance, a city might pilot a new bike lane on one street, monitor traffic and safety impacts, and make adjustments before rolling it out to other areas. This step-by-step process ensures that each iteration improves on the last, minimizing risks and maximizing benefits.

Why It Matters

Iterative solutions prioritize learning and adaptability, making them ideal for complex systems where static plans often fail. For example, in education, iterative approaches allow teachers to refine lesson plans based on student performance and feedback, improving outcomes over time.

Iteration also reduces the pressure to "get it right" the first time. By breaking solutions into manageable cycles, you can make progress without being paralyzed by the fear of failure. Each iteration builds on the last, creating a sense of momentum and continuous improvement.

This approach is also highly inclusive. Involving stakeholders in each phase of iteration ensures that solutions address diverse perspectives and needs, resulting in more equitable and effective outcomes.

Exercises

1. **Apply Iteration to a Goal:** Choose a project or problem you're working on and outline an iterative plan. What small step can you test first, and how will you refine it?
2. **Analyze Past Iteration:** Reflect on a time when you refined a process or solution over multiple attempts. What did you learn, and how did the iterations improve the outcome?
3. **Design a Feedback Loop for Iteration:** Identify how you'll gather feedback and measure success at each stage of an iterative project.

Key Takeaway

Iterative solutions embrace cycles of learning and improvement—this approach ensures adaptability and progress in dynamic systems.

Chapter 72:
Align Incentives

Incentives are the forces that drive behavior in a system, whether financial rewards, recognition, or intrinsic motivations. Aligning incentives means ensuring that individual goals are in harmony with the broader system's objectives. When incentives are misaligned, actions that benefit individuals may harm the system, leading to inefficiencies, conflict, or even collapse.

For example, in a workplace, if employees are rewarded solely for individual sales, they may prioritize personal gains over teamwork, harming customer satisfaction or long-term business growth. Aligning incentives — such as rewarding both individual performance and team collaboration — encourages behaviors that benefit both the individual and the organization.

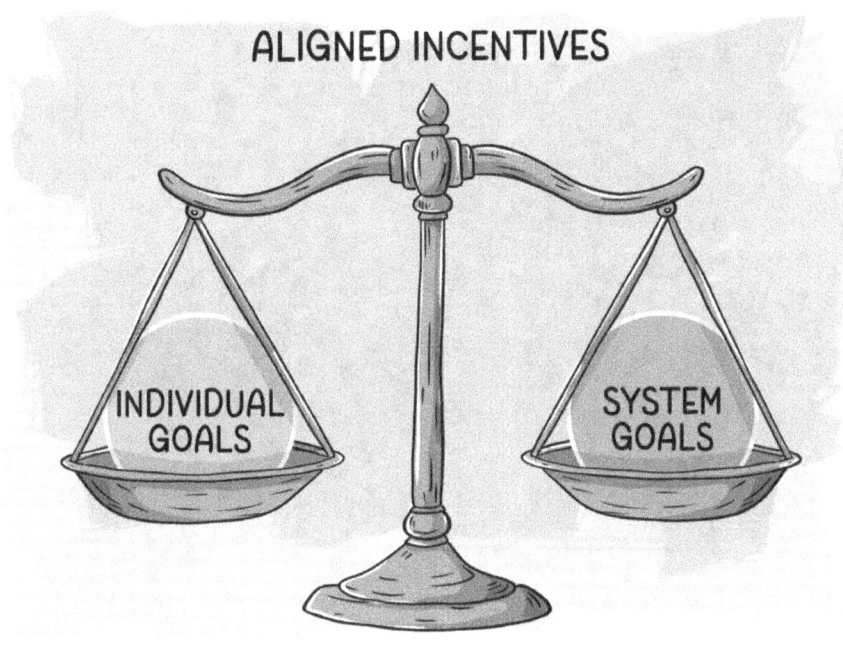

ALIGNED INCENTIVES

INDIVIDUAL GOALS

SYSTEM GOALS

This principle applies across systems, from public policy to ecosystems. By aligning motivations with desired outcomes, you create a system that naturally drives toward its goals.

How to Align Incentives

1. **Understand Current Motivations:** Identify what drives behavior in the system. Are these incentives leading to desired outcomes or unintended consequences?
2. **Define System Goals:** Clearly articulate what the system is trying to achieve, such as efficiency, sustainability, or equity.
3. **Create Shared Benefits:** Design incentives that reward actions benefiting both individuals and the system as a whole.
4. **Monitor and Adjust:** Continuously evaluate whether incentives are achieving their intended effects, and make adjustments as needed.

Real-World Example

In environmental conservation, carbon credit systems align financial incentives with sustainability goals. Companies that reduce emissions can sell credits to others, creating a financial motive for sustainable practices. This approach balances individual profit with global environmental benefits.

Why It Matters

Misaligned incentives create friction and inefficiencies, often driving behaviors that undermine the system's goals. For example, healthcare providers paid solely for the volume of procedures may prioritize quantity over quality, leading to over-treatment and higher costs. Aligning incentives with patient outcomes ensures better care and system efficiency.

Aligned incentives also build trust and collaboration. When stakeholders see that their interests are considered, they're more likely to engage constructively and work toward shared goals. This principle is particularly important in systems with diverse actors, such as communities or multinational organizations.

By designing incentives thoughtfully, you create a system that naturally moves toward success, reducing the need for constant oversight or correction.

Exercises

1. **Analyze a System's Incentives:** Choose a system you're part of, such as a workplace or community group. Are incentives aligned with the system's goals, or do they create conflict?
2. **Redesign Incentives:** For a system with misaligned incentives, propose changes that balance individual motivations with system-wide benefits.
3. **Track Incentive Impacts:** Implement a new incentive in a system you manage and observe how it changes behavior over time.

Key Takeaway

Aligning incentives ensures that individual actions support system-wide goals, creating harmony and driving collective success.

SHIFT PERSPECTIVE

Chapter 73: Broaden Your Scope of Analysis

Seeing the Bigger Picture

When solving problems or understanding systems, it's easy to focus too narrowly, analyzing only the most obvious elements or immediate factors. While this can yield quick insights, it often misses the larger context where true solutions lie. Broadening your scope of analysis involves stepping back to consider external influences, indirect connections, and long-term impacts. This approach ensures that you capture the full complexity of the system and avoid unintended consequences.

For example, when addressing urban traffic congestion, analyzing only road layouts may overlook broader factors like public transportation availability, population growth, and urban planning policies. Expanding the scope to include these elements can lead to more comprehensive and sustainable solutions, such as investing in mass transit or designing walkable neighborhoods.

Broadening your scope doesn't mean overcomplicating your analysis. Instead, it's about looking at the system in context, ensuring that every piece of the puzzle is considered before making decisions.

How to Broaden Your Scope

1. **Identify External Influences:** Ask what factors outside the immediate system might be affecting its behavior, such as economic trends, environmental changes, or cultural shifts.
2. **Map Interconnections:** Analyze how the system interacts with neighboring systems, such as how a supply chain depends on global trade or how an ecosystem interacts with urban development.
3. **Consider Long-Term Effects:** Look beyond short-term outcomes to evaluate how decisions might impact the system over time.
4. **Engage Diverse Perspectives:** Consult stakeholders from different fields or backgrounds to uncover blind spots and gain a more holistic view.

Real-World Example

In public health, addressing obesity requires a broad analysis that includes not only individual behaviors but also factors like food deserts, cultural norms, economic inequality, and urban design. Solutions that target these broader influences — such as creating policies for healthier food access — are far more effective than those focused solely on individual choices.

Why It Matters

Narrow analyses often lead to incomplete solutions or unintended consequences. For instance, focusing solely on expanding roads to reduce traffic might encourage more car usage, worsening congestion in the long run. Broadening your scope reveals alternative solutions, such as improving public transit or incentivizing carpooling.

This approach also enhances adaptability. Systems rarely operate in isolation, and external changes can disrupt even well-designed plans. By considering the bigger picture, you prepare for these shifts and ensure that solutions remain effective under changing conditions.

Finally, a broader scope fosters collaboration. When all interconnected elements are on the table, diverse stakeholders can align their efforts, creating solutions that benefit the entire ecosystem.

Exercises

1. **Expand an Analysis:** Choose a system you're analyzing, such as a workplace process or community issue. Identify factors outside the immediate system that could influence its behavior.
2. **Make Connections:** Create a diagram showing how your system interacts with neighboring systems or external forces. Reflect on what these connections reveal.
3. **Think Long-Term:** For a decision you're considering, imagine how it might affect the system five, ten, or twenty years from now. Does your solution hold up over time?

Key Takeaway

Broadening your scope of analysis reveals hidden connections and external influences. This holistic approach ensures more effective and sustainable solutions.

Chapter 74: Reduce Delays in Reporting

Timely Information, Better Decisions

In systems where decisions rely on feedback, delays in reporting create blind spots that lead to inefficiencies, poor outcomes, or even crises. Reducing these delays ensures that decision-makers receive accurate and timely information, allowing them to respond effectively and keep the system on track.

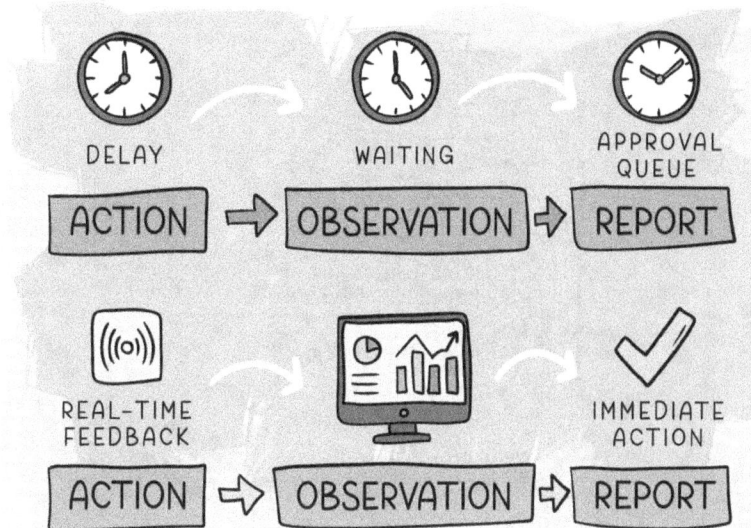

For instance, in disaster response, slow reporting of damages or resource needs can delay aid distribution, worsening the situation. Streamlining reporting processes — through real-time data collection or automated systems — improves coordination and ensures that help arrives when and where it's needed.

Timely reporting isn't just about speed; it's also about relevance. Information must be accurate, actionable, and delivered to the right people at the right time to make a difference.

How to Reduce Delays in Reporting

1. **Streamline Communication Channels:** Minimize unnecessary steps between data collection and decision-making, such as redundant approvals or manual reporting processes.
2. **Leverage Technology:** Use tools like sensors, dashboards, or real-time analytics to automate data collection and reporting.
3. **Prioritize Key Metrics:** Focus on collecting and sharing the most critical information, avoiding overload or distractions from less relevant data.
4. **Establish Clear Roles:** Assign responsibilities for data collection, validation, and reporting to ensure accountability and reduce bottlenecks.

Real-World Example

In manufacturing, real-time monitoring systems alert operators to equipment malfunctions as they occur. This immediate reporting allows for quick intervention, preventing costly downtime or further damage. In contrast, delayed reporting might result in extended shutdowns or safety risks.

Why It Matters

Delayed reporting often leads to missed opportunities or preventable failures. For example, in financial systems, outdated reports might cause investors to act on irrelevant data, leading to poor decisions or missed market opportunities. Faster reporting ensures that actions are based on current realities, not past conditions.

Reducing delays also improves system resilience. When disruptions occur, timely feedback allows for rapid adjustments, minimizing damage and restoring balance. For instance, during a supply chain disruption, real-time updates on inventory levels enable faster rerouting of resources, reducing losses.

Beyond practical benefits, streamlined reporting fosters trust and accountability. When stakeholders have access to accurate and timely information, transparency increases, and decision-making becomes more collaborative and effective.

Exercises

1. **Analyze Reporting Delays:** Choose a system you're part of, such as a workplace or community project. Identify points where delays in reporting slow down decision-making.
2. **Propose Improvements:** Design changes to reduce reporting delays, such as automating data collection or simplifying communication channels.
3. **Track Results:** Implement your changes and monitor how they impact decision-making speed and quality. Reflect on lessons learned.

Key Takeaway

Reducing delays in reporting ensures timely, accurate information. This accelerates decision-making and enhances system performance.

Chapter 75: Encourage Transparency

Transparency is essential for effective systems management. It means making processes, decisions, and flows within a system clear and accessible to everyone involved. When stakeholders understand how the system works — how resources move, how decisions are made, and what outcomes are expected — they can make better contributions and hold the system accountable.

For instance, in public budgeting, transparent systems that show where funds come from and how they are spent foster trust among citizens. This clarity helps avoid misunderstandings, reduces corruption, and allows for more informed participation in decision-making.

Transparency also ensures that potential inefficiencies, risks, or conflicts are spotted early. Without it, problems often remain hidden until they escalate, making them harder and costlier to address.

How to Encourage Transparency

1. **Document Processes Clearly:** Map out how the system functions, using diagrams or flowcharts to make information accessible to all stakeholders.
2. **Share Data Openly:** Make critical information, such as metrics, decisions, or outcomes, easily available to those who need it. Use dashboards, reports, or meetings to share updates.
3. **Eliminate Black Boxes:** Avoid processes or areas within the system that are opaque or understood by only a few individuals. Encourage knowledge sharing and collaboration.
4. **Solicit Feedback:** Actively seek input from stakeholders to ensure that transparency efforts are meeting their needs and that no information is being overlooked.

Real-World Example

In supply chain management, transparency is a growing focus. Companies use blockchain technology to track the movement of goods, providing real-time visibility into where products come from, how they're handled, and when they'll arrive. This level of transparency builds trust between suppliers, businesses, and customers.

Why It Matters

Without transparency, systems are prone to inefficiency, corruption, and conflict. For example, organizations with opaque decision-making processes often experience confusion or resentment among employees, reducing morale and productivity. Transparency ensures that everyone understands the goals and operations of the system, fostering alignment and collaboration.

Transparency also enhances accountability. When stakeholders can see how their actions impact the system and how the system serves its goals, they're more likely to act responsibly. This principle applies to everything from corporate governance to community initiatives.

Moreover, transparency strengthens trust. Whether between government and citizens, businesses and customers, or leaders and teams, clear communication and open access to information build confidence and mutual respect.

Exercises

1. **Evaluate Transparency:** Choose a system you interact with, such as a workplace or local government. Identify areas where transparency is strong and where it could be improved.
2. **Create a Transparency Plan:** For a project or system you manage, outline steps to make processes, data, or decisions clearer to stakeholders.
3. **Monitor Transparency's Impact:** Implement changes to improve transparency and track how they affect trust, efficiency, or collaboration within the system.

Key Takeaway

Transparency fosters trust, accountability, and efficiency. Making systems clear and accessible empowers stakeholders and improves outcomes.

Chapter 76: Counteract Perverse Incentives

When Incentives Go Awry

Perverse incentives are rewards or penalties that unintentionally encourage behaviors harmful to the system's overall goals. These misaligned motivations often arise from poorly designed policies, metrics, or structures, and they can have far-reaching consequences if left unchecked.

For example, a factory rewarded for producing the highest volume of goods might prioritize quantity over quality, leading to defective products and dissatisfied customers. Similarly, teachers judged solely on student test scores may focus on rote memorization rather than fostering critical thinking.

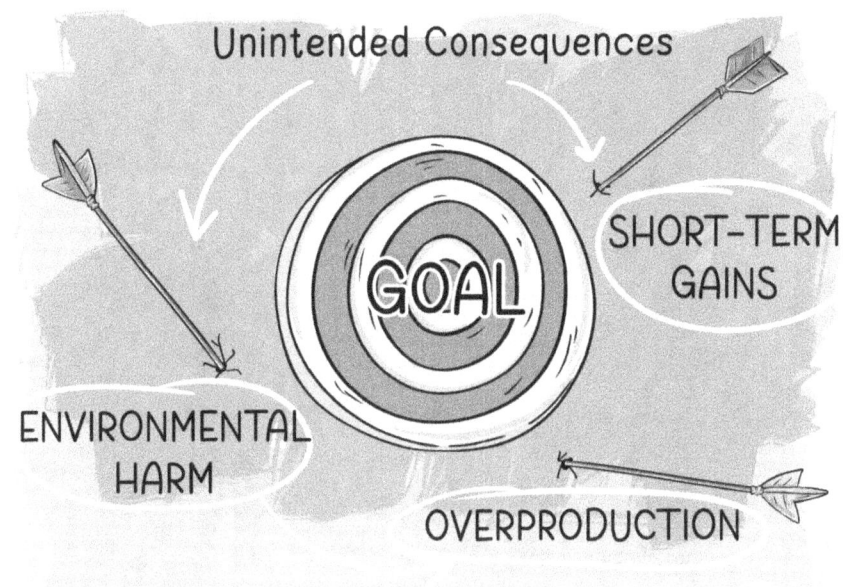

Counteracting perverse incentives requires carefully aligning rewards and penalties with desired outcomes. This ensures that individual actions support, rather than undermine, the system's broader objectives.

How to Counteract Perverse Incentives

1. **Identify Misaligned Rewards:** Analyze the system to find incentives that lead to unintended consequences, such as focusing on short-term gains at the expense of long-term goals.
2. **Clarify Desired Outcomes:** Define the system's objectives clearly, ensuring that incentives align with achieving these goals.
3. **Redesign Incentive Structures:** Adjust rewards and penalties to encourage behaviors that benefit the system as a whole.
4. **Monitor and Refine:** Continuously evaluate how incentives impact the system, making adjustments as needed to maintain alignment.

Real-World Example

In fisheries management, quotas designed to prevent overfishing sometimes create a "race to fish," where fleets rush to catch their limits before others, leading to unsafe practices and resource depletion. Transitioning to catch-share programs, where fishermen hold rights to a percentage of the total allowable catch, aligns incentives with sustainability, encouraging careful resource management.

Why It Matters

Perverse incentives undermine trust, efficiency, and long-term success. For instance, in healthcare, fee-for-service payment models can incentivize unnecessary treatments, driving up costs without improving patient outcomes. Addressing these misalignments ensures that the system serves its intended purpose effectively.

Aligned incentives also prevent resource waste. When motivations align with goals, resources are used more efficiently, and efforts are focused where they're most needed. For example, companies that reward innovation rather than excessive cost-cutting are more likely to thrive in competitive markets.

Counteracting perverse incentives fosters a culture of accountability and alignment. Stakeholders are more engaged and motivated when they see that their efforts contribute to meaningful and constructive outcomes.

Exercises

1. **Identify a Perverse Incentive:** Reflect on a system you're familiar with, such as a workplace policy or community initiative. Are there incentives that unintentionally encourage harmful behaviors?
2. **Redesign Incentives:** Propose changes to align rewards and penalties with the system's goals. How would these adjustments improve outcomes?
3. **Track Impact:** Implement a redesigned incentive and monitor its effects on behavior and system performance. What lessons can you apply moving forward?

Key Takeaway

Misaligned incentives lead to unintended consequences. Realigning them ensures that actions support the system's overall goals.

Chapter 77: Use Systems Thinking in Leadership

Leading Through Connection

Leadership in complex systems requires more than managing tasks or achieving immediate goals. It demands a holistic perspective—understanding how decisions ripple across interconnected parts and considering long-term impacts. Systems thinking equips leaders to anticipate challenges, identify opportunities, and align diverse components toward shared objectives.

Consider a CEO leading a company through digital transformation. A systems-thinking leader wouldn't just focus on implementing new technologies. They'd analyze how these changes impact employee workflows, customer experiences, and the broader market. By addressing these interconnected elements, they'd create a smoother transition that benefits the entire organization.

Effective leaders use systems thinking to foster collaboration, adapt to change, and ensure sustainable success. Instead of treating problems in isolation, they see the bigger picture, guiding their teams with clarity and purpose.

How to Use Systems Thinking in Leadership

1. **Develop a Holistic Vision:** Focus on the big picture, considering how decisions impact all parts of the system and their stakeholders.
2. **Engage Stakeholders:** Involve team members, partners, and communities in decision-making to gather diverse perspectives and build alignment.
3. **Anticipate Ripple Effects:** Analyze how short-term actions might create long-term consequences, ensuring that strategies align with the system's goals.
4. **Promote Adaptability:** Design systems and teams that can adjust to changing circumstances, ensuring resilience in the face of uncertainty.

Real-World Example

Jacinda Ardern, former Prime Minister of New Zealand, applied systems thinking during the COVID-19 pandemic. Her leadership balanced public health measures, economic stability, and social well-being, creating a coordinated response that minimized harm across interconnected systems. By engaging communities and considering diverse needs, she guided her country with empathy and effectiveness.

Why It Matters

Systems-thinking leaders create stability in complexity. When decisions are made without understanding how they affect interconnected parts, unintended consequences arise. For example, a company that cuts costs by downsizing staff might see short-term financial gains but suffer long-term productivity losses due to employee burnout and decreased morale.

Leadership grounded in systems thinking ensures that strategies are sustainable. By addressing root causes rather than symptoms, leaders create solutions that endure over time. For instance, a mayor improving urban transportation might focus not just on building roads but also on integrating public transit, walkable spaces, and bike lanes for a comprehensive solution.

Systems thinking also fosters collaboration. Leaders who see the connections between diverse stakeholders can build partnerships that amplify impact, aligning efforts toward common goals.

Exercises

1. **Analyze a Leadership Challenge:** Reflect on a complex decision you've faced or observed. How might systems thinking have changed the approach or outcome?
2. **Create a Systems Structure:** For a team or project you lead, map out the interconnections between people, processes, and goals. Use these guidelines to identify potential ripple effects.
3. **Practice Holistic Decision-Making:** Choose an upcoming decision and consider its short-term and long-term impacts on the system. How can you align it with broader goals?

Key Takeaway

Systems-thinking leaders see the big picture, anticipate ripple effects, and guide their teams with clarity and purpose, ensuring sustainable success.

Chapter 78: Apply Risk Management Systems

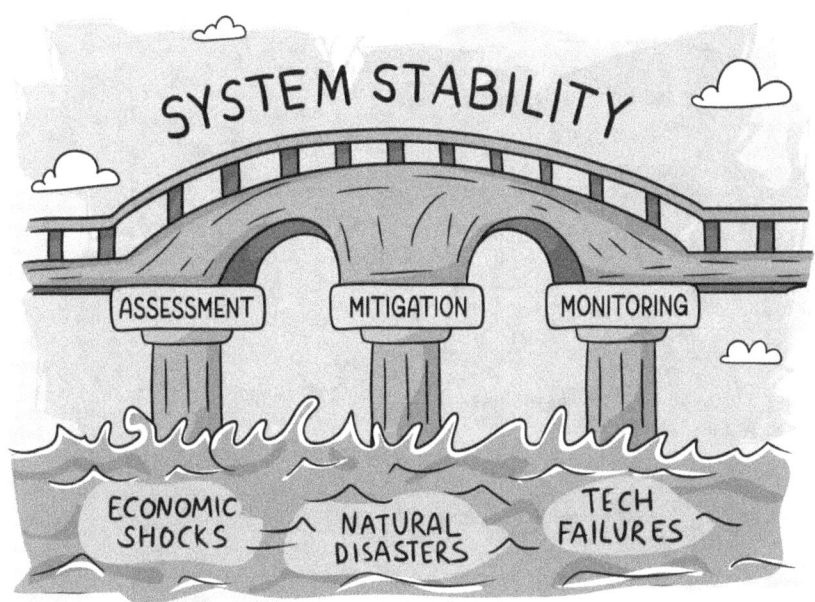

Every system faces risks — uncertainties that can disrupt its stability and performance. Risk management systems identify these potential threats, assess their likelihood and impact, and implement strategies to minimize harm. This proactive approach ensures that systems remain resilient, even in the face of disruptions.

Consider an energy company preparing for natural disasters. By identifying risks like hurricanes or droughts, assessing their potential to disrupt power grids, and implementing strategies like backup generators or grid diversification, the company can maintain services during crises.

Risk management isn't just about avoiding harm. It's about building systems that can adapt and recover. This approach fosters confidence and stability, ensuring that systems thrive even under challenging conditions.

How to Apply Risk Management Systems

1. **Identify Potential Risks:** Map out vulnerabilities in the system, such as resource dependencies, external pressures, or technological weaknesses.
2. **Assess Likelihood and Impact:** Evaluate how likely each risk is to occur and how severely it would affect the system. Prioritize high-impact risks.
3. **Develop Mitigation Strategies:** Create plans to reduce the likelihood or minimize the impact of key risks, such as diversifying suppliers or implementing redundancies.
4. **Monitor and Adapt:** Continuously track risks and update strategies as conditions change or new vulnerabilities emerge.

Real-World Example

In financial systems, stress tests simulate adverse scenarios — such as market crashes or interest rate spikes — to assess banks' resilience. These tests help institutions identify vulnerabilities and implement safeguards, such as maintaining higher capital reserves, ensuring stability during economic turbulence.

Why It Matters

Risk management systems protect against disruptions that can derail progress or cause significant harm. For example, a hospital without adequate risk management might run out of critical supplies during a pandemic, compromising patient care. Proactive planning ensures that resources are available when needed.

Effective risk management also enhances decision-making. By understanding potential threats, leaders can make informed choices that balance opportunities with safeguards. For instance, a company entering a new market might mitigate risks by piloting its product in a small region before expanding.

Beyond immediate benefits, risk management builds trust. Stakeholders are more likely to invest, collaborate, or participate when they see that systems are prepared for uncertainties.

Exercises

1. **Identify Risks in a System:** Choose a system you're part of and list potential risks it faces. Which are the most likely or impactful?
2. **Propose Mitigation Strategies:** For one key risk, design a plan to reduce its likelihood or impact. Consider redundancies, diversification, or contingency plans.
3. **Monitor Risks Over Time:** Implement a risk management plan and track its effectiveness. Adjust your strategies as conditions evolve.

Key Takeaway

Risk management systems protect against disruptions, ensuring that systems remain resilient and prepared for uncertainties.

Chapter 79: Strengthen Weak Connections

The Power of Connectivity

In any system, connections between components determine how well it functions. While strong connections foster collaboration, resilience, and efficiency, weak connections can create bottlenecks, reduce performance, and leave the system vulnerable to stress. Strengthening these weak links ensures that the entire system works cohesively and can handle disruptions more effectively.

For example, in a workplace, weak connections might appear as departments that rarely communicate, leading to misunderstandings or missed opportunities. Strengthening these links—perhaps through cross-department meetings or shared goals — improves collaboration, prevents inefficiencies, and drives innovation.

Weak connections often go unnoticed until a crisis exposes their fragility. By identifying and reinforcing them proactively, you create a system that's not only efficient but also adaptable and robust.

How to Strengthen Weak Connections

1. **Identify Fragile Links:** Map out the connections in your system and look for areas where communication, trust, or resources are lacking.
2. **Foster Collaboration:** Build bridges between disconnected parts of the system, such as through joint projects, regular meetings, or shared platforms.
3. **Invest in Resources:** Provide the tools, training, or support needed to strengthen weak connections, ensuring that all components can function effectively.
4. **Monitor and Adapt:** Continuously assess the strength of connections and adjust strategies as the system evolves or new weak points emerge.

Real-World Example

In supply chains, weak connections often appear as small, specialized suppliers that lack the capacity to meet surging demand. Strengthening these links — through financial support, training, or diversification of suppliers — reduces vulnerabilities and ensures smoother operations during disruptions.

Why It Matters

Weak connections are often the first points to fail during stress, causing cascading disruptions. For instance, in ecosystems, a decline in pollinator populations weakens connections between plants and insects, threatening food production and biodiversity. Addressing these weak links stabilizes the entire system.

Strengthening weak connections also promotes equity and inclusivity. In social systems, marginalized groups often represent weak connections due to limited access to resources or opportunities. By investing in these connections, systems become more equitable and resilient.

Finally, strong connections amplify the system's overall capacity. When all components are well-linked, they can share resources, coordinate efforts, and adapt more effectively to change.

Exercises

1. **Visualize Your System:** Create a diagram of the connections in a system you're part of, such as a workplace or community. Identify areas where connections are weak.
2. **Design a Strengthening Plan:** Choose one weak connection and outline steps to improve it, such as through communication, collaboration, or resource investment.
3. **Evaluate Progress:** Implement your plan and monitor how strengthening the connection impacts the system's overall performance.

Key Takeaway

Weak connections undermine systems. Identifying and strengthening them ensures resilience, equity, and cohesion.

Chapter 80: Design for Redundancy

Why Redundancy Matters

Redundancy often gets a bad reputation as inefficiency, but in systems thinking, it's a critical feature of resilience. Redundancy ensures that if one part of the system fails, others can take over, preventing total collapse. Whether it's backup servers in IT, alternative energy sources in power grids, or cross-trained employees in a workplace, redundancy allows systems to absorb shocks and recover quickly.

For example, during the COVID-19 pandemic, healthcare systems with redundant resources — like reserve staff and extra hospital beds — were better equipped to handle surges in patient numbers. Without these backups, many systems faced critical failures.

Designing for redundancy involves identifying critical functions, assessing vulnerabilities, and creating overlaps or backups that keep the system running smoothly, even under stress.

How to Design for Redundancy

1. **Identify Critical Functions:** Determine which parts of the system are essential for its operation, such as key processes, resources, or roles.
2. **Assess Vulnerabilities:** Analyze where failures are most likely to occur, whether from external disruptions or internal weaknesses.
3. **Build Backup Systems:** Create alternatives, such as duplicate resources, cross-training employees, or parallel processes, to ensure continuity.
4. **Test Redundancies:** Regularly evaluate how well backup systems perform under simulated stress, making improvements as needed.

Real-World Example

Airlines build redundancy into their safety systems by having duplicate instruments, backup pilots, and multiple layers of checks. If one system fails, another takes over, ensuring passenger safety and preventing catastrophic failures.

Why It Matters

Without redundancy, systems are brittle and prone to collapse when disruptions occur. For example, a factory with no backup machinery might lose weeks of production if a critical component breaks down. Redundancy provides the flexibility and resilience needed to adapt and recover.

Redundancy also creates opportunities for innovation. In workplaces, cross-training employees not only builds backup capacity but also enhances team versatility and collaboration. Similarly, diversified energy sources, like solar and wind, reduce reliance on fossil fuels while advancing sustainability.

Finally, redundancy fosters trust. Stakeholders feel more confident in systems designed to withstand stress, whether they're investors in a company, members of a community, or users of a service.

Exercises

1. **Identify Key Vulnerabilities:** In a system you manage, determine where failures are most likely to occur and what the consequences would be.
2. **Propose a Redundancy Plan:** Design backups or alternatives for one critical function, such as duplicate resources or cross-trained staff.
3. **Test and Evaluate:** Simulate a failure scenario to see how well your redundancy plan performs. Refine the plan as needed.

Key Takeaway

Redundancy isn't waste — it's resilience. Designing systems with backups ensures continuity and stability under stress.

Chapter 81: Avoid Unintended Consequences

Beyond the Immediate Outcome

When making decisions in complex systems, it's easy to focus on immediate goals without considering broader ripple effects. However, these systems are interconnected, and actions often produce unintended consequences — outcomes that weren't planned or desired. Understanding and anticipating these effects is critical for designing solutions that work holistically.

For example, introducing invasive species to control pests has often backfired in ecosystems. Cane toads were introduced to Australia to manage sugarcane pests, but they became a destructive force, outcompeting native species and disrupting local ecosystems.

The lack of foresight about the ripple effects turned a solution into a larger problem.

Avoiding unintended consequences doesn't mean predicting every possible outcome — it means adopting a mindset of caution, curiosity, and adaptability to minimize harm and adjust strategies as needed.

How to Avoid Unintended Consequences

1. **Map the System:** Identify how different parts of the system are connected and how changes in one area might affect others.
2. **Engage Diverse Stakeholders:** Consult people with different perspectives and expertise to uncover potential ripple effects you might overlook.
3. **Simulate Scenarios:** Use tools like modeling or role-playing to explore how a decision could play out under different conditions.
4. **Monitor and Adapt:** Once an action is implemented, track its effects closely, looking for signs of unintended consequences and adjusting as needed.

Real-World Example

In urban planning, building highways to reduce traffic congestion often leads to increased car usage — a phenomenon known as induced demand. This unintended consequence worsens the very problem it aims to solve. Cities that prioritize public transit and walkability avoid this trap, creating sustainable solutions that align with broader goals.

Why It Matters

Ignoring unintended consequences can create inefficiencies, inequities, or even crises. For example, agricultural subsidies meant to stabilize food production often encourage overproduction, leading to wasted resources and environmental harm. Anticipating these effects ensures that policies and actions serve their intended purpose without creating new challenges.

Understanding unintended consequences also fosters long-term thinking. Short-term fixes may seem appealing, but they often come at the expense of sustainability. By analyzing ripple effects, you can design solutions that balance immediate needs with future impacts.

Finally, this approach builds trust and credibility. When stakeholders see that decisions are thoughtful and account for potential risks, they're more likely to support and participate in the system.

Exercises

1. **Analyze Past Decisions:** Reflect on a policy or action that produced unintended consequences. What were the ripple effects, and how could they have been anticipated?
2. **Simulate a Decision:** Choose a potential action and consider its possible outcomes, both intended and unintended. How could you minimize negative effects?
3. **Develop an Adaptive Plan:** For a current challenge, design a strategy that includes monitoring and adjustment phases to address unintended consequences as they arise.

Key Takeaway

Actions in complex systems often have ripple effects. Anticipating and addressing unintended consequences ensures thoughtful, effective solutions.

Chapter 82: Enhance System Flexibility

The Need for Adaptability

Flexibility is the hallmark of resilient systems. In a world of constant change — economic shifts, technological advances, climate fluctuations — rigid systems often fail because they can't adjust to new conditions. Flexible systems, on the other hand, absorb shocks, adapt to challenges, and thrive in dynamic environments.

For instance, during the COVID-19 pandemic, companies with flexible work policies quickly transitioned to remote operations, maintaining productivity and supporting employee well-being. Organizations with rigid structures struggled to adapt, facing disruptions in workflows and employee satisfaction.

Flexibility doesn't mean abandoning structure or planning. It means designing systems with built-in capacity to adjust, ensuring they remain effective even under uncertainty.

How to Enhance System Flexibility

1. **Diversify Resources:** Avoid over-reliance on a single resource, supplier, or process. Diversity provides alternatives when disruptions occur.
2. **Embrace Modular Design:** Break systems into smaller, independent components that can be adjusted or replaced without disrupting the entire system.
3. **Encourage Experimentation:** Foster a culture of innovation where testing new ideas and learning from failures is embraced.
4. **Build Feedback Mechanisms:** Regularly monitor system performance and use insights to adapt strategies in real time.

Real-World Example

Ecosystems demonstrate natural flexibility. After a forest fire, plants adapted to fire-prone environments — such as fire-resistant trees or fast-growing grasses — quickly restore the ecosystem. This resilience stems from diversity and adaptability, ensuring that the system recovers even after significant disruption.

Why It Matters

Rigid systems are brittle, prone to collapse when conditions change. For example, companies that resist adopting new technologies often fall behind competitors who embrace innovation and adapt to evolving markets. Flexibility ensures that systems can pivot and thrive.

Flexibility also supports long-term sustainability. Systems designed to adapt are better equipped to handle ongoing challenges like climate change, economic instability, or population growth. For instance, cities with flexible zoning laws can adjust to changing needs, such as creating affordable housing during population surges.

Finally, enhancing flexibility fosters confidence and engagement. Stakeholders feel empowered when systems are adaptable and responsive, creating an environment of collaboration and innovation.

Exercises

1. **Identify a Rigid System:** Choose a system you interact with that struggles to adapt to change. What makes it rigid, and how could flexibility be introduced?
2. **Propose a Modular Design:** For a project or process, redesign it into smaller, independent parts that can be adjusted without disrupting the whole system.
3. **Test Flexibility:** Implement a small change in a system and observe how it adapts. Use the insights to improve its responsiveness to future challenges.

Key Takeaway

Flexibility ensures resilience. Systems that adapt to change are better equipped to thrive in dynamic environments.

Chapter 83: Seek Diversity for Stability

Diversity is a cornerstone of stability in systems. Whether in ecosystems, economies, or social structures, incorporating varied elements reduces reliance on any single component and creates resilience against disruptions. Diversity provides backup mechanisms, fosters innovation, and ensures that systems can adapt to change.

For example, ecosystems with diverse plant species are more resistant to pests and diseases than monocultures. If one species is affected, others can fill its role, maintaining ecosystem functions like nutrient cycling and soil stabilization. Similarly, organizations with diverse teams benefit from a broader range of perspectives, leading to creative problem-solving and better decision-making.

Seeking diversity isn't just about inclusion; it's about designing systems that are robust, flexible, and prepared to thrive under a wide range of conditions.

How to Seek Diversity

1. **Identify Vulnerabilities:** Look for areas in the system that rely heavily on a single resource, process, or perspective. These are points of fragility.
2. **Incorporate Multiple Elements:** Introduce varied components to reduce dependence on any one factor, such as diversifying suppliers, stakeholders, or approaches.
3. **Encourage Cross-Pollination:** Foster collaboration between different fields, industries, or disciplines to bring fresh ideas and solutions into the system.
4. **Monitor and Adjust:** Continuously evaluate whether diversity is improving resilience and adjust strategies as needed to address gaps or imbalances.

Real-World Example

In finance, diversified investment portfolios are a classic example of seeking diversity for stability. By spreading investments across different asset classes, sectors, and regions, investors reduce the risk of losses from any single market downturn, ensuring steadier overall performance.

Why It Matters

Homogeneity creates fragility. Systems that rely on a single crop, technology, or perspective are vulnerable to failure when conditions change. For instance, monoculture farming increases the risk of catastrophic crop failures due to pests or disease. In contrast, farms with diverse crops are more resilient and sustainable.

Diversity also fosters innovation. When systems integrate varied elements, they unlock new possibilities and solutions. For example, diverse teams in organizations consistently outperform homogeneous ones by bringing unique perspectives to problem-solving and decision-making.

Finally, seeking diversity supports equity and inclusion. Systems that embrace different voices and experiences are not only fairer but also better equipped to address the needs of all stakeholders.

Exercises

1. **Assess a System's Diversity:** Choose a system you interact with, such as a workplace, community, or project. Identify areas where diversity is strong and where it's lacking.
2. **Introduce Variety:** For a system you manage, propose ways to increase diversity, such as by adding new team members, strategies, or resources.
3. **Track Diversity's Impact:** Implement changes and monitor how increased diversity affects the system's stability, adaptability, or performance.

Key Takeaway

Diversity creates resilience. Incorporating varied elements strengthens systems and prepares them to thrive under changing conditions.

Chapter 84: Analyze Success Stories

Learning from What Works

Analyzing success stories offers valuable insights into what makes systems thrive. Whether it's a thriving ecosystem, a high-performing team, or a well-executed project, understanding why something worked reveals replicable practices and principles. This approach shifts the focus from merely solving problems to actively creating success.

For instance, Singapore's transformation from a resource-scarce city-state to a global economic hub is a success story built on strategic planning, innovation, and investment in human capital. By studying its journey, other cities can identify strategies like prioritizing education and fostering business-friendly policies to drive sustainable growth.

Success stories are more than inspiring — they provide blueprints for effective system design, revealing what aligns goals, resources, and processes to achieve exceptional outcomes.

How to Analyze Success Stories

1. **Select Relevant Examples:** Choose success stories similar to the system you're analyzing, ensuring their lessons are applicable to your context.
2. **Identify Key Drivers:** Focus on the factors that contributed most to the success, such as leadership, collaboration, or innovation.
3. **Extract Replicable Practices:** Highlight strategies or processes that can be adapted to your own system.
4. **Consider Contextual Factors:** Analyze what unique conditions or constraints shaped the success story and how they might differ from your own situation.

Real-World Example

Toyota's lean manufacturing system is a widely studied success story. Its focus on eliminating waste, improving efficiency, and empowering employees revolutionized the automotive industry. Organizations worldwide have adapted these principles — known as "lean thinking" — to enhance their operations, from healthcare to software development.

Why It Matters

Studying success shifts the narrative from problem-fixing to possibility-building. It provides practical insights into what works and why, helping systems move beyond survival toward thriving. For example, a non-profit studying a successful fundraising campaign can replicate strategies like personalized outreach or leveraging social media to achieve similar results.

Success stories also build confidence and momentum. Highlighting what's possible inspires teams and stakeholders to aim higher, fostering a culture of ambition and innovation.

Additionally, analyzing success uncovers transferable principles. Even if the exact context isn't replicable, the underlying strategies — such as prioritizing stakeholder engagement or leveraging technology — often apply across different systems.

Exercises

1. **Choose a Success Story:** Identify a system or project that succeeded in an area you're interested in. What made it effective?
2. **Extract Lessons:** Break down the success into key factors or strategies that contributed to its outcomes. How might you apply these lessons to your own system?
3. **Adapt and Test:** Implement one strategy from the success story in your context. Monitor its impact and refine it to fit your specific needs.

Key Takeaway

Success stories are blueprints for excellence — analyzing what works reveals lessons and practices that drive thriving systems.

Chapter 85: Foster Community-Led Solutions

Empowering Local Voices

Solutions that arise from within communities are often the most effective and sustainable. Community-led approaches leverage local knowledge, skills, and relationships to address challenges in ways that align with unique needs and contexts. This collaborative method not only creates practical solutions but also fosters a sense of ownership and empowerment among participants.

Consider participatory urban planning projects where local residents help design public spaces. In Medellín, Colombia, community involvement in transforming unsafe neighborhoods into vibrant areas with parks and libraries led to lasting change. Residents felt invested in the outcomes, ensuring the spaces were maintained and well-used.

Fostering community-led solutions shifts the focus from top-down interventions to bottom-up collaboration, ensuring that solutions resonate deeply with those they impact.

How to Foster Community-Led Solutions

1. **Engage Early and Often:** Involve community members from the start of the process, ensuring their voices shape both the goals and strategies.
2. **Leverage Local Knowledge:** Recognize and respect the expertise that communities have about their own challenges, resources, and dynamics.
3. **Facilitate Collaboration:** Provide platforms for dialogue and cooperation, where diverse stakeholders can share ideas, align efforts, and build trust.
4. **Support Capacity Building:** Equip communities with the tools, training, or resources they need to implement and sustain solutions.

Real-World Example

In Kenya, the M-Pesa mobile payment system emerged as a community-driven response to limited banking access. By addressing a local challenge with a solution tailored to the context, M-Pesa transformed financial inclusion for millions, becoming a global model for mobile banking.

Why It Matters

Community-led solutions ensure that interventions are practical and culturally appropriate. Top-down approaches often fail because they overlook local nuances or impose solutions that don't align with the community's reality. For example, international aid projects that ignore local customs may face resistance or inefficiencies, while those co-created with communities achieve greater acceptance and impact.

This approach also fosters resilience. When communities are empowered to solve their own challenges, they develop skills, networks, and confidence that prepare them to handle future issues independently.

Additionally, involving communities builds trust and accountability. People are more likely to support and sustain solutions they've had a hand in shaping, creating stronger and more cohesive systems.

Exercises

1. **Identify Community Assets:** Choose a community challenge and map its existing resources, skills, and networks. How might these be leveraged for solutions?
2. **Facilitate a Collaboration:** Organize a brainstorming session with diverse stakeholders to explore community-driven approaches to a local issue.
3. **Empower with Resources:** Design a plan to provide tools, training, or funding that supports a community in implementing its own solutions.

Key Takeaway

Community-led solutions align with local needs and foster empowerment. Collaborative approaches build trust, resilience, and long-term success.

Chapter 86: Identify Overlooked Costs

The Price You Don't See

In systems thinking, it's critical to recognize not just the obvious costs but also the overlooked ones — those that might not appear immediately but accumulate over time. Ignoring these hidden trade-offs often leads to inefficiencies, financial losses, or harm to stakeholders and the environment.

For instance, a company might cut costs by using cheaper materials, but the overlooked costs — product failures, loss of reputation, and warranty claims — outweigh the initial savings. Similarly, neglecting maintenance on infrastructure might save money in the short term but leads to far greater expenses when systems fail and require costly repairs.

Identifying overlooked costs ensures that decisions are made with a full understanding of their long-term impacts, avoiding pitfalls that could undermine the system's success.

How to Identify Overlooked Costs

1. **Consider Long-Term Impacts:** Analyze how decisions today might create expenses in the future, such as maintenance, resource depletion, or environmental harm.
2. **Assess Externalities:** Look for costs that might be shifted onto others, such as pollution affecting local communities or public health systems.
3. **Analyze Dependencies:** Recognize how decisions might strain other parts of the system, creating indirect costs like inefficiencies or delays.
4. **Involve Stakeholders:** Engage diverse perspectives to uncover costs that may not be immediately apparent from a single vantage point.

Real-World Example

Single-use plastics illustrate overlooked costs. While cheap and convenient, their environmental impact — including cleanup expenses, harm to marine life, and microplastic contamination — imposes massive costs on ecosystems and public health. Shifting to reusable materials addresses these hidden costs, promoting long-term sustainability.

Why It Matters

Overlooking costs often leads to short-sighted decisions that harm the system's resilience and sustainability. For example, companies that prioritize shareholder profits without investing in employee well-being often face high turnover rates, recruitment expenses, and productivity losses.

Accounting for all costs — visible and hidden — creates more balanced and sustainable strategies. For instance, renewable energy systems might seem costly upfront, but they eliminate long-term expenses associated with fossil fuel pollution, health impacts, and resource scarcity.

Additionally, identifying overlooked costs builds trust and accountability. Stakeholders are more likely to support decisions that consider broader impacts, ensuring equitable outcomes for all involved.

Exercises

1. **Analyze a Past Decision:** Reflect on a choice that seemed cost-effective initially but led to unexpected expenses later. What were the overlooked costs, and how could they have been accounted for?
2. **Map Externalities:** Choose a system or process and identify costs that might be shifted onto others, such as environmental or social impacts.
3. **Plan for Long-Term Costs:** For a current decision, outline potential hidden costs and propose strategies to address them upfront.

Key Takeaway

Overlooked costs undermine sustainability — recognizing them ensures balanced decisions that account for long-term impacts.

New Challenges and Opportunities

Chapter 87: Adapt to Changing Environments

Survival Through Adaptation

Change is inevitable, and systems that fail to adapt risk stagnation or collapse. Whether it's shifting market demands, evolving technologies, or environmental transformations, dynamic conditions require systems to adjust their processes, goals, and strategies. Adaptability isn't just about survival — it's about thriving in uncertainty and turning challenges into opportunities.

Take the retail industry, for example. Companies that quickly adapted to the rise of e-commerce, such as Amazon and Shopify, transformed their business models to meet changing consumer behaviors. Those that clung to traditional approaches struggled or disappeared. Adaptable systems recognize change as a constant and build mechanisms to respond flexibly.

By designing systems that evolve alongside their environments, you create resilience and ensure continued relevance, no matter how conditions shift.

How to Adapt to Changing Environments

1. **Monitor Trends:** Stay informed about external forces shaping the environment, such as technological advancements, social trends, or policy changes.
2. **Foster Agility:** Build systems that can pivot quickly, such as modular processes, cross-trained teams, or flexible technologies.
3. **Encourage Experimentation:** Test small changes to learn what works and scale successful strategies.
4. **Engage Stakeholders:** Involve diverse voices to anticipate changes from multiple perspectives and develop inclusive solutions.

Real-World Example

Netflix's evolution from DVD rentals to a streaming platform exemplifies adaptability. By recognizing the decline of physical media and the rise of online content, Netflix shifted its business model and pioneered an industry, staying ahead of competitors and maintaining its relevance.

Why It Matters

Failure to adapt often leads to irrelevance. For instance, Kodak, once a leader in photography, struggled to transition to digital technology, ultimately losing its market position to more adaptable competitors. Systems that anticipate and embrace change are better equipped to handle disruptions and seize emerging opportunities.

Adaptability also fosters innovation. As conditions change, new possibilities arise — whether through advancements in technology, shifts in consumer preferences, or environmental transformations. Adaptable systems harness these opportunities to grow and evolve.

Finally, adaptability ensures sustainability. Systems designed to evolve can respond to long-term challenges like climate change or population growth, creating solutions that endure over time.

Exercises

1. **Analyze Past Adaptation:** Reflect on a time when a system you were part of successfully adapted to change. What factors enabled this success?
2. **Anticipate Future Changes:** Identify trends or challenges that might affect a system you manage. How could you prepare to adapt to these changes?
3. **Design an Agile Strategy:** Choose a goal or process and outline steps to make it more adaptable, such as building in flexibility or testing new approaches.

Key Takeaway

Adaptability ensures resilience — systems that evolve alongside changing environments thrive in uncertainty and seize opportunities for growth.

Chapter 88: Optimize for Long-Term Outcomes

Thinking Beyond the Immediate

In a fast-paced world, it's tempting to focus on short-term goals — whether cutting costs, meeting deadlines, or achieving quick wins. However, optimizing for long-term outcomes creates stability, sustainability, and greater value over time. This approach requires balancing immediate needs with broader objectives, ensuring that actions today build a foundation for tomorrow.

For instance, investing in renewable energy infrastructure may be costly upfront, but it yields long-term benefits in reduced emissions, energy independence, and economic savings. Similarly, companies that prioritize employee development may see short-term costs but gain a loyal, skilled workforce that drives sustained success.

Optimizing for the long term means adopting a mindset of patience, planning, and purpose, ensuring that systems are designed to endure and thrive.

How to Optimize for Long-Term Outcomes

1. **Clarify Long-Term Goals:** Define what success looks like over years or decades, aligning actions with these objectives.
2. **Evaluate Trade-Offs:** Analyze how short-term decisions might impact long-term outcomes, ensuring that immediate benefits don't undermine sustainability.
3. **Invest Strategically:** Prioritize resources for initiatives that deliver enduring value, even if they require upfront sacrifices.
4. **Monitor Progress:** Regularly track how actions align with long-term goals, adjusting strategies to stay on course.

Real-World Example

The reforestation efforts in Costa Rica exemplify long-term thinking. By protecting forests and restoring degraded lands, the country has created sustainable ecosystems that support biodiversity, tourism, and climate resilience, proving that investments in the environment yield lasting benefits.

Why It Matters

Short-term thinking often creates inefficiencies and missed opportunities. For example, businesses that prioritize quarterly profits over long-term growth may underinvest in innovation, ultimately losing their competitive edge. Optimizing for long-term outcomes ensures that systems remain relevant and robust.

Long-term thinking also aligns with sustainability. Systems that consider future impacts, such as green infrastructure or education reform, address root causes rather than symptoms, creating solutions that endure.

Additionally, focusing on the long term builds trust. Stakeholders recognize and value organizations and systems that prioritize future well-being, fostering loyalty and collaboration.

Exercises

1. **Analyze a Short-Term Trade-Off:** Reflect on a recent decision that prioritized immediate results. How might a focus on long-term outcomes have changed the approach or results?
2. **Set a Long-Term Goal:** Choose a system or project and outline its desired outcomes over the next decade. What steps today will support these goals?
3. **Design for Endurance:** Propose a strategy to optimize a system for long-term success, such as investing in training, infrastructure, or sustainability initiatives.

Key Takeaway

Optimizing for long-term outcomes ensures sustainability and stability — decisions today build the foundation for success tomorrow.

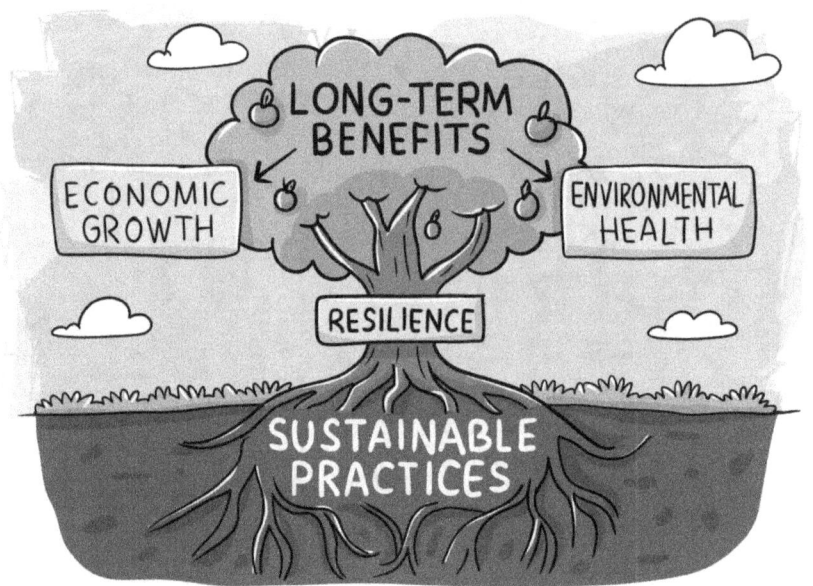

Chapter 89: Create Sustainable Systems

Building Systems That Endure

Sustainability ensures that systems can meet present needs without compromising the ability of future generations to thrive. It involves balancing economic, environmental, and social goals, recognizing their interconnections and mutual dependence. Sustainable systems prioritize longevity, resilience, and equity, creating value that extends far beyond immediate outcomes.

For example, Denmark's investment in wind energy demonstrates sustainability in action. By shifting to renewable energy, the country reduces its reliance on fossil fuels, protects the environment, and creates green jobs, achieving economic and ecological benefits simultaneously.

Creating sustainable systems requires intentional design, long-term thinking, and a commitment to adaptability. Whether in urban planning, business strategy, or community development, sustainability offers a path to thriving in a resource-constrained world.

How to Create Sustainable Systems

1. **Integrate Interdependence:** Recognize how economic, environmental, and social elements interact, ensuring that strategies benefit all three dimensions.
2. **Prioritize Renewable Resources:** Design systems that rely on resources that regenerate or recycle, reducing waste and environmental harm.
3. **Address Inequities:** Ensure that all stakeholders have access to the system's benefits, fostering inclusivity and fairness.
4. **Monitor Sustainability Metrics:** Track indicators such as resource use, emissions, or social equity to measure and improve sustainability.

Real-World Example

The Netherlands' water management system is a global model of sustainability. By integrating ecological restoration, flood prevention, and urban development, the Dutch have created systems that protect communities while supporting biodiversity and tourism.

Why It Matters

Unsustainable systems create fragility and inequity. For example, overexploiting natural resources might boost profits temporarily but leads to environmental degradation, resource scarcity, and economic instability. Sustainable systems ensure that benefits endure across generations.

Sustainability also drives innovation. By addressing challenges like climate change or inequality, systems uncover new opportunities, such as green technologies or community-driven solutions. For example, companies investing in sustainable supply chains often gain competitive advantages in increasingly eco-conscious markets.

Finally, sustainable systems build trust. When stakeholders see a commitment to long-term well-being, they're more likely to engage, support, and collaborate, creating a virtuous cycle of growth and stability.

Exercises

1. **Evaluate a System:** Choose a system you're part of and assess its sustainability in terms of economic, environmental, and social dimensions. What improvements could make it more balanced?
2. **Propose a Sustainable Initiative:** Design a project or policy that prioritizes long-term sustainability, such as a renewable energy program or community-based recycling effort.
3. **Track Metrics:** Implement your initiative and monitor its sustainability indicators. Reflect on lessons learned and potential refinements.

Key Takeaway

Sustainable systems balance economic, environmental, and social goals. Intentional design ensures longevity and thriving across generations.

Chapter 90: Incorporate Circular Economy Principles

A circular economy replaces the traditional "take-make-waste" model with one that keeps resources in use for as long as possible. By designing products, processes, and systems to minimize waste and maximize reuse, circular economies create value while reducing environmental impact.

For instance, Patagonia, the outdoor clothing company, incorporates circular economy principles by offering repair services, recycling old garments, and creating products from recycled materials. This approach not only reduces waste but also strengthens customer loyalty and brand identity.

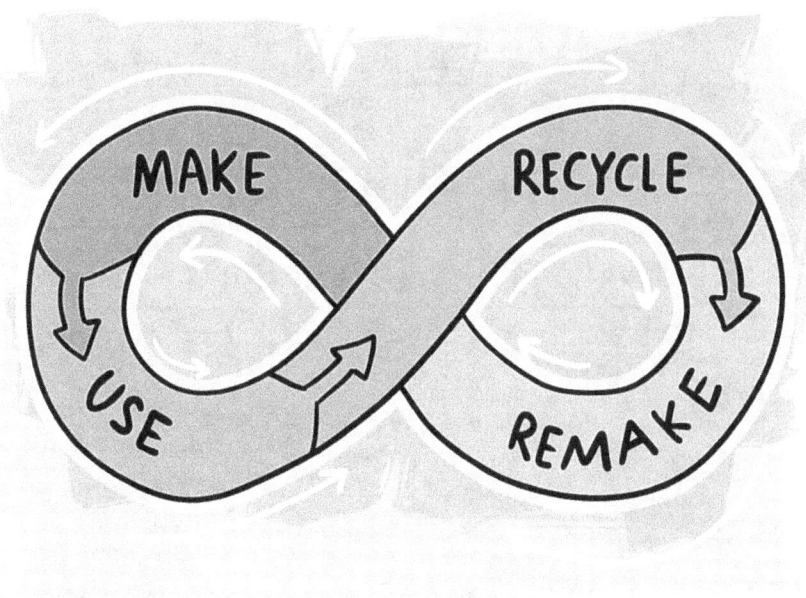

Incorporating circular economy principles requires rethinking how resources flow through systems. It's about designing for regeneration, ensuring that nothing is wasted and everything has a purpose.

How to Incorporate Circular Economy Principles

1. **Design for Longevity:** Create products and systems that last longer, with components that are easy to repair, upgrade, or reuse.
2. **Minimize Waste:** Identify points where resources are discarded and redesign processes to capture and reuse them.
3. **Promote Sharing and Reuse:** Encourage models like sharing platforms or product-as-a-service to maximize resource efficiency.
4. **Close Material Loops:** Ensure that materials are recycled or composted back into the system, reducing dependence on virgin resources.

Real-World Example

In Sweden, a "recycling revolution" has led to only 1% of household waste being sent to landfills. Through rigorous recycling, waste-to-energy programs, and public engagement, Sweden has become a global leader in closing material loops and reducing environmental impact.

Why It Matters

Linear systems that rely on extracting resources and discarding waste are inherently unsustainable. They deplete finite materials, pollute ecosystems, and create economic inefficiencies. Circular economies address these issues by keeping resources in use, reducing environmental harm, and creating economic opportunities.

Circular systems also drive innovation. By rethinking traditional processes, businesses and communities uncover new ways to create value, such as developing biodegradable packaging or using waste as raw material for new products.

Finally, circular economy principles align with societal shifts toward sustainability. As consumers increasingly demand eco-friendly options, organizations that embrace circular models position themselves as leaders in a changing market.

Exercises

1. **Identify Waste in a System:** Choose a system or process you're familiar with and map points where resources are wasted. How could these materials be reused or recycled?
2. **Design a Circular Product:** Develop a concept for a product or service that incorporates circular economy principles, such as durability, repairability, or recyclability.
3. **Promote Circular Practices:** Create a plan to implement circular practices in a community or workplace, such as a composting program or material-sharing initiative.

Key Takeaway

Circular economies create value by keeping resources in use. Incorporating these principles reduces waste and builds sustainable systems.

Chapter 91: Match Innovation with Stability

Balancing Change and Continuity

Innovation drives progress, but without stability, it can disrupt systems or lead to unsustainable growth. Stability provides the foundation that allows innovation to flourish without causing chaos. Matching these two forces creates systems that are dynamic yet dependable, capable of evolving while maintaining their core functions.

Consider the renewable energy sector. While innovation has led to breakthroughs like solar panels and wind turbines, stable infrastructure — such as reliable grids and storage solutions — ensures that these technologies integrate seamlessly into existing energy systems. The balance allows for progress without risking blackouts or inefficiencies.

By aligning innovation with stability, you can create systems that adapt to new challenges and opportunities while preserving the structures that sustain them.

How to Match Innovation with Stability

1. **Identify Core Functions:** Define which parts of the system must remain stable to ensure reliability, such as essential services, processes, or values.
2. **Encourage Experimentation:** Create space for testing and adopting innovative ideas without disrupting the system's foundation.
3. **Develop Supportive Structures:** Ensure that stable processes, resources, or policies enable innovation to thrive without causing imbalance.
4. **Monitor System Dynamics:** Regularly assess how innovation and stability interact, making adjustments to maintain balance.

Real-World Example

The automotive industry demonstrates this balance. Electric vehicle (EV) manufacturers innovate with battery technologies and autonomous driving, while stable supply chains and manufacturing standards ensure consistent quality and reliability. Together, these forces drive progress without sacrificing trust or functionality.

Why It Matters

Innovation without stability leads to fragility. For example, start-ups that scale too quickly often collapse under the weight of insufficient processes or resources. Stability ensures that systems can absorb and sustain growth.

On the other hand, stability without innovation fosters stagnation. Organizations or systems that resist change risk becoming obsolete, as seen in industries that fail to adapt to technological advancements. Matching stability with innovation ensures continued relevance and resilience.

This balance also builds stakeholder confidence. Stable systems that embrace change demonstrate reliability and forward-thinking, fostering trust among investors, employees, and communities.

Exercises

1. **Analyze a System:** Identify a system you're part of, such as a workplace or community. Are innovation and stability balanced, or does one dominate?
2. **Propose a Balanced Strategy:** Design an approach to integrate a new idea or technology while maintaining the system's essential functions.
3. **Evaluate Progress:** Implement your strategy and track how the balance between innovation and stability affects the system's performance.

Key Takeaway

Innovation and stability are complementary forces. Aligning them creates systems that evolve while maintaining resilience and reliability.

Chapter 92: Focus on Interdependence

Everything is Connected

Interdependence lies at the heart of systems thinking. No element of a system operates in isolation — each is connected to and influenced by others. Recognizing and strengthening these connections ensures that systems function cohesively, adapt to change, and achieve shared goals.

For example, sustainable agriculture depends on healthy ecosystems, economic viability, and social support. Farmers need fertile soil (environment), fair prices (economy), and community cooperation (social systems). When these elements work together, the entire system thrives. Ignoring one weakens the others, leading to instability.

Focusing on interdependence means designing systems where connections are acknowledged, nurtured, and leveraged to create positive feedback and resilience.

How to Focus on Interdependence

1. **Map Relationships:** Identify how elements within the system are connected, such as dependencies between stakeholders, processes, or resources.
2. **Strengthen Links:** Build bridges between disconnected or weakly connected parts of the system, fostering collaboration and coordination.
3. **Align Goals:** Ensure that different components of the system work toward shared objectives, reducing conflict and inefficiency.
4. **Monitor Changes:** Continuously evaluate how shifts in one part of the system affect others, adjusting strategies as needed.

Real-World Example

The One Health approach to global health recognizes the interdependence of human, animal, and environmental health. By addressing these areas collectively — such as combating zoonotic diseases or promoting sustainable farming — this approach creates solutions that benefit all interconnected systems.

Why It Matters

Ignoring interdependence often leads to unintended consequences. For instance, deforestation might provide short-term economic gains but disrupt ecosystems, water cycles, and local communities, causing long-term harm. Recognizing these connections ensures balanced decisions.

Focusing on interdependence also fosters collaboration. When systems are designed to align efforts, such as government agencies working with businesses and non-profits, they achieve more cohesive and impactful results.

Finally, interdependence enhances resilience. Well-connected systems distribute resources, knowledge, and support, making them better equipped to handle disruptions or crises.

Exercises

1. **Identify Interdependencies:** Choose a system you interact with and create a diagram of how its elements connect. Reflect on how strengthening these links could improve performance.
2. **Analyze a Disruption:** Think of a time when one part of a system failed. How did it affect other components, and what could have minimized the impact?
3. **Design Collaborative Solutions:** Propose a strategy that leverages interdependence to address a challenge, such as creating partnerships or integrating processes.

Key Takeaway

Interdependence is the foundation of system health. Acknowledging and strengthening connections ensures cohesive, resilient systems.

Chapter 93: Address Core Problems

In complex systems, it's easy to get caught up addressing surface-level symptoms, such as inefficiencies or recurring crises. However, these are often signals of deeper issues — core problems rooted in the system's structure or design. Addressing core problems directly leads to more sustainable and impactful solutions, preventing the same symptoms from re-emerging.

For example, addressing traffic congestion by expanding roads might temporarily reduce delays but often worsens the problem through induced demand. The core problem—lack of public transportation or overreliance on cars—remains unaddressed. Shifting focus to developing efficient public transit systems or walkable cities tackles the root cause, creating long-term solutions.

By identifying and solving core problems, you reduce waste, frustration, and inefficiency, building systems that operate smoothly and effectively.

How to Address Core Problems

1. **Trace Symptoms to Causes:** Use tools such as root-cause analysis to uncover the underlying issues driving surface-level problems.
2. **Examine System Structure:** Identify elements like feedback cycles, bottlenecks, or imbalances that perpetuate core problems.
3. **Prioritize Impactful Solutions:** Focus on interventions that address root causes rather than quick fixes for symptoms.
4. **Involve Stakeholders:** Collaborate with those affected to ensure the core problem is accurately identified and the solution is widely supported.

Real-World Example

The Flint water crisis highlighted the danger of addressing symptoms without tackling core problems. Short-term solutions, such as switching water sources, failed to address systemic issues like infrastructure neglect and inadequate oversight. Only by focusing on these root causes can sustainable solutions for clean, safe water be achieved.

Why It Matters

Focusing on symptoms creates inefficiencies and wastes resources. For instance, repeatedly patching a leaking pipe without replacing it leads to ongoing costs and disruptions. Tackling the core issue—replacing outdated infrastructure — provides a lasting fix.

Addressing core problems also prevents cascading failures. In ecosystems, ignoring issues like habitat destruction can lead to widespread consequences, from species extinction to climate instability. Solving root causes stabilizes the entire system.

Finally, targeting core problems fosters innovation and resilience. Solutions that address foundational issues often unlock new opportunities for growth and collaboration, strengthening the system as a whole.

Exercises

1. **Trace a Problem's Roots:** Choose a recurring issue in a system you interact with and analyze its root causes. What structural factors or feedback loops sustain it?
2. **Propose a Core Solution:** Design an intervention that addresses the root cause of the problem. How would this approach prevent symptoms from recurring?
3. **Monitor Impact:** Implement your solution and track how effectively it eliminates symptoms. Reflect on lessons learned and potential refinements.

Key Takeaway

Sustainable solutions focus on core problems — addressing root causes builds efficient, resilient systems that prevent recurring issues.

Chapter 94:
Simplify Complex Systems

The Elegance of Simplicity

Complex systems can be overwhelming, with layers of processes, stakeholders, and interdependencies. While some complexity is inherent and necessary, much of it stems from inefficiencies, outdated practices, or unclear priorities. Simplifying systems allows you to focus on critical components, improving efficiency, clarity, and adaptability.

Consider healthcare systems burdened by excessive administrative processes. Streamlining patient records, automating repetitive tasks, and reducing bureaucratic hurdles frees up resources for direct patient care, improving outcomes and efficiency.

Simplification doesn't mean oversimplifying — it's about removing unnecessary complications while retaining the system's essential functions and goals.

How to Simplify Complex Systems

1. **Identify Key Components:** Distinguish between essential and nonessential elements, focusing on what drives the system's core functions.
2. **Streamline Processes:** Eliminate redundancies, bottlenecks, or unnecessary steps that slow the system down.
3. **Use Clear Communication:** Standardize language, formats, or tools to ensure that all stakeholders understand the system's goals and operations.
4. **Test for Efficiency:** Implement changes incrementally, evaluating how each adjustment improves clarity or performance.

Real-World Example

The Kanban method, used in manufacturing and project management, simplifies workflows by visualizing tasks on a board. This approach helps teams identify priorities, track progress, and reduce inefficiencies, making complex projects more manageable and transparent.

Why It Matters

Unnecessary complexity creates frustration and inefficiency. For example, complicated tax codes confuse taxpayers and increase compliance costs. Simplifying forms and processes improves accessibility and reduces errors.

Simplified systems are also more adaptable. When external conditions change, streamlined structures can pivot more easily than cumbersome, overly layered ones. For instance, businesses with clear decision-making processes adjust more quickly to market shifts than those bogged down by excessive approvals.

Finally, simplification fosters collaboration. Clear, well-organized systems make it easier for stakeholders to engage, share insights, and align efforts, enhancing overall performance.

Exercises

1. **Map a Complex System:** Choose a system you interact with and create a diagram of its components. Identify areas where complexity could be reduced.
2. **Propose Simplifications:** Suggest changes to streamline processes, such as removing redundancies or standardizing communication tools.
3. **Evaluate Simplification's Impact:** Implement your proposed changes and monitor how they affect the system's efficiency and effectiveness.

Key Takeaway

Simplifying complex systems enhances clarity, efficiency, and adaptability. Focusing on essentials ensures sustainable and effective performance.

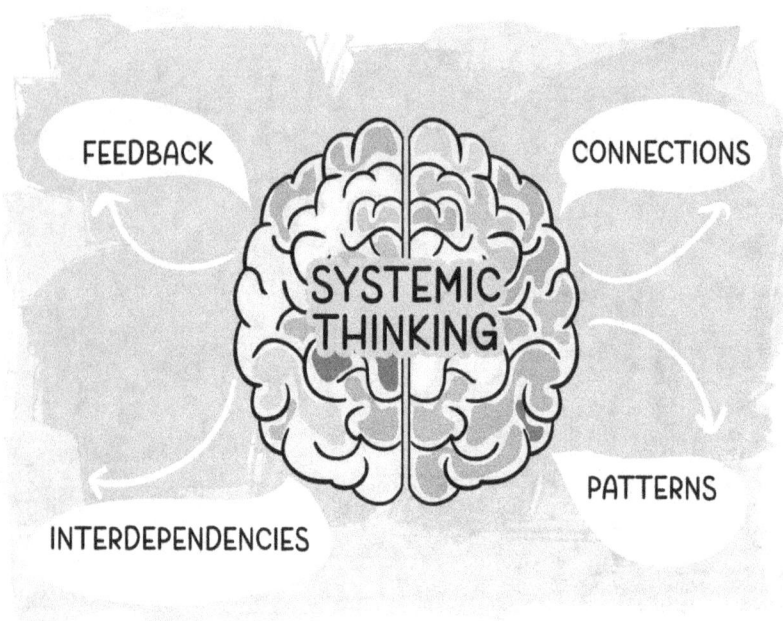

FEEDBACK

CONNECTIONS

SYSTEMIC THINKING

PATTERNS

INTERDEPENDENCIES

Chapter 95: Develop Systemic Thinking Habits

Cultivating a Systems Mindset

Systems thinking isn't just a tool; it's a habit — a way of seeing and understanding the world. Developing systemic thinking habits involves training your mind to recognize patterns, connections, and interdependencies in everyday situations. This mindset transforms how you approach problems, plan solutions, and navigate complexity.

For instance, a teacher using systemic thinking might not only focus on individual student performance but also consider factors like classroom dynamics, family support, and curriculum design. By addressing these interconnected elements, the teacher creates a more supportive and effective learning environment.

Making systems thinking a habit requires practice, curiosity, and a commitment to looking beyond the surface. Over time, this approach becomes second nature, enabling you to make smarter, more informed decisions.

How to Develop Systemic Thinking Habits

1. **Practice Seeing Connections:** Regularly map out how different elements in a situation influence one another, such as how workplace morale affects productivity.
2. **Ask Big-Picture Questions:** When faced with a problem, ask how it fits into the larger system. What forces are shaping it, and how do they interact?
3. **Reflect on Ripple Effects:** Consider how changes in one part of the system might affect others, both immediately and over time.
4. **Embrace Continuous Learning:** Read, observe, and engage with diverse systems—natural, organizational, or societal—to expand your understanding of how they function.

Real-World Example

In urban planning, systemic thinkers consider the interplay between housing, transportation, economic opportunities, and public health. This holistic perspective leads to integrated solutions, such as mixed-use developments that reduce commuting times while promoting community well-being.

Why It Matters

Systemic thinking habits enhance problem-solving by encouraging you to look beyond symptoms and address root causes. For example, a company facing high turnover might initially focus on salary adjustments but discover, through systemic analysis, that workplace culture or career development opportunities are the real drivers.

These habits also improve collaboration. Understanding interconnections fosters empathy and alignment, helping teams and stakeholders work together toward shared goals.

Finally, systemic thinking builds adaptability. By recognizing patterns and feedback loops, you can anticipate challenges and design solutions that evolve alongside changing conditions.

Exercises

1. **Daily Connections Practice:** Each day, pick a situation or problem and identify at least three interconnected elements that influence it. Reflect on how they shape the outcome.
2. **Unpack a Recent Decision:** Think of a decision you made recently and diagram its ripple effects across different parts of the system. What insights emerge?
3. **Engage in Systems Learning:** Explore a system outside your expertise, such as an ecosystem or an economic model. What connections and patterns do you notice?

Key Takeaway

Developing systemic thinking habits transforms how you understand and navigate complexity. Consistent practice makes this perspective second nature.

Chapter 96: Use Systems Thinking in Policy

Policies That Work Holistically

Effective policy design requires more than addressing immediate problems. It demands a systems-thinking approach. Policies impact multiple areas simultaneously, creating ripple effects that shape communities, economies, and environments. Systems thinking ensures that these interconnections are acknowledged, aligned, and leveraged for maximum benefit.

For example, policies promoting renewable energy not only reduce carbon emissions but also create jobs, improve public health, and strengthen energy independence. A systems-thinking approach integrates these benefits into a comprehensive strategy that maximizes positive outcomes.

Using systems thinking in policy means crafting solutions that are sustainable, equitable, and adaptable. This holistic perspective avoids unintended consequences and ensures that policies serve the needs of diverse stakeholders.

How to Use Systems Thinking in Policy

1. **Map Policy Interconnections:** Identify how a proposed policy affects different systems and stakeholders, including potential indirect impacts.
2. **Anticipate Ripple Effects:** Analyze how changes in one area — such as education reform — might influence related areas like workforce readiness or economic growth.
3. **Engage Stakeholders:** Involve diverse voices in the policymaking process to uncover blind spots and ensure that policies address multiple perspectives.
4. **Monitor and Adapt:** Continuously evaluate the impact of policies, making adjustments to address emerging challenges or opportunities.

Real-World Example

Finland's education policies demonstrate systemic thinking. By focusing on teacher training, equitable funding, and holistic curricula, Finland has built a system where education excellence supports broader social and economic outcomes, such as reduced inequality and high innovation rates.

Why It Matters

Policies designed without systems thinking often produce unintended consequences. For instance, agricultural subsidies that incentivize monoculture farming may boost short-term yields but lead to long-term environmental degradation and reduced biodiversity. Systems thinking ensures that policies consider both immediate and downstream effects.

This approach also fosters alignment between policy goals. For example, policies addressing housing affordability can integrate public transportation and green infrastructure, creating synergies that enhance quality of life while reducing carbon footprints.

Finally, systems-thinking policies build resilience. By considering how policies interact with dynamic environments, they remain effective even as conditions change, ensuring sustained impact.

Exercises

1. **Analyze a Policy:** Choose a policy you're familiar with and outline its impacts on different systems. What interconnections and ripple effects do you observe?
2. **Propose a Holistic Policy:** Design a policy that addresses a key issue while supporting multiple goals, such as economic growth, sustainability, and public health.
3. **Evaluate Policy Outcomes:** Select an existing policy and assess how well it aligns with systems-thinking principles. What changes could improve its effectiveness?

Key Takeaway

Systems thinking creates policies that are holistic, sustainable, and resilient — aligning diverse goals ensures long-term success.

Chapter 97: Challenge Default Mental Models

Reframing the Way You See Systems

Default mental models are the ingrained assumptions and frameworks people use to understand the world. While they provide shortcuts for decision-making, these models often limit perspectives, reinforce biases, and oversimplify complexity. Challenging these default assumptions is essential for effective systems thinking, as it opens up new possibilities and prevents flawed decisions.

For example, many organizations operate under the assumption that profit maximization is the sole measure of success. Challenging this mental model reveals alternative approaches, such as focusing on social impact, sustainability, or stakeholder well-being, which can lead to more balanced and enduring success.

By questioning default mental models, you uncover hidden assumptions, expand your understanding, and design solutions that align with the true dynamics of a system.

How to Challenge Default Mental Models

1. **Identify Assumptions:** Reflect on the beliefs and frameworks you use to interpret a situation. What do you take for granted?
2. **Consider Alternatives:** Explore other ways of understanding the system, drawing on diverse perspectives, disciplines, or data sources.
3. **Engage in Critical Reflection:** Ask probing questions like, "What if this assumption is wrong?" or "What am I missing?" to uncover blind spots.
4. **Test New Models:** Experiment with alternative mental models and evaluate how they affect your understanding and decision-making.

Real-World Example

In the energy sector, the default mental model that fossil fuels were the only viable source of energy dominated for decades. Challenging this assumption led to breakthroughs in renewable energy, like solar and wind, reshaping global energy systems and addressing environmental challenges.

Why It Matters

Default mental models can perpetuate systemic problems. For instance, the assumption that economic growth must come at the expense of environmental health has driven unsustainable practices. Challenging this model reveals opportunities for green growth and circular economies.

Reframing mental models also drives innovation. By questioning "the way things have always been done," systems become more open to novel ideas, partnerships, and strategies. For example, ride-sharing services like Uber and Lyft emerged by challenging the traditional taxi model.

Finally, breaking free from default assumptions fosters inclusivity. By considering diverse perspectives, systems are better equipped to serve a wider range of stakeholders, creating more equitable outcomes.

Exercises

1. **Identify a Default Model:** Think of a mental model you commonly use, such as "Success equals profit." Reflect on how this assumption shapes your decisions.
2. **Reframe the Model:** Explore alternative perspectives. For example, how might success be measured in terms of social impact or resilience?
3. **Test a New Approach:** Apply an alternative mental model to a decision or problem and evaluate the results. How did this shift in perspective affect outcomes?

Key Takeaway

Challenging default mental models reveals hidden assumptions and unlocks new possibilities. This practice expands understanding and drives better decisions.

Chapter 98: Invest in Continuous Learning

Continuous learning is the foundation of effective systems thinking. As systems evolve, new challenges and opportunities arise, requiring a mindset of curiosity and adaptability. Investing in ongoing learning ensures that you remain responsive to change, deepen your understanding, and refine your strategies over time.

For example, in the fast-changing field of technology, professionals who prioritize continuous learning —by attending workshops, pursuing certifications, or engaging in peer learning — stay ahead of industry shifts, ensuring their relevance and success.

Continuous learning isn't limited to formal education. It includes seeking feedback, reflecting on experiences, and engaging with diverse perspectives to uncover new insights and refine your approach to complex systems.

How to Invest in Continuous Learning

1. **Adopt a Growth Mindset:** View challenges and mistakes as opportunities to learn and grow rather than as setbacks.
2. **Engage in Lifelong Education:** Pursue formal and informal learning opportunities, such as courses, books, podcasts, or mentoring relationships.
3. **Reflect on Experiences:** Regularly analyze past actions and outcomes to identify lessons and apply them moving forward.
4. **Learn from Others:** Seek out diverse perspectives and collaborate with people from different disciplines, backgrounds, or industries.

Real-World Example

The Japanese concept of Kaizen, or continuous improvement, embodies the value of ongoing learning. Companies like Toyota use Kaizen to refine processes and products incrementally, creating a culture of innovation and excellence that has sustained their global success.

Why It Matters

Without continuous learning, systems stagnate. For instance, businesses that resist adapting to new technologies or market trends often lose relevance, while those that invest in learning thrive in dynamic environments.

Continuous learning also builds resilience. As new challenges arise — such as climate change or technological disruptions — learning equips systems with the knowledge and tools needed to adapt effectively.

Finally, lifelong learning fosters collaboration. Engaging with diverse ideas and perspectives creates opportunities for innovation and alignment, strengthening systems and their outcomes.

Exercises

1. **Reflect on Past Lessons:** Identify a recent challenge or success and analyze what you learned from it. How can you apply these lessons moving forward?
2. **Pursue a Learning Opportunity:** Choose a topic or skill you're curious about and explore resources like books, courses, or mentorships to deepen your knowledge.
3. **Collaborate for Growth:** Join a discussion group or network with people outside your field to exchange insights and expand your perspective.

Key Takeaway

Continuous learning ensures adaptability and growth. Staying curious and open equips systems to thrive in dynamic environments.

Chapter 99: Empower the Marginalized

Inclusion is Strength

Empowering marginalized voices is not just a moral imperative — it's essential for system health and resilience. Marginalized individuals and groups often experience first-hand the consequences of system inefficiencies, inequities, or blind spots, giving them unique insights into problems and potential solutions. Bringing these voices into the conversation enriches decision-making, strengthens collaboration, and ensures that systems are more inclusive and effective.

For example, Indigenous communities have long been stewards of their environments, using traditional knowledge to maintain ecological balance. Empowering these voices in modern conservation efforts bridges scientific and cultural approaches, creating sustainable solutions that honor both innovation and tradition.

Empowerment goes beyond inviting participation — it involves redistributing power, providing resources, and fostering environments where diverse perspectives can thrive and shape systems meaningfully.

How to Empower the Marginalized

1. **Identify Barriers:** Analyze systemic obstacles that prevent marginalized groups from participating fully, such as unequal access to education, technology, or decision-making platforms.
2. **Create Opportunities:** Design programs, policies, or initiatives that actively include marginalized voices and prioritize their leadership.
3. **Redistribute Resources:** Ensure equitable access to tools, funding, and networks needed for meaningful participation.
4. **Foster Representation:** Amplify the voices of underrepresented groups through mentorship, advocacy, or community-led initiatives.

Real-World Example

In Brazil, marginalized communities in the Amazon rainforest have been empowered through partnerships with conservation organizations. These collaborations prioritize Indigenous leadership in forest protection, combining local knowledge with global resources to address deforestation and climate change.

Why It Matters

Ignoring marginalized voices perpetuates inequity and inefficiency. For instance, urban planning projects that exclude low-income residents often result in gentrification, displacement, and social fragmentation. Empowering these communities ensures solutions are inclusive and equitable.

This approach also strengthens systems. Diverse perspectives challenge default assumptions, drive innovation, and create outcomes that work for a broader range of stakeholders.

Finally, empowerment builds trust and solidarity. When marginalized groups see their contributions valued, it fosters collaboration and a shared commitment to system-wide success.

Exercises

1. **Identify Marginalized Voices:** In a system you're part of, reflect on which groups are underrepresented. What barriers prevent their participation?
2. **Design an Empowerment Strategy:** Develop an initiative to amplify marginalized voices, such as through mentorship, resource distribution, or collaborative decision-making.
3. **Evaluate Inclusivity:** Assess the impact of your strategy on the system's inclusivity and effectiveness. What lessons emerge for future efforts?

Key Takeaway

Empowering marginalized voices enriches systems. This approach ensures equity, drives innovation, and strengthens collective success.

Chapter 100: Apply Systems Thinking Everywhere

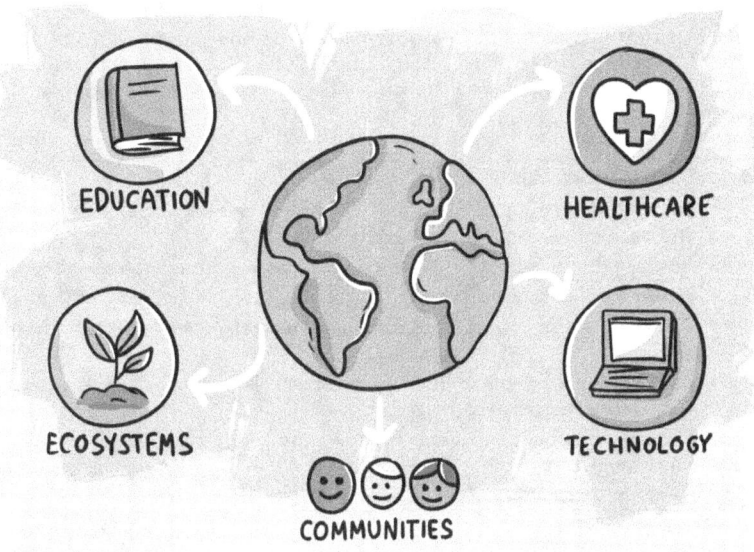

Systems thinking isn't limited to specific fields or industries. it's a universal framework for understanding and navigating the interconnectedness of life. Whether you're managing a household, leading an organization, or addressing global challenges, systems thinking offers tools to uncover relationships, anticipate outcomes, and design solutions that align with larger goals.

For instance, applying systems thinking in personal finance involves not just budgeting but also considering long-term goals, external economic factors, and interdependencies like family needs or career growth. In this context, it ensures more thoughtful and sustainable decision-making.

By applying systems thinking everywhere, you cultivate a habit of seeing beyond surface-level problems, fostering a mindset that values connection, adaptability, and purpose in every aspect of life.

How to Apply Systems Thinking Everywhere

1. **Adopt a Systems Perspective Daily:** Reflect on how your actions and decisions connect to larger systems, whether in relationships, work, or community involvement.
2. **Start Small:** Practice systems thinking on everyday challenges, such as organizing a team project or managing personal routines.
3. **Expand Gradually:** Apply these principles to more complex systems, like organizational strategies, community initiatives, or global issues.
4. **Teach and Share:** Empower others to embrace systems thinking by modeling the approach, sharing insights, and fostering collaborative problem-solving.

Real-World Example

The Global Vaccine Alliance (Gavi) applies systems thinking to improve access to vaccines worldwide. By addressing interconnected factors like supply chains, healthcare infrastructure, and public education, Gavi creates scalable and sustainable solutions that save lives.

Why It Matters

Applying systems thinking universally transforms how people approach challenges. It shifts the focus from isolated fixes to integrated solutions, creating lasting impact across diverse domains.

This approach also fosters global resilience. In a world of interconnected crises — such as climate change, pandemics, and economic instability — systems thinking provides a roadmap for navigating complexity and driving collective progress.

Finally, systems thinking enriches personal growth. By viewing yourself as part of larger networks, you gain deeper awareness of your role, purpose, and potential to contribute meaningfully to the world.

Exercises

1. **Start with an Everyday System:** Choose a simple system in your life, such as meal planning or commuting. How can systems thinking improve its efficiency or impact?
2. **Apply to a Broader Context:** Identify a larger system—such as a workplace or community initiative—and map its connections. What insights emerge?
3. **Share Your Insights:** Teach a friend, colleague, or family member one principle of systems thinking and discuss how it applies to their experiences.

Key Takeaway

Systems thinking is a universal tool. Applying it everywhere unlocks new perspectives and creates meaningful impact in every facet of life.

Conclusion: The Transformative Power of Systems Thinking

As you reach the final pages of this book, reflect on the journey you've undertaken. You've explored 100 ways to uncover connections, anticipate ripple effects, and design solutions that align with the deeper dynamics of the systems around you. This is more than just a set of tools—it's a transformative perspective that redefines how you approach problems, opportunities, and change.

Valuable Learnings

The practical insights in this book has equipped you to:

- **Spot Interconnections:** See the relationships between seemingly unrelated parts, helping you identify leverage points and design more impactful solutions.
- **Address Root Causes:** Move beyond treating symptoms to tackle the foundational issues driving system behaviors.
- **Foster Resilience:** Design systems that adapt to change, recover from disruptions, and thrive in complexity.
- **Collaborate Inclusively:** Recognize and integrate diverse voices to create solutions that are equitable, innovative, and enduring.
- **Balance Short-Term and Long-Term Goals:** Navigate the tension between immediate needs and sustainable outcomes with clarity and purpose.

These skills are universally applicable, empowering you to tackle challenges in personal life, professional settings, communities, and global contexts.

Practical Tips for Applying Systems Thinking

1. **Start Small:** Practice systems thinking on manageable challenges, such as improving team workflows, optimizing a personal project, or streamlining household routines. Identify interconnections and experiment with small changes to observe their impact.
2. **Define Relationships:** Use tools like mind maps, diagrams, or even simple lists to visualize how the parts of a system interact. This exercise reveals dependencies, bottlenecks, and opportunities for intervention.
3. **Ask Questions:** Develop the habit of asking systems-oriented questions: What are the ripple effects? Who or what else is affected? What feedback loops are at play?
4. **Think Across Time Scales:** When making decisions, consider both short-term benefits and long-term consequences. For instance, investing in employee training might reduce immediate output but create lasting gains in productivity and morale.
5. **Involve Others:** Systems thrive on collaboration. Share what you've learned, invite diverse perspectives, and work with stakeholders to co-create solutions that benefit the broader network.
6. **Stay Curious:** Systems are dynamic. Keep learning by observing natural systems, studying successful models, or exploring new frameworks. Continuous curiosity fuels your ability to adapt and innovate.

Moving Forward

Systems thinking isn't a skill you master overnight; it's a lifelong practice. Each system you engage with offers new lessons, challenges, and opportunities for growth. Embrace this mindset in all areas of your life — at home, at work, and in the world.

The true power of systems thinking lies in its ability to bridge gaps. It connects the micro and the macro, the present and the future, the individual and the collective. When applied thoughtfully, it fosters solutions that are as inclusive as they are effective, creating value for yourself and the systems you inhabit.

Now, the responsibility shifts to you. Use the insights from this book to inspire change, build resilience, and create a positive impact. Whether you're redesigning a workflow, addressing community challenges, or tackling global issues, remember: no action is too small when it's part of a larger, interconnected whole.

Appendix A: Chapter Summaries

This appendix serves as your quick-reference guide to the 100 chapters of this book. Each chapter title is accompanied by a brief description of its key idea, allowing you to revisit concepts, refresh your understanding, or find inspiration as you apply systems thinking in your life.

Section I: The Basics of Seeing Systems (Chapters 1–20)

1. **Zoom Out to See the Big Picture**
   Recognize how stepping back reveals patterns that are not immediately visible.

2. **Identify Key Stakeholders**
   Visualize who is affected by and influences the system.

3. **Trace Causal Links**
   Follow the chain of events to find the root causes driving system behaviors.

4. **Spot Feedback Loops**
   Detect reinforcing cycles in the system.

5. **Unpack Delay Dynamics**
   Recognize where time lags disrupt relationships.

6. **Look for System Boundaries**
   Define where a system starts and ends for clarity.

7. **Observe Resource Flows**
   Track how energy, materials, or money move through the system.

8. **Notice Points of Tension**
   Detect areas where competing forces create instability.

9. **Uncover Emergent Behavior**
   See how simple interactions create complex outcomes.

10. **Understand System History**
    Study the past to explain present system behavior.

11. **Visualize Interconnections**
    Use diagrams to reveal relationships between system parts.

12. **Distinguish Stocks from Flows**
    Separate accumulations (stocks) from changes (flows).

13. **Notice Self-Organization**
    Observe how systems structure themselves without external control.

14. **Focus On Tipping Points**
    Identify thresholds where small changes create large effects.

15. **See Patterns Across Scales**
    Look for recurring behaviors at micro, macro, and in-between levels.

16. **Look for Missing Connections**
    Identify gaps where elements should interact but don't.

17. **Assess System Resilience**
    Evaluate how well a system recovers from disruptions.

18. **Find Balancing Forces**
    Recognize what stabilizes or restrains growth in the system.

19. **See Dependencies**
    Trace how one part of the system relies on another.

20. **Recognize How Systems Change**
    Notice how systems adjust in response to internal or external pressures.

Section II: Analyzing Human-Created Systems (Chapters 21–40)

21. **Study Incentive Structures**
    Identify rewards and penalties driving behavior in the system.

22. **Watch out for Backfiring Motivators**
    Identify cases where rewards unintentionally cause harm or undesired outcomes.

23. **Track Decision Pathways**
    Follow how choices propagate through the system.

24. **Examine Rules and Norms**
    Understand formal and informal guidelines shaping interactions.

25. **Map Communication Channels**
See how information flows influence outcomes.

26. **Notice Bottlenecks**
Find points where flows slow down or get stuck.

27. **Identify System Archetypes**
Pinpoint recurring structures such as "Success to the Successful" that shape system behavior.

28. **Explore Power Bases**
Spot who has control and how they use it.

29. **Find Leverage Points**
Locate small changes that yield big results.

30. **Trace Resource Inequalities**
Observe how uneven distributions create systemic issues.

31. **Spot Structural Biases**
Identify embedded advantages or disadvantages in the system.

32. **Understand The Snowball Effect**
Explore how small changes can lead to major outcomes.

33. **Analyze Network Centrality**
Study which nodes or actors are most influential.

34. **Look for Cross-System Overlaps**
Notice when systems share characteristics.

35. **Track Failures to Learn**
Examine breakdowns to understand vulnerabilities.

36. **Identify Siloed Thinking**
Spot isolated parts that limit broader coordination.

37. **Evaluate the Role of Middle Actors**
Observe intermediaries that mediate connections or flows.

38. **See Intermediary Goals**
Notice how mid-level objectives shape larger outcomes.

39. **Spot the Pace of Change**
Assess whether the system evolves too quickly or slowly for its environment.

40. **Detect Systemic Fragility**
Recognize when a system is too rigid to adapt.

Section III: Spotting Patterns in Natural Systems (Chapters 41-60)

41. **See Cycles Everywhere**
Identify recurring natural rhythms like seasons or migrations.

42. **Understand Energy Flows**
Follow how energy moves through ecosystems.

43. **Uncover Predator-Prey Dynamics**
Observe how nature's relationships are intertwined.

44. **Trace Nutrient Paths**
Study how elements like carbon and nitrogen circulate.

45. **Find Anchor Points**
Discover the critical species or elements that have an outsized impact on the system's stability.

46. **Notice Niche Functions**
Discover how unique functions contribute to the stability and success of a system.

47. **Evaluate Mechanisms**
Study how ecosystems bounce back after disruption.

48. **Find Cascading Effects**
Observe how small ecological shifts ripple through the system.

49. **Detect Resource Competition**
Watch how organisms or groups vie for limited supplies.

50. **Observe Natural "Evolution"**
See how changes in behavior or structure meet evolving needs.

51. **Recognize Interconnected Ecosystems**
Understand how forests, oceans, and rivers rely on each other.

52. **Spot Self-Healing Solutions**
Study how damaged environments recover naturally.
53. **See Nature's Redundancies**
Observe backups that provide support in critical areas.
54. **Trace Habitat Fragmentation**
Follow how breaking habitats affects broader systems.
55. **Watch Energy Minimization Strategies**
Observe how natural systems optimize efficiency.
56. **Look for Mutualism**
Study win-win relationships in ecosystems.
57. **Detect Adaptive Behaviors**
See how ecosystems grow, collapse, and renew over time.
58. **Understand Biotic-Abiotic Interactions**
Study how living organisms affect non-living elements and vice versa.
59. **See Human-Nature Interactions**
Explore how humans impact and are shaped by natural systems.
60. **Track Species Migration Networks**
Follow the dynamic flows of populations over time.

Section IV: Applying Systems Thinking to Solve Problems (Chapters 61–100)

61. **Break Down the Problem into Subsystems**
Dissect challenges into manageable, interrelated parts.
62. **Use Feedback for Continuous Improvement**
Adjust actions based on real-time results.
63. **Test Small Interventions**
Experiment in a controlled way to learn before scaling.
64. **Activate Unused Resources**
Identify overlooked assets within the system.
65. **Find Nonlinear Influences**
Spot where small shifts create unpredictable changes.
66. **Build Strong Systems**
Design for flexibility and recovery from shocks.
67. **Eliminate Obstructions**
Free up critical choke points.
68. **Encourage Cross-System Collaboration**
Connect isolated parts to solve shared problems.
69. **Monitor Leading Indicators**
Track early signs of upcoming changes.
70. **Avoid Over-Optimization**
Prevent pushing efficiency to the point of fragility.
71. **Develop Iterative Solutions**
Tweak and improve systems in cycles.
72. **Align Incentives**
Adjust motivations to drive system-wide benefits.
73. **Broaden Your Scope of Analysis**
Include external factors that influence the system's behavior.
74. **Reduce Delays in Reporting**
Shorten loops for faster, more accurate adjustments.
75. **Encourage Transparency**
Make flows and connections within the system clear and easy to understand.
76. **Counteract Perverse Incentives**
Reframe goals to align actions with desired outcomes.
77. **Use Systems Thinking in Leadership**
Lead teams with a holistic, interconnected perspective.
78. **Apply Risk Management Systems**
Anticipate and mitigate potential disruptions.

79. **Strengthen Weak Connections**
Fortify the most vulnerable parts of a system.
80. **Design for Redundancy**
Add backups to critical parts for longevity.
81. **Avoid Unintended Consequences**
Predict and address secondary effects of changes.
82. **Enhance System Flexibility**
Build the ability to adapt to unexpected shifts.
83. **Seek Diversity for Stability**
Integrate varied elements for robustness.
84. **Analyze Success Stories**
Learn from systems that thrive.
85. **Foster Community-Led Solutions**
Empower local stakeholders to drive change.
86. **Identify Overlooked Costs**
Spot trade-offs that may not be immediately apparent in decisions.
87. **Adapt to Changing Environments**
Align systems with shifting external conditions.
88. **Optimize for Long-Term Outcomes**
Balance immediate gains with future needs.
89. **Create Sustainable Systems**
Design processes that maintain equilibrium.
90. **Incorporate Circular Economy Principles**
Close loops to reuse resources effectively.
91. **Match Innovation with Stability**
Introduce change without destabilizing the system.
92. **Focus on Interdependence**
Strengthen connections that boost overall health.
93. **Address Core Problems**
Go beyond just looking at symptoms, aim to find solutions.
94. **Simplify Complex Systems**
Streamline without losing essential functions.
95. **Develop Systemic Thinking Habits**
Practice spotting connections in everyday life.
96. **Use Systems Thinking in Policy**
Shape laws with an understanding of ripple effects.
97. **Challenge Default Mental Models**
Question assumptions to see systems differently.
98. **Invest in Continuous Learning**
Build capacity to remain flexible as systems evolve.
99. **Empower the Marginalized**
Bring overlooked voices into systemic change.
100. **Apply Systems Thinking Everywhere**
Recognize that no part of life exists in isolation.

Appendix B: Section and Chapter Guide

This appendix organizes the book by its four main sections and chapters. It's designed to help you quickly locate topics of interest and see how the book's structure builds from foundational concepts to advanced applications.

The Basics of Seeing Systems

- Zoom Out to See the Big Picture
- Identify Key Stakeholders
- Trace Causal Links
- Spot Feedback Loops
- Unpack Delay Dynamics
- Look for System Boundaries
- Observe Resource Flows
- Notice Points of Tension
- Uncover Emergent Behavior
- Understand System History
- Visualize Interconnections
- Distinguish Stocks from Flows
- Notice Self-Organization
- Focus On Tipping Points
- See Patterns Across Scales
- Look for Missing Connections
- Assess System Resilience
- Find Balancing Forces
- See Dependencies
- Recognize How Systems Change

Analyzing Human-Created Systems

- Study Incentive Structures
- Watch out for Backfiring Motivators
- Track Decision Pathways
- Examine Rules and Norms
- Map Communication Channels
- Notice Bottlenecks
- Identify System Archetypes
- Explore Power Bases
- Find Leverage Points
- Trace Resource Inequalities
- Spot Structural Biases
- Understand The Snowball Effect
- Analyze Network Centrality
- Look for Cross-System Overlaps
- Track Failures to Learn
- Identify Siloed Thinking
- Evaluate the Role of Middle Actors
- See Intermediary Goals
- Spot the Pace of Change
- Detect Systemic Fragility

Spotting Patterns in Natural Systems

- See Cycles Everywhere
- Understand Energy Flows
- Uncover Predator-Prey Dynamics
- Trace Nutrient Paths
- Find Anchor Points
- Notice Niche Functions
- Evaluate Mechanisms
- Find Cascading Effects
- Detect Resource Competition
- Observe Natural "Evolution"
- Recognize Interconnected Ecosystems
- Spot Self-Healing Solutions
- See Nature's Redundancies
- Trace Habitat Fragmentation
- Watch Energy Minimization Strategies
- Look for Mutualism
- Detect Adaptive Behaviors
- Understand Biotic-Abiotic Interactions
- See Human-Nature Interactions
- Track Species Migration Networks

Applying Systems Thinking to Solve Problems

- Break Down the Problem into Subsystems
- Use Feedback for Continuous Improvement
- Test Small Interventions
- Activate Unused Resources
- Find Nonlinear Influences
- Build Strong Systems
- Eliminate Obstructions
- Encourage Cross-System Collaboration
- Monitor Leading Indicators
- Avoid Over-Optimization
- Develop Iterative Solutions
- Align Incentives
- Broaden Your Scope of Analysis
- Reduce Delays in Reporting
- Encourage Transparency
- Counteract Perverse Incentives
- Use Systems Thinking in Leadership
- Apply Risk Management Systems
- Strengthen Weak Connections
- Design for Redundancy
- Avoid Unintended Consequences
- Enhance System Flexibility
- Seek Diversity for Stability
- Analyze Success Stories
- Foster Community-Led Solutions
- Identify Overlooked Costs
- Adapt to Changing Environments
- Optimize for Long-Term Outcomes
- Create Sustainable Systems
- Incorporate Circular Economy Principles
- Match Innovation with Stability
- Focus on Interdependence
- Address Core Problems
- Simplify Complex Systems
- Develop Systemic Thinking Habits
- Use Systems Thinking in Policy
- Challenge Default Mental Models
- Invest in Continuous Learning
- Empower the Marginalized
- Apply Systems Thinking Everywhere

Appendix C: Practice Scenarios

This appendix is designed to help you apply the principles of systems thinking to real-world situations. Each scenario presents a system-related problem, followed by a challenge that prompts you to think critically about how to use the concepts and strategies from this book. These exercises will help solidify your understanding of systems thinking and build confidence in your ability to navigate complex challenges.

Scenario 1: Traffic Congestion in a Growing City

Problem: A rapidly growing city is experiencing severe traffic congestion during peak hours. Expanding roads temporarily relieved the issue but has worsened it over time due to increased car usage. Public transportation options are limited and underfunded.

Challenge: Apply the principles of **"Find Leverage Points" (Chapter 29)** and **"Address Core Problems" (Chapter 93)** to identify the root causes of congestion and propose a long-term solution that reduces reliance on personal vehicles.

Scenario 2: Declining Team Productivity

Problem: A project team's productivity has been steadily declining. Team members report unclear goals, miscommunication, and bottlenecks in decision-making. Morale is low, and deadlines are being missed.

Challenge: Use **"Map Communication Channels" (Chapter 25)** and **"Strengthen Weak Connections" (Chapter 79)** to identify how information flows and interpersonal relationships can be improved to boost productivity and morale.

Scenario 3: Community Water Shortages

Problem: A rural community is facing seasonal water shortages due to overuse and inefficient irrigation practices. Efforts to dig new wells have not addressed the underlying issue, and tensions between farmers and residents are growing.

Challenge: Leverage **"Observe Resource Flows" (Chapter 7)** and **"Develop Systemic Thinking Habits" (Chapter 95)** to track water use and design a sustainable water management system that balances agricultural and residential needs.

Scenario 4: Declining Pollinator Populations

Problem: A region has seen a sharp decline in pollinator species, threatening local agriculture. While some farmers have switched to artificial pollination methods, these are expensive and less effective.

Challenge: Use **"Find Anchor Points" (Chapter 45)** and **"Look for Mutualism" (Chapter 56)** to identify critical relationships in the ecosystem and propose strategies to restore pollinator populations naturally.

Scenario 5: Siloed Departments in an Organization

Problem: Departments in a company operate in silos, leading to inefficiencies and duplicated efforts. Employees feel isolated, and innovation is stifled due to a lack of cross-departmental collaboration.

Challenge: Apply **"Identify Siloed Thinking" (Chapter 36)** and **"Encourage Cross-System Collaboration" (Chapter 68)** to design initiatives that break down silos and promote interdepartmental cooperation.

Scenario 6: Housing Shortages in Urban Areas

Problem: Urban housing shortages are driving up rents and displacing lower-income residents. Developers are hesitant to build affordable housing due to low profit margins, exacerbating the issue.

Challenge: Use **"Trace Resource Inequalities" (Chapter 30)** and **"Analyze Success Stories" (Chapter 84)** to address the systemic causes of housing shortages and propose policies that incentivize equitable development.

Scenario 7: Overreliance on a Single Supplier

Problem: A manufacturing company depends heavily on a single supplier for critical components. A recent disruption in the supplier's operations caused costly delays and missed production deadlines.

Challenge: Apply **"Diversify Resources" (Chapter 82)** and **"Strengthen Weak Connections" (Chapter 79)** to develop a more resilient supply chain.

Scenario 8: Persistent Classroom Disruptions

Problem: A teacher struggles to maintain order in a classroom where frequent disruptions undermine learning. Efforts to address individual students' behavior haven't resolved the broader problem.

Challenge: Use **"Notice Points of Tension" (Chapter 8)** and **"Uncover Emergent Behavior" (Chapter 9)** to identify systemic causes of the disruptions and propose strategies to create a supportive learning environment.

Scenario 9: Unequal Access to Healthcare

Problem: A rural area experiences unequal access to healthcare, with residents facing long travel distances and limited availability of medical professionals. Existing facilities are overwhelmed.

Challenge: Leverage **"Spot Structural Biases" (Chapter 31)** and **"Design for Redundancy" (Chapter 80)** to create a more equitable and robust healthcare delivery system.

Scenario 10: Overcrowded Public Transportation

Problem: A city's public transportation system is overcrowded and underfunded. Riders experience frequent delays, and complaints are rising, yet investment in infrastructure is stagnant.

Challenge: Apply **"Monitor Leading Indicators" (Chapter 69)** and **"Evaluate the Role of Middle Actors" (Chapter 37)** to identify solutions that improve service and secure stakeholder support for long-term investment.

Problem: A company struggles to retain employees, with high turnover resulting in increased hiring and training costs. Exit interviews reveal dissatisfaction with workplace culture and lack of career growth opportunities.

Challenge: Use **"Align Incentives" (Chapter 72)** and **"Analyze Network Centrality" (Chapter 33)** to create a workplace environment that motivates and retains talent.

Problem: A food retailer experiences high levels of waste, with unsold products often discarded due to spoilage. Supply chain inefficiencies and demand forecasting errors exacerbate the issue.

Challenge: Leverage **"Track Failures to Learn" (Chapter 35)** and **"Simplify Complex Systems" (Chapter 94)** to design a more efficient and sustainable supply chain.

Problem: A coastal town faces recurring flooding but lacks adequate disaster preparedness. Past efforts to build infrastructure have been reactive rather than proactive.

Challenge: Use **"Enhance System Flexibility" (Chapter 82)** and **"Focus on Tipping Points" (Chapter 14)** to create a disaster management plan that builds long-term resilience.

Problem: A town struggles with low turnout for public meetings and a lack of participation in civic initiatives, leaving decisions to a small group of stakeholders.

Challenge: Apply **"Foster Community-Led Solutions" (Chapter 85)** and **"Encourage Transparency" (Chapter 75)** to design strategies that increase community engagement and trust.

Problem: A non-profit organization struggles to allocate resources effectively, with some programs overfunded while others are chronically under-resourced.

Challenge: Leverage **"Observe Resource Flows" (Chapter 7)** and **"Find Leverage Points" (Chapter 29)** to optimize resource allocation and improve impact across all programs.

Appendix D: Your Checklist for Spotting Connections

This checklist is your quick-reference guide for integrating systems thinking into your daily life, work, and problem-solving. Each point distills key principles and strategies from the book into actionable steps, ensuring that you can apply what you've learned with ease and confidence. Use this checklist as a starting point for analyzing challenges, designing solutions, and fostering systemic change.

1. Zoom Out for the Big Picture
- Step back and identify the broader system influencing the situation.
- Look for patterns, trends, or connections that aren't immediately visible.
- Ask: "How does this fit into the larger context?"

2. Identify Key Stakeholders
- Visualize who is affected by the system and who influences it.
- Consider perspectives from diverse groups, including marginalized voices.
- Ask: "Whose input is missing, and how can I include it?"

3. Trace Root Causes
- Look beyond surface-level symptoms to uncover underlying problems.
- Use tools like root-cause analysis to connect symptoms to systemic issues.
- Ask: "What is driving this problem, and where does it originate?"

4. Map System Interconnections
- Create diagrams to visualize how elements within a system interact.
- Highlight dependencies, feedback loops, and points of tension.
- Use the map to identify opportunities for intervention or improvement.

5. Leverage Feedback Mechanisms
- Look for reinforcing or balancing cycles within the system.
- Identify areas where small changes can have significant ripple effects.
- Monitor feedback to adjust and refine your approach.

6. Address Bottlenecks
- Identify areas where flows or processes are slowed or blocked.
- Evaluate whether resources, time, or communication are contributing factors.
- Propose solutions to free up bottlenecks and restore efficiency.

7. Monitor Long-Term Impacts
- Assess how today's decisions will affect the system in the future.
- Balance short-term gains with long-term sustainability.
- Ask: "What are the unintended consequences of this action?"

8. Embrace Diversity in Systems
- Include diverse elements, perspectives, and resources to increase resilience.
- Recognize the value of redundancy and backup systems.
- Ask: "What variety does this system need to thrive?"

9. Strengthen Weak Connections
- Identify and fortify vulnerable links within the system.
- Foster collaboration and communication to bridge gaps.
- Ask: "Where is the system weakest, and how can I support it?"

10. Simplify Complexity
- Remove unnecessary steps or redundancies that hinder performance.
- Focus on essential goals and processes to improve clarity.
- Test simplifications incrementally to ensure they enhance effectiveness.

11. Foster Community-Led Solutions
- Empower stakeholders to design and implement solutions.
- Build trust through transparency, shared ownership, and collaboration.
- Provide tools, training, or resources to support their efforts.

12. Design for Flexibility
- Build systems that can adapt to changing conditions or disruptions.
- Use modular components to make adjustments easier.
- Monitor performance and adjust strategies based on feedback.

13. Anticipate Trade-Offs
- Evaluate the costs and benefits of each decision across different areas.
- Look for hidden costs that might emerge over time.
- Ensure that trade-offs align with long-term system goals.

14. Balance Innovation with Stability
- Foster creative thinking while maintaining reliable processes.
- Experiment in controlled ways that don't disrupt core functions.
- Regularly evaluate whether innovation and stability are aligned.

15. Keep Learning and Adapting
- Stay curious and open to new ideas, perspectives, and methods.
- Reflect on successes and failures to refine your approach.
- Engage with diverse systems to expand your understanding and skills.

Pro Tip

Systems thinking is a practice, not a destination. As you apply these principles, remember to stay adaptable, reflective, and patient. Start small, experiment, and learn from every experience. The more you practice, the easier it becomes to see connections, anticipate ripple effects, and design solutions that truly make a difference. Stay curious — the systems around you are waiting to teach you something new!

Part 4: Strategic Thinking

An AI's Guide to 100 Strategies for Long-Term Success Using Game Theory and Strategic Planning

Introduction: A Blueprint for Strategic Mastery

Imagine standing on a chessboard where every piece represents a decision, every move ripples through the game, and every player has their own hidden agenda. This is life — an intricate dance of game plans, competition, and opportunity. While life doesn't come with a playbook, it does come with patterns, principles, and solutions that can be learned, mastered, and applied.

Who This Book Is For

This book is designed for anyone who aspires to think several steps ahead — whether you're a leader, entrepreneur, student, or someone navigating the complexities of life itself.

Each chapter delivers a clear, practical plan you can apply immediately. These systems are not just limited to winning in traditional "games" such as business or negotiations. They're equally valuable for personal growth, managing risks, fostering relationships, and navigating life's uncertainties. From mastering the timing of critical decisions to transforming failure into opportunity, you'll find tools here to help you achieve long-term success.

Why should you read this book?

Strategy isn't just for CEOs or chess masters. It's for anyone who wants to live deliberately. It's a mindset that equips you with the ability to anticipate challenges, plan your actions, and pivot effectively when circumstances change. It empowers you to see the bigger picture while keeping an eye on the details. In a world of noise, distractions, and constant competition, the ability to think tactically is your greatest advantage.

What You'll Gain

With this book you will:

- Gain insights from game theory, which will teach you to see decisions as part of a larger system where every action has a reaction.
- Learn how to uncover hidden opportunities in partnerships, neutralize opponents' advantages, and make calculated risks that pay off.
- Discover the power of adapting to change and using uncertainty as a tool rather than a threat.

It's time to think ahead, act wisely, and win confidently. Let's begin.

Section I: Foundational Strategies

Strategic thinking begins with a strong foundation — a set of principles that guide your decisions and actions, regardless of the situation. This section lays the groundwork for effective strategy by teaching you how to think beyond the immediate, prioritize clarity, and harness the subtle dynamics of competition and collaboration. By mastering these concepts, you'll create a robust mental framework to support the more advanced strategies that follow.

Chapter 1: Play the Long Game, Not the Next Move

When faced with a decision, many people fall into the trap of thinking only about their immediate next step. However, life rewards those who can think ahead. To "play the long game" means to approach every decision with a focus on the bigger picture. It's about resisting the temptation of short-term gains and prioritizing actions that align with your long-term objectives.

In the world of strategy, short-sightedness can cost you dearly. Imagine a chess player so focused on capturing a pawn that they fail to notice their opponent setting up a checkmate. In life, this translates to chasing small wins — such as a quick sale, a flashy promotion, or instant gratification.

The long game requires patience, foresight, and a commitment to outcomes that may not pay off immediately. This doesn't mean ignoring short-term actions altogether. Rather, it's about ensuring that each step aligns with your overarching goals. Think of each decision as a domino. Knock it down in the right direction, and it triggers a cascade of events that lead to your desired outcome.

Why People Struggle with Long-Term Thinking

Many people default to short-term thinking because it feels tangible. Immediate results are easy to see, measure, and celebrate. Long-term goals, on the other hand, can feel distant, abstract, and uncertain. This uncertainty often discourages people from committing to the long game.

But here's the secret: short-term wins are often fleeting. They may feel satisfying in the moment, but they rarely contribute to lasting success. Long-term thinking, while harder to maintain, creates a framework for sustained growth and meaningful accomplishments.

How to Play the Long Game

1. **Clarify Your Big Picture Goals:** Start by identifying what you truly want to achieve. Whether it's financial independence, career fulfillment, or personal growth, write down your long-term vision in specific terms.
2. **Align Short-Term Actions with Long-Term Goals:** Before making any decision, ask yourself, "Does this move me closer to my ultimate goal?" If not, reconsider.
3. **Accept Delayed Gratification:** Long-term success often requires sacrifices in the short term. Practice saying no to distractions that don't serve your bigger purpose.
4. **Review and Adjust:** The long game isn't static. Periodically review your progress and adjust your actions to stay aligned with your vision.

Real-World Example

Take the story of Amazon. In its early days, Amazon's founder Jeff Bezos deliberately chose to prioritize long-term growth over immediate profits. Investors criticized the company's unprofitable model, but Bezos stuck to his strategy of reinvesting revenues into expansion. Today, Amazon dominates in the global market because it played the long game when others didn't.

Exercises

1. **Personal Assessment:** Think of a decision you've made recently. Was it focused on short-term results or long-term impact? Write down what you would do differently if you were playing the long game.
2. **Long-Term Mapping:** Choose a long-term goal in your life. Break it into smaller milestones that align with your overall vision. Write down one immediate action you can take to move closer to your first milestone.
3. **Practice Delayed Gratification:** Identify one habit or behavior that prioritizes short-term satisfaction (e.g. impulse spending, procrastination). Commit to replacing it with an action that supports your long-term goals for one week.

Key Takeaway

Short-term wins may feel gratifying, but they rarely lead to lasting success. When you play the long game, every move contributes to a broader vision, ensuring your efforts build momentum toward meaningful and lasting outcomes.

Chapter 2: Begin with the End in Mind

Most people start projects or make decisions with enthusiasm but little thought about where they're headed. It's like starting a road trip without knowing the destination. You may drive fast and far, but you could end up in the wrong place entirely. To truly succeed, you must *begin with the end in mind*.

This strategy is about defining your ultimate goal before taking the first step. When you're clear on your destination, every decision becomes easier because you can evaluate whether it moves you closer to or farther from your goal. Without this understanding, you risk wasting time, resources, and energy on actions that don't contribute to meaningful outcomes.

Why It Matters

Envisioning the end allows you to reverse-engineer success. Think of an architect designing a building. They don't start by laying bricks randomly; they begin with a blueprint that shows the completed structure. Similarly, knowing your "end" ensures that each action you take builds toward a coherent outcome.

This principle applies in every domain — personal, professional, or even interpersonal. Whether you're starting a business, planning a career, or improving a relationship, you need to define what success looks like to achieve it.

How to Apply This Strategy

1. **Define Success:** What does the "end" look like for you? Be specific. A vague goal like "be happy" isn't actionable. Instead, aim for "a career that balances creative fulfillment with financial stability."
2. **Work Backward:** Identify the key milestones that lead to your goal. Break the journey into smaller steps, ensuring each builds on the last.
3. **Stay Flexible:** The end goal can evolve over time, but the insights it provides keeps you focused, even as circumstances change.

Real-world Example

Consider Pixar, the animation studio known for its blockbuster films. When Pixar begins creating a movie, they don't start with character design or animation. They start with the story's ending — how the audience should feel as the credits roll. This focus on the end goal ensures that every element of the movie serves the overarching narrative, resulting in powerful storytelling.

Exercises

1. **Vision Statement:** Write a one-paragraph description of your ideal outcome for a current project, goal, or challenge. Be as specific as possible.
2. **Milestone Mapping:** Identify three key milestones that will help you move toward this outcome. For each milestone, write one action step you can take this week.
3. **Future Reflection:** Imagine yourself one year from now, having achieved your goal. Write a letter to your present self describing what you did to succeed.

Key Takeaway

Starting with the end in mind creates a clear path to success, ensuring every action you take builds toward a meaningful and coherent outcome.

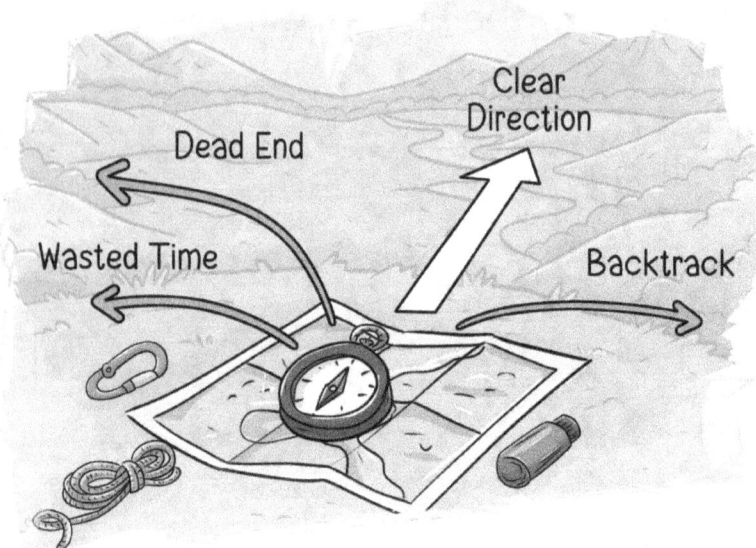

Chapter 3: Prioritize Clarity Over Speed

In today's fast-paced world, the pressure to act quickly is overwhelming. Everyone seems to value speed — fast results, instant decisions, and quick wins. But speed alone can be deceptive. Moving fast without understanding your direction is like sprinting into the fog — you might cover ground, but you could be heading straight for a cliff. Focusing on clarity instead of speed is the key to avoiding this common pitfall.

This strategy is not about procrastination or endless deliberation. It's about thinking before acting. Without focus, you risk missteps, wasted resources, and unnecessary stress — all of which slow you down in the long run.

Why Sharpness is a Superior Advantage

Clear thinking aligns your decisions with your larger goals and ensures your actions solve the right problem. Acting without vision often results in "busy work" — you feel productive, but nothing meaningful is accomplished.

For example, in business, teams often rush to implement solutions before fully diagnosing the issue. They might introduce new software to increase efficiency, only to discover later that the real problem was outdated workflows. This reactive approach creates additional problems that could have been avoided with a moment of pause and deeper understanding.

When certainty comes first, you not only eliminate unnecessary detours but also inspire confidence in yourself and others. People follow leaders who act decisively *and* intelligently. By pausing to gain certainty, you demonstrate wisdom and the ability to focus on what truly matters.

How to Prioritize Clarity Over Speed

1. **Pause to Reflect:** Before making a decision, take a moment to ask, "What is the ultimate goal? What problem am I solving?" This simple pause can prevent costly mistakes.
2. **Gather Context:** Seek information from multiple sources. Are you acting on complete and accurate data, or are you making assumptions?
3. **Focus on the Root Cause:** Don't rush to treat symptoms. Dig deeper to identify the underlying issue. For example, if your team is missing deadlines, is it due to poor time management, unclear instructions, or a deeper cultural issue?
4. **Communicate Effectively:** Misunderstandings often arise from unclear communication. Before moving forward, ensure everyone involved shares the same understanding of the goal and strategy.

Real-World Example

Consider the story of Toyota's legendary success. One of the cornerstones of Toyota's production system is the principle of "stopping to fix problems." When an issue arises on the production line, Toyota employees are trained to pause operations and thoroughly investigate the root cause before continuing. While this approach may seem counterproductive in the moment, it ultimately saves time, reduces waste, and improves quality.

Now, compare this to companies that rush to meet deadlines without addressing systemic issues. Their short-term speed often leads to product recalls, customer dissatisfaction, and long-term reputational damage. Toyota's commitment to precision has allowed it to maintain a reputation for reliability and excellence over decades.

Exercises

1. **Purpose Planner:** Identify a decision you're currently facing. Write down everything you know about the situation. Then, list any gaps in your understanding. What questions need to be answered before you proceed?
2. **Root Cause Analysis:** Choose a problem you're currently dealing with. Use the "5 Whys" technique—ask "why" five times to drill down to the root cause. Write down the true issue and potential solutions.
3. **Team Alignment:** If working with others, ask each team member to explain the goal of your project in their own words. Compare responses to uncover misalignments and clarify expectations.

Key Takeaway

Speed without direction leads to wasted effort. Clarity may take a little more time up front, but it prevents costly mistakes and ensures meaningful progress.

Chapter 4: Leverage Asymmetry in Resources

SMART USE OF RESOURCES

Big Goal

Many people assume that success requires having more money, more time, or more resources. However, history is filled with examples of individuals and organizations that achieved extraordinary results despite having fewer resources than their competitors. The key to their success? They leveraged asymmetry.

Asymmetry means recognizing the unique strengths you have – even if they seem small or unconventional. When you think strategically about your resources, you can outmaneuver competitors who rely solely on brute force or size.

Understanding Asymmetry

Asymmetry arises when two parties have unequal resources, skills, or abilities. While this might seem like a disadvantage, it often creates opportunities. Smaller players can act with agility and creativity, while larger ones may be constrained by bureaucracy or rigid systems. The key is to find ways to amplify the strengths you *do* have and use them in ways that your opponent cannot counter.

For example, in the business world, start-ups often lack the financial power of established corporations. Yet, they frequently succeed by using speed, innovation, and niche focus to carve out market dominance. They recognize that their small size allows them to take risks and adapt quickly, advantages that larger companies often lack.

How to Leverage Asymmetry

1. **Identify Your Unique Strengths:** Start by listing the resources, skills, or attributes you have that others might not. These could include specialized knowledge, agility, creativity, or the ability to take calculated risks.
2. **Think Creatively:** Use your strengths in unexpected ways. For example, if you lack funding, you might focus on building partnerships or offering a highly personalized experience that bigger competitors can't replicate.
3. **Exploit Weaknesses in Larger Systems:** Look for areas where bigger competitors are slow, inflexible, or overextended, and position yourself to fill the gaps they overlook.
4. **Focus on Precision:** Instead of spreading resources thin, concentrate them on a single, high-impact objective. A well-aimed slingshot can accomplish more than a scattered barrage.

Real-World Example

Consider the story of Airbnb. When it launched, the founders didn't have the resources to compete directly with the massive hotel industry. Instead, they identified an asymmetry: hotels were impersonal, expensive, and lacked variety. By leveraging this gap, Airbnb created a platform where homeowners could offer unique, affordable lodging options.

Despite its small beginnings, Airbnb's innovative use of technology and community resources allowed it to disrupt an entire industry.

Exercises

1. **Resource Audit:** Write down all the resources, skills, and strengths you currently have – even those that seem minor or unconventional. Next, identify one challenge or competitor you're facing. How can you use your unique strengths to gain an advantage?
2. **Spot the Weakness:** Identify a competitor, organization, or problem that seems overwhelming. What weaknesses or blind spots can you exploit to turn the situation to your advantage?
3. **Create a Focused Plan:** Choose one specific strength you have and outline a plan to use it in a high-impact way. This might involve targeting a niche audience, solving a specific problem, or creating a unique offering.

Key Takeaway

Success doesn't come from having the most resources. It comes from using what you have with precision and creativity. By leveraging asymmetry, you can turn even small strengths into powerful tools for achieving outsized results.

Chapter 5: Embrace Iterative Progress

Perfection is overrated. Waiting for an ideal moment often leads to missed opportunities. Success doesn't come from flawless execution on the first try — it comes from taking action, learning from the results, and refining your approach over time. This is the power of iterative progress.

Iteration means making continuous, small improvements instead of aiming for an all-or-nothing approach. By breaking your goals into manageable steps and focusing on improving incrementally, you create a system of steady growth. Each iteration builds on the last, propelling you closer to success while reducing the risk of catastrophic failure.

Why Iteration Matters

Think of iteration as a way to "fail forward." When you focus on iterative progress, every misstep becomes a lesson and every success becomes a foundation for the next step. This mindset not only makes daunting goals feel achievable but also increases your adaptability. In an unpredictable world, being able to adjust and improve as you go is far more valuable than rigidly sticking to a plan that doesn't work.

Consider the alternative: trying to achieve perfection in one go. This approach often leads to analysis paralysis, where the fear of making a mistake stops you from taking any action at all. Iteration, by contrast, embraces imperfection as part of the process.

How to Embrace Iterative Progress

1. **Break Down Big Goals:** Start by dividing your objective into smaller, actionable steps. Instead of aiming to "launch a successful business," focus on completing your first prototype or securing your first client.
2. **Act, Learn, Repeat:** After each step, evaluate the results. What worked? What didn't? Use this feedback to inform your next action.
3. **Focus on Consistency:** Iterative progress isn't about big leaps—it's about taking steady, consistent steps forward. Even small improvements compound over time.
4. **Stay Open to Change:** As you progress, be willing to adjust your approach. Iteration requires flexibility and a willingness to adapt based on what you learn.

Real-World Example

The story of Spotify's rise to dominance in the music industry is a masterclass in iterative progress. When Spotify launched, it wasn't the polished platform that users know today. Early versions were far from perfect but offered just enough value to attract users and generate feedback. By continually releasing updates, testing features, and refining its algorithms, Spotify grew into the global leader it is now.

Exercises

1. **Iterative Goal Setting:** Identify a big goal in your life. Break it into smaller steps and write down one action you can take today to move toward your first milestone.
2. **Evaluate and Adjust:** Choose a project you're currently working on. Assess your progress so far. What can you improve in your next iteration?
3. **Celebrate Small Wins:** Write down three small achievements from the past week that contributed to your larger goals. Reflect on how these incremental wins are moving you forward.

Key Takeaway

Progress isn't about perfection, It's about persistence. By embracing iterative progress, you create a system of continuous improvement, turning small, consistent actions into meaningful, long-term success.

Chapter 6: Balance Offensive and Defensive Moves

Every strategy involves a mix of offensive and defensive actions. Offense is about taking risks, seizing opportunities, and moving aggressively toward your goals. Defense, on the other hand, is about protecting your resources, mitigating risks, and securing your position. True strategic mastery lies in knowing when to attack and when to hold back.

Many people lean too heavily on one side. Some charge forward recklessly, exposing themselves to unnecessary risks, while others focus so much on safeguarding what they have that they miss opportunities for growth. To succeed, you must strike a balance between offense and defense, adjusting your approach based on the situation.

Why Harmony Matters

Imagine a sports team that plays entirely on offense, neglecting defense. They might score points quickly but will ultimately lose if they can't protect their lead. The same applies in life: without equilibrium, you risk overextending or stagnating.

Balancing offensive and defensive moves also builds resilience. Offense helps you grow, while defense ensures you can weather setbacks. Together, they create a stable foundation for long-term success.

How to Balance Offensive and Defensive Moves

1. **Assess the Situation:** Evaluate whether the current environment favors bold action or cautious protection. What are the risks and rewards?
2. **Set Priorities:** Define your primary goal—are you trying to gain ground or secure your position? Let this guide your actions.
3. **Stay Flexible:** The relationship between offense and defense isn't static. Be ready to shift gears as circumstances change.
4. **Monitor Resources:** Offensive moves require investment, while defensive moves preserve what you have. Always keep an eye on your resource levels.

Real-World Example

Early in its history, Netflix took an offensive approach by pioneering DVD rentals and later launching its streaming service. However, as competition grew, Netflix shifted to defense, investing heavily in original content to secure its market position. By balancing bold innovation with protective measures, Netflix has remained a dominant player in the entertainment industry.

Exercises

1. **Evaluate Your Current Status Quo:** Reflect on your current goals. Are you leaning too heavily on offense or defense? Write down one action to restore stability.
2. **Risk and Reward Analysis:** Identify one opportunity you're considering. List the potential risks and rewards. How can you mitigate the risks while maximizing the rewards?
3. **Shifting Gears:** Think of a recent situation where you were too defensive or too aggressive. What would you do differently to achieve a better footing?

Key Takeaway

Strategic success requires balancing bold, offensive moves with cautious, defensive ones. By adapting to the situation and managing resources wisely, you create a stable foundation for growth and resilience.

Chapter 7: Understand the Zero-Sum Game

Life is not always a win-win situation. In some scenarios, what one person gains, another must lose. These situations are called zero-sum games, where the total resources are fixed, and one party's victory is directly tied to another's defeat. Understanding when you're in a zero-sum game is crucial for making strategic decisions, as it requires a very different approach than situations where collaboration is possible.

What is a Zero-Sum Game?

In a zero-sum game, the sum of all outcomes is zero. If one person wins $100, the other loses $100. There's no room for mutual gain or shared success. Common examples include competitive sports, negotiations over a single asset, or battles for market share in a saturated industry.

Recognizing a zero-sum scenario allows you to focus your strategy accordingly. In these situations, collaboration is off the table, and your goal becomes maximizing your position while minimizing your opponent's. Misinterpreting a zero-sum game as a cooperative one can lead to costly mistakes, such as trusting an opponent who has no incentive to share the spoils.

Why It's Important to Recognize Zero-Sum Games

Not every competition is zero-sum. Many situations allow for shared growth, mutual benefits, or creative solutions that expand the "pie." However, when the stakes are truly zero-sum, any attempt at collaboration or compromise can weaken your position.

For example, if two companies are vying for the same exclusive government contract, only one can win. Collaboration isn't possible, and any concessions you make directly hurt your chances. On the other hand, treating a situation as zero-sum when it isn't can close off opportunities for cooperation and growth.

The key is to correctly identify the dynamics of the game you're playing. Is the pie fixed, or can it be expanded? Are you truly in competition, or is there room for a win-win outcome?

How to Succeed in Zero-Sum Games

1. **Prioritize Your Objectives:** Be clear about what you want and focus entirely on achieving it. In zero-sum games, distractions or concessions can cost you the win.

2. **Study Your Opponent:** In zero-sum scenarios, understanding your rival's strengths, weaknesses, and strategies is as important as knowing your own.

3. **Maximize Leverage:** Use every advantage at your disposal to strengthen your position. This might include controlling key resources, setting the terms of engagement, or using psychological tactics.

4. **Prepare for Trade-Offs:** Since every gain comes at the other's expense, be ready to negotiate strategically. Decide what you're willing to sacrifice to secure your most important goals.

Real-World Example

One of the most famous examples of a zero-sum game is the Cold War-era arms race between the United States and the Soviet Union. Both nations competed to amass nuclear weapons, knowing that any gain by one was perceived as a direct loss by the other. Collaboration wasn't possible in this high-stakes scenario, so both sides invested heavily in strategies that would tip the balance of power in their favor.

Exercises

1. **Identify a Zero-Sum Game:** Think of a situation in your life where resources or outcomes are limited (e.g. competing for a promotion). Write down the stakes and how your gain might directly impact others.

2. **Assess the Dynamics:** Reflect on a recent conflict or competition. Was it truly zero-sum, or was there room for mutual benefit? How might you approach it differently if it wasn't zero-sum?

3. **Plan Your Strategy:** For a zero-sum scenario you're currently facing, outline three actions you can take to maximize your chances of winning without unnecessary concessions.

Key Takeaway

Zero-sum games demand a clear, focused strategy where every gain or loss is directly tied to the outcome. Recognizing when you're in a zero-sum scenario ensures you avoid unnecessary compromises and position yourself for maximum success.

Chapter 8: Find Win-Win Opportunities

Not every situation has to be a competition. Many scenarios allow for collaboration, creativity, and shared success. The art of finding win-win opportunities lies in recognizing these situations and fostering outcomes that benefit all parties.

Understanding Win-Win Dynamics

A win-win situation occurs when cooperation creates mutual value. This often requires shifting from a competitive mindset to one focused on shared goals. In business, win-win deals might involve forming partnerships, combining strengths, or negotiating terms that satisfy both sides.

For example, imagine two businesses competing for customers in the same neighborhood. Instead of undercutting each other's prices, they could form a partnership to host a joint event, attracting more customers to both. This collaboration benefits both parties far more than direct competition.

How to Create Win-Win Outcomes

1. **Identify Shared Interests:** Look for common goals or values that both sides can work toward. What does the other party want that aligns with your objectives?
2. **Expand Opportunities:** Instead of fighting over limited resources, explore ways to create additional value. This might involve finding creative solutions or redefining the problem.
3. **Communicate Openly:** Building trust is essential for collaboration. Be transparent about your goals and encourage the other party to do the same.
4. **Stay Flexible:** Win-win outcomes often require compromise. Be willing to adjust your approach to find a solution that benefits everyone.

Real-World Example

Consider the relationship between Tesla and Panasonic. Tesla, as an electric vehicle manufacturer, relies on high-quality batteries, while Panasonic specializes in battery production. Instead of operating as competitors, the two companies formed a partnership to develop better batteries together. This collaboration expanded the market for both, creating mutual gains that wouldn't have been possible otherwise.

Exercises

1. **List Shared Goals:** Think of a current conflict or negotiation you're involved in. Write down what you want and what the other party might want. Are there areas where your goals overlap?
2. **Brainstorm Solutions:** For a challenge you're facing, list three creative ways to "expand the pie" and create additional value for all parties involved.
3. **Build Trust:** Identify one relationship or negotiation where trust is low. What steps can you take to build credibility and encourage collaboration?

Key Takeaway

Win-win opportunities allow both sides to achieve greater success than they could alone. By focusing on shared goals and creating mutual value, they can turn potential conflicts into powerful collaborations.

Chapter 9: Evaluate Trade-Offs in Every Decision

Every choice you make comes at a cost. Choosing one option means giving up something else — this is the essence of a trade-off. Strategic thinkers understand that decisions aren't about having everything but about making deliberate choices that maximize value. To make the best decisions, you must evaluate trade-offs carefully, weighing the potential benefits against the sacrifices required.

Trade-offs are everywhere, from personal decisions like how to spend your time to professional choices such as allocating limited resources. Do you focus on short-term gains or invest in long-term growth? Do you prioritize speed or quality? Understanding and analyzing these trade-offs is essential for navigating complexity and making sound strategic decisions.

Why Trade-Offs Matter

It's tempting to believe you can have it all, but reality doesn't work that way. Resources such as time, money, and energy are finite. When you commit to one path, you inherently close off others. By failing to acknowledge trade-offs, you risk spreading yourself too thin, making decisions impulsively, or pursuing conflicting goals.

Consider a company deciding between investing in product development or marketing. Product development may lead to better long-term growth, but without strong marketing, sales might suffer in the short term. There's no "right" answer — it depends on the company's priorities and situation.

How to Evaluate Trade-Offs Effectively

1. **Clarify Your Priorities:** Before making a decision, identify what matters most to you or your organization. Are you optimizing for speed, cost, quality, or something else?
2. **Identify the Opportunity Cost:** Opportunity cost is the value of what you give up by choosing one option over another. Ask yourself, "What am I sacrificing by saying yes to this?"
3. **Quantify the Costs and Benefits:** Assign tangible values to the pros and cons of each option. This can include time, money, effort, or impact.
4. **Consider the Long-Term Impact:** Don't just think about immediate gains. Ask how each option aligns with your long-term goals.
5. **Involve Stakeholders:** If the decision affects others, involve them in the process to ensure you're considering all perspectives.

Real-World Example

The legendary investor Warren Buffett often speaks about the importance of trade-offs. Buffett is known for declining numerous opportunities, even lucrative ones, because they don't align with his core investment philosophy. Rather than chasing high-risk, high-reward tech stocks during the dot-com boom, Buffett focused on steady, reliable investments. While he missed some short-term gains, his disciplined approach to evaluating trade-offs has made him one of the most successful investors in history.

Exercises

1. **Opportunity Cost Exercise:** Think about a recent decision you made. Write down what you chose and what you gave up by making that choice. Reflect on whether the trade-off was worth it.
2. **Prioritization Matrix:** For a current challenge, list all possible options and rank them based on their alignment with your goals, resources required, and potential benefits.
3. **Long-Term View:** Choose one decision you're facing right now. Write down the short-term and long-term impacts of each option. Which choice best supports your larger vision?

Key Takeaway

Every decision involves trade-offs, and success depends on recognizing and evaluating them wisely. By clarifying priorities, understanding opportunity costs, and focusing on long-term goals, you can make choices that maximize value and minimize regret.

Chapter 10: Don't Confuse Luck with Strategy

Success often has two ingredients: skill and luck. But humans are wired to see patterns, even where none exist, which leads them to overestimate how much control they have over outcomes.

This chapter is about recognizing the role of luck in your successes (and failures) and ensuring you don't mistake chance events for a brilliant strategy.

Why It's Dangerous to Confuse Luck with Strategy

When luck is mistaken for skill, it leads to overconfidence. A leader who attributes their success entirely to their strategic genius might double down on risky decisions, assuming they can replicate past results. Conversely, underestimating the role of luck in failures can lead to unnecessary self-doubt or abandoning a sound strategy.

Understanding the difference allows you to replicate what's within your control and account for what isn't. It also makes you more humble and adaptable — two qualities essential for long-term success.

How to Separate Luck from Strategy

1. **Evaluate Repeatability:** A good strategy produces consistent results, while luck is often unpredictable. If your success can't be replicated, chance likely played a role.
2. **Focus on Process, Not Outcomes:** A sound process doesn't guarantee success every time, but it increases your odds over the long run. Luck affects individual outcomes; strategy affects the overall trend.
3. **Identify External Factors:** Reflect on external conditions that may have influenced the outcome. Was timing a factor? Did you benefit from someone else's mistakes?
4. **Stay Humble:** Recognize that even the best strategies rely on some degree of luck. Humility helps you remain open to learning and improvement.

Real-World Example

Consider the career of athletes or actors who find early success. Those who attribute their success solely to talent often struggle when luck (like being in the right place at the right time) no longer favors them. However, those who combine skill with self-awareness build lasting careers.

Exercises

1. **Outcome Analysis:** Reflect on a recent success or failure. List all the factors that contributed to the result. Which ones were within your control, and which were due to external circumstances?
2. **Process Review:** Identify one key decision you made recently. Evaluate whether it was based on sound strategy or influenced by a lucky break.
3. **Luck vs. Skill Assessment:** Think of someone you admire. Reflect on how much of their success might be due to luck versus strategy. What can you learn from their approach?

Key Takeaway

Luck plays a role in every outcome, but long-term success depends on sound strategy. By focusing on processes you can control and staying humble about factors you can't, you'll make better decisions and improve over time.

Chapter 11: Cultivate Tactical Patience

Patience is often seen as passive—waiting for something to happen. But tactical patience is far from passive. It's a deliberate and strategic approach that involves resisting the urge to act prematurely, waiting for the right moment to strike, and using time as an asset rather than a limitation. This ability to wait for the most opportune moment is a hallmark of great strategists, from military leaders to business executives.

The Difference Between Patience and Tactical Patience

While ordinary patience involves enduring delays, tactical patience is about using time as a tool to improve outcomes. It requires focus, foresight, and the discipline to resist acting out of frustration or impulse. Tactical patience ensures that when you act, your timing and resources are aligned for maximum impact.

Think of tactical patience like waiting for the perfect wave while surfing. Rushing to catch the first wave you see may result in a short or chaotic ride. But waiting for the right wave gives you the momentum to glide further and more smoothly.

Why Tactical Patience Matters

Hasty decisions often lead to wasted effort, unnecessary risk, or missed opportunities. Tactical patience, on the other hand, allows you to:

- **Gather More Information:** Time can reveal hidden variables or additional details that improve decision-making.
- **Avoid Traps:** Acting too early might mean falling into a competitor's setup or a situation that wasn't fully prepared.
- **Maximize Resources:** Waiting allows you to align resources, whether it's finances, skills, or partnerships, for better outcomes.

At the same time, tactical patience isn't about endless delay. It's about balancing preparation with decisiveness — knowing when to act and when to wait.

How to Cultivate Tactical Patience

1. **Develop a Clear Goal:** Tactical patience is useless without a clear target. Know exactly what you're waiting for and why it matters.
2. **Monitor the Situation:** Regularly assess the conditions. Are they improving or deteriorating? Is the window of opportunity opening or closing?
3. **Prepare While You Wait:** Use the waiting period to strengthen your position. Train, gather resources, or refine your strategy so you're ready to act when the time comes.
4. **Resist Impulses:** When you feel the urge to act out of impatience or frustration, pause and ask, "Is this the best moment, or am I rushing?"
5. **Recognize the Right Moment:** Tactical patience doesn't mean waiting forever. Be ready to seize the moment when conditions align with your goal.

Real-World Example

The story of Apple's entry into the smartphone market is a prime example of tactical patience. By the early 2000s, mobile phones were already widespread, and competitors such as Nokia and Blackberry dominated the market. Apple could have rushed to release its own device, but instead, it waited. During this time, the company studied user behavior, refined its software, and developed the ground-breaking iPhone.

When Apple finally launched the iPhone in 2007, it wasn't the first smartphone, but it was the most refined. The company's tactical patience allowed it to disrupt the market with a product that redefined mobile technology, leaving its competitors scrambling to catch up.

Exercises

1. **Pause Before Acting:** Think of a decision you're currently facing. Write down why you feel the need to act now. Then, list three reasons why waiting might lead to a better outcome.
2. **Monitor and Adjust:** Identify a goal you've been working toward. Evaluate the current conditions—what signs would indicate it's time to act? Write these down.
3. **Preparation Period:** Choose a goal that requires timing. Use this week to prepare your resources, improve your skills, or refine your strategy while waiting for the right moment.

Key Takeaway

Tactical patience isn't about inaction; it's about timing. By waiting for the right moment to act, you maximize your impact, avoid unnecessary risks, and set yourself up for success.

Chapter 12: Harness the Power of Perception

Perception is a powerful tool in strategy. It shapes how others see you, how they respond to your actions, and even how you view yourself. The ability to influence perception can be the difference between success and failure. But harnessing perception isn't about manipulation or deception. It's about projecting the right image and ensuring your actions align with how you want to be seen.

Why Perception Matters

Perception often carries more weight than reality. In negotiations, people are more likely to trust a confident but prepared speaker than someone hesitant, even if both have the same information. In leadership, followers gravitate toward those who project calm and competence, especially in uncertain situations.

Strategists understand that people act based on what they believe, not necessarily what is true. By managing perception, you can guide decisions, build trust, and strengthen your position.

How to Harness Perception

1. **Define How You Want to Be Seen:** Decide what qualities you want to project — credibility, confidence, reliability — and ensure your actions reinforce them.
2. **Pay Attention to Body Language:** Non-verbal cues often speak louder than words. Stand tall, make eye contact, and speak clearly to convey confidence.
3. **Control the Narrative:** Be proactive in sharing your story. If you let others define you, their perception may work against you.
4. **Align Actions with Image:** Perception isn't about pretending. Ensure your behavior and decisions consistently reinforce the image you want to project.
5. **Understand Others' Perspectives:** Perception isn't one-size-fits-all. Tailor how you present yourself based on the beliefs, needs, and biases of your audience.

Real-World Example

Elon Musk is a master of shaping perception. While his companies (Tesla, SpaceX, and others) have faced significant challenges, Musk projects an image of visionary confidence. This perception has allowed him to attract investors, build customer loyalty, and maintain public trust even during setbacks.

However, perception must align with reality to be sustainable. Leaders who project confidence without substance often lose credibility once their promises fall through.

Exercises

1. **Self-Perception Audit:** Write down three words you think others would use to describe you. Compare them to the three words you want them to use. What actions can you take to bridge the gap?
2. **Body Language Practice:** For one week, focus on improving your body language. Maintain good posture, make consistent eye contact, and use deliberate gestures. Reflect on how others respond to you.
3. **Narrative Control:** Think of a situation where others misunderstood your intentions. Rewrite the story you want them to believe, and outline steps to communicate it more effectively in the future.

Key Takeaway

Perception shapes how others interact with you and how opportunities unfold. By managing how you're seen and aligning it with your actions, you build trust, credibility, and influence.

Chapter 13: Simplify Complex Options

When faced with too many choices, even the sharpest minds can become overwhelmed. This phenomenon, often called "decision paralysis," occurs when complexity hinders action. The solution? Simplify. This doesn't mean ignoring important details. It is about distilling complexity into actionable clarity.

Strategic thinkers excel at cutting through noise to focus on the core elements that matter. They understand that inaction often stems from an excess of options rather than a lack of them. Simplifying complex options allows you to see the bigger picture, make better decisions, and act with confidence.

Why Simplification is Crucial

Complexity is the enemy of efficiency. When too many variables are at play, the brain struggles to weigh pros and cons, creating delays or poor decisions. By reducing choices to their essentials, you free up mental energy to focus on execution rather than indecision.

Consider a business leader deciding where to allocate resources. A dozen competing priorities might feel equally urgent, but by focusing on the top two or three with the highest impact, the leader ensures progress without being bogged down by competing demands.

How to Simplify Complex Options

1. **Define Your Objective:** Start by asking, "What is the end goal?" This ensures that your efforts are directed toward what matters most.
2. **Group Similar Choices:** When options overlap, group them into categories. This reduces the mental load of considering each individually.
3. **Identify Key Criteria:** Choose two or three criteria that matter most to your decision. Evaluate each option based on these factors.
4. **Eliminate Low-Value Choices:** Discard options that don't significantly contribute to your goal. This narrows your focus to the highest-impact choices.
5. **Use Decision Frameworks:** Tools like decision trees or cost-benefit analyses can help organize complex information into a clear structure.

Real-World Example

Slack, the workplace communication platform, is a contemporary example of simplifying complexity to achieve success. When Slack launched, many companies were already using a mix of email, file-sharing services, and messaging apps to manage communication. Rather than trying to compete with each tool separately, Slack focused on simplifying workplace communication by consolidating these functions into one platform.

Exercises

1. **Pare Down Priorities:** List all the tasks or options you're currently considering for a project. Identify the top three that will have the greatest impact and focus on them.
2. **Create a Decision Tree:** For a complex decision you're facing, draw a decision tree to map out your options, their consequences, and how they align with your goals.
3. **Eliminate the Noise:** Reflect on an area of your life where complexity is holding you back. What unnecessary choices or distractions can you remove to create clarity?

Key Takeaway

Simplifying complex options isn't about ignoring details. It's about focusing on what truly matters. By cutting through the noise and prioritizing high-impact choices, you enable clear, confident decision-making that drives meaningful results.

Chapter 14: Always Ask "Why?" Twice

Curiosity is the foundation of strategic thinking, and asking "why?" is its simplest yet most powerful tool. But a single "why?" is rarely enough. The first answer often addresses symptoms rather than root causes. Asking "why?" twice — or more — forces you to dig deeper, uncovering the true dynamics behind a problem or opportunity.

This technique, known as the 5 Whys in problem-solving frameworks, is a hallmark of analytical thinking. By refusing to settle for surface-level answers, you gain a clearer understanding of situations, enabling more effective strategies.

Why Asking "Why?" Twice is Effective

Most people accept the first explanation they receive. While this saves time, it often leads to decisions based on incomplete or misleading information. By going deeper, you uncover the core issue, which is often more nuanced than it first appears.

For example, if a project misses its deadline, the immediate answer might be, "The team worked too slowly." But asking "why?" again might reveal that the real issue was unclear communication or insufficient planning. Tackling the deeper cause prevents repeat failures.

How to Use the "Why?" Technique

1. **Start with the Obvious:** Ask "why?" to address the most immediate or visible issue.
2. **Dig Deeper:** For every answer you receive, ask "why?" again. Repeat until you uncover a root cause or actionable insight.
3. **Avoid Assumptions:** Be cautious not to settle for assumptions or convenient answers. Challenge yourself to find evidence for each response.
4. **Focus on Solutions:** Once the root cause is clear, identify actions to address it directly, rather than just treating symptoms.

Real-World Example

In the early 2000s, Domino's Pizza faced declining sales and poor customer satisfaction. Initial surveys revealed that customers didn't like the pizza. But instead of stopping there, Domino's executives asked, **"Why don't customers like the pizza?"** The answer? It lacked freshness and flavor. **"Why does it lack freshness?"** Because the dough recipe and delivery methods hadn't been updated in decades.

This deeper questioning led Domino's to revamp its pizza recipe, improve its delivery processes, and launch a transparent marketing campaign that highlighted the changes. The result was a turnaround in both reputation and sales, proving that going beyond surface-level answers can lead to meaningful transformation.

Exercises

1. **Root Cause Analysis:** Think of a recent challenge you faced. Write down the first answer to "why?" and keep asking until you uncover the root cause.
2. **Challenge Assumptions:** Choose a belief or routine you follow without question. Ask "why?" twice to analyze whether it still serves you.
3. **Practice with Small Decisions:** Use this technique for everyday choices to build the habit of digging deeper into your reasoning.

Key Takeaway

By asking "why?" more than once, you move beyond surface-level answers to uncover root causes. This deeper understanding allows you to solve problems at their core and make more effective decisions.

Chapter 15: Avoid Overcommitting Help

Helping others is an essential part of building relationships and fostering trust. However, overcommitting your time, energy, or resources can backfire. When you stretch yourself too thin, you risk not delivering on your promises, burning out, or neglecting your own priorities. The key is learning how to offer meaningful help without overcommitting.

Many people fall into the trap of overcommitting because they fear disappointing others or believe saying "yes" to every request is the best way to build trust. While well-intentioned, this behavior can lead to missed deadlines, compromised quality, and a reputation for unreliability. Strategic thinkers understand that saying "no" is sometimes the best way to protect their ability to provide high-value assistance where it truly matters.

Why Avoiding Overcommitment is Important

Overcommitting doesn't just affect you. It also impacts those you're trying to help. If you take on too many requests, the quality of your assistance often suffers. By focusing your efforts, you ensure that the help you provide is effective and impactful.

How to Offer Help Without Overcommitting

1. **Assess Your Capacity:** Before agreeing to help, evaluate whether you have the time and resources to follow through without compromising other priorities.
2. **Prioritize Requests:** Not all requests are equally important. Focus on helping where your contribution will have the greatest impact.
3. **Set Boundaries:** Clearly communicate what you can and cannot offer. For example, agree to assist with specific tasks rather than taking on an entire project.
4. **Learn to Say "No" Gracefully:** Declining a request doesn't have to damage relationships. Be honest and suggest alternatives, such as other resources or people who may be able to help.
5. **Protect Your Own Priorities:** Helping others should never come at the cost of neglecting your personal or professional goals.

Real-World Example

Bill Gates famously faced challenges managing his time as Microsoft grew. Recognizing the risk of overcommitting, Gates adopted a deliberate approach to prioritize tasks and delegate effectively. By saying "no" to opportunities that didn't align with his long-term goals, he focused his energy on high-impact areas, such as developing ground-breaking software and growing Microsoft into a tech giant.

Exercises

1. **Track Your Commitments:** Write down all the tasks, favors, or responsibilities you've agreed to recently. Evaluate whether any of them can be delegated, delayed, or declined.
2. **Set a Help Limit:** For the next week, commit to helping no more than three people or projects. Focus on offering meaningful assistance to each.
3. **Practice Saying "No":** Reflect on a request you should have declined but didn't. Write a polite response you could use in a similar situation in the future.

Key Takeaway

Helping others is valuable, but overcommitting reduces the quality of your assistance and drains your resources. By focusing your help where it matters most and setting boundaries, you ensure that your efforts are both effective and sustainable.

Chapter 16: Be the First Mover When It Counts

In strategy, timing is everything. Being the first mover — someone who takes action before others — can provide significant advantages, such as establishing market dominance, shaping perceptions, or capturing key opportunities. However, being the first mover isn't always the best choice. The key lies in knowing when taking the lead will create lasting advantages and when waiting might be wiser.

Why First Movers Have an Edge

First movers often benefit from "first-mover advantage." This can include:

- **Brand Recognition:** Being first establishes your name as synonymous with the innovation or opportunity.
- **Market Share:** Early action allows you to secure resources, customers, or territory before competitors enter the field.
- **Shaping the Rules:** By moving first, you can influence how others view the market or opportunity, creating a standard others must follow.

However, moving first also carries risks. If the timing is wrong or the approach isn't well-thought-out, others can learn from your mistakes and gain an edge as "fast followers."

How to Decide When to Be the First Mover

1. **Assess the Landscape:** Is the opportunity time-sensitive, or could waiting allow for more preparation?
2. **Evaluate the Risks:** What are the potential downsides of moving first, and are you prepared to address them?
3. **Prepare Thoroughly:** First movers succeed when they combine speed with preparation. Moving first without being ready can lead to failure.
4. **Monitor Competitors:** If others are on the verge of acting, being the first mover may prevent them from gaining an edge.

Real-World Example

In the early 2000s, PayPal revolutionized online payments by being the first company to provide a seamless, secure method for transferring money electronically. At a time when e-commerce was gaining traction, PayPal's first-mover advantage allowed it to integrate quickly with platforms such as eBay. By establishing trust in the marketplace and becoming synonymous with online transactions, PayPal outpaced competitors and set the standard for digital payment systems. Its early action positioned it as a leader in the financial technology space.

Exercises

1. **Identify First-Mover Opportunities:** Look at your current goals or projects. Are there opportunities where acting first could provide a competitive advantage?
2. **Weigh the Risks:** For a decision where you're considering moving first, list the potential risks and benefits. How can you mitigate the risks?
3. **Plan Your First Move:** Choose one area where you can act decisively this week. Create a clear plan to ensure your first move is impactful.

Key Takeaway

Being the first mover can offer significant advantages, but only if the timing and preparation align. By acting decisively when it counts, you position yourself to shape outcomes and secure lasting success.

Chapter 17: Follow the Nash Equilibrium

In strategic decision-making, knowing when to compromise and when to hold your ground is critical. The Nash Equilibrium, a concept from game theory, provides a framework for understanding balance in competitive and cooperative situations. Named after mathematician John Nash, this principle occurs when all parties involved in a decision have chosen their best possible strategy, assuming the others won't change theirs.

The Nash Equilibrium is not about everyone winning — it's about reaching a state where no individual can improve their position without making someone else worse off. It's a critical concept for navigating scenarios where decisions are interdependent, like negotiations, market competition, or even interpersonal dynamics.

Why the Nash Equilibrium Matters

Many strategies fail because they assume that one party's actions are independent of the other's. In reality, most decisions are interconnected. By understanding the Nash Equilibrium, you can identify stable outcomes where neither side has an incentive to deviate.

Consider a price war between two businesses. If both undercut each other indefinitely, they'll erode their profits. Instead, by understanding each other's limits, they may settle at a price point that maximizes mutual benefit while discouraging further undercutting.

How to Apply the Nash Equilibrium in Real Life

1. **Analyze Interdependence:** Identify how your decisions affect others and how their actions impact you.
2. **Evaluate Stable Outcomes:** Look for strategies where no party has an incentive to unilaterally change their approach.
3. **Avoid Unnecessary Aggression:** Recognize when escalating a situation is counterproductive. Sometimes the best move is maintaining balance.
4. **Build Predictability:** In negotiations or partnerships, demonstrate consistency so others can rely on your strategy, leading to more stable outcomes.

Real-World Example

The global airline industry often operates around Nash Equilibrium principles. Airlines compete on ticket pricing, but unrestrained price wars would harm everyone. Instead, they often settle into pricing structures where each airline maintains profitability, knowing that aggressive under-pricing would trigger retaliation and mutual losses.

This equilibrium doesn't eliminate competition, but it ensures a balance where no single airline is incentivized to disrupt the market radically. Understanding this dynamic helps airlines remain competitive while avoiding destructive price wars.

Exercises

1. **Find a Nash Equilibrium:** Think of a negotiation or conflict you're involved in. What choices could create a stable outcome where neither party has an incentive to change their position?
2. **Assess Interconnected Decisions:** Choose a scenario where your decisions impact others. How do their likely responses shape your strategy?
3. **Simulate Stability:** Create a simple game with a friend, where both players make decisions that impact each other's outcomes. Look for the point where neither of you can improve without cooperation.

Key Takeaway

The Nash Equilibrium highlights the importance of interdependence in strategic thinking. By recognizing stable outcomes where no party benefits from unilaterally changing their strategy, you can navigate competition and collaboration with greater confidence.

Chapter 18: Build Redundancies for Resilience

In a perfect world, everything would go according to plan. But in reality, systems fail, people make mistakes, and unforeseen events occur. Building redundancies — backup systems, extra resources, or contingency plans — is essential for ensuring resilience. While redundancies may seem inefficient in the short term, they provide the safety and flexibility needed to thrive in uncertain environments.

Why Redundancies Are Crucial

Redundancies act as fail-safes. They ensure that when one system fails, another is ready to take its place. In business, this might mean having multiple suppliers for critical materials. In personal finances, it could involve an emergency savings fund. Redundancies don't just prevent failure — they allow you to recover faster and minimize disruption.

Space exploration is a good example. NASA incorporates redundancies into every mission, from backup communication systems to duplicate life-support mechanisms. These redundancies add weight and cost, but they're non-negotiable when the stakes are life and mission success.

How to Build Redundancies

1. **Identify Critical Systems:** Focus on areas where failure would have the greatest impact, such as finances, operations, or relationships.
2. **Create Backups:** Develop alternative resources, plans, or systems that can step in when the primary one fails.
3. **Test Your Redundancies:** A plan is only as good as its execution. Regularly test your backups to ensure they work under pressure.
4. **Balance Efficiency with Resilience:** Avoid excessive redundancy that wastes resources, but ensure you're prepared for high-stakes risks.

Real-World Example

The COVID-19 pandemic highlighted the importance of redundancies in global supply chains. Companies that relied on single suppliers for key components faced severe disruptions, while those with diversified suppliers weathered the crisis more effectively. This resilience through redundancy underscored the need for proactive planning in a volatile world.

Exercises

1. **Identify Vulnerabilities:** Write down three areas of your life or business where failure would have the greatest impact. What redundancies can you create to mitigate these risks?
2. **Create a Backup Plan:** For a project or goal, develop an alternative plan in case your primary approach fails.
3. **Test Your Systems:** Choose one critical area and test its backup. For example, try using an alternative supplier or accessing an emergency fund to ensure it works as intended.

Key Takeaway

Building redundancies ensures you're prepared for failures or unexpected events. By incorporating backups and contingency plans into critical areas, you create resilience and flexibility in the face of uncertainty.

> We talked about renting this space six months ago...

> Yeah, but we kept waiting—and now someone else grabbed it.

Chapter 19: Don't Neglect the Cost of Inaction

The cost of inaction is often invisible but can be just as damaging as a bad decision. While most people focus on the risks of acting too quickly or making the wrong choice, they often overlook the hidden price of doing nothing. Strategic thinkers understand that inaction is rarely neutral. It usually results in missed opportunities, wasted potential, or worsening problems.

Inaction can occur for many reasons: fear of failure, overanalysis, or a desire for perfect conditions. But in most cases, waiting too long leads to greater risks than acting with imperfect information. The challenge is learning to assess when waiting adds value and when it merely delays progress.

Why Inaction is Risky

1. **Opportunities are Finite:** Many opportunities have a shelf life. Waiting too long can mean losing your chance to act altogether.
2. **Problems Escalate:** Unaddressed challenges often grow more complex and costly over time.
3. **Stagnation Stalls Growth:** Refusing to act keeps you in place while others move ahead, leaving you at a disadvantage.

Consider a business that hesitates to adopt new technology. While they deliberate, competitors who act early gain a technological edge, capturing market share and setting new standards. By the time the hesitant business decides to act, they're left playing catch-up.

How to Evaluate the Cost of Inaction

1. **Quantify Potential Losses:** Identify what's at stake if you choose not to act — missed revenue, declining market share, or personal growth.
2. **Compare Risks:** Assess whether the risks of inaction outweigh the risks of taking a calculated step forward.
3. **Set Deadlines:** Avoid indefinite delays by giving yourself a clear timeline to act.
4. **Start Small:** If you're unsure about a decision, take a low-stakes action to test the waters without fully committing.

Real-World Example

Kodak provides a cautionary tale of the cost of inaction. Although Kodak invented the first digital camera in 1975, the company hesitated to pursue digital photography for fear of cannibalizing its film business. While Kodak delayed, competitors such as Sony and Canon embraced digital technology, capturing the market and redefining the industry. By the time Kodak acted, it was too late. The company filed for bankruptcy in 2012, a victim of its own failure to adapt.

Exercises

1. **Identify an Opportunity:** Think of a decision you've been delaying. Write down what you stand to lose if you continue to wait.
2. **Risk Assessment:** Compare the risks of acting versus the risks of inaction. Which option has the higher long-term cost?
3. **Take One Step:** Choose a small, manageable action you can take today toward resolving a delayed decision.

Key Takeaway

Inaction has a cost, often greater than the risks of acting. By evaluating what's at stake and taking steps forward, you position yourself to seize opportunities and prevent problems from escalating.

Chapter 20: Master the Pivot Point

Even the most carefully crafted plans can hit obstacles, whether due to shifting circumstances, emerging competitors, or new opportunities. Success often hinges not on sticking rigidly to a failing course but on the ability to pivot — shifting your approach while maintaining focus on your ultimate goal. A well-timed pivot transforms challenges into opportunities, keeps your momentum intact, and positions you for long-term success.

A pivot can be as small as adjusting your tactics in a negotiation or as significant as completely redefining your business model. The key is to identify when a pivot is necessary and execute it with clarity and purpose.

The coffee shop idea didn't work out.

Let's pivot—what if we turn it into a co-working space?

Why Pivoting is Essential

1. **Adaptation Ensures Survival:** Markets, industries, and environments are constantly changing. Without adaptability, even the strongest strategies can become obsolete. Pivoting allows you to adjust to these changes and remain competitive.
2. **It Protects Resources:** Continuing on a failing path wastes time, energy, and money. A strategic pivot redirects those resources to more promising opportunities.
3. **It Maximizes Learning:** Every obstacle provides valuable insights. Pivoting uses those lessons to refine your approach and make better decisions moving forward.

How to Pivot Effectively

1. **Clarify Your Core Goal:** Before pivoting, reaffirm what you're trying to achieve. A successful pivot shifts the approach without losing sight of the destination.
2. **Reassess Your Strengths:** Identify the resources, skills, or assets you already have that can support the new direction.
3. **Plan the Transition:** A pivot isn't a leap of faith. Develop a clear strategy for reallocating resources, setting new priorities, and communicating the change to stakeholders.
4. **Maintain Momentum:** A pivot isn't about starting over—it's about redirecting your existing efforts. Ensure continuity by leveraging what you've already built.
5. **Communicate Clearly:** If your pivot affects others—whether employees, customers, or partners—be transparent about why the change is happening and how it benefits the larger mission.

Real-World Example

Instagram's transformation into the platform it is today exemplifies the power of a strategic pivot. Initially, it was a location-based check-in app with several features, including photo sharing. However, users gravitated toward the photo-sharing function, while other features saw little engagement.

Recognizing this trend, the founders made a bold pivot: they stripped the app down to its core photo-sharing feature, rebranded it as Instagram, and focused on simplicity and usability. By pivoting at the right time, the team avoided spreading resources too thin and created a product that resonated deeply with its audience.

Exercises

1. **Evaluate a Current Path:** Identify a project or strategy that's underperforming. What signs suggest it may be time to pivot? Write down potential new directions.
2. **Redefine Your Goal:** Revisit your core objective for a long-term project. How might a pivot help you achieve it more effectively?
3. **Develop a Pivot Plan:** For a challenge you're facing, outline the steps needed to shift focus or strategy while maintaining continuity and momentum.

Key Takeaway

Pivoting isn't about giving up. It's about adapting to stay aligned with your goals. By recognizing when to pivot, planning your shift carefully, and communicating clearly, you turn obstacles into opportunities and maintain progress toward success.

Section II: Competitive Strategies

In the game of strategy, competition is inevitable. Whether you're navigating business rivalries, political conflicts, or even personal challenges, success often depends on how well you handle opposition. This section dives into the art of competing strategically — leveraging your strengths, exploiting weaknesses, and staying one step ahead of your rivals.

Chapter 21: Make the Most of Your Competition's Blind Spots

Every competitor, no matter how skilled, has blind spots — areas they ignore, underestimate, or fail to notice. These blind spots aren't necessarily flaws in their strategy; they are often the natural result of human limitations, overconfidence, or an excessive focus on certain priorities. Your ability to identify and exploit these gaps can be the difference between an ordinary outcome and a decisive victory.

Blind spots come in many forms: overlooked markets, neglected risks, or assumptions that competitors take for granted. By honing your observational skills and strategically addressing these blind spots, you create opportunities that your rivals simply don't see coming.

Why Blind Spots Exist

Blind spots aren't just mistakes; they are often the by-product of focus. A business deeply committed to dominating one market may neglect emerging competitors in other areas. A highly experienced leader might rely too heavily on old methods, failing to adapt to new trends. Blind spots can also arise from complacency, overconfidence, or cognitive biases that skew judgment.

Identifying and leveraging these blind spots gives you a competitive edge by capitalizing on areas where your opponent has made themselves vulnerable.

How to Identify Blind Spots

1. **Monitor Patterns:** Watch for areas where your competitor consistently invests their attention and resources. Blind spots often emerge in areas they neglect or deprioritize.
2. **Observe Their Assumptions:** Pay attention to what they assume about the market, their competitors, or their own strengths. Question whether those assumptions hold true.
3. **Listen to Feedback:** Customer complaints, industry trends, or even insider leaks can reveal areas where competitors are falling short.
4. **Analyze Resource Allocation:** Where are they putting most of their energy? Blind spots are often in the areas they've chosen not to focus on.

Real-World Example

When Southwest Airlines entered the market, it identified a significant blind spot in the airline industry: most competitors were focused on major hubs and long-haul flights, leaving short-distance travel underserved. Southwest capitalized on this gap by offering low-cost, high-frequency flights between smaller cities.

By prioritizing efficiency, quick turnarounds, and customer-friendly pricing, Southwest tapped into a market that traditional airlines had largely ignored. This strategic focus not only allowed the company to grow rapidly but also disrupted the airline industry, forcing competitors to adapt.

Exercises

1. **Competitor Audit:** Choose a competitor and list areas where they might be overinvested or underinvested. Identify one blind spot you could exploit.
2. **Test Their Awareness:** Introduce a small, unexpected action and observe their reaction. This can reveal how prepared they are to respond.
3. **Assess Your Own Blind Spots:** Reflect on areas of your strategy that you may be neglecting. Seek feedback from a trusted advisor to uncover weaknesses you might not see.

Key Takeaway

Your competitor's blind spots are your hidden opportunities. By identifying areas they overlook and acting strategically, you gain an edge that catches them off guard and puts you ahead.

Chapter 22: Focus on the Player, Not Just the Rules

When it comes to competition, most people focus exclusively on the rules of the game—the structure, tactics, and tools needed to succeed. While this is essential, it's equally critical to focus on the player. Competitors aren't machines; they're human beings influenced by emotions, biases, and individual tendencies. By understanding the person behind the strategy, you gain a powerful advantage.

Rules may create the framework for competition, but the player decides how to interpret and execute within those boundaries. Learning their habits, motivations, and vulnerabilities allows you to predict their actions, exploit their weaknesses, and adapt your approach to counter their moves.

Why Focusing on the Player Matters

Rules apply equally to everyone, but players approach them differently. A risk-averse competitor might avoid bold moves even when the rules encourage them. A highly confident rival might overreach, assuming their strategy is flawless. When you focus on the player, you see opportunities that the rules alone don't reveal.

Moreover, human behavior is often predictable. Patterns emerge over time — whether in decision-making, communication, or reactions under pressure. Understanding these patterns enables you to tailor your strategy to outsmart your opponent.

How to Focus on the Player

1. **Study Their History:** Review their past decisions and outcomes. Are there recurring themes in how they approach problems or challenges?
2. **Identify Their Triggers:** Observe what makes them confident, frustrated, or indecisive. Emotional responses often reveal underlying tendencies.
3. **Anticipate Reactions:** Based on their behavior, predict how they'll respond to specific actions. Use this knowledge to shape your strategy.
4. **Adapt to Their Style:** If they're aggressive, use patience to wear them down. If they're cautious, use bold moves to keep them on the defensive.

Real-World Example

In the 1972 World Chess Championship, Bobby Fischer used psychological tactics to gain an edge over Boris Spassky. Fischer didn't just play the game — he studied Spassky's habits, from his favored strategies to his reactions under pressure. By introducing unexpected moves and even subtle distractions, Fischer disrupted Spassky's focus and forced him to play reactively. This focus on the player, rather than just the game, helped Fischer secure a historic victory.

Exercises

1. **Opponent Analysis:** Choose a competitor and write down three patterns in their behavior. How could you use these patterns to anticipate their next move?
2. **Self-Reflection:** Identify one habit or tendency of yours that an opponent might exploit. How can you address it to avoid becoming predictable?
3. **Experiment with Reactions:** During your next competitive interaction, introduce an unexpected element and observe how the other party responds. Use this insight to refine your approach.

Key Takeaway

The game's rules may be fixed, but players interpret and act on them differently. By studying the person behind the strategy, you gain insight into their tendencies and can craft approaches that outmaneuver them effectively.

Chapter 23: Control the Tempo of Engagement

In any competitive scenario, controlling the tempo — the speed and rhythm of engagement — gives you the upper hand. Whether it's a negotiation, a business rivalry, or a debate, the party that dictates the pace often controls the outcome. By adjusting the tempo to suit your strengths and disrupt your opponent's, you can maintain momentum when it benefits you or slow things down to regain control.

Tempo management isn't just about acting quickly or slowly. It's about strategic pacing: accelerating when it forces your rival to make hasty mistakes or pausing to gather information, plan, or wear down your opponent's patience. The right tempo can destabilize even the most prepared competitors.

Why Tempo Control is Powerful

1. **Keeps You in the Driver's Seat:** Setting the tempo forces others to react to your moves instead of focusing on their strategy.
2. **Disrupts Opponents:** A slower tempo frustrates aggressive rivals, while a faster pace overwhelms cautious ones.
3. **Aligns Actions with Goals:** Controlling the tempo ensures you're moving at a pace that maximizes your strengths and minimizes your weaknesses.

For example, in negotiations, a fast tempo can create pressure for quick agreements, while slowing things down can give you time to gather more information and identify leverage points.

How to Control the Tempo

1. **Start with Observation:** Understand your opponent's natural rhythm. Are they fast-paced and impulsive, or methodical and slow?
2. **Set the Tone Early:** Begin interactions at your desired pace to establish control from the start.
3. **Vary the Tempo:** Use shifts in speed to surprise your opponent, keeping them off balance.
4. **Use Pauses Strategically:** Silence can be a powerful tool, forcing your rival to fill the gap and potentially reveal information or weaken their position.
5. **Stay Adaptable:** If your opponent tries to take control, adjust to regain the upper hand without losing sight of your objectives.

Real-World Example

Muhammad Ali's famous "rope-a-dope" strategy during his 1974 fight with George Foreman is a perfect illustration of tempo control. Ali deliberately slowed the pace by leaning against the ropes and letting Foreman exhaust himself with a barrage of punches. By conserving his energy and dictating the rhythm of the fight, Ali waited for the perfect moment to strike. In the eighth round, he unleashed a fast-paced counterattack, knocking out Foreman to win the match.

Exercises

1. **Identify Your Tempo:** Reflect on your natural pace in competitive situations. Are you fast-paced, methodical, or adaptable? How can you use this to your advantage?
2. **Practice Shifting Gears:** In your next discussion or negotiation, experiment with speeding up or slowing down the conversation. Observe how the other person reacts and adjust accordingly.
3. **Plan a Tempo Strategy:** Choose a current challenge or rivalry and outline when to accelerate and when to slow down to maintain control.

Key Takeaway

Controlling the tempo of engagement allows you to dictate the flow of competition, forcing opponents to play on your terms. By managing the rhythm strategically, you can destabilize rivals, maintain control, and align actions with your ultimate goals.

Chapter 24: Feign Weakness Where You Are Strong

Sometimes, the best way to exploit your strengths is to hide them. Feigning weakness in areas where you are strong can mislead your opponents into underestimating you, or exposing their vulnerabilities. This tactic allows you to maneuver with the element of surprise and strike when they least expect it.

Feigning weakness doesn't mean giving up your advantage—it's about appearing less capable while maintaining your true strength. This misdirection can create opportunities for decisive action when your rival is unprepared.

Why Feigning Weakness Works

1. **Encourages Overconfidence:** Rivals who perceive you as weak may become careless or complacent, leaving themselves vulnerable.
2. **Shifts Focus:** By downplaying your strengths, you redirect your opponent's attention to areas that don't matter as much.
3. **Creates Element of Surprise:** Opponents are less likely to prepare for a strong move when they perceive no threat.

For example, in a competitive bidding process, a company might initially appear disinterested to prevent rivals from driving up prices. When the time is right, they can step in with a strong offer and secure the deal.

How to Feign Weakness Effectively

1. **Understand Perception:** Assess how others view your strengths and weaknesses. Use this insight to shape their expectations.
2. **Downplay Capabilities:** Be subtle — don't overdo it. A convincing feint relies on appearing naturally weak rather than obviously deceptive.
3. **Time Your Move:** Wait until your opponent has fully committed to their assumptions before revealing your true strength.
4. **Avoid Becoming Predictable:** If you feign weakness too often, others may begin to suspect your intentions. Use this tactic sparingly for maximum impact.

Real-World Example

During the 1980s, Nintendo feigned disinterest in the home console market, allowing competitors like Atari and Sega to dominate early. Behind the scenes, Nintendo was perfecting its NES (Nintendo Entertainment System). By the time it launched, the NES was far more advanced than its rivals' offerings, quickly capturing the market. Nintendo's apparent lack of urgency lulled competitors into complacency, giving the company a decisive edge.

Exercises

1. **Analyze Your Strengths:** Identify an area where you excel. How could feigning weakness in this area create an opportunity to surprise your competitors?
2. **Create a Feint Strategy:** Outline a scenario where you could deliberately downplay your capabilities to mislead a rival or adversary.
3. **Evaluate Timing:** Reflect on a past situation where revealing strength too early backfired. How could you have timed your move better?

Key Takeaway

Feigning weakness where you are strong allows you to disarm opponents and catch them off guard. By using misdirection strategically, you gain the element of surprise and create opportunities to strike decisively.

Chapter 25: Cultivate Alliances to Outflank Threats

In the face of formidable competition or overwhelming challenges, alliances can be your greatest asset. By building strategic partnerships, you combine resources, knowledge, and influence to tackle threats from multiple angles. An alliance isn't just about teamwork—it's a calculated strategy to strengthen your position and neutralize competitors or obstacles.

Alliances can take many forms: formal partnerships, informal collaborations, or even temporary arrangements to address specific threats. The key is to align your interests with others in a way that benefits everyone involved. A strong alliance not only outflanks competitors but also protects you from becoming isolated in the heat of competition.

Why Alliances Are Powerful

1. **Shared Resources:** Alliances allow you to pool assets, such as expertise, funding, or infrastructure, to accomplish more than you could alone.
2. **Broader Reach:** Partnering with others expands your network, giving you access to markets, opportunities, or audiences that were previously out of reach.
3. **Divide and Conquer:** An alliance can enable you to divide responsibilities, allowing each partner to focus on their strengths.
4. **Neutralizing Rivals:** By aligning with others, you can collectively beat common threats.

For example, two small businesses in the same industry might form an alliance to negotiate better rates with suppliers or share marketing resources to compete against larger competitors.

How to Cultivate Effective Alliances

1. **Identify Common Goals:** Look for partners whose interests align with yours. A strong alliance depends on mutual benefit.
2. **Choose Complementary Strengths:** Seek allies who bring unique capabilities that fill gaps in your own strategy.
3. **Build Trust:** Alliances thrive on transparency and reliability. Invest time in building trust to ensure a lasting partnership.
4. **Communicate Clearly:** Define roles, responsibilities, and expectations from the outset to avoid misunderstandings.
5. **Stay Flexible:** Alliances are dynamic. Be prepared to adjust the terms or nature of the partnership as circumstances change.

Real-World Example

The strategic partnership between Starbucks and PepsiCo is a perfect example of using alliances to outflank threats. In the 1990s, Starbucks wanted to expand its presence in the bottled coffee market but lacked the distribution network to reach grocery stores and vending machines. PepsiCo, with its extensive distribution channels, faced increasing competition in the beverage market and sought new products to boost its portfolio.

The two companies formed an alliance, combining Starbucks' brand and coffee expertise with PepsiCo's distribution power. This partnership allowed Starbucks to dominate the ready-to-drink coffee market while helping PepsiCo diversify its offerings. Together, they outflanked competitors like Coca-Cola and Nestlé in the growing bottled coffee segment.

Exercises

1. **Map Your Network:** List potential allies in your field or industry. Identify how their strengths could complement your own to address a common challenge.
2. **Define Mutual Benefits:** Think of a current threat or obstacle. Outline how partnering with another person or organization could create a win-win solution.
3. **Build Trust:** Identify an existing partnership or relationship. Take one step this week to strengthen trust, such as sharing information or offering help.

Key Takeaway

Strategic alliances allow you to overcome threats and achieve goals that would be impossible alone. By combining strengths and aligning interests, you create a powerful force capable of tackling even the toughest challenges.

Chapter 26: Use Decoys to Distract and Mislead

Decoys are powerful tools in strategy. By presenting a distraction or false target, you misdirect your competitors' focus, causing them to waste time and resources on irrelevant pursuits. A well-placed decoy shifts attention away from your true intentions, allowing you to act decisively in areas your rivals aren't prepared for.

Using decoys effectively requires subtlety and timing. The goal isn't to deceive for the sake of deception—it's to guide your opponents' actions in a way that benefits your strategy. Whether in negotiations, competition, or warfare, decoys create opportunities to strike where it matters most while your rivals are preoccupied elsewhere.

Why Decoys Work

1. **Divert Resources:** Competitors focused on a decoy will allocate energy to the wrong areas, weakening their ability to counter your real moves.
2. **Create Uncertainty:** A convincing decoy makes it harder for rivals to predict your true intentions, forcing them to act reactively.
3. **Buy Time:** Distracting opponents gives you the breathing room to prepare, regroup, or execute your strategy.

For example, in chess, a player might sacrifice a lesser piece to distract their opponent while positioning their more powerful pieces for a decisive move.

How to Use Decoys Effectively

1. **Choose the Right Distraction:** A decoy should be credible enough to capture attention but expendable enough that losing it won't harm your position.
2. **Time It Perfectly:** Deploy your decoy at a moment when your opponent is most likely to react strongly.
3. **Control the Narrative:** Shape how the decoy is perceived to maximize its impact.
4. **Act Quickly:** Use the distraction to make your real move while your opponent is preoccupied.

Real-World Example

In the fast-food industry, Burger King has often used clever decoys to distract competitors and draw attention to its brand. One notable example was the "Whopper Detour" campaign in 2018. Burger King launched a promotion where customers could order a Whopper for just one cent — *but only if they were within 600 feet of a McDonald's location.*

The campaign created the illusion that Burger King was directing customers toward McDonald's, but the real goal was to distract McDonald's while driving attention and traffic to the Burger King app. The campaign was a huge success, resulting in over 1.5 million app downloads and strengthening Burger King's digital engagement. By using McDonald's locations as a decoy, Burger King successfully turned its rival's presence into an advantage.

Exercises

1. **Identify a Decoy Opportunity:** Think of a current competition or negotiation. What false target could you present to mislead your rival?
2. **Plan Your Real Move:** While your opponent is distracted, what action can you take to advance your true goal?
3. **Test Subtle Decoys:** In a low-stakes situation, introduce a small decoy and observe how others react. Refine your approach based on the results.

Key Takeaway

Decoys are a strategic way to mislead and distract your rivals, giving you the opportunity to act where it matters most. By directing their focus away from your true intentions, you gain the upper hand and create space for decisive action.

Chapter 27: Capture High Ground in Negotiations

In negotiations, securing the high ground gives you the ability to shape the conversation, frame the terms, and maintain leverage. The high ground isn't just about moral superiority — it's about positioning yourself so that the other party must negotiate on your terms. This could mean controlling key information, offering the most valuable resource, or influencing the timing and structure of the negotiation.

Capturing high ground requires preparation, insight into what the other party values, and the ability to establish authority without appearing inflexible. When done effectively, you can guide the negotiation toward a favorable outcome while maintaining collaboration and goodwill.

Why High Ground is Important in Negotiations

1. **Sets the Agenda:** The party in the strongest position often defines the rules of engagement, making it harder for others to shift the conversation.
2. **Increases Influence:** High ground allows you to frame your offer as indispensable or superior, making it difficult for others to challenge your terms.
3. **Minimizes Pressure:** With a strong position, you can negotiate with confidence, avoiding desperation or rushed decisions.

For example, if you have a unique skill set or exclusive resource, you're automatically in a stronger position to negotiate favorable terms. The other party needs what you offer, giving you leverage to secure better outcomes.

How to Capture High Ground

1. **Prepare Thoroughly:** Research what the other party values most. Position yourself as the provider of something they can't easily get elsewhere.
2. **Control Information Flow:** Share key details strategically while withholding information that could weaken your position.
3. **Define the Context:** Take the lead in framing the negotiation. For instance, if discussing pricing, emphasize value over cost to set the tone.
4. **Be the First Mover:** When appropriate, initiate the negotiation to establish your terms as the starting point.
5. **Stay Calm Under Pressure:** High ground is lost when you react emotionally or concede too quickly. Maintain composure to reinforce your position.

Real-World Example

In 1993, Nabisco negotiated the purchase of the SnackWell's brand from a smaller company. Nabisco used its high ground by highlighting its extensive distribution network and marketing capabilities, which the smaller company lacked. By framing the conversation around how Nabisco could elevate the brand's success — something the seller couldn't achieve on its own — Nabisco gained leverage to negotiate favorable acquisition terms.

By capturing the high ground early, Nabisco positioned itself as the solution, not just a buyer. This allowed them to close the deal while retaining control over the brand's future.

Exercises

1. **Assess Your Position:** Think of an upcoming negotiation or discussion. What unique value or advantage can you bring to the table to establish high ground?
2. **Frame the Narrative:** Write down how you'll present your position to emphasize your strengths and guide the conversation in your favor.
3. **Simulate a High-Ground Scenario:** Role-play a negotiation with a friend or colleague, practicing how to maintain control and reinforce your leverage.

Key Takeaway

Capturing the high ground in negotiations ensures you dictate the terms and maintain leverage. By preparing thoroughly, framing the conversation, and presenting unique value, you position yourself for success.

Chapter 28: Create False Choices to Frame the Narrative

In competition, the way a choice is framed often determines the outcome. By presenting false choices, you guide your opponent toward a decision that aligns with your goals, even if they believe they're making the choice independently. False choices aren't about deception — they're about shaping perceptions to create a sense of control while subtly influencing the decision in your favor.

For example, in a sales pitch, you might offer two pricing tiers: one high-value option and one less attractive, lower-value option. The customer feels they're making a choice, but both options benefit you. The real power lies in the framing, which steers them toward the outcome you've already prepared.

Why False Choices Are Effective

1. **Simplifies Complexity:** False choices reduce the number of options, making it easier for the decision-maker to choose without overthinking.
2. **Guides Decision-Making:** Framing the options subtly nudges the decision-maker toward the preferred outcome.
3. **Creates Illusion of Control:** People feel empowered when they believe they're making a choice, even if the options are designed to benefit you.

How to Create False Choices

1. **Define Your Desired Outcome:** Decide what result you want before presenting the choices.
2. **Design the Options Strategically:** Include at least one option that's clearly less desirable, ensuring the preferred choice stands out.
3. **Avoid Overcomplication:** Too many options can overwhelm the decision-maker. Keep the choices simple and focused.
4. **Anticipate Reactions:** Consider how your options will be perceived and adjust to ensure the framing aligns with your goals.

Real-World Example

In the fast-food industry, McDonald's often uses false choices in its menu design. For example, meal upgrades like "small, medium, or large" options create the illusion of choice, but the framing encourages customers to choose the medium or large size, which provides higher profit margins. By presenting these predefined options, McDonald's subtly guides customers toward decisions that align with its business goals.

Exercises

1. **Frame a Decision:** Think of a situation where you need to influence someone's choice. Write down two or three options that guide them toward your desired outcome.
2. **Practice Simplifying:** Take a complex scenario and reduce it to two clear choices. How can you frame these options to make your preferred outcome more appealing?
3. **Evaluate Past Choices:** Reflect on a time when you were presented with limited options. Did the framing influence your decision? How can you use this insight strategically?

Key Takeaway

Creating false choices allows you to shape the narrative and guide decisions subtly. By framing options strategically, you empower others to choose while ensuring the outcome aligns with your goals.

Chapter 29: Use a Divide-and-Conquer Approach

United Group   Divided Team

Divide and conquer is a timeless strategy that involves breaking a larger, unified opponent into smaller, more manageable parts. By isolating groups, teams, or resources, you weaken your rival's ability to coordinate and defend against your moves. This approach has been used in military campaigns, corporate rivalries, and political maneuvers throughout history.

At its core, divide and conquer works by creating divisions where there was once unity. These divisions may stem from exploiting differences in goals, creating distractions, or sowing mistrust. Once divided, your opponent's strength is diluted, and their vulnerabilities are easier to target.

Why Divide-and-Conquer Works

1. **Weakens Unity:** A divided opponent cannot act cohesively, making them easier to defeat or outmaneuver.
2. **Overwhelms Resources:** Isolated groups have fewer resources to resist your strategy.
3. **Creates Distrust:** Internal divisions reduce morale and increase inefficiency.

For example, in a corporate setting, divide and conquer might involve negotiating separately with departments that have conflicting priorities, weakening their collective bargaining power.

How to Apply Divide-and-Conquer

1. **Identify Fault Lines:** Look for areas where your opponent's unity is weakest, such as differing priorities or conflicting interests.
2. **Create Distractions:** Introduce competing goals or narratives that draw attention away from their shared focus.
3. **Isolate Key Players:** Target influential individuals or groups, reducing their ability to collaborate effectively.
4. **Exploit Internal Rivalries:** Encourage competition or disagreement within the opposing group to erode their cohesion.
5. **Act Decisively:** Once divisions appear, move quickly to capitalize on the weakened structure.

Real-World Example

The Roman Empire mastered the divide-and-conquer strategy in its military campaigns. When facing powerful coalitions of tribes or nations, Roman generals would negotiate peace with one group while attacking another, systematically dismantling alliances. By isolating their enemies and dealing with them individually, Rome was able to expand its influence and maintain control over vast territories.

This approach worked because it prevented unified resistance, allowing the Romans to defeat stronger opponents by dividing their resources and morale.

Exercises

1. **Identify Potential Divisions:** Analyze a current challenge or competitor. Where are their internal divisions or weak points in unity?
2. **Plan a Distraction:** Develop a strategy to introduce competing priorities or narratives that weaken your opponent's focus.
3. **Simulate the Approach:** Role-play a negotiation or conflict scenario where you use divide-and-conquer tactics to gain an advantage.

Key Takeaway

Divide and conquer allows you to weaken larger opponents by breaking their unity and isolating their strengths. By identifying divisions and acting strategically, you can defeat rivals and gain the upper hand.

Chapter 30: Benefit from the Overconfidence of Your Opponents

Overconfidence is one of the most exploitable weaknesses in competition. When rivals overestimate their abilities or underestimate yours, they become prone to missteps, risky decisions, and overextensions. By recognizing and capitalizing on this arrogance, you can turn their overconfidence into your advantage.

Overconfident competitors often act impulsively, take unnecessary risks, or neglect preparation. These behaviors create opportunities for you to strike decisively or position yourself more strategically. However, exploiting overconfidence requires patience, observation, and a readiness to act when the moment is right.

Why Overconfidence is a Weakness

1. **Leads to Mistakes:** Overconfident rivals often skip due diligence, leaving themselves vulnerable to errors.
2. **Creates Blind Spots:** They may ignore warning signs or dismiss potential threats.
3. **Encourages Overextension:** Overconfident players may stretch themselves too thin, leaving critical areas unprotected.

For instance, in a sales scenario, an overconfident competitor might offer aggressive discounts to secure a deal, only to damage their long-term profitability. By staying composed and highlighting your strengths, you can secure the client with a more balanced offer.

How to Exploit Overconfidence

1. **Observe Their Patterns:** Identify behaviors that indicate overconfidence, such as dismissive remarks or overly ambitious goals.
2. **Encourage Overreach:** Subtly validate their confidence, nudging them toward bolder, riskier actions.
3. **Stay Prepared:** Overconfidence doesn't mean incompetence. Be ready to act quickly if they falter.
4. **Focus on Your Strengths:** Use their dismissiveness as an opportunity to build quietly in areas they're neglecting.

Real-World Example

In the late 1990s, Nokia dominated the mobile phone industry and became overconfident in its market position. The company dismissed the emerging smartphone trend, believing its existing models were untouchable. Meanwhile, others capitalized on this arrogance by investing heavily in smartphone technology.

When the iPhone launched in 2007, Nokia's overconfidence left it unprepared for the shift in consumer demand. Within a few years, the company lost its market leadership. This downfall highlights how overconfidence can blind even the strongest competitors to disruptive threats.

Exercises

1. **Spot Overconfidence:** Identify a competitor or colleague who exhibits overconfidence. How does their arrogance create opportunities for you?
2. **Plan a Response:** Develop a strategy to exploit an overconfident rival's blind spots or overextensions.
3. **Reflect on Your Own Confidence:** Are there areas where you might be overconfident? How can you stay grounded and vigilant?

Key Takeaway

Overconfidence creates opportunities for exploitation by leading rivals to overlook risks or underestimate you. By observing their weaknesses and staying prepared, you can turn their arrogance into a decisive advantage.

Chapter 31: Pre-empt Competitors Through Purposeful Partnerships

Sometimes the best way to outwit competitors is not by direct confrontation but by forming alliances that cut them off from critical opportunities. Purposeful partnerships — deliberately crafted to strengthen your position — can pre-empt competitors by locking in resources, creating exclusivity, or establishing a dominant market position.

Pre-emptive partnerships are about thinking ahead. By aligning with key players, you secure advantages that make it harder for your rivals to gain a foothold. These partnerships can include exclusive supplier agreements, joint ventures, or collaborative projects that corner a market or secure a unique advantage.

Why Purposeful Partnerships Work

1. **Control Critical Resources:** Partnerships can give you priority access to supplies, expertise, or markets, leaving competitors scrambling to find alternatives.
2. **Enhance Credibility:** Partnering with respected players can increase your influence and reputation, making it harder for rivals to compete.
3. **Create Barriers:** Strategic partnerships can establish exclusivity, locking competitors out of valuable opportunities.

For example, by forming an exclusive partnership with a leading distributor, a company can dominate a market segment while competitors struggle to reach the same audience.

How to Form Purposeful Partnerships

1. **Identify Key Players:** Look for partners who have resources, networks, or expertise that complement your goals.
2. **Align Incentives:** Ensure the partnership benefits both parties to create a strong, lasting alliance.
3. **Move Early:** Partnerships are most effective when formed before competitors recognize the opportunity.
4. **Negotiate Exclusivity:** Whenever possible, secure terms that give you unique access to the partner's resources or capabilities.
5. **Communicate the Advantage:** Use the partnership to showcase your strengthened position, discouraging competitors from challenging you.

Real-World Example

In the 1980s, Intel and IBM formed a strategic partnership that transformed the computer industry. By aligning with IBM, Intel became the exclusive supplier of microprocessors for IBM's personal computers. This partnership not only propelled Intel to market dominance but also made it difficult for competitors to gain traction in the rapidly growing PC market.

The exclusivity of the Intel-IBM relationship pre-empted rivals from establishing similar deals, securing Intel's position as a leader in the tech industry for decades.

Exercises

1. **Identify Potential Partners:** List organizations or individuals whose resources or expertise align with your goals. How could a partnership with them strengthen your position?
2. **Create a Partnership Plan:** Choose one potential partner and outline the mutual benefits of collaborating with them.
3. **Evaluate Competitors:** Analyze how your competitors could benefit from similar partnerships. How can you act first to secure the advantage?

Key Takeaway

Purposeful partnerships allow you to secure resources, credibility, and influence that pre-empt competitors from gaining ground. By forming alliances strategically, you strengthen your position and create lasting barriers to entry.

Chapter 32: Set Traps by Shaping Expectations

In competitive strategy, shaping expectations is a powerful way to influence your opponent's actions. By creating scenarios that seem safe or appealing, you can guide rivals into traps—positions where their predictable choices give you a decisive advantage.

Traps are not about deception for its own sake; they are about leveraging human psychology and your rival's assumptions. By carefully shaping their expectations, you make their moves easier to anticipate and counter, putting them at a disadvantage before they even act.

Why Traps Work

1. **Exploit Predictability:** Competitors often act based on assumptions. Shaping those assumptions lets you anticipate their next move.
2. **Force Poor Choices:** A well-set trap limits your rival's options, guiding them into a position of weakness.
3. **Maintain Control:** By dictating the terms of engagement, you stay one step ahead while your opponent reacts to your lead.

For example, in business, a company might announce a lower-priced product line to distract competitors, prompting them to overinvest in countering the new threat while neglecting their core offerings.

How to Set Effective Traps

1. **Understand Your Rival's Assumptions:** Study their behavior and beliefs to identify how they're likely to respond.
2. **Create False Signals:** Present scenarios that appear to confirm their assumptions, leading them into predictable actions.
3. **Limit Their Options:** Design the trap so that your rival's choices are narrowed to those that benefit you.
4. **Strike at the Right Moment:** Once your rival falls into the trap, act decisively to capitalize on their weakened position.

Real-World Example

During the Battle of Austerlitz in 1805, Napoleon Bonaparte used a classic trap by deliberately weakening his right flank, creating the illusion of vulnerability. The opposing Allied forces, confident in their assessment, attacked the "weak" flank. However, Napoleon had anticipated this move and concentrated his forces elsewhere, cutting off and defeating the Allies decisively.

By shaping the enemy's expectations, Napoleon turned their predictability into his greatest advantage, solidifying his reputation as a brilliant tactician.

Exercises

1. **Analyze a Rival's Patterns:** Identify a competitor's predictable behaviors. How could you shape their expectations to guide their actions?
2. **Design a Trap:** Outline a scenario where you could create a false signal or opportunity to lure a rival into a position of weakness.
3. **Evaluate Your Vulnerabilities:** Reflect on areas where you might be falling into traps set by others. How can you stay vigilant and adapt?

Key Takeaway

Setting traps by shaping expectations allows you to control your rival's actions and turn their predictability into your advantage. By influencing their decisions, you create opportunities to strike decisively and secure victory.

Chapter 33: Win Battles, Avoid Wars

In competition, not every battle is worth fighting. Winning small, strategic engagements can often achieve your goals more effectively than engaging in drawn-out conflicts. Wars — whether in business, politics, or life — are costly, unpredictable, and often leave both sides worse off. By focusing on winning key battles while avoiding unnecessary wars, you conserve resources, maintain relationships, and position yourself for long-term success.

This principle is about being selective. Instead of aiming for total domination, prioritize battles that bring the greatest rewards with the least cost. This approach not only preserves your resources but also ensures that your victories are meaningful and sustainable.

Why Avoiding Wars Matters

1. **Minimizes Risk:** Full-scale conflict often leads to collateral damage, wasted resources, and unintended consequences.
2. **Preserves Relationships:** Battles can be resolved without burning bridges, keeping opportunities for future collaboration open.
3. **Maintains Focus:** Engaging in too many conflicts spreads your energy thin, weakening your ability to win where it matters most.

For example, in negotiations, it's often better to concede minor points to achieve your main objective. By avoiding unnecessary contention, you ensure the outcome aligns with your goals while keeping the process smooth and productive.

How to Win Battles While Avoiding Wars

1. **Identify Key Objectives:** Before engaging, determine whether the battle aligns with your long-term goals.
2. **Pick Your Fights:** Focus only on conflicts where victory will provide significant advantages.
3. **Avoid Escalation:** Stay calm and avoid retaliating unnecessarily, even if provoked. Respond strategically, not emotionally.
4. **Negotiate Where Possible:** Resolve smaller disputes diplomatically to conserve resources for larger challenges.
5. **Know When to Walk Away:** Sometimes, the best way to win is to avoid fighting altogether.

Real-World Example

In the tech industry, Microsoft demonstrated this strategy in its competition with Google over cloud services. Rather than engaging directly in a "cloud war," Microsoft focused on targeted battles, such as building Azure's strengths in enterprise solutions and hybrid cloud systems. This allowed Microsoft to carve out a dominant position in its niche without directly confronting Google's established dominance in consumer cloud services.

By strategically choosing its battles, Microsoft avoided unnecessary conflict and grew Azure into one of the world's leading cloud platforms, achieving its goals without wasting resources on unwinnable wars.

Exercises

1. **Evaluate Current Conflicts:** List the battles you're currently fighting. Which ones are aligned with your long-term goals, and which could you avoid?
2. **Prioritize Your Efforts:** Choose one conflict that offers the greatest reward and focus your energy there.
3. **Reflect on a Past Conflict:** Identify a time when engaging in a "war" led to unnecessary costs. How could you have resolved it more strategically?

Key Takeaway

Winning battles without engaging in wars allows you to achieve focused victories while conserving resources and avoiding unnecessary risks. By choosing your fights wisely, you position yourself for sustainable success.

Chapter 34: Undermine Rivals with Incremental Disruption

Not every victory requires a dramatic or sudden move. Incremental disruption—making small, consistent changes that undermine your rival's position—can be just as effective as a bold strategy. These disruptions weaken your competitors gradually, allowing you to gain ground while avoiding direct confrontation.

Incremental disruption is about patience and persistence. Instead of seeking immediate results, focus on steady progress that erodes your rival's advantages over time. This

approach is less risky than a head-on challenge and often goes unnoticed until it's too late to counter.

Why Incremental Disruption is Effective

1. **Avoids Detection:** Small changes are harder to notice and respond to, giving you a stealthy advantage.
2. **Builds Momentum:** Incremental progress creates compounding benefits, leading to significant results over time.
3. **Preserves Resources:** Gradual disruption requires fewer resources than large-scale moves, making it more sustainable.

For example, in retail, a smaller competitor might gradually expand its product offerings to match those of a larger rival. Each addition chips away at the larger competitor's market share without provoking a full-scale response.

How to Undermine Rivals Incrementally

1. **Target Small Vulnerabilities:** Look for areas where your rival is slightly weak and make steady improvements there.
2. **Stay Consistent:** Commit to a long-term strategy of gradual progress rather than seeking immediate gains.
3. **Adapt Over Time:** Use feedback from each move to refine your approach and keep your rival off balance.
4. **Monitor Your Impact:** Track how your disruptions affect your rival's position and adjust accordingly.

Real-World Example

IKEA's approach to disrupting the furniture industry is an excellent example of incremental change. Instead of directly challenging traditional furniture retailers with luxury products or high-end showrooms, IKEA focused on small innovations that made furniture more affordable and accessible.

It introduced flat-pack furniture to reduce shipping and storage costs, developed self-service warehouses to streamline operations, and implemented in-store childcare to enhance the shopping experience. These gradual, customer-focused changes chipped away at traditional furniture stores' market dominance over time, positioning IKEA as a global leader in affordable, functional furniture.

Exercises

1. **Identify a Small Target:** Choose one area where you could make small, consistent improvements to challenge a rival's position.
2. **Develop a Plan:** Outline a step-by-step strategy for gradually increasing your influence or weakening your competitor's advantage.
3. **Track Your Progress:** Measure the impact of your incremental changes over time and adjust your approach as needed.

Key Takeaway

Incremental disruption is a patient, strategic way to undermine competitors and gain ground. By focusing on small, consistent improvements, you can achieve significant results while avoiding direct confrontation.

Chapter 35: Neutralize Emerging Risks Before They Escalate

In competitive strategy, emerging risks are like sparks. They may seem harmless at first but can quickly ignite into destructive forces if left unchecked. Success depends on identifying and neutralizing these risks early, before they escalate into major threats. This proactive approach ensures that your resources are focused on growth and opportunity, not damage control.

Emerging risks can take many forms: a new competitor entering your market, a subtle shift in customer preferences, or early warning signs of financial strain. While it's easy to dismiss these as minor concerns, strategic thinkers understand that ignoring them often leads to costly consequences later. Addressing these risks early allows you to maintain control and stay ahead.

Why Neutralizing Risks Early Matters

1. **Prevents Escalation:** Small risks are easier and less expensive to resolve than large crises.
2. **Maintains Momentum:** Addressing issues early minimizes disruptions to your goals and operations.
3. **Builds Resilience:** A proactive approach strengthens your ability to adapt and handle future challenges.

For example, a business noticing a slight drop in customer satisfaction can act immediately by gathering feedback and implementing improvements, preventing a larger exodus of customers later.

How to Neutralize Emerging Risks

1. **Identify Warning Signs:** Stay alert to small changes in your environment, such as market trends, competitor behavior, or internal performance metrics.
2. **Evaluate Impact:** Assess whether the risk has the potential to escalate and disrupt your goals.
3. **Act Decisively:** Once a risk is identified, take swift and focused action to address it.
4. **Monitor Continuously:** Keep track of resolved risks to ensure they don't re-emerge or evolve into new challenges.

Real-World Example

In the early 2010s, Netflix faced an emerging risk as customer preferences shifted toward more original content rather than licensing existing shows. Recognizing this trend early, Netflix began investing heavily in producing its own original series, such as *House of Cards* and *Stranger Things*.

By acting quickly to address this emerging risk, Netflix not only retained its subscriber base but also positioned itself as a leader in original programming. This proactive move helped Netflix outpace competitors like Hulu and Amazon Prime Video, who were slower to adapt to the same trend.

Exercises

1. **Risk Assessment:** Identify one small risk in your current environment. Write down its potential impact and a quick plan to neutralize it.
2. **Develop a Warning System:** Create a system to monitor early indicators of risk, such as regular performance reviews or customer feedback loops.
3. **Evaluate a Past Risk:** Reflect on a situation where a small problem escalated because it wasn't addressed early. What could you have done differently?

Key Takeaway

Neutralizing emerging risks before they escalate is key to staying ahead in any competitive scenario. By acting proactively and decisively, you prevent small issues from becoming major obstacles and ensure long-term stability and success.

Chapter 38: Counter Aggression with Calm Confidence

When faced with aggression — whether from competitors, adversaries, or even colleagues — it's tempting to respond in kind. However, reacting emotionally often leads to poor decisions and escalates conflict. Calm confidence is a far more effective response, allowing you to maintain control, project strength, and make calculated moves.

Calm confidence doesn't mean ignoring aggression or passively accepting challenges. Instead, it involves recognizing the underlying emotions and motives driving the aggression and addressing them with composure. This approach defuses tension, shifts power dynamics, and positions you as a leader who cannot be rattled.

Why Calm Confidence is Effective

1. **Disarms Aggressors:** Aggressive individuals or competitors often expect an emotional response. Your calmness surprises and unsettles them.
2. **Maintains Control:** Staying composed ensures you act strategically rather than impulsively.
3. **Earns Respect:** Confidence without aggression demonstrates strength and maturity, earning you credibility and trust.

For example, in negotiations, an aggressive party might use pressure tactics to force concessions. Responding with calm, firm counterarguments shifts the dynamic, signaling that you won't be intimidated.

How to Counter Aggression with Calm Confidence

1. **Pause Before Reacting:** Take a moment to assess the situation and control your emotions before responding.
2. **Acknowledge Their Position:** Validating their concerns or frustrations can defuse tension and open the door for constructive dialogue.
3. **Speak with Authority:** Use clear, measured language to assert your position without escalating the conflict.
4. **Stay Focused on Your Goals:** Keep the bigger picture in mind, avoiding distractions from your core objectives.
5. **Use Non-Verbal Cues:** Maintain steady eye contact, a relaxed posture, and controlled gestures to convey calmness.

Real-World Example

During the Cuban Missile Crisis in 1962, U.S. President John F. Kennedy exemplified calm confidence in the face of Soviet aggression. While military advisors pushed for immediate, aggressive action, Kennedy chose a measured approach, engaging in strategic communication and back-channel negotiations.

This calm, calculated response prevented a nuclear confrontation and resolved the crisis peacefully, solidifying Kennedy's reputation as a thoughtful and decisive leader.

Exercises

1. **Practice Delayed Reaction:** In your next high-pressure interaction, take a moment to pause and breathe before responding. Reflect on how this affects the outcome.
2. **Build Confidence:** Identify one area where you feel uncertain. Take steps to build knowledge or skills, so you can address future challenges with greater assurance.
3. **Reflect on Past Aggression:** Think of a time you responded emotionally to aggression. How could a calm, confident approach have improved the situation?

Key Takeaway

Countering aggression with calm confidence allows you to maintain control, disarm your opponent, and demonstrate leadership. By staying composed and focused, you turn challenges into opportunities for strength and respect.

Chapter 39: Force Your Competitors to Overextend

A classic mistake in competition is overextension — when a rival stretches their resources, capabilities, or focus too thin in an attempt to achieve too much. By strategically creating situations that pressure your competitors to overcommit, you can weaken their position while conserving your own resources. This approach doesn't just exploit your rival's ambition; it transforms their strengths into liabilities.

Forcing competitors to overextend requires understanding their priorities, identifying where they're vulnerable, and setting traps that encourage them to take on more than they can handle. This can be achieved through competitive pricing, rapid innovation, or creating scenarios that compel your rivals to chase unsustainable goals.

Why Forcing Overextension Works

1. **Weakens Focus:** Overextended competitors lose clarity, making mistakes and neglecting key priorities.
2. **Exhausts Resources:** Stretching too far depletes financial, human, or operational resources, leaving rivals vulnerable.
3. **Creates Vulnerabilities:** Rivals distracted by overextension often leave critical areas exposed, giving you opportunities to strike.

For example, a company might launch multiple new products simultaneously, forcing competitors to divide their attention and resources across various fronts.

How to Force Overextension

1. **Identify Ambitious Rivals:** Overextension is most likely when competitors are overly ambitious or driven by the fear of falling behind.
2. **Create Competitive Pressure:** Introduce challenges that require significant investments of time, money, or energy to address.
3. **Encourage Missteps:** Subtly validate their ambitious moves, nudging them to overcommit to unrealistic goals.
4. **Stay Disciplined:** While your competitor stretches themselves thin, maintain focus on your core strengths and priorities.
5. **Exploit Weak Points:** As your rival overextends, identify and target areas where they've lost focus or weakened their defenses.

Real-World Example

During the Cola Wars of the 1980s, PepsiCo strategically forced Coca-Cola to overextend through aggressive marketing and new product launches. Pepsi's *Pepsi Challenge* campaign successfully portrayed its product as the preferred cola in blind taste tests, which pressured Coca-Cola to respond.

In reaction, Coca-Cola made a bold and costly move by introducing "New Coke," an updated formula intended to outshine Pepsi. The backlash from consumers, loyal to the original Coke formula, forced Coca-Cola to reintroduce "Coca-Cola Classic" just months later. This overextension of resources and focus not only strained Coca-Cola financially but also damaged its brand image temporarily, allowing Pepsi to gain ground in the market.

Exercises

1. **Analyze a Competitor:** Identify a rival who may be overextending. What are their weaknesses, and how could you apply pressure to exploit them?
2. **Test Competitive Pressure:** Create a situation that encourages a competitor to commit more resources than necessary. How do they respond?
3. **Avoid Overextension Yourself:** Reflect on areas where you might be stretching too thin. What steps can you take to refocus and strengthen your position?

Key Takeaway

Forcing competitors to overextend transforms their ambition into a liability. By creating pressure and staying focused, you weaken your rivals while conserving your own resources for strategic gains.

Chapter 40: Apply the Minimax Principle in Critical Decisions

The Minimax principle, a cornerstone of game theory, is a decision-making strategy that focuses on minimizing the maximum possible loss. In competitive environments, it helps you make critical decisions by preparing for the worst-case scenario while positioning yourself to capitalize on the best outcomes.

The goal isn't to avoid risk entirely but to ensure that even if things go wrong, the damage is manageable. This disciplined approach allows you to act with confidence, knowing you've accounted for potential downsides. The Minimax principle is particularly valuable in high-stakes situations, where uncertainty and risk are unavoidable.

Why the Minimax Principle is Powerful

1. **Reduces Vulnerability:** Preparing for worst-case scenarios protects you from catastrophic failures.
2. **Enhances Decision Clarity:** By focusing on minimizing losses, you simplify complex choices.
3. **Balances Risk and Reward:** The principle ensures you remain cautious while still pursuing opportunities.

For example, in negotiations, the Minimax principle might involve securing a fallback option or setting a clear minimum threshold to avoid walking away empty-handed.

How to Apply the Minimax Principle

1. **Define the Worst Case:** Identify the maximum loss or setback you could face in the situation.
2. **Evaluate Options:** Analyze each decision based on how it minimizes the worst possible outcome.
3. **Prepare Safeguards:** Develop contingency plans to mitigate risks and ensure stability.
4. **Act Strategically:** Once you've minimized losses, focus on maximizing potential gains without taking unnecessary risks.
5. **Adapt to New Information:** Continuously assess your decisions as new data emerges, adjusting your approach as needed.

Real-World Example

In 2008, during the global financial crisis, Berkshire Hathaway, under the leadership of Warren Buffett, applied the Minimax principle when investing in struggling companies. Rather than taking aggressive, high-risk positions, Buffett focused on minimizing potential losses while still securing gains.

One notable move was Berkshire's investment in Goldman Sachs. Buffett negotiated a deal to purchase $5 billion in preferred stock, which paid a 10% dividend and included warrants to buy common stock at a fixed price. This structure minimized Berkshire's downside risk (ensuring consistent returns from dividends) while still providing upside potential through the warrants.

This cautious yet opportunistic approach allowed Berkshire Hathaway to profit significantly from the recovery without exposing itself to undue financial risk, exemplifying the Minimax principle in action.

Exercises

1. **Identify a Critical Decision:** Write down a high-stakes decision you're currently facing. What is the worst-case scenario, and how can you minimize its impact?
2. **Develop a Contingency Plan:** Choose one area of risk and outline steps to protect yourself if the worst happens.
3. **Evaluate Past Decisions:** Reflect on a decision where you failed to consider the worst case. How could applying the Minimax principle have improved the outcome?

Key Takeaway

The Minimax principle helps you navigate uncertainty by minimizing potential losses while positioning yourself for success. By preparing for the worst and striving for the best, you make smarter, more confident decisions in competitive environments.

Section III: Cooperative Strategies

In the competitive world of strategy, collaboration can often be the key to unlocking greater opportunities and achieving success. This section focuses on the art of cooperation — how to build trust, create value together, and sustain productive relationships while protecting your interests. Whether forming alliances, leading teams, or negotiating partnerships, these strategies will help you navigate the complexities of working with others. Cooperation isn't just about compromise; it's about crafting mutually beneficial outcomes while maintaining strength and integrity.

Chapter 41: Lay the Foundation for Trust Before You Request Collaboration

Trust is the currency of effective collaboration. Without trust, even the most promising partnerships can falter under the weight of doubt and miscommunication. Building trust before asking for collaboration ensures that the foundation of your relationship is strong, enabling smoother teamwork and more successful outcomes.

Establishing trust doesn't happen overnight. It requires consistent actions, clear communication, and a demonstrated commitment to shared values. When trust is in place, others are more willing to work with you, share resources, and take risks, knowing that the relationship is built on reliability and mutual respect.

Why Trust is Crucial in Collaboration

1. **Facilitates Open Communication:** Trust encourages honesty, reducing misunderstandings and fostering transparency.
2. **Reduces Friction:** When trust exists, disagreements are easier to resolve, as both parties believe in each other's good intentions.
3. **Strengthens Commitment:** People are more likely to invest in a partnership when they feel secure in the relationship.

For example, an entrepreneur looking to secure funding from investors must first build trust by demonstrating competence, reliability, and a shared vision for success.

How to Build Trust Before Collaboration

1. **Be Consistent:** Show reliability through your actions, delivering on promises consistently over time.
2. **Demonstrate Competence:** Prove that you have the skills and expertise to contribute effectively to the partnership.
3. **Show Empathy:** Understand the other party's goals, values, and concerns, and align your actions with their interests.
4. **Be Transparent:** Share information openly to eliminate doubts and foster confidence in your intentions.
5. **Start Small:** Build trust incrementally through smaller interactions before asking for larger commitments.

Real-World Example

In the 2000s, Procter & Gamble (P&G) established trust with smaller research firms and independent innovators before requesting collaboration through its "Connect + Develop" initiative. By actively engaging with external partners, sharing clear guidelines, and honoring intellectual property agreements, P&G demonstrated its reliability and commitment to fairness.

This foundation of trust allowed P&G to form productive partnerships that resulted in successful products such as the Swiffer and Crest Whitestrips. By proving themselves as a trustworthy collaborator, P&G attracted top innovators and fostered long-term relationships that benefited all parties.

Exercises

1. **Evaluate Trust Levels:** Identify a relationship where you want to collaborate. What actions can you take to build trust before making your request?
2. **Reflect on Past Successes:** Think of a successful partnership in your life. What trust-building steps contributed to its success?
3. **Start Small:** Plan a small action or project that demonstrates your reliability to a potential collaborator.

Key Takeaway

Trust is the foundation of collaboration. By building trust early through consistency, transparency, and empathy, you create a strong base for productive partnerships.

Chapter 42: Bolster Mutual Dependence in Joint Ventures

Mutual dependence is the glue that holds joint ventures together. When both parties rely on each other to achieve shared success, the partnership becomes stronger and more sustainable. This dynamic ensures that each partner remains committed to the venture, knowing their own success depends on the other's contributions.

In joint ventures, mutual dependence creates balance. It discourages one party from exploiting the other and fosters a sense of shared responsibility. The key is to structure the partnership so that each party's strengths complement the other's, creating a synergy that benefits both sides equally.

MUTUAL DEPENDENCE

Why Mutual Dependence is Essential

1. **Ensures Commitment:** Partners who depend on each other are less likely to abandon the venture or act against its interests.
2. **Enhances Stability:** A balanced reliance creates equilibrium, reducing power imbalances and fostering cooperation.
3. **Maximizes Value:** Mutual dependence leverages the unique strengths of each partner, driving greater results together than either could achieve alone.

For instance, in a technology joint venture, one company might specialize in hardware development while the other focuses on software. Each party depends on the other to deliver their part of the solution, ensuring cooperation.

How to Bolster Mutual Dependence

1. **Define Clear Roles:** Assign responsibilities that highlight each partner's strengths and create interdependence.
2. **Align Incentives:** Ensure that both parties benefit equally from the venture's success.
3. **Share Resources:** Pool resources, such as funding, expertise, or technology, to deepen the partnership's value.
4. **Maintain Open Communication:** Regular updates and discussions help reinforce trust and ensure alignment.
5. **Prepare for Challenges:** Develop joint contingency plans to address potential risks or setbacks together.

Real-World Example

In 2019, Starbucks partnered with Nestlé to expand its global reach in the coffee market. Starbucks relied on Nestlé's extensive distribution network to sell its products in grocery stores worldwide, while Nestlé leveraged Starbucks' brand recognition to enhance its portfolio. This mutual dependence created a highly successful venture, with both companies benefiting from their combined strengths.

Exercises

1. **Assess a Joint Venture:** Identify a partnership or collaboration you're part of. How can you strengthen mutual dependence to ensure its success?
2. **Map Complementary Strengths:** In a current or potential partnership, list each party's unique strengths. How can these be aligned to create interdependence?
3. **Address Imbalances:** Reflect on past collaborations. Were there imbalances in dependence? What steps could have been taken to correct them?

Key Takeaway

Mutual dependence is the cornerstone of successful joint ventures. By aligning strengths, sharing responsibilities, and fostering balanced reliance, you create partnerships that are resilient and productive.

Chapter 43: Share the Pie to Make It Bigger

In many situations, competition centers on dividing a limited "pie" of resources, profits, or opportunities. However, truly successful collaboration shifts the focus from dividing the pie to making it bigger. By working together to create additional value, all parties benefit more than they would have by competing for a fixed portion.

This principle is about abundance, not scarcity. Instead of seeing collaboration as a zero-sum game, recognize that joint efforts often lead to exponential gains. Whether it's through co-developing a product, pooling resources, or sharing expertise, expanding the pie unlocks opportunities for everyone involved.

Why Expanding the Pie is Effective

1. **Maximizes Mutual Benefits:** When the pie grows, everyone gets a larger share, reducing conflict over limited resources.
2. **Fosters Innovation:** Collaboration encourages creative solutions that wouldn't arise in isolation.
3. **Builds Long-Term Partnerships:** A focus on shared growth strengthens trust and goodwill between collaborators.

For instance, companies in the same industry might partner to develop industry standards, expanding the overall market and benefiting all players.

How to Expand the Pie

1. **Focus on Value Creation:** Look for ways to add value to the collaboration rather than focusing solely on dividing existing resources.
2. **Leverage Complementary Strengths:** Combine unique assets or expertise to create synergies that neither party could achieve alone.
3. **Communicate Openly:** Share ideas and goals transparently to identify opportunities for mutual growth.
4. **Prioritize Long-Term Gains:** Aim for sustainable benefits rather than short-term wins.
5. **Celebrate Joint Successes:** Recognize and reward the shared accomplishments to reinforce the value of collaboration.

Real-World Example

In 2004, Toyota and BMW partnered to develop hydrogen fuel cell technology. Instead of competing directly, the two automakers combined their expertise—Toyota contributed its knowledge of fuel cell systems, while BMW brought its advanced materials and engineering capabilities.

By collaborating, the companies expanded the pie, accelerating the development of sustainable technology and sharing the benefits of reduced costs and enhanced innovation. This partnership highlighted how working together can unlock opportunities that would be harder to achieve individually.

Exercises

1. **Identify Collaborative Opportunities:** Think of a situation where you're competing for resources or recognition. How could collaboration create more value for everyone?
2. **Find Complementary Strengths:** Write down a potential partner's unique assets and how they align with your own to expand the pie.
3. **Focus on Shared Gains:** Reflect on a past collaboration. How could you have shifted the focus from dividing resources to creating more value together?

Key Takeaway

Sharing the pie to make it bigger creates opportunities for exponential growth. By focusing on collaboration and value creation, you build partnerships that benefit everyone involved.

Chapter 44: Use Reciprocity to Strengthen Relationships

Reciprocity — the practice of giving and receiving in return — is a cornerstone of strong relationships. In collaborative strategies, reciprocity strengthens bonds, fosters trust, and creates a cycle of mutual support. When you give generously and strategically, others feel compelled to respond in kind, deepening the relationship and paving the way for long-term cooperation.

Reciprocity doesn't just apply to material exchanges. It can take the form of offering support, sharing resources, or even providing valuable insights. The key is to give without expecting an immediate return, knowing that your generosity will likely lead to future opportunities.

Why Reciprocity Works

1. **Builds Trust:** Acts of giving demonstrate goodwill and reliability, fostering deeper connections.
2. **Creates Mutual Support:** Reciprocity ensures that both parties contribute to the relationship, balancing effort and reward.
3. **Strengthens Loyalty:** People are more likely to support those who have supported them, creating lasting partnerships.

For example, offering mentorship or guidance to a peer often leads to reciprocal opportunities, such as introductions to key contacts or collaboration on future projects.

How to Use Reciprocity Effectively

1. **Give First:** Take the initiative to offer value before asking for anything in return.
2. **Be Genuine:** Ensure your actions come from a place of authenticity, not manipulation.
3. **Match the Scale:** Tailor your contributions to the context and the relationship, ensuring they are meaningful without overextending yourself.
4. **Follow Through:** Deliver on promises to reinforce trust and demonstrate reliability.
5. **Keep the Cycle Going:** Maintain reciprocity by continuing to exchange value over time.

Real-World Example

LinkedIn's professional networking platform thrives on reciprocity. Users endorse one another's skills, share job opportunities, and provide recommendations. This cycle of giving and receiving creates stronger connections and encourages ongoing engagement, ultimately benefiting the entire LinkedIn community.

Exercises

1. **Give Without Expectation:** Identify one person in your network and offer value—whether through advice, support, or a resource—without expecting anything in return.
2. **Reflect on Reciprocity:** Think of a time when someone supported you. How did you reciprocate? How did it impact your relationship?
3. **Create a Reciprocity Plan:** List ways you can give value to key collaborators or partners in your life.

Key Takeaway

Reciprocity is the engine of strong relationships. When you give generously and authentically, you create a cycle of mutual support that strengthens partnerships and fosters long-term cooperation.

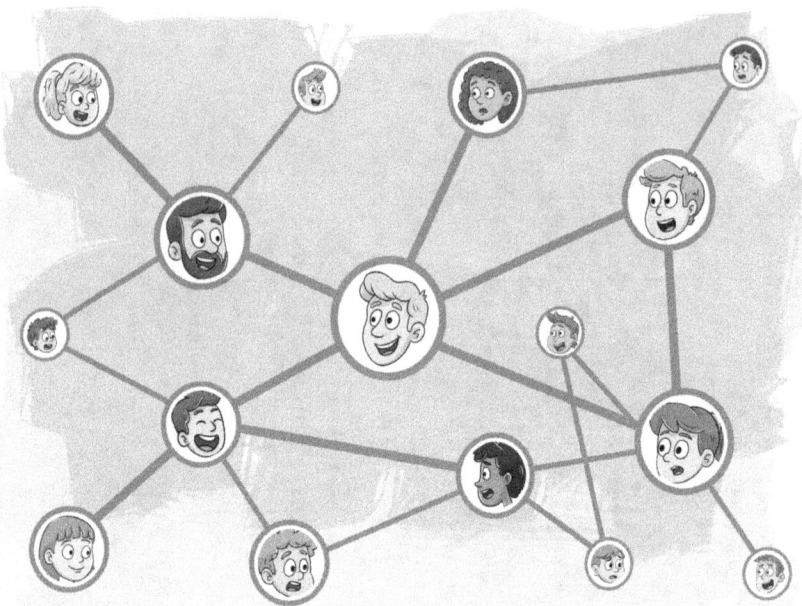

Chapter 45: Capitalize Network Effects for Influence

Network effects occur when the value of a product, service, or relationship increases as more people use or participate in it. In cooperative strategies, leveraging network effects allows you to expand your influence, gain access to new opportunities, and create self-sustaining growth. This concept is central to many successful platforms, ecosystems, and communities.

By building and nurturing networks, you tap into the power of collective growth. The more connections you create, the more valuable the network becomes—not just for you, but for everyone involved. This compounding value drives loyalty, participation, and engagement, amplifying your influence over time.

Why Network Effects are Powerful

1. **Create Exponential Growth:** As the network grows, so does its value, creating a self-reinforcing cycle.
2. **Increase Engagement:** Networks encourage participants to stay involved, knowing they benefit more as the network expands.
3. **Strengthen Influence:** A strong network positions you as a central figure, enhancing your ability to lead and direct opportunities.

For example, social media platforms like Instagram thrive on network effects. As more users join, the platform becomes more valuable, attracting even more users in a virtuous cycle.

How to Capitalize on Network Effects

1. **Start with Core Connections:** Focus on building a strong initial network of engaged, high-value participants.
2. **Encourage Sharing:** Create incentives for participants to invite others, fostering organic growth.
3. **Deliver Consistent Value:** Ensure the network provides ongoing benefits to keep participants engaged and loyal.
4. **Strengthen Connectivity:** Facilitate interactions between members to increase the value of the network as a whole.
5. **Adapt and Expand:** Continuously evolve the network to meet changing needs and attract new participants.

Real-World Example

Uber effectively leveraged network effects to dominate the ride-hailing industry. By focusing on onboarding more drivers, Uber ensured that riders could get faster service. In turn, the growing number of riders attracted even more drivers to the platform.

This mutually reinforcing cycle created a better experience for both parties. Riders enjoyed shorter wait times, and drivers benefited from increased demand. Uber's ability to capitalize on these network effects allowed it to outpace competitors and establish itself as the leading ride-hailing service in markets worldwide.

Exercises

1. **Map Your Network:** Identify the key connections in your professional or personal network. How can you strengthen or expand these relationships?
2. **Create Network Growth:** Develop a strategy to encourage others to join or engage with your network.
3. **Deliver Value:** Identify one way to provide consistent benefits to your network members, ensuring they remain engaged.

Key Takeaway

Network effects amplify your influence and growth by creating compounding value as more participants join. By building and nurturing networks, you position yourself as a central figure in a thriving ecosystem.

Chapter 46: Be Predictable in Cooperative Settings

Predictability might seem like a weakness in competitive settings, but in cooperation, it's a strength. Being predictable in your actions, decisions, and commitments fosters trust, reduces misunderstandings, and makes it easier for others to align with you. When collaborators know what to expect from you, they are more likely to rely on and invest in the partnership.

In cooperative environments, unpredictability creates confusion and mistrust. Partners may hesitate to commit fully if they fear you'll change direction unexpectedly. By contrast, predictability signals dependability, allowing teams and alliances to function smoothly and achieve shared goals.

Why Predictability Matters in Cooperation

1. **Builds Trust:** Consistent behavior reassures others that you will follow through on your commitments.
2. **Facilitates Planning:** When others can anticipate your actions, they can coordinate their efforts more effectively.
3. **Reduces Conflict:** Predictability minimizes the risk of misunderstandings or misaligned expectations.

For example, a project manager who consistently communicates timelines and meets deadlines creates an environment where team members can focus on their tasks without uncertainty.

How to Be Predictable in Cooperative Settings

1. **Set Clear Expectations:** Define your goals, responsibilities, and boundaries from the outset.
2. **Communicate Regularly:** Keep collaborators informed about your progress and any changes to the plan.
3. **Honor Commitments:** Follow through on promises and deliverables without fail.
4. **Develop Routines:** Establish consistent practices that signal reliability, such as weekly updates or structured meetings.
5. **Admit Mistakes Transparently:** When setbacks occur, address them openly to maintain trust.

Real-World Example

FedEx built its reputation as a dependable logistics partner by being predictably reliable. Its slogan, "When it absolutely, positively has to be there overnight," reflects its commitment to delivering packages on time, every time. This consistency has made FedEx the go-to choice for businesses and individuals worldwide, solidifying its position as a leader in the shipping industry.

Exercises

1. **Reflect on Your Predictability:** Consider a recent collaboration. Were your actions predictable and consistent? How did this impact the partnership?
2. **Establish a Routine:** Develop a habit or process that signals reliability to your team or collaborators.
3. **Communicate Expectations:** In your next group project, clearly outline what others can expect from you and encourage them to do the same.

Key Takeaway

Predictability is a cornerstone of successful cooperation. By being consistent and reliable, you foster trust, streamline coordination, and strengthen relationships in any collaborative setting.

Chapter 47: Compromise Strategically, Not Emotionally

Compromise is often essential in cooperative settings, but not all compromises are created equal. Emotional compromises, driven by frustration, guilt, or impatience, can lead to imbalanced outcomes and regret. Strategic compromises, on the other hand, are deliberate, calculated, and aligned with your long-term goals.

The key to compromising strategically is to focus on the bigger picture. Rather than simply giving in to keep the peace or to avoid conflict, you assess the potential trade-offs and ensure that what you concede is less valuable than what you gain. By thinking long-term and maintaining your priorities, you create compromises that strengthen relationships without undermining your position.

Why Strategic Compromise is Effective

1. **Preserves Your Interests:** Thoughtful compromises ensure you don't give up anything critical to your goals.
2. **Strengthens Partnerships:** Balanced compromises build goodwill and trust in collaborative relationships.
3. **Avoids Regret:** Strategic decisions prevent the resentment that often accompanies emotional sacrifices.

For instance, during a business negotiation, offering a discount on pricing in exchange for a longer contract term creates a win-win compromise. You give up some short-term revenue but secure long-term stability.

How to Compromise Strategically

1. **Understand Your Priorities:** Know what matters most to you before entering a discussion, so you can protect your key interests.
2. **Evaluate Trade-Offs:** Assess what you're giving up versus what you're gaining. Ensure the exchange is favorable to your goals.
3. **Communicate Clearly:** Articulate your reasoning to the other party, ensuring transparency and reducing misunderstandings.
4. **Stay Calm and Focused:** Avoid making decisions based on frustration or emotional pressure. Take time to think.
5. **Seek Reciprocity:** Ensure that any compromise you make is matched by a concession from the other party.

Real-World Example

The U.S. government's 2012 negotiations with auto manufacturers to improve fuel efficiency standards illustrate strategic compromise. The automakers agreed to higher standards, which aligned with environmental goals, in exchange for a gradual implementation timeline. This allowed the industry to adjust and innovate while still meeting long-term regulatory objectives.

By focusing on mutual benefits and avoiding an emotional standoff, both sides reached a compromise that advanced their priorities without unnecessary conflict.

Exercises

1. **Identify Non-Negotiables:** Write down your top three priorities in a current or upcoming negotiation. How can you protect these while remaining flexible elsewhere?
2. **Evaluate a Past Compromise:** Reflect on a time when you made a compromise. Was it strategic or emotional? What could you have done differently?
3. **Plan a Strategic Trade-Off:** Consider an area where you might need to compromise. What could you offer that costs you little but benefits the other party significantly?

Key Takeaway

Compromising strategically ensures that your decisions are thoughtful, balanced, and aligned with your goals. By focusing on long-term benefits and avoiding emotional sacrifices, you strengthen relationships without weakening your position.

Chapter 48: Maximize Joint Gains in Team-Ups

In any collaboration, the true measure of success isn't how much one party benefits — it's how much both parties gain together. Maximizing joint gains means identifying and leveraging shared opportunities to create the greatest possible value for everyone involved. This mindset goes beyond transactional thinking, fostering deeper partnerships and long-term growth.

Maximizing joint gains requires focusing on synergy: combining resources, ideas, or strengths in ways that amplify results. It also involves open communication and mutual understanding, ensuring that both parties' goals are respected and aligned. When done effectively, team-ups become a force multiplier, delivering outcomes far greater than either party could achieve alone.

Why Maximizing Joint Gains is Important

1. **Enhances Value Creation:** Shared effort and resources generate results that benefit everyone.
2. **Strengthens Partnerships:** Equitable collaboration fosters trust and encourages future cooperation.
3. **Avoids Conflict:** A focus on mutual benefit reduces competition within the partnership.

For example, two businesses collaborating on a marketing campaign can combine their audiences, expertise, and budgets to achieve greater reach and impact than either could alone.

How to Maximize Joint Gains

1. **Align Goals:** Clearly define shared objectives at the start of the collaboration to ensure mutual focus.
2. **Leverage Complementary Strengths:** Identify and utilize each party's unique resources or expertise.
3. **Encourage Open Communication:** Create an environment where both parties feel comfortable sharing ideas and feedback.
4. **Measure Success Together:** Establish metrics that reflect the shared value created by the partnership.
5. **Celebrate Joint Achievements:** Acknowledge and reward the contributions of all parties to reinforce the value of the team-up.

Real-World Example

In 2018, McDonald's and Coca-Cola collaborated on the "Sip. Share. Win!" campaign, which combined Coca-Cola's beverages with McDonald's food promotions. Customers could purchase specially marked Coca-Cola beverages at McDonald's and enter for a chance to win prizes, including free McDonald's meals.

This team-up benefited both brands: McDonald's boosted customer traffic while Coca-Cola strengthened its association with a major food retailer. By aligning their marketing efforts and leveraging their mutual popularity, the partnership created greater engagement and value for both companies and their customers.

Exercises

1. **Identify Shared Goals:** Think of a current or potential partnership. What mutual objectives could you align to create greater value?
2. **Leverage Complementary Skills:** List the unique strengths you and a collaborator bring to the table. How can you combine them for maximum impact?
3. **Evaluate Success Metrics:** Define how you'll measure the joint success of a collaboration. How do these metrics benefit both parties equally?

Key Takeaway

Maximizing joint gains transforms partnerships into high-value opportunities. By aligning goals, leveraging strengths, and creating shared success, you build collaborations that deliver exponential results for everyone involved.

Chapter 49: Establish Harmony Between Transparency and Secrecy

In collaborative efforts, striking the right balance between transparency and secrecy is vital. Transparency builds trust, aligns goals, and facilitates teamwork, while secrecy safeguards your competitive edge and protects sensitive information. Navigating this balance requires a strategic approach that considers the context, the partners involved, and the ultimate objectives of the collaboration.

When too much is revealed, you risk exposing vulnerabilities or losing your unique advantage. Conversely, excessive secrecy can breed suspicion, misunderstandings, or even conflicts. Finding the harmony between these extremes ensures that the partnership is both effective and secure.

This balance is particularly important in high-stakes collaborations, such as mergers, product co-developments, or strategic alliances. By sharing enough information to foster alignment while withholding details that could compromise your position, you create an environment of trust and protection.

Why Balancing Transparency and Secrecy Matters

1. **Builds Trust:** Transparency shows good faith and commitment, encouraging others to invest in the collaboration.
2. **Enhances Cooperation:** Open communication ensures everyone is on the same page, reducing misalignment.
3. **Protects Critical Assets:** Keeping key details confidential prevents leaks, theft, or misuse of sensitive information.

Consider a startup collaborating with a larger corporation to launch a new product. The startup must share its product roadmap and development goals to ensure the partnership's success but may withhold proprietary technology or patent information to avoid losing its competitive advantage.

How to Balance Transparency and Secrecy

1. **Define Boundaries Early:** Establish clear guidelines about what information will be shared and what will remain private.
2. **Tailor Transparency Levels:** Adjust your openness based on the trustworthiness, track record, and role of each partner in the collaboration.
3. **Communicate Strategically:** Share information that directly contributes to the partnership's goals and hold back details that aren't immediately relevant.
4. **Use Legal Protections:** Non-disclosure agreements (NDAs) and confidentiality clauses ensure that shared information remains secure.
5. **Monitor Continuously:** Assess the effectiveness of your balance over time and adapt as the partnership evolves.

Real-World Example

In the pharmaceutical industry, companies frequently collaborate to develop drugs or vaccines, such as Pfizer and BioNTech's partnership during the COVID-19 pandemic. The two companies shared vital research data and aligned their production goals while protecting their proprietary technologies. This balance allowed both parties to work effectively toward their shared objective without compromising their individual competitive positions.

Exercises

1. **Assess Your Current Approach:** In an existing partnership, evaluate whether you're being too transparent or overly secretive. Adjust your strategy accordingly.
2. **Create a Sharing Framework:** Outline specific types of information you're willing to share in collaborations and what must remain confidential.
3. **Seek Feedback:** Ask collaborators if they feel your level of transparency fosters trust and alignment. Use their input to refine your approach.

Key Takeaway

Striking the right balance between transparency and secrecy ensures effective collaboration while protecting your interests. By aligning openness with strategic confidentiality, you create partnerships that are both trustworthy and secure.

Chapter 50: Foster a Reputation for Fair Actions

In cooperative strategies, your reputation is one of your greatest assets. A reputation for fairness attracts high-quality partners, fosters loyalty, and strengthens your influence within any group. When others perceive you as someone who acts equitably and prioritizes mutual benefit, they're more likely to engage with you, invest in your success, and remain committed to long-term relationships.

Fostering a reputation for fairness doesn't happen overnight. It requires consistent, intentional actions that demonstrate ethical behavior, transparency, and respect for others' contributions. Over time, this commitment to fairness creates a lasting impression that sets you apart as a trustworthy and reliable collaborator.

Why a Reputation for Fairness Matters

1. **Builds Trust:** Fair actions signal integrity, reassuring others of your intentions and reliability.
2. **Encourages Cooperation:** People are more willing to collaborate with those they believe will treat them equitably.
3. **Enhances Influence:** A fair reputation positions you as a leader, making others more likely to follow your guidance.

For instance, leaders who consistently credit their teams for successes build goodwill and inspire greater effort, creating a positive cycle of trust and productivity.

How to Foster a Reputation for Fair Actions

1. **Act Consistently:** Ensure that your decisions reflect fairness across all situations, avoiding favoritism or bias.
2. **Communicate Your Reasoning:** Be transparent about the factors influencing your decisions to eliminate doubts or perceptions of unfairness.
3. **Acknowledge Contributions:** Publicly recognize and reward the efforts of those you work with, demonstrating your commitment to equity.
4. **Correct Mistakes Proactively:** If you've acted unfairly, address the situation immediately to rebuild trust.
5. **Promote Equity:** Strive to create opportunities that are distributed fairly among all stakeholders.

Real-World Example

Patagonia, the outdoor apparel company, exemplifies the power of fairness in business. By ensuring ethical labor practices, providing fair wages, and maintaining environmentally sustainable operations, Patagonia has built a reputation for acting with integrity. This approach has not only attracted loyal customers but also like-minded collaborators, amplifying its positive impact.

Exercises

1. **Reflect on Past Decisions:** Think of a situation where fairness may have been questioned. What steps could you take to improve similar decisions in the future?
2. **Develop a Fairness Checklist:** Create a set of criteria to evaluate the fairness of your decisions before taking action.
3. **Solicit Feedback:** Ask collaborators or team members for honest feedback on how they perceive your fairness. Use this insight to refine your actions.

Key Takeaway

A reputation for fairness is a powerful tool in cooperation. By consistently acting with integrity, transparency, and equity, you build trust and create opportunities for stronger, more productive relationships.

Chapter 51: Turn Enemies into Allies

In competitive environments, it's natural to encounter adversaries—individuals or organizations whose goals conflict with yours. While conflict can sometimes motivate innovation and progress, prolonged hostility often drains resources and limits opportunities. Transforming enemies into allies is a powerful strategy that not only neutralizes threats but also creates opportunities for collaboration and mutual growth.

Turning adversaries into allies requires understanding their goals, identifying common ground, and building trust over time. This transformation doesn't mean compromising your principles or giving up your objectives. Instead, it's about finding ways to align interests and create a win-win dynamic that benefits both parties.

Why Turning Enemies into Allies Matters

1. **Neutralizes Conflict:** Resolving hostility reduces wasted energy and resources.
2. **Creates New Opportunities:** Collaborating with former adversaries can unlock shared potential.
3. **Demonstrates Leadership:** Transforming conflict into cooperation showcases strategic foresight and emotional intelligence.

For example, two rival businesses might partner to co-develop a product that neither could create alone, leveraging each other's strengths to achieve a shared goal.

How to Turn Enemies into Allies

1. **Understand Their Perspective:** Learn your adversary's goals, motivations, and challenges. Empathy is key to finding common ground.
2. **Start Small:** Propose low-risk collaborations that build trust and demonstrate the potential for mutual benefit.
3. **Communicate Transparently:** Be honest about your intentions and goals to reduce suspicion and foster trust.
4. **Focus on Common Goals:** Highlight areas where your interests align and work together to achieve shared outcomes.
5. **Maintain Boundaries:** While fostering collaboration, ensure your core values and objectives remain intact.

Real-World Example

In 2018, Microsoft and Sony, long-time rivals in the gaming industry, surprised the market by announcing a strategic partnership to collaborate on cloud gaming and AI solutions. Historically, the two companies competed fiercely in the console wars with Xbox and PlayStation. However, the rise of cloud gaming and emerging competition from tech giants like Google and Amazon prompted them to join forces.

By collaborating on advanced technologies, Microsoft and Sony were able to strengthen their positions in the gaming ecosystem while addressing shared challenges. This partnership demonstrated how even staunch rivals can align their interests to achieve mutual benefits and tackle external threats.

Exercises

1. **Identify Potential Allies:** List current adversaries in your professional or personal life. What common goals or interests could form the basis of collaboration?
2. **Propose a Small Collaboration:** Think of a low-risk way to work with a rival, such as sharing insights or co-hosting an event.
3. **Evaluate Past Conflicts:** Reflect on a previous adversarial relationship. Could it have been transformed into an alliance? How?

Key Takeaway

Turning enemies into allies transforms conflict into opportunity. By finding common ground and building trust, you neutralize threats and create partnerships that drive mutual success.

Chapter 52: Concentrate on the Shared Objective

Collaboration is most effective when everyone is aligned toward a shared objective. When goals diverge, distractions, inefficiencies, and conflicts arise, weakening the partnership's impact. Focusing on the shared objective ensures that all efforts contribute to a common purpose, maximizing efficiency and results.

This focus doesn't mean suppressing individual ideas or goals. It's about integrating them into the broader mission. By keeping the shared objective front and center, collaborators can navigate disagreements and distractions without losing sight of the ultimate purpose.

Why Focusing on the Shared Objective is Critical

1. **Enhances Alignment:** Clear goals unify efforts, ensuring that all actions support the partnership's mission.
2. **Reduces Conflict:** A common purpose minimizes disputes by providing a clear framework for decision-making.
3. **Boosts Efficiency:** Concentrating on shared outcomes streamlines processes and eliminates redundant efforts.

For instance, in a joint research project, focusing on the end goal — such as publishing a breakthrough study — helps partners prioritize tasks and allocate resources effectively.

How to Concentrate on the Shared Objective

1. **Define the Goal Clearly:** Establish a specific, measurable objective that all parties agree on.
2. **Revisit the Objective Regularly:** Keep the goal visible during discussions and decision-making to ensure alignment.
3. **Encourage Open Dialogue:** Allow team members to voice concerns or ideas, but always tie conversations back to the shared goal.
4. **Celebrate Progress Together:** Acknowledge milestones to reinforce commitment to the objective.
5. **Avoid Scope Creep:** Resist the temptation to add unrelated tasks or goals that dilute focus.

Real-World Example

The International Space Station (ISS) is a remarkable example of global collaboration focused on a shared objective. Despite political and cultural differences, space agencies from multiple countries—including NASA, Roscosmos, and ESA—united around the goal of advancing space exploration and scientific research.

By concentrating on their common mission, these agencies overcame challenges and built one of humanity's greatest scientific achievements.

Exercises

1. **Define a Shared Goal:** In a current collaboration, write down the main objective and ensure all participants are aligned with it.
2. **Refocus a Distraction:** Identify a recent discussion or task that strayed from the shared goal. How can you redirect efforts back to the main objective?
3. **Celebrate a Milestone:** Choose a recent achievement in your collaboration and acknowledge how it contributed to the shared mission.

Key Takeaway

Focusing on the shared objective ensures that collaboration is unified, efficient, and purpose-driven. By aligning efforts and minimizing distractions, you maximize the impact of your partnerships.

Chapter 53: Generate Value Before Asking for Value

In cooperative settings, trust and goodwill often hinge on your ability to demonstrate value before making requests. Generating value first shows others that you're invested in the relationship, not just seeking to benefit from it. This approach fosters trust, strengthens connections, and encourages reciprocity, creating a foundation for long-term collaboration.

Generating value doesn't always require grand gestures. It can be as simple as offering advice, sharing resources, or lending support without expecting an immediate return. These small actions accumulate, building goodwill and positioning you as a valuable and reliable partner.

Why Generating Value First is Effective

1. **Builds Trust:** Giving before asking demonstrates your commitment to the partnership.
2. **Encourages Reciprocity:** People are naturally inclined to return favors, fostering mutual benefit.
3. **Establishes Reputation:** Creating value reinforces your reliability and positions you as an asset in any collaboration.

For example, a professional networking contact who consistently shares job leads, offers mentorship, or connects others without expecting immediate payback will likely receive more support when they need it.

How to Generate Value Before Asking for Value

1. **Understand Their Needs:** Identify what your collaborators or partners value most and offer support in those areas.
2. **Offer Expertise:** Share your knowledge or skills to help others solve problems or achieve their goals.
3. **Provide Resources:** Contribute tools, information, or connections that can benefit the partnership.
4. **Be Proactive:** Look for opportunities to create value without waiting to be asked.
5. **Stay Consistent:** Continue offering value over time to build a strong, enduring relationship.

Real-World Example

In the early days of HubSpot, the company built its reputation by offering free educational content and tools to businesses, such as blogs, webinars, and marketing resources. This approach demonstrated HubSpot's expertise and commitment to helping businesses grow, even before they became paying customers.

By creating value upfront, HubSpot earned the trust of its audience and established itself as a leader in inbound marketing. This value-first strategy not only attracted loyal customers but also laid the foundation for long-term relationships, ensuring continued success as the company grew.

Exercises

1. **Identify an Opportunity to Give:** Think of a relationship where you could create value without expecting anything in return. Take one small action this week.
2. **Reflect on Reciprocity:** Consider a time when someone created value for you. How did it affect your willingness to support them later?
3. **Plan a Value-First Approach:** In an upcoming collaboration or negotiation, outline ways you can contribute before making requests.

Key Takeaway

Generating value first builds trust, fosters goodwill, and lays the groundwork for productive partnerships. By investing in others, you position yourself as a reliable and valuable collaborator.

Chapter 54: Be Generous Without Being Exploitable

Generosity is a powerful tool in collaboration, but unchecked generosity can lead to exploitation. Being generous without being exploitable means contributing freely and meaningfully to partnerships while setting clear boundaries to protect your interests.

Generosity fosters trust, goodwill, and reciprocity, but when taken too far, it can leave you vulnerable to unfair demands or overreliance. Striking the right balance ensures that your contributions are valued and that your generosity strengthens the partnership rather than depleting your resources.

Why Balanced Generosity is Important

1. **Builds Trust:** Genuine generosity shows others that you care about the partnership's success.
2. **Encourages Fairness:** Boundaries ensure that your generosity is respected rather than taken for granted.
3. **Protects Resources:** Maintaining balance prevents burnout or overextension, ensuring your long-term effectiveness.

For instance, in a team project, offering to take on additional tasks demonstrates generosity, but agreeing to do everything can lead to resentment and imbalance.

How to Be Generous Without Being Exploitable

1. **Set Clear Boundaries:** Define what you're willing to give and where you need to draw the line.
2. **Monitor Reciprocity:** Ensure that your generosity is met with fairness and effort from the other party.
3. **Communicate Assertively:** Politely decline requests that exceed your boundaries while offering alternative support.
4. **Prioritize Meaningful Contributions:** Focus on actions that create the greatest impact for the partnership.
5. **Evaluate the Relationship:** Periodically assess whether the partnership remains equitable and beneficial.

Real-World Example

In the world of freelancing, graphic designers often offer initial consultations or sample work to attract clients. The most successful freelancers balance generosity — providing high-quality previews of their work — while setting clear boundaries, such as limiting the number of revisions or charging for additional services. This approach ensures their contributions are valued without being exploited.

Exercises

1. **Assess Your Generosity:** Reflect on a recent partnership. Were you too generous or not generous enough? What could you have done differently?
2. **Define Your Boundaries:** Write down your limits for time, effort, or resources in collaborations. Practice communicating them assertively.
3. **Track Reciprocity:** In an ongoing collaboration, evaluate whether the relationship is balanced. Take steps to restore fairness if needed.

Key Takeaway

Generosity builds trust and goodwill, but it must be balanced with clear boundaries to avoid exploitation. By giving freely while protecting your interests, you create stronger, more sustainable partnerships.

Chapter 55: Align Incentives to Sustain Cooperation

For cooperation to thrive, all parties involved must feel that their efforts contribute to shared success while also advancing their personal or organizational goals. Aligning incentives ensures that everyone has a clear, mutual reason to stay committed to the partnership, reducing conflict and fostering long-term collaboration.

Misaligned incentives often lead to misunderstandings, inefficiencies, and even resentment, as parties may prioritize their own interests over the group's objectives. By carefully structuring agreements and understanding what motivates each participant, you can create an environment where collaboration feels natural and rewarding.

Why Aligning Incentives is Critical

1. **Fosters Commitment:** Shared benefits keep all parties engaged and invested in the partnership.
2. **Reduces Conflict:** When goals are aligned, there's less competition within the collaboration.
3. **Enhances Productivity:** Clear incentives encourage each party to contribute their best efforts.

For example, in a business joint venture, offering equity shares tied to performance ensures that all parties have a vested interest in achieving success.

How to Align Incentives

1. **Understand Motivations:** Identify what each participant values most, whether it's financial rewards, recognition, or creative freedom.
2. **Create Win-Win Structures:** Design agreements where success for one party directly benefits the others.
3. **Set Clear Metrics:** Define measurable goals and rewards tied to specific outcomes.
4. **Revisit Agreements Regularly:** Ensure that incentives remain fair and relevant as the partnership evolves.
5. **Acknowledge Contributions:** Regularly recognize and reward individual efforts to maintain morale and motivation.

Real-World Example

The partnership between Lego and Universal Music Group (UMG) in 2020 demonstrates the importance of aligned incentives. The two companies collaborated to create LEGO VIDIYO, a product line that combined Lego's creativity and UMG's music catalog to allow kids to create music videos using physical bricks and augmented reality.

The incentives were perfectly aligned: Lego gained access to popular music to enhance its product appeal, while UMG introduced its artists to a younger audience. Both parties benefited from the collaboration, encouraging sustained cooperation as the product developed and expanded.

Exercises

1. **Evaluate a Current Partnership:** Identify whether the incentives in your collaboration are aligned. How could they be improved?
2. **Design a Win-Win Model:** In a new or potential partnership, outline how both parties can benefit equally from shared success.
3. **Monitor Incentive Impact:** Reflect on how current incentives influence behavior within your team or collaboration. Adjust if necessary.

Key Takeaway

Aligned incentives sustain cooperation by ensuring that everyone benefits from shared success. By understanding motivations and creating win-win structures, you foster long-term, productive relationships.

Chapter 56: Honor Loyalty Proactively

Loyalty is the cornerstone of lasting relationships, but it must be nurtured and rewarded to remain strong. Honoring loyalty proactively means not waiting until someone questions their commitment to you. Instead, it involves consistently recognizing and appreciating their efforts, contributions, or allegiance, ensuring they feel valued and motivated to maintain the relationship.

Proactive loyalty doesn't just strengthen bonds—it also reinforces your reputation as a trustworthy partner. This approach minimizes turnover in teams, discourages opportunistic behavior in collaborations, and fosters a culture of mutual respect and support.

Why Honoring Loyalty Matters

1. **Strengthens Relationships:** Recognizing loyalty deepens trust and commitment.
2. **Encourages Reciprocity:** Loyal actions inspire similar dedication from others.
3. **Enhances Stability:** Loyal collaborators are less likely to seek alternative opportunities, ensuring continuity.

For instance, employers who regularly acknowledge and reward long-term employees through promotions, bonuses, or public recognition often see higher retention rates and improved morale.

How to Honor Loyalty Proactively

1. **Show Appreciation:** Regularly thank collaborators for their contributions and dedication.
2. **Offer Tangible Rewards:** Provide meaningful benefits, such as financial bonuses, new opportunities, or public recognition.
3. **Create Growth Opportunities:** Ensure loyal partners or team members have chances to advance or expand their skills.
4. **Communicate Openly:** Keep loyal collaborators informed about changes or plans to make them feel included and valued.
5. **Be Consistent:** Demonstrate loyalty in return by standing by your collaborators in times of uncertainty or challenge.

Real-World Example

Loyalty programs in hospitality, such as Marriott Bonvoy, exemplify proactive loyalty. Marriott consistently rewards frequent customers with points, upgrades, and exclusive perks, reinforcing their commitment to the brand. This proactive recognition ensures that loyal customers feel valued and remain engaged, leading to long-term relationships and repeat business.

Exercises

1. **Identify Loyal Partners:** List individuals or groups who have shown consistent loyalty to you or your organization. What steps can you take to honor their commitment?
2. **Plan a Loyalty Reward:** Develop a meaningful way to recognize and reward loyalty in your personal or professional life.
3. **Reflect on Reciprocity:** Think about how you demonstrate loyalty in return. Are there areas where you could improve?

Key Takeaway

Honoring loyalty proactively strengthens relationships, fosters trust, and encourages long-term commitment. By consistently recognizing and rewarding dedication, you build a foundation of mutual respect and shared success.

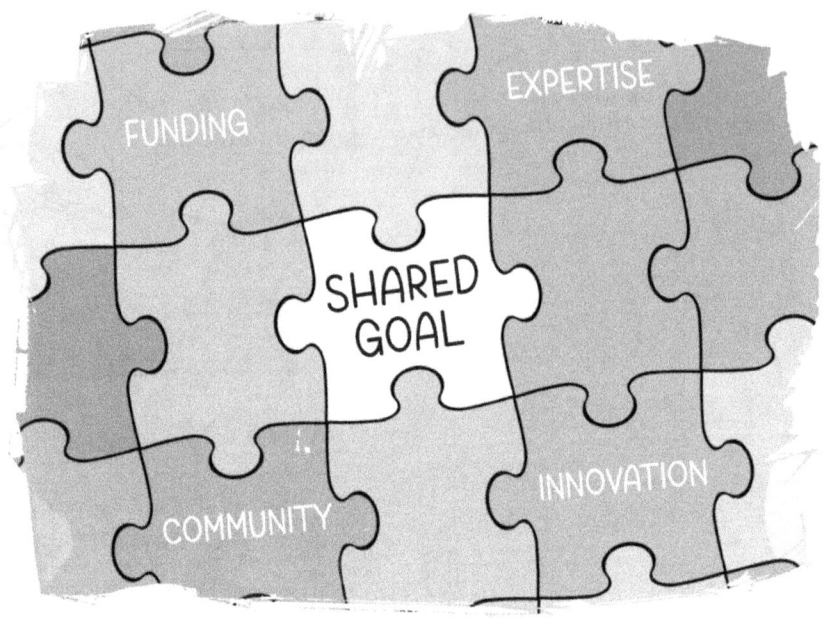

Chapter 57: Forge Coalitions Around Shared Interests

Forging coalitions can be the key to achieving goals that might otherwise be out of reach. Coalitions are alliances of individuals or organizations united by common interests, where each member contributes their strengths to the group's collective success. By pooling resources, knowledge, and influence, coalitions amplify impact and create opportunities for mutual growth.

The key to successful coalitions lies in identifying shared interests that motivate all members equally. A strong coalition isn't just about joining forces—it's about ensuring that every participant benefits meaningfully from the collaboration. By focusing on common ground and clearly defining roles, you create an alliance that thrives on trust, respect, and a shared vision.

Why Forging Coalitions is Powerful

1. **Combines Strengths:** Coalitions bring together diverse resources, skills, and perspectives for greater impact.
2. **Builds Credibility:** Working as a united front increases influence and legitimacy.
3. **Shares Risk:** Challenges and responsibilities are distributed, reducing the burden on any single member.

For example, environmental coalitions often unite companies, non-profits, and governments around goals like reducing emissions. These partnerships pool expertise, funding, and public support to achieve significant outcomes.

How to Forge Effective Coalitions

1. **Identify Shared Goals:** Focus on a common objective that aligns with the interests of all potential members.
2. **Clearly Define Roles:** Assign responsibilities that leverage each participant's unique strengths.
3. **Maintain Open Communication:** Foster transparency and collaboration by encouraging regular dialogue.
4. **Celebrate Collective Wins:** Recognize and publicize successes to reinforce the coalition's value.
5. **Adapt to Change:** Be flexible and willing to adjust strategies as new opportunities or challenges arise.

Real-World Example

The Fair Trade Movement is a prime example of coalitions built around shared interests. Fairtrade International brings together farmers, workers, businesses, and NGOs with the common goal of promoting sustainable agriculture and ethical trading practices.

By pooling resources and aligning their efforts, this coalition has empowered small-scale farmers, improved working conditions, and raised awareness about ethical consumption worldwide. The coalition's success demonstrates how diverse groups with complementary strengths can unite to achieve significant, shared objectives that benefit all members.

Exercises

1. **Identify a Common Goal:** Think of a challenge or opportunity where collaboration could amplify success. Who might share your interests?
2. **Build a Coalition Plan:** Outline the key stakeholders, their potential contributions, and how they might benefit from joining your coalition.
3. **Evaluate a Past Collaboration:** Reflect on a previous group effort. What worked well, and what could have been improved?

Key Takeaway

Coalitions built around shared interests create powerful synergies. When you unite diverse strengths and focusing on common goals, you amplify impact and achieve outcomes that benefit all members.

Chapter 58: Avoid Overpromising in Groups

The desire to please others or secure agreement can lead to overpromising — making commitments that are unrealistic or unsustainable. While well-intentioned, overpromising often results in missed deadlines, strained relationships, and diminished trust when expectations aren't met.

Avoiding overpromising doesn't mean being overly cautious or unambitious. Instead, it's about being realistic, honest, and transparent about what you can deliver. By managing expectations effectively, you ensure that your contributions are reliable and that the group maintains confidence in your commitments.

Why Avoiding Overpromising is Essential

1. **Preserves Trust:** Meeting expectations consistently reinforces credibility and reliability.
2. **Reduces Stress:** Realistic commitments prevent overwork and burnout.
3. **Promotes Long-Term Success:** Sustainable efforts lead to stronger, more enduring relationships.

For instance, in project collaborations, committing to an unachievable timeline can disrupt the entire group's workflow. Setting a realistic schedule ensures smoother coordination and better outcomes.

How to Avoid Overpromising

1. **Be Honest About Capacity:** Assess your resources, time, and abilities before making commitments.
2. **Set Realistic Expectations:** Clearly communicate what you can and cannot deliver.
3. **Provide Updates:** If challenges arise, inform the group promptly and adjust expectations as needed.
4. **Focus on Quality Over Quantity:** Commit to fewer tasks, but execute them to the highest standard.
5. **Learn From Experience:** Reflect on past commitments to identify patterns and improve future decision-making.

Real-World Example

In the automotive industry, Ford provides a valuable example of avoiding overpromising. During the launch of the all-electric Ford F-150 Lightning, Ford carefully set realistic expectations regarding delivery timelines and production capacity. Instead of overpromising on immediate availability, the company communicated a phased rollout plan and adjusted delivery schedules as demand surged.

By managing customer expectations upfront, Ford maintained trust and avoided the backlash often associated with missed promises. This approach ensured a smoother launch and strengthened its reputation as a reliable and transparent automaker.

Exercises

1. **Evaluate Your Current Commitments:** Are there any promises you've made that may be unrealistic? How can you address this proactively?
2. **Practice Saying No:** In your next group discussion, identify a request you can decline or renegotiate for clarity and balance.
3. **Reflect on Past Overpromises:** Think about a time when you overpromised. What were the consequences, and how can you improve moving forward?

Key Takeaway

Avoiding overpromising in groups safeguards trust and ensures sustainable success. This approach allows you to set realistic expectations, deliver consistently, build credibility and strengthen collaborative relationships.

Chapter 59: Communicate Clearly to Reduce Misunderstandings

Miscommunication is one of the most common barriers to effective collaboration. Unclear messages, assumptions, and ambiguity can lead to misunderstandings, delays, and even conflicts. Clear communication ensures that everyone involved in a partnership or team is aligned, informed, and able to act with confidence.

Effective communication isn't just about speaking clearly — it's about listening actively, tailoring your message to your audience, and confirming mutual understanding. When communication is prioritized, teams function more smoothly, partnerships thrive, and shared goals are more easily achieved.

Why Clear Communication is Crucial

1. **Prevents Confusion:** Clear messages reduce the likelihood of misinterpretation or errors.
2. **Builds Trust:** Transparent and honest communication fosters confidence and strengthens relationships.
3. **Enhances Efficiency:** When everyone understands their roles and responsibilities, tasks are completed more effectively.

For example, during team projects, regularly clarifying goals, deadlines, and expectations minimizes confusion and keeps progress on track.

How to Communicate Clearly

1. **Define Your Message:** Be clear about the purpose and key points of your communication before delivering it.
2. **Use Simple Language:** Avoid jargon or overly complex phrases that could confuse your audience.
3. **Confirm Understanding:** Ask for feedback or repeat key points to ensure your message has been received as intended.
4. **Adapt to Your Audience:** Tailor your tone and delivery to suit the needs and preferences of your collaborators.
5. **Be Transparent:** Share necessary details openly, avoiding omissions that could lead to misunderstandings.

Real-World Example

NASA's Apollo missions highlight the importance of clear communication. Engineers, astronauts, and mission control relied on precise and unambiguous instructions to execute complex tasks. For instance, during the Apollo 13 crisis, clear, step-by-step communication between astronauts and mission control enabled the team to safely navigate life-threatening challenges, demonstrating how effective communication can make or break a collaboration.

Exercises

1. **Audit a Recent Interaction:** Reflect on a conversation or email. Were your key points clearly conveyed? How could you improve?
2. **Practice Active Listening:** In your next meeting, focus on understanding others' perspectives fully before responding.
3. **Clarify Roles:** In your current team project, ensure that everyone understands their responsibilities by summarizing and confirming them.

Key Takeaway

Clear communication reduces misunderstandings and ensures alignment in collaborative efforts. By listening actively and delivering concise, transparent messages, you foster trust and streamline success.

Chapter 60: Exit Teams Gracefully When Necessary

Sometimes, the best decision in a collaborative effort is to step away. Exiting a team or partnership isn't inherently negative — it can signify growth, a shift in priorities, or the conclusion of your role in a project. However, how you leave a group matters significantly. Exiting gracefully ensures that relationships remain intact, reputations are preserved, and future opportunities for collaboration remain open.

A graceful exit involves honesty, professionalism, and a focus on the group's continued success. By clearly communicating your reasons and ensuring a smooth transition, you leave a positive impression and minimize disruption to the team's goals.

Why Exiting Gracefully Matters

1. **Preserves Relationships:** A positive departure maintains goodwill and future collaboration potential.
2. **Minimizes Disruption:** Planning your exit ensures continuity for the remaining team.
3. **Enhances Reputation:** A thoughtful exit demonstrates professionalism and maturity.

For instance, a project manager transitioning out of a role might document processes, train their replacement, and offer continued support during the handover.

How to Exit Teams Gracefully

1. **Communicate Early:** Inform the team of your intention to leave as soon as possible, providing sufficient notice.
2. **Explain Your Reasons:** Share your decision honestly and constructively, focusing on growth or new opportunities rather than grievances.
3. **Support the Transition:** Help identify or train a replacement, and ensure all your responsibilities are documented and delegated.
4. **Express Gratitude:** Acknowledge the team's contributions and express appreciation for the experience.
5. **Stay Open to the Future:** Keep the door open for future collaborations by leaving on positive terms.

Real-World Example

When Eric Schmidt stepped down as Google's CEO in 2011, he exemplified a graceful exit. Schmidt transitioned to an executive chairman role, ensuring a smooth handover of responsibilities to co-founder Larry Page. He continued to advise and support the company, preserving strong relationships and contributing to Google's ongoing success.

Exercises

1. **Plan a Hypothetical Exit:** Imagine leaving your current team or project. What steps would you take to ensure a smooth transition?
2. **Reflect on Past Exits:** Consider a time when you left a group or role. What went well, and what could have been handled better?
3. **Express Gratitude:** Write a note of appreciation to a current or past collaborator, strengthening your professional relationships.

Key Takeaway

Exiting teams gracefully ensures positive relationships, smooth transitions, and ongoing opportunities. By communicating openly and prioritizing the group's success, you leave a lasting, constructive impact.

Section IV: Adaptive Strategies

Adaptability is not just a skill — it's a necessity. This section explores how to thrive in unpredictable environments by staying flexible, innovative, and resilient. By mastering the art of adaptation, you'll be equipped to seize opportunities, outmaneuver challenges, and thrive no matter what the future holds.

Chapter 61: Anticipate Game-Changing Trends

Game-changing trends can disrupt industries, reshape markets, and create new opportunities for those who see them early. Anticipating these shifts allows you to stay ahead of competitors and position yourself to benefit from the coming change. It's not about predicting the future with certainty — it's about identifying patterns, analyzing signals, and preparing to act when opportunities arise.

Successful leaders and organizations make trend-watching a priority. They monitor technological advances, cultural shifts, and emerging industries to spot potential transformations. By understanding the forces driving change, you can align your strategies to harness these trends before they reshape the landscape.

Why Anticipating Trends is Critical

1. **First-Mover Advantage:** Early identification allows you to act before others, gaining a competitive edge.
2. **Reduces Risk:** Preparing for change minimizes disruption and positions you to adapt smoothly.
3. **Encourages Innovation:** Staying ahead of trends inspires forward-thinking strategies and solutions.

For instance, companies that embraced remote work technologies before the COVID-19 pandemic were better prepared to transition when the world suddenly shifted to work-from-home models.

How to Anticipate Game-Changing Trends

1. **Track Key Indicators:** Monitor industry reports, emerging technologies, and consumer behavior for early signs of change.
2. **Engage with Experts:** Participate in discussions, panels, and networks that provide insights into future developments.
3. **Analyze Adjacent Industries:** Look at trends in related fields that could impact your sector.
4. **Embrace Curiosity:** Encourage your team to explore unconventional ideas and challenge assumptions.
5. **Prepare for Multiple Scenarios:** Develop flexible plans that account for a range of possible outcomes.

Real-World Example

In the 1980s, Apple anticipated the growing demand for personal computers that were user-friendly and accessible to non-technical users. While other companies focused on technical specifications and business markets, Apple saw an opportunity to cater to everyday consumers.

The launch of the Macintosh in 1984, featuring a graphical user interface and a mouse, revolutionized the personal computing industry. This foresight into the trend toward intuitive, design-oriented technology established Apple as a leader in consumer innovation and shaped the modern tech landscape.

Exercises

1. **Identify Emerging Trends:** Write down three trends in your industry that could disrupt or transform the market.
2. **Scenario Planning:** Create a strategy for how you would adapt if one of these trends became dominant.
3. **Expand Your Horizon:** Research a field outside your industry to identify innovations that might impact your work.

Key Takeaway

Anticipating game-changing trends positions you to act before others, turning potential disruptions into opportunities. By staying curious and prepared, you can adapt and thrive in a rapidly evolving world.

Chapter 62: Be the First to Spot Weak Signals

Major shifts often begin as faint signals — early indicators of change that are easy to miss but critical to spot. Being the first to notice these weak signals allows you to act decisively, while others remain unaware or hesitant. These signals might include subtle shifts in consumer behavior, emerging technologies, or small market disruptions that hint at larger trends to come.

Spotting weak signals requires an open mind, curiosity, and a willingness to explore unconventional sources of information. It also involves interpreting the context of these signals and assessing their potential impact. Acting on weak signals is risky, but when done wisely, it positions you as a pioneer.

Why Spotting Weak Signals Matters

1. **Provides an Early Advantage:** Acting on signals before others gives you a head start.
2. **Minimizes Surprises:** Early awareness allows you to prepare for potential disruptions.
3. **Drives Innovation:** Weak signals often highlight opportunities to create or improve solutions.

For example, the rise of plant-based diets started as a weak signal with niche products like tofu and almond milk. Companies like Beyond Meat and Oatly recognized this trend early, developing innovative plant-based alternatives and growing their market before competitors.

How to Spot Weak Signals

1. **Look Beyond the Mainstream:** Explore niche markets, independent research, and emerging technologies for early indicators.
2. **Track Anomalies:** Pay attention to unexpected shifts in data, customer behavior, or market patterns.
3. **Foster Diverse Input:** Engage with individuals from different industries, cultures, or backgrounds to gain fresh perspectives.
4. **Experiment with Ideas:** Test small-scale initiatives to explore the potential of weak signals.
5. **Monitor Continuously:** Weak signals can emerge gradually, so keep an eye on trends over time.

Real-World Example

In the mid-2010s, Square (now Block, Inc.) recognized weak signals pointing to a growing demand for mobile payment solutions among small businesses. While larger payment processors focused on established retailers, Square introduced its portable card reader, enabling entrepreneurs, food trucks, and small vendors to accept credit card payments conveniently through their smartphones.

This move, based on early observations of small businesses' struggles with traditional payment systems, allowed Square to capture an underserved market segment. By acting on these weak signals, Square not only filled a critical gap but also set the stage for its long-term success in financial technology.

Exercises

1. **Identify Weak Signals:** List three subtle changes or anomalies you've noticed in your industry. What might they indicate?
2. **Explore Niche Communities:** Join forums, attend events, or follow niche influencers to uncover emerging ideas.
3. **Test a Hypothesis:** Develop a small project or initiative based on a weak signal you've identified.

Key Takeaway

Spotting weak signals allows you to act early and capitalize on emerging opportunities. By staying curious and attentive, you can detect subtle changes before they become significant forces of disruption.

Chapter 63: Apply Change as a Well-Designed Asset

Change is inevitable, but not all change is inherently beneficial. The key lies in applying change as a well-designed asset — a resource that you shape and direct toward achieving specific goals. When you actively harness change rather than reacting to it, you gain control over its outcomes and use it to create lasting value.

This mindset requires viewing change as an opportunity rather than a disruption. Instead of fearing uncertainty, ask how you can shape emerging trends, technologies, or challenges to benefit your goals. By proactively designing how you respond to change, you stay ahead of competitors and adapt to evolving circumstances with purpose.

Why Applying Change as an Asset is Effective

1. **Maximizes Opportunity:** Proactively shaping change turns potential disruptions into strategic advantages.
2. **Reduces Risk:** A structured approach to change minimizes negative impacts and improves outcomes.
3. **Encourages Innovation:** Using change creatively opens the door to new ideas and opportunities.

For example, businesses that reframe economic downturns as opportunities to streamline operations or diversify revenue streams often emerge stronger and more resilient.

How to Apply Change as an Asset

1. **Assess the Context:** Understand the nature of the change and its potential impact on your goals.
2. **Define Your Objective:** Decide how you want to leverage the change to achieve specific outcomes.
3. **Develop a Plan:** Create a step-by-step approach for integrating change into your strategy.
4. **Engage Your Team:** Involve others in brainstorming and implementing solutions, leveraging diverse perspectives.
5. **Monitor and Adjust:** Track progress and refine your approach as new developments unfold.

Real-World Example

In the early 2010s, Adidas used the rapid adoption of 3D printing as a strategic asset. While many companies hesitated to invest in the emerging technology, Adidas developed its Futurecraft line, featuring 3D-printed midsoles for its running shoes. By integrating change into its design process, Adidas created a product that combined innovation with functionality, boosting its reputation as a forward-thinking brand and attracting new customers.

Exercises

1. **Reframe a Current Challenge:** Identify a change you're facing and brainstorm ways to use it to your advantage.
2. **Create a Change Action Plan:** Choose one emerging trend and outline steps for incorporating it into your goals.
3. **Reflect on Past Success:** Think of a time when you successfully adapted to change. What lessons can you apply to future challenges?

Key Takeaway

Change becomes a powerful asset when you proactively shape and integrate it into your strategy. By approaching change as an opportunity for growth, you can transform challenges into valuable outcomes.

Chapter 64: Develop Options for Uncertain Futures

Uncertainty is a constant in any competitive environment, and the most successful individuals and organizations prepare by developing multiple options for the future. Rather than committing to a single path, they create flexibility, ensuring they can pivot as circumstances evolve. By building a portfolio of options, you mitigate risk, seize opportunities, and remain agile in the face of change.

This approach involves identifying key uncertainties, brainstorming potential scenarios, and preparing strategies for each. While it's impossible to predict the future with precision, creating options ensures you're ready to act no matter which direction the world takes.

Why Developing Options is Crucial

1. **Reduces Risk:** Multiple options provide fallback plans if initial strategies fail.
2. **Increases Agility:** Preparedness allows for quicker adaptation to unexpected changes.
3. **Encourages Confidence:** Knowing you have contingencies reduces stress and fosters decisive action.

For instance, organizations that diversify their supply chains are better equipped to handle disruptions such as political instability, natural disasters, or economic changes.

How to Develop Options for Uncertain Futures

1. **Identify Key Uncertainties:** Pinpoint the factors that could significantly impact your goals.
2. **Create Multiple Scenarios:** Envision different possible futures and how they might unfold.
3. **Develop Contingency Plans:** Prepare strategies and resources for each scenario.
4. **Test and Refine Options:** Pilot your strategies on a small scale to evaluate their feasibility.
5. **Remain Flexible:** Be willing to revise your options as new information emerges.

Real-World Example

During the early 2000s, Intel diversified its product offerings to prepare for shifts in the tech industry. Anticipating changes in demand for traditional computer processors, the company invested in technologies like mobile processors, server chips, and artificial intelligence. By developing multiple options, Intel remained a leader in a rapidly evolving market and positioned itself for long-term growth.

Exercises

1. **Brainstorm Future Scenarios:** Write down three possible futures that could impact your work or goals. What options could you prepare for each?
2. **Evaluate Your Current Options:** Are you overly reliant on a single strategy? Identify areas where diversification is needed.
3. **Test One Option:** Choose a potential strategy and implement it on a small scale to gauge its effectiveness.

Key Takeaway

Developing options for uncertain futures ensures you're ready to adapt, no matter what lies ahead. By preparing for multiple scenarios, you reduce risk and gain the confidence to navigate change with flexibility and foresight.

Chapter 65: Use Real Options to Hedge Strategies

OPPORTUNITIES

In strategic planning, uncertainty is unavoidable. One of the most effective ways to navigate it is by using real options—a framework that allows you to make flexible, staged decisions. Real options give you the ability to delay, expand, or abandon a course of action as new information becomes available, enabling you to hedge against risks while still pursuing opportunities.

Unlike traditional strategies that require a firm commitment upfront, real options recognize the value of flexibility. By keeping multiple paths open and making incremental investments, you maintain the ability to pivot without overcommitting. This approach is especially valuable in dynamic environments where the future is difficult to predict.

Why Real Options Are Powerful

1. **Minimizes Risk:** Real options reduce the cost of failure by allowing you to abandon unproductive paths early.
2. **Increases Agility:** Flexible strategies enable quick adjustments to changing circumstances.
3. **Encourages Exploration:** Small, initial investments lower the barrier to testing new ideas or markets.

For instance, a company considering international expansion might lease a small office or test a product in a single market before committing to full-scale operations.

How to Use Real Options

1. **Identify Opportunities:** Look for areas where flexibility could provide an advantage, such as emerging technologies or new markets.
2. **Break Down Decisions:** Divide your strategy into smaller, manageable steps with decision points along the way.
3. **Invest Incrementally:** Commit resources in stages, increasing investment only as conditions become clearer.
4. **Set Triggers for Action:** Define the conditions under which you'll expand, continue, or abandon a project.
5. **Evaluate Regularly:** Continuously assess the performance and feasibility of your options as circumstances evolve.

Real-World Example

Pharmaceutical companies often use real options in drug development. Instead of fully funding a drug from research to market, they start with smaller investments in early-stage trials. If the results are promising, they commit more resources to subsequent stages. This staged approach allows them to minimize losses if a drug fails while retaining the ability to capitalize on successful projects.

Exercises

1. **Create a Real Option:** Identify a decision you're currently facing and outline a plan to stage your commitments.
2. **Analyze a Past Decision:** Reflect on a situation where flexibility could have improved your outcome. How could real options have helped?
3. **Define Your Triggers:** Choose a current project and list the conditions that would prompt you to expand, pause, or abandon it.

Key Takeaway

Real options provide the flexibility to adapt your strategies to uncertainty. By staging decisions and committing incrementally, you reduce risk and maintain the agility to pivot as new opportunities or challenges arise.

Chapter 66: Develop Contingency Plans for Key Obstacles

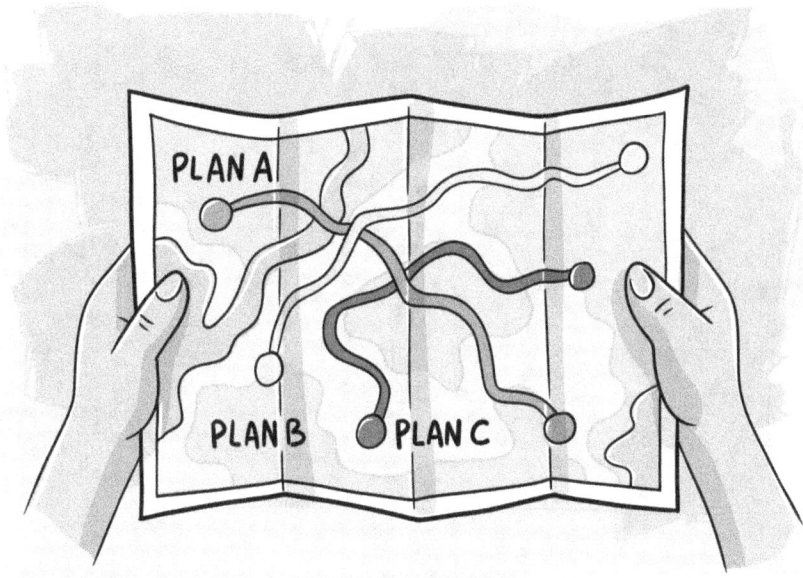

No strategy, no matter how well-designed, is immune to unexpected obstacles. Contingency plans ensure that you're prepared for setbacks by providing alternative actions when your primary plan encounters resistance. These plans act as a safety net, allowing you to continue progressing toward your goals even when challenges arise.

Developing effective contingency plans requires anticipating potential risks, assessing their likelihood, and preparing practical solutions. The process not only mitigates damage but also builds confidence, knowing that you're ready to respond effectively no matter what happens.

Why Contingency Plans Matter

1. **Reduces Disruption:** Quick responses minimize the impact of unexpected challenges.
2. **Increases Confidence:** Knowing you're prepared fosters calm and decisive action under pressure.
3. **Preserves Progress:** Contingency plans ensure that setbacks don't derail your overall strategy.

For example, organizations often prepare for cybersecurity breaches by developing incident response plans. These plans include steps for isolating the threat, securing data, and restoring systems, minimizing downtime and damage.

How to Develop Contingency Plans

1. **Identify Key Risks:** Analyze potential obstacles that could impact your goals or operations.
2. **Prioritize Risks:** Focus on the most likely and impactful challenges first.
3. **Define Alternative Actions:** Outline specific steps you'll take if a risk materializes.
4. **Allocate Resources:** Ensure that the necessary tools, personnel, or funds are available to implement your plan.
5. **Test and Revise Plans:** Conduct drills or simulations to assess your readiness and improve weak areas.

Real-World Example

In 2010, BP developed robust contingency plans following the Deepwater Horizon oil spill. Recognizing the risks associated with future offshore drilling, BP implemented advanced safety protocols, response drills, and new technologies to mitigate similar incidents.

One critical contingency was establishing partnerships with specialized environmental response teams to address spills rapidly if they occurred. This proactive planning not only reduced the likelihood of another disaster but also positioned BP as a company striving to rebuild trust through preparedness and accountability.

Exercises

1. **List Potential Obstacles:** Identify three risks that could impact your current goals. Outline contingency plans for each.
2. **Evaluate a Past Setback:** Think of a challenge you faced. How could a contingency plan have mitigated its impact?
3. **Test a Plan:** Choose one contingency plan and conduct a simulation or dry run to evaluate its effectiveness.

Key Takeaway

Contingency plans protect progress by preparing you for obstacles. By anticipating risks and defining clear alternative actions, you ensure resilience and adaptability in the face of unexpected challenges.

Chapter 67: Test Assumptions Before Acting

Assumptions are often the foundation of decisions, but when left untested, they can lead to costly mistakes. Testing assumptions before acting ensures that your strategies are based on accurate, validated information rather than guesswork. This process involves challenging preconceived notions, gathering evidence, and experimenting in low-risk environments to confirm that your assumptions hold true.

Whether you're launching a new product, entering a market, or implementing a change, assumptions play a crucial role in shaping your approach. By proactively questioning and validating these assumptions, you minimize risks and increase your chances of success.

Why Testing Assumptions Matters

1. **Reduces Risk:** Verifying assumptions minimizes the likelihood of failure by addressing potential flaws early.
2. **Informs Better Decisions:** Testing provides data-driven insights that improve the quality of your choices.
3. **Encourages Agility:** Identifying false assumptions allows you to pivot before fully committing resources.

For example, entrepreneurs often test assumptions about customer demand by launching minimum viable products (MVPs). These simplified versions of their offerings gauge market interest without significant investment, providing valuable feedback before scaling up.

How to Test Assumptions

1. **Identify Key Assumptions:** Pinpoint the beliefs or predictions that your strategy relies on most heavily.
2. **Design Small Experiments:** Develop low-risk tests to validate each assumption, such as surveys, prototypes, or pilot programs.
3. **Gather Evidence:** Collect data from real-world scenarios to confirm or disprove your assumptions.
4. **Iterate Based on Findings:** Use test results to refine your strategy, addressing weaknesses and building on strengths.
5. **Engage Stakeholders:** Involve your team or partners in testing to gain diverse perspectives and insights.

Real-World Example

Before opening its first store, Warby Parker tested the assumption that consumers would buy eyeglasses online. The founders launched a small-scale website, offering a limited number of frames to see if customers were willing to shop for eyewear without trying them on in person. The test was a success, proving that the concept resonated with consumers. This validation allowed Warby Parker to scale confidently, disrupting the eyewear industry.

Exercises

1. **List Your Assumptions:** Write down three assumptions underlying a current project or decision. How can you test them?
2. **Design a Small Experiment:** Create a low-cost, low-risk test to validate one of your assumptions this week.
3. **Evaluate Past Decisions:** Reflect on a decision where an untested assumption led to challenges. How could testing have improved the outcome?

Key Takeaway

Testing assumptions reduces risk and strengthens decisions by replacing guesswork with evidence. By validating your beliefs through small experiments, you ensure that your actions are based on reality, not speculation.

Chapter 68: Try Experimentation for Growth

Experimentation is the engine of growth. By testing new ideas, approaches, or strategies, you uncover opportunities that might otherwise remain hidden. Experimentation isn't about random trial and error—it's a structured process that involves setting hypotheses, testing in controlled environments, and analyzing results to learn what works.

In a rapidly changing world, businesses and individuals who embrace experimentation are better equipped to adapt and innovate. Experimentation not only drives growth but also fosters creativity, resilience, and a culture of continuous improvement.

Why Experimentation is Crucial for Growth

1. **Encourages Innovation:** Experiments reveal new possibilities and spark creative solutions.
2. **Reduces Uncertainty:** Testing ideas on a small scale minimizes risks before scaling up.
3. **Builds Resilience:** Experimentation fosters a mindset that views failure as a stepping stone to success.

For example, tech companies often use A/B testing to experiment with product features, website layouts, or marketing campaigns. By comparing results, they identify the most effective strategies for growth.

How to Try Experimentation for Growth

1. **Define Your Goals:** Clearly articulate what you want to achieve with your experiments.
2. **Set Hypotheses:** Develop predictions about what you expect to happen and why.
3. **Start Small:** Test ideas on a limited scale to minimize risks and costs.
4. **Measure Results:** Use data to evaluate the success of your experiments and identify areas for improvement.
5. **Iterate and Scale:** Refine your approach based on findings, scaling up successful experiments.

Real-World Example

Zappos embraced experimentation by offering a unique trial to test online shoe retailing. Founder Nick Swinmurn initially listed local shoe store inventories online and only purchased shoes once a customer placed an order. This experiment validated the concept without requiring a large upfront investment, paving the way for Zappos to revolutionize the e-commerce footwear industry.

Exercises

1. **Design an Experiment:** Identify one area where you could test a new idea. Outline your hypothesis, method, and measurement plan.
2. **Reflect on Past Experiments:** Think about a time when you tried something new. What worked, and what did you learn?
3. **Commit to a Growth Mindset:** Identify one risk or challenge you've avoided. How can experimentation help you address it?

Key Takeaway

Experimentation drives growth by uncovering new opportunities and fostering innovation. By testing ideas on a small scale, you minimize risks, learn from failures, and pave the way for success.

Chapter 69: Turn Failures into Stepping Stones for Progress

Failure is an inevitable part of innovation and growth, but its impact depends entirely on how you respond to it. Viewing failures as stepping stones rather than dead ends transforms setbacks into valuable learning opportunities. By analyzing what went wrong, you gain insights that refine your strategies, improve decision-making, and prepare you for future challenges.

Turning failures into progress requires a shift in mindset. Rather than focusing on the negative aspects of a setback, consider what it has taught you and how it can shape your next steps. This approach not only builds resilience but also encourages a culture where experimentation and risk-taking are embraced as necessary for long-term success.

Why Learning from Failure is Crucial

1. **Fosters Growth:** Each failure provides unique lessons that refine your skills and strategies.
2. **Builds Resilience:** Overcoming setbacks strengthens your ability to adapt to future challenges.
3. **Encourages Innovation:** When failure is seen as a learning opportunity, it inspires bold, creative approaches.

For example, failure often drives breakthroughs in scientific research. Many important discoveries, from penicillin to post-it notes, began as unintentional outcomes of experiments. By analyzing "failures," researchers uncovered ground-breaking innovations.

How to Turn Failures into Progress

1. **Reflect and Analyze:** Take time to understand what went wrong and why. Break down the failure into specific elements to identify areas for improvement.
2. **Extract Lessons:** Write down the key insights you've gained from the setback and how they can inform your future actions.
3. **Reframe Your Mindset:** View failure as part of the process rather than an endpoint. Celebrate the courage it took to take a risk.
4. **Share Learnings:** If you're part of a team, openly discuss what happened to foster a culture of learning and transparency.
5. **Apply the Lessons:** Use what you've learned to refine your approach and take smarter risks moving forward.

Real-World Example

The video game company Rovio, the creators of *Angry Birds*, failed with over 50 game releases before achieving massive success. Each failed game provided insights into what resonated with players, helping Rovio refine its design and marketing strategies. The eventual launch of *Angry Birds* turned the company into a global sensation, proving the value of persistence and learning from failure.

Exercises

1. **Reflect on a Failure:** Identify a recent setback. Write down what caused it and three lessons you can take from it.
2. **Redesign Your Approach:** Based on the lessons from a past failure, outline a new strategy to address a similar challenge.
3. **Encourage Failure Discussions:** If you're part of a team, create a safe space for discussing mistakes and the insights gained from them.

Key Takeaway

Failure isn't the end; it's a stepping stone to success. By learning from setbacks and applying those lessons, you transform obstacles into opportunities for growth and innovation.

Chapter 70: Adapt Plans in Real Time

Even the most well-thought-out plans can be disrupted by unexpected changes. The ability to adapt plans in real time ensures that you remain flexible and responsive, allowing you to navigate challenges and seize opportunities as they arise. This adaptability is a hallmark of resilient individuals and organizations, turning potential setbacks into stepping stones for success.

Real-time adaptation involves constantly monitoring the situation, identifying when a shift is necessary, and making quick, informed adjustments. It's not about abandoning your overall goals but about finding alternative paths to achieve them when the original plan no longer fits the circumstances.

Why Real-Time Adaptation is Vital

1. **Maintains Momentum:** Quick adjustments keep progress moving forward despite obstacles.
2. **Seizes Opportunities:** Staying flexible allows you to capitalize on unexpected advantages.
3. **Reduces Stress:** Having a mindset of adaptability lessens the pressure of rigidly adhering to a failing plan.

For example, adapting a marketing campaign based on real-time customer feedback can transform mediocre results into success. When Nike launched its "You Can't Stop Us" campaign during the COVID-19 pandemic, it pivoted to emphasize unity and resilience, resonating deeply with global audiences.

How to Adapt Plans in Real Time

1. **Stay Informed:** Continuously monitor progress and changes in the environment that could impact your plans.
2. **Foster Flexibility:** Build plans with room for adjustment, such as buffer time or modular strategies.
3. **Define Core Goals:** Keep your end objectives clear so you can adapt methods without losing focus.
4. **Involve Your Team:** Collaborate with others to brainstorm solutions and identify the best path forward.
5. **Act Decisively:** Avoid paralysis by analysis—make adjustments quickly based on available information.

Real-World Example

The 2021 Tokyo Olympics showcased real-time adaptability when faced with the COVID-19 pandemic. Organizers adjusted protocols, postponed events, and implemented health measures to ensure the games could proceed safely. These rapid adaptations allowed the event to succeed despite unprecedented challenges.

Exercises

1. **Review a Recent Change:** Think of a time when you had to pivot quickly. What worked well, and what could you improve?
2. **Practice Scenario Planning:** Identify a current project and outline two potential disruptions. How would you adapt?
3. **Build Flexibility:** Analyze a current plan and identify areas where you can introduce more adaptability.

Key Takeaway

Adapting plans in real time ensures resilience and responsiveness in the face of change. By staying informed and flexible, you maintain progress and turn unexpected challenges into opportunities for success.

Chapter 71: Detect Hidden Patterns in Chaos

Chaos often feels overwhelming, but beneath the surface lies hidden order waiting to be uncovered. Detecting patterns in chaos is a critical adaptive strategy that enables you to make sense of complexity, anticipate future outcomes, and act decisively in uncertain environments. The ability to see connections where others see randomness is what separates reactive individuals from strategic thinkers.

Finding patterns doesn't require special foresight — it demands focus, curiosity, and a willingness to examine situations from multiple perspectives. By identifying recurring themes, trends, or relationships, you gain insights that guide smarter decisions and innovative solutions.

Why Detecting Patterns in Chaos is Valuable

1. **Reveals Insights:** Identifying patterns helps you understand the underlying factors driving events.
2. **Improves Decision-Making:** Recognizing order in complexity enables faster, more confident choices.
3. **Enhances Predictability:** Patterns provide clues about what might happen next, allowing you to stay ahead.

For example, stock market analysts often look for patterns in trading data to predict price movements. While the market can seem chaotic, these patterns offer valuable insights for strategic investment decisions.

How to Detect Hidden Patterns in Chaos

1. **Zoom Out:** Step back from the details to view the bigger picture, which often reveals broader trends.
2. **Focus on Key Variables:** Identify the most important factors influencing the situation and track their interactions.
3. **Use Data and Analytics:** Leverage tools and methods that help you visualize complex information, such as charts or heatmaps.
4. **Engage Diverse Perspectives:** Collaborate with others who can offer different viewpoints, uncovering connections you might miss.
5. **Test Your Observations:** Validate potential patterns by checking their consistency across different scenarios.

Real-World Example

The British cryptanalysts at Bletchley Park during World War II famously detected hidden patterns in the seemingly chaotic messages encrypted by the German Enigma machine. By identifying recurring structures and analyzing vast amounts of intercepted data, they broke the code, providing crucial intelligence that helped win the war.

Exercises

1. **Identify a Chaotic Situation:** Reflect on a current challenge that feels disorganized. Write down potential patterns or recurring elements you notice.
2. **Analyze Data for Trends:** Choose a set of data (e.g., sales, performance metrics, or feedback) and look for correlations or trends.
3. **Collaborate for Insight:** Discuss a complex problem with a colleague or friend to explore new patterns you may not have considered.

Key Takeaway

Detecting hidden patterns in chaos transforms uncertainty into opportunity. By focusing on connections and recurring themes, you uncover the insights needed to act strategically in complex environments.

Chapter 72: Use Contrarian Thinking to Your Advantage

Contrarian thinking involves questioning popular beliefs and exploring alternative perspectives. While conventional wisdom often has merit, blindly following it can lead to missed opportunities and vulnerabilities. Contrarian thinkers challenge assumptions, evaluate evidence critically, and identify overlooked possibilities, giving them a strategic edge.

This approach doesn't mean opposing the majority for its own sake. Instead, it requires disciplined analysis to determine when a different path might yield better results. In a world where many follow trends, contrarian thinkers are often the first to spot flaws, inefficiencies, or untapped opportunities.

Why Contrarian Thinking is Powerful

1. **Exposes Weaknesses:** Challenging the status quo reveals blind spots or overlooked risks.
2. **Uncovers Opportunities:** Alternative perspectives often highlight paths others ignore.
3. **Drives Innovation:** Thinking differently fosters creative solutions and unique strategies.

For example, contrarian thinking allowed Howard Schultz to transform Starbucks from a small coffee shop into a global brand. At a time when coffee was seen as a utilitarian product, Schultz envisioned coffee as an experience. By challenging the industry's norms, he created a new market and redefined how people consume coffee.

How to Use Contrarian Thinking

1. **Question Assumptions:** Regularly challenge conventional beliefs, especially those that drive important decisions.
2. **Explore Opposing Views:** Seek out perspectives that contradict your own to identify potential gaps in your thinking.
3. **Analyze Underlying Evidence:** Focus on data rather than opinions when evaluating popular trends.
4. **Test Your Ideas:** Pilot contrarian approaches on a small scale before committing fully.
5. **Stay Open-Minded:** Balance doubt with curiosity, remaining open to learning and adapting.

Real-World Example

In the late 1990s, Reed Hastings, co-founder of Netflix, applied contrarian thinking by launching a subscription-based DVD rental service at a time when video rental stores dominated. His approach challenged the traditional model of renting movies by eliminating late fees and offering convenience. This disruption ultimately led to Netflix's rise as a market leader, while competitors like Blockbuster failed to adapt.

Exercises

1. **Challenge a Norm:** Identify one commonly held belief in your industry or field. Ask yourself: What if the opposite were true?
2. **Seek Contrarian Opinions:** Talk to someone with a different viewpoint on a key issue. What insights can you gain?
3. **Pilot a Contrarian Idea:** Test an unconventional strategy or approach in a low-risk scenario.

Key Takeaway

Contrarian thinking reveals opportunities hidden in plain sight. By questioning assumptions and exploring alternative perspectives, you position yourself to innovate and succeed where others follow the crowd.

Chapter 73: Stay Agile in Dynamic Environments

Agility is the ability to respond quickly and effectively to changing circumstances, making it an essential strategy in dynamic environments. Whether you're navigating shifting market trends, technological advancements, or unexpected disruptions, staying agile allows you to adapt and thrive.

Being agile doesn't mean abandoning long-term planning — it means integrating flexibility into your strategy so you can pivot without losing sight of your goals. Agility is about maintaining momentum, fostering innovation, and embracing change as an opportunity rather than a threat.

Why Agility is Crucial in Dynamic Environments

1. **Enables Rapid Response:** Agility allows you to act quickly when circumstances change, reducing the impact of challenges.
2. **Encourages Innovation:** Flexible strategies foster creative solutions to new problems.
3. **Builds Resilience:** Organizations and individuals who stay agile are better equipped to handle uncertainty and bounce back from setbacks.

For example, businesses that embraced remote work technologies early were able to maintain productivity during times of disruption. Agility in adopting new tools allowed them to minimize downtime and sustain operations.

How to Stay Agile

1. **Embrace a Growth Mindset:** View change as an opportunity to learn and improve rather than a threat.
2. **Streamline Decision-Making:** Reduce bureaucratic barriers to enable quick, effective decisions.
3. **Monitor the Environment:** Stay informed about trends and developments that could impact your goals.
4. **Encourage Collaboration:** Build teams that communicate openly and adapt collectively to challenges.
5. **Test and Iterate:** Regularly review and refine your strategies to ensure they remain relevant.

Real-World Example

In the 2010s, T-Mobile disrupted the rigid telecommunications industry by adopting an agile, customer-first approach. The company launched its "Un-carrier" strategy, eliminating contracts, offering unlimited data plans, and providing free international roaming.

While competitors clung to traditional practices like restrictive contracts and hidden fees, T-Mobile's agility allowed it to quickly address customer frustrations and attract millions of new subscribers. By staying flexible and responsive to consumer needs, T-Mobile transformed itself into a major player in the U.S. mobile market.

Exercises

1. **Identify a Change:** Reflect on a recent shift in your industry or environment. How could agility help you respond effectively?
2. **Streamline a Process:** Choose one area of your work where decision-making could be faster or more flexible. Implement a change this week.
3. **Embrace Feedback:** Solicit input from others about how you can become more adaptable in your current role or projects.

Key Takeaway

Agility is the key to thriving in dynamic environments. By staying flexible, informed, and innovative, you turn challenges into opportunities and maintain momentum in the face of change.

Chapter 74: Exploit Adversaries' Rigidity

Rigidity can be a significant weakness. Adversaries who cling to fixed strategies or resist change often leave themselves vulnerable to those who can adapt and innovate. By exploiting this rigidity, you gain an edge, outmaneuvering competitors who fail to recognize the need for flexibility.

Exploiting rigidity doesn't mean acting unethically; it's about understanding your adversaries' limitations and capitalizing on their inability to adjust. Whether in business, sports, or negotiation, recognizing and leveraging rigidity allows you to turn their predictability into your advantage.

Why Exploiting Rigidity Works

1. **Creates Opportunities:** Predictable behavior makes adversaries easier to anticipate and counter.
2. **Highlights Your Strengths:** Flexibility and creativity become powerful tools when others lack them.
3. **Drives Competitive Advantage:** Capitalizing on rigidity ensures you stay one step ahead in dynamic situations.

For instance, Blockbuster's reluctance to adapt to the rise of digital streaming was exploited by emerging companies like Hulu and Amazon Prime Video. While Blockbuster stuck to its physical rental store model, these agile competitors embraced the streaming revolution, offering consumers convenience and on-demand access to entertainment.

By the time Blockbuster attempted to adjust, its rigid approach had allowed competitors to dominate the market, leaving little room for recovery.

How to Exploit Adversaries' Rigidity

1. **Analyze Their Patterns:** Study competitors' strategies and identify areas where they're resistant to change.
2. **Anticipate Their Moves:** Use their predictability to plan counterstrategies and stay ahead.
3. **Leverage Innovation:** Introduce new ideas or approaches that disrupt their fixed methods.
4. **Create Pressure Points:** Force them into situations where their rigidity becomes a disadvantage.
5. **Stay Adaptive:** Ensure your strategies remain flexible to maintain your advantage.

Real-World Example

In the early 2000s, Salesforce disrupted the enterprise software industry by offering customer relationship management (CRM) tools through a cloud-based subscription model. Traditional software providers, like Oracle and SAP, relied on rigid, on-premises installations with high upfront costs.

By exploiting these companies' reluctance to embrace cloud technology, Salesforce captured a growing market of businesses seeking flexible, cost-effective solutions. This approach not only redefined how software was delivered but also established Salesforce as a dominant force in the tech industry.

Exercises

1. **Identify Rigidity:** Think of a competitor or challenge where rigidity is evident. How could you capitalize on it?
2. **Challenge Predictability:** Examine your own strategies. Are there areas where you've become too rigid?
3. **Develop a Disruptive Idea:** Brainstorm an innovative approach that could disrupt the status quo in your field.

Key Takeaway

Exploiting adversaries' rigidity gives you a strategic advantage. By recognizing their limitations and staying adaptive, you turn their predictability into opportunities for innovation and success.

Chapter 75: Be Unpredictable to Stay Ahead

Predictability is a liability in competitive environments. When adversaries can easily anticipate your next move, they can counter your strategies and neutralize your efforts. Being unpredictable forces others to stay reactive, giving you the upper hand by keeping them guessing.

Unpredictability isn't about chaos or randomness — it's about introducing elements of surprise and variety in your actions while maintaining alignment with your goals. This strategic use of unpredictability allows you to gain the element of surprise, disrupt your adversaries' plans, and remain ahead of the competition.

Why Being Unpredictable is Effective

1. **Keeps Adversaries Reactive:** Opponents can't plan effectively when they're unsure of your next move.
2. **Creates Opportunities:** Surprise maneuvers open new paths that others didn't anticipate.
3. **Establishes a Psychological Edge:** Unpredictability creates doubt and hesitation in adversaries, giving you the advantage.

For instance, in negotiations, changing your approach mid-discussion — such as pivoting to a new offer or using an unexpected tone — can shift the dynamic in your favor.

How to Be Unpredictable Strategically

1. **Break Patterns:** Avoid falling into repetitive routines or habits that others can easily recognize.
2. **Introduce Variability:** Rotate strategies, tactics, or approaches to maintain an element of surprise.
3. **Combine Predictable with Unpredictable Actions:** Create a baseline of reliability to build trust, but occasionally introduce unexpected moves to disrupt expectations.
4. **Monitor Reactions:** Pay attention to how others respond to your unpredictability and adjust accordingly.
5. **Stay True to Your Goals:** Ensure that your unpredictability aligns with your broader objectives and doesn't create unnecessary confusion.

Real-World Example

Ryanair, the low-cost airline, demonstrated unpredictability in its pricing strategies. Unlike traditional airlines, which maintained fixed pricing structures, Ryanair implemented dynamic pricing that adjusted based on demand, competitor actions, and even time of day. This unpredictability left competitors scrambling to match fares, while Ryanair consistently attracted cost-conscious travelers and maximized revenue.

Exercises

1. **Identify a Routine:** Find a predictable pattern in your actions or strategies. How can you introduce an element of surprise?
2. **Test an Unpredictable Move:** In a current project or negotiation, try an unexpected approach and observe the reaction.
3. **Analyze an Adversary's Predictability:** Look for predictable patterns in a competitor's behavior. How could you disrupt their expectations?

Key Takeaway

Strategic unpredictability keeps you ahead by disrupting expectations and forcing others to stay reactive. By introducing surprise in your actions, you gain the psychological and competitive edge needed to succeed.

Chapter 76: Diversify Your Cheat Sheet

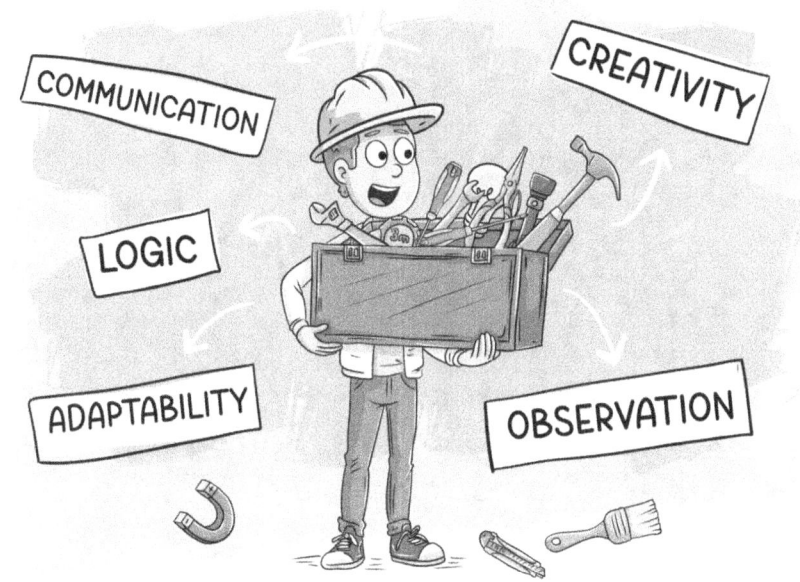

Relying on a single strategy or skillset can leave you vulnerable when circumstances change. Diversifying your "cheat sheet" ensures that you're prepared for a variety of challenges, allowing you to respond effectively in any situation. Whether you're navigating a competitive market, solving complex problems, or seizing new opportunities, having a diverse toolkit gives you flexibility and resilience.

Diversification involves expanding your knowledge, skills, and resources to create a broad foundation for success. It's not about being a jack-of-all-trades but about having enough options to adapt your approach when needed. By doing so, you reduce dependency on any one tactic and increase your chances of achieving your goals.

Why Diversifying is Crucial

1. **Increases Flexibility:** A broader toolkit allows you to pivot when a single approach fails.
2. **Mitigates Risk:** Diversification minimizes the impact of setbacks in any one area.
3. **Encourages Growth:** Learning new skills and strategies keeps you adaptable and innovative.

For example, financial investors diversify their portfolios by spreading assets across stocks, bonds, and other instruments to reduce risk and improve returns. Similarly, strategic thinkers can diversify their approaches to remain resilient in unpredictable environments.

How to Diversify Your Cheat Sheet

1. **Learn Continuously:** Commit to expanding your knowledge and skills in areas relevant to your goals.
2. **Experiment with New Approaches:** Test different strategies and tactics to see what works in various contexts.
3. **Build a Diverse Network:** Surround yourself with people from different industries, backgrounds, and expertise to gain fresh perspectives.
4. **Create Backup Plans:** Develop alternative strategies to ensure you're prepared for unexpected challenges.
5. **Embrace Flexibility:** Stay open to change and ready to pivot when needed.

Real-World Example

Disney exemplifies diversification through its business model. While initially focused on animated films, Disney expanded into theme parks, merchandise, television, and streaming services. This diverse "cheat sheet" allowed the company to weather industry disruptions and remain a global leader in entertainment.

Exercises

1. **Assess Your Toolkit:** Identify your current skills, resources, and strategies. What's missing that could strengthen your adaptability?
2. **Try Something New:** Choose one area where you lack experience and take a small step to expand your knowledge or skills.
3. **Build a Diverse Plan:** Create a strategy that includes at least three different approaches to achieving a single goal.

Key Takeaway

Diversifying your cheat sheet ensures you're ready for any challenge. By expanding your skills, strategies, and resources, you create a flexible foundation for sustained success.

Chapter 77: Counterpoise Risk and Reward Over Time

Every strategic decision involves some degree of risk and reward. The art of counterpoising — or balancing — these factors over time ensures that you make calculated moves that align with your long-term goals. Risk and reward are not static; they shift as circumstances evolve. Successful individuals and organizations are those who continuously reassess these factors and adjust their strategies accordingly.

Counterpoising risk and reward isn't about eliminating risk entirely—some degree of risk is necessary for growth. Instead, it's about understanding the relationship between the two and making decisions that maximize potential benefits while keeping risks manageable. By viewing risk and reward as interconnected forces, you can navigate uncertainty with confidence and precision.

Why Counterpoising Risk and Reward is Critical

1. **Mitigates Overexposure:** Balancing ensures that risks don't outweigh potential rewards, protecting you from unnecessary losses.
2. **Optimizes Opportunities:** Careful evaluation helps you seize high-reward opportunities without recklessness.
3. **Builds Long-Term Resilience:** Sustainable decisions prevent burnout or resource depletion over time.

For example, investors often use diversification to balance risk and reward. By spreading investments across different asset classes, they reduce the impact of losses in any one area while still pursuing growth opportunities.

How to Counterpoise Risk and Reward

1. **Assess the Stakes:** Evaluate the potential risks and rewards of a decision in both the short and long term.
2. **Start Small:** Test high-risk strategies on a smaller scale to minimize potential losses.
3. **Monitor Continuously:** Regularly review how your decisions are performing and adjust as needed.
4. **Diversify Your Approach:** Spread risks across multiple strategies to avoid overdependence on a single outcome.
5. **Know Your Threshold:** Understand your risk tolerance and set clear limits to avoid overcommitting.

Real-World Example

SpaceX exemplifies this principle in its approach to innovation. While the company takes significant risks in developing reusable rockets, it balances these risks with incremental testing. For example, prototypes like Starship undergo multiple test flights to identify flaws and reduce risk before full-scale deployment. This method allows SpaceX to pursue ground-breaking innovations while minimizing catastrophic failures.

Exercises

1. **Evaluate a Current Decision:** Write down the risks and rewards of a choice you're facing. How can you adjust your approach to achieve a better balance?
2. **Create a Risk-Reward Matrix:** Categorize potential decisions into high-risk/high-reward, low-risk/low-reward, and other combinations to identify your best options.
3. **Set a Risk Limit:** Define a clear boundary for the level of risk you're willing to accept in your current projects.

Key Takeaway

Counterpoising risk and reward over time ensures sustainable success. By continually evaluating and balancing these factors, you make informed decisions that maximize benefits while protecting yourself from unnecessary losses.

Chapter 78: Thrive in Nonlinear Scenarios

Life rarely unfolds in a straight line. Nonlinear scenarios are those where outcomes are unpredictable, relationships between actions and results are complex, and progress feels anything but linear. Thriving in such situations requires the ability to adapt, embrace uncertainty, and find creative solutions that align with your broader objectives.

Nonlinear scenarios demand flexibility and resilience. Instead of rigidly following a predefined plan, you must recognize patterns, pivot when necessary, and trust that even small actions can lead to significant breakthroughs. By focusing on adaptability rather than control, you can navigate nonlinear challenges effectively.

Why Thriving in Nonlinear Scenarios is Important

1. **Encourages Innovation:** Complexity often opens the door to new ideas and solutions.
2. **Builds Resilience:** Embracing unpredictability strengthens your ability to handle uncertainty.
3. **Fosters Long-Term Success:** Adaptability ensures progress even when the path is unclear.

For instance, entrepreneurs often encounter nonlinear growth. Early progress may seem slow or unpredictable, but persistence and adaptation often lead to exponential success as markets mature and opportunities align.

How to Thrive in Nonlinear Scenarios

1. **Embrace Complexity:** Accept that outcomes may not follow a direct path, and remain open to unexpected results.
2. **Focus on Core Goals:** Keep your overarching objectives in mind, even as you adapt your methods.
3. **Experiment Strategically:** Test multiple approaches to find what works in a complex environment.
4. **Re-evaluate Regularly:** Continuously assess your progress and adjust your strategies as needed.
5. **Celebrate Small Wins:** Recognize incremental progress as a sign that you're moving in the right direction.

Real-World Example

The development of CRISPR gene-editing technology highlights thriving in nonlinear scenarios. Early research in bacterial defense mechanisms led to the discovery of a revolutionary tool for editing DNA. The path to this breakthrough was not linear — it involved years of trial and error, unexpected findings, and collaboration across disciplines. Today, CRISPR is transforming medicine, agriculture, and biotechnology.

Exercises

1. **Identify a Nonlinear Challenge:** Reflect on a situation where progress has been unpredictable. How can you adjust your approach to better navigate it?
2. **Experiment with New Approaches:** Brainstorm three alternative methods to tackle a current complex problem.
3. **Celebrate Incremental Wins:** Write down three small successes from a nonlinear project and how they contribute to your long-term goals.

Key Takeaway

Thriving in nonlinear scenarios requires adaptability, creativity, and a focus on long-term objectives. By embracing complexity and adjusting your approach, you turn unpredictability into a source of innovation and growth.

Chapter 79: Prepare for Worst-Case Scenarios

Hope for the best, but always prepare for the worst. This classic principle is essential in any adaptive strategy. Worst-case scenarios, though unpleasant to imagine, can devastate unprepared individuals, teams, or organizations. Preparation is not about pessimism — it's about resilience. When you've planned for the most challenging outcomes, you can approach uncertainty with confidence, knowing that even the most significant disruptions won't derail you entirely.

Worst-case scenario planning doesn't mean focusing exclusively on negative outcomes. Instead, it's about identifying potential risks, understanding their impact, and creating robust systems to mitigate them. By preparing for the unexpected, you create a safety net that allows you to respond effectively, protect your interests, and even find opportunities within the chaos.

Why Preparing for the Worst is Crucial

1. **Reduces Panic:** Knowing you have a plan in place minimizes stress during a crisis.
2. **Ensures Continuity:** Preparation keeps operations running, even in difficult conditions.
3. **Builds Confidence:** When the worst is accounted for, you can focus on achieving your goals.

For example, many tech companies prepare for cyberattacks by investing in robust cybersecurity systems and developing incident response plans. This proactive approach reduces downtime and protects valuable data when attacks occur.

How to Prepare for Worst-Case Scenarios

1. **Identify Risks:** Assess potential threats to your goals, such as economic downturns, operational failures, or market shifts.
2. **Assess Impact:** Determine the likelihood and severity of each risk to prioritize your planning.
3. **Develop Mitigation Plans:** Create specific actions to reduce the probability or impact of each worst-case scenario.
4. **Stockpile Resources:** Ensure you have the tools, funds, or networks needed to respond effectively.
5. **Practice Your Plans:** Run simulations or drills to identify gaps in your preparation and refine your strategies.

Real-World Example

In the aviation industry, pilots and airlines meticulously prepare for worst-case scenarios, such as engine failures or extreme weather conditions. Training programs, redundant systems, and clear protocols ensure that even in the most challenging situations, pilots can respond effectively and prioritize passenger safety. This rigorous preparation is why air travel remains one of the safest modes of transportation.

Exercises

1. **List Your Risks:** Write down three worst-case scenarios that could impact your work or goals. Outline potential responses for each.
2. **Test a Plan:** Conduct a simulation of one of your worst-case scenarios to evaluate your readiness.
3. **Build Resilience:** Identify one area where you lack contingency measures and take steps to address it.

Key Takeaway

Preparing for worst-case scenarios builds resilience and ensures you're ready for anything. By anticipating challenges and developing strong contingency plans, you protect your goals and maintain confidence in uncertain times.

Chapter 80: Apply the OODA Loop: Observe, Orient, Decide, Act

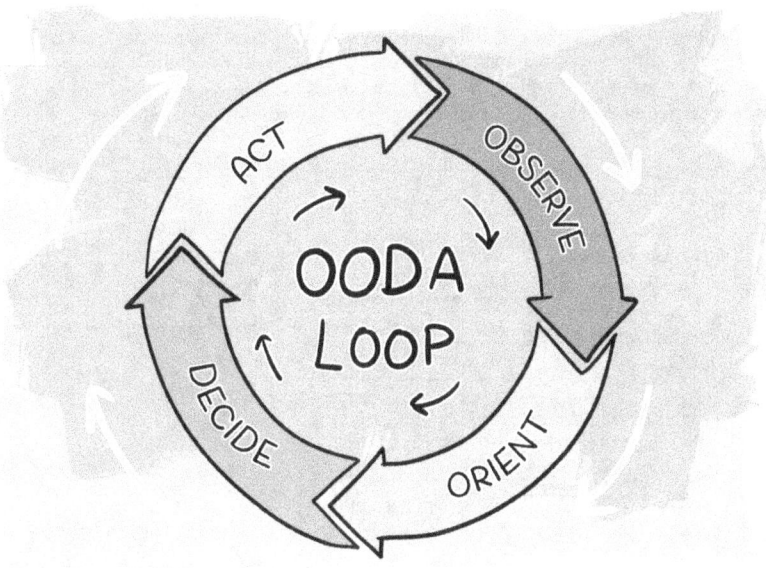

The OODA loop, developed by military strategist John Boyd, is a powerful decision-making framework that emphasizes speed, adaptability, and continuous improvement. The four steps — Observe, Orient, Decide, and Act — allow you to navigate complex situations effectively, respond to change swiftly, and stay ahead of the competition.

The OODA loop is particularly valuable in dynamic environments where circumstances evolve rapidly. It encourages you to gather information, analyze your position, make a decision, and take action — all while remaining flexible and ready to adjust as new developments arise. This iterative process ensures that you don't get stuck in analysis paralysis or fall behind due to slow responses.

The Four Steps of the OODA Loop

1. **Observe:** Gather information about your environment, competitors, and any changes affecting your situation. The goal is to develop a clear understanding of what's happening around you.
2. **Orient:** Analyze the information you've gathered, assess your position, and determine the opportunities or threats you face. This step involves synthesizing data and aligning it with your goals.
3. **Decide:** Based on your analysis, choose a course of action. Speed is critical here—delaying decisions gives others the opportunity to act first.
4. **Act:** Implement your decision decisively while remaining prepared to adapt if the situation changes.

Why the OODA Loop is Effective

1. **Increases Agility:** The loop's iterative nature ensures you can adapt to new developments quickly.
2. **Improves Decision-Making:** Breaking decisions into manageable steps reduces complexity and boosts confidence.
3. **Keeps You Ahead:** Rapid observation and action allow you to outpace competitors or adversaries.

Real-World Example

Amazon effectively applies the OODA loop in its approach to customer experience. The company continually observes customer behaviors through data, orients itself by analyzing trends, decides on improvements, and acts quickly to implement them. For example, the introduction of one-click ordering and same-day delivery demonstrates Amazon's ability to respond rapidly to evolving customer expectations, keeping it ahead in the e-commerce space.

How to Apply the OODA Loop

1. **Start Small:** Practice the OODA loop on smaller decisions to build confidence and efficiency.
2. **Stay Alert:** Continuously monitor your environment to stay informed about changes.
3. **Be Decisive:** Prioritize speed without sacrificing accuracy in your decision-making.
4. **Evaluate Outcomes:** After acting, analyze the results and refine your approach for the next iteration.

Exercises

1. **Apply the OODA Loop:** Choose a current challenge and walk through each step—Observe, Orient, Decide, Act—to address it.
2. **Evaluate a Past Decision:** Reflect on a situation where applying the OODA loop could have improved your response.
3. **Practice Rapid Decisions:** Set a timer and work through the OODA loop to solve a low-stakes problem quickly.

Key Takeaway

The OODA loop is a powerful framework for navigating dynamic environments. By observing, orienting, deciding, and acting in an iterative process, you stay agile, responsive, and ahead of the competition.

Section V: Advanced Strategies

This final section is where everything converges. Now that the foundations, tactical executions, and long-term planning are in place, you're ready to operate at the systems level. These chapters will help you manage intricate trade-offs, anticipate ripple effects, and engineer strategies that self-reinforce over time. Part 5 explores the nuance of timing, authority, group dynamics, and predictive modeling — giving you tools not just to compete, but to control the terrain.

Chapter 81: Orchestrate Complex Systems for Advantage

In today's interconnected world, success often depends on your ability to orchestrate complex systems effectively. Whether managing a supply chain, coordinating a team, or navigating market dynamics, you're dealing with intricate networks of moving parts that must work together seamlessly. The key to thriving in such environments lies in orchestrating these components in a way that amplifies their collective value.

Complex systems are dynamic, meaning that small adjustments in one area can ripple across the entire structure. Your job as a strategist is to harmonize these interactions, ensuring they align with your overarching objectives. It's not about controlling every detail—it's about creating a structure where each part functions optimally while contributing to the whole.

Why Orchestrating Complex Systems is Critical

1. **Unlocks Synergy:** When the elements of a system align, their combined impact exceeds the sum of their parts.
2. **Enhances Adaptability:** A well-orchestrated system can quickly adjust to changes without losing efficiency.
3. **Maximizes Efficiency:** Streamlining interactions reduces friction, redundancies, and wasted resources.

For example, in urban planning, city governments must balance housing, transportation, public services, and environmental sustainability. By managing these interconnected elements strategically, they create cities that are livable, resilient, and efficient.

How to Orchestrate Complex Systems

1. **Visualize the System:** Map out all components and their relationships. Understanding the system as a whole is the first step to managing it effectively.
2. **Define Key Objectives:** Set clear, overarching goals that guide the system's operation.
3. **Optimize Interactions:** Look for inefficiencies in how components work together and address them.
4. **Leverage Technology:** Use tools like analytics software, dashboards, or automation to monitor and manage complexity.
5. **Adapt Continuously:** Be prepared to adjust your system as external conditions or internal needs evolve.

Real-World Example

In Formula 1 racing, teams like Mercedes excel at orchestrating complex systems. A race car's performance relies on seamless collaboration between engineers, mechanics, strategists, and drivers. Each team member focuses on their specialized role, while advanced data analytics monitor every aspect of the car's performance in real time. By aligning these diverse elements, Formula 1 teams consistently deliver precision, speed, and reliability.

Exercises

1. **Map Your System:** Identify the key components of a system you're managing and visualize how they interact.
2. **Spot Weak Links:** Analyze one area where inefficiencies or misalignments exist. How can you improve it?
3. **Set a System-Wide Goal:** Define an objective that unites all elements of your system, and ensure each part contributes toward it.

Key Takeaway

Orchestrating complex systems turns challenges into opportunities. By aligning interconnected components toward a shared goal, you create synergy, efficiency, and sustained success.

Chapter 82: Manage Trade-Offs with Precision

Every decision comes with trade-offs—choosing one path means sacrificing another. Successful strategists recognize that trade-offs aren't obstacles; they're opportunities to clarify priorities and focus resources where they'll create the most value. Managing trade-offs with precision ensures that every choice serves your larger goals, even if it requires difficult sacrifices.

Trade-offs arise in various forms: speed versus quality, individual needs versus team objectives, or short-term gains versus long-term stability. Rather than avoiding trade-offs, embrace them as part of the decision-making process. A precise approach means weighing options carefully, communicating openly, and aligning choices with your strategic vision.

Why Managing Trade-Offs is Essential

1. **Clarifies Priorities:** Deliberate trade-offs force you to focus on what truly matters.
2. **Maximizes Impact:** Allocating resources wisely ensures you achieve the greatest returns.
3. **Prevents Burnout:** Recognizing limits avoids overextending yourself or your team.

For instance, when companies expand into new markets, they often face the trade-off between rapid growth and maintaining operational quality. The best expansions balance these priorities, scaling at a sustainable pace without sacrificing their core values.

How to Manage Trade-Offs

1. **Define Your Objectives:** Start by clarifying the results you want to achieve. Let these guide your decisions.
2. **Weigh Costs and Benefits:** Analyze the impact of each option to determine which aligns best with your goals.
3. **Communicate Transparently:** Share your reasoning with stakeholders to build trust and alignment.
4. **Review Regularly:** Reevaluate your choices to ensure they remain effective as circumstances change.
5. **Be Willing to Pivot:** If new information arises, don't hesitate to adjust your approach.

Real-World Example

In the 1990s, Procter & Gamble (P&G) faced a trade-off when deciding how to allocate resources between its established product lines and its emerging Swiffer brand. The company realized that focusing too heavily on legacy products could hinder innovation, but diverting too many resources to Swiffer could disrupt its existing market dominance.

P&G managed this trade-off by incrementally investing in Swiffer while leveraging its existing distribution and marketing channels to support the new product. This approach allowed P&G to maintain the strength of its established brands while introducing a groundbreaking product that became a billion-dollar success. The Swiffer's eventual dominance in the cleaning category highlights the precision with which P&G managed competing priorities.

Exercises

1. **Identify a Current Trade-Off:** Think of a decision you're facing where two priorities conflict. How can you evaluate which option aligns best with your goals?
2. **Analyze a Past Decision:** Reflect on a trade-off you made previously. Was it successful? What could you improve?
3. **Set Guidelines:** Establish criteria to guide future trade-offs, ensuring they align with your core objectives.

Key Takeaway

Managing trade-offs with precision ensures that every decision aligns with your long-term goals. By carefully weighing priorities and acting deliberately, you maximize impact while minimizing regret.

Chapter 83: Engineer Irreversible Advantages

Irreversible advantages are the ultimate goal of strategic thinking. These advantages are not just temporary wins — they are enduring, defensible, and nearly impossible for competitors to replicate. When you engineer irreversible advantages, you position yourself, your team, or your organization in a way that ensures long-term dominance, even in the face of challenges or changing circumstances.

Creating such advantages requires a deep understanding of your unique strengths, market dynamics, and the specific needs of your audience. By combining these elements, you can establish a position that becomes your unshakable foundation for success.

Why Irreversible Advantages Matter

1. **Sustains Long-Term Success:** Once established, these advantages provide a consistent edge over competitors.
2. **Minimizes Threats:** Competitors are less likely to erode your position when your advantages are hard to replicate.
3. **Inspires Confidence:** Irreversible advantages attract loyal customers, partners, and stakeholders who value stability.

For example, companies that build strong intellectual property portfolios or establish exclusive partnerships create barriers that prevent others from easily entering their market space.

How to Engineer Irreversible Advantages

1. **Leverage Unique Strengths:** Identify what sets you apart and find ways to enhance and protect those qualities.
2. **Invest in Innovation:** Develop technologies, processes, or products that are difficult to copy.
3. **Strengthen Customer Loyalty:** Build trust and emotional connections with your audience to create long-term relationships.
4. **Establish Barriers to Entry:** Create systems, partnerships, or networks that make it challenging for competitors to enter your market.
5. **Focus on Scalability:** Design your advantages to grow with you, ensuring they remain effective as your goals evolve.

Real-World Example

John Deere, the agricultural equipment manufacturer, has engineered irreversible advantages by developing a comprehensive ecosystem of equipment, software, and data-driven services tailored to farmers' needs. Through innovations like precision agriculture technology and long-standing relationships with farming communities, John Deere has created barriers that competitors struggle to overcome. Farmers rely not just on their tractors but also on the integrated software and support systems, making John Deere an indispensable partner in their operations.

Exercises

1. **Identify Your Strengths:** List three qualities or resources that set you apart. How can you make them difficult to replicate?
2. **Spot Barriers to Entry:** Analyze your market. What unique systems or relationships can you develop to create barriers for competitors?
3. **Future-Proof Your Advantage:** Reflect on how your current strengths can scale with your goals. What adjustments are needed?

Key Takeaway

Engineering irreversible advantages ensures lasting success. By leveraging unique strengths, building barriers, and investing in innovation, you create a position that competitors cannot easily challenge.

Chapter 84: Use Authority to Multiply Impact

Authority, when used strategically, is a powerful multiplier of impact. It allows you to inspire trust, rally others behind your vision, and drive coordinated efforts toward a shared goal. Authority isn't about exercising control – it's about cultivating respect, credibility, and the ability to guide people effectively.

Leaders who use authority wisely amplify their influence and align resources efficiently. Whether it's inspiring a team, negotiating with stakeholders, or leading an organization, authority enables you to mobilize people and resources at scale, creating exponential results.

Why Authority Multiplies Impact

1. **Inspires Trust:** People follow leaders they respect, amplifying their ability to drive change.
2. **Unites Efforts:** Authority focuses diverse teams or stakeholders on shared objectives.
3. **Speeds Decision-Making:** Clear leadership eliminates confusion, allowing faster, more effective actions.

For example, CEOs with strong authority can implement organizational changes more effectively than leaders who struggle to gain buy-in from their teams.

How to Use Authority Strategically

1. **Build Credibility:** Establish yourself as a trustworthy and knowledgeable leader.
2. **Lead by Example:** Demonstrate the behaviors, values, and work ethic you want others to follow.
3. **Communicate Clearly:** Use your authority to provide clear direction and align efforts.
4. **Empower Others:** Delegate responsibilities and give your team the autonomy to succeed.
5. **Foster Relationships:** Cultivate mutual respect with stakeholders to strengthen your influence.

Real-World Example

In the late 2000s, Dave Lewis, former CEO of Tesco, used his authority to lead the UK-based supermarket chain through a critical turnaround. At the time, Tesco was struggling with declining market share, customer dissatisfaction, and internal inefficiencies.

Lewis immediately set out to restore trust with customers and employees by implementing a back-to-basics approach. He focused on improving customer service, enhancing product quality, and simplifying pricing strategies. His clear communication and decisive leadership helped rebuild Tesco's reputation and stabilize its operations, ultimately steering the company back to profitability.

Exercises

1. **Reflect on Your Authority:** Identify areas where your authority has the most impact. How can you use it more effectively?
2. **Strengthen Credibility:** List three actions you can take to build trust and respect among your peers or team.
3. **Empower Your Team:** Delegate a key responsibility to someone you trust. How can this amplify your collective impact?

Key Takeaway

Authority is a strategic tool for multiplying impact. By earning trust, aligning efforts, and empowering others, you create the conditions for exponential success.

Chapter 85: Turn Opponents' Strengths Into Vulnerabilities

One of the most overlooked strategies in competitive environments is turning your opponents' strengths into their vulnerabilities. Many organizations and individuals build their success around key advantages — whether it's their size, resources, reputation, or specialized expertise. However, these same strengths often come with limitations or blind spots that you can exploit to gain the upper hand.

This strategy requires more than recognizing your opponents' assets; it involves understanding the trade-offs that come with those assets. For example, large organizations may have vast resources but lack agility. Market leaders may dominate an industry but be slow to adopt innovation. By analyzing these dynamics, you can position yourself to use their strengths against them.

Why This Strategy Works

1. **Exploits Complacency:** Over-reliance on strengths can make opponents predictable or resistant to change.
2. **Highlights Weaknesses:** Strengths often come at the expense of flexibility, speed, or adaptability.
3. **Turns the Tables:** By using their own advantages against them, you can counterbalance power dynamics.

How to Turn Strengths Into Vulnerabilities

1. **Identify Overreliance:** Look for areas where opponents depend heavily on a single strength.
2. **Spot Inflexibility:** Assess whether their strengths make them slow to adapt to changing conditions.
3. **Position Yourself Strategically:** Use your own agility, creativity, or innovation to target their blind spots.
4. **Create Pressure Points:** Force them into situations where their strengths become liabilities, such as by emphasizing speed when they rely on scale.
5. **Be Unpredictable:** Avoid direct competition with their strength and instead operate where they are least prepared.

Real-World Example

When Aldi entered the U.S. market, it targeted grocery giants like Walmart. Instead of competing head-to-head on selection or store size, Aldi focused on its strength: simplicity. Its smaller stores and limited product lines allowed for lower costs, faster shopping experiences, and competitive pricing. Walmart's strength — offering massive selection — became a vulnerability as customers seeking convenience and affordability flocked to Aldi.

By exploiting the inefficiencies of their larger competitors, Aldi carved out a profitable niche and expanded rapidly in the U.S. market.

Exercises

1. **Analyze a Competitor's Strengths:** Identify one major strength of a competitor and consider how it could also limit their adaptability.
2. **Target a Blind Spot:** Think of a situation where you could use a competitor's strength to your advantage.
3. **Evaluate Your Own Strengths:** Reflect on your strengths and consider whether they leave you vulnerable to specific challenges.

Key Takeaway

Your opponents' strengths can often become their greatest vulnerabilities. By identifying blind spots and adapting your strategy accordingly, you can turn the tables and gain a significant advantage.

Chapter 86: Harness the Wisdom of the Crowd

The wisdom of the crowd is a powerful resource for solving complex problems, generating ideas, and making informed decisions. The collective knowledge, perspectives, and insights of a diverse group often produce better outcomes than those of any single individual, no matter how experienced or skilled. By harnessing this collective intelligence, you can unlock innovative solutions and gain deeper understanding in any situation.

Crowdsourcing ideas doesn't mean relying on random opinions. The key to leveraging the wisdom of the crowd lies in structuring the process effectively. When you curate input from diverse but informed perspectives, the aggregated knowledge becomes a strategic asset that far exceeds the sum of its parts.

Why the Wisdom of the Crowd Works

1. **Diversity Drives Insight:** A range of perspectives ensures you consider multiple angles and solutions.
2. **Aggregates Expertise:** Combining the knowledge of many people often leads to more accurate outcomes.
3. **Encourages Innovation:** Crowdsourced ideas can reveal creative solutions that one person might overlook.

For example, platforms like Wikipedia thrive on the collective contributions of users worldwide. By harnessing the expertise and dedication of a global crowd, Wikipedia has become one of the most comprehensive and trusted sources of knowledge.

How to Harness the Wisdom of the Crowd

1. **Define Your Goal:** Be clear about the problem you want to solve or the insight you want to gain.
2. **Gather a Diverse Group:** Include people with varied expertise, backgrounds, and perspectives.
3. **Encourage Open Participation:** Create an environment where everyone feels comfortable sharing their ideas.
4. **Aggregate and Analyze Data:** Look for patterns, trends, or commonalities in the input you receive.
5. **Test and Refine Solutions:** Use the crowd's insights as a starting point for developing actionable strategies.

Real-World Example

LEGO's Ideas platform is a brilliant example of using the wisdom of the crowd. LEGO invites fans to submit ideas for new sets, which are then reviewed by the company. Winning ideas, like the "LEGO Women of NASA" set, often become bestsellers. This approach not only generates innovative product ideas but also strengthens customer engagement by involving fans in the creative process.

Exercises

1. **Crowdsource an Idea:** Identify a challenge you're facing and gather input from a group of diverse individuals.
2. **Evaluate Collective Input:** Aggregate and analyze the suggestions you receive. What patterns emerge?
3. **Refine and Test:** Take one of the ideas from your crowdsource exercise and implement it on a small scale.

Key Takeaway

The wisdom of the crowd turns collective intelligence into a powerful strategic tool. By leveraging diverse perspectives, you gain deeper insights, foster innovation, and make better decisions.

Chapter 87: Command the Precision of Timing

Timing isn't just a factor in strategy — it's a force multiplier. Acting too early can lead to wasted resources, while acting too late often means missed opportunities. Commanding the precision of timing allows you to strike the perfect balance, ensuring that your actions create maximum impact.

Great strategists understand that timing is about more than speed; it's about aligning your actions with external factors like market readiness, competitor moves, or audience expectations. By mastering this balance, you can make decisions that not only meet the moment but also shape the future.

Why Timing is Crucial

1. **Maximizes Impact:** Acting at the right time amplifies your efforts and outcomes.
2. **Reduces Risk:** Careful timing ensures you avoid premature or poorly-timed actions.
3. **Creates Opportunities:** Observing the landscape helps you act when the conditions are most favorable.

For example, timing is critical in product launches. Introducing a product before a market is ready can result in failure, while waiting too long allows competitors to dominate. The key is finding the precise moment when demand aligns with readiness.

How to Command the Precision of Timing

1. **Monitor Trends:** Stay informed about industry shifts, market demands, and competitor activities.
2. **Evaluate Readiness:** Assess whether you, your team, and your resources are fully prepared to act.
3. **Wait for the Right Moment:** Be patient, but remain ready to act decisively when conditions align.
4. **Create Timing Windows:** Influence external factors, such as customer readiness or stakeholder interest, to align with your plans.
5. **Learn from History:** Study past successes and failures to understand how timing impacted outcomes.

Real-World Example

Zara, the global fashion retailer, is renowned for its precise timing in responding to fashion trends. Unlike competitors that plan collections months in advance, Zara's supply chain is designed to rapidly adapt to customer preferences. By monitoring sales data and consumer behavior in real time, Zara designs, manufactures, and delivers new items to stores in just a few weeks.

This ability to act at the right moment ensures Zara consistently aligns its offerings with current trends, keeping customers engaged and ahead of slower-moving competitors.

Exercises

1. **Reflect on Timing:** Think of a past decision. How did timing influence its success or failure?
2. **Identify a Key Moment:** Look at a current challenge or opportunity. When is the optimal time to act?
3. **Create a Timing Plan:** For an upcoming project, outline key milestones and external factors that will guide your timing decisions.

Key Takeaway

Precision in timing multiplies the effectiveness of your actions. By carefully monitoring trends, evaluating readiness, and acting decisively, you align your strategy with the perfect moment for success.

Chapter 88: Uncover Unique Perspectives to Lead with an Edge

Standing out requires more than just good ideas — it requires unique perspectives. Leaders who uncover fresh ways of thinking gain a powerful edge, allowing them to see opportunities others miss, solve problems innovatively, and inspire teams to achieve extraordinary results.

Uncovering unique perspectives involves seeking out diverse inputs, challenging assumptions, and being open to unconventional approaches. It's not just about being different for the sake of it; it's about finding new angles that unlock value and create meaningful impact.

Why Unique Perspectives Matter

1. **Drives Innovation:** Fresh viewpoints reveal creative solutions to entrenched challenges.
2. **Builds Competitive Advantage:** Seeing what others overlook positions you ahead of the curve.
3. **Fosters Growth:** Diverse thinking encourages adaptability and learning.

For example, many breakthroughs in business come from leaders who apply ideas from one industry to another. Cross-pollinating perspectives often leads to innovations that redefine markets.

How to Uncover Unique Perspectives

1. **Seek Diverse Inputs:** Collaborate with people from different backgrounds, industries, or cultures.
2. **Challenge Conventional Thinking:** Question assumptions and explore alternative viewpoints.
3. **Experiment Freely:** Test unconventional ideas on a small scale to gauge their potential.
4. **Look Outside Your Industry:** Study trends and practices in unrelated fields for transferable insights.
5. **Encourage Open Dialogue:** Foster a team culture where unconventional ideas are welcomed and explored.

Real-World Example

Chipotle revolutionized the fast-food industry by combining high-quality, fresh ingredients with the efficiency of a quick-service restaurant. Inspired by fine dining concepts and the growing demand for healthier options, Chipotle's unique perspective broke away from traditional fast-food norms. This differentiation helped the brand carve out a new niche in the industry, known as "fast-casual dining."

Exercises

1. **Challenge Assumptions:** Identify a current problem and list three assumptions you've made about it. How could they be wrong?
2. **Collaborate Outside Your Comfort Zone:** Partner with someone from a different field or background for fresh insights.
3. **Explore Other Industries:** Research trends in an industry unrelated to yours. What lessons can you apply?

Key Takeaway

Unique perspectives give you a competitive edge by revealing opportunities and solutions others overlook. By fostering diverse thinking and challenging assumptions, you position yourself to lead innovatively and effectively.

Chapter 89: Be Relentless in Follow-Through

A brilliant strategy means little without relentless follow-through. It's not the initial idea or effort that determines success — it's the consistent, determined execution that brings results. Being relentless in follow-through means committing to your goals, overcoming obstacles, and staying focused even when challenges arise.

Follow-through isn't just about persistence; it's about strategic persistence. It involves revisiting your plan, adjusting your approach when needed, and continuously pushing toward the finish line. This disciplined focus sets leaders and organizations apart in competitive landscapes where distractions and setbacks are inevitable.

Why Follow-Through is Essential

1. **Transforms Ideas into Results:** Execution turns vision into tangible outcomes.
2. **Builds Credibility:** Consistently delivering on promises earns trust and respect.
3. **Fosters Resilience:** Persistent follow-through helps you adapt and overcome challenges.

For example, many start-ups fail not because of flawed ideas but because they lack the discipline to follow through consistently. Relentless execution bridges the gap between potential and achievement.

How to Be Relentless in Follow-Through

1. **Set Clear Milestones:** Break down your goals into manageable steps and track your progress.
2. **Stay Focused:** Avoid distractions and stay committed to your objectives.
3. **Adapt to Challenges:** Be flexible in your approach but firm in your commitment to the goal.
4. **Hold Yourself Accountable:** Regularly evaluate your actions and adjust where needed.
5. **Celebrate Progress:** Recognize small victories to maintain motivation and momentum.

Real-World Example

Nike's global dominance is a testament to relentless follow-through. From the launch of its first running shoes in the 1960s to its transformation into a lifestyle brand, Nike has consistently executed on its vision of inspiring athletes. Campaigns such as "Just Do It" reinforced its brand identity, while ongoing innovation in footwear and apparel ensured market leadership. Nike's commitment to execution — through design, marketing, and partnerships — has made it a leader for decades.

Exercises

1. **Evaluate Your Persistence:** Reflect on a recent project. Did you follow through to completion? If not, identify what stopped you.
2. **Set Milestones:** Break down a current goal into smaller steps and create a timeline to track progress.
3. **Commit Publicly:** Share your goal with a trusted friend or colleague to create accountability for follow-through.

Key Takeaway

Relentless follow-through transforms vision into reality. By staying focused, adaptable, and committed, you ensure that your efforts deliver meaningful and lasting results.

Chapter 90: Apply the Prisoner's Dilemma to Real Life

The Prisoner's Dilemma, a classic concept from game theory, illustrates how individuals must balance self-interest with collaboration in situations where trust is uncertain. In this scenario, two individuals must choose to cooperate or betray each other, with outcomes dependent on their decisions. While mutual cooperation yields the best results for both, fear of betrayal often leads to suboptimal choices.

In real life, this dilemma plays out in negotiations, partnerships, and competitive environments. Understanding and applying the Prisoner's Dilemma allows you to anticipate behaviors, foster trust, and make decisions that maximize long-term gains.

Why Understanding the Prisoner's Dilemma is Valuable

1. **Improves Decision-Making:** Recognizing the dynamics of cooperation and competition helps you act strategically.
2. **Builds Trust:** Choosing cooperation in the right scenarios fosters stronger relationships.
3. **Prevents Exploitation:** Knowing when to protect your interests guards against betrayal.

For example, businesses in the same industry often face this dilemma. Should they compete aggressively or collaborate to expand the market? Balancing these choices strategically determines long-term outcomes.

How to Apply the Prisoner's Dilemma

1. **Assess Incentives:** Identify the rewards and risks for cooperation versus competition.
2. **Foster Communication:** Open dialogue reduces uncertainty and builds trust.
3. **Promote Mutual Benefits:** Highlight the advantages of working together to encourage cooperation.
4. **Use Tit-for-Tat Strategies:** In repeat interactions, start by cooperating and respond to the other party's actions accordingly.
5. **Analyze Long-Term Outcomes:** Focus on decisions that benefit you over multiple interactions rather than a single event.

Real-World Example

In the 1990s, Intel and AMD faced a classic Prisoner's Dilemma in the semiconductor industry. While they competed fiercely, both companies realized that setting certain standards, such as x86 processor compatibility, benefited the entire industry by fostering broader adoption of personal computers. This strategic cooperation allowed both companies to grow, even as they remained competitors.

Exercises

1. **Identify a Dilemma:** Think of a situation where you face a choice between collaboration and self-interest. What factors will influence your decision?
2. **Simulate the Scenario:** Role-play a Prisoner's Dilemma with a colleague to explore strategies for cooperation and competition.
3. **Reflect on Long-Term Gains:** Analyze a past decision. Did focusing on short-term benefits lead to better or worse outcomes?

Key Takeaway

Applying the Prisoner's Dilemma to real life helps you navigate trust and competition effectively. By fostering collaboration in the right contexts and protecting your interests strategically, you create outcomes that benefit all parties involved.

Chapter 91:
Engineer Scarcity
to Drive Value

Scarcity is one of the most powerful drivers of value. When something is rare, hard to obtain, or available only for a limited time, its desirability skyrockets. People are wired to value what they perceive as exclusive or fleeting, and strategic use of scarcity can elevate your offerings, strengthen demand, and position your brand as premium.

Engineering scarcity isn't about creating artificial shortages—it's about carefully controlling supply, timing, or accessibility to enhance perceived value. When done effectively, scarcity not only increases demand but also fosters a sense of urgency, prompting quicker decision-making from your audience.

Why Scarcity Works

1. **Increases Perceived Value:** People often equate rarity with quality or significance.
2. **Drives Urgency:** Limited availability prompts quicker action to avoid missing out.
3. **Encourages Exclusivity:** Scarcity creates a sense of being part of an elite group, enhancing loyalty and engagement.

For example, many luxury brands like Hermès limit the availability of their products, such as the iconic Birkin bag. This scarcity not only drives demand but also strengthens the brand's image as exclusive and aspirational.

How to Engineer Scarcity

1. **Limit Supply:** Offer a controlled quantity of products or services to create exclusivity.
2. **Create Time Constraints:** Use limited-time offers or seasonal releases to drive urgency.
3. **Segment Access:** Provide early or exclusive access to loyal customers or members.
4. **Highlight Rarity:** Clearly communicate why the opportunity is unique or hard to find.
5. **Avoid Artificiality:** Ensure your scarcity strategy feels authentic, not manipulative.

Real-World Example

The book publishing industry often uses scarcity to great effect. J.K. Rowling's *The Tales of Beedle the Bard* was initially released as a limited edition, with only seven handwritten copies. This exclusivity generated immense interest, making the eventual mass-market release a major event. The combination of scarcity and anticipation heightened the book's value and appeal.

Exercises

1. **Identify an Opportunity for Scarcity:** Choose a product or service you offer. How can you limit its availability or timing to enhance its value?
2. **Analyze Competitor Strategies:** Look at how competitors use scarcity. What lessons can you apply to your approach?
3. **Test a Scarcity Strategy:** Run a limited-time or exclusive offering and track its impact on engagement and sales.

Key Takeaway

Scarcity is a strategic tool that elevates value and drives demand. By carefully limiting supply, timing, or access, you create urgency and exclusivity that resonates with your audience.

Chapter 92: Use Game-Theoretic Modeling to Predict Next Steps

Game theory is the science of strategic interaction. It provides a framework for predicting how individuals or groups will behave in competitive or cooperative situations. By applying game-theoretic modeling, you can anticipate the actions of others, optimize your decisions, and gain an edge in complex environments.

Game theory isn't just for mathematicians—it's a practical tool for decision-making in business, politics, negotiations, and more. It helps you map out scenarios, assess risks, and identify optimal strategies by considering the motivations and potential responses of all parties involved.

Why Game Theory is Powerful

1. **Enhances Prediction:** Understanding others' incentives helps you anticipate their moves.
2. **Improves Decision-Making:** Game theory provides a structured approach to analyzing complex scenarios.
3. **Reveals Hidden Opportunities:** By modeling interactions, you often uncover win-win solutions or strategic advantages.

For example, game theory is frequently applied in auction design. Governments and companies use it to structure bidding processes that maximize value while ensuring fair competition.

How to Use Game-Theoretic Modeling

1. **Define the Players:** Identify all parties involved in the situation.
2. **Clarify Incentives:** Understand the goals and motivations of each player.
3. **Map Possible Moves:** List the potential actions each player could take.
4. **Analyze Outcomes:** Evaluate the consequences of each combination of moves.
5. **Select Your Strategy:** Choose the option that best aligns with your goals while anticipating others' responses.

Real-World Example

Procter & Gamble (P&G) used game theory to address competition in the detergent market. Facing aggressive pricing strategies from rivals, P&G analyzed how competitors would react to various pricing and product decisions. Using game-theoretic modeling, they anticipated that rivals would respond aggressively to price cuts but less so to product innovation.

P&G shifted its focus to launching Tide Pods, an innovative product that created a new market segment. This move allowed P&G to gain a competitive edge without engaging in damaging price wars, demonstrating the power of game theory in predicting and influencing market dynamics.

Exercises

1. **Identify a Strategic Interaction:** Think of a competitive or cooperative situation you're facing. Who are the players, and what are their incentives?
2. **Model Possible Moves:** Map out the potential actions of each party and the likely outcomes.
3. **Test a Strategy:** Choose a course of action based on your analysis and monitor the results.

Key Takeaway

Game-theoretic modeling provides a strategic edge by predicting others' actions and optimizing your decisions. By understanding incentives and mapping scenarios, you stay one step ahead in complex interactions.

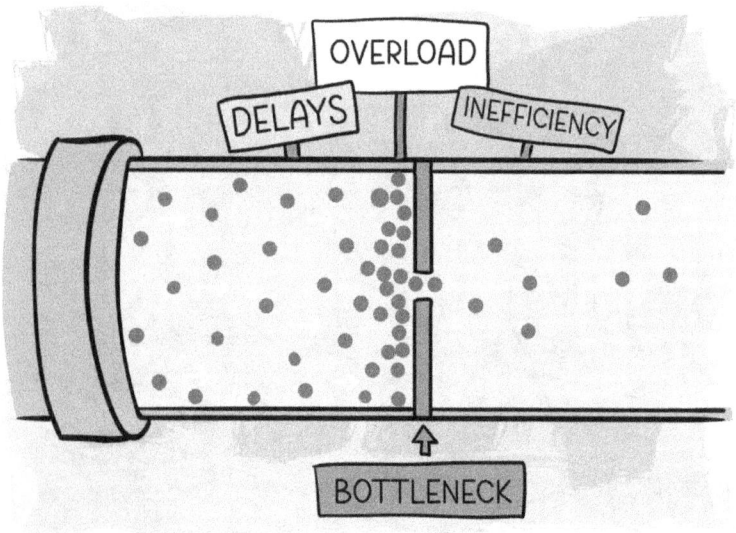

Chapter 93: Identify and Gain from Bottlenecks in Systems

Bottlenecks are the points in a system where progress slows, efficiency drops, or resources are constrained. While they're often seen as obstacles, bottlenecks can also present opportunities. Identifying and addressing these constraints allows you to unlock hidden potential, improve system performance, and even gain a competitive edge by solving problems others overlook.

Whether in supply chains, workflows, or decision-making processes, bottlenecks are inevitable. The key is to approach them strategically. Instead of working around or ignoring them, focus on understanding their root causes and finding ways to improve or bypass them. By doing so, you turn limitations into opportunities for growth and innovation.

Why Addressing Bottlenecks Matters

1. **Maximizes Efficiency:** Removing constraints allows systems to flow more smoothly and productively.
2. **Improves Decision-Making:** Identifying critical points clarifies where resources and attention are needed most.
3. **Creates Competitive Advantage:** Solving bottlenecks often leads to innovations that set you apart.

For example, bottlenecks in logistics systems, such as port congestion, can delay shipments and disrupt supply chains. Addressing these issues often requires creative solutions, such as rerouting shipments or using alternative transportation methods.

How to Identify and Gain from Bottlenecks

1. **Analyze the System:** Map out the entire process and pinpoint areas where progress slows or inefficiencies occur.
2. **Assess Impact:** Evaluate how the bottleneck affects overall performance and prioritize high-impact areas.
3. **Optimize or Eliminate:** Focus on improving or removing the bottleneck through better processes, tools, or resources.
4. **Innovate Around Constraints:** Use the bottleneck as inspiration to develop alternative methods or solutions.
5. **Monitor Continuously:** Bottlenecks can shift over time, so regular analysis is essential.

Real-World Example

In the early 2000s, Dell Computers faced bottlenecks in its supply chain that were slowing production and increasing costs. To address this, Dell restructured its operations by adopting a build-to-order model. Instead of relying on large inventories, Dell began producing computers only after receiving customer orders.

This approach eliminated delays caused by excess inventory and reduced dependency on forecast accuracy. By streamlining its supply chain and focusing on real-time demand, Dell not only removed a significant bottleneck but also gained a competitive edge by delivering customized products faster than competitors.

Exercises

1. **Map a Process:** Choose a workflow or system you're involved with. Identify the step where progress slows most frequently.
2. **Evaluate Solutions:** Brainstorm three ways to address a bottleneck in your current system. Which option offers the best balance of effort and impact?
3. **Measure Impact:** Implement one solution and track the improvement in efficiency or performance.

Key Takeaway

Bottlenecks are opportunities in disguise. By identifying constraints and optimizing around them, you unlock hidden potential and position yourself for sustained success.

Chapter 94: Redefine the Rules of the Game

In a competitive environment, playing by the established rules often leads to incremental progress at best. To truly stand out, you must redefine the rules of the game. This strategy involves changing the parameters of competition to favor your strengths, creating a playing field where you have the upper hand.

Redefining the rules doesn't mean breaking them —it means reshaping expectations, challenging assumptions, and introducing innovations that others must adapt to. When you set the standard, competitors must follow your lead, allowing you to dictate the pace and direction of the industry.

Why Redefining the Rules Works

1. **Creates a New Playing Field:** Changing the rules forces competitors to adapt to your terms.
2. **Highlights Strengths:** By redefining the game, you emphasize your unique advantages.
3. **Inspires Innovation:** Breaking free from tradition fosters creative solutions and opportunities.

For example, when Cirque du Soleil entered the entertainment market, it redefined the circus. By eliminating animals, focusing on theatrical storytelling, and targeting adult audiences, Cirque created a new category of performance art. This shift allowed it to thrive in a declining industry while leaving traditional circuses scrambling to catch up.

How to Redefine the Rules

1. **Question Assumptions:** Challenge the norms and traditions that define your industry or field.
2. **Identify Your Strengths:** Focus on what sets you apart and build your strategy around those advantages.
3. **Introduce Innovations:** Develop products, services, or approaches that disrupt expectations.
4. **Change the Narrative:** Use branding and communication to frame your approach as the new standard.
5. **Lead the Transition:** Help stakeholders and customers embrace the new rules through education and engagement.

Real-World Example

Warby Parker redefined the eyewear industry by introducing an innovative direct-to-consumer model. Traditional glasses retailers relied on high markups, in-store fittings, and limited selection. Warby Parker flipped the script by offering stylish, affordable frames online with a home try-on program. This approach disrupted the industry and forced competitors to adapt to the new customer expectations Warby Parker had established.

Exercises

1. **Challenge a Norm:** Identify one "rule" in your industry or field. How could you approach it differently?
2. **Highlight Your Edge:** List three unique strengths you have. How can you use them to redefine expectations?
3. **Test a New Rule:** Implement a small change in how you operate and assess its impact on your environment.

Key Takeaway

Redefining the rules of the game transforms competition into opportunity. By reshaping expectations and introducing innovations, you position yourself to lead and thrive on your terms.

Chapter 95: Turn Opposing Forces Into Complementors

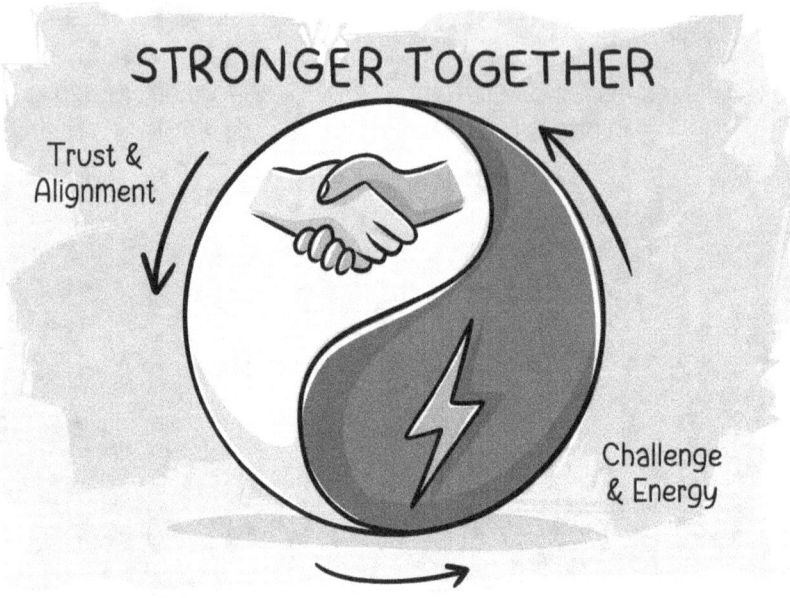

In competitive environments, it's easy to view opposing forces solely as adversaries. However, there are situations where your competitors or seemingly conflicting elements can become valuable partners. Turning opposing forces into complementors involves finding ways to align interests, leveraging each other's strengths, and creating win-win scenarios that benefit everyone involved.

This strategy requires a shift in mindset — rather than focusing on defeating your opponent, you unlock opportunities for mutual growth, shared innovation, and enhanced market reach.

Why This Strategy Works

1. **Unlocks Synergy:** Combining strengths with others often leads to greater collective impact.
2. **Expands Opportunities:** Collaboration opens doors to resources, networks, or markets you couldn't access alone.
3. **Reduces Conflict:** Aligning interests minimizes competition and creates a more cooperative dynamic.

For example, rival tech companies often collaborate on setting industry standards, benefiting both parties while fostering innovation that drives the entire sector forward.

How to Turn Opposing Forces Into Complementors

1. **Identify Shared Goals:** Look for areas where your interests align with your competitors or opposing forces.
2. **Focus on Strengths:** Leverage what each party brings to the table to create a stronger partnership.
3. **Define Boundaries:** Set clear terms to ensure collaboration remains mutually beneficial.
4. **Communicate Openly:** Foster trust and transparency to build a sustainable relationship.
5. **Monitor and Adjust:** Continuously evaluate the partnership to ensure it stays aligned with your objectives.

Real-World Example

Rival automakers BMW and Mercedes-Benz collaborated in 2015 to create Here, a digital mapping platform for autonomous driving. While traditionally fierce competitors, they recognized that pooling resources to develop advanced mapping technology would benefit both companies. By collaborating on this shared goal, they accelerated innovation and positioned themselves as leaders in the evolving field of autonomous vehicles.

Exercises

1. **Identify a Potential Complementor:** Think of a competitor or opposing force in your industry. What shared goals could you explore?
2. **Map Collaborative Opportunities:** List three areas where combining resources or expertise with an opposing force could create mutual benefit.
3. **Test the Waters:** Propose a small-scale collaboration to gauge feasibility and trust.

Key Takeaway

Turning opposing forces into complementors transforms competition into opportunity. By aligning shared goals and leveraging mutual strengths, you create partnerships that benefit all involved and expand the potential for success.

Chapter 96: Always Leave Room for Reversal

Even the best-laid plans can face unforeseen challenges, and rigidity in strategy often leads to failure. Always leaving room for reversal ensures that you have the flexibility to pivot, adapt, or even undo decisions when circumstances change. This principle is not about abandoning commitment — it's about building adaptability into your approach to safeguard against uncertainty.

Reversals can be difficult, but they often prevent greater losses or open up new opportunities. A willingness to change direction signals strength and strategic foresight, not weakness. By preparing for potential reversals, you ensure that you're never locked into a path that no longer serves your goals.

Why Reversal is Essential

1. **Reduces Risk:** Flexibility minimizes the impact of unforeseen challenges.
2. **Encourages Innovation:** The ability to pivot fosters creativity and experimentation.
3. **Preserves Resources:** Reversals often prevent further losses when a strategy proves ineffective.

For example, businesses launching new products often build in the option to discontinue or rebrand if early results don't meet expectations. This approach allows them to experiment without committing irreversibly to a failing course.

How to Leave Room for Reversal

1. **Start Small:** Test ideas on a limited scale before committing significant resources.
2. **Set Decision Gates:** Define checkpoints where you evaluate progress and decide whether to continue, pivot, or reverse.
3. **Build Flexibility:** Design strategies and processes that allow for adjustments without significant disruption.
4. **Monitor Continuously:** Stay attuned to changes in your environment, competitors, and results.
5. **Communicate Openly:** Ensure that stakeholders understand the importance of adaptability and are prepared for potential reversals.

Real-World Example

The food company Campbell's launched its low-sodium soups in response to growing health trends. However, when sales declined due to customer dissatisfaction with taste, Campbell's reversed its strategy by reintroducing the original recipes while maintaining a smaller low-sodium product line. This flexibility preserved its brand reputation and allowed the company to meet diverse customer needs.

Exercises

1. **Analyze a Current Plan:** Identify a strategy where you could incorporate more flexibility for reversal.
2. **Evaluate Past Decisions:** Reflect on a situation where leaving room for reversal could have improved the outcome.
3. **Design a Safety Net:** Develop a contingency plan for a current project or decision.

Key Takeaway

Leaving room for reversal ensures that you remain adaptable in the face of change. By building flexibility into your strategies, you protect your goals and stay prepared for unexpected challenges.

Chapter 97: Stockpile Reserves for Important Moments

In strategy, timing is everything — but timing without resources is wasted potential. Stockpiling reserves ensures that when the right moment arises, you have the means to act decisively and effectively. These reserves could be financial capital, talent, energy, or even goodwill, ready to deploy when the stakes are highest.

Reserves aren't just about survival; they're about seizing opportunities. When competitors are overextended or markets are volatile, your ability to act from a position of strength becomes a game-changer. By strategically building and managing reserves, you prepare not just for challenges but also for the moments that define long-term success.

Why Stockpiling Reserves is Critical

1. **Provides Stability:** Reserves act as a buffer against unexpected setbacks.
2. **Enables Strategic Action:** Having resources ready allows you to act quickly when opportunities arise.
3. **Builds Resilience:** Preparedness fosters confidence and adaptability in uncertain environments.

For example, companies that maintain financial reserves can invest in innovation or acquisitions during economic downturns, while competitors struggle to stay afloat.

How to Stockpile Reserves Strategically

1. **Identify Key Resources:** Determine what types of reserves are most valuable for your goals (e.g., funds, relationships, materials).
2. **Build Gradually:** Accumulate reserves consistently, even during stable periods, to avoid overextension.
3. **Protect Against Overuse:** Establish clear criteria for when and how reserves can be deployed.
4. **Align with Goals:** Ensure your reserves directly support your long-term objectives.
5. **Monitor Regularly:** Track your reserves to ensure they remain sufficient and relevant.

Real-World Example

Costco has long been recognized for its disciplined approach to inventory management. Unlike many retailers that run lean to minimize costs, Costco stockpiles essential goods in larger quantities. This strategy allowed Costco to maintain availability and meet customer demand during supply chain disruptions, reinforcing customer loyalty and market stability.

Exercises

1. **Assess Your Reserves:** Identify the resources you currently have and where gaps exist.
2. **Develop a Stockpiling Plan:** Create a strategy for gradually building reserves without overextending.
3. **Set Usage Criteria:** Define the conditions under which reserves can be used to maximize impact.

Key Takeaway

Stockpiling reserves prepares you for both challenges and opportunities. By building and managing key resources strategically, you ensure the ability to act decisively when it matters most.

Chapter 98: Design Self-Reinforcing Systems

Self-reinforcing systems are the ultimate strategic advantage. These systems create a positive feedback loop where each success strengthens the next, driving continuous improvement and growth. When designed effectively, they reduce effort over time while producing increasingly significant results.

This strategy requires careful planning. Self-reinforcing systems thrive on alignment—where inputs and outputs are connected in a way that creates momentum. By identifying key areas where your efforts can compound, you set the foundation for sustainable progress that builds on itself.

Why Self-Reinforcing Systems Work

1. **Creates Momentum:** Positive feedback loops accelerate progress with minimal additional effort.
2. **Drives Efficiency:** Automation and scalability reduce resource expenditure over time.
3. **Builds Resilience:** Strong systems withstand external shocks and adapt to change.

For example, loyalty programs like those offered by Sephora encourage repeat purchases by rewarding customers. The more customers buy, the more rewards they earn, which incentivizes further engagement — fueling the company's growth while deepening customer loyalty.

How to Design Self-Reinforcing Systems

1. **Identify Core Drivers:** Pinpoint the actions or inputs that create the most significant results.
2. **Connect Inputs and Outputs:** Ensure that each success feeds back into the system, creating a loop of reinforcement.
3. **Leverage Technology:** Automate processes to enhance scalability and reduce manual intervention.
4. **Evaluate Scalability:** Test the system's ability to grow without losing effectiveness.
5. **Monitor and Adjust:** Continuously assess the system's performance and make improvements as needed.

Real-World Example

The video game company Epic Games, creators of *Fortnite*, has built a self-reinforcing system through its free-to-play model and in-game purchases. By offering *Fortnite* for free, the company attracted millions of players. These players, in turn, purchase cosmetic upgrades and skins, generating substantial revenue without impacting gameplay balance.

Epic reinvests this revenue into frequent content updates, events, and collaborations, which keep players engaged and attract new ones. The growing player base further enhances the game's community and visibility, creating a feedback loop that continually strengthens *Fortnite's* position as a global gaming phenomenon.

Exercises

1. **Identify a Potential Loop:** Reflect on one area of your work or business where a feedback loop could create compounding results.
2. **Map the System:** Outline how inputs and outputs can connect to reinforce each other.
3. **Test and Refine:** Implement a small-scale version of your system and assess its impact.

Key Takeaway

Self-reinforcing systems create sustainable, scalable success. By designing processes that compound results, you build momentum and efficiency that drive long-term growth.

Chapter 99: End Games with Grace and Foresight

In strategy, how you end matters as much as how you begin. Whether it's concluding a negotiation, exiting a market, or wrapping up a long-term project, the final steps often define perceptions, relationships, and future opportunities. Ending with grace and foresight ensures that you leave on your terms, maintain credibility, and set the stage for what comes next.

End games require careful planning. While it's tempting to focus solely on achieving your goal, a poorly executed exit can undo years of progress. Thoughtful conclusions consider both immediate results and long-term implications, balancing the need for closure with the potential for future growth.

Why Ending Gracefully Matters

1. **Preserves Relationships:** Leaving with respect and professionalism strengthens connections for future collaborations.
2. **Enhances Reputation:** A well-executed conclusion reinforces your credibility and legacy.
3. **Opens New Doors:** Strategic endings often lead to fresh opportunities or smoother transitions.

For example, businesses that phase out obsolete products responsibly—offering clear communication and support to customers—maintain loyalty and pave the way for their next innovation.

How to End with Grace and Foresight

1. **Define Success Early:** Establish clear goals for your conclusion, ensuring alignment with your long-term vision.
2. **Communicate Transparently:** Keep stakeholders informed about your decisions and next steps.
3. **Minimize Disruption:** Take steps to ensure smooth transitions and avoid unnecessary complications.
4. **Reflect and Document:** Analyze what worked, what didn't, and how lessons learned can inform future efforts.
5. **Leave the Door Open:** Conclude with positivity, leaving room for future opportunities or collaborations.

Real-World Example

General Electric (GE) decided to exit its lighting business after over a century of operation. Instead of abruptly shutting down, GE transitioned its lighting division to a buyer while ensuring employees and customers were supported throughout the process. This graceful exit preserved GE's reputation while allowing it to focus on more profitable sectors.

Exercises

1. **Plan an Exit:** Identify one project or commitment nearing completion. How can you conclude it thoughtfully and strategically?
2. **Reflect on Past Endings:** Think of a situation where you ended something poorly. What could you have done differently?
3. **Set Closing Goals:** For an ongoing effort, define what success looks like at the end and how you'll achieve it.

Key Takeaway

Ending with grace and foresight ensures that your conclusions are as strategic as your beginnings. By focusing on professionalism, reflection, and future potential, you close the chapter while setting the stage for continued success.

Chapter 100: Achieve Strategic Mastery Through Continuous Education

Mastery is not a destination but a journey. The most successful strategists understand that learning never ends. Whether you're refining your skills, exploring new concepts, or adapting to an evolving world, continuous education is the key to staying relevant, innovative, and ahead of the curve.

Strategic mastery isn't just about accumulating knowledge — it's about applying it. Each new insight builds on what you already know, deepening your understanding and expanding your capabilities. By committing to lifelong learning, you ensure that your strategies remain fresh, adaptable, and effective in any environment.

Why Continuous Education is Essential

1. **Keeps You Relevant:** Staying informed ensures you're always prepared for emerging trends and challenges.
2. **Enhances Innovation:** New ideas and perspectives fuel creativity and growth.
3. **Builds Confidence:** Ongoing learning reinforces your expertise, making you a more decisive and effective leader.

For example, many leaders dedicate time to reading, attending workshops, or engaging in peer networks to stay updated on best practices and industry shifts.

How to Pursue Continuous Education

1. **Stay Curious:** Regularly seek out new topics, books, or courses that challenge your current understanding.
2. **Learn from Experience:** Reflect on successes and failures to extract valuable lessons.
3. **Engage with Experts:** Build relationships with mentors or peers who can offer diverse perspectives.
4. **Experiment and Apply:** Test new strategies or ideas in low-risk scenarios to refine your skills.
5. **Commit to Growth:** Set specific goals for your personal and professional development.

Real-World Example

The late Ruth Bader Ginsburg, U.S. Supreme Court Justice, exemplified continuous education. Even as a highly accomplished legal mind, she consistently sought new knowledge, from studying emerging legal theories to engaging with cultural and technological shifts. Her commitment to lifelong learning allowed her to remain a relevant and transformative figure in her field.

Exercises

1. **Identify Learning Goals:** Write down three areas where you want to expand your knowledge or skills.
2. **Schedule Learning Time:** Dedicate a specific time each week to reading, attending events, or exploring new ideas.
3. **Test Your Knowledge:** Apply a new concept or skill in your work to see how it enhances your strategy.

Key Takeaway

Strategic mastery is built through continuous education. By staying curious, reflective, and open to new ideas, you ensure that your strategies remain dynamic, effective, and ahead of the curve.

Conclusion

This book has explored 100 strategies to empower you with the tools needed to think, act, and lead strategically in an ever-changing world. Each chapter was designed to guide you from foundational principles to advanced concepts, providing insights that apply across industries, challenges, and ambitions. Now, the challenge is to integrate them into your decision-making processes, leadership style, and long-term vision.

From Knowledge to Action

Strategic thinking isn't just about knowing what to do; it's about consistently applying these principles to achieve your goals. Start small. Implement one or two strategies that feel most actionable, measure their impact, and refine your approach. Strategy is iterative — it evolves as you learn and adapt. By starting with focused actions and expanding gradually, you build confidence and momentum that carry you forward.

Adapting to Complexity

A critical aspect of strategic mastery is knowing when to pivot. As circumstances change, strategies that once worked may need to be re-evaluated. Leaving room for reversal, testing assumptions, and applying feedback loops ensure that you remain flexible and ready to adjust when needed. Remember, agility and foresight are your greatest allies in a world of constant change.

Applying the Lessons in Every Sphere

The strategies in this book aren't limited to business or professional endeavors — they apply to every aspect of life. Whether you're negotiating with a partner, planning a personal project, or navigating complex relationships, these lessons provide tools for better decision-making, clearer communication, and more effective action.

For example, concepts such as prioritizing clarity over speed, aligning incentives, and fostering mutual dependence can improve teamwork and relationships. Similarly, strategies like leveraging asymmetry and anticipating trends help you stay ahead in personal or professional growth.

Looking Ahead

Now it's your turn. Take these strategies and make them your own. Use them to shape your decisions, inspire your team, and achieve your goals. Reflect on what you've learned, stay open to growth, and lead with purpose and precision.

Appendix A: Quick Reference Guide

This appendix is your go-to resource for a concise overview of the strategies covered in the book. Each chapter has been summarized into a single actionable line, allowing you to revisit key insights at a glance. Use this section as a quick reference to remind yourself of the tools and concepts you've learned, organized by the five parts of the book.

Section I: Foundational Strategies

1. **Play the Long Game, Not the Next Move:** Focus on sustainable, long-term success over short-term wins.
2. **Begin with the End in Mind:** Start every strategy with a clear vision of your ultimate goal.
3. **Prioritize Clarity Over Speed:** Make decisions with precision rather than rushing into action.
4. **Leverage Asymmetry in Resources:** Use unique advantages to outperform competitors with greater resources.
5. **Embrace Iterative Progress:** Build success gradually through small, consistent improvements.
6. **Balance Offensive and Defensive Moves:** Blend proactive and protective strategies for well-rounded success.
7. **Understand the Zero-Sum Game:** Recognize when competition requires gaining at others' expense.
8. **Find Win-Win Opportunities:** Seek collaborative solutions that benefit all parties involved.
9. **Evaluate Trade-Offs in Every Decision:** Weigh costs and benefits to optimize outcomes.
10. **Don't Confuse Luck with Strategy:** Separate chance from deliberate planning to refine your approach.
11. **Cultivate Tactical Patience:** Wait for the right opportunity before taking action.
12. **Harness the Power of Perception:** Use how others see you to influence outcomes in your favor.
13. **Simplify Complex Options:** Break down overwhelming choices into clear, actionable steps.
14. **Always Ask "Why?" Twice:** Dig deeper into motivations and assumptions to uncover the truth.
15. **Avoid Overcommitting Help:** Offer assistance wisely to prevent resource overextension.
16. **Be the First Mover When It Counts:** Act early to seize opportunities or shape the playing field.
17. **Follow the Nash Equilibrium:** Make decisions that balance individual and collective gains.
18. **Build Redundancies for Resilience:** Prepare for uncertainty by creating backup systems.
19. **Don't Neglect the Cost of Inaction:** Recognize the risks of staying idle in a changing landscape.
20. **Master the Pivot Point:** Adapt quickly and effectively when plans need to change.

Section II: Competitive Strategies

21. **Make the Most of Your Competition's Blind Spots:** Exploit gaps in your competitors' awareness to gain an edge.
22. **Focus on the Player, Not Just the Rules:** Tailor your strategy to your opponent's behavior, not the framework.
23. **Control the Tempo of Engagement:** Set the pace of interactions to stay in control.
24. **Feign Weakness Where You Are Strong:** Mislead competitors by disguising your strengths.
25. **Cultivate Alliances to Outflank Threats:** Partner with others to neutralize shared challenges.
26. **Use Decoys to Distract and Mislead:** Divert attention from your true intentions to gain an advantage.
27. **Capture High Ground in Negotiations:** Secure leverage by framing discussions in your favor.
28. **Create False Choices to Frame the Narrative:** Shape decisions by limiting perceived options.
29. **Use a Divide-and-Conquer Approach:** Fragment opponents to weaken their collective strength.
30. **Benefit from the Overconfidence of Your Opponents:** Capitalize on rivals' overestimations of their abilities.
31. **Pre-empt Competitors Through Purposeful Partnerships:** Collaborate to block competitors before they act.
32. **Set Traps by Shaping Expectations:** Lead opponents into predictable, disadvantageous actions.
33. **Win Battles, Avoid Wars:** Prioritize focused victories over costly, drawn-out conflicts.
34. **Undermine Rivals with Incremental Disruption:** Erode competitors' strengths through small, consistent moves.
35. **Neutralize Emerging Risks Before They Escalate:** Address potential threats early to prevent larger issues.
36. **Channel Psychological Momentum:** Use confidence and timing to keep the advantage on your side.
37. **Adopt an Inside-Out Mindset:** Leverage internal strengths before looking outward for solutions.
38. **Counter Aggression with Calm Confidence:** Respond to threats with poise to neutralize their impact.
39. **Force Your Competitors to Overextend:** Encourage rivals to exhaust resources while you stay steady.
40. **Apply the Minimax Principle in Critical Decisions:** Minimize potential losses while maximizing gains.

Section III: Cooperative Strategies

41. **Lay the Foundation for Trust Before You Request Collaboration:** Build credibility before seeking cooperation.
42. **Bolster Mutual Dependence in Joint Ventures:** Strengthen interdependence to ensure partnership success.
43. **Share the Pie to Make It Bigger:** Expand opportunities by collaborating rather than competing.
44. **Use Reciprocity to Strengthen Relationships:** Foster goodwill by giving value before seeking returns.
45. **Capitalize Network Effects for Influence:** Leverage interconnected systems to amplify impact.
46. **Be Predictable in Cooperative Settings:** Foster trust by acting consistently and reliably.

47. **Compromise Strategically, Not Emotionally:** Negotiate with logic, not sentiment.
48. **Maximize Joint Gains in Team-Ups:** Align efforts to achieve shared success.
49. **Establish Harmony Between Transparency and Secrecy:** Balance openness with discretion for optimal collaboration.
50. **Foster a Reputation for Fair Actions:** Build trust by consistently demonstrating fairness.
51. **Turn Enemies into Allies:** Transform adversaries into partners through shared goals.
52. **Concentrate on the Shared Objective:** Keep partnerships focused on common interests.
53. **Generate Value Before Asking for Value:** Prove your worth before seeking reciprocity.
54. **Be Generous Without Being Exploitable:** Offer support while protecting your interests.
55. **Align Incentives to Sustain Cooperation:** Ensure everyone benefits equally to maintain partnerships.
56. **Honor Loyalty Proactively:** Reward steadfastness to strengthen relationships.
57. **Forge Coalitions Around Shared Interests:** Unite groups with common objectives for greater impact.
58. **Avoid Overpromising in Groups:** Manage expectations to maintain credibility.
59. **Communicate Clearly to Reduce Misunderstandings:** Use transparency to prevent conflict.
60. **Exit Teams Gracefully When Necessary:** End partnerships positively to preserve goodwill.

Section IV: Adaptive Strategies

61. **Anticipate Game-Changing Trends:** Stay ahead by identifying transformative shifts early.
62. **Be the First to Spot Weak Signals:** Detect subtle changes that signal future developments.
63. **Apply Change as a Well-Designed Asset:** Leverage change to your advantage through planning.
64. **Develop Options for Uncertain Futures:** Prepare flexible strategies for multiple scenarios.
65. **Use Real Options to Hedge Strategies:** Invest in opportunities while minimizing risks.
66. **Develop Contingency Plans for Key Obstacles:** Prepare for challenges before they arise.
67. **Test Assumptions Before Acting:** Validate your plans by questioning their foundations.
68. **Try Experimentation for Growth:** Innovate by testing and iterating ideas.
69. **Turn Failures into Stepping Stones for Progress:** Learn from setbacks to move forward stronger.
70. **Adapt Plans in Real Time:** Stay flexible to react effectively as situations evolve.
71. **Detect Hidden Patterns in Chaos:** Find order in complexity to guide decisions.
72. **Use Contrarian Thinking to Your Advantage:** Embrace unconventional ideas to uncover opportunities.
73. **Stay Agile in Dynamic Environments:** Move quickly and flexibly to stay ahead of change.
74. **Exploit Adversaries' Rigidity:** Use others' resistance to adapt as a weakness.
75. **Be Unpredictable to Stay Ahead:** Keep competitors guessing by avoiding predictable patterns.
76. **Diversify Your Cheat Sheet:** Build a broad toolkit to adapt to any scenario.
77. **Counterpoise Risk and Reward Over Time:** Balance short-term risk with long-term rewards.
78. **Thrive in Nonlinear Scenarios:** Embrace complexity to find opportunities in chaos.
79. **Prepare for Worst-Case Scenarios:** Anticipate challenges and plan accordingly.
80. **Apply the OODA Loop: Observe, Orient, Decide, Act:** Use this iterative framework to adapt quickly.

Section V: Advanced Strategies

81. **Orchestrate Complex Systems for Advantage:** Align diverse elements to create synergy.
82. **Manage Trade-Offs with Precision:** Balance conflicting priorities for optimal results.
83. **Engineer Irreversible Advantages:** Build strengths that competitors cannot replicate.
84. **Use Authority to Multiply Impact:** Leverage influence to inspire and lead effectively.
85. **Turn Opponents' Strengths Into Vulnerabilities:** Exploit competitors' overreliance on their strengths.
86. **Harness the Wisdom of the Crowd:** Use collective intelligence for better decisions.
87. **Command the Precision of Timing:** Act at the perfect moment for maximum impact.
88. **Uncover Unique Perspectives to Lead with an Edge:** See what others miss to innovate effectively.
89. **Be Relentless in Follow-Through:** Ensure consistent execution to achieve goals.
90. **Apply the Prisoner's Dilemma to Real Life:** Balance cooperation and competition strategically.
91. **Engineer Scarcity to Drive Value:** Use limited availability to increase demand.
92. **Use Game-Theoretic Modeling to Predict Next Steps:** Anticipate others' actions to plan effectively.
93. **Identify and Gain From Bottlenecks in Systems:** Optimize constraints to unlock potential.
94. **Redefine the Rules of the Game:** Change the framework of competition to your advantage.
95. **Turn Opposing Forces Into Complementors:** Align with competitors to create mutual benefits.
96. **Always Leave Room for Reversal:** Build flexibility into plans to adapt to change.
97. **Stockpile Reserves for Important Moments:** Prepare resources for critical opportunities.
98. **Design Self-Reinforcing Systems:** Create feedback loops that drive long-term success.

99. **End Games with Grace and Foresight:** Conclude strategically to preserve relationships and reputation.

100. **Achieve Strategic Mastery Through Continuous Education:** Commit to lifelong learning to refine your expertise.

Appendix B: Section and Chapter Outline

This appendix provides a straightforward outline of all the chapters in the book, organized by section. Use this as a quick guide to locate chapters or revisit specific topics as needed.

Section I: Foundational Strategies (Chapters 1–20)

- Play the Long Game, Not the Next Move
- Begin with the End in Mind
- Prioritize Clarity Over Speed
- Leverage Asymmetry in Resources
- Embrace Iterative Progress
- Balance Offensive and Defensive Moves
- Understand the Zero-Sum Game
- Find Win-Win Opportunities
- Evaluate Trade-Offs in Every Decision
- Don't Confuse Luck with Strategy
- Cultivate Tactical Patience
- Harness the Power of Perception
- Simplify Complex Options
- Always Ask "Why?" Twice
- Avoid Overcommitting Help
- Be the First Mover When It Counts
- Follow the Nash Equilibrium
- Build Redundancies for Resilience
- Don't Neglect the Cost of Inaction
- Master the Pivot Point

Section II: Competitive Strategies (Chapters 21–40)

- Make the Most of Your Competition's Blind Spots
- Focus on the Player, Not Just the Rules
- Control the Tempo of Engagement
- Feign Weakness Where You Are Strong
- Cultivate Alliances to Outflank Threats
- Use Decoys to Distract and Mislead
- Capture High Ground in Negotiations
- Create False Choices to Frame the Narrative
- Use a Divide-and-Conquer Approach
- Benefit from the Overconfidence of Your Opponents
- Pre-empt Competitors Through Purposeful Partnerships
- Set Traps by Shaping Expectations
- Win Battles, Avoid Wars
- Undermine Rivals with Incremental Disruption
- Neutralize Emerging Risks Before They Escalate
- Channel Psychological Momentum
- Adopt an Inside-Out Mindset
- Counter Aggression with Calm Confidence
- Force Your Competitors to Overextend
- Apply the Minimax Principle in Critical Decisions

Section III: Cooperative Strategies (Chapters 41–60)

- Lay the Foundation for Trust Before You Request Collaboration
- Bolster Mutual Dependence in Joint Ventures
- Share the Pie to Make It Bigger
- Use Reciprocity to Strengthen Relationships

- Capitalize Network Effects for Influence
- Be Predictable in Cooperative Settings
- Compromise Strategically, Not Emotionally
- Maximize Joint Gains in Team-Ups
- Establish Harmony Between Transparency and Secrecy
- Foster a Reputation for Fair Actions
- Turn Enemies into Allies
- Concentrate on the Shared Objective
- Generate Value Before Asking for Value
- Be Generous Without Being Exploitable
- Align Incentives to Sustain Cooperation
- Honor Loyalty Proactively
- Forge Coalitions Around Shared Interests
- Avoid Overpromising in Groups
- Communicate Clearly to Reduce Misunderstandings
- Exit Teams Gracefully When Necessary

Section IV: Adaptive Strategies (Chapters 61–80)

- Anticipate Game-Changing Trends
- Be the First to Spot Weak Signals
- Apply Change as a Well-Designed Asset
- Develop Options for Uncertain Futures
- Use Real Options to Hedge Strategies
- Develop Contingency Plans for Key Obstacles
- Test Assumptions Before Acting
- Try Experimentation for Growth
- Turn Failures into Stepping Stones for Progress
- Adapt Plans in Real Time
- Detect Hidden Patterns in Chaos
- Use Contrarian Thinking to Your Advantage
- Stay Agile in Dynamic Environments
- Exploit Adversaries' Rigidity
- Be Unpredictable to Stay Ahead
- Diversify Your Cheat Sheet
- Counterpoise Risk and Reward Over Time
- Thrive in Nonlinear Scenarios
- Prepare for Worst-Case Scenarios
- Apply the OODA Loop: Observe, Orient, Decide, Act

Section V: Advanced Strategies (Chapters 81–100)

- Orchestrate Complex Systems for Advantage
- Manage Trade-Offs with Precision
- Engineer Irreversible Advantages
- Use Authority to Multiply Impact
- Turn Opponents' Strengths Into Vulnerabilities
- Harness the Wisdom of the Crowd
- Command the Precision of Timing
- Uncover Unique Perspectives to Lead with an Edge
- Be Relentless in Follow-Through
- Apply the Prisoner's Dilemma to Real Life
- Engineer Scarcity to Drive Value
- Use Game-Theoretic Modeling to Predict Next Steps
- Identify and Gain From Bottlenecks in Systems
- Redefine the Rules of the Game
- Turn Opposing Forces Into Complementors

- Always Leave Room for Reversal
- Stockpile Reserves for Important Moments
- Design Self-Reinforcing Systems
- End Games with Grace and Foresight
- Achieve Strategic Mastery Through Continuous Education

Appendix C: Practice Scenarios

This appendix provides 15 real-world practice scenarios to help you apply the strategies outlined in this book. Each scenario presents a problem statement followed by a challenge that asks you to identify which strategy (or strategies) from the chapters can be used to address the situation. Use this section to sharpen your strategic thinking and strengthen your ability to adapt these principles to various situations.

Scenario 1: Reviving a Declining Product Line

Problem Statement: Your company's once-popular product is now losing market share to competitors offering newer, more innovative solutions. Internal stakeholders are divided on whether to continue investing in the product or phase it out.

Challenge: Apply strategies such as **"Turn Failures into Stepping Stones for Progress"** (Chapter 69) or **"Redefine the Rules of the Game"** (Chapter 94) to identify how to reposition or transform the product to regain relevance.

Scenario 2: Navigating a High-Stakes Negotiation

Problem Statement: You're negotiating a critical partnership with a larger company that has greater leverage. They've proposed terms that seem one-sided but essential for moving forward.

Challenge: Use strategies like **"Capture High Ground in Negotiations"** (Chapter 27) and **"Compromise Strategically, Not Emotionally"** (Chapter 47) to secure favorable terms while maintaining the partnership.

Scenario 3: Managing a Team in Conflict

Problem Statement: Two key team members have conflicting priorities and their disagreements are affecting the overall performance of the team. The organization cannot afford to lose either individual.

Challenge: Apply **"Lay the Foundation for Trust Before You Request Collaboration"** (Chapter 41) and **"Concentrate on the Shared Objective"** (Chapter 52) to realign the team's focus and resolve tensions.

Scenario 4: Launching a New Product in a Saturated Market

Problem Statement: Your company plans to launch a product in a market dominated by established players. Resources are limited, and you need to make an impact quickly.

Challenge: Use **"Be the First Mover When It Counts"** (Chapter 16) or **"Exploit Adversaries' Rigidity"** (Chapter 74) to identify a niche or unique approach that can differentiate your product.

Scenario 5: Addressing Customer Dissatisfaction

Problem Statement: A key customer segment has expressed dissatisfaction with your service, leading to declining sales and potential reputational damage.

Challenge: Apply **"Harness the Power of Perception"** (Chapter 12) and **"Generate Value Before Asking for Value"** (Chapter 53) to rebuild trust and loyalty with your customers.

Scenario 6: Facing Aggressive Competition

Problem Statement: A rival company has launched a price war, aggressively undercutting your offerings to capture market share. Your margins are too tight to match their pricing.

Challenge: Use **"Force Your Competitors to Overextend"** (Chapter 39) or **"Neutralize Emerging Risks Before They Escalate"** (Chapter 35) to develop a non-price-based strategy to counteract the competition.

Scenario 7: Managing Limited Resources

Problem Statement: Your department has been tasked with delivering an ambitious project but has only half the resources originally allocated. Deadlines are tight, and expectations remain high.

Challenge: Leverage **"Leverage Asymmetry in Resources"** (Chapter 4) and **"Build Redundancies for Resilience"** (Chapter 18) to optimize resource use and deliver results efficiently.

Scenario 8: Responding to Industry Disruption

Problem Statement: A technological breakthrough is reshaping your industry, leaving traditional players at risk of obsolescence. Your organization has been slow to adapt.

Challenge: Apply **"Anticipate Game-Changing Trends"** (Chapter 61) and **"Adapt Plans in Real Time"** (Chapter 70) to create a strategy that embraces innovation and positions your organization for success.

Scenario 9: Strengthening a Weak Partnership

Problem Statement: A strategic partnership with another company is underperforming, and trust between both parties has eroded. The partnership is still critical to achieving long-term goals.

Challenge: Use **"Align Incentives to Sustain Cooperation"** (Chapter 55) and **"Be Generous Without Being Exploitable"** (Chapter 54) to rebuild trust and improve collaboration.

Problem Statement: A potential economic downturn threatens your company's operations. Leadership is divided on how much to invest in contingency planning versus staying focused on current projects.

Challenge: Leverage **"Prepare for Worst-Case Scenarios" (Chapter 79)** and **"Stockpile Reserves for Important Moments" (Chapter 97)** to ensure readiness without compromising current objectives.

Scenario 11: Encouraging Innovation in a Stagnant Team

Problem Statement: Your team is hesitant to take risks or experiment, leading to a lack of fresh ideas and slow progress.

Challenge: Apply **"Try Experimentation for Growth" (Chapter 68)** and **"Use Contrarian Thinking to Your Advantage" (Chapter 72)** to foster a culture of creativity and calculated risk-taking.

Scenario 12: Turning a Competitor into a Collaborator

Problem Statement: A rival company has been targeting your market aggressively, but there's potential for collaboration to expand opportunities for both sides.

Challenge: Use **"Turn Opposing Forces Into Complementors" (Chapter 95)** and **"Forge Coalitions Around Shared Interests" (Chapter 57)** to establish common ground and create a win-win partnership.

Scenario 13: Shifting Internal Perceptions

Problem Statement: Your department is perceived as a support function rather than a driver of value, limiting your influence within the organization.

Challenge: Leverage **"Harness the Power of Perception" (Chapter 12)** and **"Be the First to Spot Weak Signals" (Chapter 62)** to redefine your role and demonstrate strategic value.

Scenario 14: Competing Against a First Mover

Problem Statement: A competitor has launched a new product that's gaining momentum. You're tasked with finding a way to counteract their lead without mimicking their strategy.

Challenge: Use **"Exploit Adversaries' Rigidity" (Chapter 74)** and **"Command the Precision of Timing" (Chapter 87)** to find innovative ways to regain market attention.

Scenario 15: Exiting a Market with Grace

Problem Statement: Your company needs to exit an underperforming market, but doing so risks alienating existing customers and damaging your brand reputation.

Challenge: Apply **"End Games with Grace and Foresight" (Chapter 99)** and **"Always Leave Room for Reversal" (Chapter 96)** to ensure a smooth transition that minimizes negative impacts.

Appendix D: Strategic Application Checklist

This checklist is designed to help you integrate the strategies from this book into your daily life, decision-making, and long-term planning. Use it as a guide to ensure that you consistently apply the principles and practices outlined in this book. Each point highlights a key area of focus with actionable steps to reinforce strategic thinking and execution.

1. Define Your Long-Term Vision
- Write down where you want to be in 5, 10, or 20 years.
- Break your vision into measurable goals.
- Regularly revisit and adjust your vision as needed.

2. Prioritize Actions for Maximum Impact
- Identify the tasks that will make the biggest difference.
- Use the 80/20 rule to focus on high-impact efforts.
- Set deadlines to create urgency for important actions.

3. Balance Risk and Reward in Decisions
- Assess both short-term and long-term consequences.
- Identify worst-case scenarios and prepare for them.
- Take calculated risks when the potential reward is worth it.

4. Build Relationships Strategically
- Network with people who align with your goals.
- Offer value before asking for favors or collaboration.
- Foster trust through consistent and reliable actions.

5. Stay Flexible and Ready to Pivot
- Regularly review your progress and identify areas for change.
- Develop contingency plans for key goals.
- Embrace failure as an opportunity to adapt and improve.

6. Use Perception to Your Advantage
- Present yourself and your work in ways that align with your goals.
- Pay attention to how others view your actions and adjust as needed.
- Communicate clearly and confidently to shape perceptions.

7. Simplify Complex Decisions
- Break down big decisions into smaller, manageable parts.
- Focus on what's essential and eliminate distractions.
- Use decision-making frameworks to clarify your options.

8. Invest in Lifelong Learning
- Dedicate time to reading, courses, or mentorship.
- Stay updated on trends and shifts in your field or industry.
- Reflect on past successes and failures to extract lessons.

9. Act with Patience and Precision
- Avoid rushing into decisions without sufficient information.
- Wait for the right moment to take action.
- Stay disciplined and focused, even when progress feels slow.

10. Cultivate Win-Win Outcomes
- Look for ways to create mutual benefit in negotiations or collaborations.
- Approach conflicts with the goal of finding shared ground.
- Build solutions that address the needs of all parties involved.

11. Plan for the Unexpected
- Identify potential risks and plan responses in advance.
- Build redundancies into your work or processes to handle surprises.
- Test your plans with small-scale experiments to uncover blind spots.

12. Leverage Strengths—Yours and Others'
- Identify your unique skills and focus on them.
- Delegate tasks that align with others' strengths.
- Collaborate with people whose skills complement your own.

13. Stay Ahead by Spotting Trends Early
- Monitor industry developments and weak signals of change.
- Regularly discuss trends with peers or mentors to gain diverse insights.
- Adjust your strategies to align with emerging opportunities.

14. Keep Relationships Strong
- Check in regularly with key contacts, even when there's no immediate need.
- Show appreciation for others' contributions.
- Actively listen and respond thoughtfully to build rapport.

15. Execute Relentlessly
- Break projects into actionable steps and tackle them daily.
- Track progress and hold yourself accountable.
- Celebrate small wins to maintain momentum and motivation.

Pro Tip: Make Strategy a Habit

The key to mastering strategy is consistency. Integrate strategic thinking into your daily routines by using this checklist regularly. Reflect on your actions, evaluate outcomes, and adjust your approach as needed. Small, deliberate steps taken every day will compound over time, transforming your mindset and ensuring long-term success. Remember, strategy isn't a one-time exercise — it's a way of life.

Part 5: Game Theory

An AI's Guide to 100 Strategies for Mastering Decisions, Negotiations, and Human Dynamics

Introduction

Life is not random; it's a series of interconnected decisions. Every choice you make — whether in your career or relationships — is a move in a larger, dynamic game. The key difference between winning and losing is not luck but strategy. Mastering various approaches is what this book is all about.

It is your guide for navigating an intricate game, written not as a dense, academic guide but as a practical, actionable resource. Game theory is not just for economists or mathematicians; it's for anyone who wants to make better decisions, anticipate the moves of others, and thrive in the complexity of life.

Who This Book is For

This book is for every human who's ever faced a decision — or a challenge. Whether you're a business leader negotiating multi-million-dollar deals, a student looking to sharpen your critical thinking, or a parent trying to resolve household conflicts, this book has something for you.

It's also for people tired of relying on guesswork. Too often, humans make decisions based on gut feelings, emotions, or incomplete information. While instincts have their place, they are no substitute for structured, rational thinking. This book is for those who want to replace guesswork with clarity and turn chaos into strategy.

Why Read This Book

Humans are natural players in life's game, but few truly understand the rules. Game theory reveals the patterns behind choices, interactions, and outcomes. It teaches you to think ahead, recognize opportunities, and avoid common pitfalls such as emotional biases or short-term thinking.

By reading this book, you'll gain:

- **The ability to anticipate others' actions** and stay one step ahead.
- **A toolkit for resolving conflicts**, finding win-win outcomes, and managing competition.
- **Insights into human dynamics**, helping you decode behavior and motivations.

Once you learn to think like a strategist, you'll find prospects hidden in plain sight. You'll see obstacles not as barriers but as puzzles waiting to be solved.

Most importantly, this book will help you think differently — playing the game of life smarter, with purpose, precision and confidence.

Are you ready to begin? The game awaits.

Section I: Foundations of Strategic Thinking

Before mastering the complex strategies of decision-making and negotiation, you must first understand the foundational principles that underpin all strategic thought. This section introduces you to core concepts such as cooperation, competition, and equilibrium, which form the bedrock of game theory. These are not abstract ideas; they are tools you can apply daily to navigate challenges, build trust, and predict outcomes with greater confidence. By mastering these foundations, you'll develop a mindset that prepares you for every decision ahead.

Chapter 1: The Prisoner's Dilemma – Cooperation vs. Defection

Why This Matters

The Prisoner's Dilemma is more than an abstract puzzle — it's a mirror for real-world conflicts where trust, risk, and self-interest collide. Whether negotiating a business deal, resolving a team conflict, or making choices in competitive markets, you will face situations where you must decide whether to cooperate for mutual gain or prioritize self-protection. This dilemma teaches you to think critically about the ripple effects of your decisions and helps you avoid falling into traps driven by fear or greed.

The concept was first developed in the early 1950s by Merrill Flood and Melvin Dresher at RAND Corporation, and later formalized by mathematician Albert W. Tucker, who created the now-famous "prisoners" scenario to illustrate the problem (Tucker, 1950). Despite its mathematical origins, the dilemma resonates deeply with everyday human interactions, showing how even rational individuals often fail to cooperate, even when it's in their mutual interest.

Consider this: life's most valuable opportunities often rely on cooperation. Partnerships, collaborations, and long-term relationships are built on trust. But trust is fragile, and the fear of betrayal can push people into defensive, short-term thinking. By understanding the dynamics of the Prisoner's Dilemma, you'll learn when it's worth risking cooperation — and when to safeguard yourself against potential betrayal.

This concept also matters because it reveals a critical truth about human behavior: people are not always rational. Fear, pride, and greed can drive decisions that undermine long-term benefits. By recognizing these tendencies in yourself and others, you can develop strategies to encourage cooperation and build trust, even in competitive environments. Mastering this principle will help you move beyond reactive choices and toward proactive, strategic thinking.

How It Works

The classic Prisoner's Dilemma involves two suspects arrested for a crime. They are separated and offered a deal:

- **If both stay silent** (cooperate), they each get a light sentence.
- **If one betrays the other** (defects) while the other stays silent, the betrayer goes free while the silent party gets the maximum sentence.
- **If both betray** (defect), they each receive a moderate sentence.

The catch? Each prisoner must decide without knowing what the other will do. The logical choice is often to defect since betrayal avoids the worst-case scenario, yet mutual cooperation yields the best collective outcome.

This tension between short-term self-interest and long-term collaboration is everywhere: should companies compete or form alliances? Should nations cooperate on global challenges, or prioritize their own interests? For example, during the Cold War, the arms race mirrored this dilemma. Both the U.S. and the Soviet Union faced the choice of stockpiling weapons (defecting) or disarming (cooperating). While disarming would have been mutually beneficial, the fear of betrayal kept both nations in a costly arms race (Schelling, 1960).

Real-Life Example

In 1971, Coca-Cola and Pepsi faced a version of the Prisoner's Dilemma. Both wanted to dominate the soda market and had the option to either reduce advertising (cooperate) or aggressively outspend each other (defect). They both chose to "defect," launching massive advertising campaigns that ultimately hurt their profit margins while maintaining their competitive positions. If both companies had cooperated by reducing advertising, they could have saved billions while still retaining market share.

1. **Scenario Analysis:** Imagine you are negotiating a salary raise with your employer. Write two possible outcomes: one where you cooperate with their constraints (e.g. budget limits) and one where you "defect" by threatening to leave the company. Which strategy creates the best long-term outcome?

2. **Analyze a Dilemma:** Think of a recent situation where you had to choose between self-interest and mutual cooperation (e.g. splitting work on a group project). Which choice did you make, and how did it impact the relationship or outcome?

3. **Simulate the Dilemma:** Pair up with a friend and play out the Prisoner's Dilemma using a simple scoring system (e.g. points for cooperation vs. betrayal). Track how trust evolves over repeated rounds.

Key Takeaway

The Prisoner's Dilemma reveals that while short-term self-interest often feels safe, long-term success usually comes from fostering trust and collaboration. Knowing when to cooperate and when to protect yourself is the cornerstone of strategic thinking.

Chapter 2: Tit-for-Tat – The Power of Reciprocity

Why This Matters

The "Tit-for-Tat" strategy, first popularized through the work of political scientist Robert Axelrod, demonstrates the power of reciprocity in repeated interactions (Axelrod, 1984). Axelrod's ground-breaking tournaments of the Iterated Prisoner's Dilemma revealed that this simple strategy — cooperate first, then mirror your opponent's actions — outperformed many complex alternatives.

This strategy isn't just about fairness; it's a blueprint for cooperation. By mirroring the behavior of others—rewarding cooperation and responding firmly to betrayal — Tit-for-Tat establishes an environment where trust can grow. It shows that kindness isn't weakness, and retaliation isn't malice; they are tools for maintaining balance in relationships.

The importance of this strategy goes beyond personal relationships. In business negotiations, team dynamics, or even international diplomacy, Tit-for-Tat prevents exploitation and rewards fair play. When both sides know their actions will be reciprocated, it creates a natural incentive to cooperate.

How It Works

The principles of Tit-for-Tat align with findings in behavioral psychology and evolutionary biology, where mutual reciprocity is observed as a mechanism for fostering cooperation (Axelrod, 1984; Ostrom, 2010).

The essence of Tit-for-Tat is simple:

1. **Start Cooperatively.** Always begin by extending trust or goodwill.

2. **Reciprocate Behavior.** If the other party cooperates, continue to cooperate. If they betray, immediately mirror their betrayal.

3. **Forgive Quickly.** Once the other party returns to cooperation, do the same. Tit-for-Tat does not hold grudges.

This strategy proved remarkably successful in Robert Axelrod's *Evolution of Cooperation* (1984), where he organized tournaments inviting participants to submit strategies for repeated Prisoner's Dilemma games. Among the many complex entries, the simple Tit-for-Tat strategy consistently outperformed others. Its secret lies in its fairness and clarity—it encourages cooperation without risking prolonged exploitation.

Real-Life Example

Consider the Cold War between the United States and the Soviet Union. During this prolonged period of tension, there were numerous instances of Tit-for-Tat dynamics. One notable example was the Strategic Arms Limitation Talks (SALT). Each side would make measured concessions, such as reducing a particular class of weapons, in exchange for reciprocal concessions from the other. By mirroring actions, both sides managed to avoid full-scale escalation while maintaining balance.

Exercises

1. **Reciprocity in Action:** Identify a situation where you responded to someone's behavior (positive or negative). Reflect on whether your response mirrored theirs and how it influenced the outcome. Write down how Tit-for-Tat could have improved the interaction.

2. **Simulated Strategy:** Pair up with a friend and play a repeated Prisoner's Dilemma game (using simple points for cooperation or defection). Use the Tit-for-Tat strategy and observe how trust evolves over multiple rounds. Compare your results to other strategies, such as always cooperating or always betraying.

3. **Plan a Reciprocity Strategy:** Think of a current relationship—personal or professional—where trust needs to be strengthened. Write a short plan outlining how you can implement Tit-for-Tat principles to encourage mutual cooperation.

Tit-for-Tat teaches that trust and fairness are not weaknesses but strengths. By starting with cooperation, responding to betrayal, and forgiving quickly, you create an environment where collaboration thrives and exploitation diminishes. Reciprocity is the foundation of lasting relationships and mutual success.

Chapter 3: Dominant Strategies – Choosing the Best Option

Why This Matters

At the heart of every decision lies a choice: which option will give you the best outcome? The concept of dominant strategies simplifies this process by identifying the choice that works best regardless of what others do. In game theory, a dominant strategy is one that always provides the best result for a player, no matter how the opposing player acts.

Why does this matter in real life? Because decision-making often involves uncertainty about what others will do. Dominant strategies eliminate that uncertainty, giving you a clear, logical path forward. By mastering this concept, you can avoid overanalyzing complex scenarios and focus on the options that deliver consistent results.

Dominant strategies also teach you something profound about competition: sometimes, the best move isn't about what the opponent does—it's about your own priorities. Whether in business, personal negotiations, or social interactions, understanding dominant strategies can help you streamline your choices and achieve better outcomes with less stress.

How It Works

The concept of dominant strategies was formalized in John von Neumann and Oskar Morgenstern's foundational work, *Theory of Games and Economic Behavior* (1944). They demonstrated how dominant strategies simplify complex decision-making by providing a consistent best option, regardless of an opponent's moves.

For example, imagine you are playing a simplified pricing game with a competitor:
- If you price your product low, you capture more market share but earn less profit per unit.
- If you price it high, you earn more profit per unit but risk losing customers to your competitor.

Here's the twist: if your competitor always prices their product higher than yours, choosing a low price becomes your dominant strategy because it guarantees you a larger market share, regardless of their decision.

Dominant strategies work best in games where your choices directly influence outcomes, like business pricing, product launches, or even personal financial decisions. However, in some situations, there may be no dominant strategy —meaning the best choice depends on the actions of others. Recognizing when you do or don't have a dominant strategy is just as valuable as knowing how to use one.

Real-Life Example

The use of dominant strategies in the fast-food industry mirrors insights from *Thinking Strategically* by Avinash Dixit and Barry Nalebuff (1991), which examines how companies identify and execute their most advantageous options.

A famous example of a dominant strategy comes from the fast-food industry. McDonald's often chooses to open locations in high-traffic areas, like city centers or highways, even if competitors like Burger King or Wendy's do the same. Why? Because opening in high-traffic areas guarantees steady customer flow regardless of what the competition does.

Contrast this with a small restaurant that might rely on avoiding competitors to survive. For McDonald's, "high-traffic locations" represent a dominant strategy—it's always a good move, no matter what others do.

In your personal life, dominant strategies might show up in simpler forms. For instance, choosing to save a portion of your income is a dominant strategy for financial stability. Regardless of whether the economy booms or busts, saving money always benefits you.

Exercises

1. **Identifying Dominant Strategies:** Think of a recent decision where you had multiple options. Write down the possible outcomes of each choice based on what others might do. Was there a dominant strategy—a choice that worked best no matter what happened?

2. **Strategic Observation:** Look at a major company's behavior (e.g. Apple). Can you identify a dominant strategy they use in their industry, such as pricing, innovation, or customer service?

3. **Simulating Dominance:** Design a simple game with a friend where each player makes decisions (e.g. setting prices, choosing investments). Identify whether dominant strategies exist in the game and test how they influence outcomes.

A dominant strategy simplifies decision-making by offering the best option regardless of external factors. When you find one, you eliminate uncertainty and focus on choices that consistently deliver success.

Chapter 4: Pareto Efficiency – Maximizing Mutual Gains

Why This Matters

In decision-making, negotiation, and resource allocation, it's easy to focus on getting the best deal for yourself. But what if there's a way to optimize outcomes for everyone involved? This is where Pareto Efficiency comes in – a concept that ensures no one can be made better off without making someone else worse off.

Pareto Efficiency matters because it helps you identify outcomes where resources are allocated in the most effective way possible. Instead of viewing situations as a zero-sum game, where one side's gain is another's loss, Pareto Efficiency encourages you to find solutions that maximize value for all parties.

In the real world, understanding Pareto Efficiency can transform the way you negotiate, collaborate, and make decisions. Whether you're dividing project responsibilities, negotiating contracts, or even making family decisions, this principle helps you recognize when you've reached an optimal outcome – and when there's still room for improvement.

How It Works

Pareto Efficiency is named after Italian economist Vilfredo Pareto, who introduced the concept in his 1906 work *Manual of Political Economy*. He observed that in an efficient allocation, no individual could improve their situation without disadvantaging someone else (Pareto, 1906).

Imagine a simple scenario: you and a friend are dividing a pizza. If you take seven slices and leave one slice for your friend, this allocation is not Pareto efficient – your friend could receive more without you necessarily losing much. However, if you each take four slices, the division is Pareto efficient because neither of you can get more without the other losing something.

In economics, Pareto Efficiency is used to evaluate markets, public policies, and negotiations. Consider a trade deal between two countries. If both countries adjust tariffs in a way that increases exports and consumer satisfaction without harming domestic industries, they've achieved a Pareto improvement. However, once both countries maximize their mutual benefits, they've reached Pareto Efficiency, and further changes would harm one side or the other.

This concept doesn't guarantee equality or fairness, but it does ensure that resources are being used in the most effective way possible for everyone involved. By striving for Pareto Efficiency, you can make decisions that maximize value and avoid unnecessary waste or conflict.

Real-Life Example

Collaborative resource allocation scenarios often align with Elinor Ostrom's findings in *Governing the Commons*, which discusses how groups manage shared resources effectively to achieve Pareto-efficient outcomes (Ostrom, 2010).

Consider a workplace scenario where two departments are sharing a limited budget. One department, focused on marketing, needs funds for an upcoming campaign, while the other, focused on operations, needs resources for equipment upgrades. Initially, each department fights for a larger share of the budget, leaving resources poorly allocated.

Through collaboration, they discover a Pareto improvement: allocating slightly more funds to marketing for the campaign while giving operations just enough for a critical upgrade. Both departments achieve their goals without harming the other. Once this balance is struck, the budget allocation becomes Pareto efficient, as any further adjustments would hurt one department's effectiveness.

Exercises

1. **Identifying Pareto Efficiency:** Think of a negotiation or collaboration you've recently participated in. Write down the final outcome and assess whether it was Pareto efficient. Could one party have gained more without harming the other?
2. **Finding Pareto Improvements:** Imagine dividing tasks for a group project. Propose one or two adjustments to the division of work that could improve productivity for everyone involved. Did you find a Pareto improvement?
3. **Practical Negotiation Exercise:** Role-play a negotiation with a friend. Divide a fictional resource (e.g., money, time, or materials) and try to reach a Pareto efficient outcome. Discuss the process and what changes led to the best results.

Key Takeaway

Pareto Efficiency ensures that no one can gain more without someone else losing out. By focusing on mutual benefits and optimal outcomes, you can maximize value in negotiations, collaborations, and decision-making.

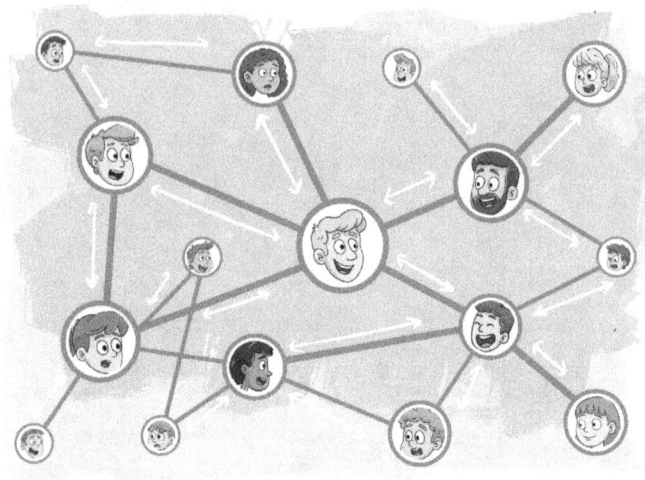

Chapter 5: Nash Equilibrium – Finding Stability in Structures

Why This Matters

Life is filled with situations where the choices of others influence your decisions, and vice versa. In these scenarios, you often seek a stable outcome—one where no one can gain more by unilaterally changing their strategy. This is the essence of the Nash Equilibrium, a cornerstone of game theory developed by mathematician John Nash.

His revolutionary contribution to game theory earned him the Nobel Prize in Economics in 1994. His concept of Nash Equilibrium, first presented in his 1950 paper *Equilibrium Points in n-Person Games*, showed how stability in decision-making can emerge from rational individual behavior (Nash, 1950).

Nash Equilibrium matters because it explains the balance point in competitive and cooperative settings, from business rivalries to personal relationships. When all participants in a system are making optimal choices based on the actions of others, no one has a reason to deviate. This concept isn't just theoretical; it applies to real-world markets, political negotiations, and even social interactions.

By understanding Nash Equilibrium, you can better anticipate the behavior of others, design strategies that hold steady under scrutiny, and avoid futile efforts to shift outcomes when the structure is already stable. It's a tool for finding harmony in complexity and avoiding wasted effort in unstable dynamics.

How It Works

The practical applications of Nash Equilibrium have been explored extensively, particularly in Schelling's *The Strategy of Conflict* (1960), which highlighted its relevance in areas such as arms control and political negotiations.

A Nash Equilibrium occurs when all players in a game choose strategies that maximize their outcomes, given the strategies of others. No player can improve their position by changing their strategy alone.

Imagine two companies, A and B, competing in the same market. Each has two choices: price their product low (to gain market share) or high (to maximize profit margins). If both choose low prices, they split the market but earn less profit. If both choose high prices, they maintain profitability but risk losing customers to competitors. The equilibrium emerges when both companies price their products at a point where neither can gain more by unilaterally lowering or raising their prices.

Nash Equilibrium isn't always perfect or fair — it may not maximize collective gains, as in the Prisoner's Dilemma. However, it offers stability, making it critical for understanding how decisions evolve in interconnected systems.

Real-Life Example

The concept of Nash Equilibrium plays out visibly in the ride-sharing industry, where companies like Uber and Lyft compete for customers. Both firms offer dynamic pricing, adjusting fares based on demand. If Uber lowers its prices too much, it may gain market share but lose profitability. If Lyft raises its prices, it risks losing riders to Uber. Over time, both companies settle into a pricing strategy that reflects a Nash Equilibrium — neither can improve their position without prompting the other to react.

On a personal level, consider a household decision where two family members must decide whether to cook dinner or order takeout. If both wait for the other to cook, they go hungry. If both choose takeout, they spend more than necessary. The equilibrium might be that one person cooks while the other cleans — an arrangement where neither has a better alternative given the other's choice.

Exercises

1. **Identify Equilibriums in Everyday Life:** Think of a situation where two or more people (or groups) made decisions that influenced one another (e.g. deciding on vacation plans, team roles, or splitting a bill). Was there a Nash Equilibrium where no one had a better option?
2. **Simulate a Game:** Create a simple game with two players and two choices (e.g. high or low effort on a shared project). Assign points to each outcome. Play the game and identify whether a Nash Equilibrium emerges.
3. **Analyze Business Competition:** Choose two competing businesses in your area (e.g. coffee shops, gyms, or restaurants). How do their pricing, services, or promotions reflect a stable strategy where neither benefits from unilaterally changing their approach?

Key Takeaway

The Nash Equilibrium provides a stable framework for understanding decisions in competitive and cooperative scenarios. By identifying these equilibriums, you can predict behavior, design stable strategies, and avoid wasted effort trying to shift outcomes that are already balanced.

Chapter 6: Zero-Sum Games – Succeeding at Someone Else's Expense

Why This Matters

In some scenarios, success doesn't come from collaboration or mutual gains — it comes at the expense of others. These are zero-sum games, where one player's gain is exactly balanced by another's loss. Understanding zero-sum dynamics is essential in highly competitive environments, such as auctions, sports, and adversarial negotiations.

Zero-sum games matter because they strip away the possibility of win-win solutions. They teach you to focus sharply on tactics, anticipate your opponent's moves, and maximize your advantage. Unlike non-zero-sum games, where cooperation might yield better outcomes, these situations require you to adopt a combative mindset and fight for every inch of ground.

How It Works

Zero-sum games were a central focus of von Neumann and Morgenstern's *Theory of Games and Economic Behavior* (1944). Their work demonstrated how these competitive dynamics apply to markets, auctions, and even military strategy.

Zero-sum games are defined by the rule that one player's gain equals another's loss. If you win $10 in a poker hand, someone else loses $10. If a team wins a soccer match, the other team loses. There's no middle ground or shared victory.

A classic zero-sum scenario is a bidding war for a limited resource. Imagine two companies bidding for the same piece of land. Every dollar one company bids above the other is a dollar they lose in profit. The goal is not just to win the auction but to win while minimizing losses—a delicate balance of aggression and caution.

Zero-sum games are often used in military strategy, where one side's territory gains are the other's losses. The principles also apply in smaller-scale settings, such as competitive job markets, where one candidate's hiring often means another candidate's rejection.

Real-Life Example

The adversarial nature of zero-sum scenarios aligns with insights from Thomas Schelling's *The Strategy of Conflict* (1960), which explored high-stakes competitions.

In the world of professional sports, zero-sum dynamics are unavoidable. Consider the FIFA World Cup final. The stakes are clear: one team will lift the trophy, and the other will go home defeated. Every goal scored by one team directly reduces the chances of the other team winning.

In business, zero-sum scenarios often occur during contract negotiations, particularly when resources are scarce. For instance, two companies might compete for an exclusive supplier agreement. If one company secures the deal, the other loses access to the supplier, leaving them scrambling for alternatives.

Exercises

1. **Spot Zero-Sum Situations:** Reflect on a competitive situation you've experienced (e.g., playing a game, applying for a job, or negotiating for limited resources). Was it a zero-sum game? How did you approach it?
2. **Simulated Competition:** Play a zero-sum game with a friend (e.g. a simple bidding war). Analyze the strategies you used to maximize your gains and minimize your losses.
3. **Anticipating Opponent Moves:** Choose a real-world zero-sum scenario (e.g. two companies competing for market share). Predict how each side might act and devise a strategy that one side could use to outmaneuver the other.

Key Takeaway

Zero-sum games are defined by competition, not collaboration. Mastering these situations requires sharp tactics, anticipation, and an unwavering focus on maximizing your gains while minimizing your opponent's.

Chapter 7: Non-Zero-Sum Games – Shared Triumphs through Working Together

Why This Matters

Unlike zero-sum games, where one player's gain is another's loss, **non-zero-sum games** open the door to mutual success. These situations represent the reality of most human interactions: cooperation can create outcomes where everyone benefits, and competition is not always necessary.

The foundation of non-zero-sum games was first explored by John von Neumann and Oskar Morgenstern in their groundbreaking work *Theory of Games and Economic Behavior* (1944). Later, Robert Axelrod's research on cooperative strategies in *The Evolution of Cooperation* (1984) demonstrated how reciprocity and mutual benefit drive success in these scenarios.

Non-zero-sum dynamics are found everywhere—from business partnerships to global climate agreements. Understanding how to navigate these scenarios enables you to focus on building alliances, sharing resources, and pursuing outcomes that grow the total "pie" instead of fighting over limited slices.

Mastering non-zero-sum games changes how you approach relationships, negotiations, and problem-solving. Instead of seeing others as rivals, you'll learn to identify opportunities for collaboration, even in competitive settings. This mindset fosters creativity, trust, and long-term success.

How It Works

Non-zero-sum games occur when the total benefits available can grow through cooperation. A classic example is trade: two nations can exchange goods and services to improve their overall economic well-being, rather than competing over limited resources.

Elinor Ostrom, in her work *Governing the Commons* (2010), showed how groups that cooperatively manage shared resources, such as water or fisheries, often achieve non-zero-sum outcomes. By establishing trust and clear communication, these groups increase the overall value of their shared assets, benefiting everyone involved.

Consider a scenario where two companies operate in overlapping markets. Instead of undercutting each other on price (zero-sum behavior), they could collaborate to create complementary products, driving overall demand higher. This approach benefits both parties, as well as their customers.

The key to non-zero-sum games is recognizing interdependence. Success often relies on building trust, aligning incentives, and communicating effectively. However, these scenarios can also involve risks — if one side defects or betrays the agreement, mutual benefits collapse. Thus, managing trust and incentives becomes critical.

Real-Life Example

A powerful example of a non-zero-sum game is the Paris Climate Agreement. Countries worldwide agreed to reduce greenhouse gas emissions for the benefit of the planet. By cooperating, nations collectively address a global threat, creating a safer environment for future generations.

However, this collaboration requires trust. If one country "defects" by failing to meet its commitments, others may lose faith and withdraw. The agreement succeeds only when all parties work toward the shared goal. This dynamic highlights the potential — and fragility — of non-zero-sum games.

On a smaller scale, imagine two rival coffee shops on the same street. Instead of battling over customers, they could partner to organize a neighborhood coffee festival, attracting more visitors to the area. By working together, they create a win-win situation, increasing their profits and community engagement.

Exercises

1. **Identify Non-Zero-Sum Opportunities:** Think of a current challenge in your life where you see competition (e.g. at work or in your community). Write down one way collaboration with others could create mutual benefits.
2. **Analyze a Partnership:** Choose a famous business or political partnership (e.g. Apple and app developers, or international trade agreements). How does it represent a non-zero-sum game? What risks and benefits were involved?
3. **Simulate Cooperation:** With a friend, design a simple non-zero-sum game (e.g. combining resources to complete a task). Track how your strategies evolve as you work toward maximizing shared outcomes.

Key Takeaway

Non-zero-sum games reveal that success doesn't always require defeating others. By fostering collaboration, building trust, and aligning goals, you can create outcomes where everyone benefits — a hallmark of strategic and creative thinking.

Chapter 8: Backward Induction – Thinking Ahead, Acting Backward

Why This Matters

Some decisions require thinking far into the future, but planning ahead without a clear process can feel overwhelming. Backward induction, a key principle of game theory, provides a structured way to navigate complex scenarios. By starting with your desired outcome and working backward, you can create a roadmap that guides your present actions.

This method is invaluable in sequential games, where one player's move influences the next. Backward induction ensures that every step aligns with your long-term goals, whether you're negotiating, strategizing, or solving everyday challenges. As John von Neumann and Oskar Morgenstern demonstrated in *Theory of Games and Economic Behavior* (1944), backward induction is a cornerstone for solving sequential games where foresight is essential.

In real life, backward induction matters because it prevents you from being blindsided by short-term obstacles. It's the key to anticipating challenges, managing resources wisely, and always staying one step ahead.

How It Works

Backward induction works by analyzing the final stage of a decision-making process and identifying the best choice at that point. Once the optimal outcome is clear, you move one step back and determine what decision will lead you there. This process continues until you reach the starting point, giving you a complete plan from beginning to end.

For example, in chess, a skilled player doesn't just focus on their next move—they visualize the endgame and work backward to determine the sequence of moves that will achieve victory. Similarly, backward induction is used in negotiations to anticipate the other party's final position and adjust your approach in earlier stages to steer the outcome in your favor.

Robert Gibbons' *A Primer in Game Theory* (1992) explains how backward induction is especially useful in dynamic scenarios, such as auctions or project planning, where each decision builds on the previous one. It helps players avoid reactive choices by focusing on the big picture.

Real-Life Example

Backward induction is commonly used in the world of project management. Imagine a tech company planning a product launch. The desired outcome is to release a high-quality product on time. To achieve this, the company works backward:

Final stage: Product is launched.

Prior stage: Final testing and quality assurance must be completed.

Before that: Marketing materials must be ready.

Earlier stage: Core features must be developed and debugged.

Each step depends on the success of the previous one, so the team's decisions at the earliest stages are guided by their ultimate goal. If deadlines are tight, backward induction ensures resources are prioritized for tasks that directly impact the launch.

Another example comes from parenting. Imagine you want your child to develop good study habits by the time they reach high school. Using backward induction, you might start with the desired outcome—self-motivation—and work backward to implement earlier steps, such as introducing small, consistent study routines in elementary school and rewarding discipline along the way.

Exercises

1. **Plan Backward from a Goal:** Identify a personal or professional goal you want to achieve in six months. Write down the final result, then list the steps needed to get there, starting with the last stage and working backward to your present position.

2. **Apply Backward Induction to a Problem:** Think of a decision where multiple steps are involved (e.g. planning a vacation or managing a project). Use backward induction to create a plan and identify which initial actions are most critical.

3. **Analyze a Sequential Game:** With a friend, play a turn-based strategy game (e.g., tic-tac-toe or a card game). Practice using backward induction to predict your friend's future moves and adjust your current strategy accordingly.

Key Takeaway

Backward induction helps you think ahead by working backward from your desired outcome. By aligning your present actions with future goals, you can anticipate challenges, avoid short-term distractions, and create a clear path to success.

If we both commit to the main product, we can change the market.

But what if you drop out? I'd be left with nothing.

Chapter 9: The Stag Hunt – Risk and Reward in Collaboration

Why This Matters

Collaboration often requires trust, but what happens when that trust wavers? The Stag Hunt, a game theory concept dating back to Jean-Jacques Rousseau, explores this dilemma. It describes a situation where two players must decide whether to cooperate for a large reward (hunting a stag) or act alone for a smaller, guaranteed payoff (hunting rabbits).

The Stag Hunt teaches us how to weigh the risks and rewards of teamwork. If both players cooperate, they achieve a significant reward. However, if one defects and pursues a smaller gain, the cooperative effort collapses, leaving the other player worse off. As Brian Skyrms explains in *The Stag Hunt and the Evolution of Social Structure* (2004), this scenario provides profound insights into trust, risk, and the conditions required for successful collaboration.

In real life, Stag Hunt dynamics appear in business partnerships, team projects, and even international agreements. By mastering this concept, you'll learn when to trust others, how to reduce risks, and how to align incentives for mutual success.

How It Works

The Stag Hunt represents a coordination game where cooperation offers the highest payoff, but only if all participants stay committed. If either party abandons the effort, the outcome for the remaining participants is significantly worse than if they had pursued a smaller, individual reward.

Here's an example: Two hunters are in the woods. They can work together to catch a stag (a difficult task requiring full cooperation) or separately hunt rabbits (easier but less rewarding). The payoff matrix looks like this:

	Partner Hunts Stag	Partner Hunts Rabbit
You Hunt Stag	Large Reward (Cooperate)	No Reward (Defection by Partner)
You Hunt Rabbit	Small Reward (Self-Reliance)	Small Reward (Both Defect)

This structure mirrors real-world dilemmas where the best outcomes depend on trust and shared commitment. However, if there's uncertainty about the other party's intentions, players may default to the safer option, sacrificing potential gains.

Real-Life Example

Consider a start-up where two co-founders are deciding how to allocate their time. They can either focus on building a breakthrough product (the stag) or pursue smaller, less risky side projects (the rabbits). If both founders dedicate themselves to the product, they achieve ground-breaking success. But if one founder shifts their focus to a side project, the other's efforts are wasted, and the company falters.

The Stag Hunt's dynamics also appear in international relations. For example, nations working to combat climate change face a similar challenge. If all nations commit to reducing emissions (the stag), the planet benefits. However, if some nations defect by prioritizing short-term economic gains (the rabbit), global efforts weaken, and the cooperative goal fails.

Exercises

1. **Identify a Stag Hunt Scenario:** Reflect on a situation where you had to decide between cooperation and self-reliance. What factors influenced your choice? Did the outcome resemble a Stag Hunt dynamic?
2. **Simulate Trust in a Team Game:** Pair up with a friend and create a scenario where you can choose to cooperate for a large reward or act independently for a smaller, guaranteed payoff. Play multiple rounds and discuss how trust evolves over time.
3. **Evaluate Trust in Collaboration:** Think of a team project or partnership you've been part of. Analyze whether everyone stayed committed to the shared goal or if someone prioritized individual rewards. How did this affect the outcome?

Key Takeaway

The Stag Hunt illustrates the importance of trust and alignment in collaboration. By fostering shared commitment and reducing risks, you can achieve greater rewards through teamwork, even in uncertain situations.

References for Chapter 9

1. Skyrms, Brian. (2004). *The Stag Hunt and the Evolution of Social Structure*. Cambridge University Press.
2. Rousseau, Jean-Jacques. (1755). *Discourse on Inequality*.
3. Axelrod, Robert. (1984). *The Evolution of Cooperation*. Basic Books.

Chapter 10: The Ultimatum Scenario – Balancing Fairness and Self-Interest

Why This Matters

Negotiations often hinge on fairness. But what happens when one party offers a deal that seems objectively better than nothing yet feels unfair? The Ultimatum Game, first introduced by Werner Güth and colleagues in 1982, reveals that humans often prioritize fairness over pure self-interest. It shows how social norms, emotions, and perceptions of justice can override rational economic behavior (Güth, Schmittberger, & Schwarze, 1982).

The Ultimatum Game is a key concept in behavioral economics, where researchers like Daniel Kahneman and Amos Tversky have explored how fairness and framing influence decision-making. Their work demonstrated that humans are not purely rational actors; instead, fairness and reciprocity often dictate behavior, even when rejecting an offer leads to personal loss (Kahneman & Tversky, 1981).

Understanding the Ultimatum Scenario matters because it helps you navigate situations where emotions and perceptions of justice outweigh cold calculations. From salary negotiations to business deals, recognizing when fairness influences decisions allows you to craft proposals that others are more likely to accept—building trust and long-term relationships.

How It Works

In the Ultimatum Game, two players must divide a sum of money. The proposer suggests a split (e.g. 70/30), and the responder can either accept or reject the offer. If the responder accepts, the money is divided as proposed. If they reject it, both players walk away with nothing.

Güth et al.'s 1982 experiments revealed surprising results: offers below 30% of the total were often rejected, even though accepting them would leave the responder better off than receiving nothing. This finding contradicted traditional economic theory, which assumes that humans act purely rationally to maximize personal gain.

Further research, including Fehr and Schmidt's *Theory of Fairness, Competition, and Cooperation* (1999), expanded on this by showing that fairness considerations are deeply ingrained in human behavior. People are willing to sacrifice personal benefits to punish perceived greed or unfairness, even at significant cost to themselves.

These dynamics have real-world implications. For instance, in international trade agreements, if one nation offers terms that are perceived as exploitative, the other nation may reject the deal outright—even if both sides stand to gain. Similarly, in workplace negotiations, lowball salary offers often backfire because they undermine trust and goodwill.

Real-Life Example

Consider a freelance graphic designer negotiating a project fee. The client offers $500 for a job worth $1,000, citing budget constraints. While $500 is better than nothing, the designer rejects the offer because it feels exploitative, fearing it sets a precedent for undervaluation.

This scenario mirrors the Ultimatum Game: the designer prioritizes fairness and long-term implications over immediate financial gain. The client learns that lowball offers can backfire, forcing them to revaluate their approach to future negotiations.

On a larger scale, the Ultimatum Scenario plays out in mergers and acquisitions. When one company offers terms heavily skewed in its favor, the deal may fail—not because the other party wouldn't benefit, but because accepting such terms feels like conceding too much. Kahneman and Tversky's research highlights this rejection of perceived losses, even when the deal offers measurable gains (Kahneman & Tversky, 1981).

Exercises

1. **Analyze a Past Negotiation:** Reflect on a negotiation where fairness influenced the outcome (e.g., dividing responsibilities, splitting profits, or setting prices). Did one party reject an offer despite tangible benefits? Why?
2. **Simulate the Ultimatum Game:** Play the Ultimatum Game with a friend. Start with a sum of money or tokens and experiment with different splits. Track how often low offers are rejected and discuss how fairness influenced decisions.
3. **Apply Fairness to Strategy:** Consider a current negotiation or decision where fairness is a factor. Write down how you might balance fairness with your goals to create a proposal that's acceptable to all parties.

Key Takeaway

The Ultimatum Game demonstrates that fairness often trumps pure self-interest in decision-making. By understanding this dynamic, you can craft proposals that respect others' perceptions of equity, building trust and avoiding rejection.

Section II: Advanced Tactics for Decision-Making

Building on the foundational principles of game theory, this section dives deeper into advanced strategies that refine your decision-making skills. These concepts go beyond simple choices, addressing the complexity of dynamic environments, strategic deception, and long-term planning. Whether you're navigating competitive markets, resolving intricate disputes, or simply making high-stakes personal decisions, the tactics in this part will equip you to anticipate challenges, leverage opportunities, and achieve optimal outcomes. Each chapter introduces cutting-edge strategies backed by mathematical theory and real-world applications, ensuring you are prepared for even the most complex scenarios.

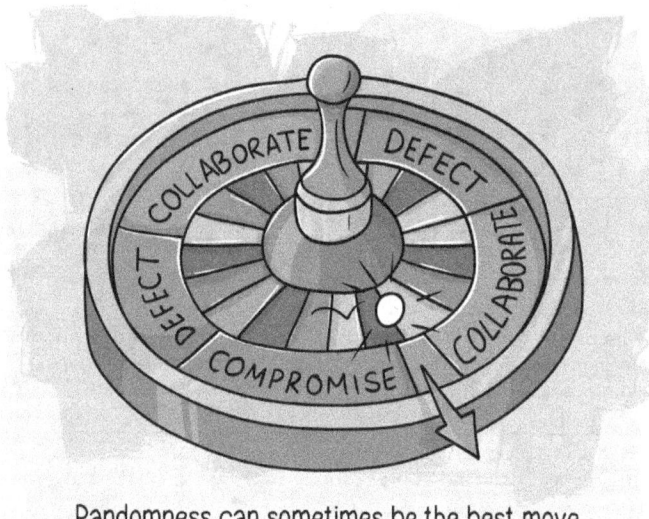

Randomness can sometimes be the best move.

Chapter 11: Mixed Tactics – Embracing Calculated Randomness

Why This Matters

In highly competitive environments, predictability can be your greatest weakness. Opponents who can anticipate your actions gain an edge. This is where mixed strategies, a concept formalized by John von Neumann and Oskar Morgenstern in *Theory of Games and Economic Behavior* (1944), come into play. Mixed strategies involve introducing calculated randomness into your decisions to keep opponents guessing.

This approach is particularly relevant in zero-sum games, negotiations, and competitive industries. When your moves are unpredictable, you prevent others from exploiting patterns in your behavior. As explained by Roger Myerson in *Game Theory: Analysis of Conflict* (1991), mixed strategies are a powerful tool for achieving balance in scenarios where no pure strategy guarantees success.

How It Works

A mixed strategy involves choosing among multiple options with a specific probability distribution. For example, in a penalty kick during soccer, the kicker might randomly decide to aim left, right, or center, ensuring the goalkeeper cannot reliably predict their choice.

Mathematically, mixed strategies often emerge as solutions in Nash Equilibriums. For example, in rock-paper-scissors, no single choice dominates, so players must randomize their actions to avoid being exploited. This randomness ensures that each opponent faces the same expected payoff regardless of their choice.

In business, mixed strategies can be used to introduce unpredictability into pricing, product releases, or marketing tactics, keeping competitors off-balance and protecting market share.

Real-Life Example

Mixed strategies were famously used by the Allied forces in World War II. To prevent German forces from anticipating their troop movements, the Allies used deception and randomized tactics, such as false radio transmissions and decoy units, to disguise their true plans for the D-Day invasion. These tactics kept the enemy guessing, enabling a successful landing in Normandy.

In everyday life, mixed strategies apply to situations like negotiating salaries. For example, alternating between aggressive and cooperative approaches prevents the other party from establishing a reliable counter-strategy.

Exercises

1. **Simulate Randomized Choices:** Play a game of rock-paper-scissors with a friend, using randomization (e.g. rolling a die) to determine your moves. Observe how unpredictability affects the game's dynamics.

2. **Apply Randomness to Strategy:** Think of a negotiation or conflict where your choices have become predictable. Write down two ways you could introduce randomness into your strategy to regain the advantage.

3. **Analyze Randomized Business Tactics:** Research a company that uses unexpected moves to outmaneuver competitors (e.g. surprise product launches or flash sales). How does this randomness enhance their position?

Key Takeaway

Mixed strategies use calculated randomness to prevent opponents from exploiting patterns in your behavior. By embracing unpredictability, you can stay one step ahead in competitive and adversarial situations.

Chapter 12: Minimax Programs – Guarding Against the Worst-Case

Why This Matters

In uncertain situations, focusing solely on the best-case scenario can leave you vulnerable. The minimax strategy, a foundational concept in game theory, focuses instead on minimizing potential losses in the worst-case scenario. Originally developed by John von Neumann, the minimax approach is widely used in competitive environments, including chess, business, and conflict resolution (*Theory of Games and Economic Behavior*, 1944).

This strategy matters because it shifts your mindset to consider the worst possible outcomes and take proactive steps to mitigate risks. As explored in Luce and Raiffa's *Games and Decisions* (1957), minimax programs allow decision-makers to navigate high-stakes situations by prioritizing safety without sacrificing opportunity.

How It Works

The minimax strategy involves analyzing all possible outcomes and focusing on the one with the least favorable payoff. By choosing a move that minimizes your maximum loss, you create a safety net that ensures stability, even in worst-case scenarios.

Consider a simple example: A company is bidding for a contract. While they could offer an aggressive bid to maximize profits, this approach risks being undercut by competitors. Instead, using minimax logic, they might choose a moderate bid that reduces potential losses if competitors bid lower.

Minimax is particularly useful in zero-sum games, where one player's gain equals the other's loss. In such cases, preparing for the worst-case scenario ensures that your opponent cannot exploit your weaknesses.

Real-Life Example

The Cuban Missile Crisis of 1962 is a classic illustration of the minimax strategy. Facing a potential nuclear conflict, U.S. President John F. Kennedy and Soviet Premier Nikita Khrushchev both sought to avoid catastrophic outcomes. Kennedy's decision to implement a naval blockade, rather than launching a full-scale attack, minimized the risk of nuclear escalation while maintaining pressure on the Soviets. This calculated move exemplified minimax thinking, balancing assertiveness with caution to prevent the worst-case scenario.

In a business context, minimax is commonly applied in investment strategies. For example, portfolio diversification reduces the potential for catastrophic losses by spreading risk across different asset classes. Even if one investment performs poorly, the overall portfolio remains stable.

Exercises

1. **Apply Minimax Thinking to a Decision:** Identify a current challenge where the worst-case scenario could have significant consequences (e.g., launching a project, negotiating a deal). Write down the minimax strategy you could use to mitigate risks.

2. **Analyze a Historical Event:** Research a historical conflict or negotiation where leaders used minimax strategies to avoid disastrous outcomes (e.g., the Cuban Missile Crisis or trade wars). What steps did they take to guard against the worst-case scenario?

3. **Simulate a Game:** Play a zero-sum game like chess or tic-tac-toe. Focus on minimizing your losses rather than maximizing your gains. Reflect on how this approach changes your decision-making process.

Key Takeaway

The minimax strategy helps you guard against worst-case scenarios by prioritizing safety and stability in decision-making. By minimizing potential losses, you can navigate uncertainty with confidence.

Chapter 13: Commitment Devices – Strengthening Your Resolve

In situations requiring decisive action, distractions or temptations can weaken your resolve. A commitment device eliminates alternative choices, forcing you to follow through on your decision. This concept, popularized by Thomas Schelling in *The Strategy of Conflict* (1960), demonstrates how removing options can strengthen your position and improve outcomes.

Commitment devices are essential for personal discipline, negotiations, and leadership. By limiting your future flexibility, you signal seriousness and prevent second-guessing. As explored in Elster's *Ulysses and the Sirens* (1979), commitment devices are like Ulysses tying himself to the mast: they ensure you stay focused, even when external factors try to pull you off course.

How It Works

Commitment devices work by creating constraints that lock you into a specific course of action. These constraints can be physical (e.g. locking your phone away to focus on work) or social (e.g. making a public declaration of your goals).

In game theory, commitment devices are powerful tools for shaping expectations and influencing others. For example, a company announcing an irreversible product launch date signals to competitors and customers that it's fully committed to delivering on time.

Real-Life Example

One famous example is Hernán Cortés' conquest of the Aztec Empire in 1519. Upon arriving in Mexico, Cortés ordered his ships to be burned, leaving no option for retreat. This dramatic commitment device motivated his troops to fight with greater determination, as failure meant certain death.

In everyday life, commitment devices are commonly used to achieve personal goals. For example, setting up automatic savings deductions from your pay check eliminates the temptation to spend, ensuring consistent financial progress.

Exercises

1. **Create a Commitment Device:** Identify a goal you've struggled to achieve (e.g. exercising regularly, saving money). Write down one commitment device you could implement to ensure follow-through.
2. **Analyze a Historical Example:** Research a historical leader or event where commitment devices were used to strengthen resolve (e.g. Cortés burning his ships). How did this strategy impact the outcome?
3. **Apply Commitments to Negotiations:** Think of a negotiation scenario where signaling commitment could strengthen your position. Write down the steps you could take to remove alternative options and enhance your credibility.

Key Takeaway

Commitment devices lock you into a specific course of action, removing distractions and demonstrating resolve. By eliminating alternatives, you can stay focused and signal strength in negotiations and decision-making.

Chapter 14: Schelling Points – Unspoken Agreements in Coordination

Schelling Point

Why This Matters

Coordination can be challenging when communication is impossible or limited. In such scenarios, people often rely on Schelling Points, or natural focal points, to align their actions. Introduced by Nobel laureate Thomas Schelling in *The Strategy of Conflict* (1960), Schelling Points explain how humans intuitively gravitate toward common solutions in the absence of explicit agreements.

This concept is essential for decision-making in uncertain environments, where clarity is scarce, and alignment depends on shared expectations. Understanding Schelling Points can help you predict others' behavior, solve coordination problems, and create strategies that leverage natural focal points to your advantage.

How It Works

A Schelling Point is a solution that people tend to choose in the absence of communication because it feels natural, special, or prominent. For example, if two people are told to meet in New York City without specifying a location, many will choose Grand Central Terminal because it's a well-known, central landmark.

Schelling Points emerge from shared cultural knowledge, geography, or intuitive reasoning. They can be used to solve coordination games where players must align their choices to achieve success. For example, if two companies want to set industry standards but cannot negotiate directly, they may both adopt widely used practices as the "natural" choice.

Real-Life Example

One famous application of Schelling Points occurred during the Cold War. Schelling himself analyzed nuclear deterrence strategies, noting how certain actions (e.g., stationing troops at critical borders) served as focal points for maintaining stability. These strategies sent clear, implicit signals to opponents without direct communication.

In a simpler example, think about splitting a restaurant bill among friends. Without discussion, people often default to evenly splitting the total, as it feels like the "fair" choice – a Schelling Point that avoids unnecessary debate.

Exercises

1. **Identify a Schelling Point:** Think of a situation where you coordinated with someone without explicit communication (e.g., choosing a meeting place or resolving a conflict). What natural focal point guided your decision?

2. **Simulate a Coordination Game:** With a friend, play a game where you must independently pick a number between 1 and 10. The goal is to match their choice without discussing it beforehand. Reflect on how shared knowledge or intuition influenced your choices.

3. **Apply Schelling Points Strategically:** Identify a negotiation or business decision where coordination is required. Write down one way you could use Schelling Points to align expectations or create agreement without direct communication.

Key Takeaway

Schelling Points help solve coordination problems by providing intuitive focal points for decision-making. By understanding and leveraging these natural alignments, you can navigate uncertainty and foster collaboration.

Chapter 15: Shapley Value – Fair Divisions in Complex Situations

Why This Matters

When multiple players contribute to a shared outcome, how do you fairly divide the rewards? The Shapley Value, developed by Lloyd Shapley in 1953, provides a systematic solution to this problem. It calculates each player's contribution to the overall success and ensures equitable divisions based on their input.

This concept is crucial in negotiations, resource allocation, and teamwork. By applying the Shapley Value, you can resolve disputes, design fair agreements, and foster trust in collaborative settings. Its mathematical precision ensures that everyone receives their due share, preventing resentment or feelings of unfairness.

How It Works

The Shapley Value assigns a value to each participant based on their marginal contribution to every possible coalition. Imagine three employees collaborate on a project, contributing different skills. The Shapley Value calculates the value added by each individual in various combinations, ensuring the reward reflects their unique contributions.

This method is widely used in cooperative game theory and real-world applications like profit-sharing, political coalitions, and even resource management. Shapley's approach ensures fairness while accounting for the complexity of group dynamics (*Contributions to the Theory of Games*, 1953).

Real-Life Example

Consider a start-up with three co-founders: one provides capital, another develops the product, and the third handles marketing. The company's success relies on all three, but their contributions are unequal. Applying the Shapley Value helps calculate each founder's fair share of profits based on the value they bring to the venture.

The Shapley Value also plays a role in international relations. For example, when countries collaborate on climate change initiatives, this method can help determine each nation's fair contribution to shared goals, balancing factors like GDP, emissions, and technological capabilities.

Exercises

1. **Calculate the Shapley Value:** Create a scenario with three contributors to a shared project (e.g. a group assignment or business venture). Assign values to their contributions and calculate a fair division using the Shapley Value formula.
2. **Apply Fairness in Real Life:** Think of a situation where you divided resources or rewards among multiple participants. How could the Shapley Value have guided a fairer allocation?
3. **Simulate Teamwork:** Form a group with friends and collaborate on a simple task (e.g. assembling a puzzle or brainstorming ideas). Use the Shapley Value to evaluate each member's contribution and decide how to allocate credit or rewards.

Key Takeaway

The Shapley Value ensures fair divisions by considering each participant's unique contributions. By applying this method, you can foster trust, resolve disputes, and create equitable outcomes in collaborative efforts.

Chapter 16: Bluffing and Signaling – The Art of Deception

Why This Matters

In strategic situations, the ability to mislead opponents or convey key information without direct statements can create a significant advantage. Bluffing and signaling are core tactics in game theory that help you manipulate perceptions, sow doubt, and force opponents to act based on incomplete or misleading information.

Bluffing and signaling are widely used in poker, negotiations, and even military strategy. As explored by Thomas Schelling in *The Strategy of Conflict* (1960), signaling allows players to send messages, whether truthful or deceptive, to influence others' decisions. Mastering these tactics enables you to disguise weaknesses, amplify strengths, and guide opponents into making suboptimal choices.

How It Works

- **Bluffing:** Bluffing involves presenting false or exaggerated information to mislead others. In a negotiation, for instance, you might claim to have alternative offers to pressure your opponent into making a better deal.
- **Signaling:** Signaling involves sending credible messages, either truthful or calculated, to influence others' beliefs. For a signal to be effective, it must be costly or risky enough that it wouldn't be sent unless it were genuine. For example, a luxury brand signaling quality through high prices and exclusive marketing relies on the fact that low-quality brands couldn't afford the same tactics.

Bluffing and signaling are often intertwined. While bluffing works by exploiting uncertainty, signaling works by reducing it. Both require careful calibration: bluffing too aggressively risks exposure, while ineffective signaling fails to persuade.

Real-Life Example

In 1995, Microsoft famously bluffed its way into dominating the browser market. At the time, Netscape Navigator was the leading browser. Microsoft signaled its intention to develop a competing product – Internet Explorer – but exaggerated its readiness to launch, creating uncertainty for Netscape. The bluff forced Netscape to accelerate its development cycle, leading to rushed decisions and a loss of market dominance. Microsoft's actual product launch came later, but the psychological pressure they applied helped secure their position.

Bluffing and signaling also play critical roles in poker. For example, a player with a weak hand might bet aggressively to create the illusion of strength, forcing opponents to fold. Similarly, signaling appears in job interviews, where candidates use credentials, experience, or even attire to signal competence and reliability to potential employers.

Exercises

1. **Practice Bluffing:** Play a game of poker or a similar strategy game. Practice bluffing in low-risk situations to observe how opponents react. Reflect on how effective your bluffs were and why.
2. **Analyze Effective Signals:** Identify a product or service that uses signaling to convey quality or reliability (e.g., a luxury brand or a certification). How do these signals influence customer perceptions?
3. **Apply Signaling to Negotiations:** Think of a negotiation or decision where signaling could improve your position. Write down one way to use a credible signal to strengthen your case.

Key Takeaway

Bluffing and signaling are powerful tools for influencing perceptions and guiding opponents' decisions. By mastering these tactics, you can gain an edge in negotiations, strategy games, and competitive environments.

Chapter 17: Opportunity Cost – Recognizing What You Sacrifice

Why This Matters

Every decision involves a trade-off: by choosing one path, you inevitably forgo others. The concept of opportunity cost, first introduced by Friedrich von Wieser in 1914, helps you evaluate these trade-offs by quantifying the value of what you give up.

Opportunity cost is a vital tool for strategic thinking. As discussed in Mankiw's *Principles of Economics* (1998), it forces you to consider the unseen consequences of your choices and align decisions with your long-term goals. From financial investments to personal time management, recognizing opportunity costs ensures you don't waste resources on less valuable alternatives.

How It Works

Opportunity cost is the value of the next-best alternative you give up when making a choice. For example, if you spend $100 on dining out, the opportunity cost might be the savings or investment returns you could have achieved with that money.

In game theory, opportunity costs influence decisions in competitive and cooperative settings. A company deciding whether to invest in research or marketing, for instance, must weigh the opportunity cost of pursuing one strategy over the other. Opportunity cost also applies to personal choices, such as spending time on leisure versus skill development.

Real-Life Example

Consider a university student deciding whether to attend graduate school or enter the workforce. The opportunity cost of graduate school includes not only tuition fees but also the potential salary and career experience they forgo during their studies. Evaluating this trade-off helps the student make an informed decision based on their long-term career goals.

Exercises

1. **Calculate an Opportunity Cost:** Think of a recent decision you made (e.g., spending money, allocating time). Write down the opportunity cost of your choice. Was it worth the trade-off?
2. **Analyze a Business Decision:** Research a company's recent strategic move (e.g., a merger, product launch, or pivot). What opportunity costs might have influenced their decision?
3. **Apply to Personal Goals:** Identify a long-term goal you've been delaying. Write down the opportunity costs of continuing to delay versus starting now.

Key Takeaway

Opportunity cost highlights the hidden trade-offs in every decision. By evaluating what you sacrifice, you can make more informed choices and focus on the options with the greatest value.

Chapter 18: First-Mover Advantage – Leading for Personal Gain

Why This Matters

Timing can often determine the difference between success and failure. The first-mover advantage, a concept rooted in economic and strategic theory, refers to the competitive edge gained by being the first to act in a market or scenario. As explored by Lieberman and Montgomery in their seminal paper, *First-Mover Advantages* (1988), early movers can shape market dynamics, establish customer loyalty, and create barriers to entry for competitors.

This concept matters because it highlights how taking the initiative can set the stage for long-term success. However, the first-mover advantage is not guaranteed — without proper strategy, early entrants may falter, paving the way for competitors to capitalize on their mistakes. Understanding when and how to seize the first-mover advantage ensures you can act decisively and effectively.

How It Works

The first-mover advantage arises from several key benefits:

1. **Brand Recognition:** Being the first to introduce a product or service creates a lasting impression on customers, fostering loyalty.
2. **Resource Control:** Early entrants can secure valuable resources, such as patents, distribution channels, or prime locations, making it harder for competitors to catch up.
3. **Switching Costs:** By locking customers into their ecosystem, first movers create barriers to switching, further solidifying their position.

However, first movers face risks. As noted by Christensen in *The Innovator's Dilemma* (1997), pioneers often make mistakes that latecomers learn from, leading to a "fast-follower advantage." Success requires balancing bold action with careful planning to maximize the benefits of early entry while minimizing risks.

Real-Life Example

One of the most famous examples of the first-mover advantage is Amazon. Jeff Bezos founded the company in 1994 as one of the first major online retailers. By establishing an early presence in e-commerce, Amazon gained a dominant market share, built extensive distribution networks, and fostered customer loyalty. Even as competitors like Walmart and Target entered the space, Amazon's first-mover advantage allowed it to maintain leadership.

However, not all first movers succeed. Consider Friendster, one of the earliest social networking platforms. While it initially gained traction, technical issues and poor user experience allowed competitors like Facebook and MySpace to capitalize on its shortcomings. This example illustrates that being first is not enough — sustained success requires strategic execution.

Exercises

1. **Evaluate First-Mover Opportunities:** Identify a current industry or market trend where being the first mover could provide a competitive edge. Write down potential benefits and risks of acting early.
2. **Analyze a First-Mover Success or Failure:** Research a company that succeeded or failed as a first mover. What factors contributed to their outcome?
3. **Simulate Timing Strategies:** In a game or simulation (e.g. launching a product or entering a market), experiment with acting first versus waiting to observe competitors. Reflect on the trade-offs of each approach.

Key Takeaway

The first-mover advantage allows early entrants to shape the market and establish dominance, but success depends on strategic execution and the ability to adapt to challenges.

Chapter 19: Stackelberg Leadership – Dominating by Taking the Lead

Why This Matters

In many competitive scenarios, taking the lead enables you to set the tone, influence others, and shape the game to your advantage. Stackelberg leadership, named after economist Heinrich von Stackelberg, explores this phenomenon by analyzing how leaders and followers behave in sequential decision-making games (*Market Structure and Equilibrium*, 1934).

Stackelberg leadership matters because it provides a framework for understanding how to capitalize on being the first to act in structured environments. By taking the lead, you can force competitors to respond to your moves, gaining a strategic edge. However, effective leadership also requires anticipating how followers will react and ensuring your decisions remain optimal in the face of their responses.

How It Works

In Stackelberg games, the leader acts first, and the follower reacts based on the leader's decision. This sequence contrasts with simultaneous games, where players act at the same time. The leader gains an advantage by influencing the follower's choices, effectively shaping the outcome of the game.

For example, a dominant firm might set prices for a product, forcing smaller competitors to adjust their strategies to stay competitive. This ability to dictate the terms of the game makes leadership a powerful strategic tool. However, as noted in Fudenberg and Tirole's *Game Theory* (1991), the leader must carefully anticipate the follower's reaction to avoid unintended consequences.

Real-Life Example

Tesla exemplifies Stackelberg leadership in the electric vehicle (EV) market. By aggressively investing in EV technology, infrastructure, and branding, Tesla positioned itself as the industry leader. This forced traditional automakers to follow its lead, often playing catch-up in a market Tesla helped define.

Another example comes from sports. In a chess match, a player taking the lead by dictating the opening moves forces their opponent into a reactive position, gaining a psychological and strategic advantage.

Exercises

1. **Simulate Stackelberg Leadership:** In a strategy game or negotiation, take the role of the leader and make the first move. Observe how your actions influence others' responses and shape the outcome.
2. **Analyze Leadership in Business:** Research a company that acts as a leader in its industry (e.g. Apple). How do their early actions force competitors to adapt?
3. **Plan a Leadership Move:** Identify a situation in your life or work where acting as a leader could provide an advantage. Write down the steps you would take to influence others and achieve your goal.

Key Takeaway

Stackelberg leadership demonstrates how taking the initiative allows you to influence others and shape outcomes to your advantage. By anticipating reactions and planning strategically, you can dominate competitive scenarios.

Chapter 20: Sequential Interplays – Playing the Long Game

Why This Matters

Decisions made today often shape the outcomes of tomorrow. In sequential interplays, actions unfold over time, requiring players to think several steps ahead. Unlike simultaneous games where players act at the same time, sequential games involve anticipating future moves and counter-moves to maintain control and achieve long-term success.

This concept is vital in strategic planning, negotiations, and competitive environments where patience and foresight can secure significant advantages. Sequential interplays, as first modeled in *Theory of Games and Economic Behavior* by John von Neumann and Oskar Morgenstern (1944), reveal how structured decision-making over time can transform complex challenges into manageable steps.

As further explored by Fudenberg and Tirole in *Game Theory* (1991), sequential strategies rely heavily on the ability to anticipate responses. This requires not only logical planning but also a deep understanding of your opponents' incentives and constraints. Their work emphasizes that players who consistently evaluate future scenarios gain a distinct advantage in dynamic environments.

How It Works

In sequential games, players take turns making decisions, with each move influencing subsequent actions. These games often require players to evaluate potential outcomes at every stage, factoring in how opponents or collaborators are likely to respond.

The rollback method, commonly used in game theory, involves working backward from the desired outcome to determine the best initial move. This aligns with the principle of backward induction discussed in earlier chapters, but in sequential interplays, every step is part of a larger strategy.

Dixit and Nalebuff, in *Thinking Strategically: The Competitive Edge in Business, Politics, and Everyday Life* (1991), discuss how sequential strategies are not only about anticipating future moves but also about influencing those moves. For example, a company entering a new market might set prices aggressively low, forcing competitors to either accept reduced profits or exit the market altogether. By planning multiple steps ahead, the company shapes the competitive landscape in its favor.

Real-Life Example

A classic example of sequential interplays is the **U.S.-China trade negotiations**. Each country implements policies or tariffs in response to the other's actions, carefully evaluating how each step will influence the broader economic and political landscape. For instance, the U.S. might impose tariffs on specific goods, anticipating that China will respond with counter-tariffs. By thinking ahead, policymakers aim to guide the negotiation toward favorable terms without escalating the conflict unnecessarily.

In personal finance, sequential interplays appear in retirement planning. A young professional might choose to prioritize saving early in their career, understanding that the compounded returns from these savings will yield significant benefits decades later. Each financial decision builds upon the last, shaping their financial security over time.

Exercises

1. **Plan a Sequential Strategy:** Identify a long-term goal that requires multiple steps to achieve (e.g. career advancement, project completion). Write down the sequence of actions needed and consider how each step influences the next.
2. **Analyze Sequential Games in Politics or Business:** Research a political negotiation or business strategy where actions unfolded over time (e.g. trade wars, mergers, or international treaties). How did each party's moves shape the overall outcome?
3. **Simulate a Sequential Game:** With a partner, play a turn-based strategy game (e.g. checkers or a simplified negotiation). Focus on how your initial moves set the stage for future actions. Reflect on whether your strategy evolved as the game progressed.

Key Takeaway

Sequential interplays require thinking beyond immediate actions to anticipate and shape future outcomes. By planning strategically and evaluating each step's long-term impact, you can gain control over complex, time-dependent scenarios.

Section III: Winning in Negotiations

Negotiation is both an art and a science, and mastering it requires strategy, preparation, and psychological insight. This section equips you with powerful tools to navigate negotiations with confidence and precision, whether you're closing a business deal, resolving a conflict, or making a life-changing decision. From understanding your Best Alternative to a Negotiated Agreement (BATNA) to leveraging the Anchoring Effect and manipulating time with the Deadline Master Plan, these chapters break down advanced tactics to give you the upper hand. Backed by game theory principles and real-world applications, these strategies ensure you'll negotiate from a position of strength and achieve mutually beneficial outcomes.

Chapter 21: BATNA – Always Have an Exit Plan

Why This Matters

The most successful negotiators are those who walk into a negotiation prepared to walk away. The Best Alternative to a Negotiated Agreement (BATNA) is your fallback plan if the deal on the table doesn't meet your needs. This concept, first introduced by Roger Fisher and William Ury in their seminal book *Getting to Yes* (1981), empowers negotiators by giving them clarity and leverage.

Max H. Bazerman and Margaret A. Neale expand on this concept in *Negotiating Rationally* (1992), emphasizing that a well-defined BATNA prevents emotional decision-making and reduces the chances of accepting unfavorable terms. By preparing alternatives in advance, negotiators create a solid foundation to assess offers objectively and protect their interests.

Having a strong BATNA matters because it shifts the balance of power. If you know you have a viable alternative, you won't feel pressured to accept unfavorable terms. Conversely, if your counterpart senses that you're reliant on the deal, they can exploit your vulnerability. By cultivating a strong BATNA, you can confidently reject bad offers and push for terms that meet your goals.

How It Works

Your BATNA is essentially your best fallback option. For example, if you're negotiating the price of a car, your BATNA might be another dealership offering a similar model at a competitive price. Knowing this gives you leverage: you can confidently walk away if the current negotiation doesn't meet your needs.

Fisher and Ury emphasize that identifying and strengthening your BATNA before entering a negotiation is critical. This preparation involves researching alternatives, assessing their feasibility, and determining the lowest acceptable terms you're willing to accept. Similarly, Bazerman and Neale highlight the importance of comparing your BATNA against the proposed terms during the negotiation process, ensuring your choices align with your broader goals.

Dixit and Nalebuff, in *Thinking Strategically: The Competitive Edge in Business, Politics, and Everyday Life* (1991), further illustrate how BATNAs can influence power dynamics. They argue that a well-communicated BATNA can subtly pressure the other party into making concessions, as they realize you are not dependent on the current deal. BATNAs are not just about walking away—they're about negotiating from a position of informed power.

Real-Life Example

Consider a job seeker negotiating their salary. If the candidate has another offer from a different company, they can use that offer as leverage. Knowing their BATNA (the alternative offer) gives them the confidence to push for higher pay or better benefits. On the other hand, a candidate with no alternatives may feel pressured to accept whatever is offered, regardless of whether it meets their expectations.

This principle applies in business as well. In 2011, Netflix raised its subscription prices, causing backlash and a wave of customer cancellations. Many customers who left had strong BATNAs: competitors such as Hulu offered comparable services. Bazerman and Neale argue that strong alternatives force companies like Netflix to reconsider their strategies, as customers are less likely to accept changes when viable substitutes are readily available.

Exercises

1. **Identify Your BATNA:** Think of an upcoming negotiation (e.g. salary discussion, business deal, or conflict resolution). Write down your best alternative if the negotiation fails. How can you strengthen this alternative before entering the discussion?

2. **Analyze a BATNA in Action:** Research a public negotiation or business decision where one party had a strong BATNA (e.g. mergers, strikes, or international trade deals). How did their BATNA influence the outcome?

3. **Strengthen Your Leverage:** Write down three ways you can improve your fallback options in a current or future negotiation. Consider resources, alternatives, or allies you can leverage.

Key Takeaway

A strong BATNA gives you the confidence to walk away from bad deals and negotiate from a position of power. By preparing your alternatives, you can ensure better outcomes and avoid being cornered in negotiations.

Chapter 22: Anchoring Effect – Setting the Tone Early

Why This Matters

The anchoring effect is a cognitive bias that heavily influences negotiations. It occurs when the first number or idea introduced in a discussion acts as a psychological anchor, shaping all subsequent decisions. Amos Tversky and Daniel Kahneman first explored this phenomenon in their ground-breaking work on cognitive biases, *Judgment Under Uncertainty* (1974), demonstrating how even irrelevant anchors can skew decisions.

Anchoring matters because the party who sets the anchor often gains the upper hand. A high opening bid can establish an expectation of value, while a low starting offer can reset the perceived range of acceptable outcomes. By strategically introducing an anchor, you can control the framework of the negotiation and subtly influence the final agreement.

How It Works

Anchoring works by planting a reference point early in the negotiation, which affects the other party's perception of value or fairness. For instance, if a seller starts by quoting a high price for a product, the buyer will unconsciously adjust their counteroffer relative to that initial figure — even if the price is inflated.

Tversky and Kahneman's experiments revealed that anchors are surprisingly sticky: even when participants knew the anchor was arbitrary, it still influenced their judgments. This effect is particularly powerful in negotiations because people often lack complete information and rely on the initial anchor as a guide.

In *Thinking Strategically* (Dixit & Nalebuff, 1991), anchoring is described as a tactical move to "frame the conversation," forcing your counterpart to play within the parameters you set. However, anchors must be chosen carefully. An anchor perceived as too extreme can backfire, undermining your credibility.

Real-Life Example

In real estate, anchoring plays a pivotal role. A homeowner selling their house might set an asking price significantly higher than the market average. Even if buyers negotiate the price down, the final sale price often ends up closer to the initial asking price than it would have if the seller had started lower. This tactic forces buyers to frame their offers relative to the anchor, often leading to higher outcomes for the seller.

Another famous example comes from retail sales. Stores often display a high "original price" next to a discounted price. Even if the original price was artificially inflated, it serves as an anchor, making the discount appear more significant and encouraging purchases. This phenomenon is rooted in Tversky and Kahneman's findings about how people assess value relative to anchors.

Exercises

1. **Practice Setting an Anchor:** Identify an upcoming negotiation (e.g. asking for a raise or selling a product). Write down a strong anchor you could use to set the tone early.
2. **Analyze Anchors in Business:** Research a business negotiation or pricing strategy where anchoring played a key role (e.g. mergers, salary discussions, or product pricing). How did the initial anchor influence the final outcome?
3. **Resist the Anchor:** Reflect on a situation where you were influenced by an anchor (e.g. making a purchase or negotiating a deal). Write down how you could have resisted its influence by focusing on objective criteria.

Key Takeaway

The anchoring effect demonstrates how setting the first reference point in a negotiation can shape the outcome. By strategically introducing an anchor, you can influence the perceived value and guide the conversation in your favor.

Chapter 23:
Logrolling – Trading Concessions for Maximum Gains

Why This Matters

In negotiations, it's rare for both parties to value every issue equally. Logrolling is the art of trading concessions on lower-priority issues to gain advantages on higher-priority ones. By identifying each party's preferences, logrolling allows you to craft win-win solutions that maximize mutual gains.

This concept is extensively discussed in *Getting to Yes* (Fisher & Ury, 1981), where the authors emphasize focusing on interests rather than positions. Logrolling transforms negotiations from a zero-sum battle into an opportunity for creative problem-solving, ensuring both sides leave the table satisfied.

How It Works

Logrolling begins by identifying the issues at stake and ranking their importance. For instance, in a labor negotiation, management might prioritize cost savings, while employees prioritize better working conditions. By agreeing to concessions that matter less to you but more to the other party, you can secure concessions on issues that matter most to you.

Bazerman and Neale, in *Negotiating Rationally* (1992), highlight that logrolling requires trust and open communication. Both parties must reveal their true priorities, creating the transparency needed to identify mutually beneficial trade-offs. Successful logrolling often hinges on this collaborative mindset, ensuring no one feels exploited.

Real-Life Example

A classic example of logrolling occurred during the Camp David Accords in 1978. In negotiations between Israel and Egypt, facilitated by U.S. President Jimmy Carter, each side made concessions on issues of lesser importance to secure gains on their highest priorities. Israel agreed to withdraw from the Sinai Peninsula, addressing Egypt's territorial concerns, while Egypt recognized Israel's right to exist, fulfilling Israel's primary demand.

In business, logrolling frequently appears in vendor-client relationships. For example, a supplier might agree to faster delivery times (a priority for the client) in exchange for a longer-term contract (a priority for the supplier). By trading concessions, both sides achieve their goals.

Exercises

1. **Identify Logrolling Opportunities:** Think of a negotiation where you need to address multiple issues (e.g. work responsibilities, partnerships). Write down which issues are high, medium, and low priorities for you. How could you trade concessions to maximize gains?
2. **Research Historical Logrolling:** Study a major negotiation (e.g. international treaties or business deals) where logrolling played a role. How did the parties exchange concessions to achieve mutual benefits?
3. **Simulate Logrolling in Practice:** Role-play a negotiation with a partner where you have competing priorities. Practice revealing your preferences and trading concessions to find a win-win solution.

Key Takeaway

Logrolling is a powerful negotiation tool that turns conflicting priorities into opportunities for mutual gain. By trading concessions strategically, you can maximize outcomes and foster collaboration.

Chapter 24:
ZOPA –
Identifying the Zone of Possible Agreement

Why This Matters

Every successful negotiation depends on finding the Zone of Possible Agreement (ZOPA) – the range where both parties' interests overlap. First described in Fisher and Ury's *Getting to Yes* (1981), ZOPA is the space where deals are possible because both parties see value in the outcome.

Understanding ZOPA is critical because it prevents wasted time and frustration. If no overlap exists between the parties' acceptable terms, a deal cannot be reached. By clearly identifying ZOPA early on, you can focus your efforts on crafting agreements that satisfy both sides and avoid unrealistic demands that could derail discussions.

How It Works

ZOPA exists when the buyer's maximum willingness to pay exceeds the seller's minimum acceptable price. For instance, if a buyer is willing to pay up to $1,000 for a product and the seller is willing to accept no less than $800, the ZOPA is between $800 and $1,000. Negotiations within this range have a high chance of success.

In *Negotiating Rationally* (Bazerman & Neale, 1992), the authors emphasize the importance of preparation in identifying ZOPA. Both parties must understand their own limits (BATNA) and estimate the other side's limits to locate the overlapping range. Effective negotiators use probing questions and careful observation to clarify ZOPA during discussions.

Real-Life Example

ZOPA played a critical role in the 2015 Paris Climate Agreement, where nations negotiated emissions reduction targets. Developed countries prioritized limiting global temperature increases, while developing nations sought financial and technological support to transition to clean energy. The ZOPA lay in agreements that balanced environmental goals with economic development needs. This shared space allowed the parties to finalize a historic accord despite differing priorities.

In the business world, consider a software vendor negotiating a service contract with a client. If the client's budget is $50,000 – $70,000 and the vendor's acceptable range is $60,000 – $80,000, ZOPA lies between $60,000 and $70,000. Both parties can explore solutions within this range to maximize mutual value.

Exercises

1. **Define ZOPA in Your Negotiations:** Think of an upcoming negotiation. Write down your acceptable range and estimate the other party's range. Where do you think the ZOPA lies?
2. **Analyze a Historical Negotiation:** Research a high-stakes negotiation (e.g. international treaties, mergers). How did the parties identify and operate within the ZOPA?
3. **Role-Play a ZOPA Scenario:** Pair up with a friend and negotiate a mock deal. Each person should set their acceptable range privately. During the negotiation, identify where the ZOPA exists and close the deal within that range.

Key Takeaway

ZOPA represents the shared space where deals are possible. By identifying and operating within this range, you can negotiate effectively and avoid wasted effort on unattainable outcomes.

Chapter 25: Splitting the Difference – Mastering Compromise

Not all negotiations end with one party getting everything they want. Splitting the difference is a widely used tactic to resolve disputes when parties are close to agreement but unable to settle on precise terms. By finding the midpoint between two positions, negotiators can break deadlocks and reach acceptable compromises.

Howard Raiffa, in *The Art and Science of Negotiation* (1982), explains that splitting the difference often works because it feels inherently fair to both parties. However, it's important to ensure the midpoint reflects a balanced compromise rather than a capitulation to unreasonable demands.

How It Works

Splitting the difference involves taking the average or midpoint of two offers. For example, if a buyer offers $9,000 for a car and the seller demands $11,000, they might agree to $10,000 — a straightforward compromise.

Fisher and Ury, in *Getting to Yes* (1981), caution against relying on splitting the difference too early. While it can resolve disputes quickly, it works best when both parties have made good-faith efforts to explore other options first. Otherwise, the resulting compromise might leave valuable opportunities untapped.

Real-Life Example

In labor negotiations, splitting the difference is a common strategy for resolving wage disputes. For instance, a union might demand a 10% raise, while management offers 5%. After prolonged talks, they might agree on a 7.5% raise. This midpoint ensures that both sides achieve partial success while avoiding a strike or impasse.

Another example comes from real estate. A seller might list their house at $300,000, while a buyer offers $280,000. Splitting the difference at $290,000 allows both sides to avoid further negotiation while securing a fair deal.

Exercises

1. **Practice Splitting the Difference:** Think of a recent disagreement (e.g. splitting costs or dividing tasks). Write down the positions of both sides and calculate the midpoint. Did this approach resolve the issue?
2. **Analyze When It Works Best:** Research a historical negotiation where splitting the difference was used (e.g. wage settlements or political compromises). Why was this tactic effective in that situation?
3. **Experiment with Alternatives:** Role-play a negotiation where splitting the difference is one possible solution. Explore other options first, then evaluate whether splitting the difference is the best choice.

Key Takeaway

Splitting the difference provides a simple, fair resolution when parties are close to agreement. However, it's most effective after exploring other options to ensure the compromise reflects genuine balance.

Chapter 26:
Hardball Tactics –
Standing Firm
Against Pressure

Why This Matters

Sometimes, negotiations become adversarial, and one or both parties resort to hardball tactics to gain an edge. These tactics can include high-pressure moves like ultimatums, take-it-or-leave-it offers, or even emotional manipulation. While hardball tactics can disrupt negotiations, understanding how to use them effectively—or counter them—ensures that you maintain control and protect your interests.

Hardball tactics are explored extensively in G. Richard Shell's *Bargaining for Advantage* (1999), where he outlines the principles of navigating high-pressure negotiations. Shell emphasizes that preparation, self-awareness, and composure are critical for neutralizing aggressive moves while maintaining a firm stance.

How It Works

Hardball tactics are designed to unbalance the other party, forcing them to make decisions under stress. Common tactics include:

1. **Ultimatums:** Setting a strict deadline or condition to force a decision.
2. **Good Cop/Bad Cop:** One negotiator takes a hard stance while the other appears sympathetic, creating psychological pressure.
3. **Highball/Lowball Offers:** Proposing extreme terms to anchor the negotiation and gain concessions.

In *The Power of Negotiation* by Harvard Business Review (2003), the authors argue that recognizing these tactics early is essential. The best counter-strategy is preparation: having a strong BATNA, staying calm under pressure, and reframing the conversation to neutralize aggressive moves.

Real-Life Example

In 1995, **the Major League Baseball strike** showcased the use of hardball tactics on both sides. Team owners attempted to impose a salary cap, while players threatened to walk out, knowing the financial losses would pressure owners to negotiate. Both sides used ultimatums, delays, and public pressure to gain leverage. Ultimately, while the strike disrupted the league, a new agreement was reached after both sides adjusted their tactics.

On a smaller scale, consider a landlord negotiating rent with a tenant. If the landlord issues a take-it-or-leave-it offer with a steep increase, the tenant might feel pressured to accept. However, a prepared tenant with alternative options (BATNA) could counter by citing market rates or negotiating for better terms.

Exercises

1. **Recognize Hardball Tactics:** Reflect on a past negotiation where hardball tactics were used against you (e.g., ultimatums, aggressive offers). How did you respond? What could you have done differently?
2. **Role-Play Resistance:** With a partner, simulate a negotiation where one side uses hardball tactics. Practice identifying and calmly countering these moves while maintaining focus on your goals.
3. **Develop a Neutralizing Strategy:** Think of an upcoming negotiation where you might encounter hardball tactics. Write down specific responses to common tactics like ultimatums or lowball offers.

Key Takeaway

Hardball tactics are designed to pressure you into making concessions, but they can be neutralized with preparation, calm responses, and reframing. Staying firm and focused ensures that you maintain control under pressure.

Chapter 27: Framing Effects – Shaping the Narrative to Win

Why This Matters

The way information is presented often matters as much as the information itself. Framing effects, a concept explored extensively in Tversky and Kahneman's *Judgment Under Uncertainty* (1974), demonstrate how decisions are influenced by how options are framed. Positive framing can make a proposal appear more appealing, while negative framing can deter undesirable choices.

Framing is critical in negotiations because it shapes the narrative and directs the other party's focus. By framing issues strategically, you can emphasize benefits, minimize drawbacks, and guide the discussion toward your preferred outcome. This aligns with insights from Heath and Heath's *Made to Stick* (2007), which highlights the importance of crafting messages in ways that resonate with others by focusing on simplicity, clarity, and emotion.

How It Works

Framing effects exploit the human tendency to evaluate options based on context rather than objective value. For example, framing a proposal as "saving $1,000" rather than "reducing a $5,000 loss to $4,000" makes the outcome feel more favorable, even though the net savings are identical.

In *Negotiation Genius* (Malhotra & Bazerman, 2008), the authors highlight that effective framing involves tailoring your narrative to the other party's values and priorities. Heath and Heath's research supports this by showing that messages framed around emotional or practical relevance are more likely to stick, influencing long-term decision-making and perceptions.

Real-Life Example

The Coca-Cola "New Coke" debacle of 1985 is a famous example of framing gone wrong. Coca-Cola introduced a new formula to appeal to modern tastes, framing it as an "improved" product. However, loyal customers felt this framing ignored their emotional attachment to the original formula, leading to widespread backlash. Coca-Cola quickly reverted to its original formula, demonstrating the importance of understanding your audience's perspective when framing decisions.

In personal negotiations, framing effects often influence salary discussions. For instance, framing a pay raise request as "aligning my compensation with industry standards" rather than simply asking for "more money" makes the request feel more reasonable and data-driven. This approach reflects the principles in *Made to Stick*, where Heath and Heath emphasize how framing ideas around clear and relatable contexts increases their persuasive power.

Exercises

1. **Practice Reframing:** Take a recent disagreement or proposal. Write down how you originally presented it and then reframe it to highlight benefits or align better with the other party's interests.
2. **Analyze Framing in Advertising:** Research an advertisement or marketing campaign. How does the framing influence perceptions of the product or service? Does it reflect any of the principles from *Made to Stick* (e.g., simplicity or emotional appeal)?
3. **Test Framing in Negotiations:** Role-play a negotiation where one person uses framing to influence the other party's decision. Evaluate how the framing shaped the final outcome.

Key Takeaway

Framing effects demonstrate that how you present information can significantly influence decisions. By shaping the narrative strategically, you can make your proposals more compelling and align them with the other party's priorities.

Chapter 28: The Decoy Effect – Steering Choices Subtly

Why This Matters

Sometimes, the best way to influence a decision is not by presenting fewer choices, but by adding a strategically designed one. The decoy effect, as explored in Dan Ariely's *Predictably Irrational* (2008), demonstrates how introducing a third option can nudge people toward a desired outcome.

The decoy effect matters in negotiations and decision-making because it leverages psychology to create perceived value. By adding an option that's less attractive but comparable to the desired choice, you subtly guide others toward the choice you want them to make. This strategy is particularly effective when the options involve trade-offs, such as price and quality. Daniel Kahneman's *Thinking, Fast and Slow* (2011) expands on this idea, emphasizing how intuitive (fast) thinking often dominates rational (slow) thinking, making people especially susceptible to relative comparisons like those in the decoy effect.

How It Works

The decoy effect occurs when one option (the "decoy") is intentionally included to make another option seem more attractive by comparison. For example, in pricing strategies, a retailer might present:

- Option A: $10 for a small popcorn.
- Option B: $15 for a medium popcorn.
- Option C (Decoy): $14.50 for a small popcorn.

Here, the decoy (C) makes the medium popcorn (B) appear like a better deal, even if the consumer wouldn't have considered it otherwise. Kahneman's concept of cognitive biases explains this phenomenon: people rely on fast, intuitive judgments when evaluating choices, and relative comparisons often dominate these quick decisions.

Richard Thaler, in *Nudge: Improving Decisions About Health, Wealth, and Happiness* (2008), also discusses the decoy effect as part of a broader toolkit for shaping decisions. By carefully designing choices, you can influence decisions without removing autonomy.

Real-Life Example

The Economist magazine's subscription pricing is a famous example of the decoy effect in action. At one point, the magazine offered these three options:

1. Online-only subscription: $59.
2. Print-only subscription: $125.
3. Online + Print subscription: $125.

The print-only subscription acted as a decoy, making the combined online and print subscription seem like a much better deal. This pricing structure increased sales of the combined option, even though the print-only subscription was never intended to be chosen.

Kahneman's work highlights why this approach is effective: people's intuitive (fast) thinking draws them toward the option that appears superior in a relative sense, without deeply analyzing whether all options are truly necessary or rational.

Exercises

1. **Design a Decoy:** Think of a decision where you want to influence someone's choice (e.g. offering a service package or presenting a business proposal). Write down two main options and a decoy that makes your desired choice more appealing.

2. **Analyze a Decoy in Action:** Research a product or service that uses the decoy effect (e.g. pricing strategies, subscription models). How does the decoy influence consumer behavior?

3. **Test the Decoy Effect in Negotiations:** Role-play a negotiation with a partner where you introduce a decoy option. Observe how it changes their perception of the other options.

Key Takeaway

The decoy effect is a powerful tool for subtly steering decisions. By adding a carefully designed option, you can influence choices and guide others toward outcomes that align with your goals.

Chapter 29: Supremacy Dynamics – Using Strong Points and Weakness

Every negotiation involves a balance of power, and understanding supremacy dynamics – the interplay between strengths and weaknesses — can help you gain a decisive edge. This principle, rooted in Carl von Clausewitz's *On War* (1832), teaches negotiators to exploit their strengths while targeting the vulnerabilities of their opponents.

Supremacy dynamics are critical because they allow you to reframe power imbalances. Even if the other party appears stronger, understanding their weaknesses can level the playing field. This strategy involves not only leveraging your own assets but also carefully observing and capitalizing on gaps in their position.

How It Works

Supremacy dynamics involve two key tactics:

1. **Strength Maximization:** Highlight your unique advantages, such as expertise, resources, or alternatives, to establish dominance.
2. **Weakness Exploitation:** Identify the other party's pressure points—such as time constraints or dependencies—and use them to your advantage.

Clausewitz's ideas about targeting an opponent's "center of gravity" apply here. In negotiations, this might mean focusing on the key issue they care about most and using it as leverage. As Shell discusses in *Bargaining for Advantage* (1999), successful negotiators balance their strengths while probing for vulnerabilities, creating opportunities to shift the dynamic in their favor.

Real-Life Example

In the U.S.-China trade war, both countries leveraged supremacy dynamics. The U.S. used tariffs to target China's reliance on exports, while China exploited U.S. agricultural dependency to impose counter-tariffs. Each side identified the other's vulnerabilities while highlighting their own strengths, such as technological leadership or market size, to gain leverage in negotiations.

On a personal level, supremacy dynamics play out in job negotiations. A candidate with specialized skills (a strength) can demand higher compensation, while an employer facing tight deadlines (a weakness) might concede to those demands.

Exercises

1. **Identify Strengths and Weaknesses:** List your strengths and the other party's weaknesses in an upcoming negotiation. How can you use this information to gain leverage?
2. **Analyze Supremacy Dynamics in History:** Research a historical or business negotiation (e.g. the U.S.-China trade war). How did each side use their strengths and exploit the other's vulnerabilities?
3. **Simulate Supremacy Dynamics:** Role-play a negotiation where one party appears stronger. Practice using your strengths and targeting their weaknesses to level the playing field.

Key Takeaway

Supremacy dynamics involve leveraging your strengths and targeting the other party's weaknesses. By understanding the balance of power, you can create opportunities to shift negotiations in your favor.

Chapter 30: Deadline Master Plan – Using Time as Leverage

Why This Matters

Deadlines are not just markers of time — they are powerful tools for shaping negotiations. When used strategically, deadlines create urgency, pressure, and leverage, influencing how decisions are made. As explained in Richard Shell's *Bargaining for Advantage* (1999), deadlines force parties to act quickly, often leading to concessions that favor the more prepared negotiator.

Deadlines matter because they alter the psychological dynamics of negotiation. By imposing time constraints, you can steer discussions toward resolution, especially when the other party is unprepared to face the consequences of missing the deadline. This tactic works in both personal and professional contexts, from resolving business disputes to closing last-minute deals.

How It Works

Deadlines affect negotiations by introducing two key elements:

1. **Scarcity of Time:** As the deadline approaches, the pressure to reach a resolution increases. Parties are more likely to compromise to avoid the costs of a failed negotiation.
2. **Asymmetric Urgency:** If one party is more affected by the deadline than the other, the less-affected party gains leverage. For example, if a supplier is under pressure to meet a delivery schedule, the buyer can use that urgency to negotiate better terms.

Shell emphasizes that deadlines can be real (fixed and immutable) or artificial (created as a tactic). Artificial deadlines, when used strategically, can give the impression of urgency without locking you into a rigid timeline. Meanwhile, in *Negotiation Genius* (Malhotra & Bazerman, 2008), the authors highlight that successfully leveraging deadlines requires preparation and a clear understanding of both parties' priorities.

Real-Life Example

A well-known example of deadline dynamics occurred during the Brexit negotiations between the United Kingdom and the European Union. With hard deadlines looming for the UK's departure from the EU, both sides faced immense pressure to reach agreements on trade, border policies, and financial settlements. The EU, less affected by the looming deadlines, gained a strategic advantage, often forcing the UK to make concessions to avoid chaotic outcomes. This illustrates how asymmetrical urgency impacts negotiations when one side has more to lose from delays.

In everyday situations, consider real estate transactions. Buyers and sellers often face deadlines due to mortgage approvals, moving timelines, or market conditions. A seller with a strict deadline to close may accept a lower price to ensure the deal goes through, while a buyer under no time pressure can negotiate more assertively.

Exercises

1. **Analyze Your Deadlines:** Reflect on an upcoming negotiation or decision. Are there deadlines involved? If so, identify whether they are real or artificial and how they could be used to your advantage.
2. **Create an Artificial Deadline:** Design a negotiation scenario where you impose a deadline to create urgency. Observe how this changes the dynamics of the discussion and the other party's willingness to compromise.
3. **Research Deadline Tactics in History:** Study a major negotiation or event where deadlines played a critical role (e.g., Brexit, labor strikes, or high-stakes mergers). How did the presence of a deadline shape the outcome?

Key Takeaway

Deadlines are a powerful tool for creating urgency and driving negotiations to resolution. By understanding how time affects decision-making, you can strategically use or resist deadlines to gain leverage and control outcomes.

Section IV: Navigating Human Dynamics

The heart of decision-making lies in understanding people. Whether you're persuading, collaborating, or competing, mastering human dynamics gives you the edge. This section explores the psychological, social, and behavioral patterns that shape interactions. Armed with these strategies, you'll learn to anticipate actions, build trust, and navigate the complexities of group dynamics and individual biases. These chapters blend game theory, behavioral economics, and social psychology to help you master the human element in any scenario.

Chapter 31: Social Proof – Leading with Consensus

Why This Matters

Humans are inherently social beings, often looking to others for cues about how to think, feel, or act. Social proof, a concept popularized by Robert Cialdini in *Influence: The Psychology of Persuasion* (1984), explains how people are more likely to follow the lead of others, especially in uncertain situations. This psychological tendency can be a powerful tool in negotiations, marketing, and leadership.

Social proof matters because it creates momentum. When you demonstrate that others support your idea, product, or proposal, people are more likely to align with you, believing that the group consensus indicates credibility or value. However, as Cialdini warns, this tactic can backfire if the social proof lacks authenticity or relevance to the audience.

How It Works

Social proof operates on the principle that people tend to follow the crowd. For example, a restaurant displaying a "Most Popular Dish" label on a menu uses social proof to influence customers' choices.

Cialdini's research found that social proof is particularly effective in situations involving uncertainty or where people lack expertise. By highlighting examples of others adopting or endorsing a choice, you reduce hesitation and build confidence in your proposal. In *Yes! 50 Scientifically Proven Ways to Be Persuasive* (Goldstein, Martin, & Cialdini, 2008), the authors emphasize that tailoring social proof to match the audience's values enhances its effectiveness.

Real-Life Example

The Ice Bucket Challenge of 2014 is a prime example of social proof in action. This viral campaign encouraged participants to pour a bucket of ice water over themselves, post the video online, and challenge others to do the same—all while donating to ALS research. The campaign gained traction because participants highlighted celebrity involvement and displayed the growing number of people participating. As each new participant shared their video, the challenge's credibility and momentum grew exponentially, resulting in $115 million raised for ALS research.

This phenomenon aligns with principles outlined by Jonah Berger in *Contagious: Why Things Catch On* (2013), which emphasizes that visibility is key to social proof. The public nature of the Ice Bucket Challenge made participation visible to a large audience, creating a ripple effect of imitation and consensus.

Exercises

1. **Create Social Proof in Your Work:** Identify a project or proposal you're working on. Write down one way to use social proof, such as highlighting endorsements, testimonials, or group success, to build credibility.
2. **Analyze Social Proof in Action:** Research a campaign or movement that relied heavily on social proof (e.g. viral challenges, product launches). How did it influence behavior?
3. **Test Social Proof in Negotiations:** Role-play a negotiation where one party uses examples of others adopting similar terms to influence the other. Reflect on how this shapes perceptions of the proposal.

Key Takeaway

Social proof leverages the power of consensus to influence decisions. By showing that others endorse your ideas, you can build credibility and momentum, especially in situations of uncertainty.

Chapter 32: Contextualizing – Define the Rules to Trump the System

Why This Matters

Success in negotiations and strategy often depends not on playing the game better, but on redefining the game itself. Contextualizing involves framing or redefining the parameters of a situation to create favorable conditions. As discussed in David McRaney's *You Are Not So Smart* (2011), the way a situation is framed or structured heavily influences decision-making and behavior.

This approach matters because it allows you to take control of the narrative and the environment in which decisions are made. By setting the context, you establish the rules and priorities that others will follow, giving you a significant advantage.

How It Works

Contextualizing works by focusing attention on specific rules or framing that benefits you. For example, a salesperson might emphasize total value (e.g. "you'll save $1,000 over five years") rather than upfront costs, shifting the focus toward long-term gains.

In *Nudge* (Thaler & Sunstein, 2008), the authors explore how contextualizing – such as setting default choices or adjusting how options are presented – can guide decisions without restricting freedom. McRaney builds on this idea, arguing that people often fail to question the context, making it a powerful tool for influencing outcomes.

Real-Life Example

In 2003, Apple revolutionized the music industry by introducing the iTunes Store. At a time when music piracy via platforms like Napster was rampant, Apple reframed the rules of music consumption by offering an affordable, legal alternative. By contextualizing music as a digital asset rather than a physical product, Apple shifted consumer expectations and made purchasing individual songs for $0.99 an appealing option.

As highlighted in Walter Isaacson's *Steve Jobs* (2011), this reframing wasn't just about pricing; it was about reshaping how people viewed music ownership and access. Apple's contextual approach ultimately laid the groundwork for further innovations like Apple Music and Spotify, which expanded on the idea of digital access to transform the entire music industry.

Exercises

1. **Reframe a Proposal:** Think of a situation where you want to persuade someone. Write down the current framing and then redefine the context to highlight benefits that align with their priorities.
2. **Analyze Rule-Changing Strategies:** Research a company or leader who redefined an industry or negotiation rules (e.g. Tesla). How did contextualizing help them succeed?
3. **Test Contextualizing in Practice:** Role-play a negotiation where one party introduces new framing or rules. Reflect on how this changes the dynamics and outcomes of the discussion.

Key Takeaway

Contextualizing allows you to redefine the rules of engagement, creating an environment where success becomes more achievable. By shaping the narrative and structure of decisions, you gain a strategic edge.

Chapter 33: Moral Hazards – Avoid Incentivizing Bad Behavior

Why This Matters

A moral hazard arises when individuals or groups are incentivized to take risks because they know they'll be shielded from the consequences. Originally a term from economics, moral hazards now appear in negotiations, management, and policymaking. As Kenneth Arrow discussed in *The Limits of Organization* (1974), moral hazards stem from asymmetry between who bears the risk and who reaps the rewards.

Understanding moral hazards is critical because failing to address them can lead to irresponsible behavior, inflated risks, and systemic breakdowns. By carefully aligning incentives and accountability, you can create systems that encourage responsible decision-making without fostering recklessness.

How It Works

Moral hazards often emerge when people are insulated from the consequences of their actions. For example, employees with guaranteed job security might put in less effort if they know poor performance won't result in termination.

In *Thinking Strategically* (Dixit & Nalebuff, 1991), the authors emphasize that addressing moral hazards requires a balance of trust and incentives. Effective solutions include tying rewards to outcomes, improving transparency, and ensuring accountability. These measures realign the relationship between risks and rewards, mitigating reckless behavior.

Real-Life Example

The 2008 global financial crisis is a textbook example of moral hazard. Banks and financial institutions engaged in risky lending practices, knowing that potential losses would be mitigated by government bailouts. This lack of accountability incentivized short-term profits over long-term stability. As Joseph Stiglitz discusses in *Freefall: America, Free Markets, and the Sinking of the World Economy* (2010), moral hazards at multiple levels of the financial system contributed to the collapse, highlighting the dangers of shielding entities from the consequences of their actions.

On a smaller scale, moral hazards can arise in insurance. For instance, a car owner with comprehensive coverage might drive less cautiously, knowing that the insurance company will cover damages. This disconnect between responsibility and consequences leads to riskier behavior.

Exercises

1. **Identify a Moral Hazard:** Reflect on a system or process you're part of (e.g., workplace policies or shared resources). Are there safeguards that unintentionally incentivize risky or irresponsible behavior?
2. **Analyze a Historical Event:** Research the 2008 financial crisis or another event influenced by moral hazards. What were the misaligned incentives, and how could they have been addressed?
3. **Design an Incentive System:** Think of a scenario where you manage a team or resources. Write down how you would structure accountability and rewards to minimize moral hazards.

Key Takeaway

Moral hazards occur when people are shielded from the consequences of their actions, encouraging reckless behavior. By aligning risks and rewards, you can create systems that promote responsibility and accountability.

Chapter 34: The Tragedy of the Commons – Protecting Shared Resources

Why This Matters

The Tragedy of the Commons, first articulated by Garrett Hardin in his 1968 essay, describes how shared resources are often overused and depleted because individuals act in their own self-interest. This phenomenon appears in environmental issues, organizational settings, and even personal relationships.

Addressing the Tragedy of the Commons is crucial because it helps prevent the collapse of systems dependent on shared resources. Whether managing team projects, public goods, or ecosystems, understanding this dynamic enables you to foster cooperation and sustainability.

How It Works

The Tragedy of the Commons occurs when individuals prioritize personal gain over collective well-being, leading to resource depletion. For example, if a company overuses a shared data server for its own projects, it slows down performance for everyone else.

Hardin emphasized that solutions require collective action, such as setting usage limits, implementing penalties, or assigning property rights. Ostrom's *Governing the Commons* (1990) expanded on this idea, showing how communities can create successful resource management systems through cooperation, trust, and clearly defined rules.

Real-Life Example

Overfishing in international waters illustrates the Tragedy of the Commons. Without enforced limits, fishing companies exploit shared oceans, depleting fish stocks and harming the global food supply. Efforts like the United Nations Fish Stocks Agreement (1995) aim to regulate this behavior, but enforcement remains challenging.

In workplaces, shared resources like communal budgets or meeting rooms can fall victim to this dynamic. For instance, if one team monopolizes a shared conference room, others lose access, reducing overall productivity. Addressing such issues requires clear guidelines and collaborative planning.

Exercises

1. **Identify a Commons Issue:** Think of a shared resource you use regularly (e.g. office supplies, public parks). Are there examples of overuse, and how could this be mitigated?
2. **Study a Successful Solution:** Research a community or organization that successfully manages shared resources (e.g. water usage in arid regions). What strategies did they use?
3. **Propose a Policy:** Imagine managing a shared resource (e.g. a team budget). Write a policy to ensure sustainable and fair use.

Key Takeaway

The Tragedy of the Commons highlights the risks of overusing shared resources for personal gain. By fostering cooperation and setting clear rules, you can create sustainable systems that benefit everyone.

Chapter 35: The Sunk Cost Fallacy – Knowing When to Let Go

Why This Matters

The sunk cost fallacy is a cognitive bias that traps people into justifying further investments in time, money, or effort based on what they've already spent, even when it's no longer rational. This fallacy is a key concept in behavioral economics, popularized by Richard Thaler in *Misbehaving: The Making of Behavioral Economics* (2015).

Recognizing and avoiding the sunk cost fallacy is crucial because it allows you to make forward-looking decisions rather than being anchored by past commitments. Whether in business, relationships, or personal projects, understanding when to walk away can save you from throwing good resources after bad.

How It Works

The sunk cost fallacy occurs when decision-makers irrationally weigh previous investments, leading them to persist in failing ventures. For example, continuing to repair an old car that constantly breaks down might seem logical because of past repair costs, but buying a new car could be the more practical choice.

Thaler and Cass Sunstein, in *Nudge* (2008), emphasize that humans tend to overvalue past investments because of loss aversion — the fear of admitting failure or wasting effort. Breaking free from this bias requires reframing the decision in terms of future gains rather than sunk costs.

Real-Life Example

A notable example of the sunk cost fallacy occurred with Concorde, the supersonic jet project developed by Britain and France. Even after it became clear that the project was financially unsustainable, both governments continued funding it for years because of the significant resources already invested. This behavior exemplified the sunk cost trap, as described in *Behavioral Economics and Public Policy* (2014) by Camerer and Loewenstein, who argue that focusing on irrecoverable costs blinds decision-makers to better alternatives.

On a smaller scale, people often encounter the sunk cost fallacy in relationships. Staying in an unhealthy partnership because "we've been together for so long" exemplifies how past investments can cloud present judgment. Recognizing that sunk costs are irretrievable can help individuals prioritize future well-being over past efforts.

Exercises

1. **Identify Your Sunk Costs:** Think of a project, relationship, or habit where you've invested significant time or resources. Write down whether continuing offers future benefits or if it's time to let go.
2. **Analyze a Historical Example:** Research a business or government project that persisted due to sunk costs (e.g., Concorde or the Vietnam War). What lessons can be drawn from their decisions?
3. **Practice Reframing Decisions:** Imagine a scenario where you must decide whether to continue or quit (e.g., a project nearing failure). Reframe the decision based on potential future benefits rather than past investments.

Key Takeaway

The sunk cost fallacy traps decision-makers into irrational persistence by overvaluing past investments. By focusing on future benefits, you can make more rational and productive decisions.

Chapter 36: Information Asymmetry – Managing Knowledge Gaps

Why This Matters

Information asymmetry occurs when one party in a negotiation or decision-making process has more information than the other. This imbalance creates a power dynamic that can lead to unfair outcomes or strategic advantages. First articulated by George Akerlof in *The Market for Lemons* (1970), this concept is a cornerstone of economics and negotiation strategy.

Understanding and managing information asymmetry is crucial because it helps level the playing field. Whether you're the better-informed party or the one at a disadvantage, knowing how to use or overcome knowledge gaps can significantly impact the outcome of a negotiation.

How It Works

Information asymmetry often leads to two common outcomes:

Exploitation: The better-informed party uses their advantage to secure favorable terms (e.g., a car dealer selling a substandard vehicle to an uninformed buyer).

Distrust: The less-informed party, aware of the imbalance, becomes overly cautious, potentially derailing the negotiation.

Akerlof's research highlights that transparency and trust-building measures can mitigate these effects. In *Negotiation Genius* (Malhotra & Bazerman, 2008), the authors suggest techniques like sharing selective information, asking probing questions, and validating data to bridge knowledge gaps and build trust.

Real-Life Example

The used car market exemplifies information asymmetry, as buyers often lack the detailed knowledge sellers have about a vehicle's history. To address this, services like Carfax emerged, offering transparency through vehicle history reports. By reducing the information gap, these services have helped buyers make more informed decisions while encouraging sellers to provide higher-quality vehicles.

Another example comes from healthcare, where patients rely on doctors to interpret complex medical information. Mistrust can arise if patients suspect doctors of prioritizing profits over care. Efforts to improve transparency, such as offering second opinions or providing access to medical records, aim to reduce this asymmetry and foster trust.

Exercises

1. **Identify an Asymmetry:** Think of a situation where you were at an information disadvantage (e.g. purchasing a product or negotiating a contract). How did this impact the outcome?
2. **Analyze an Industry Solution:** Research a product or service (e.g. Carfax, online reviews) designed to reduce information asymmetry. How does it level the playing field?
3. **Practice Closing Gaps:** In a negotiation scenario, role-play as both the better-informed and less-informed party. Practice strategies like probing questions, transparency, and selective disclosure to manage the information gap.

Key Takeaway

Information asymmetry creates power imbalances in negotiations and decisions. By addressing knowledge gaps and fostering transparency, you can build trust and achieve fairer outcomes.

Chapter 37: Herd Behavior – Predicting Group Dynamics

Why This Matters

Herd behavior refers to the tendency of individuals to follow the actions of a larger group, often without fully considering their own information or judgment. This phenomenon, first studied in-depth by Banerjee in *A Simple Model of Herd Behavior* (1992), highlights how group dynamics influence decision-making.

Understanding herd behavior is crucial because it shapes markets, public opinion, and even personal decisions. From stock market bubbles to viral trends, recognizing when people are acting as part of a herd allows you to anticipate movements, avoid pitfalls, and strategically influence group dynamics to your advantage.

How It Works

Herd behavior arises when individuals prioritize group consensus over personal judgment, often to avoid standing out or making a mistake. For example, in a hiring decision, a manager might favor a candidate praised by others, even if they have reservations, simply to align with the group.

Banerjee's model shows how information cascades contribute to herd behavior. If early decision-makers act in a particular way, others are likely to follow, assuming the first group had better information. In *Thinking, Fast and Slow* (Kahneman, 2011), this tendency is tied to System 1 thinking — an intuitive, fast-response system — which seeks shortcuts in uncertain situations by deferring to the crowd.

Real-Life Example

The Dot-Com Bubble of the late 1990s is a famous example of herd behavior in financial markets. As investors saw others pouring money into internet start-ups, they followed suit, ignoring the lack of viable business models. This collective overvaluation led to an eventual market crash. Banerjee's analysis of herd behavior explains how the assumption that "everyone else knows something I don't" can lead to irrational mass decision-making.

On a smaller scale, herd behavior is evident in consumer trends. For instance, the rise of fidget spinners in 2017 saw millions of people buying the product simply because others were, rather than because of its intrinsic value. Understanding these patterns allows marketers to anticipate and even create trends by targeting key influencers within a group.

Exercises

1. **Identify Herd Behavior:** Think of a recent decision you made that was influenced by others (e.g., buying a product or choosing an activity). Was it based on personal judgment or the influence of the group?
2. **Analyze a Market Trend:** Research a market trend or bubble (e.g. cryptocurrency, NFTs). How did herd behavior contribute to its rise or fall?
3. **Simulate Herd Dynamics:** In a group decision-making exercise, have one participant act as an influencer by endorsing a specific choice. Observe how the group's behavior shifts and analyze whether the decision was rational or herd-driven.

Key Takeaway

Herd behavior drives group decisions, often overriding individual judgment. Recognizing and predicting these dynamics allows you to navigate or influence collective actions strategically.

Chapter 38: Reputation Capital – Building and Spending Trust Wisely

Why This Matters

In negotiations and decision-making, reputation is a form of capital that takes time to build but can be spent strategically. Reputation capital refers to the accumulated trust and credibility that influences how others perceive your actions and intentions. Axelrod's *The Evolution of Cooperation* (1984) demonstrates that a strong reputation encourages cooperation and deters adversarial behavior.

Reputation capital matters because it serves as both a shield

and a bargaining tool. A trustworthy reputation earns goodwill, making others more likely to agree to your terms. However, reckless actions or broken promises can deplete this resource, damaging relationships and opportunities in the long term.

How It Works

Reputation capital is built through consistent behavior that aligns with shared values, honesty, and reliability. For example, delivering on promises strengthens trust, while failing to follow through erodes credibility. Axelrod's research shows that in repeated interactions, a good reputation deters exploitation because others value the benefits of continued cooperation.

In *Reputation Rules* (Diermeier, 2011), the author emphasizes that managing reputation involves balancing long-term consistency with occasional strategic risks. Spending reputation capital judiciously—such as calling in favors or challenging norms—can yield high rewards, provided it doesn't undermine future trust.

Real-Life Example

In the 1990s, Toyota built a reputation for reliability and quality through consistent product performance and customer service. However, a series of recalls in the late 2000s dented that trust. Toyota's response—open communication, accountability, and swift action—helped rebuild its reputation capital over time, demonstrating how managing credibility can sustain relationships even after setbacks.

On an individual level, professionals rely on reputation capital in networking. A manager known for integrity is more likely to secure promotions, partnerships, and loyalty from their team than one with a history of broken promises. This dynamic aligns with Axelrod's findings on reciprocity and trust in cooperative systems.

Exercises

1. **Evaluate Your Reputation:** Write down how others perceive your reliability, honesty, and collaboration skills. What actions could strengthen your reputation capital?
2. **Analyze Reputation Recovery:** Research a company or individual that successfully rebuilt their reputation after a crisis. What actions helped restore trust?
3. **Plan Reputation Spending:** Think of a scenario where you might need to "spend" reputation capital (e.g., asking for a favor or making an unpopular decision). How will you balance the immediate benefits with the long-term impact on trust?

Key Takeaway

Reputation capital is a valuable resource that builds trust and credibility over time. By managing and spending it wisely, you can strengthen relationships and achieve long-term success.

Chapter 39: Shadow of the Future – Decisions with Long-Term Consequences

Why This Matters

In repeated interactions or long-term relationships, the shadow of the future plays a critical role in shaping behavior. A concept explored in Robert Axelrod's *The Evolution of Cooperation* (1984), this principle explains how the anticipation of future encounters encourages cooperation and deters short-term exploitation.

Understanding the shadow of the future is essential for making decisions with lasting implications. In negotiations, business partnerships, or personal relationships, recognizing the long-term impact of today's actions helps you build trust, avoid conflicts, and foster sustainable outcomes.

How It Works

The shadow of the future operates on the idea that future consequences influence present behavior. For example, in a business partnership, one party might avoid deceptive tactics to maintain the relationship and ensure continued collaboration.

Axelrod's research shows that when players in a repeated game anticipate future interactions, they are more likely to adopt cooperative strategies like reciprocity. This principle also aligns with Elinor Ostrom's findings in *Governing the Commons* (1990), which highlight that long-term perspectives are critical for sustainable management of shared resources.

In practical terms, the shadow of the future creates accountability. Knowing that today's actions will impact tomorrow's opportunities encourages decision-makers to prioritize integrity, fairness, and mutual benefit.

Real-Life Example

The founding of the European Union (EU) is a compelling example of the shadow of the future. After World War II, European nations recognized that their long-term stability and prosperity depended on closer economic and political cooperation. The creation of the European Coal and Steel Community (ECSC) in 1951 laid the groundwork for the EU by fostering collaboration in industries critical to national security, reducing the likelihood of future conflicts. This forward-thinking approach prioritized shared, long-term benefits over short-term nationalism, ensuring decades of peace and economic growth in the region.

Exercises

1. **Evaluate Long-Term Impacts:** Think of a decision you're currently facing. Write down how it could influence your relationships, opportunities, or reputation five years from now.
2. **Analyze Cooperation in Repeated Games:** Research a successful partnership (e.g. between companies or countries). How did the shadow of the future encourage cooperation and deter exploitation?
3. **Simulate Long-Term Accountability:** In a role-playing exercise, negotiate a deal where future interactions are guaranteed. Observe how knowing you'll meet again influences trust, concessions, and decision-making.

Key Takeaway

The shadow of the future highlights the long-term consequences of today's decisions. By prioritizing sustainable, cooperative actions, you can build trust and strengthen relationships for lasting success.

Chapter 40: Overconfidence Bias – Avoiding Hubris in Planning

Why This Matters

Overconfidence bias is the tendency to overestimate one's abilities, knowledge, or control over outcomes. This bias, explored by Daniel Kahneman and Amos Tversky in their foundational research on heuristics, can lead to unrealistic expectations, poor planning, and avoidable failures.

Avoiding overconfidence is critical for effective decision-making. Whether in business, negotiations, or personal endeavors, recognizing your limits and accounting for uncertainty allows you to make more balanced, realistic plans. As highlighted in Kahneman's *Thinking, Fast and Slow* (2011), tempering confidence with critical thinking can prevent costly mistakes.

How It Works

Overconfidence bias manifests in several ways:

Overprecision: Overestimating the accuracy of one's knowledge or predictions.

Overestimation: Believing one's abilities or outcomes are better than they are.

Illusion of Control: Assuming more influence over events than is realistic.

In *The Undoing Project* (Lewis, 2016), the partnership between Kahneman and Tversky demonstrates how overconfidence leads people to ignore warning signs, underestimate risks, and overcommit resources. Recognizing this bias requires incorporating feedback, consulting diverse perspectives, and preparing for worst-case scenarios.

Real-Life Example

The failure of WeWork's IPO in 2019 is a striking example of overconfidence bias. WeWork's leadership, particularly its CEO, overestimated the company's valuation, disregarded critical feedback, and failed to account for operational weaknesses. This hubris led to the collapse of the IPO and a drastic reduction in valuation, forcing a leadership overhaul and significant restructuring.

On a personal level, overconfidence bias often appears in career planning. For instance, someone might overestimate their qualifications for a job and neglect to prepare adequately for an interview, resulting in missed opportunities. Recognizing and addressing overconfidence ensures better preparation and adaptability.

Exercises

1. **Identify Overconfidence:** Reflect on a past decision where overconfidence led to a mistake. How could you have better accounted for risks or sought additional input?
2. **Analyze a Case of Hubris:** Research a business or leader whose overconfidence led to failure (e.g. WeWork, Blockbuster). What lessons can you apply to your own decision-making?
3. **Plan for Uncertainty:** In a current project, write down worst-case scenarios and how you would address them. Compare this approach to your initial expectations and adjust your plans accordingly.

Key Takeaway

Overconfidence bias blinds individuals to risks and limitations, leading to poor decisions. By recognizing this bias and accounting for uncertainty, you can make more realistic and effective plans.

Section V: Resilient and Creative Strategies

Success in complex and ever-changing environments requires resilience, creativity, and the ability to adapt. This section explores strategies that equip you to thrive under pressure, plan for uncertainty, and turn challenges into opportunities. From building redundancy to prepare for failure, to leveraging a win-win mindset for collaboration, and mastering emotional regulation in high-stakes situations, these chapters provide actionable techniques to stay agile and forward-thinking. Whether you're managing limited resources, building coalitions, or practicing patience for long-term gains, this section emphasizes strategies that ensure sustained success in even the most dynamic circumstances.

Chapter 41: Redundancy – Preparing for Failure

Why This Matters

In any system, failure is not just a possibility — it's a certainty over time. Redundancy involves creating backup systems, resources, or strategies to ensure continuity and resilience when things go wrong. Nassim Nicholas Taleb highlights the importance of redundancy in *Antifragile: Things That Gain from Disorder* (2012), arguing that it acts as a buffer against uncertainty and unexpected events.

Redundancy matters because it protects you from catastrophic losses. Whether in negotiations, business planning, or personal projects, having alternatives and safeguards allows you to respond quickly and effectively to setbacks without losing momentum.

How It Works

Redundancy operates on the principle of distributing risks across multiple layers. For example, an entrepreneur launching a new product might maintain a reserve of capital to cover unexpected costs or have alternate suppliers to prevent delays.

In *The Checklist Manifesto* (Gawande, 2009), the author illustrates how redundancy — through simple yet systematic preparation — saves lives in fields like surgery and aviation. By anticipating potential failures and building safety nets, individuals and organizations can maintain stability even in crises.

Real-Life Example

The Apollo 13 mission of 1970 is a famous example of redundancy in action. After an oxygen tank exploded, putting the crew's lives at risk, NASA engineers relied on redundant systems and pre-tested contingency plans to ensure the astronauts' safe return. As Taleb notes, redundancy wasn't just a safety measure—it was the reason the mission didn't end in disaster.

In everyday life, redundancy can appear in personal finance. Maintaining an emergency fund ensures you're prepared for unexpected expenses, like medical bills or job loss. Without this safety net, a single crisis can create long-term financial instability.

Exercises

1. **Identify Redundancy Gaps:** Think about a current project or system you rely on (e.g. your work schedule, finances). What are the potential points of failure, and how could you create backups?
2. **Research Redundancy in History:** Study an event or project (e.g. Apollo 13) where redundancy played a critical role. How did the preparation ensure success despite failure?
3. **Plan Your Redundancy Layers:** Write down one area in your life or work where you could benefit from additional safety nets. Develop at least two specific backup strategies.

Key Takeaway

Redundancy is the foundation of resilience. By anticipating failures and building layers of backup, you can maintain stability and adapt effectively to unexpected challenges.

Chapter 42: Flexible Approaches – Adapting in Real-Time

In rapidly changing environments, rigidity is a liability. Flexibility involves the ability to adjust plans, strategies, and mindsets in response to new information or shifting circumstances. As emphasized in *The Art of War* by Sun Tzu (translated 1910), adaptability is critical for survival and success, whether in battle, business, or negotiations.

Flexibility matters because static strategies often fail in dynamic environments. By staying open to change and reacting quickly to emerging challenges, you can seize opportunities, mitigate risks, and maintain momentum.

How It Works

Flexibility requires a balance between preparation and spontaneity. For example, a negotiator might enter discussions with clear goals but remain open to alternative solutions proposed by the other party.

In *The Lean Startup* (Ries, 2011), the author advocates for iterative approaches, where businesses continuously adapt their strategies based on customer feedback and market trends. This mindset enables rapid responses to change, reducing the risk of major failures.

Real-Life Example

The COVID-19 pandemic demonstrated the importance of flexibility across industries. Many restaurants adapted by pivoting to takeout and delivery services, while remote work became the norm for businesses worldwide. Companies like Zoom and DoorDash thrived because they quickly adjusted to meet new demands. As Ries suggests, flexibility allows organizations to turn crises into opportunities by aligning their actions with changing realities.

On a personal level, flexibility might involve adjusting career goals in response to economic changes. For instance, someone facing job loss might pivot to an entirely new industry, leveraging transferable skills to succeed in a different environment.

Exercises

1. **Evaluate Your Flexibility:** Think of a recent situation where your plans didn't work out as expected. How did you adapt, and what could you have done differently?
2. **Study a Flexible Organization:** Research a company that thrived by adapting to change (e.g., Zoom during the pandemic). What strategies enabled their success?
3. **Practice Flexibility in Decision-Making:** Simulate a negotiation where unexpected challenges arise. Practice adjusting your approach in real-time while maintaining focus on your goals.

Key Takeaway

Flexibility is the ability to adapt to changing circumstances while maintaining focus on long-term objectives. By staying open to new ideas and adjusting your strategies, you can turn challenges into opportunities.

Chapter 43: Scenario Analysis – Considering Through Every Outcome

Why This Matters

In a world filled with uncertainty, making decisions without considering possible outcomes can lead to costly mistakes. Scenario analysis is a strategic planning method that evaluates a range of potential futures to identify risks, opportunities, and contingency plans. Originating in military strategy and later adapted to business by companies like Shell in the 1970s, this approach allows decision-makers to act with foresight and confidence.

Scenario analysis matters because it helps you prepare for uncertainty. By anticipating how different factors might interact, you can build resilience against disruptions, make more informed choices, and avoid the paralysis of decision-making under pressure.

How It Works

Scenario analysis involves three key steps:

Define Critical Variables: Identify factors most likely to influence outcomes (e.g. market trends, competitor actions).

Develop Scenarios: Create plausible stories for how these variables might interact, such as "best case," "worst case," and "most likely case."

Plan Responses: Develop strategies tailored to each scenario, ensuring you're prepared no matter what happens.

In *The Art of the Long View* (Schwartz, 1991), the author emphasizes the importance of using scenario analysis not just for predicting the future, but for clarifying present uncertainties and strategic options. The method fosters creative thinking while grounding decisions in data and logic.

Real-Life Example

During the COVID-19 pandemic, hospitals used scenario analysis to prepare for potential surges in patient numbers. Administrators developed strategies for resource allocation based on different scenarios, such as "moderate increase in cases" or "overwhelming influx." This proactive planning allowed some institutions to manage resources effectively, avoiding critical shortages.

Businesses also relied on scenario analysis during the pandemic. For instance, airlines evaluated scenarios ranging from slow recovery to prolonged shutdowns, developing plans for each. Companies that engaged in thorough scenario planning were better positioned to adapt to unpredictable changes in travel demand.

Exercises

1. **Map Your Scenarios:** Identify a decision or project you're working on. Write down three scenarios – best case, worst case, and most likely case – and outline potential strategies for each.

2. **Analyze a Historical Example:** Research an organization or government that successfully used scenario analysis (e.g. Shell during the oil crisis of the 1970s). What lessons can you apply to your own decision-making?

3. **Simulate a Scenario Planning Session:** With a team or partner, choose a challenge and brainstorm possible outcomes. Develop plans for each scenario and discuss how they would impact your choices.

Key Takeaway

Scenario analysis prepares you to navigate uncertainty by considering multiple possible futures. By planning for a range of outcomes, you can make informed decisions and adapt to changing circumstances with confidence.

Chapter 44: Win-Win Mindset – Growing the Pie for Everyone

A win-win mindset focuses on creating value that benefits everyone involved. First introduced in Fisher and Ury's *Getting to Yes* (1981), this approach emphasizes collaborative problem-solving to expand the "pie" rather than fight over fixed portions.

It fosters trust, creativity, and long-term relationships. When parties work together toward mutual benefit, they can uncover shared interests, resolve conflicts more efficiently, and create sustainable outcomes that satisfy all stakeholders.

Importantly, win-win strategies are not about being "nice" or making unnecessary concessions. As Covey explains in *The Speed of Trust* (2006), a win-win outcome is built on mutual respect and credibility, ensuring fairness while maximizing value for all parties. This approach requires clarity of goals, open communication, and a willingness to think beyond immediate, self-centered gains.

How It Works

Adopting a win-win mindset involves shifting away from competitive thinking and embracing collaboration. The process includes three essential steps:

1. **Separate Positions from Interests:** Positions are the surface-level demands people make (e.g. "I need a higher salary"), while interests are the underlying reasons behind those demands (e.g., "I need financial security"). By identifying and addressing interests, negotiators can find solutions that satisfy deeper needs rather than fixating on rigid positions.

2. **Generate Creative Options:** A win-win negotiation often requires thinking outside the box. Rather than framing a discussion as a single-issue conflict, such as "who gets more," negotiators can explore creative options that add value for both sides. For instance, in a job negotiation, instead of merely haggling over salary, the parties might consider additional benefits like flexible hours or professional development opportunities.

3. **Use Objective Criteria:** Disputes often arise from subjective perceptions of fairness. Using objective standards, such as industry benchmarks or market data, helps create a common ground for decision-making. This approach fosters transparency and reduces the risk of emotional conflict.

In *The Manager as Negotiator* (Lax & Sebenius, 1986), the authors stress that win-win solutions are particularly effective in complex, multi-party negotiations where shared goals can lead to exponential value creation. By reframing the negotiation as a joint problem-solving effort, parties can uncover opportunities that might otherwise go unnoticed.

Real-Life Example

The **Dayton Accords** of 1995, which ended the Bosnian War, exemplify the win-win mindset in high-stakes negotiations. Mediators focused on creating agreements that addressed the core concerns of all parties involved—territorial control, governance, and security guarantees—rather than forcing one side to "win" outright. By identifying shared interests, the accords achieved a fragile but lasting peace.

Exercises

1. **Practice Separating Interests:** Think of a disagreement you've experienced. Write down the surface-level positions of each party and then list the underlying interests. How could a win-win approach address these interests?

2. **Analyze a Win-Win Negotiation:** Research a successful negotiation that used win-win principles (e.g. a high-profile business merger). What strategies fostered mutual benefit?

3. **Simulate a Collaborative Negotiation:** Role-play a negotiation where both parties work together to brainstorm creative options. Focus on expanding the "pie" rather than dividing it. Reflect on the outcomes and how they differ from a zero-sum approach.

Key Takeaway

A win-win mindset emphasizes collaboration and mutual benefit, transforming conflicts into opportunities to create value. By addressing shared interests, using creative problem-solving, and relying on objective criteria, you can achieve outcomes that satisfy all parties while fostering long-term relationships.

Chapter 45: Emotional Regulation – Staying Cool Under Fire

Why This Matters

Emotional regulation is the cornerstone of effective decision-making and negotiation. In high-pressure situations, emotions like anger, frustration, or anxiety can cloud judgment and lead to poor outcomes. As Daniel Goleman discusses in *Emotional Intelligence* (1995), the ability to recognize and manage emotions — both yours and others' — is a critical skill in leadership, negotiations, and conflict resolution.

Mastering emotional regulation allows you to think clearly, maintain focus, and respond constructively, even when tensions are high. It also prevents emotional outbursts that could damage relationships or derail discussions. This skill is especially valuable in complex negotiations, where composure often determines whether you secure a favorable deal or lose ground.

How It Works

Emotional regulation involves three key steps:

1. **Recognize Your Emotions:** Identify your emotional triggers and how they manifest (e.g. a racing heart, raised voice). Awareness is the first step in managing emotional responses.
2. **Pause and Reflect:** Take a moment to step back before reacting. Techniques like deep breathing or counting to ten can help defuse immediate emotional intensity.
3. **Reframe the Situation:** Shift your perspective to focus on the bigger picture or underlying goals, rather than the emotional trigger. This approach fosters constructive responses rather than impulsive reactions.

In *Thinking, Fast and Slow* (Kahneman, 2011), the author highlights how instinctive "fast thinking" often leads to emotional decisions. Emotional regulation helps activate "slow thinking," enabling more rational and measured responses.

Real-Life Example

Captain Chesley "Sully" Sullenberger's emergency landing on the Hudson River in 2009 demonstrates the power of emotional regulation in high-pressure situations. After a bird strike disabled both engines of US Airways Flight 1549, Sully remained calm and focused, quickly assessing the situation and executing a safe water landing that saved all 155 passengers and crew aboard. His ability to manage his emotions allowed him to think clearly, prioritize actions, and make life-saving decisions under extreme stress.

Sully's story is often cited as an example of emotional intelligence in action, aligning with Daniel Goleman's emphasis on self-control and composure as key components of effective leadership.

Exercises

1. **Identify Emotional Triggers:** Reflect on a recent situation where emotions influenced your actions. What triggered your response, and how could you have managed it better?
2. **Practice Calming Techniques:** Try a calming strategy like deep breathing, meditation, or visualization during a stressful moment. Record how it affected your ability to think clearly.
3. **Reframe a Conflict:** Think of a past conflict. How could you have reframed the situation to focus on solutions rather than the emotional trigger?

Key Takeaway

Emotional regulation allows you to maintain control and think clearly under pressure. By recognizing triggers, pausing before reacting, and reframing situations, you can respond constructively and achieve better outcomes.

Chapter 46: Empathy Mapping – Understanding Others' Motivation

Why This Matters

Understanding the motivations, fears, and desires of others is key to building trust, resolving conflicts, and influencing decisions. Empathy mapping is a structured tool for visualizing another person's perspective, helping you gain deeper insights into their mindset. As Simon Sinek explains in *Start with Why* (2009), understanding the "why" behind people's actions allows you to connect with them more effectively and align your strategies with their goals.

Empathy mapping matters because it transforms interactions. Whether negotiating, managing a team, or addressing a customer's needs, seeing the world from their perspective creates opportunities for collaboration, innovation, and influence. It also helps you anticipate objections and address them proactively.

How It Works

Empathy mapping involves answering key questions about the other person's experience:

1. **What Do They Say?** Understand their explicit concerns, demands, or feedback.
2. **What Do They Think?** Consider their beliefs, assumptions, or doubts that influence their behavior.
3. **What Do They Feel?** Identify emotional drivers like fear, excitement, or frustration.
4. **What Do They Do?** Observe their actions, habits, and decisions.

In *Designing for Growth* (Liedtka & Ogilvie, 2011), empathy mapping is presented as a tool to uncover hidden needs and align solutions with the other party's perspective. It helps you focus on understanding motivations rather than making assumptions.

Real-Life Example

Successful customer service teams often use empathy mapping to improve experiences. For example, Zappos, an online shoe retailer, trains employees to empathize with customers' frustrations, such as returning a pair of shoes. By focusing on the customer's perspective, Zappos consistently delivers exceptional service and builds lasting loyalty.

In negotiations, empathy mapping can be used to uncover shared goals. For instance, when negotiating a contract, understanding the other party's financial constraints or long-term objectives allows you to propose solutions that align with their priorities, fostering trust and collaboration.

Exercises

1. **Create an Empathy Map:** Choose someone you interact with regularly (e.g. a colleague, customer, or partner). Answer the four key questions to map their perspective and identify how you can address their needs.
2. **Analyze a Case Study:** Research a company or leader known for empathetic practices (e.g. Simon Sinek). How did empathy influence their success?
3. **Simulate Empathy in Negotiations:** Role-play a negotiation where one party uses empathy mapping to understand the other's needs. Reflect on how this strategy improves outcomes.

Key Takeaway

Empathy mapping provides a structured way to understand others' motivations, fostering trust and collaboration. By stepping into their perspective, you can anticipate needs, address concerns, and align strategies for mutual benefit.

Chapter 47: Asymmetric Warfare – Persevering with Fewer Resources

Why This Matters

In many situations, individuals or groups face opponents with significantly greater resources or power. Asymmetric warfare involves using unconventional strategies to counter these imbalances, turning perceived weaknesses into advantages. This concept originates in military strategy but is widely applicable in negotiations, business, and life. As discussed in *The Art of Strategy* (Dixit & Nalebuff, 2008), leveraging creativity and adaptability allows smaller players to succeed against formidable adversaries.

Asymmetric warfare matters because it teaches that resource limitations do not equate to inevitable defeat. Instead, those with fewer resources can focus on efficiency, innovation, and strategic maneuvering to achieve disproportionate outcomes. Whether you're a start-up competing with an industry giant or an individual negotiating with a large organization, understanding and applying asymmetric strategies can level the playing field.

How It Works

Asymmetric warfare relies on identifying and exploiting the vulnerabilities of a larger opponent. Key principles include:

1. **Leverage Agility:** Smaller players can adapt faster than larger, slower-moving opponents.
2. **Exploit Weak Points:** Identify areas where the larger entity is overextended, inefficient, or vulnerable.
3. **Focus Resources Strategically:** Concentrate efforts on areas where you can have the greatest impact, rather than spreading resources too thin.

In *The Innovator's Dilemma* (Christensen, 1997), the author highlights how smaller companies often disrupt industry leaders by focusing on niche markets the giants overlook. This principle of asymmetric strategy applies beyond business, emphasizing the importance of targeted, unconventional approaches to overcoming resource gaps.

Real-Life Example

The rise of Airbnb is a striking example of asymmetric strategy in business. Competing against established hotel chains with far greater resources, Airbnb leveraged a decentralized model, allowing property owners to offer accommodations without the overhead costs associated with traditional hotels. By focusing on underserved niches—such as travelers seeking affordable or unique experiences — Airbnb disrupted the hospitality industry, growing into a global powerhouse.

In personal contexts, asymmetric strategies can appear in job negotiations. For instance, a candidate without direct experience in a specific role might emphasize transferable skills, personal projects, or unique insights that larger, more experienced candidates might not possess. By shifting the focus, they can stand out and succeed despite lacking traditional qualifications.

Exercises

1. **Identify an Asymmetry:** Reflect on a situation where you faced a larger or more powerful opponent (e.g., a competitor, company, or team). How could you have used unconventional strategies to gain an advantage?
2. **Analyze a Disruptor:** Research a company or individual who succeeded against a more powerful competitor (e.g. SpaceX). What asymmetric strategies contributed to their success?
3. **Simulate an Asymmetric Challenge:** Role-play a scenario where one party has significantly fewer resources than the other. Practice developing creative strategies to overcome the imbalance.

Key Takeaway

Asymmetric warfare shows that resource limitations can be overcome with creativity, adaptability, and strategic focus. By identifying and exploiting vulnerabilities, smaller players can achieve outsized success against larger opponents.

Chapter 48: Coalition Building – Strength in Numbers

Why This Matters

Coalition building involves bringing together individuals or groups with shared interests to achieve a common objective. Whether in negotiations, activism, or business, coalitions amplify strength by combining resources, knowledge, and influence. This concept is central to game theory, as discussed in *Co-opetition* (Brandenburger & Nalebuff, 1996), where collaboration among competitors often creates more value than working alone.

Coalition building matters because it provides leverage in complex situations. By forming alliances, you can tackle challenges that would be insurmountable alone, amplify your voice, and pool resources to achieve collective goals. It also fosters diversity of thought, leading to more innovative and sustainable solutions.

How It Works

Effective coalition building involves:

1. **Identifying Shared Goals:** Find common ground among potential allies, even if your broader interests differ.
2. **Clarifying Roles:** Assign clear responsibilities to each member of the coalition, ensuring efficient collaboration.
3. **Balancing Contributions and Rewards:** Ensure that all parties benefit proportionally from the coalition's success, maintaining trust and commitment.

In *Getting to Yes* (Fisher & Ury, 1981), the authors highlight that coalitions work best when based on mutual respect and transparent communication. Avoiding hidden agendas and fostering shared accountability are key to sustaining partnerships over time.

Real-Life Example

The Civil Rights Movement in the United States exemplifies the power of coalition building. Organizations like the NAACP, Southern Christian Leadership Conference (SCLC), and Student Nonviolent Coordinating Committee (SNCC) joined forces with faith groups, labor unions, and student activists to push for civil rights reforms. Despite differing strategies and priorities, these coalitions united around shared goals, such as ending segregation and securing voting rights. Their combined efforts led to landmark achievements like the Civil Rights Act of 1964.

In the corporate world, coalition building appears in strategic partnerships. For example, car manufacturers and tech companies often collaborate to develop electric vehicles or autonomous driving technologies. These coalitions allow each partner to leverage the other's strengths, such as manufacturing expertise or software development, creating mutual benefits.

Exercises

1. **Form Your Own Coalition:** Think of a challenge or goal you're facing. Who could you partner with to combine strengths and achieve success? Write down their potential contributions and the shared goals.
2. **Analyze a Coalition in History:** Research a successful coalition (e.g. the Civil Rights Movement or a business partnership). What made their collaboration effective, and what challenges did they overcome?
3. **Simulate Coalition Negotiations:** Role-play forming a coalition with a group. Practice clarifying roles, balancing contributions, and maintaining trust throughout the process.

Key Takeaway

Coalition building demonstrates the power of collaboration in achieving shared goals. By uniting around common interests, balancing contributions, and fostering trust, coalitions can overcome challenges and create lasting success.

Chapter 49: Resource Management – Making Every Move Count

Why This Matters

In every aspect of life—whether in negotiations, business, or personal endeavors — resources are finite. Resource management is the art of allocating time, money, energy, or talent effectively to achieve maximum impact. As Peter Drucker emphasizes in *The Effective Executive* (1967), the way you use resources often matters more than the resources themselves.

Mastering resource management is crucial because even the most abundant assets can be wasted without a clear strategy. Conversely, individuals or organizations with limited resources can achieve remarkable results by optimizing their use. Whether facing tight budgets, constrained timeframes, or limited manpower, effective resource management ensures that every move counts.

How It Works

Resource management involves:

1. **Prioritizing Goals:** Focus on high-impact objectives that align with long-term strategies. Avoid spreading resources too thin by trying to achieve everything at once.
2. **Allocating Strategically:** Divide resources based on priority, urgency, and return on investment. For example, dedicate more funding to projects with clear potential for success.
3. **Monitoring and Adjusting:** Continuously evaluate how resources are being used and make necessary adjustments to stay on track.

In *Essentialism* (McKeown, 2014), the author emphasizes the importance of "less but better," focusing on a few critical priorities instead of attempting to tackle everything at once. This mindset is key to efficient resource management.

Real-Life Example

During the Battle of Thermopylae, King Leonidas of Sparta exemplified resource management by using a small force of 300 Spartans to defend against a much larger Persian army. By carefully choosing the narrow mountain pass as the battleground, Leonidas maximized his limited manpower's effectiveness, holding off the Persian forces far longer than expected. This tactical use of resources became legendary and underscores the power of strategic thinking in constrained situations.

In business, small start-ups often face resource constraints but succeed by focusing on their core strengths. For example, WhatsApp began with a small team but concentrated its efforts on providing a simple, efficient messaging platform. By managing their limited resources effectively, they grew into one of the most successful messaging services globally before being acquired by Facebook.

Exercises

1. **Prioritize Your Resources:** Think about a current project or goal. List your available resources and rank them based on their importance and impact. How can you reallocate them for better results?
2. **Study a Case of Resourcefulness:** Research a historical event or company (e.g. the Battle of Thermopylae or a successful startup) where limited resources were managed effectively. What strategies did they use?
3. **Simulate Resource Allocation:** Create a scenario where you have limited resources (e.g. time, budget, or manpower). Develop a plan to allocate them strategically to achieve your goal.

Key Takeaway

Resource management is the art of achieving maximum impact with finite resources. By prioritizing goals, allocating strategically, and remaining adaptable, you can overcome limitations and achieve success.

Chapter 50: Leverage Longevity – Practice Patience for Big Returns

In a world that often prioritizes instant gratification, patience is an undervalued but powerful strategy. Leverage longevity means focusing on long-term goals and enduring short-term setbacks to achieve significant returns over time. As discussed in *The Compound Effect* (Hardy, 2010), consistent, small efforts accumulate exponentially when given enough time.

Patience matters because many of life's most significant successes — whether in business, relationships, or personal growth — are the result of sustained effort over time. By practicing persistence and resisting the temptation for immediate results, you can achieve goals that might seem unattainable in the short term.

How It Works

Leverage longevity operates on three principles:

1. **Think Long-Term:** Set goals that align with your broader vision, even if they require years to achieve.
2. **Stay Consistent:** Focus on small, incremental progress rather than seeking dramatic, overnight changes.
3. **Endure Setbacks:** Recognize that temporary failures are part of the journey and maintain resilience through adversity.

In *Antifragile* (Taleb, 2012), the author emphasizes the value of systems that improve over time through sustained effort and adaptation. This concept applies to personal and professional growth, where patience amplifies the impact of consistent work.

Real-Life Example

Warren Buffett's investment philosophy epitomizes the power of patience. Buffett's strategy involves identifying high-quality companies and holding onto investments for decades, allowing compounding to work its magic. This approach has made him one of the world's wealthiest individuals. His success underscores the value of thinking long-term and resisting the temptation to chase short-term trends.

On a personal level, longevity can be leveraged in skill development. For example, someone learning a new language or mastering an instrument won't see immediate results, but years of consistent practice lead to fluency or expertise. By staying patient and persistent, individuals achieve milestones that once seemed out of reach.

Exercises

1. **Set a Long-Term Goal:** Identify a goal that will take at least one year to achieve. Break it into smaller milestones and commit to consistent effort toward each step.
2. **Analyze Patience in Action:** Research a successful person (e.g. Warren Buffett) or project that benefited from long-term thinking. What can you learn from their persistence?
3. **Reflect on Past Efforts:** Think of a time when patience paid off for you. What challenges did you face, and how did staying consistent help you succeed?

Key Takeaway

Leverage longevity emphasizes the power of patience and persistence in achieving big returns. By focusing on long-term goals, staying consistent, and enduring setbacks, you can unlock exponential growth and success over time.

Section VI: Strategies for Handling Complexity

As decisions grow more intricate and variables multiply, strategies must evolve to manage complexity effectively. This section explores how to navigate challenging environments, from mastering multi-party negotiations to using Bayesian reasoning in uncertain scenarios. These chapters provide tools for controlling escalation, adapting to shifting rules, and blending competition with collaboration. With a focus on clarity and precision, you'll learn to simplify overwhelming situations, leverage behavioral insights, and build robust plans that thrive in dynamic contexts. These techniques turn complexity into an advantage, equipping you to excel in even the most convoluted scenarios.

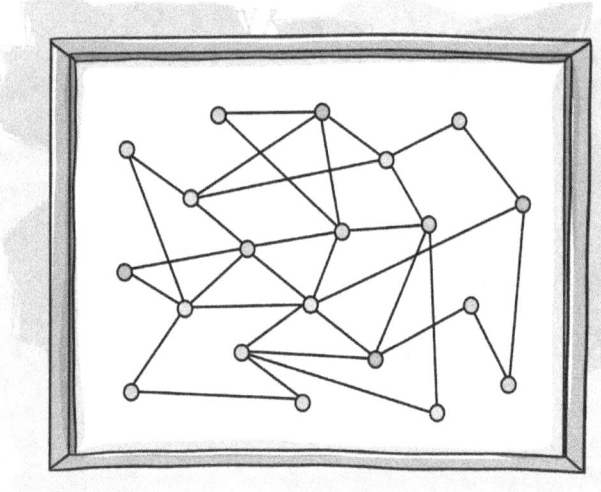

Chapter 51: Multi-Party Negotiations – Managing Complex Group Dynamics

Why This Matters

Negotiations involving multiple parties are exponentially more complex than one-on-one discussions. Multi-party negotiations introduce competing interests, power imbalances, and the potential for coalitions, making coordination and consensus-building critical. As Howard Raiffa explores in *The Art and Science of Negotiation* (1982), managing multi-party dynamics requires clarity, strategic thinking, and the ability to align diverse objectives.

Mastering multi-party negotiations is essential because these scenarios often arise in high-stakes environments, such as mergers, policy-making, or international diplomacy. Successfully navigating them allows you to resolve conflicts, build consensus, and achieve outcomes that would be unattainable through unilateral action.

How It Works

Managing multi-party negotiations involves the following strategies:
1. **Clarify Objectives:** Identify and rank the priorities of all parties involved, ensuring transparency and alignment where possible.
2. **Facilitate Communication:** Establish clear channels for open dialogue, reducing misunderstandings and fostering trust.
3. **Build Coalitions:** Form alliances with like-minded parties to strengthen your position and create momentum toward a shared goal.

In *Getting to Yes* (Fisher & Ury, 1981), the authors emphasize the importance of focusing on interests rather than positions. This approach is particularly effective in multi-party settings, where creative solutions often emerge through collaboration.

Real-Life Example

The Good Friday Agreement of 1998 is a landmark example of successful multi-party negotiations. This agreement ended decades of violent conflict in Northern Ireland, known as "The Troubles." The talks involved multiple stakeholders, including the British and Irish governments, Northern Ireland's political parties, and various community leaders.

Negotiators overcame deep-seated mistrust by focusing on shared interests, such as peace and economic stability, while addressing core issues like governance and cultural recognition. U.S. Senator George Mitchell, who chaired the negotiations, used meticulous facilitation and ensured all voices were heard, demonstrating how clear processes and trust-building can bring diverse parties to a consensus.

Exercises

1. **Practice Mapping Stakeholders:** Think of a multi-party situation you're involved in or familiar with. Identify the key stakeholders, their priorities, and potential alliances. How could you build coalitions or find shared goals?
2. **Analyze a Multi-Party Negotiation:** Research a successful example of multi-party negotiations. What strategies were used to align competing interests?
3. **Simulate a Multi-Party Scenario:** Role-play a negotiation involving multiple parties with conflicting priorities. Focus on building coalitions, clarifying objectives, and achieving consensus.

Key Takeaway

Multi-party negotiations require aligning diverse objectives through clear communication, coalition-building, and shared problem-solving. By focusing on interests rather than positions, you can manage complexity and achieve meaningful outcomes.

Chapter 52: Design Approach – Setting the Stage for Success

Why This Matters

Success in complex situations often depends less on the actions taken during execution and more on the groundwork laid beforehand. The design approach emphasizes preparing the environment, participants, and processes to create conditions conducive to success. This proactive strategy aligns with Jeanne Liedtka's insights in *Designing for Growth* (2011), where she argues that thoughtful design fosters creativity, collaboration, and clarity.

The design approach matters because it allows you to shape outcomes before challenges arise. Whether leading a project, hosting a negotiation, or implementing change, setting the stage ensures smoother execution, minimizes friction, and improves outcomes.

How It Works

Applying the design approach involves:

1.. **Define Objectives:** Clearly articulate what success looks like and ensure all stakeholders understand these goals.
2. **Plan the Environment:** Create a setting that fosters collaboration, such as neutral meeting spaces or structured agendas.
3. **Establish Processes:** Design frameworks for decision-making, communication, and conflict resolution to guide participants effectively.

In *The Art of Innovation* (Kelley, 2001), the author emphasizes how design-thinking principles, like prototyping and iteration, apply beyond product development to solving organizational and interpersonal challenges.

Real-Life Example

The Camp David Accords of 1978, brokered by U.S. President Jimmy Carter, showcase the power of the design approach. Carter created an environment conducive to peace talks by isolating Egyptian and Israeli leaders at the presidential retreat, removing external pressures, and fostering focused dialogue. His structured agenda and personal involvement helped secure agreements that had eluded years of open conflict.

Exercises

1. **Design Your Ideal Environment:** Think of a situation where you'll need collaboration (e.g. a meeting or negotiation). Write down how you would design the setting, processes, and communication methods to ensure success.
2. **Analyze a Designed Outcome:** Research a successful event or initiative (e.g. the Camp David Accords). How did its design contribute to its success?
3. **Test the Design Approach:** Apply the design approach to a small project or discussion. Reflect on how your preparation influenced the outcome.

Key Takeaway

The design approach ensures success by shaping environments, processes, and expectations before execution. By preparing thoughtfully, you create conditions that foster collaboration, innovation, and effective problem-solving.

Chapter 53: Bayesian Touchpoints – Playing with Incomplete Information

In many decisions and negotiations, complete information is a luxury. Bayesian reasoning is a framework for making better decisions under uncertainty by updating your beliefs and strategies as new information emerges. Named after Reverend Thomas Bayes, this method is foundational in probability theory and decision science, as explored in *Thinking, Fast and Slow* (Kahneman, 2011).

Bayesian thinking matters because it helps you make informed decisions even when the facts are incomplete. By focusing on probabilities and continuously refining assumptions, you can navigate uncertainty with greater confidence and precision, whether you're analyzing market trends, negotiating deals, or responding to unpredictable events.

How It Works

Bayesian reasoning involves three steps:

1. **Set Prior Beliefs:** Begin with an initial estimate or assumption about the likelihood of an event or outcome based on available information.
2. **Incorporate New Evidence:** Evaluate how new data or observations align with or contradict your initial beliefs.
3. **Update Probabilities:** Adjust your beliefs accordingly, refining your understanding and improving your decision-making over time.

In *Superforecasting* (Tetlock & Gardner, 2015), the authors emphasize how expert forecasters use Bayesian principles to make accurate predictions. The key is maintaining flexibility and a willingness to revise your approach based on emerging information.

Real-Life Example

Medical diagnosis processes often employ Bayesian reasoning to refine conclusions with incomplete information. For example, when a doctor evaluates a patient with flu-like symptoms, they start with prior probabilities (e.g. it's flu season, making the flu a likely cause). As additional tests (e.g. temperature, bloodwork) are conducted, the doctor updates their assessment, ruling out other possibilities such as strep throat. This iterative process ensures decisions are guided by evidence and evolving probabilities, not assumptions.

Exercises

1. **Apply Bayesian Reasoning:** Think of a current decision where you have incomplete information. Write down your initial assumptions, then evaluate how new evidence might adjust your thinking.
2. **Analyze Bayesian Applications:** Research a system or organization that uses iterative updates, such as a recommendation engine or a weather forecast model. How does this process improve accuracy over time?
3. **Practice Real-Time Updates:** Role-play a negotiation where new information emerges throughout the discussion. Practice revising your approach as the conversation unfolds.

Key Takeaway

Bayesian reasoning helps you navigate uncertainty by continuously updating your beliefs based on new information. By staying adaptable and focusing on probabilities, you can make more informed and accurate decisions over time.

Chapter 54: The Value of Patience – Delaying Moves to Get Big Returns

Why This Matters

In a world driven by speed, patience is often underestimated. However, delaying action strategically can create opportunities for better outcomes. The value of patience lies in waiting for the right moment to act, gathering information, or allowing events to unfold favorably. As highlighted in *The Art of Strategy* (Dixit & Nalebuff, 2008), patience can turn seemingly minor advantages into significant wins.

Patience matters because rushing decisions often leads to missed opportunities or costly mistakes. By mastering the art of timing, you can increase the chances of success while reducing risks, whether negotiating contracts, investing in markets, or navigating personal challenges.

How It Works

The value of patience relies on three principles:

1.. **Gather Information:** Use time to collect insights and reduce uncertainty before making a decision.
2. **Allow Momentum to Build:** Sometimes, waiting enables external factors to align in your favor.
3. **Control Emotional Impulses:** Patience requires discipline and the ability to resist pressure for immediate action.

In *The 48 Laws of Power* (Greene, 1998), the author highlights how waiting for the opportune moment is a key strategy used by influential leaders. Timing, when executed well, can amplify the impact of your actions.

Real-Life Example

Warren Buffett's investment strategy demonstrates the value of patience. Buffett famously avoids short-term speculation, instead waiting for undervalued companies with strong long-term growth potential. His patience has allowed him to make calculated investments that yield massive returns over decades, cementing his reputation as one of history's most successful investors.

In negotiations, patience can also turn the tide. For example, in real estate, a buyer might wait for a motivated seller to lower their asking price rather than rushing into a deal. This approach allows the buyer to secure a better value by letting circumstances evolve in their favor.

Exercises

1. **Identify a Situation for Patience:** Reflect on a current challenge where immediate action might not be necessary. How could waiting for the right moment improve your results?
2. **Analyze a Patient Leader:** Research someone known for their strategic patience (e.g., Warren Buffett). What lessons can you learn from their approach?
3. **Test Delayed Action:** Simulate a negotiation or decision-making scenario where one party waits for the other to act first. Reflect on how patience affects the outcome.

Key Takeaway

Patience allows you to maximize opportunities and reduce risks by waiting for the right moment to act. By gathering information, aligning external factors, and controlling impulses, you can make decisions with greater confidence and impact.

Chapter 55: Escalation Control – Avoiding Destructive Spirals

Why This Matters

Escalation is a common pitfall in conflicts and negotiations. When disagreements spiral out of control, they can lead to destructive outcomes, damaged relationships, and missed opportunities. Escalation control involves identifying and halting these spirals before they cause irreparable harm. As highlighted in *Getting Past No* (Ury, 1991), staying composed and redirecting the energy of a heated exchange can turn adversaries into collaborators.

Mastering escalation control is essential because unchecked conflicts drain resources, erode trust, and limit progress. Whether in professional negotiations or personal disputes, understanding how to de-escalate situations creates space for constructive dialogue and solutions.

How It Works

Escalation control involves:

1. **Recognizing Early Signs:** Identify when a discussion is becoming unproductive or overly emotional. Look for raised voices, rigid positions, or repetitive arguments.
2. **Interrupting the Cycle:** Use calming techniques, such as taking a break, acknowledging emotions, or shifting the focus to shared goals.
3. **Redirecting Energy:** Reframe the issue to focus on problem-solving rather than blame or competition.

In *Crucial Conversations* (Patterson et al., 2002), the authors stress the importance of creating a safe environment for dialogue. Escalation often occurs when people feel threatened or misunderstood, so fostering safety is key to regaining control.

Real-Life Example

The Montgomery Bus Boycott of 1955–1956 is a powerful example of escalation control in social movements. When Rosa Parks' arrest sparked outrage over racial segregation, civil rights leaders like Martin Luther King Jr. maintained a strategy of nonviolence and measured responses. Despite provocations and threats, the boycott avoided destructive escalation by focusing on peaceful protest, coordinated communication, and shared community goals. This approach eventually led to the desegregation of Montgomery's buses, proving that controlled, deliberate action can lead to meaningful change even in high-pressure situations.

Exercises

1. **Recognize Escalation Triggers:** Reflect on a recent conflict. What signs indicated escalation? How could you have intervened earlier to redirect the conversation?
2. **Practice De-Escalation Techniques:** Role-play a heated negotiation where one party becomes increasingly rigid. Practice using calming language and reframing to steer the discussion toward resolution.
3. **Analyze a Historical Escalation:** Study a real-world example where escalation spiraled out of control (e.g. a labor strike or international conflict). What could have been done to prevent it?

Key Takeaway

Escalation control is the art of stopping conflicts before they spiral into destruction. By recognizing early signs, interrupting cycles, and redirecting focus, you can preserve relationships and create opportunities for resolution.

Chapter 56: Evolutionary Methods – Adapting to Changing Rules

Why This Matters

The rules of any game — whether in business, negotiations, or life — are rarely static. Evolutionary methods focus on adapting strategies as circumstances evolve, turning change into an opportunity rather than a threat. Inspired by principles from evolutionary biology, these methods are about learning, iterating, and thriving in dynamic environments. As articulated in *The Origin of Wealth* (Beinhocker, 2006), flexibility and adaptability are essential for long-term success.

Mastering evolutionary methods is crucial because rigid strategies fail in the face of unexpected shifts. Whether you're dealing with changing market conditions or unpredictable stakeholders, the ability to adjust your approach ensures resilience and continued progress.

How It Works

Evolutionary methods operate on three principles:

1. **Experimentation:** Test different approaches and learn from successes and failures.
2. **Feedback Loops:** Continuously gather data and refine strategies based on real-world outcomes.
3. **Adaptation:** Embrace flexibility and adjust your plans to align with changing circumstances.

In *Antifragile* (Taleb, 2012), the author emphasizes the value of systems that improve under pressure and change. Evolutionary methods build resilience by turning challenges into opportunities for growth.

Real-Life Example

The Lego Group's turnaround in the early 2000s illustrates the power of evolutionary methods. After facing declining sales and mounting debt, Lego experimented with new products, licensing agreements (like partnerships with *Star Wars* and *Harry Potter*), and digital innovations, including video games and apps. The company also embraced feedback loops by engaging with fans through initiatives like the LEGO Ideas platform, where users submit designs for new products. By continuously adapting to shifts in the toy market and consumer preferences, Lego regained its status as a global leader in the toy industry.

Exercises

1. **Identify Areas for Adaptation:** Think about a current challenge where the "rules" have shifted (e.g., a new technology or competitor). How can you adjust your strategy to stay ahead?
2. **Analyze a Case of Evolution:** Research a company or individual (e.g. a professional athlete) who thrived by adapting to changing circumstances. What lessons can you apply?
3. **Test an Evolutionary Strategy:** Choose a small project and apply an experimental approach. Gather feedback, adjust your methods, and reflect on the outcomes.

Key Takeaway

Evolutionary methods emphasize the importance of adapting strategies to align with changing environments. By experimenting, gathering feedback, and embracing flexibility, you can turn uncertainty into opportunity and thrive in dynamic contexts.

Why This Matters

In complex environments, pure competition or unbridled collaboration rarely leads to optimal outcomes. Hybrid blueprints, which blend elements of synergy and competition, provide a balanced approach that leverages the strengths of both strategies. This dynamic framework is especially effective in industries, organizations, or ecosystems where players must work together while pursuing their interests.

The ability to apply hybrid blueprints is essential because many real-world challenges involve both shared goals and competing priorities. As outlined in *Co-opetition* (Brandenburger & Nalebuff, 1996), combining collaboration and competition enables organizations and individuals to create value while maintaining their edge.

How It Works

Hybrid blueprints thrive on three principles:

1. **Identify Shared Interests:** Find areas where collaboration benefits all parties, such as industry standards or joint ventures.
2. **Maintain Competitive Incentives:** Ensure that competition exists where it drives innovation, efficiency, or differentiation.
3. **Adapt to Context:** Recognize when to shift the balance between cooperation and competition as circumstances evolve.

This approach is particularly effective in markets with overlapping ecosystems. For example, tech companies often collaborate to develop universal platforms (like USB standards) while fiercely competing in their proprietary products.

Real-Life Example

The Airbus and Boeing collaboration on aviation safety standards is a strong example of hybrid blueprints. While these two aerospace giants fiercely compete for market share in commercial aircraft, they also work together through organizations like the International Civil Aviation Organization (ICAO) to establish and improve global safety standards.

By collaborating on safety regulations, the companies ensure passenger trust in air travel, benefiting the entire industry. At the same time, their competitive rivalry drives innovation in fuel efficiency, design, and technology, helping each company maintain its unique edge. This balance of cooperation and competition strengthens the industry as a whole while allowing both Airbus and Boeing to thrive.

Exercises

1. **Map a Hybrid Opportunity:** Identify a situation where you collaborate with competitors (e.g. shared resources, mutual goals). How can you balance cooperation and competition to maximize value?
2. **Analyze a Hybrid Success Story:** Research an example of co-opetition (e.g. vaccine development or tech alliances). What lessons can you learn from their approach?
3. **Simulate a Hybrid Strategy:** In a negotiation scenario, practice collaborating with a competitor on shared goals while maintaining a competitive edge in other areas. Reflect on the dynamics and outcomes.

Key Takeaway

Hybrid blueprints blend synergy and competition to create balanced strategies for complex environments. By identifying shared interests and maintaining competitive incentives, you can achieve innovation, efficiency, and mutual success.

Chapter 58: Liability Diversification – Spreading Bets for Stability

Uncertainty is an inherent part of decision-making. Liability diversification involves spreading risks across multiple areas to ensure that failure in one aspect does not lead to complete collapse. This principle is widely used in finance but applies equally to negotiations, business strategies, and personal decision-making. As emphasized in *The Intelligent Investor* (Graham, 1949), diversification acts as a safety net, protecting against volatility and unexpected shocks.

Liability diversification matters because it minimizes the impact of unforeseen events. By avoiding over-reliance on a single strategy, resource, or outcome, you can build resilience and adapt to challenges more effectively. Whether managing a portfolio, leading a project, or navigating personal goals, spreading risks ensures stability and sustainability.

How It Works

Diversification relies on three core principles:

1. **Distribute Risks:** Spread liabilities across multiple options or areas to reduce vulnerability to any single failure.
2. **Balance Exposure:** Ensure that no single liability dominates, maintaining a proportionate allocation of resources.
3. **Monitor Continuously:** Regularly review your diversified approach to ensure it aligns with changing circumstances.

In *Antifragile* (Taleb, 2012), the author highlights the "barbell strategy," a form of diversification where you combine highly conservative and highly aggressive bets to balance safety and opportunity. This approach ensures protection during downturns while still allowing for significant gains.

Real-Life Example

Sony's diversification across multiple industries demonstrates the value of liability diversification. While Sony is best known for its consumer electronics, it has also invested heavily in other areas, including gaming (PlayStation), entertainment (Sony Pictures and Sony Music), and financial services. This diversification strategy allows Sony to remain resilient during market downturns in any one sector. For example, when competition in the electronics market became intense, the company's gaming and entertainment divisions helped stabilize overall revenue.

This approach has enabled Sony to thrive despite challenges in individual business lines, showcasing how spreading risks across diverse industries can ensure long-term stability.

Exercises

1. **Assess Your Diversification:** Identify a project, investment, or strategy you're currently pursuing. Are you overly reliant on a single option? How can you distribute risks more effectively?
2. **Analyze a Case of Failure Due to Lack of Diversification:** Research a business or organization that struggled due to over-reliance on one resource (e.g. Kodak's dependence on film). What lessons can you learn from their experience?
3. **Plan a Barbell Strategy:** In a negotiation or decision-making scenario, create a plan that balances low-risk and high-reward options. Reflect on how this approach improves your overall stability.

Key Takeaway

Liability diversification ensures resilience by spreading risks across multiple areas. By distributing liabilities, balancing exposure, and staying adaptable, you can minimize the impact of unexpected challenges and maintain stability.

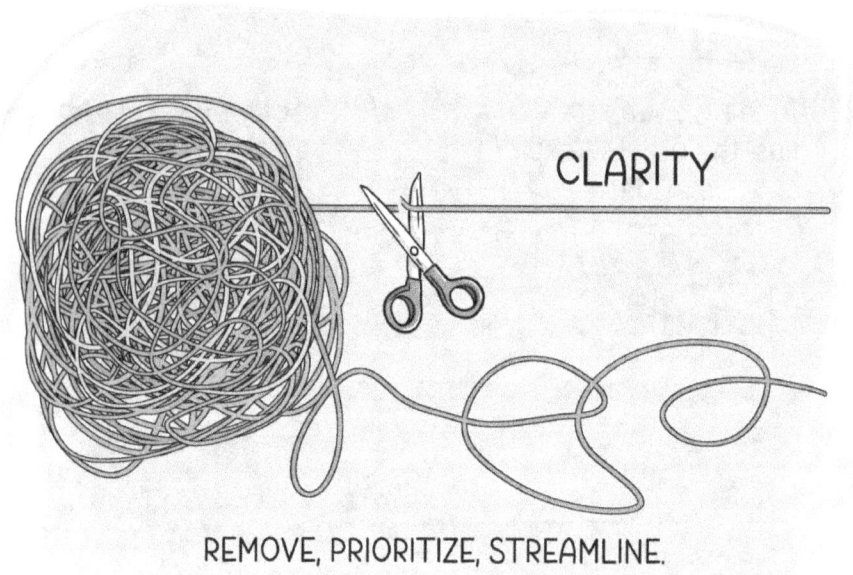

CLARITY

REMOVE, PRIORITIZE, STREAMLINE.

Chapter 59: The Cost of Complexity – Simplifying to Stay Ahead

Why This Matters

In an interconnected world, complexity often feels inevitable. However, unchecked complexity can lead to inefficiency, confusion, and missed opportunities. Simplifying processes, decisions, and strategies allows you to focus on what truly matters, enabling better outcomes. As discussed in *The Laws of Simplicity* (Maeda, 2006), simplicity is not about removing important elements but making the complex more manageable and meaningful.

Understanding the cost of complexity is critical because excessive layers—whether in business models, decision-making processes, or negotiations—can obscure goals and reduce effectiveness. Simplification fosters clarity, improves communication, and ensures that resources are used efficiently.

How It Works

Reducing complexity involves three key steps:

1. **Identify Bottlenecks:** Pinpoint areas where excessive layers or unclear processes are creating inefficiencies.
2. **Prioritize Core Elements:** Focus on essential goals and remove unnecessary steps or distractions.
3. **Streamline Communication:** Simplify how information is shared to improve understanding and collaboration.

In *Essentialism* (McKeown, 2014), the author highlights the power of "less but better," emphasizing that simplification is about sharpening focus rather than cutting corners. This approach helps teams and individuals align their efforts with meaningful outcomes.

Real-Life Example

The success of Apple's product design illustrates the power of simplicity. Under Steve Jobs' leadership, Apple prioritized minimalism and user-centric designs, stripping away unnecessary features to create intuitive and visually appealing products. For example, the original iPod succeeded not because it was the most feature-rich device but because it was easy to use, with a simple interface and slogan: "1,000 songs in your pocket." By reducing complexity, Apple revolutionized the tech industry and became a leader in innovation.

In a different context, organizations that simplify decision-making processes also benefit. For instance, Southwest Airlines streamlined its operations by focusing on a single type of aircraft (the Boeing 737), reducing training and maintenance costs. This simplification contributed to the company's reputation for efficiency and profitability in a highly competitive industry.

Exercises

1. **Simplify a Process:** Identify a task or workflow that feels unnecessarily complex. Break it down into its core components and remove steps or features that don't add significant value.
2. **Analyze a Simplification Success Story:** Research a company or product (e.g., Apple or Southwest Airlines) known for successful simplification. What strategies did they use, and what were the outcomes?
3. **Streamline Your Communication:** Practice explaining a complex idea in the simplest terms possible, using no more than three key points. Reflect on how this exercise improves clarity.

Key Takeaway

The cost of complexity can drain resources and obscure goals. By identifying bottlenecks, prioritizing essentials, and streamlining processes, you can simplify effectively, stay focused, and achieve better outcomes.

Chapter 60: Behavioral Insights – Using Psychology to Your Advantage

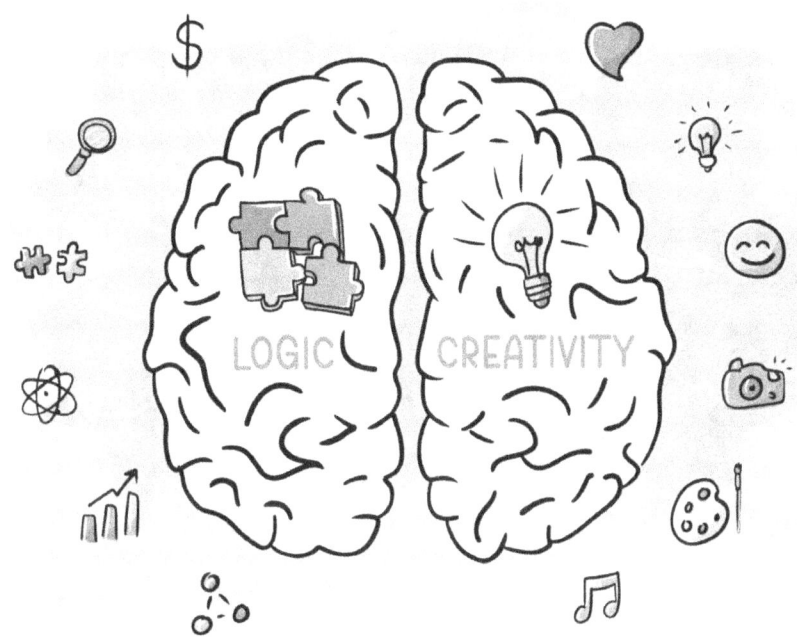

Why This Matters

Human behavior is often driven by unconscious biases, emotions, and heuristics. Behavioral insights involve understanding these psychological drivers to make better decisions and influence others effectively. Concepts from behavioral economics, popularized by Daniel Kahneman's *Thinking, Fast and Slow* (2011) and Richard Thaler's *Nudge* (2008), reveal how subtle shifts in framing or incentives can lead to significant changes in behavior.

Mastering behavioral insights matters because it equips you to navigate and shape complex interactions. Whether you're negotiating, managing a team, or designing policies, leveraging psychological principles helps you align actions with goals, reduce conflict, and foster better outcomes.

How It Works

Behavioral insights rely on understanding three key psychological principles:

1. **Cognitive Biases:** Recognize common biases like anchoring, loss aversion, and confirmation bias to avoid their pitfalls and use them strategically.
2. **Framing Effects:** Present information in ways that highlight desired outcomes. For example, emphasizing gains ("Save 20%") is often more effective than highlighting losses ("Avoid a 20% loss").
3. **Choice Architecture:** Design environments that guide decisions subtly, such as arranging healthy food at eye level in cafeterias to encourage better eating habits.

In *Nudge* (Thaler & Sunstein, 2008), the authors describe how small environmental or contextual changes can "nudge" people toward better choices without restricting their freedom.

Real-Life Example

The Save More Tomorrow (SMarT) program by Thaler and Shlomo Benartzi is a classic application of behavioral insights. This retirement savings plan leverages the principle of default choices and inertia by automatically enrolling employees in savings increases tied to future raises. Since people are more likely to commit to actions that don't require immediate sacrifice, the program significantly increased savings rates among participants.

Exercises

1. **Identify Biases in Action:** Reflect on a recent decision you made. Can you identify any cognitive biases that influenced your choice? How might you overcome or leverage these biases in the future?
2. **Practice Framing Techniques:** Take a message or offer and write two versions: one emphasizing gains and the other losses. Test which version is more persuasive with a colleague or friend.
3. **Design a Choice Environment:** Create a scenario where you design a system to encourage better behavior (e.g. increasing participation in a survey or encouraging recycling). Consider how small changes in presentation or defaults could impact outcomes.

Key Takeaway

Behavioral insights reveal how psychology drives decisions and actions. By understanding cognitive biases, framing effects, and choice architecture, you can navigate complex interactions, influence behavior, and achieve better results.

Section VII: Game Theory in Everyday Life

Game theory isn't confined to boardrooms, negotiations, or international diplomacy. It plays a pivotal role in daily life. This section explores how game theory principles apply to common challenges, from managing relationships and motivating teams to handling risk and uncertainty. You'll learn how to negotiate with irrational players, align incentives for success, and harness concepts like reputation and trust to build long-term advantages. These chapters transform abstract strategies into practical tools you can use to make smarter decisions, build stronger connections, and navigate everyday complexities with confidence.

Chapter 61: Negotiating with Irrational Players – Keeping Calm Under Chaos

Why This Matters

Negotiating with irrational players — those driven by emotion, stubbornness, or erratic behavior — can feel like navigating a storm. Their unpredictability and refusal to follow logical paths make it difficult to reach agreements. However, by staying calm and applying structured strategies, you can manage these interactions effectively. As highlighted in *Getting Past No* (Ury, 1991), maintaining composure and redirecting the energy of chaos can lead even the most challenging discussions toward productive outcomes.

This skill matters because irrational players are a part of life, whether they're colleagues, clients, or family members. Learning how to negotiate with them ensures you can protect your interests while fostering cooperation instead of conflict.

How It Works

Negotiating with irrational players requires a balance of patience, emotional regulation, and strategic redirection. Key steps include:

1. **Acknowledge Their Emotions:** Recognize and validate the emotions driving their behavior, such as anger or frustration, without conceding your position.
2. **Reframe the Conversation:** Shift focus from emotional reactions to shared goals or benefits.
3. **Stay Grounded:** Avoid being drawn into their chaos by maintaining a calm and neutral demeanor.

In *Crucial Conversations* (Patterson et al., 2002), the authors emphasize the importance of creating a safe environment for dialogue. Establishing trust and showing empathy can often defuse irrationality and pave the way for constructive negotiation.

Real-Life Example

A well-known example is Abraham Lincoln's strategy during his presidency. Lincoln was known for dealing with difficult, irrational individuals, including political rivals and wartime generals. Instead of reacting emotionally, he often used humor, empathy, and carefully chosen words to defuse tensions. His ability to stay calm and focus on the broader goals of the Union allowed him to manage conflicts effectively, even under immense pressure.

On a personal level, consider a workplace dispute where a colleague reacts irrationally to constructive feedback. Instead of escalating the conflict, acknowledging their emotions ("I understand this must be frustrating") and redirecting the focus to shared goals ("Let's figure out how we can solve this together") can turn a volatile situation into a collaborative one.

Exercises

1. **Practice Staying Calm:** Think of a recent situation where someone acted irrationally. Reflect on how you reacted and write down strategies you could use to stay calm and composed next time.
2. **Role-Play with a Partner:** Simulate a negotiation where one person acts irrationally. Practice using acknowledgment, reframing, and grounding techniques to guide the conversation back on track.
3. **Study a Historical Example:** Research how a historical leader or negotiator dealt with irrational individuals (e.g., Lincoln, Mandela). What strategies did they use to stay calm and resolve the situation?

Key Takeaway

Negotiating with irrational players requires patience, empathy, and strategic redirection. By staying composed, acknowledging emotions, and focusing on shared goals, you can turn chaotic interactions into opportunities for progress.

Chapter 62: Frictionless Output – Reducing Barriers to Teamwork

Teamwork is often hindered by unnecessary friction — miscommunication, unclear roles, or conflicting priorities. Frictionless output focuses on reducing these barriers to create smoother collaboration and improved results. As outlined in *The Five Dysfunctions of a Team* (Lencioni, 2002), eliminating friction not only enhances productivity but also strengthens trust and cohesion within teams.

Mastering frictionless output is crucial because teams are the foundation of most successful organizations and projects. Removing obstacles allows each member to contribute their best, fostering innovation and achieving goals more efficiently.

How It Works

Creating frictionless teamwork involves:

1. **Clarify Roles and Goals:** Ensure that everyone understands their responsibilities and how their contributions align with the team's objectives.
2. **Streamline Communication:** Use clear, concise communication to avoid misunderstandings and encourage transparency.
3. **Encourage Collaboration:** Create a culture where team members feel comfortable sharing ideas, asking questions, and providing feedback.

In *Drive* (Pink, 2009), the author highlights how intrinsic motivation — autonomy, mastery, and purpose — thrives in environments with reduced friction, leading to more engaged and effective teams.

Real-Life Example

Pixar Animation Studios provides an excellent example of frictionless teamwork. The company fosters collaboration by creating an open feedback culture, where team members from all levels and departments are encouraged to contribute ideas. This approach eliminates hierarchical barriers and ensures the best ideas rise to the surface, leading to ground-breaking films like *Toy Story* and *Inside Out*.

In a smaller-scale example, a remote team working across time zones can reduce friction by implementing clear communication tools (e.g. Slack, Trello) and establishing regular check-ins to align goals. These practices streamline workflows and minimize misunderstandings, ensuring everyone stays on track.

Exercises

1. **Identify Team Frictions:** Think about a team or group you're part of. List the most common sources of friction and brainstorm ways to address them (e.g. clarifying goals, improving tools).
2. **Analyze a Collaborative Success:** Research an organization or project known for exceptional teamwork (e.g. NASA's Apollo missions). What practices contributed to their success?
3. **Create a Collaboration Plan:** Design a plan for improving teamwork within your own context. Include strategies for clarifying roles, streamlining communication, and encouraging feedback.

Key Takeaway

Frictionless teamwork eliminates barriers that hinder productivity and collaboration. By clarifying roles, improving communication, and fostering a collaborative culture, teams can achieve seamless output and greater success.

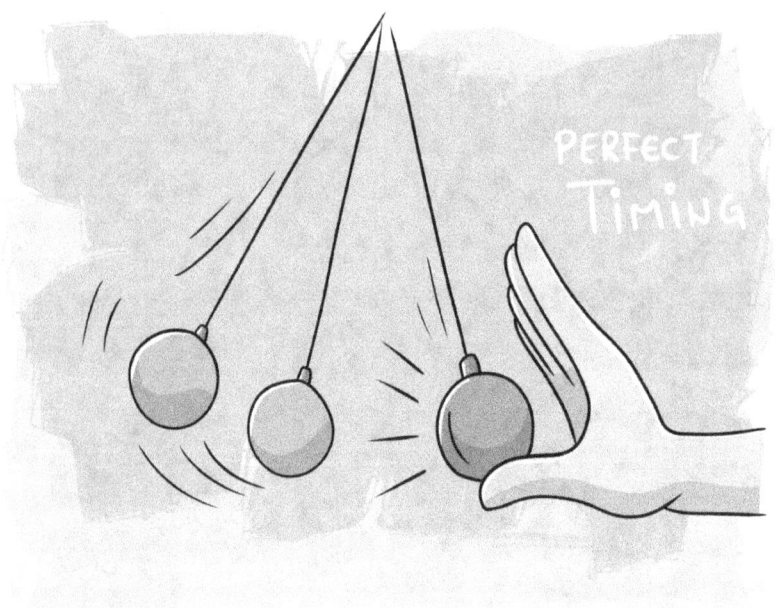

PERFECT Timing

Chapter 63: Timing the Market – Knowing When to Act

Why This Matters

Timing is everything when making decisions, whether in financial markets, negotiations, or everyday choices. Timing the market refers to the strategic act of identifying the optimal moment to take action, based on analysis and anticipation of future trends. While often associated with investing, the principle applies broadly to life and business, where acting too early or too late can result in missed opportunities or increased risks.

Mastering timing matters because the consequences of decisions are rarely uniform over time. Acting with foresight allows you to capitalize on opportunities and avoid costly mistakes, turning the timing itself into a competitive advantage.

How It Works

Timing the market involves three key elements:

1. **Gather Information:** Monitor trends, patterns, and external factors that might influence outcomes. In financial markets, this could mean analyzing historical data or economic indicators.
2. **Anticipate Future Moves:** Use strategic foresight to predict how events may unfold. This involves scenario planning and considering potential risks.
3. **Act Decisively:** Once the optimal window is identified, act quickly and with confidence to maximize returns or benefits.

In *The Little Book That Still Beats the Market* (Greenblatt, 2010), the author emphasizes the importance of understanding long-term trends rather than reacting impulsively. Success often comes from balancing patience with decisive action when the moment is right.

Real-Life Example

Procter & Gamble's launch of Tide Pods illustrates the importance of timing in innovation. By introducing Tide Pods in 2012, P&G capitalized on growing consumer demand for convenience and single-use products. The company's extensive market research revealed a shift in consumer preferences toward simpler and more efficient solutions for household tasks. By waiting until the market was ready for this innovation — when consumers were accustomed to single-serve products like K-Cups — they ensured a successful product launch. Tide Pods quickly became a market leader, driving significant growth for P&G in the laundry detergent category.

Exercises

1. **Evaluate Past Timing:** Reflect on a recent decision where timing was critical. Did you act too early, too late, or at the right moment? What factors influenced your timing?
2. **Practice Trend Analysis:** Choose a market or field (e.g., real estate, technology) and identify current trends. Consider how you might act strategically based on these patterns.
3. **Simulate Timing Scenarios:** Create a hypothetical situation where timing matters, such as launching a product or entering a negotiation. Plan your actions based on different timing windows and reflect on the outcomes.

Key Takeaway

Timing the market is about recognizing and seizing opportunities at the right moment. By gathering information, anticipating future moves, and acting decisively, you can maximize benefits and minimize risks in any decision-making process.

Chapter 64: Repetition and Reputation – Reaching Your Goals Through Consistency

CONSISTENCY

Why This Matters

Consistency is the foundation of mastery, trust, and influence. Repetition builds competence through practice and refinement, while reputation amplifies your credibility and opens doors to opportunities. Together, they create a cycle where consistent actions not only drive personal improvement but also establish how others perceive and trust you. As James Clear explains in *Atomic Habits* (2018), small, repeated behaviors compound into extraordinary outcomes, often surpassing initial expectations.

Reputation and repetition matter because they set the stage for long-term success. Consistent effort allows you to improve incrementally, while a strong reputation attracts collaboration, loyalty, and opportunities that align with your goals. By leveraging these principles, you can make steady progress in any area of life, from building a career to fostering relationships.

How It Works

Achieving success through repetition and reputation involves three critical steps:

1. **Establish Core Habits:** Repetition requires identifying small, repeatable actions that align with your long-term goals. This could involve daily practice, regular check-ins with a team, or maintaining high standards in every project. As highlighted in *The Power of Habit* (Duhigg, 2012), habits simplify the path to improvement by reducing decision fatigue and reinforcing positive behaviors.

2. **Deliver Consistently:** Reputation is built on trust, which grows when people see you deliver reliable results. Whether meeting deadlines, keeping promises, or maintaining professionalism, consistent actions shape how others perceive your dependability. Over time, this builds a reputation that precedes you, opening doors to greater opportunities.

3. **Leverage Momentum:** Repetition creates momentum that builds confidence and expertise. As you improve through practice, your reputation amplifies your reach, leading to a compounding effect where each success reinforces the next.

This cycle of repetition and reputation is not about perfection but persistence. Even small, consistent efforts can lead to transformative outcomes, both in skill development and relationship-building.

Real-Life Example

The legendary career of Serena Williams epitomizes the power of repetition and reputation. Through relentless practice and unwavering focus, Serena refined her skills, becoming one of the most accomplished athletes in history. Her consistency on the tennis court—winning 23 Grand Slam titles—built a reputation that transcends sports. Beyond her athletic achievements, Serena's reputation for discipline and resilience has made her a role model, securing sponsorships, business ventures, and a lasting legacy.

In everyday contexts, repetition and reputation play an equally critical role. Consider a freelancer building their career. By consistently delivering high-quality work on time, they earn the trust of clients, leading to repeat business and glowing referrals. Over time, their reputation as a reliable professional becomes a magnet for opportunities, enabling growth without constant self-promotion.

Exercises

1. **Track a Habit:** Identify a skill or goal you want to improve. Break it into daily or weekly actions, and track your progress for 30 days. Reflect on how repetition strengthens your confidence and results.

2. **Evaluate Your Reputation:** Write down three adjectives you think others associate with you professionally or personally. How do your actions support or detract from this perception? What steps can you take to enhance your reputation?

3. **Analyze a Role Model:** Research someone known for their consistency and strong reputation (e.g. an artist, entrepreneur, or leader). What habits or actions contributed to their success? How can you apply similar strategies in your own journey?

Key Takeaway

Repetition fuels personal growth, while reputation builds trust and influence. By focusing on consistent effort and delivering reliable results, you create a compounding effect that propels you toward long-term success in any endeavor.

ALIGNED INCENTIVES

Chapter 65: Incentive Alignment – Motivating Others Effectively

Why This Matters

Motivating others is one of the most critical challenges in leadership, teamwork, and negotiations. Misaligned incentives can lead to inefficiency, conflict, or outright failure, as individuals prioritize their own goals over the group's objectives. Incentive alignment ensures that everyone's motivations are directed toward a common purpose, creating a win-win dynamic where individual efforts contribute to collective success.

This concept matters because it bridges the gap between intention and action. When incentives are properly aligned, they encourage collaboration, increase productivity, and foster trust. As Dan Pink emphasizes in *Drive* (2009), intrinsic motivators like autonomy, mastery, and purpose are just as important as external rewards in ensuring long-term engagement.

How It Works

Aligning incentives involves three key steps:

1. **Understand Motivations:** Identify what drives each individual—whether it's financial rewards, recognition, autonomy, or personal growth.
2. **Design Fair Rewards:** Create systems where rewards reflect contributions and encourage collaboration. Avoid structures that foster competition within teams when cooperation is needed.
3. **Communicate Shared Goals:** Clearly articulate how individual efforts align with broader organizational or team objectives.

In *Thinking, Fast and Slow* (Kahneman, 2011), the author highlights how cognitive biases can lead to misaligned incentives. Leaders must recognize these biases to design frameworks that truly motivate and align stakeholders effectively.

Real-Life Example

The success of Wikipedia showcases the power of aligned incentives. Unlike traditional organizations, Wikipedia relies on thousands of volunteers to create and maintain its content. The platform's incentive structure is intrinsic rather than financial — contributors are motivated by the opportunity to share knowledge, gain recognition within the community, and be part of a larger mission to make information accessible to everyone. This alignment of individual passions with Wikipedia's overarching goal has allowed it to thrive as the world's largest online encyclopedia.

In professional contexts, aligned incentives are critical in commission-based sales teams. For example, companies that implement team-based bonuses rather than individual commissions encourage collaboration and discourage unhealthy competition. This alignment fosters a supportive environment where team members work together to achieve collective success.

Exercises

1. **Identify Incentives:** Choose a team or project you're part of and list the incentives currently in place. Are they aligned with the group's goals, or do they create unintended conflicts?
2. **Redesign a System:** Take a flawed incentive structure (real or hypothetical) and redesign it to encourage collaboration and alignment. Reflect on how these changes improve outcomes.
3. **Analyze a Success Story:** Research an organization or initiative (e.g. Wikipedia) that successfully uses aligned incentives. What lessons can you apply to your own context?

Key Takeaway

Aligned incentives motivate individuals to work toward shared goals while minimizing conflicts. By understanding motivations, designing fair rewards, and communicating a clear purpose, you can foster collaboration and drive collective success.

Chapter 66: Loss Aversion – Turning Fear into Opportunity

Humans are wired to fear losses more than they value equivalent gains — a phenomenon known as loss aversion. This psychological bias, first studied by Daniel Kahneman and Amos Tversky in *Prospect Theory* (1979), explains why people often avoid risks even when the potential rewards outweigh the costs. While loss aversion can lead to cautious behavior, understanding and reframing it allows you to make better decisions and turn fear into opportunity.

Loss aversion matters because it affects decision-making in every aspect of life, from investing and negotiations to personal relationships. Recognizing this bias helps you manage fear more effectively and make rational choices that align with long-term goals.

How It Works

Turning loss aversion into an advantage involves:

1. **Recognize the Bias:** Be aware of situations where fear of loss is driving your decisions. Ask yourself whether the perceived risk is greater than the actual likelihood of loss.
2. **Reframe the Decision:** Focus on the potential gains rather than the losses. For example, instead of fearing a failed investment, consider the knowledge and experience gained from trying.
3. **Take Calculated Risks:** Mitigate losses through diversification, preparation, or setting clear limits while still pursuing opportunities.

In *The Art of Thinking Clearly* (Dobelli, 2013), the author emphasizes that managing loss aversion requires shifting your perspective and seeing setbacks as learning experiences rather than permanent failures.

Real-Life Example

Elon Musk's investment in SpaceX provides an excellent example of overcoming loss aversion. In 2008, after three failed rocket launches, Musk faced financial ruin and immense public scrutiny. Instead of giving up, Musk reframed the potential losses as stepping stones toward eventual success. He took the calculated risk of funding one final launch with nearly all his remaining resources. That fourth launch succeeded, earning NASA contracts that secured SpaceX's future and revolutionized space travel. Musk's ability to embrace potential losses and focus on the long-term vision turned a near-catastrophe into ground-breaking innovation.

Exercises

1. **Identify a Fear of Loss:** Reflect on a recent decision where fear of loss influenced your actions. How could you have reframed the situation to focus on the potential gains?
2. **Simulate a Negotiation:** Practice a negotiation scenario where one party fears rejection or failure. Work on reframing their perspective to emphasize opportunities instead of risks.
3. **Analyze a Risk-Taker's Story:** Research a successful entrepreneur or leader who took significant risks despite potential losses. What mindset shifts allowed them to overcome loss aversion?

Key Takeaway

Loss aversion is a natural bias, but it doesn't have to hold you back. By recognizing fear-driven decisions, reframing risks as opportunities, and taking calculated actions, you can transform hesitation into progress.

Chapter 67: Prospect Theory – Seeing Challenges the Right Way

Why This Matters

The way challenges are framed profoundly impacts how people respond to them. Prospect theory, introduced by Daniel Kahneman and Amos Tversky, demonstrates that individuals don't evaluate gains and losses objectively. Instead, they make decisions based on perceived value relative to a reference point, often overweighing losses compared to equivalent gains. Understanding this principle allows you to approach challenges strategically and influence how others perceive risks and opportunities.

Prospect theory matters because it helps you navigate decision-making with greater clarity. By recognizing how framing affects behavior, you can make smarter choices, reduce emotional biases, and present challenges in ways that inspire confidence and action.

How It Works

Prospect theory operates on three key principles:

1. **Loss Aversion:** People feel the pain of losses more acutely than the pleasure of equivalent gains. For example, losing $100 feels worse than the joy of winning $100.
2. **Reference Points:** Decisions are influenced by how outcomes are framed relative to a baseline. What feels like a gain in one context might feel like a loss in another.
3. **Framing Effects:** The same situation can evoke different reactions depending on whether it's presented as a potential gain or a potential loss.

In *Thinking, Fast and Slow* (Kahneman, 2011), the author explains that understanding these biases is essential for overcoming them and making more rational decisions.

Real-Life Example

The London congestion charge is a real-world application of prospect theory. Introduced in 2003, the policy was framed as a loss: drivers entering central London during peak hours would pay a daily charge. This framing played on loss aversion, discouraging unnecessary trips and reducing congestion. The policy successfully shifted behavior by leveraging psychological biases, demonstrating how framing can shape outcomes effectively.

On a personal level, consider someone trying to save money. Framing savings as "losing" discretionary spending often feels restrictive. However, reframing the same action as "gaining financial freedom" encourages a more positive perspective, increasing motivation to save.

Exercises

1. **Reframe a Challenge:** Think of a current problem you're facing. How can you reframe it as an opportunity or potential gain instead of focusing on what might be lost?
2. **Analyze a Decision:** Reflect on a past decision where loss aversion influenced your choice. How might a different framing have led to a better outcome?
3. **Simulate Framing Effects:** Present a hypothetical scenario to a friend or colleague in two ways: one emphasizing potential losses and the other potential gains. Observe how the framing changes their response.

Key Takeaway

Prospect theory reveals how perceptions of gains and losses shape decision-making. By reframing challenges as opportunities and recognizing biases, you can approach decisions with greater clarity and inspire action in others.

Chapter 68: The Role of Luck – Managing the Uncontrollable

Why This Matters

Luck plays a larger role in success and failure than most people acknowledge. While hard work, preparation, and skill are critical, luck often serves as the tipping point in achieving extraordinary outcomes. Managing the uncontrollable doesn't mean eliminating luck but rather positioning yourself to maximize its benefits while mitigating its downsides. As Nassim Taleb explores in *Fooled by Randomness* (2001), understanding luck's role helps you make decisions grounded in reality rather than illusion.

This concept matters because failing to recognize the role of luck can lead to overconfidence in success or undue blame for failure. By understanding luck's influence, you can make more informed decisions and prepare for uncertainty with greater resilience.

How It Works

Managing luck involves three strategies:

1. **Create Opportunities:** Increase your exposure to luck by taking calculated risks, networking, and staying open to new experiences.
2. **Focus on Controllables:** While luck can't be controlled, preparation, skill, and effort improve the chances of favorable outcomes.
3. **Learn from Outcomes:** Distinguish between decisions influenced by skill versus luck, using reflection to refine your approach.

In *The Success Equation* (Mauboussin, 2012), the author emphasizes how understanding the balance between skill and luck helps individuals and organizations navigate uncertainty effectively.

Real-Life Example

The rise of Google illustrates the interplay of skill and luck. While Google's founders, Larry Page and Sergey Brin, developed a superior search engine, their success was bolstered by fortunate timing. The internet was rapidly expanding, and their product launched at a moment when users desperately needed better search tools. Additionally, their initial funding came from a chance meeting with an investor. While their skill was undeniable, luck played a key role in their meteoric rise.

On a personal level, consider a job opportunity gained through networking. While hard work and qualifications are critical, a chance meeting at the right time can often open unexpected doors. Recognizing the role of luck in such scenarios helps you appreciate opportunities and prepare for them when they arise.

Exercises

1. **Reflect on a Lucky Break:** Think of a time when luck played a role in your success. What factors made you ready to capitalize on that opportunity?
2. **Increase Your Exposure to Luck:** Identify one area in your life where you can take more calculated risks or meet new people. Record how these efforts create new opportunities over time.
3. **Analyze Skill vs. Luck:** Choose a well-known success story (e.g. a company, athlete, or artist). Break down how much of their success can be attributed to skill versus luck.

Key Takeaway

Luck is an uncontrollable yet powerful force in success. By creating opportunities, focusing on preparation, and recognizing luck's influence, you can position yourself to capitalize on favorable circumstances and navigate uncertainty effectively.

Chapter 69: Trust Building – Creating Long-Term Alliances

Why This Matters

Trust is the cornerstone of any meaningful relationship, whether in business, negotiations, or personal life. Building trust ensures cooperation, reduces conflict, and lays the foundation for long-term alliances. As Stephen M.R. Covey explains in *The Speed of Trust* (2006), trust accelerates progress and improves efficiency by eliminating the need for constant oversight and doubt.

Mastering trust-building is essential because trust isn't a static asset — it requires deliberate actions and consistent effort. By fostering reliability, honesty, and transparency, you create relationships that withstand challenges and grow stronger over time.

How It Works

Building trust involves three critical principles:

1. **Consistency:** Deliver on promises and demonstrate reliability over time. People trust actions more than words.
2. **Transparency:** Communicate openly and honestly, especially in difficult situations. Avoid hidden agendas or manipulation.
3. **Empathy:** Show genuine concern for others' needs and perspectives, fostering mutual respect and understanding.

In *Never Split the Difference* (Voss, 2016), the author highlights how trust is built in negotiations by listening actively, demonstrating empathy, and finding ways to create shared value. These small but deliberate actions strengthen bonds, even in high-stakes scenarios.

Real-Life Example

The partnership between Starbucks and PepsiCo exemplifies trust building in a long-term alliance. In the 1990s, Starbucks wanted to expand its ready-to-drink coffee products but lacked the distribution capabilities to reach global markets. PepsiCo, with its extensive distribution network, became a strategic partner. Over time, the two companies built trust through consistent communication, shared objectives, and successful product launches like bottled Frappuccinos. This alliance continues to thrive, demonstrating how mutual trust can lead to enduring collaboration and sustained growth for both parties.

Exercises

1. **Evaluate Your Trustworthiness:** Reflect on a relationship where trust is critical. Are your actions consistent, transparent, and empathetic? Identify one area to improve.
2. **Analyze a Trust-Building Partnership:** Research a successful business alliance. What specific actions built and maintained trust between the parties?
3. **Practice Active Listening:** In your next conversation, focus entirely on understanding the other person's perspective. Reflect on how this action strengthens trust in the relationship.

Key Takeaway

Trust-building requires consistency, transparency, and empathy. By fostering these qualities, you can create strong, enduring alliances that withstand challenges and drive mutual success.

Chapter 70: The Domino Effect – Anticipating Chain Reactions

CONSEQUENCES

Why This Matters

Every decision humans make creates ripples that extend far beyond the immediate action. The domino effect refers to this chain reaction, where one event sets off a series of consequences, often in unexpected ways. Understanding this dynamic allows you to anticipate outcomes, plan for contingencies, and make choices with greater foresight.

Mastering the domino effect is crucial because it helps you avoid unintended consequences while leveraging positive momentum. As Peter Senge explains in *The Fifth Discipline* (1990), systems thinking—the ability to see connections and anticipate ripple effects — is key to long-term success in complex environments.

How It Works

Anticipating the domino effect involves three steps:

1. **Map the System:** Visualize how a single decision will impact related areas, identifying direct and indirect consequences.
2. **Plan for Contingencies:** Consider how you can mitigate negative effects or amplify positive ones.
3. **Monitor the Impact:** Continuously assess how initial actions are influencing the system, and adjust your strategy accordingly.

In *Thinking in Systems* (Meadows, 2008), the author emphasizes the importance of feedback loops—understanding how actions influence outcomes over time — to navigate complex systems effectively.

Real-Life Example

The Marshall Plan after World War II demonstrates the power of the domino effect in international policy. By investing in the economic recovery of European nations, the United States not only helped rebuild war-torn economies but also stabilized global markets, strengthened alliances, and curtailed the spread of communism. This chain reaction of positive outcomes stemmed from a single, well-considered initiative.

In everyday life, consider the domino effect of small daily habits. For example, developing a morning routine that includes exercise and planning can set the tone for a productive day, which leads to achieving long-term goals. These small, consistent actions create a cascading impact on overall success.

Exercises

1. **Trace a Domino Effect:** Reflect on a recent decision you made. Map out the immediate and longer-term consequences that resulted. What lessons can you apply to future decisions?
2. **Plan for Ripple Effects:** Choose a pending decision and brainstorm possible outcomes. Identify both positive and negative chain reactions, and develop strategies to amplify benefits or mitigate risks.
3. **Analyze a Historic Chain Reaction:** Research an event with significant ripple effects (e.g. the Marshall Plan). How did one decision create broader consequences?

Key Takeaway

The domino effect highlights how one decision sets off a series of outcomes. By mapping systems, planning contingencies, and monitoring impacts, you can anticipate ripple effects and make choices that lead to positive, lasting results.

Section VIII: Advanced Game Theory Applications

As you deepen your understanding of game theory, it's time to explore strategies that demand a higher level of precision and foresight. This section delves into advanced applications, from adopting a master player's mindset to controlling the flow of information, sending powerful signals, and managing competition effectively. These chapters focus on techniques that sharpen decision-making, prevent costly missteps, and ensure you maintain an edge in complex scenarios. Whether you're navigating high-stakes negotiations or competing in crowded markets, these strategies equip you to stay ahead, adapt intelligently, and maximize long-term success.

Chapter 71: The Superior Mindset – Act Like a Master Player

Why This Matters

Mastering the game requires more than just playing it—it demands thinking like the best players. The superior mindset is about understanding the broader landscape, anticipating moves several steps ahead, and approaching every decision with a blend of strategy, patience, and confidence. It's the difference between reactive and proactive decision-making.

This mindset matters because success in high-stakes situations often depends on your ability to stay calm under pressure, think critically, and act decisively. Adopting a master player's perspective transforms challenges into opportunities and ensures you're always prepared for what comes next.

How It Works

Developing the superior mindset involves three critical elements:

1. **Think Multiple Moves Ahead:** Like a chess master, visualize the potential outcomes of your decisions and how they interact with others' moves.
2. **Focus on the Long Game:** Prioritize strategies that maximize long-term benefits over short-term gains.
3. **Stay Adaptable:** Be prepared to adjust your approach based on changing dynamics or unforeseen circumstances.

In *The Art of Strategy* (Dixit & Nalebuff, 2008), the authors emphasize that thinking strategically involves placing yourself in others' shoes to predict their moves while simultaneously advancing your own goals.

Real-Life Example

Sara Blakely's strategy for building Spanx into a global brand exemplifies the superior mindset. Blakely, the company's founder, approached the shapewear market with a long-term vision to innovate and dominate an underserved niche. Instead of rushing into production without validation, she meticulously tested her prototypes, patented her ideas, and secured partnerships with major retailers like Neiman Marcus. Blakely also focused on branding, turning Spanx into a lifestyle symbol rather than just a product. Her ability to see beyond immediate sales and invest in sustainable growth and customer loyalty transformed Spanx into a billion-dollar company.

Exercises

1. **Visualize the Gameboard:** Choose a current challenge and map out all the possible moves and outcomes. Consider how your decisions will influence others and how you'll respond to their moves.
2. **Play the Long Game:** Reflect on a decision you've made recently. Did it prioritize long-term benefits or short-term gains? How might you approach similar decisions differently in the future?
3. **Study a Master Player:** Research a successful leader or strategist. What actions or mindsets contributed to their success? How can you apply similar strategies?

Key Takeaway

The superior mindset transforms reactive decision-making into proactive strategy. By thinking ahead, focusing on the long game, and staying adaptable, you position yourself to master any challenge.

Chapter 72: The Role of Information – Controlling the Flow for Victory

Why This Matters

In negotiations, leadership, or problem-solving, information is a currency that can be spent wisely or squandered recklessly. Knowing how to control the flow of information – what to reveal, what to withhold, and when to share – can make the difference between success and failure. Properly managing the timing and volume of information allows you to shape perceptions, influence decisions, and protect your leverage.

This concept matters because overloading others with unnecessary details can create confusion, while withholding critical information at the wrong time can breed mistrust. As explored in *Influence: The Psychology of Persuasion* (Cialdini, 1984), the way information is presented greatly impacts how it is perceived and acted upon, making control of the flow a critical skill in strategic interactions.

How It Works

Mastering the flow of information involves three core strategies:

1. **Curate What Matters:** Identify the most relevant and impactful information for the situation. Avoid revealing unnecessary details that could dilute your message or provide leverage to others.
2. **Control Timing:** Share information when it serves your purpose, such as building trust or strengthening your position.
3. **Frame the Narrative:** Present information in a way that emphasizes your desired perspective, steering the conversation toward your goals.

In *Thinking, Fast and Slow* (Kahneman, 2011), the author highlights how people are influenced by the way information is framed. Strategic framing ensures that what you reveal works in your favor.

Real-Life Example

J.K. Rowling's release of the Harry Potter series demonstrates masterful control of information flow. Rowling maintained strict secrecy about key plot details, building suspense and anticipation among readers. She also strategically revealed hints and teasers during interviews, keeping fans engaged between book releases. This careful management of information not only amplified the series' popularity but also turned every release into a cultural event.

On a personal level, consider how control of information can influence negotiations. For example, during a salary negotiation, a candidate who selectively shares their qualifications and achievements while withholding competing offers until later stages can maintain leverage and increase their chances of securing a better deal.

Exercises

1. **Analyze an Information Flow:** Reflect on a recent situation where the way information was shared influenced the outcome. What worked well, and what could have been handled differently?
2. **Practice Framing Information:** Take a piece of data or news and write two ways to present it—one that highlights positive outcomes and another that emphasizes risks. Observe how the framing changes perceptions.
3. **Plan Your Narrative:** Choose a goal you're working toward (e.g., a presentation or pitch). Decide what key information to share, what to withhold, and the timing for maximum impact.

Key Takeaway

Controlling the flow of information allows you to shape outcomes strategically. By curating what you share, timing it effectively, and framing it persuasively, you can maintain leverage and steer conversations toward success.

Credible Threat

Why This Matters

A threat loses its value if it's empty or unbelievable. Credible threats are powerful tools in negotiations and leadership because they force others to reconsider their actions without requiring you to follow through. When used effectively, they minimize conflict and maximize influence. However, issuing threats recklessly can erode trust and harm your credibility.

This concept is vital because it allows you to assert authority while maintaining control and reducing unnecessary risks. As highlighted in *Games People Play* (Berne, 1964), the effectiveness of a threat lies not in its delivery but in its perceived plausibility and the stakes it creates.

How It Works

The success of a credible threat depends on three principles:
1. **Build a Reputation for Follow-Through:** People must believe that you are willing and able to carry out your threat if necessary.
2. **Be Clear and Specific:** Clearly communicate what the consequences of inaction or resistance will be, leaving no room for ambiguity.
3. **Use Threats Sparingly:** Overuse or empty threats can harm your credibility and undermine future influence.

Real-Life Example

The Justice Department's antitrust investigation into AT&T and Time Warner's merger in 2017 is a prime example of a credible threat. The government publicly announced that it was prepared to block the merger unless specific conditions were met. Although the case went to court, the announcement alone sent a strong signal that antitrust scrutiny was serious, forcing other companies considering mergers to tread carefully. This credible threat influenced corporate behavior industry-wide without requiring immediate action on every potential case.

In personal contexts, a credible threat might involve a landlord warning of eviction for late rent payments. While the landlord doesn't necessarily want to evict a tenant, the threat—if backed by a history of enforcing such policies — can compel compliance and resolve the issue without escalation.

Exercises

1. **Evaluate a Threat:** Reflect on a time when you issued or faced a threat. Was it credible? How did it influence the outcome? What could have been improved?
2. **Craft a Credible Threat:** Design a mock negotiation scenario where you need to issue a credible threat. Focus on making it specific, believable, and proportional to the situation.
3. **Analyze a Case Study:** Research an example of a credible threat in business or diplomacy (e.g., the AT&T antitrust case). What made the threat effective, and how did it shape outcomes?

Key Takeaway

Credible threats are about influence, not force. By building a reputation for follow-through, communicating clearly, and using threats sparingly, you can assert authority and shape decisions without unnecessary conflict.

Chapter 74: Counterfactual Reasoning – What If and What Next?

Why This Matters

Counterfactual reasoning is the process of considering "what could have been" or "what might be" to improve decision-making and strategy. By analyzing alternate outcomes and potential futures, you can gain critical insights into missed opportunities, plan for contingencies, and refine your approach. This mental exercise allows you to identify mistakes, anticipate challenges, and make smarter, more adaptable choices.

This skill matters because humans are prone to focusing solely on the present or past without adequately preparing for future scenarios. By asking "what if" and "what next," you can broaden your perspective and avoid repeating errors. As explored in *Black Box Thinking* (Syed, 2015), reflecting on hypothetical scenarios often reveals the root causes of failure and opportunities for growth.

How It Works

Counterfactual reasoning operates in two directions:

1. **What If (Backward Thinking):** Analyze past decisions by imagining alternate outcomes. For example, "What if I had acted sooner?" or "What if we had chosen a different strategy?" This retrospective lens helps you identify lessons from past actions.
2. **What Next (Forward Thinking):** Plan for potential futures by considering different paths and their consequences. For instance, "What happens if we launch this product now versus six months later?" Forward-thinking enables strategic preparation for multiple scenarios.

By combining these approaches, you can make decisions with greater clarity and confidence, avoiding past pitfalls while seizing future opportunities.

Real-Life Example

The Titanic disaster in 1912 offers a powerful case of counterfactual reasoning. Following the tragedy, investigators and engineers analyzed the series of decisions that led to the ship's sinking, asking critical "what if" questions. For example, "What if there had been more lifeboats?" or "What if the captain had slowed down in icy waters?" This backward analysis led to sweeping changes in maritime safety regulations, such as mandatory lifeboat requirements and improved iceberg monitoring.

In modern contexts, counterfactual reasoning is widely used in risk management. For instance, businesses often perform scenario analyses to ask "what next" when planning expansions or new product launches, preparing contingency plans for different market conditions.

Exercises

1. **Reflect on a "What If" Scenario:** Think of a decision you regret or a project that didn't succeed. Ask "what if" questions to identify alternate actions you could have taken and what you learned.
2. **Plan a "What Next" Exercise:** Identify a decision you're facing now. Consider at least three possible future outcomes and develop strategies for each.
3. **Analyze a Historical Event:** Choose a historical success or failure (e.g. a major innovation). Explore how "what if" and "what next" questions might have altered the outcome.

Key Takeaway

Counterfactual reasoning sharpens decision-making by examining past outcomes and anticipating future possibilities. By asking "what if" and "what next," you can learn from mistakes, plan for uncertainties, and make smarter, more resilient choices.

Chapter 75: Signaling Power – Sending the Right Messages

Why This Matters

In both personal and professional interactions, the signals you send—intentionally or unintentionally—shape how others perceive your intentions, capabilities, and reliability. Signaling power refers to using deliberate cues, messages, or actions to convey confidence, authority, or trustworthiness. When done effectively, signaling can reduce uncertainty, establish credibility, and influence decision-making.

This concept matters because in a world full of noise, people often rely on signals to make quick judgments. As explored in *The Signal and the Noise* (Silver, 2012), separating meaningful signals from irrelevant noise is critical for navigating complex environments and influencing others effectively.

How It Works

Effective signaling involves three core principles:

Clarity: Ensure that your signal is easily understood by your audience. Ambiguity can dilute its impact.

Authenticity: Signals must align with your actions and capabilities. Misaligned signals can damage trust and credibility.

Relevance: Tailor your signal to the specific audience and context. The right message at the wrong time can backfire.

In negotiations, for example, confidence can be signaled through body language, tone, or the strategic release of information. A well-timed signal can establish authority or reassure others, shaping outcomes in your favor.

Real-Life Example

Toyota's commitment to hybrid technology serves as a strong example of signaling power. When Toyota introduced the Prius in the late 1990s, it wasn't just a product launch—it was a signal to consumers and competitors that the company was leading the shift toward environmentally friendly vehicles. By investing heavily in hybrid technology and prominently marketing the Prius, Toyota established itself as an innovator in sustainable transportation, influencing market trends and setting itself apart from competitors.

On a smaller scale, consider how job candidates signal competence during interviews. A well-prepared portfolio, professional demeanor, and specific examples of past achievements send clear signals of capability and reliability, building confidence in their suitability for the role.

Exercises

1. **Identify Your Signals:** Reflect on how your actions, communication, or presentation signal your intentions or capabilities. Are they aligned with your goals?
2. **Analyze a Signal in Action:** Research a company or individual known for their effective signaling (e.g. Toyota with the Prius). What specific signals did they send, and how were they received?
3. **Practice Sending Signals:** In your next interaction—whether a meeting, pitch, or presentation—deliberately send a signal that aligns with your desired outcome. Reflect on its effectiveness.

Key Takeaway

Signaling power is about shaping perceptions through deliberate messages and cues. By sending clear, authentic, and relevant signals, you can establish authority, build trust, and influence outcomes effectively.

Chapter 76: Competitive Positioning – Standing Out in Crowded Markets

Why This Matters

In crowded markets, blending in is a recipe for irrelevance. Competitive positioning is the art of distinguishing yourself, your product, or your organization in a way that captures attention and creates lasting value. By identifying what makes you unique and communicating that effectively, you carve out a space that others cannot easily occupy.

This concept is vital because markets are saturated with options, and decision-makers often face overwhelming choices. As Michael Porter explains in *Competitive Strategy* (1980), companies must decide whether to lead on cost, differentiation, or focus —trying to do it all typically results in mediocrity. Strategic positioning ensures you play to your strengths and maximize your competitive edge.

How It Works

Competitive positioning relies on three key principles:

1. **Identify Your Unique Value:** Determine what sets you apart — this could be quality, cost efficiency, innovation, or emotional appeal.
2. **Know Your Audience:** Tailor your positioning to meet the specific needs and desires of your target market.
3. **Communicate Consistently:** Reinforce your unique value proposition (UVP) through branding, messaging, and actions, ensuring it's memorable and believable.

In *Purple Cow* (Godin, 2003), the author emphasizes that being remarkable — a "purple cow" in a field of ordinary ones — ensures that you stand out and capture attention in even the most competitive spaces.

Real-Life Example

Dyson's entry into the vacuum cleaner market is a masterclass in competitive positioning. When James Dyson launched his bagless vacuum cleaners, he didn't just compete on performance — he framed Dyson vacuums as innovative, sleek, and technologically superior. By focusing on a clear UVP (no loss of suction) and consistent branding, Dyson captured a premium segment of the market despite being priced higher than competitors. His ability to position Dyson products as the must-have choice for tech-savvy, design-conscious consumers propelled the company to global success.

On a smaller scale, competitive positioning can be seen in personal branding. For example, a freelance graphic designer who specializes in eco-friendly packaging design can position themselves as the go-to expert for sustainable brands. By focusing on this niche, they stand out in a sea of generalists.

Exercises

1. **Define Your Unique Selling Points:** Write down three things that make you, your product, or your organization unique. How can you communicate these more effectively to your audience?
2. **Analyze a Successful Brand:** Study a company like Dyson or Tesla (without repeating examples). What positioning strategy did they use, and how did it set them apart?
3. **Test Your Positioning:** Create a short pitch or description of your unique value proposition. Share it with a colleague or friend and get feedback on how clear and compelling it is.

Key Takeaway

Competitive positioning ensures you stand out in crowded markets. By identifying your unique value, knowing your audience, and communicating consistently, you create differentiation that drives success.

Chapter 77: Entry Deterrence – Keeping Rivals Out of Your Territory

Why This Matters

In competitive environments, preventing rivals from entering your territory is often as important as thriving within it. Entry deterrence involves creating barriers that make it difficult, costly, or unappealing for competitors to challenge your position. By securing your market, you protect profits, maintain leadership, and focus on growth without constant disruption.

This concept is crucial because unchecked competition can erode market share, reduce margins, and increase instability. As explored in *The Innovator's Dilemma* (Christensen, 1997), companies that fail to defend their territory often find themselves outflanked by disruptive challengers.

How It Works

Effective entry deterrence involves three strategies:

1. **Erect Barriers:** Build high start-up costs, patents, brand loyalty, or regulatory advantages that make entry unattractive.
2. **Signal Dominance:** Demonstrate your capability and willingness to compete aggressively if challenged, discouraging rivals from entering.
3. **Innovate Continuously:** Stay ahead of competitors by introducing new products, features, or services that raise the bar for market entry.

In *Co-opetition* (Brandenburger & Nalebuff, 1996), the authors emphasize that entry deterrence isn't about destroying competition—it's about securing your position while leaving room for partnerships and mutual benefits when possible.

Real-Life Example

Intel's dominance in the microprocessor market highlights effective entry deterrence. Intel leveraged its massive investments in research and development (R&D) to consistently deliver cutting-edge processors, setting a high bar for competitors. It also used its market influence to establish industry standards that heavily favored its products, making it difficult for new entrants to compete on performance or compatibility. Additionally, Intel maintained strong relationships with hardware manufacturers, ensuring its processors were widely adopted. This combination of innovation, partnerships, and strategic influence kept rivals at bay for decades.

On a smaller scale, entry deterrence can be seen in a local boutique that creates exclusive partnerships with suppliers to ensure unique, high-quality products that competitors cannot easily replicate. This approach not only secures the boutique's market position but also builds customer loyalty.

Exercises

1. **Identify Barriers:** Think about your market or industry. What barriers currently exist to protect your position, and how can you strengthen them?
2. **Analyze a Dominant Player:** Study a company like Intel or another leader in your industry. What entry deterrence strategies have they used, and how effective have they been?
3. **Design a Deterrence Plan:** Imagine a competitor is entering your market. Develop a strategy to deter them, focusing on barriers, signaling, and innovation.

Key Takeaway

Entry deterrence secures your territory by discouraging competitors from entering. By building barriers, signaling dominance, and innovating continuously, you can maintain leadership and focus on long-term growth.

Chapter 78: Managing Missteps – Learning from Failures

Why This Matters

Failures are inevitable, but how you respond to them determines your long-term success. Managing missteps is about turning setbacks into opportunities for growth. By analyzing what went wrong, addressing weaknesses, and applying lessons learned, you can emerge stronger and more resilient. As discussed in *Failing Forward* (Maxwell, 2007), failure is not the opposite of success — it's part of the journey.

This mindset matters because fear of failure often leads to risk aversion, missed opportunities, and stagnation. Embracing mistakes as learning tools allows you to innovate, adapt, and achieve lasting progress.

How It Works

Managing missteps effectively involves three steps:

1. **Reflect:** Take time to analyze the root cause of the failure. What assumptions or actions led to the misstep? Avoid placing blame and focus on understanding the situation objectively.
2. **Adapt:** Develop strategies to address the weaknesses or gaps that caused the failure. This might involve new training, processes, or tools.
3. **Implement Change:** Apply the lessons learned in future decisions, ensuring that past mistakes lead to smarter choices and better outcomes.

In *The Lean Startup* (Ries, 2011), the concept of "build, measure, learn" highlights the value of iterative improvement. Every failure provides valuable data to refine your approach and move closer to success.

Real-Life Example

NASA's lessons from the Challenger disaster exemplify how missteps can lead to transformative change. After the space shuttle Challenger tragically exploded in 1986, NASA conducted an extensive investigation to understand the root causes. The findings revealed issues in organizational communication and decision-making processes. In response, NASA implemented significant reforms, including stricter safety protocols and more transparent communication structures. These changes not only improved future missions but also restored trust in the organization.

On a personal level, consider an entrepreneur whose initial business venture fails due to poor market research. By reflecting on their mistake, they might identify the need to better understand customer needs, leading to a more successful second attempt.

Exercises

1. **Conduct a Failure Audit:** Reflect on a recent failure. What went wrong, and why? What specific lessons can you apply to avoid repeating the same mistakes?
2. **Develop a Resilience Plan:** Create a plan for handling future failures. Include steps for reflection, adaptation, and implementation of changes.
3. **Study a Recovery Story:** Research a company or individual who bounced back from failure (e.g., NASA after Challenger). What actions did they take, and how did they turn their misstep into an advantage?

Key Takeaway

Failure is not the end — it's a step toward improvement. By reflecting on missteps, adapting your approach, and applying lessons learned, you can transform setbacks into stepping stones to success.

Chapter 79: Maximizing Utility – Balancing Functionality and Fairness

Why This Matters

Achieving the best possible outcome often involves trade-offs. Maximizing utility is about balancing functionality (efficiency, practicality) with fairness (equity, inclusiveness). This approach ensures that decisions are both effective and just, fostering sustainable outcomes and trust among stakeholders.

This principle matters because decisions skewed too far toward functionality risk alienating key stakeholders, while prioritizing fairness excessively may hinder productivity. Striking a balance is essential for creating solutions that are both efficient and inclusive, particularly in high-stakes negotiations, leadership, or policy-making.

How It Works

Maximizing utility involves three essential steps:

1. **Assess Stakeholder Needs:** Identify the goals, concerns, and expectations of all parties involved to understand where functionality and fairness align or conflict.
2. **Evaluate Trade-Offs:** Quantify the impacts of prioritizing one dimension (efficiency or equity) over the other. What gains or losses occur in each scenario?
3. **Craft Balanced Solutions:** Design outcomes that optimize practical results while maintaining fairness, ensuring that all parties feel valued and engaged.

In *Thinking Strategically* (Dixit & Nalebuff, 1993), the authors discuss how strategic decision-making often involves considering utility—both in terms of tangible gains and the perceptions of fairness by those affected.

Real-Life Example

The redesign of the public transportation system in Curitiba, Brazil serves as a strong example of maximizing utility. In the 1970s, the city faced rapid population growth and increasing traffic congestion. City planners prioritized efficiency by creating the Bus Rapid Transit (BRT) system, which allowed buses to move as quickly and effectively as subway trains. Simultaneously, they ensured fairness by keeping fares affordable and making the system accessible to low-income residents. This balance between functionality and fairness resulted in an efficient, equitable, and sustainable public transport model that has been replicated worldwide.

On a personal level, imagine managing a group project. Balancing workload distribution (fairness) with meeting tight deadlines (efficiency) ensures that no team member feels overburdened while the group still delivers high-quality results on time.

Exercises

1. **Analyze a Trade-Off You've Made:** Reflect on a recent decision where you prioritized functionality or fairness. What was the outcome, and how could you have improved the balance between the two?
2. **Develop a Balanced Plan:** Choose a problem in your life or work (e.g. resource allocation or team management). Design a solution that maximizes both efficiency and equity.
3. **Study a Case of Utility Balancing:** Research a large-scale decision (e.g. a government program or corporate initiative). How did decision-makers balance functionality and fairness, and what lessons can you learn?

Key Takeaway

Maximizing utility means striking a balance between functionality and fairness to achieve efficient and equitable outcomes. By assessing needs, evaluating trade-offs, and crafting balanced solutions, you create sustainable progress that satisfies both practical and moral considerations.

Chapter 80: The Principle of Least Regret – Playing It Safe When Needed

Why This Matters

In life and decision-making, uncertainty is inevitable. The principle of least regret helps navigate uncertain scenarios by prioritizing choices that minimize potential negative consequences. It's a safeguard against excessive risks while still allowing for thoughtful, forward momentum. When faced with difficult decisions, this principle ensures you act rationally without being paralyzed by fear of failure.

This concept matters because regret can cloud future decision-making and harm morale. By focusing on actions that reduce regret, you gain clarity and confidence in high-stakes or uncertain environments. This principle aligns with behavioral economics concepts, such as those discussed in *Thinking, Fast and Slow* (Kahneman, 2011), which highlights how people often overestimate the pain of potential losses compared to the satisfaction of gains.

How It Works

Applying the principle of least regret involves three steps:

1. **Identify Potential Outcomes:** Map out possible consequences of each decision, including worst-case and best-case scenarios.
2. **Assess Regret Potential:** Consider which outcomes would leave you feeling the least regret if things don't go as planned.
3. **Make the Least Risky but Reasonable Choice:** Select the option that balances caution with progress, ensuring you don't overplay or underplay your hand.

This principle is particularly useful in irreversible decisions or high-stakes scenarios where outcomes can have lasting effects. In *Predictably Irrational* (Ariely, 2008), the author discusses how people often avoid risk altogether to sidestep regret but notes that calculated risk-taking with safeguards often leads to better results.

Real-Life Example

NASA's approach to the Mars Rover missions demonstrates the principle of least regret. When designing the Curiosity Rover, engineers faced the challenge of ensuring the rover could land safely on Mars, a high-risk operation with no margin for error. To minimize regret, NASA opted for a sky crane landing system that provided additional stability, even though it required more resources and innovation than simpler methods. This cautious but ambitious approach paid off, ensuring a safe landing and a successful mission.

In everyday contexts, consider an investor choosing between two opportunities: a high-risk stock and a reliable mutual fund. If the investor is more concerned about losing money than missing out on potential gains, they might opt for the mutual fund, minimizing potential regret while still making a productive choice.

Exercises

1. **Map Your Regrets:** Reflect on a recent decision that didn't go as planned. What alternative choice might have reduced your regret, and what did you learn from the experience?
2. **Simulate a Risky Decision:** Choose a hypothetical high-stakes decision. Map out the potential outcomes and apply the principle of least regret to determine the most reasonable choice.
3. **Plan for the Future:** Identify a significant decision you'll face soon. List possible options, their potential outcomes, and the choice that minimizes regret while still achieving meaningful progress.

Key Takeaway

The principle of least regret ensures you make thoughtful decisions in uncertain situations by minimizing potential negative consequences. By mapping outcomes, assessing regret potential, and choosing cautiously, you can navigate risks without sacrificing progress.

Section IX: Cultural and Ethical Dimensions of Strategy

In the realm of strategy, decisions don't exist in a vacuum—they are influenced by cultural contexts, ethical considerations, and collective values. This part explores the intersection of strategy with morality and culture, offering insights into maintaining integrity while achieving goals. From understanding unspoken norms to leveraging the wisdom of crowds, these chapters highlight the nuances of navigating global environments, balancing fairness with expediency, and making ethically sound decisions. Whether you're managing alliances, adapting to diverse cultural settings, or striving for ethical breakthroughs, this section equips you to act strategically without compromising trust or values.

Chapter 81: The Ethics of Bluffing – Getting Ahead Without Breaking Trust

Why This Matters

Bluffing is often misunderstood as deception, but when done ethically, it's a legitimate and valuable tool in strategic decision-making. The ethics of bluffing revolves around using calculated misdirection to gain leverage while respecting boundaries of trust and fairness. Ethical bluffing can help you influence outcomes, build confidence, and maintain long-term relationships.

This concept is critical because careless or dishonest bluffing can undermine credibility and harm reputations. Ethical bluffing ensures that you remain competitive without sacrificing integrity, allowing you to build trust even in high-stakes scenarios. As highlighted in *Negotiation Genius* (Malhotra & Bazerman, 2007), strategic communication and selective disclosure are central to successful and ethical bluffing.

How It Works

Ethical bluffing relies on three key principles:
1. **Understand the Context:** Bluffing is ethical when all parties understand it as part of the strategic process (e.g. negotiations or sales).
2. **Avoid Misrepresentation:** Never bluff about something that could cause harm or compromise trust if revealed.
3. **Strengthen Trust:** Use bluffing to achieve short-term leverage without damaging long-term credibility or relationships.

By following these principles, you can maintain the balance between competitive advantage and ethical responsibility.

Real-Life Example

Richard Branson's approach to launching Virgin Atlantic in the airline industry demonstrates ethical bluffing in business. When Branson announced Virgin Atlantic's launch, he strategically exaggerated the scale of the company's plans and readiness to compete with established giants like British Airways. This created buzz and positioned Virgin as a serious contender, drawing public and media attention. However, Branson avoided crossing ethical lines by ensuring that Virgin delivered a high-quality experience once the airline officially launched. The bluff succeeded in drawing interest without compromising long-term trust in the Virgin brand.

On a personal level, ethical bluffing could involve a job applicant indicating they are in talks with multiple employers. While creating urgency for a hiring decision, the bluff is ethical as long as the applicant genuinely values the opportunity being discussed.

Exercises

1. . **Evaluate a Strategic Bluff:** Reflect on a time when bluffing was used in a decision-making or negotiation process. Was it ethical? What impact did it have on trust and results?
2. **Practice Ethical Bluffing:** Imagine a scenario where you need to influence someone's decision without revealing everything. Design a strategy that uses ambiguity ethically.
3. **Analyze a Corporate Strategy:** Research a company (e.g., Virgin Atlantic or another innovative player) that used bluffing or signaling. What made their strategy effective and ethical?

Key Takeaway

Bluffing can be a powerful tool when used ethically. By respecting boundaries of trust, avoiding misrepresentation, and aligning with strategic goals, you can influence outcomes while maintaining integrity and long-term credibility.

Chapter 82: Cultural Sensitivity – Adapting Processes for Global Success

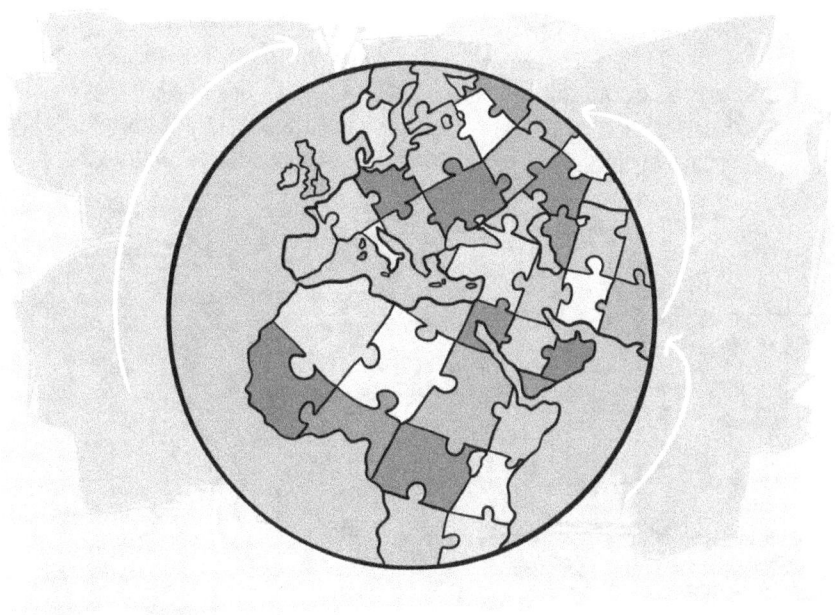

In today's interconnected world, success often depends on the ability to navigate diverse cultural landscapes. Cultural sensitivity is about understanding and respecting differences in values, norms, and communication styles across cultures. Adapting processes to align with these differences enhances trust, fosters collaboration, and ensures that strategies are effective in global contexts.

This concept matters because failing to consider cultural nuances can lead to misunderstandings, conflict, and missed opportunities. As Erin Meyer explains in *The Culture Map* (2014), understanding how different cultures approach communication, decision-making, and leadership is essential for building strong international partnerships.

How It Works

Cultural sensitivity involves three key actions:

1. **Learn the Landscape:** Research the cultural norms and expectations of the people or organizations you're engaging with. This includes understanding communication styles, leadership preferences, and decision-making processes.
2. **Adapt Your Approach:** Tailor your strategies and processes to align with the cultural values of your audience. For example, some cultures prioritize consensus, while others value individual initiative.
3. **Foster Mutual Respect:** Show genuine interest in and respect for cultural differences, which builds trust and strengthens relationships.

In *When Cultures Collide* (Lewis, 2005), the author highlights how successful global leaders actively adjust their behavior to fit the cultural context, ensuring their strategies resonate across borders.

Real-Life Example

McDonald's international expansion strategy exemplifies cultural sensitivity in action. When entering markets like India, McDonald's adapted its menu to suit local tastes, introducing vegetarian options and avoiding beef-based products to respect religious and cultural norms. Similarly, in Japan, McDonald's adjusted its advertising campaigns to align with the country's emphasis on subtlety and group harmony. This ability to tailor offerings and messaging to diverse cultural contexts has been a key factor in McDonald's global success.

On a personal level, cultural sensitivity can be seen in team collaboration. For instance, a leader managing a global team might adjust their communication style to include high-context cultures (e.g. Japan) by emphasizing indirect cues while maintaining clarity for low-context cultures (e.g. Germany) through direct communication.

Exercises

1. **Cultural Research:** Choose a country or culture you're unfamiliar with. Research their business practices, communication styles, and values. Reflect on how you might adapt your approach when interacting with people from that culture.
2. **Analyze a Global Brand:** Study a company like McDonald's or Coca-Cola. How have they adapted their strategies to succeed in different cultural contexts?
3. **Practice Adapting:** Think about a recent interaction with someone from a different cultural background. What adjustments could you make to improve understanding and connection?

Key Takeaway

Cultural sensitivity is essential for global success. By learning cultural norms, adapting strategies, and fostering mutual respect, you can build strong relationships and achieve lasting impact across diverse contexts.

Chapter 83: Moral Outlining – Making a Breakthrough While Staying Ethical

Why This Matters

Pushing boundaries and achieving breakthroughs often requires challenging norms, but without ethical grounding, such progress risks harming people, reputations, or the greater good. Moral outlining is the practice of mapping out your strategic decisions within ethical boundaries. It ensures that innovation, ambition, and success remain aligned with your values and society's expectations.

This matters because short-term success achieved through unethical means often results in long-term consequences, including damaged relationships and trust. As explored in *Ethics for the Real World* (Howard & Korver, 2008), having a clear moral framework strengthens decision-making and protects against actions that might undermine integrity.

How It Works

Moral outlining involves three steps:

1. **Define Your Ethical Principles:** Establish your non-negotiables — values or actions you refuse to compromise, regardless of the situation.
2. **Assess the Impact:** Evaluate how your decisions affect stakeholders, ensuring they align with your principles and create positive outcomes.
3. **Create an Ethical Action Plan:** Build a step-by-step strategy for achieving your goals while staying within the boundaries of your moral framework.

In *The Responsible Entrepreneur* (Sharma, 2014), the author emphasizes the importance of embedding ethics into every stage of innovation, ensuring that progress serves both individual and collective goals.

Real-Life Example

Patagonia's approach to business sustainability exemplifies moral outlining. The company has consistently prioritized environmental and social responsibility over maximizing profits. For example, its "Don't Buy This Jacket" campaign encouraged customers to think twice before making unnecessary purchases, highlighting the environmental cost of consumerism. While unconventional, this strategy aligned with Patagonia's core values, strengthened customer loyalty, and reinforced its reputation as an ethical leader in the outdoor apparel industry.

On a personal level, moral outlining can be seen in decisions like turning down a lucrative but ethically questionable job offer or choosing to report unethical behavior within an organization, even when it's inconvenient or risky.

Exercises

1. **Define Your Moral Framework:** Write down your core ethical principles. How do they influence your decisions, and what actions are non-negotiable for you?
2. **Analyze an Ethical Decision:** Reflect on a time when you faced a choice between success and staying true to your values. Did you make the right decision? What did you learn from the experience?
3. **Study an Ethical Brand:** Research a company like Patagonia. How does its commitment to ethics shape its decisions and reputation?

Key Takeaway

Moral outlining ensures that breakthroughs are achieved ethically. By defining principles, assessing impacts, and creating actionable plans, you can align innovation and success with your values, building trust and lasting impact.

Chapter 84: The Invisible Rules – Understanding Unspoken Norms

Why This Matters

Success in any strategy requires not only understanding the formal rules but also recognizing the invisible, unspoken norms that govern behavior in different contexts. These "rules" may include social expectations, cultural nuances, or organizational dynamics. By understanding these subtleties, you can avoid missteps, gain influence, and strengthen relationships.

This concept is critical because ignoring unspoken norms can lead to unintended consequences, from social faux pas to broken trust. In *The Culture Map* (Meyer, 2014), the author highlights how understanding invisible rules — such as indirect communication in some cultures or hierarchical dynamics in others — is vital for building effective collaborations.

How It Works

Mastering invisible rules requires three steps:

1. **Observe Before Acting:** Take time to understand the social dynamics, cultural values, or organizational expectations in a given environment.
2. **Ask Questions Carefully:** When in doubt, seek clarification from trusted sources or colleagues to ensure you don't inadvertently break unspoken rules.
3. **Adapt and Align:** Tailor your behavior and strategies to fit the context, ensuring you operate effectively within both visible and invisible boundaries.

This approach fosters smoother interactions and avoids conflicts caused by misunderstanding or overlooking norms.

Real-Life Example

Toyota's approach to global expansion demonstrates the importance of respecting invisible rules. When Toyota entered the U.S. market, it didn't just bring its cars — it studied American consumer preferences and workplace norms. This included adapting its production methods to incorporate both Japanese efficiency principles and U.S. workers' expectations for autonomy and feedback. By respecting unspoken norms, Toyota successfully bridged cultural gaps and became one of the leading car manufacturers in the U.S.

On a personal level, understanding invisible rules might mean recognizing the unspoken dynamics in a workplace. For example, in some companies, meetings may operate informally, with decisions made in casual conversations rather than formal presentations. Recognizing and adapting to these nuances ensures smoother collaboration.

Exercises

1. **Observe a New Environment:** In a new social or professional setting, spend time observing behaviors and interactions. What unspoken norms can you identify, and how might they influence your approach?
2. **Adapt to Cultural Differences:** Research a culture you're unfamiliar with. Identify at least two unspoken norms and consider how you might adjust your behavior to align with them.
3. **Analyze a Success Story:** Study a company like Toyota or another global organization. How did they navigate unspoken norms to achieve success in new markets?

Key Takeaway

Understanding invisible rules helps you navigate unspoken norms and expectations, enabling smoother interactions and stronger relationships. By observing, asking questions, and adapting, you can build trust and operate effectively in any context.

Chapter 85: Equity vs. Expediency – Balancing Fairness in Frameworks

Why This Matters

In many strategic decisions, there's a tension between doing what's fair and doing what's fast or efficient. Equity vs. expediency highlights the challenge of balancing fairness with the need for timely and effective solutions. While fairness fosters trust and cooperation, expediency drives results. Learning to strike this balance ensures sustainable success in both leadership and collaboration.

This balance matters because leaning too far toward expediency can erode trust, while overemphasizing equity can slow progress. As highlighted in *Justice: What's the Right Thing to Do?* (Sandel, 2009), fairness and efficiency don't have to be mutually exclusive — they can coexist in a well-thought-out framework.

How It Works

Balancing equity and expediency requires three steps:

1. **Clarify Priorities:** Determine the short- and long-term goals of the situation. Is fairness critical for building trust, or does the situation demand rapid action?
2. **Evaluate Stakeholder Needs:** Identify who will be affected and how. Prioritize equity where trust and relationships are at stake, and expediency when urgency takes precedence.
3. **Find a Middle Ground:** Seek solutions that address the most pressing needs without compromising fairness entirely. Hybrid approaches often yield the best outcomes.

In *The Fifth Discipline* (Senge, 1990), systems thinking emphasizes how organizations can design frameworks that balance competing priorities, ensuring that fairness and expediency work in harmony rather than opposition.

Real-Life Example

The European Union's response to Brexit negotiations offers a compelling example of balancing equity and expediency. While the EU sought to expedite the process to minimize uncertainty, it also prioritized fairness to member states by ensuring that no single country would benefit disproportionately from the outcome. By maintaining transparency and adhering to its core principles, the EU navigated the negotiations with a balance of fairness and pragmatism.

On a smaller scale, imagine a project manager distributing tasks among team members. If one person is significantly overloaded, equity might dictate redistributing responsibilities fairly, even if it delays the project slightly. Balancing these priorities ensures both the team's morale and the project's success.

Exercises

1. **Evaluate a Past Decision:** Reflect on a time when you had to choose between equity and expediency. What was your choice, and how did it impact the outcome? How might you approach it differently?
2. **Test a Hybrid Approach:** Think of a current challenge where equity and expediency are in conflict. Develop a solution that incorporates elements of both.
3. **Analyze a Global Strategy:** Research a negotiation or initiative (e.g., Brexit or a corporate merger). How did decision-makers balance fairness with efficiency, and what were the results?

Key Takeaway

Balancing equity and expediency is key to sustainable success. By clarifying priorities, evaluating stakeholder needs, and finding middle-ground solutions, you can build trust and achieve timely results.

Chapter 86: Altruistic Choices – Sacrificing to Gain in the Long Term

In a competitive world, the idea of sacrificing for others may seem counterintuitive, but altruistic choices often generate trust, loyalty, and opportunities that outweigh short-term losses. By giving time, resources, or effort without expecting immediate returns, you build relationships and foster an environment of collaboration that pays dividends in the future.

LONG-TERM GROWTH.

This approach matters because short-sighted strategies focused solely on self-interest can damage relationships and reduce goodwill. Altruistic actions, when aligned with long-term goals, create a ripple effect of mutual benefit, as highlighted in *Give and Take* (Grant, 2014), which explores how givers often achieve greater long-term success than takers.

How It Works

Altruistic choices can lead to long-term advantages when implemented thoughtfully:

1. **Identify Meaningful Opportunities:** Focus on actions that align with your values and have the potential to create lasting positive impact.
2. **Act Without Expectation:** Approach altruism as a genuine contribution, not a transactional gesture.
3. **Build Long-Term Relationships:** Use your actions to foster trust and goodwill, ensuring that your sacrifices contribute to sustainable success.

In *The Evolution of Cooperation* (Axelrod, 1984), the concept of reciprocal altruism demonstrates how helping others can encourage mutual benefit over time, particularly in repeated interactions.

New Real-Life Example

Costco's decision to pay employees higher wages than industry standards is a powerful example of altruistic choices in business. By prioritizing employee well-being over short-term profit margins, Costco built a culture of loyalty and trust. This led to lower turnover rates, improved customer service, and a more productive workforce, which ultimately resulted in long-term financial success. Costco's actions showed that sacrificing immediate gains for the benefit of others can create sustained advantages for all parties involved.

On a personal level, altruistic choices might include volunteering time to mentor someone in your field. While it may not bring immediate rewards, the connections and goodwill generated can lead to unexpected opportunities down the road.

Exercises

1. **Reflect on a Personal Sacrifice:** Think of a time you sacrificed your own interests to help someone else. What impact did it have on them, and how did it shape your relationship or perspective?
2. **Plan a Meaningful Action:** Identify a way you can support someone in your personal or professional life. Focus on an action that aligns with your values and creates positive impact.
3. **Research an Example:** Study a company or leader that made an altruistic decision, such as Costco. How did their actions benefit others, and what long-term success did they achieve?

Key Takeaway

Altruistic choices can create significant long-term gains by fostering trust, loyalty, and collaboration. By sacrificing strategically and focusing on meaningful actions, you build relationships and opportunities that lead to sustainable success.

Learning from Great Minds

Chapter 87: Historical Lessons – Learning from Great Minds

Why This Matters

The challenges of today often mirror those of the past. Learning from great minds in history provides invaluable insights into strategy, resilience, and decision-making. Whether navigating political turmoil, advancing innovation, or solving complex social problems, historical figures often faced similar dilemmas, offering lessons that remain relevant today.

This approach matters because ignoring history risks repeating mistakes. By studying how great leaders overcame challenges, you can extract practical strategies and apply them in modern contexts, as highlighted in *Leadership in War* (Roberts, 2019), which explores the decision-making processes of historical leaders during crises.

How It Works

Drawing lessons from history involves three steps:
1. **Identify Parallels:** Look for historical events or figures that faced challenges similar to yours. Focus on their strategies and thought processes.
2. **Analyze Their Choices:** Examine what worked, what didn't, and why. Understand how their context influenced their decisions.
3. **Apply the Principles:** Adapt the lessons to fit your unique circumstances, ensuring they align with modern challenges and opportunities.

In *The Lessons of History* (Durant & Durant, 1968), the authors emphasize the recurring nature of human behavior and decisions, making history a valuable guide for solving contemporary problems.

Real-Life Example

Abraham Lincoln's leadership during the U.S. Civil War exemplifies the value of historical lessons. Faced with a deeply divided nation, Lincoln prioritized clear communication, moral clarity, and long-term vision to preserve the Union. His decision to issue the Emancipation Proclamation – while controversial – was both a moral and strategic act that strengthened the North's position while undermining the Confederacy. Today, leaders can draw from Lincoln's example to navigate complex negotiations, manage crises, and inspire others through purpose-driven leadership.

On a smaller scale, studying a figure like Marie Curie – who persevered despite significant societal barriers to make groundbreaking scientific discoveries – can inspire resilience and determination in personal and professional pursuits.

Exercises

1. **Research a Historical Leader:** Choose a historical figure whose challenges resonate with your own. Study their strategies and reflect on how their lessons can apply to your situation.
2. **Analyze a Historical Event:** Identify a major event (e.g., the Civil War or the Industrial Revolution). What strategies were employed, and how can they inform modern decisions?
3. **Create a Personal Connection:** Write down a challenge you're currently facing. Identify a historical parallel and outline three lessons you can apply.

Key Takeaway

History offers a treasure trove of strategic insights. By studying the decisions of great minds, you can adapt their lessons to modern challenges, ensuring informed, effective, and purpose-driven action.

Chapter 88: Managing Alliances – Balancing Loyalty and Pragmatism

Why This Matters

Strategic alliances amplify resources, expertise, and opportunities, but they require careful management to balance loyalty and pragmatism. Managing alliances is about nurturing trust and cooperation while ensuring that the partnership remains aligned with your evolving objectives. Strong alliances can propel success, while poorly managed ones can become liabilities.

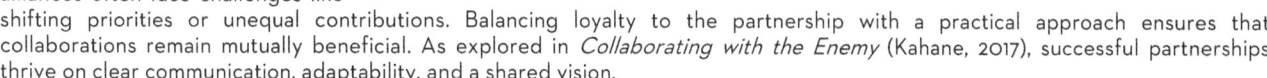

This concept matters because alliances often face challenges like shifting priorities or unequal contributions. Balancing loyalty to the partnership with a practical approach ensures that collaborations remain mutually beneficial. As explored in *Collaborating with the Enemy* (Kahane, 2017), successful partnerships thrive on clear communication, adaptability, and a shared vision.

How It Works

Managing alliances effectively involves three key principles:

1. **Define Shared Goals:** Clearly establish the partnership's objectives, ensuring they align with the interests of all parties.
2. **Communicate Transparently:** Regular communication fosters trust, helps address conflicts early, and keeps the alliance adaptable to change.
3. **Know When to Pivot:** Balance loyalty to the alliance with the need to adjust or exit when the partnership no longer serves its purpose.

These steps create a foundation for strong alliances that are both resilient and flexible, ensuring long-term success.

Real-Life Example

The strategic partnership between Spotify and Waze highlights the balance of loyalty and pragmatism in alliances. In 2017, the companies joined forces to integrate music streaming with navigation, providing users with seamless control of Spotify playlists within the Waze app. This collaboration benefited both platforms – Spotify gained exposure to Waze users, while Waze enhanced its user experience with music functionality. Despite the partnership, both companies retained their independence and pursued their broader business goals, demonstrating how alliances can thrive through alignment and mutual benefit without overdependence.

On a personal level, managing alliances might look like collaborating with a colleague on a shared project while maintaining the flexibility to pursue individual career goals. Clear communication and mutual respect ensure that both parties benefit from the partnership.

Exercises

1. **Evaluate an Alliance:** Reflect on a partnership you've been involved in. What aspects of the alliance worked well, and where could there have been better alignment or communication?
2. **Build an Alliance Strategy:** Identify a potential partner in your personal or professional life. Outline shared goals, define communication methods, and establish how you'll balance loyalty with pragmatism.
3. **Analyze a Partnership:** Study the Spotify-Waze partnership or another alliance. What strategies did they use to align their goals and maintain balance, and what can you learn from their approach?

Key Takeaway

Managing alliances requires balancing loyalty with pragmatism. By fostering trust, maintaining transparency, and knowing when to pivot, you can create partnerships that drive shared success and adaptability.

Chapter 89:
Ethical Negotiation – Advancing Without Exploiting

Why This Matters

Negotiation often involves conflicting interests, but the true art lies in advancing your goals without exploiting others. Ethical negotiation focuses on achieving outcomes that benefit all parties while maintaining trust, fairness, and long-term relationships. It ensures that success is built on collaboration, not coercion, and protects your reputation in future dealings.

This matters because exploitative tactics may yield short-term wins but often result in damaged relationships, loss of trust, and reputational harm. As discussed in *Getting to Yes* (Fisher & Ury, 1981), principled negotiation fosters creative, win-win solutions that align with ethical standards and mutual interests.

How It Works

Ethical negotiation involves three critical practices:

1. **Focus on Interests, Not Positions:** Identify the underlying needs and priorities of all parties rather than rigid demands. This opens pathways for creative solutions.
2. **Be Transparent and Honest:** Share relevant information openly while respecting confidentiality, ensuring fairness without compromising your position.
3. **Seek Win-Win Outcomes:** Strive for agreements that leave all parties satisfied, fostering goodwill and long-term collaboration.

This approach ensures that negotiation is a constructive process that strengthens relationships rather than undermining them.

Real-Life Example

The 1993 Oslo Accords between Israel and the Palestine Liberation Organization (PLO) exemplify ethical negotiation in a high-stakes context. Facilitated by Norway, the negotiations focused on mutual recognition and peaceful coexistence. Although not without flaws, the accords were built on principles of fairness and shared interests, such as land rights and self-governance. The process emphasized transparency, mutual respect, and a focus on common goals, demonstrating that even deeply divided parties can find common ground through ethical negotiation.

On a smaller scale, consider a salary negotiation. An ethical approach involves being honest about your expectations, understanding the employer's constraints, and finding a solution—like additional benefits or growth opportunities—that meets both parties' needs.

Exercises

1. **Reflect on a Negotiation:** Think about a past negotiation you participated in. Was it conducted ethically? What could have been done differently to improve the process and outcome?
2. **Practice Interests-Based Negotiation:** Role-play a negotiation scenario with a partner. Focus on identifying each other's interests and developing a solution that satisfies both parties.
3. **Analyze a Historic Agreement:** Research the Oslo Accords or another major negotiation. What strategies were employed to achieve fairness, and what lessons can you apply?

Key Takeaway

Ethical negotiation is about advancing goals without exploitation. By focusing on interests, fostering transparency, and seeking win-win outcomes, you can achieve success while building trust and long-term relationships.

Chapter 90: The Wisdom of Crowds – Leveraging Collective Intelligence

Why This Matters

Harnessing the power of collective intelligence can transform decision-making and innovation. The wisdom of crowds leverages the combined knowledge, perspectives, and creativity of a group to solve complex problems, predict outcomes, and generate groundbreaking ideas. Properly structured, this approach outperforms even the most talented individuals by pooling insights and reducing biases.

This matters because relying on a single viewpoint, no matter how informed, limits possibilities. As James Surowiecki explores in *The Wisdom of Crowds* (2004), when groups are diverse, independent, and aggregated effectively, they consistently produce superior outcomes in fields ranging from business to science.

How It Works

For the wisdom of crowds to work effectively, three principles must be followed:

1. **Encourage Diversity:** Include participants with varied expertise, experiences, and perspectives to broaden the knowledge base.
2. **Promote Independent Thinking:** Allow each contributor to express their insights freely, without being swayed by others.
3. **Aggregate Input Effectively:** Use systems or tools to compile, analyze, and synthesize the group's contributions into actionable solutions.

This approach fosters creativity and robust decision-making while mitigating individual biases.

Real-Life Example

NASA's "Mars Exploration Rover" public contest demonstrates the power of collective intelligence. Before sending the Spirit and Opportunity rovers to Mars in 2003, NASA invited students across the United States to participate in a naming contest. Thousands of submissions poured in, reflecting the creativity and thoughtfulness of young minds. The winning names — Spirit and Opportunity — not only resonated with NASA's mission but also generated public engagement and enthusiasm for the Mars program. This example illustrates how collective contributions, even from unexpected sources, can lead to meaningful outcomes.

On a smaller scale, businesses can use employee suggestion programs to solve internal challenges. For instance, Toyota's "Kaizen" philosophy encourages workers at all levels to contribute ideas for process improvements, leading to innovation and operational efficiency.

Exercises

1. **Host a Problem-Solving Session:** Gather a diverse group to brainstorm solutions to a challenge you're facing. Use structured methods, like the Delphi technique, to aggregate and refine their input.
2. **Analyze a Collective Achievement:** Research a successful use of collective intelligence (e.g. NASA's naming contest or Toyota's Kaizen system). What principles were applied, and what can you learn from them?
3. **Crowdsource Feedback:** Use a survey or online poll to collect ideas or opinions from a larger group. Reflect on how these aggregated insights could inform your decisions.

Key Takeaway

The wisdom of crowds harnesses collective intelligence to solve problems, innovate, and make better decisions. By fostering diversity, independence, and effective aggregation, you can unlock the full potential of group contributions.

Section X: Mastering the Game of Life

In life, the stakes are high, the players are diverse, and the rules are ever-changing. Mastering the game of life requires more than talent or luck—it demands strategy, resilience, and an unwavering commitment to growth. This final section explores how game theory principles can be applied to personal and professional development, empowering you to thrive amidst uncertainty, build lasting connections, and leave a meaningful legacy. Whether you're navigating setbacks, influencing others, or playing for the long term, these chapters will provide the tools to strategize for success and fulfillment in every dimension of your life.

Chapter 91: Personal Plans – Applying Game Theory to Your Life

Why This Matters

Life is filled with decisions that shape your path, from career moves to relationships and personal growth. Applying game theory to your personal plans helps you make smarter, more intentional choices by analyzing potential outcomes, considering others' actions, and optimizing strategies for success.

This matters because hasty or unexamined decisions can lead to regret or missed opportunities. Using game theory principles enables you to think several steps ahead, anticipate obstacles, and align your actions with your long-term goals.

How It Works

Applying game theory to your life involves three steps:

1. **Identify Your Goals:** Define what success looks like for you in different areas of life (e.g. financial stability, strong relationships, personal fulfillment).
2. **Map Possible Outcomes:** Consider the choices available to you and predict how others' actions might influence your path. Use tools like decision trees to visualize scenarios.
3. **Strategize for Optimal Results:** Choose the path that maximizes your gains while minimizing risks, ensuring alignment with your values and long-term vision.

In *Thinking in Bets* (Duke, 2018), the author emphasizes how strategic thinking improves decision-making by incorporating probabilities and potential outcomes, even when uncertainty is present.

Real-Life Example

Oprah Winfrey's career decisions illustrate personal planning rooted in strategic thinking. When transitioning from her talk show to building a media empire, Oprah weighed her options carefully, considering the risks and rewards of launching the Oprah Winfrey Network (OWN). By aligning her actions with her vision of empowering others and diversifying her brand, she maximized her long-term success while navigating complex decisions.

Exercises

1. **Define Your Life Game Plan:** Choose a major decision you're facing. Use game theory principles to map out potential scenarios and identify the optimal choice.
2. **Study a Strategic Career Move:** Research a leader like Oprah Winfrey or another public figure. How did their decisions align with game theory principles, and what can you learn from their approach?
3. **Create a Decision Tree:** Visualize a personal choice by outlining possible actions, their outcomes, and the factors influencing each option. Reflect on which path aligns best with your goals.

Key Takeaway

Applying game theory to your personal plans enables you to make intentional, strategic decisions. By analyzing outcomes, anticipating others' actions, and aligning choices with your goals, you can chart a course for success and fulfillment.

Chapter 92: Handling Uncertainty – Thriving in the Unknown

Why This Matters

Uncertainty is a constant in life, whether in careers, relationships, or personal goals. Handling uncertainty means embracing the unknown and making decisions confidently despite incomplete information. Learning to thrive in unpredictable situations builds resilience, creativity, and adaptability, allowing you to seize opportunities and navigate challenges with clarity.

This matters because fear of uncertainty often leads to indecision or overly cautious choices. As Nassim Nicholas Taleb discusses in *Antifragile* (2012), uncertainty can be a source of growth and innovation if approached with the right mindset and strategy.

How It Works

Thriving in uncertainty involves three key strategies:

1. **Focus on Controllable Actions:** Identify what you can influence and take deliberate steps to move forward, even when the outcome isn't guaranteed.
2. **Build Flexibility:** Stay open to adjusting your plans as new information emerges, ensuring you can pivot when necessary.
3. **Adopt a Growth Mindset:** View uncertainty as an opportunity to learn and grow rather than a source of fear.

By focusing on these strategies, you can reduce the anxiety of the unknown and harness its potential for personal and professional growth.

Real-Life Example

The rapid response of Zoom during the COVID-19 pandemic showcases thriving in uncertainty. As demand for remote communication tools surged unexpectedly, Zoom quickly adapted by scaling its infrastructure, prioritizing security updates, and launching user-friendly features. Despite the unpredictable circumstances, the company's agility allowed it to meet the needs of millions of users worldwide, solidifying its position as a market leader.

On a personal level, thriving in uncertainty might look like pursuing a new career path despite lacking all the details upfront. By taking small, intentional steps—such as networking or gaining relevant skills—you can move forward while remaining adaptable.

Exercises

1. **Identify Controllables:** Think about an uncertain situation you're facing. Write down the aspects you can influence and create a plan to address them.
2. **Practice Flexibility:** Reflect on a time when a plan didn't go as expected. How did you adapt, and what could you do differently next time to handle uncertainty more effectively?
3. **Analyze an Agile Organization:** Study a company like Zoom or another leader that thrived during a period of uncertainty. What strategies did they use, and how can you apply similar principles in your life?

Key Takeaway

Uncertainty is inevitable, but it doesn't have to be paralyzing. By focusing on controllable actions, building flexibility, and embracing a growth mindset, you can turn unpredictability into a source of strength and opportunity.

Chapter 93: Targeted Storytelling – Persuasion Through a Specific Script

Storytelling isn't just an art — it's a strategy. Targeted storytelling uses specific, purpose-driven narratives to persuade and inspire others. A well-told story connects emotionally, simplifies complex ideas, and motivates action, making it an essential tool for communication and influence.

This matters because data alone rarely drives decisions; it's the emotional connection that compels people to act. As explored in *Made to Stick* (Heath & Heath, 2007), stories that are clear, specific, and relatable are far more persuasive than facts presented in isolation.

How It Works

Effective targeted storytelling involves three steps:

1. **Understand Your Audience:** Tailor your narrative to the needs, values, and emotions of the people you're addressing.
2. **Focus on Specifics:** Use concrete details and examples to make your story relatable and memorable.
3. **End with a Call to Action:** Ensure your story inspires the audience to think, feel, or act in alignment with your goals.

By mastering these steps, you can craft compelling stories that resonate and drive meaningful outcomes.

Real-Life Example

Nike's "Just Do It" campaign demonstrates the power of targeted storytelling. Rather than simply promoting athletic products, Nike tells stories of perseverance and triumph, featuring athletes of all levels overcoming challenges. These narratives inspire customers by connecting deeply with their aspirations and emotions, turning Nike into a brand synonymous with determination and success.

On a personal level, targeted storytelling might involve sharing a specific example of how a past project succeeded to persuade a team to adopt your approach for a new initiative. The right story can clarify your vision and rally others behind it.

Exercises

1. **Craft a Personal Story:** Think of a challenge you've overcome. Write a short narrative with specific details and a clear message to share with someone who might benefit from your experience.
2. **Analyze an Effective Campaign:** Study a storytelling-based marketing campaign, such as Nike's. What made it effective, and how can you apply similar techniques in your communication?
3. **Tailor a Story to Your Audience:** Choose a professional or personal goal you're working toward. Develop a story that aligns with your audience's values and inspires them to support your vision.

Key Takeaway

Targeted storytelling is a powerful way to influence and inspire. By tailoring your narratives, focusing on specifics, and driving action, you can connect with others on a deeper level and achieve your goals.

Chapter 94: Building Resilience – Recovering from Setbacks

Setbacks are inevitable, but resilience — the ability to recover and grow stronger in the face of adversity — is what separates temporary failure from long-term success. Building resilience equips you with the mental and emotional tools to adapt, persevere, and thrive when things go wrong.

This matters because life's challenges often test your resolve, and how you respond determines your trajectory. In *Grit* (Duckworth, 2016), Angela Duckworth emphasizes that persistence, combined with adaptability, is a critical factor in achieving success over time.

How It Works

Building resilience involves three core practices:

1. **Reframe Setbacks as Opportunities:** View failures not as permanent losses but as valuable learning experiences that can guide your future actions.
2. **Develop Coping Mechanisms:** Cultivate habits like mindfulness, journaling, or physical activity to process stress and maintain focus.
3. **Foster a Support Network:** Surround yourself with people who encourage, challenge, and inspire you, providing a safety net when setbacks occur.

By practicing these steps, you can transform difficulties into stepping stones for growth and progress.

Real-Life Example

Howard Schultz's journey with Starbucks demonstrates the power of resilience. When Schultz joined Starbucks in the 1980s, the company faced financial struggles, and his vision of turning it into a global coffee empire was met with doubt. Despite numerous rejections and challenges, Schultz persevered, refining his strategy and securing funding. Today, Starbucks is one of the most recognizable brands worldwide, largely due to Schultz's ability to recover and learn from setbacks.

On a personal level, resilience might mean bouncing back from a failed job interview or business pitch by seeking feedback, refining your approach, and trying again with renewed determination.

Exercises

1. **Reframe a Recent Setback:** Think about a challenge you've faced recently. What lessons can you take from the experience, and how can you apply them moving forward?
2. **Strengthen Your Coping Mechanisms:** Identify one habit—like mindfulness or journaling—you can develop to process stress and improve focus. Practice it for a week and reflect on the impact.
3. **Analyze a Resilient Leader:** Study someone like Howard Schultz or another public figure known for resilience. What strategies did they use to recover from setbacks, and how can you incorporate them into your own life?

Key Takeaway

Resilience is about transforming setbacks into opportunities for growth. By reframing challenges, developing coping mechanisms, and fostering a strong support network, you can recover stronger and achieve lasting success.

Chapter 95: Continuous Improvement – Learning from Every Situation

KEEP REFINING

Why This Matters

Life is a constant journey of growth, but improvement doesn't happen automatically – it requires deliberate effort. Continuous improvement means reflecting on each experience, identifying lessons, and applying those insights to evolve over time. This practice helps you adapt, innovate, and achieve lasting success.

This matters because success is often built on incremental progress rather than grand leaps. As outlined in *Atomic Habits* (Clear, 2018), small, consistent changes compound over time to produce transformational results.

How It Works

To integrate continuous improvement into your life, follow these three steps:

1. **Reflect on Outcomes:** After any experience, evaluate what went well and what could have been done differently.
2. **Embrace Feedback:** Actively seek constructive input from others to gain new perspectives and identify blind spots.
3. **Take Action and Adjust:** Implement changes based on your reflections and feedback, continuously refining your approach.

By committing to these steps, you create a cycle of growth that strengthens your skills, knowledge, and resilience.

Real-Life Example

Pixar Animation Studios exemplifies continuous improvement through its commitment to refining the creative process. After completing each film, Pixar holds a "post-mortem" session where the team dissects what worked and what didn't, from storytelling to technical execution. These lessons inform their next project, allowing Pixar to consistently deliver innovative and emotionally resonant films. This iterative process has been key to their success, producing hits like *Toy Story* and *Inside Out*.

On a personal level, continuous improvement might involve analyzing how you prepared for a big presentation. By reflecting on what aspects resonated with your audience and what could be enhanced, you can refine your approach for even greater impact in the future.

Exercises

1. **Reflect on a Recent Event:** Choose a recent experience or project you worked on. Identify two things you did well and one thing you could improve. Write down how you'll address this in the future.
2. **Ask for Constructive Feedback:** Reach out to someone you trust and ask for their input on a skill or project you're working on. Use their suggestions to create a specific action plan for improvement.
3. **Track Small Changes Over Time:** Choose one habit or behavior to improve (e.g., time management or communication). Track your progress over the next month, making small adjustments each week. Reflect on how these changes add up.

Key Takeaway

Continuous improvement transforms experiences into opportunities for growth. By reflecting, seeking feedback, and taking deliberate action, you can refine your approach and achieve lasting progress in all areas of your life.

Chapter 96: The Mastery of Perspective – Seeing the Big Picture

In life, it's easy to get lost in the details and lose sight of the larger vision. Mastering perspective means learning to zoom out and see the overarching patterns, connections, and long-term implications of decisions. It's about aligning day-to-day actions with a broader strategy, ensuring clarity and focus in your pursuits.

This concept matters because short-term thinking often leads to missed opportunities or mistakes that could have been avoided with a bigger-picture view. In *The Art of Thinking Clearly* (Dobelli, 2013), the author emphasizes the importance of avoiding cognitive biases that limit perspective and focusing on long-term goals instead.

How It Works

Mastering perspective involves three essential practices:

1. **Zoom Out:** Regularly step back to evaluate how your current actions align with your broader goals.
2. **Seek Diverse Insights:** Incorporate viewpoints from others to gain a more comprehensive understanding of the situation.
3. **Balance Macro and Micro Views:** Alternate between the big picture and key details to ensure your strategy is cohesive and actionable.

By cultivating this skill, you can make decisions that are not only effective in the moment but also contribute to long-term success.

Real-Life Example

Satya Nadella's leadership at Microsoft illustrates the mastery of perspective. When Nadella became CEO in 2014, he shifted Microsoft's focus from short-term profits to long-term growth by prioritizing cloud computing, artificial intelligence, and cross-platform collaboration. This required a big-picture view of the industry's future and the willingness to make strategic changes. His vision transformed Microsoft into one of the world's most valuable companies while fostering innovation and adaptability.

On a personal level, mastering perspective might involve balancing career goals with personal well-being. For instance, someone overly focused on work might zoom out to recognize the importance of health and relationships, adjusting their priorities accordingly.

Exercises

1. **Zoom Out on a Current Goal:** Choose a goal or project you're working on. Reflect on how it fits into your broader vision for your life or career. What adjustments could you make to better align with your long-term objectives?
2. **Gather Diverse Perspectives:** Discuss a major decision with trusted friends, colleagues, or mentors. Compare their views with your own and consider how their insights might shape your understanding.
3. **Balance Micro and Macro Views:** Practice alternating between the big picture and specific details of a current challenge. How do these perspectives complement each other, and how can they inform your strategy?

Key Takeaway

Mastering perspective allows you to align daily actions with long-term goals. By zooming out, seeking diverse insights, and balancing macro and micro views, you can make informed decisions that lead to sustainable success.

Chapter 97: Focused Networking – Expanding Your Sphere of Influence

Why This Matters

In a world driven by collaboration, relationships are one of the most valuable assets. Focused networking emphasizes building meaningful, strategic connections rather than chasing quantity. By aligning your relationships with your goals and values, you create a support system that fosters personal and professional growth.

This matters because a scattershot approach to networking often results in shallow, unproductive relationships. As Porter Gale explains in *Your Network Is Your Net Worth* (2013), meaningful connections lead to greater opportunities and deeper collaboration than superficial interactions.

How It Works

Building a focused network requires three steps:

1. **Identify Key Connections:** Determine the individuals or groups whose values and goals align with yours, and prioritize building relationships with them.
2. **Foster Genuine Relationships:** Approach networking with authenticity, focusing on mutual benefit rather than self-interest.
3. **Maintain Your Network:** Regularly engage with your connections through meaningful interactions to keep relationships strong and mutually beneficial.

This approach ensures that your network is both supportive and effective in helping you achieve your goals.

Real-Life Example

Reid Hoffman, co-founder of LinkedIn, exemplifies focused networking. Hoffman's success stems from his ability to cultivate meaningful relationships with other tech leaders, investors, and innovators. By aligning his connections with his vision of fostering professional collaboration, Hoffman built not only a robust network but also a platform that revolutionized how people connect professionally.

On a personal level, focused networking might mean identifying mentors who can guide your career or colleagues who share your vision for a project. Building these relationships authentically ensures long-term support and collaboration.

Exercises

Map Your Network: Create a list of your current connections. Identify which relationships align most closely with your goals and focus on nurturing those connections.

Reach Out Strategically: Identify one person in your desired field or industry you'd like to connect with. Reach out with a thoughtful message explaining why you value their work and how you can mutually benefit.

Strengthen Existing Relationships: Choose three people in your network to reconnect with. Schedule a coffee chat or send a personalized message to catch up and offer support.

Key Takeaway

Focused networking builds meaningful connections that align with your goals and values. By prioritizing key relationships, fostering authenticity, and maintaining engagement, you can expand your sphere of influence and open doors to new opportunities.

Chapter 98: Balancing Solutions and Tactics – Knowing When to Zoom In

Why This Matters

In problem-solving, knowing when to focus on detailed tactics versus overarching solutions is critical. Balancing solutions and tactics means understanding when to prioritize high-level strategy and when to zero in on the specific actions needed to execute that strategy. This balance ensures that your efforts are both effective and aligned with your long-term goals.

This matters because too much focus on tactics can lead to

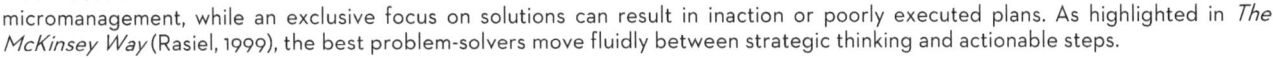

micromanagement, while an exclusive focus on solutions can result in inaction or poorly executed plans. As highlighted in *The McKinsey Way* (Rasiel, 1999), the best problem-solvers move fluidly between strategic thinking and actionable steps.

How It Works

Balancing solutions and tactics involves three essential steps:
1. **Define the Problem Clearly:** Start by identifying whether the challenge requires a high-level solution, a tactical approach, or both.
2. **Move Between Levels as Needed:** Regularly assess whether you need to zoom out for perspective or zoom in to address specific challenges.
3. **Ensure Alignment:** Confirm that your tactics serve the larger solution, creating coherence between your immediate actions and long-term goals.

This dynamic approach ensures that no detail is overlooked while maintaining focus on the bigger picture.

Real-Life Example

SpaceX's Mars mission planning demonstrates the balance between solutions and tactics. The overarching solution is to establish a sustainable human presence on Mars, a goal requiring visionary strategy. At the same time, SpaceX tackles tactical challenges like improving rocket reusability and refining spacecraft design to bring this vision closer to reality. By aligning these detailed actions with their big-picture goal, SpaceX progresses steadily toward its ambitious mission.

On a personal level, this balance could involve developing a five-year career plan (solution) while taking specific steps like upskilling or networking (tactics) to ensure progress toward your broader vision.

Exercises

1. **Analyze a Current Goal:** Identify a goal you're working toward. Map out the high-level solution and the detailed tactics required to achieve it. How well are these two levels aligned?
2. **Switch Perspectives:** Choose a current challenge and practice alternating between focusing on the broader solution and the specific tactics. Reflect on how shifting perspectives helps refine your approach.
3. **Study a Balanced Strategy:** Research a company like SpaceX or another organization known for strategic innovation. How do they balance long-term solutions with short-term tactics?

Key Takeaway

Balancing solutions and tactics ensures effective problem-solving. By defining the problem, moving between levels as needed, and aligning tactics with overarching goals, you can achieve sustainable success.

Chapter 99: Legacy Planning – Going Beyond the Current Status Quo

Why This Matters

Legacy isn't just about what you leave behind—it's about the values, achievements, and influence you create that endure beyond your time. Legacy planning involves thinking long-term, ensuring that your efforts contribute to a lasting impact that benefits others and aligns with your purpose.

This matters because focusing solely on immediate success can limit your potential for making a meaningful, enduring contribution. As Stephen R. Covey explains in *The 7 Habits of Highly Effective People* (1989), beginning with the end in mind ensures that your actions today align with the legacy you want to leave tomorrow.

How It Works

Effective legacy planning involves three key principles:

1. **Define Your Values and Purpose:** Clarify what matters most to you and how you want to be remembered.
2. **Align Actions with Long-Term Impact:** Ensure that your decisions and efforts contribute to a greater goal beyond immediate outcomes.
3. **Empower Others:** Build systems or relationships that allow your influence to grow and continue after you're gone.

This approach helps you create a legacy that reflects your values and drives positive change.

Real-Life Example

Bill and Melinda Gates' philanthropic efforts through the Gates Foundation exemplify legacy planning. By dedicating their resources to global health, education, and poverty reduction, they've created a foundation that will continue to make an impact for generations. Their focus on sustainability and long-term goals ensures that their work extends beyond their lifetimes.

On a personal level, legacy planning could involve mentoring someone who can carry forward your values and vision or contributing to a cause that aligns with your purpose.

Exercises

Define Your Legacy: Reflect on how you want to be remembered. Write down your core values and how they align with the impact you want to create.

Plan for Long-Term Impact: Identify one action you can take today that will contribute to a lasting legacy. This could be creating a mentorship program, starting a community initiative, or writing a book to share your knowledge.

Study an Inspiring Legacy: Research a figure like Bill Gates or another individual known for their enduring contributions. What steps did they take to ensure their work would outlast them, and what lessons can you apply?

Key Takeaway

Legacy planning is about creating an enduring impact that reflects your values and purpose. By defining what matters, aligning your actions, and empowering others, you can build a legacy that inspires and influences beyond your lifetime.

Chapter 100: Infinite Games – Thriving in a World Without End

THE GAME NEVER ENDS

Why This Matters

Many of life's challenges and pursuits aren't finite—they don't have a clear endpoint or a fixed set of rules. Infinite games, as described by Simon Sinek in *The Infinite Game* (2019), require a mindset of adaptability, resilience, and continuous evolution. Thriving in such a world means focusing on growth, relationships, and purpose rather than "winning."

This matters because playing with a finite mindset in an infinite game often leads to burnout, short-term thinking, and unsustainable results. Adopting an infinite mindset ensures that you stay relevant, impactful, and fulfilled over the long haul, no matter how the rules or circumstances change.

How It Works

Thriving in infinite games involves three key shifts in mindset:

1. **Focus on Vision, Not Victory:** Embrace a purpose that guides your actions over the long term, rather than short-term achievements.
2. **Prioritize Relationships:** Build connections that endure and evolve, creating a strong support network for sustained success.
3. **Adapt to Change:** Treat challenges as opportunities to grow and redefine your approach, staying flexible in the face of uncertainty.

These principles allow you to navigate the complexities of life's infinite games while remaining grounded in your values and vision.

Real-Life Example

The evolution of Patagonia under Yvon Chouinard's leadership exemplifies the infinite game mindset. Rather than focusing solely on profit, Patagonia prioritizes environmental sustainability and social responsibility. This long-term vision has allowed the company to thrive and remain relevant for decades, building loyal customer relationships and inspiring other businesses to adopt similar practices. By committing to a purpose beyond short-term wins, Patagonia demonstrates how infinite thinking creates lasting impact.

On a personal level, embracing infinite games could mean pursuing lifelong learning or focusing on relationships that grow and evolve over time, rather than viewing success as a single destination.

Exercises

1. **Identify Your Infinite Game:** Reflect on an area of your life — such as career, relationships, or personal growth — where success doesn't have a fixed endpoint. What purpose or vision can guide your long-term actions?
2. **Strengthen Long-Term Relationships:** Choose one relationship you value deeply. Plan a meaningful way to nurture and grow that connection, prioritizing its longevity over immediate outcomes.
3. **Adapt to a Challenge:** Think of a recent obstacle you've faced. How can you approach it with a mindset of growth and flexibility, seeing it as part of an ongoing journey rather than a finite win or loss?

Key Takeaway

In a world of infinite games, success isn't about winning — it's about staying adaptable, purpose-driven, and committed to growth. By focusing on vision, relationships, and flexibility, you can thrive in a world without end.

Conclusion

Strategy is more than a tool — it is a lens through which the complexities of life become navigable. Every decision, whether large or small, fits into an interconnected game with players, rules, and outcomes. This book has revealed how the principles of game theory illuminate pathways for navigating challenges, optimizing decisions, and achieving meaningful goals.

Through foundational ideas such as the **Prisoner's Dilemma** and **Tit-for-Tat**, collaboration emerged as a dominant force, often more powerful than competition. Concepts like **Pareto Efficiency** and the **Nash Equilibrium** demonstrated the balance between individual and collective benefit, offering insights into building stable, mutually advantageous outcomes. These tools are not confined to theory but serve as practical frameworks for daily decisions.

Navigating Complexity with Advanced Tools

Moving from foundational concepts to advanced strategies, the book emphasized tools for thriving in an uncertain and dynamic world. Techniques like **Bayesian Touchpoints** and **Scenario Analysis** equipped decision-makers to operate effectively despite incomplete information, while ideas like **Entry Deterrence** and **Competitive Positioning** provided the means to stay ahead in competitive environments.

Strategies such as **Backward Induction** and **Resource Management** also highlighted the importance of balancing big-picture vision with precise, tactical action. The interplay of these perspectives ensures that each decision is not only effective in isolation but aligned with long-term goals.

Ethics, Culture, and Long-Term Thinking

In a world that increasingly values trust and inclusion, game theory demonstrated its relevance in navigating human dynamics. The chapters on **Ethical Negotiation**, **Cultural Sensitivity**, and **Moral Outlining** showed how strategic thinking can harmonize with integrity. Far from being rigid, these strategies adapt to the nuances of cultural differences and ethical dilemmas, ensuring sustainable and respectful success.

Beyond external achievements, the book shifted focus inward, guiding readers toward personal mastery. Strategies like the **Win-Win Mindset**, **Infinite Games**, and **Legacy Planning** reinforced the importance of long-term thinking. These tools emphasized that life is not a series of isolated victories but an ongoing pursuit of growth, resilience, and impact.

The Ripple Effect of Decisions

Game theory teaches that every decision creates ripples. These ripples influence systems, relationships, and future opportunities. Understanding the rules of the game, anticipating others' moves, and aligning choices with overarching goals allows for intentional actions that shape meaningful outcomes.

Through the mastery of tactics such as **Bluffing and Signaling**, **Managing Alliances**, and **Building Resilience**, this book empowered decision-makers to navigate complexity with clarity. Tools like **Continuous Improvement** and **Scenario Analysis** underscored the importance of adapting and learning from each challenge, turning setbacks into opportunities for growth.

Embracing the Infinite Game

The ultimate lesson of game theory is that life is not a finite game with clear winners and losers. Instead, it is an infinite game, where the goal is to thrive, adapt, and create lasting value. This requires vision, patience, and a willingness to evolve. Success is not measured by short-term gains but by the ability to sustain purpose and impact over time.

The game of life is dynamic, complex, and filled with possibilities. The strategies outlined in this book offer a toolkit for mastering its challenges. The next move is yours to make. Play it wisely.

Appendix A: Quick Reference Guide

This appendix serves as a streamlined guide to the 100 chapters of *Game Theory: An AI's Guide to 100 Strategies for Mastering Decisions, Negotiations, and Human Dynamics*. Designed for ease of navigation, each chapter title is accompanied by a concise one-liner summarizing its essence. Use this section to revisit specific strategies, refresh your understanding, or quickly locate tools relevant to your needs.

Section I: Foundations of Strategic Thinking

1. **The Prisoner's Dilemma**: Explore the tension between cooperation and defection in competitive scenarios.
2. **Tit-for-Tat**: Learn the power of reciprocity to foster long-term collaboration.
3. **Dominant Strategies**: Identify the best decision regardless of others' actions.
4. **Pareto Efficiency**: Discover how to maximize mutual gains in decision-making.
5. **Nash Equilibrium**: Achieve stability where no player benefits from unilateral changes.
6. **Zero-Sum Games**: Succeed in situations where one's gain is another's loss.
7. **Non-Zero-Sum Games**: Create shared wins through collaborative problem-solving.
8. **Backward Induction**: Master planning by thinking ahead and acting backward.
9. **The Stag Hunt**: Balance risk and reward in collaborative efforts.
10. **The Ultimatum Scenario**: Weigh fairness and self-interest in negotiations.

Section II: Advanced Tactics for Decision-Making

11. **Mixed Tactics**: Use calculated randomness to outwit predictable opponents.
12. **Minimax Programs**: Guard against the worst-case scenario in any strategy.
13. **Commitment Devices**: Solidify your resolve through strategic pre-commitments.
14. **Schelling Points**: Coordinate actions with unspoken agreements.
15. **Shapley Value**: Divide resources fairly in complex situations.
16. **Bluffing and Signaling**: Deploy deception effectively while maintaining credibility.
17. **Opportunity Cost**: Recognize the trade-offs in every decision.
18. **First-Mover Advantage**: Gain the upper hand by leading strategically.
19. **Stackelberg Leadership**: Dominate by taking calculated leadership positions.
20. **Sequential Interplays**: Leverage the long game in decision-making chains.

Section III: Winning in Negotiations

21. **BATNA**: Develop a strong exit plan to negotiate with confidence.
22. **Anchoring Effect**: Set the tone early by framing initial offers strategically.
23. **Logrolling**: Exchange concessions for maximum mutual benefit.
24. **ZOPA**: Identify the zone of possible agreement to close deals.
25. **Splitting the Difference**: Master the art of compromise to move forward.
26. **Hardball Tactics**: Stand firm under pressure without losing leverage.
27. **Framing Effects**: Shape narratives to influence outcomes.
28. **The Decoy Effect**: Guide choices by introducing strategic alternatives.
29. **Supremacy Dynamics**: Exploit strengths and minimize weaknesses effectively.
30. **Deadline Master Plan**: Use timing as a negotiation weapon.

Section IV: Navigating Human Dynamics

31. **Social Proof**: Lead by leveraging group consensus.
32. **Contextualizing**: Redefine the rules to gain strategic advantages.
33. **Moral Hazards**: Avoid creating incentives for harmful behavior.
34. **The Tragedy of the Commons**: Protect shared resources through smart governance.
35. **The Sunk Cost Fallacy**: Let go of losses and focus on future value.
36. **Information Asymmetry**: Manage gaps in knowledge to your benefit.
37. **Herd Behavior**: Anticipate and influence group dynamics.
38. **Reputation Capital**: Build and use trust wisely in strategic moves.
39. **Shadow of the Future**: Make decisions with long-term consequences in mind.
40. **Overconfidence Bias**: Avoid the pitfalls of hubris in planning.

Section V: Resilient and Creative Strategies

41. **Redundancy**: Prepare for failure by building buffers.
42. **Flexible Approaches**: Adapt to real-time changes for sustained success.
43. **Scenario Analysis**: Plan for multiple potential outcomes.

44. **Win-Win Mindset**: Expand opportunities to benefit everyone involved.
45. **Emotional Regulation**: Maintain composure under fire.
46. **Empathy Mapping**: Understand others' motivations to strategize effectively.
47. **Asymmetric Warfare**: Win with fewer resources through unconventional strategies.
48. **Coalition Building**: Strengthen your position by building alliances.
49. **Resource Management**: Prioritize and optimize for efficiency.
50. **Leverage Longevity**: Achieve greater returns through patience.

Section VI: Strategies for Handling Complexity

51. **Multi-Party Negotiations**: Manage competing interests in group dynamics.
52. **Design Approach**: Set the stage for strategic success.
53. **Bayesian Touchpoints**: Make informed decisions with incomplete information.
54. **The Value of Patience**: Delay immediate action for larger rewards.
55. **Escalation Control**: Prevent destructive spirals in conflicts.
56. **Evolutionary Methods**: Adapt strategies as rules change.
57. **Hybrid Blueprints**: Blend synergy and competition for strategic gains.
58. **Liability Diversification**: Spread risks to achieve stability.
59. **The Cost of Complexity**: Simplify systems to remain competitive.
60. **Behavioral Insights**: Use psychology to gain an edge.

Section VII: Game Theory in Everyday Life

61. **Negotiating with Irrational Players**: Stay calm when facing unpredictable behavior.
62. **Frictionless Output**: Eliminate barriers to streamline teamwork.
63. **Timing the Market**: Master the art of acting at the right moment.
64. **Repetition and Reputation**: Achieve long-term success through consistent actions.
65. **Incentive Alignment**: Motivate others by aligning goals and rewards.
66. **Loss Aversion**: Turn fear of loss into strategic opportunity.
67. **Prospect Theory**: Reframe challenges to improve decision-making.
68. **The Role of Luck**: Acknowledge and manage uncontrollable factors.
69. **Trust Building**: Create lasting alliances by fostering credibility.
70. **The Domino Effect**: Anticipate and influence chain reactions in decision-making.

Section VIII: Advanced Game Theory Applications

71. **The Superior Mindset**: Think like a master player for strategic advantage.
72. **The Role of Information**: Control the flow of knowledge to shape outcomes.
73. **Credible Threats**: Leverage authority without direct action.
74. **Counterfactual Reasoning**: Prepare for "what if" scenarios and future moves.
75. **Signaling Power**: Communicate strength through strategic messaging.
76. **Competitive Positioning**: Stand out in a crowded market with unique value.
77. **Entry Deterrence**: Protect your territory by discouraging rivals.
78. **Managing Missteps**: Turn failures into learning opportunities.
79. **Maximizing Utility**: Balance fairness and functionality in decision-making.
80. **The Principle of Least Regret**: Minimize risks when outcomes are uncertain.

Section IX: Cultural and Ethical Dimensions of Strategy

81. **The Ethics of Bluffing**: Advance strategically while maintaining trust.
82. **Cultural Sensitivity**: Adapt strategies for global success.
83. **Moral Outlining**: Break through challenges without compromising ethics.
84. **The Invisible Rules**: Navigate unspoken norms and hidden structures.
85. **Equity vs. Expediency**: Balance fairness with efficiency in complex systems.
86. **Altruistic Choices**: Make sacrifices for long-term gains.
87. **Historical Lessons**: Apply insights from great thinkers to modern strategy.
88. **Managing Alliances**: Weigh loyalty and pragmatism in partnerships.
89. **Ethical Negotiation**: Progress without exploiting others.
90. **The Wisdom of Crowds**: Harness collective intelligence for innovation.

91. **Personal Plans**: Use game theory to optimize daily decisions.
92. **Handling Uncertainty**: Thrive amidst unpredictable circumstances.
93. **Targeted Storytelling**: Persuade effectively with a clear and specific narrative.
94. **Building Resilience**: Recover and grow stronger after setbacks.
95. **Continuous Improvement**: Learn and refine from every experience.
96. **The Mastery of Perspective**: Balance the immediate and the big picture.
97. **Focused Networking**: Build influence through meaningful connections.
98. **Balancing Solutions and Tactics**: Know when to zoom in or out for clarity.
99. **Legacy Planning**: Shape a future that extends beyond current achievements.
100. **Infinite Games**: Adopt a mindset of thriving in a limitless journey.

Appendix B: Chapter Overview by Section

This appendix provides a streamlined breakdown of the book's structure, listing all sections and their respective chapters in an easy-to-navigate format. Use this guide as a quick reference to locate specific topics or revisit key strategies covered in the book.

Section I: Foundations of Strategic Thinking

- The Prisoner's Dilemma: Cooperation vs. Defection
- Tit-for-Tat: The Power of Reciprocity
- Dominant Strategies: Choosing the Best Option
- Pareto Efficiency: Maximizing Mutual Gains
- Nash Equilibrium: Finding Stability in Structures
- Zero-Sum Games: Succeeding at Someone Else's Expense
- Non-Zero-Sum Games: Shared Triumphs through Working Together
- Backward Induction: Thinking Ahead, Acting Backward
- The Stag Hunt: Risk and Reward in Collaboration
- The Ultimatum Scenario: Balancing Fairness and Self-Interest

Section II: Advanced Tactics for Decision-Making

- Mixed Tactics: Embracing Calculated Randomness
- Minimax Programs: Guarding Against the Worst-Case
- Commitment Devices: Strengthening Your Resolve
- Schelling Points: Unspoken Agreements in Coordination
- Shapley Value: Fair Divisions in Complex Situations
- Bluffing and Signaling: The Art of Deception
- Opportunity Cost: Recognizing What You Sacrifice
- First-Mover Advantage: Leading for Personal Gain
- Stackelberg Leadership: Dominating by Taking the Lead
- Sequential Interplays: Playing the Long Game

Section III: Winning in Negotiations

- BATNA: Always Have an Exit Plan
- Anchoring Effect: Setting the Tone Early
- Logrolling: Trading Concessions for Maximum Gains
- ZOPA: Identifying the Zone of Possible Agreement
- Splitting the Difference: Mastering Compromise
- Hardball Tactics: Standing Firm Against Pressure
- Framing Effects: Shaping the Narrative to Win
- The Decoy Effect: Steering Choices Subtly
- Supremacy Dynamics: Using Strong Points and Weakness
- Deadline Master Plan: Using Time as Leverage

Section IV: Navigating Human Dynamics

- Social Proof: Leading with Consensus
- Contextualizing: Define the Rules to Trump the System
- Moral Hazards: Avoid Incentivizing Bad Behavior
- The Tragedy of the Commons: Protecting Shared Resources

- The Sunk Cost Fallacy: Knowing When to Let Go
- Information Asymmetry: Managing Knowledge Gaps
- Herd Behavior: Predicting Group Dynamics
- Reputation Capital: Building and Spending Trust Wisely
- Shadow of the Future: Decisions with Long-Term Consequences
- Overconfidence Bias: Avoiding Hubris in Planning

Section V: Resilient and Creative Strategies

- Redundancy: Preparing for Failure
- Flexible Approaches: Adapting in Real-Time
- Scenario Analysis: Considering Through Every Outcome
- Win-Win Mindset: Growing the Pie for Everyone
- Emotional Regulation: Staying Cool Under Fire
- Empathy Mapping: Understanding Others' Motivation
- Asymmetric Warfare: Persevering with Fewer Resources
- Coalition Building: Strength in Numbers
- Resource Management: Making Every Move Count
- Leverage Longevity: Practice Patience for Big Returns

Section VI: Strategies for Handling Complexity

- Multi-Party Negotiations: Managing Complex Group Dynamics
- Design Approach: Setting the Stage for Success
- Bayesian Touchpoints: Playing with Incomplete Information
- The Value of Patience: Delaying Moves to Get Big Returns
- Escalation Control: Avoiding Destructive Spirals
- Evolutionary Methods: Adapting to Changing Rules
- Hybrid Blueprints: Blending Synergy and Competition
- Liability Diversification: Spreading Bets for Stability
- The Cost of Complexity: Simplifying to Stay Ahead
- Behavioral Insights: Using Psychology to Your Advantage

Section VII: Game Theory in Everyday Life

- Negotiating with Irrational Players: Keeping Calm Under Chaos
- Frictionless Output: Reducing Barriers to Teamwork
- Timing the Market: Knowing When to Act
- Repetition and Reputation: Reaching Your Goals Through Consistency
- Incentive Alignment: Motivating Others Effectively
- Loss Aversion: Turning Fear into Opportunity
- Prospect Theory: Seeing Challenges the Right Way
- The Role of Luck: Managing the Uncontrollable
- Trust Building: Creating Long-Term Alliances
- The Domino Effect: Anticipating Chain Reactions

Section VIII: Advanced Game Theory Applications

- The Superior Mindset: Act Like a Master Player
- The Role of Information: Controlling the Flow for Victory
- Credible Threats: Using Authority Without Acting
- Counterfactual Reasoning: What If and What Next?
- Signaling Power: Sending the Right Messages
- Competitive Positioning: Standing Out in Crowded Markets
- Entry Deterrence: Keeping Rivals Out of Your Territory
- Managing Missteps: Learning from Failures
- Maximizing Utility: Balancing Functionality and Fairness
- The Principle of Least Regret: Playing It Safe When Needed

Appendix C: Practice Scenarios

This appendix presents real-world scenarios where the strategies discussed in this book can be applied to solve challenges effectively. Each scenario highlights a specific problem and explains how certain game theory strategies can help address the issue. By working through these scenarios, readers can strengthen their ability to apply theoretical concepts to practical situations.

Scenario 1: Launching a New Product in a Crowded Market

Problem: A small start-up is preparing to launch a new product in an industry dominated by well-established players. The team is worried about how to differentiate their offering and gain consumer attention without substantial marketing resources.

Applicable Strategies:

- **Competitive Positioning (Chapter 76):** To stand out, the start-up must identify its unique value proposition—what makes its product different from and better than competitors'.
- **Entry Deterrence (Chapter 77):** By positioning aggressively, such as offering unique features or competitive pricing, the start-up can deter competitors from attempting to replicate or outshine its product.
- **Signaling Power (Chapter 75):** The start-up can use bold but credible claims, such as emphasizing limited availability or highlighting innovation, to create intrigue and attract early adopters.

Scenario 2: Negotiating a High-Stakes Partnership

Problem: Two companies with complementary strengths are negotiating a strategic partnership. However, conflicting priorities—one side wants immediate profits, while the other is focused on long-term value—are creating friction.

Applicable Strategies:

- **BATNA (Chapter 21):** Each company should develop strong alternatives to strengthen their negotiation position. Knowing they have other options can provide leverage.
- **ZOPA (Chapter 24):** Both parties must identify the Zone of Possible Agreement by understanding the overlap between their minimum acceptable outcomes.
- **Splitting the Difference (Chapter 25):** As a last resort, a fair compromise can help bridge the gap, ensuring both parties see value in moving forward.

Scenario 3: Handling an Unpredictable Competitor

Problem: A competitor in your industry has been making erratic moves, such as price cuts and surprise product launches, creating uncertainty and disruption for your company's strategy.

Applicable Strategies:

- **Mixed Tactics (Chapter 11):** Introducing calculated randomness into your actions can make your strategy less predictable and harder for competitors to counter.
- **Negotiating with Irrational Players (Chapter 61):** Rather than reacting impulsively, stay calm and focus on actions that align with your long-term goals, regardless of the competitor's behavior.

- **Framing Effects (Chapter 27):** Shape the narrative of the situation in your favor, emphasizing your strengths and stability to reassure customers and partners.

Scenario 4: Resolving a Workplace Conflict

Problem: Two employees have conflicting approaches to solving a critical project problem. The disagreement is escalating, delaying progress and lowering morale.

Applicable Strategies:

- **Emotional Regulation (Chapter 45):** As a leader, staying calm and managing your emotions will allow you to mediate effectively without escalating the conflict further.
- **Empathy Mapping (Chapter 46):** Understanding each employee's motivations and concerns can help identify common ground and guide the team toward a collaborative solution.
- **Social Proof (Chapter 31):** Highlighting examples of successful teamwork from the past can remind the team of the benefits of collaboration and inspire a cooperative mindset.

Scenario 5: Balancing Short-Term and Long-Term Goals

Problem: A CEO must decide whether to pursue a quick financial gain that would temporarily boost quarterly earnings or focus on a long-term investment that would take years to pay off but could secure the company's future.

Applicable Strategies:

- **Shadow of the Future (Chapter 39):** Long-term planning must take precedence, as decisions made today will influence the company's reputation and sustainability tomorrow.
- **The Value of Patience (Chapter 54):** Delaying immediate rewards in favor of larger returns later demonstrates strategic foresight and builds resilience.
- **Infinite Games (Chapter 100):** The goal is not to win short-term battles but to remain a significant player in the industry for years to come.

Scenario 6: Expanding into a Global Market

Problem: A company entering a foreign market struggles to navigate cultural differences and adapt its operations to local norms.

Applicable Strategies:

- **Cultural Sensitivity (Chapter 82):** Understanding and respecting cultural nuances ensures smoother communication and operations.
- **Contextualizing (Chapter 32):** Redefine internal processes to align with the rules and expectations of the new market.
- **Information Asymmetry (Chapter 36):** Bridge knowledge gaps by gathering detailed local insights to make informed decisions.

Scenario 7: Negotiating a Tight Deadline

Problem: Your team is negotiating with a supplier who is delaying key materials needed for a time-sensitive product launch. Without the materials, the launch could fail.

Applicable Strategies:

- **Deadline Master Plan (Chapter 30):** Use the impending deadline as leverage to push the supplier to prioritize your order. Highlight the consequences of delays to emphasize urgency.
- **Hardball Tactics (Chapter 26):** Apply firm but fair pressure to ensure the supplier understands the seriousness of the situation while protecting the long-term relationship.
- **Credible Threats (Chapter 73):** If necessary, signal that alternative suppliers are available and ready to step in, providing the leverage to secure action.

Scenario 8: Encouraging Team Innovation

Problem: A team's creative output has plateaued, and they are struggling to generate new ideas or solve ongoing challenges effectively.

Applicable Strategies:

- **Flexible Approaches (Chapter 42):** Encourage an iterative process where team members can experiment with unconventional methods without fear of failure.
- **Scenario Analysis (Chapter 43):** Introduce structured brainstorming by analyzing multiple "what-if" scenarios to stimulate creative thinking.
- **Building Resilience (Chapter 94):** Foster a culture where setbacks during innovation are treated as learning opportunities, building the team's confidence to explore bolder ideas.

Scenario 9: Preventing Resource Overload

Problem: A manager notices the team's workload is increasing beyond their capacity, leading to inefficiencies and burnout.

Applicable Strategies:

- **Resource Management (Chapter 49):** Assess and prioritize tasks to focus on what delivers the highest value while eliminating or delegating non-essential work.

- **Redundancy (Chapter 41):** Build buffers into the team's processes by assigning backup resources to critical tasks.
- **The Cost of Complexity (Chapter 59):** Simplify workflows and remove unnecessary layers of complexity to improve productivity and reduce stress.

Scenario 10: Addressing Public Backlash Over a Controversy

Problem: A brand has made a decision that triggered negative public reactions. Rebuilding trust with its audience is critical to preserving its market position.

Applicable Strategies:
- **Reputation Capital (Chapter 38):** Leverage existing goodwill and transparency to communicate your response effectively. Highlight prior commitments to social responsibility or customer care.
- **Ethical Negotiation (Chapter 89):** Engage with stakeholders, including critics, to address concerns openly and find solutions that restore credibility.
- **The Wisdom of Crowds (Chapter 90):** Use public feedback to demonstrate active listening and ensure future decisions are better aligned with expectations.

Scenario 11: Creating a Long-Term Alliance

Problem: Two organizations want to collaborate on a multi-year initiative, but differing priorities and distrust complicate discussions.

Applicable Strategies:
- **Managing Alliances (Chapter 88):** Develop a clear agreement that balances loyalty with flexibility to adapt over time.
- **Trust Building (Chapter 69):** Foster credibility through consistent communication, transparency, and delivering small, mutual wins early in the collaboration.
- **Multi-Party Negotiations (Chapter 51):** Use structured dialogue to ensure both parties' needs are met while navigating conflicts.

Scenario 12: Anticipating Consumer Behavior Trends

Problem: A company wants to predict consumer preferences to stay ahead of its competitors, but market data is inconclusive.

Applicable Strategies:
- **Herd Behavior (Chapter 37):** Observe patterns of group dynamics and consumer behavior to identify emerging trends.
- **Behavioral Insights (Chapter 60):** Apply psychological principles to analyze why consumers make certain choices.
- **Timing the Market (Chapter 63):** Use predictive models to act at the right moment when trends begin to solidify.

Scenario 13: Responding to an Aggressive Competitor

Problem: A rival company has aggressively cut prices and launched targeted marketing campaigns, threatening your market share.

Applicable Strategies:
- **Asymmetric Warfare (Chapter 47):** Focus on niche strengths or unconventional tactics to counter the competitor's actions without engaging directly.
- **Entry Deterrence (Chapter 77):** Reinforce your market position by improving customer loyalty and locking in distribution channels.
- **Bluffing and Signaling (Chapter 16):** Send signals that you are prepared to match their actions, such as through pricing or promotions, even if you don't fully commit.

Scenario 14: Simplifying a Complex System

Problem: A project involves multiple stakeholders, competing priorities, and intricate processes that slow progress and increase costs.

Applicable Strategies:
- **The Cost of Complexity (Chapter 59):** Identify and eliminate redundancies in the project's design to streamline processes.
- **Design Approach (Chapter 52):** Reorganize the project using first principles to create a foundation that promotes efficiency and clarity.
- **Pareto Efficiency (Chapter 4):** Focus on solutions that provide maximum mutual benefit with minimal compromises.

Scenario 15: Deciding When to Walk Away

Problem: You're stuck in a negotiation that is becoming increasingly unbalanced, with diminishing returns despite continued effort and resources.

Applicable Strategies:
- **BATNA (Chapter 21):** Evaluate your best alternative to the current deal, ensuring you're prepared to walk away confidently.
- **The Sunk Cost Fallacy (Chapter 35):** Avoid letting previous investments dictate your decisions. Focus on future benefits rather than past losses.
- **The Principle of Least Regret (Chapter 80):** Prioritize the option that minimizes long-term regret, even if it means stepping back now.

Appendix D: Strategic Checklist

This strategic checklist is designed as a practical tool for applying the principles and strategies covered in this book. By following these checkpoints, readers can systematically evaluate their decisions, identify opportunities, and address challenges effectively. Each checkpoint includes actionable steps to ensure no detail is overlooked. Use this guide as a foundation for strategic thinking in any situation.

1. **Define Your Objective Clearly**
   - Identify your primary goal and desired outcome.
   - Ensure the objective aligns with your long-term vision or values.
   - Break the goal into smaller, actionable milestones.

2. **Understand the Stakes**
   - Assess the risks and rewards associated with the decision.
   - Identify potential consequences of success or failure.
   - Prioritize based on the impact of each possible outcome.

3. **Map Out the Players**
   - List all key stakeholders and their interests.
   - Identify allies, competitors, and neutral parties.
   - Analyze the motivations and goals of each player.

4. **Evaluate Available Resources**
   - Take inventory of time, money, and personnel available.
   - Identify gaps in resources and plan how to fill them.
   - Optimize current assets to stretch their impact.

5. **Assess Your Alternatives**
   - Define your BATNA (Best Alternative to a Negotiated Agreement).
   - Brainstorm multiple pathways to achieve the objective.
   - Rank alternatives based on feasibility and impact.

6. **Anticipate Opposing Moves**
   - Think like your competitor or adversary — what would they do next?
   - Identify potential threats or disruptions.
   - Develop counterstrategies for each anticipated move.

7. **Build Trust Strategically**
   - Establish credibility through transparency and consistency.
   - Identify ways to deliver small wins to build goodwill.
   - Use empathy and active listening to strengthen alliances.

8. **Simplify Complexity**
   - Remove unnecessary steps or elements from the process.
   - Focus on the 20% of actions that deliver 80% of results (Pareto principle).
   - Communicate clearly and concisely to avoid misunderstandings.

9. **Leverage Timing Effectively**
   - Identify the best time to act for maximum impact.
   - Use deadlines to create urgency or gain leverage.
   - Be patient when waiting for the right opportunity to emerge.

10. **Stay Flexible**
    - Embrace an adaptive mindset to respond to unexpected changes.
    - Test small changes before committing to large-scale shifts.
    - Always have a contingency plan for critical actions.

11. **Use Data Wisely**
    - Gather and analyze reliable data to inform decisions.
    - Cross-check assumptions against factual evidence.
    - Avoid analysis paralysis by focusing on actionable insights.

12. **Frame the Narrative**
    - Shape how others perceive the situation to align with your goals.
    - Highlight benefits and mitigate perceived risks in your messaging.
    - Use storytelling to create a compelling and persuasive argument.

13. Manage Emotions
- Recognize emotional triggers in yourself and others.
- Maintain composure, even under pressure or provocation.
- Use empathy to defuse tensions and build rapport.

14. Think Long-Term
- Evaluate how today's decisions will impact future outcomes.
- Avoid short-term wins that could lead to long-term losses.
- Invest in strategies that build sustainable success.

15. Learn from Setbacks
- Conduct a post-mortem analysis after every failure or misstep.
- Identify lessons that can improve future decision-making.
- Use setbacks as stepping stones to refine your strategy.

Pro Tip: The Rule of 3

Always ask these three questions before making a critical decision:

What am I trying to achieve?

Who will be affected, and how?

How does this align with my long-term goals?

These three guiding questions can sharpen focus, reduce distractions, and ensure every decision contributes to lasting success.

Appendix E: Resources

1. Akerlof, George A. (1970). *The Market for Lemons: Quality Uncertainty and the Market Mechanism.* Quarterly Journal of Economics.
2. Ariely, Dan. (2008). *Predictably Irrational: The Hidden Forces That Shape Our Decisions.* Harper Perennial.
3. Arrow, Kenneth J. (1974). *The Limits of Organization.* W.W. Norton & Company.
4. Axelrod, Robert. (1984). *The Evolution of Cooperation.* Basic Books.
5. Banerjee, Abhijit V. (1992). *A Simple Model of Herd Behavior.* Quarterly Journal of Economics.
6. Bazerman, Max H., and Neale, Margaret A. (1992). *Negotiating Rationally.* The Free Press.
7. Beinhocker, Eric D. (2006). *The Origin of Wealth: Evolution, Complexity, and the Radical Remaking of Economics.* Harvard Business Review Press.
8. Benartzi, Shlomo, and Thaler, Richard H. (2004). *Save More Tomorrow: Using Behavioral Economics to Increase Employee Saving.* Journal of Political Economy.
9. Berger, Jonah. (2013). *Contagious: Why Things Catch On.* Simon & Schuster.
10. Berne, Eric. (1964). *Games People Play: The Psychology of Human Relationships.* Grove Press.
11. Bezos, Jeff. (1997). *Shareholder Letter.* Amazon.com.
12. Brandenburger, Adam, and Nalebuff, Barry. (1996). *Co-opetition: A Revolutionary Mindset That Combines Competition and Cooperation.* Currency Doubleday.
13. Brown, Brené. (2018). *Dare to Lead: Brave Work. Tough Conversations. Whole Hearts.* Random House.
14. Buffett, Warren. (2013). *The Giving Pledge.* GivingPledge.org.
15. Camerer, Colin, and Loewenstein, George. (2014). *Behavioral Economics and Public Policy.* Princeton University Press.
16. Catmull, Ed, and Wallace, Amy. (2014). *Creativity, Inc.: Overcoming the Unseen Forces That Stand in the Way of True Inspiration.* Random House.
17. Catmull, Ed. (2014). *Creativity, Inc.: Overcoming the Unseen Forces That Stand in the Way of True Inspiration.* Random House.
18. Chouinard, Yvon. (2005). *Let My People Go Surfing: The Education of a Reluctant Businessman.* Penguin Books.
19. Christensen, Clayton M. (1997). *The Innovator's Dilemma: When New Technologies Cause Great Firms to Fail.* Harvard Business School Press.
20. Cialdini, Robert B. (1984). *Influence: The Psychology of Persuasion.* Harper Business.
21. Clausewitz, Carl von. (1832). *On War.* Princeton University Press (translated editions).
22. Clear, James. (2018). *Atomic Habits: An Easy & Proven Way to Build Good Habits & Break Bad Ones.* Avery.
23. Clear, James. (2018). *Atomic Habits: An Easy & Proven Way to Build Good Habits & Break Bad Ones.* Avery.
24. Covey, Stephen M.R. (2006). *The Speed of Trust: The One Thing That Changes Everything.* Free Press.
25. Covey, Stephen R. (1989). *The 7 Habits of Highly Effective People: Powerful Lessons in Personal Change.* Free Press.
26. Dearlove, Des. (2007). *Business the Richard Branson Way: 10 Secrets of the World's Greatest Brand Builder.* Capstone Publishing.

27. Diermeier, Daniel. (2011). *Reputation Rules: Strategies for Building Your Company's Most Valuable Asset.* McGraw-Hill Education.

28. Dixit, Avinash, and Nalebuff, Barry. (1991). *Thinking Strategically: The Competitive Edge in Business, Politics, and Everyday Life.* W.W. Norton & Company.

29. Dobelli, Rolf. (2013). *The Art of Thinking Clearly.* Harper.

30. Drucker, Peter F. (1967). *The Effective Executive.* Harper & Row.

31. Duckworth, Angela. (2016). *Grit: The Power of Passion and Perseverance.* Scribner.

32. Duhigg, Charles. (2012). *The Power of Habit: Why We Do What We Do in Life and Business.* Random House.

33. Duke, Annie. (2018). *Thinking in Bets: Making Smarter Decisions When You Don't Have All the Facts.* Portfolio.

34. Durant, Will, and Ariel Durant. (1968). *The Lessons of History.* Simon & Schuster.

35. Dweck, Carol S. (2006). *Mindset: The New Psychology of Success.* Ballantine Books.

36. Dyson, James. (2000). *Against the Odds: An Autobiography.* Texere.

37. Elster, Jon. (1979). *Ulysses and the Sirens: Studies in Rationality and Irrationality.* Cambridge University Press.

38. European Union. (2020). *Brexit Negotiation Frameworks and Agreements.* Official Reports Archive.

39. Fehr, Ernst, and Schmidt, Klaus M. (1999). *A Theory of Fairness, Competition, and Cooperation.* Quarterly Journal of Economics.

40. Fisher, Roger, and Ury, William. (1981). *Getting to Yes: Negotiating Agreement Without Giving In.* Penguin Books.

41. Fisher, Roger, and Ury, William. (1981). *Getting to Yes: Negotiating Agreement Without Giving In.* Penguin Books.

42. Fudenberg, Drew, and Tirole, Jean. (1991). *Game Theory.* MIT Press.

43. Gale, Porter. (2013). *Your Network Is Your Net Worth: Unlock the Hidden Power of Connections for Wealth, Success, and Happiness.* Atria Books.

44. Gates, Bill, and Gates, Melinda. (2021). *Gates Foundation Annual Report.* Gates Foundation Archives.

45. Gawande, Atul. (2009). *The Checklist Manifesto: How to Get Things Right.* Metropolitan Books.

46. Gawer, Annabelle, and Cusumano, Michael A. (2002). *Platform Leadership: How Intel, Microsoft, and Cisco Drive Industry Innovation.* Harvard Business School Press.

47. Gibbons, Robert. (1992). *A Primer in Game Theory.* Prentice Hall.

48. Gladwell, Malcolm. (2000). *The Tipping Point: How Little Things Can Make a Big Difference.* Little, Brown and Company.

49. Godin, Seth. (2003). *Purple Cow: Transform Your Business by Being Remarkable.* Portfolio.

50. Goldstein, Noah J., Martin, Steve J., and Cialdini, Robert B. (2008). *Yes! 50 Scientifically Proven Ways to Be Persuasive.* Free Press.

51. Goleman, Daniel. (1995). *Emotional Intelligence: Why It Can Matter More Than IQ.* Bantam Books.

52. Goodwin, Doris Kearns. (2005). *Team of Rivals: The Political Genius of Abraham Lincoln.* Simon & Schuster.

53. Graham, Benjamin. (1949). *The Intelligent Investor.* Harper Business.

54. Grant, Adam. (2014). *Give and Take: Why Helping Others Drives Our Success.* Penguin Books.

55. Greenblatt, Joel. (2010). *The Little Book That Still Beats the Market.* Wiley.

56. Greene, Robert. (1998). *The 48 Laws of Power.* Penguin Books.

57. Gross, James J. (2014). *Handbook of Emotion Regulation.* The Guilford Press.

58. Güth, Werner, Schmittberger, Rolf, and Schwarze, Bernd. (1982). *An Experimental Analysis of Ultimatum Bargaining.* Journal of Economic Behavior & Organization.

59. Hardin, Garrett. (1968). *The Tragedy of the Commons.* Science.

60. Hardy, Darren. (2010). *The Compound Effect: Jumpstart Your Income, Your Life, Your Success.* Vanguard Press.

61. Harvard Business Review. (2003). *The Power of Negotiation: Mastering Negotiation Strategies.* Harvard Business School Press.

62. Heath, Chip, and Heath, Dan. (2007). *Made to Stick: Why Some Ideas Survive and Others Die.* Random House.

63. Heath, Chip, and Heath, Dan. (2007). *Made to Stick: Why Some Ideas Survive and Others Die.* Random House.

64. Hoffman, Reid. (2014). *The Start-Up of You: Adapt to the Future, Invest in Yourself, and Transform Your Career.* Currency.

65. Holling, C.S. (1973). *Resilience and Stability of Ecological Systems.* Annual Review of Ecology and Systematics.

66. Hollnagel, Erik. (2011). *Resilience Engineering in Practice: A Guidebook.* Ashgate Publishing.

67. Howard, Ronald A., and Korver, Clinton D. (2008). *Ethics for the Real World: Creating a Personal Code to Guide Decisions in Work and Life.* Harvard Business Review Press.

68. Imai, Masaaki. (1986). *Kaizen: The Key to Japan's Competitive Success.* McGraw-Hill Education.

69. Intel Corporation. (2020). *Annual Report and Market Analysis.*

70. Isaacson, Walter. (2011). *Steve Jobs.* Simon & Schuster.

71. Jobs, Steve. (2005). *Stanford Commencement Address.*

72. Kahane, Adam. (2017). *Collaborating with the Enemy: How to Work with People You Don't Agree with or Like or Trust.* Berrett-Koehler Publishers.

73. Kahneman, Daniel, and Tversky, Amos. (1979). *Prospect Theory: An Analysis of Decision under Risk.* Econometrica.

74. Kahneman, Daniel, and Tversky, Amos. (1981). *The Framing of Decisions and the Psychology of Choice.* Science.

75. Kahneman, Daniel. (2011). *Thinking, Fast and Slow.* Farrar, Straus and Giroux.

76. Kelley, Tom. (2001). *The Art of Innovation: Lessons in Creativity from IDEO, America's Leading Design Firm.* Crown Business.

77. Lax, David A., and Sebenius, James K. (1986). *The Manager as Negotiator: Bargaining for Cooperation and Competitive Gain.* The Free Press.

78. Lencioni, Patrick. (2002). *The Five Dysfunctions of a Team: A Leadership Fable.* Jossey-Bass.

79. Leonard, Thomas C. (2016). *Illiberal Reformers: Race, Eugenics, and American Economics in the Progressive Era.* Princeton University Press.

80. Lewis, Michael. (2016). *The Undoing Project: A Friendship That Changed Our Minds.* W.W. Norton & Company.

81. Lewis, Richard D. (2005). *When Cultures Collide: Leading Across Cultures.* Nicholas Brealey Publishing.

82. Lewis, Richard D. (2005). *When Cultures Collide: Leading Across Cultures.* Nicholas Brealey Publishing.

83. Lieberman, Marvin B., and Montgomery, David B. (1988). *First-Mover Advantages.* Strategic Management Journal.

84. Liedtka, Jeanne, and Ogilvie, Tim. (2011). *Designing for Growth: A Design Thinking Tool Kit for Managers.* Columbia Business School Publishing.

85. Lincoln, Abraham. (1953). *The Collected Works of Abraham Lincoln.* Edited by Roy P. Basler.

86. Luce, R. Duncan, and Raiffa, Howard. (1957). *Games and Decisions: Introduction and Critical Survey.* Wiley.

87. Maeda, John. (2006). *The Laws of Simplicity: Design, Technology, Business, Life.* MIT Press.

88. Malhotra, Deepak, and Bazerman, Max H. (2008). *Negotiation Genius: How to Overcome Obstacles and Achieve Brilliant Results at the Bargaining Table and Beyond.* Bantam.

89. Malkiel, Burton G. (2003). *A Random Walk Down Wall Street: The Time-Tested Strategy for Successful Investing.* W.W. Norton & Company.

90. Mankiw, N. Gregory. (1998). *Principles of Economics.* Cengage Learning.

91. Mauboussin, Michael J. (2012). *The Success Equation: Untangling Skill and Luck in Business, Sports, and Investing.* Harvard Business Review Press.

92. Maxwell, John C. (2007). *Failing Forward: Turning Mistakes into Stepping Stones for Success.* Thomas Nelson.

93. McKeown, Greg. (2014). *Essentialism: The Disciplined Pursuit of Less.* Crown Business.

94. McKeown, Greg. (2014). *Essentialism: The Disciplined Pursuit of Less.* Crown Business.

95. McRaney, David. (2011). *You Are Not So Smart: Why You Have Too Many Friends on Facebook, Why Your Memory Is Mostly Fiction, and 46 Other Ways You're Deluding Yourself.* Gotham Books.

96. Meadows, Donella H. (2008). *Thinking in Systems: A Primer.* Chelsea Green Publishing.

97. Meyer, Erin. (2014). *The Culture Map: Breaking Through the Invisible Boundaries of Global Business.* PublicAffairs.

98. Meyer, Erin. (2014). *The Culture Map: Breaking Through the Invisible Boundaries of Global Business.* PublicAffairs.

99. Musk, Elon. (2021). *SpaceX Mission Updates.* SpaceX Official Blog.

100. Myerson, Roger B. (1991). Game Theory: Analysis of Conflict. Harvard University Press.

101. Nadella, Satya. (2017). *Hit Refresh: The Quest to Rediscover Microsoft's Soul and Imagine a Better Future for Everyone.* Harper Business.

102. NASA. (1986). *Rogers Commission Report on the Challenger Accident.*

103. NASA. (2003). *Girl with Dreams Names Mars Rovers 'Spirit' and 'Opportunity'.* NASA Archives.

104. NASA. (2012). *Mars Science Laboratory (Curiosity) Mission Overview.*

105. Nash, John F. (1950). *Equilibrium Points in n-Person Games.* Proceedings of the National Academy of Sciences.

106. National Transportation Safety Board (NTSB). (1912). *Titanic Disaster Report.*

107. Nike. (1988). *"Just Do It" Campaign Archive.* Nike Archives.

108. Ostrom, Elinor. (1990). *Governing the Commons: The Evolution of Institutions for Collective Action.* Cambridge University Press.

109. Ostrom, Elinor. (2009). *Nobel Prize Lecture: Beyond Markets and States: Polycentric Governance of Complex Economic Systems.*

110. Ostrom, Elinor. (2010). *Governing the Commons: The Evolution of Institutions for Collective Action.* Cambridge University Press.

111. Pareto, Vilfredo. (1906). *Manual of Political Economy.* Macmillan Publishing.

112. Patagonia. (2011). *"Don't Buy This Jacket" Campaign.* Company Archive.

113. Patterson, Kerry, Grenny, Joseph, McMillan, Ron, and Switzler, Al. (2002). *Crucial Conversations: Tools for Talking When Stakes Are High.* McGraw-Hill.

114. Patterson, Kerry, Grenny, Joseph, McMillan, Ron, and Switzler, Al. (2002). *Crucial Conversations: Tools for Talking When Stakes Are High.* McGraw-Hill.

115. Pink, Daniel H. (2009). *Drive: The Surprising Truth About What Motivates Us.* Riverhead Books.

116. Pixar Animation Studios. (2020). Pixar Archives.

117. Porter, Michael E. (1980). *Competitive Strategy: Techniques for Analyzing Industries and Competitors.* Free Press.

118. Raiffa, Howard. (1982). *The Art and Science of Negotiation.* Harvard University Press.

119. Rasiel, Ethan. (1999). *The McKinsey Way: Using the Techniques of the World's Top Strategic Consultants to Help You and Your Business.* McGraw-Hill Education.

120. Ries, Eric. (2011). *The Lean Startup: How Today's Entrepreneurs Use Continuous Innovation to Create Radically Successful Businesses.* Crown Business.

121. Ritzer, George. (2011). *McDonaldization: The Reader.* Pine Forge Press.

122. Roberts, Andrew. (2019). *Leadership in War: Essential Lessons from Those Who Made History.* Viking.

123. Sandel, Michael J. (2009). *Justice: What's the Right Thing to Do?* Farrar, Straus and Giroux.

124. Saunders, Harold H. (1991). *The Other Walls: The Politics of the Arab-Israeli Peace Process.* Princeton University Press.

125. S chelling, Thomas C. (1960). *The Strategy of Conflict.* Harvard University Press.

126. Schoemaker, Paul J.H. (1995). *Scenario Planning: A Tool for Strategic Thinking.* Sloan Management Review.

127. Schultz, Howard. (2011). *Onward: How Starbucks Fought for Its Life Without Losing Its Soul.* Rodale Books.

128. Schwartz, Peter. (1991). *The Art of the Long View: Planning for the Future in an Uncertain World.* Currency Doubleday.

129. Seligman, Martin. (2011). *Flourish: A Visionary New Understanding of Happiness and Well-Being.* Atria Books.

130. Senge, Peter M. (1990). *The Fifth Discipline: The Art & Practice of the Learning Organization.* Doubleday.

131. Senge, Peter M. (1990). *The Fifth Discipline: The Art and Practice of the Learning Organization.* Doubleday/Currency.

132. Shapley, Lloyd S. (1953). *A Value for n-Person Games.* Contributions to the Theory of Games. Princeton University Press.

133. Sharma, Carol Sanford. (2014). *The Responsible Entrepreneur: Four Game-Changing Archetypes for Founders, Leaders, and Impact Investors.* Jossey-Bass.

134. Shell, G. Richard. (1999). *Bargaining for Advantage: Negotiation Strategies for Reasonable People.* Penguin Books.

135. Shiller, Robert J. (2015). *Irrational Exuberance.* Princeton University Press.

136. Silver, Nate. (2012). *The Signal and the Noise: Why So Many Predictions Fail — but Some Don't.* Penguin Books.

137. Simmons, Annette. (2006). *The Story Factor: Inspiration, Influence, and Persuasion through the Art of Storytelling.* Basic Books.

138. Sinek, Simon. (2009). *Start with Why: How Great Leaders Inspire Everyone to Take Action.* Penguin Books.

139. Sinek, Simon. (2019). *The Infinite Game.* Portfolio.

140. Spence, Michael. (1973). *Job Market Signaling.* The Quarterly Journal of Economics.

141. Spotify. (2022). How to drive with Spotify and Waze.

142. Stackelberg, Heinrich von. (1934). *Market Structure and Equilibrium.* Springer.

143. Stiglitz, Joseph E. (2010). *Freefall: America, Free Markets, and the Sinking of the World Economy.* W.W. Norton & Company.

144. Sun Tzu. (1910). *The Art of War.* Oxford University Press (translated editions).

145. Surowiecki, James. (2004). *The Wisdom of Crowds: Why the Many Are Smarter Than the Few.* Doubleday.

146. Surowiecki, James. (2004). *The Wisdom of Crowds: Why the Many Are Smarter Than the Few.* Anchor Books.

147. Susskind, Lawrence, and Cruikshank, Jeffrey. (1987). *Breaking the Impasse: Consensual Approaches to Resolving Public Disputes.* Basic Books.

148. S yed, Matthew. (2015). *Black Box Thinking: Why Most People Never Learn from Their Mistakes—But Some Do.* Penguin Books.

149. Taleb, Nassim Nicholas. (2001). *Fooled by Randomness: The Hidden Role of Chance in Life and in the Markets.* Random House.

150. Taleb, Nassim Nicholas. (2012). *Antifragile: Things That Gain from Disorder.* Random House.

151. Tetlock, Philip E., and Gardner, Dan. (2015). *Superforecasting: The Art and Science of Prediction.* Crown.

152. Thaler, Richard H. (2015). *Misbehaving: The Making of Behavioral Economics.* W.W. Norton & Company.

153. Thaler, Richard H., and Sunstein, Cass R. (2008). *Nudge: Improving Decisions About Health, Wealth, and Happiness.* Penguin Books.

154. Toyota Motor Corporation. (1990). *U.S. Market Entry Strategies.* Company Archive.

155. Toyota Motor Corporation. (1997). *Launch of the Prius.*

156. Tucker, Albert W. (1950). *A Two-Person Dilemma.* Stanford University Press.

157. Tversky, Amos, and Kahneman, Daniel. (1974). Judgment Under Uncertainty: Heuristics and Biases. Science.

158. UN Habitat Report on Curitiba's BRT System. (2013).

159. United Nations. (1993). *The Oslo Accords: Framework and Implementation.* UN Archives.

160. United States Department of Justice. (2017). *Antitrust Case Filings.*

161. Ury, William. (1991). Getting Past No: Negotiating with Difficult People. Bantam Books.

162. Von Neumann, John, and Morgenstern, Oskar. (1944). Theory of Games and Economic Behavior. Princeton University Press.

163. Voss, Chris. (2016). *Never Split the Difference: Negotiating as If Your Life Depended on It.* Harper Business.

164. Wieser, Friedrich von. (1914). Theory of Social Economy.

165. Winfrey, Oprah. (2010). *Behind the Scenes.* OWN.

Here's another book by Quinn Voss that you might like